# Greater Vancouver
## & Fraser Valley Cities & Towns

**DELUXE EDITION**

W9-BQT-920

## TABLE OF CONTENTS

| | | |
|---|---|---|
| Legend | Front | map scale, symbol description |
| Key Maps | 2 - 4 | an overview of Greater Vancouver and Fraser Valley with page designations |
| Communities Index | 5 | list of municipal & local community names |
| Page Numbering System | 5 | how to use our Vancouver & Fraser Valley atlas |
| Vancouver Area maps | 6 - 9 | an overview of Greater Vancouver and Fraser Valley |
| Southwestern B.C. | 9 | road map section of the province |
| Downtown Vancouver | 10 - 11 | a large scale map of Vancouver's downtown core |
| Street Maps | 101 - 401 | detailed street level coverage |
| B.C. Ferry Information | 101 | destinations, operating schedules, crossing times |
| Park Information | 103 | B.C. Provincial & National Parks |
| Coquihalla Highway | 118 | information & rates on the provinces toll highway |
| BC Transit | 121 | transit system (Skytrain, West Coast Express) |
| Tourism British Columbia | 124 | phone number & internet information |
| Stanley Park | 142 | phone number & internet information |
| Simon Fraser University | 144 | phone number & internet information |
| University of British Columbia | 161 | phone number & internet information |
| www.mapart.com | 167 | what you'll find on our website |
| Road Information | 193 | information on road conditions for British Columbia |
| Other MapArt products | 242 | atlases, street & road maps for British Columbia |
| Whistler Accommodations | 401 | accommodations numbered right on the maps |
| Points of Interest Index | 500 - 501 | extensive list of where you can find them |
| Street Index | 501 - 516 | comprehensive list of streets |
| British Columbia Distance Chart | 516 | distances between major centres |

## How to Use this Atlas

come see us @ www.mapart.com

**MapArt.** DIRECTION + DESIGN

PRODUCTION TEAM   Lisa Alberga   Brent Carey   Michael Foell
Luna Gao   Karen Gillingham   Oksana Kutna   Werner Mantei
Carl Nanders   Jameel Ahmed Nizamani   Dave Scott
Kyu Shim   Sam Tung-Ding Ho   Matthew Wadley
Marlene Ziobrowski

© mapmobility 2010 Edition
Published by Peter Heiler Ltd.
Distribution by **MapArt Publishing Corp.**
70 Bloor St. E., Oshawa, Ontario L1H 3M2
☎ 905-436-2525   FAX 905-723-6677
Printed in Canada   Imprimé au Canada

**DESTINATIONS** - indicate the town or city the road or highway leads to.

**NORTH ARROWS** - indicate general direction pointing north.

**GRID REFERENCES** - are used to locate places, streets or roads in the index. See page 500 for further explanation.

**PAGE ARROWS** - indicate continued coverage of the map and page.

**FIXED PAGE NUMBERING** - allows for additional pages to be added without renumbering each new addition. For more information turn to page 5.

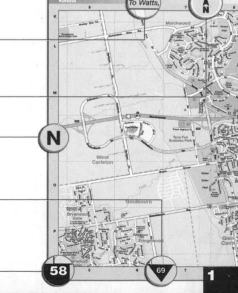

1

# Vancouver Area Key Map

Scale 1:250 000

0  2  4  6  8  10 *kilomètres* kilometres

**Maps to the North**
Squamish - Map 301
Whistler (Expanded Coverage) - Map 401

To Whistler, Squamish

To Langdale

**Lions Bay** 101

Halkett Bay Marine Provincial Park

Mt. Artaban

Port Graves

Hope Pt.

Halkett Pt.

Killarney Lake

Mount Gardner Rd.

Cripper Park

Regional

**BOWEN ISLAND**

Apodaca Provincial Park

Bowen Island Provincial Ecological Reserve

Pt. Cowan

Grafton Lake

Bowyer Island

Strachan Creek

Sunset Beach

Cypress Provincial Park

Cypress Bowl Rd.

The Lions

Hesketh

Sisters

Crown Mtn.

Hollyburn Mtn.

Goat Mtn.

Mt. Fromme

Grouse Mountain Skyride

Capilano River Regional Park

Lynn Headwaters Regional Park

The Needles

Lower Seymour Conservation Reserve

Mt. Seymour

Mount Seymour Provincial Park

Rodgers Lake

Palisade Lake

Burwell Lake

Mt. Burwell

Coliseum Mtn.

Mt. Bishop

Bishop Creek

Elsay Lake

Mt. Elsay

Indian Arm Provincial Park

Say Nuth Khaw Yum Heritage Park

Thwaytes Landing Regional Park Reserve

**Granite Falls**

Metro

Elector

American

**101**

Ferry Terminal

**Horseshoe Bay**

99

**WEST VANCOUVER**

Point Atkinson Lighthouse

Pt. Atkinson

Prospect Point Light

Capilano Suspension Bridge

Squamish Nation

Marine

Dr.

**DISTRICT OF NORTH VANCOUVER**

**Lynn Valley**

Dollarton

Deep Cove

**Belcarra**

Belcarra Regional Park

ANMORE

Brighton Beach

Buntzen Lake Recreation Area (BC Hydro)

Eagle Mtn.

**121** **122** **123** **124** **125**

**102/103**

Charlotte

Stanley Park

Stanley Park Historic

**NORTH VANCOUVER**

**142** **143** **144** **145**

**VANCOUVER**

English Bay

Vancouver Museum

BC Place Stadium

10-11

Canada Place

Powell

Hastings

Seymour Heights

Tseil-Waututh First Nation

Dollarton

Mt. Seymour Pkwy.

Deep Cove Rd.

Burnaby Mtn. Pk.

Simon Fraser University

Pt. Moody

**Moody**

Glen Dr.

**COO P**

**UNIVERSITY ENDOWMENT LANDS (METRO VANCOUVER ELECTORAL DISTRICT A)**

University of British Columbia

Pacific Spirit Regional Park

Chancellor Blvd.

NW Marine Dr.

SW Marine Dr.

Musqueam Indian Band

**161** **162** **163** **164** **165**

Broadway

Grandview Hwy.

Canada Way

**BURNABY**

Deer Lake Regional Park

Maillardville

Coquitlam

**STRAIT OF GEORGIA**

Sturgeon Bank Provincial Wildlife Management Area

Iona Beach Regional Park

Iona Island

Sea Island

Vancouver International Airport

Terminals

Sturgeon Bank

Kwantlen Poly Univ (Richmond)

Bridgeport Rd.

Marine

SE Marine

**VANCOUVER**

Imperial

Kingsway

Royal

**182** **183** **184** **185**

**NEW WESTMINSTER**

Port Mann

**Whalley**

**Guildford**

Sapperton Landing Reg. Park

Mary Hill Regional Park

Coquitlam First Nation

Colony Farm Regional Park

Richmond Art Gallery & Museum

Westminster Hwy.

**RICHMOND**

**LULU ISLAND**

Granville

Blundell

Garden

Williams Rd.

**202** **203** **204** **205**

Richmond Westminster Freeway

Annacis

Annacis Island

Fraser River

South Fraser Perimeter Road

Fraser Islands Reserve Regional Park

Kwantlen Poly Univ

**North Delta**

**Newton**

Clov

Sturgeon Bank Provincial Wildlife Management Area

Gulf of Georgia Cannery National Historic Site

**Steveston**

Moncton St.

Woodwards Landing

Finn Rd.

George Massey Tunnel

Deas Island Regional Park

Burns Bog Ecological Conservancy

Kittson

Mud Bay Regional Park

**SURREY**

**222** **223** **224** **225**

Alaksen National Wildlife Area

South Arm Marshes Provincial Wildlife Management Area

**Ladner**

Ladner Trunk Rd. (Hwy. 10)

Hornby

Mud Bay

**DELTA**

George C. Reifel National Migratory Bird Sanctuary

Westham Island

Robertson

Westham Island

Roberts

**242** **243** **244** **245**

**Crescent Beach**

Serpentine Provincial Wildlife Management Area

Sand Heads Lighthouse

Deltaport Third Berth Project

Ferry Terminal

**Tsawwassen**

Tsawwassen First Nation

Boundary Bay Regional Park

**Boundary Bay**

**BOUNDARY BAY**

Boundary Bay Provincial Wildlife Management Area

**265**

**White Rock**

Semiahmoo First Nation

Peace Arch Provincial State Park

**262/263**

**BRITISH COLUMBIA**

**WASHINGTON**

CANADA

U.S.A.

Roosevelt Rd.

Benson Rd.

A.P.A. Rd.

**Point Roberts**

Semiahmoo Bay

**Blain**

To Nanaimo

To Sidney, Victoria

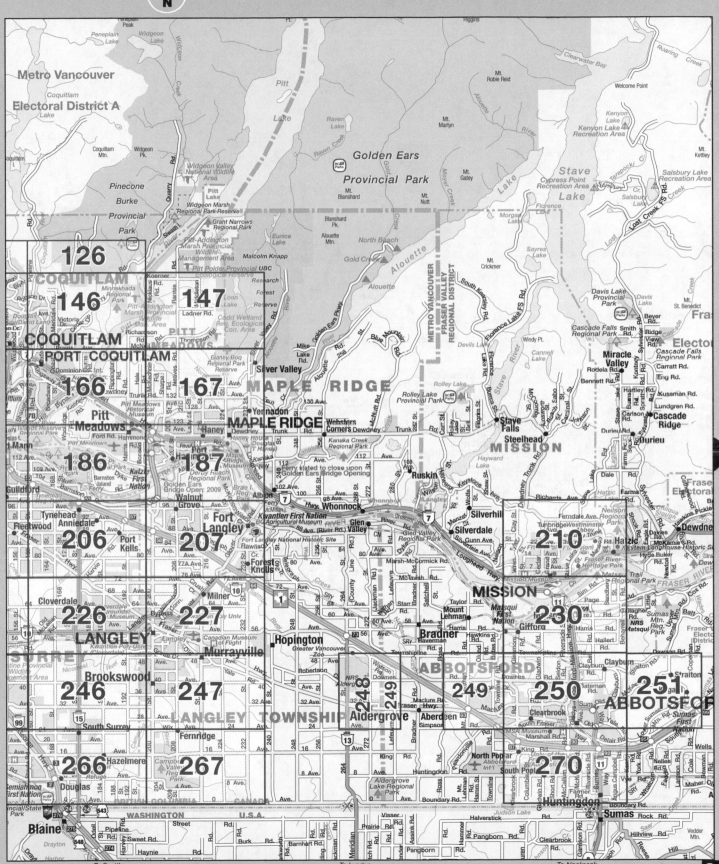

# Central Fraser Valley Key Map

Scale 1:250 000

N

0 2 4 6 8 10 kilomètres / kilometres

**Fraser Valley Electoral District C**

**Fraser Valley Electoral District F**

**Fraser Valley Electoral District G**

**Fraser Valley Electoral District H**

**Fraser Valley Electoral District E**

**Fraser Valley Electoral District D**

**Fraser Valley Electoral District B**

CHILLIWACK

CHILLIWACK

Harrison Hot Springs — **155**

Agassiz — **175**

**193**   **194**

**213**

**233**

**253**

KENT

Hemlock Valley

Harrison Mills

Scowlitz First Nation

Chehalis First Nation

Lake Errock

Deroche

Dewdney

Greendale

Yarrow

Lindell Beach

Lindell

Arnold

Sardis

Vedder Crossing

Ryder Lake

Promontory

Rosedale

Popkum Band

Bridal Falls

Cheam View

Laidlaw

Peters Band

Katz

Seabird Band

Seabird Island Band

Sasquatch Provincial Park

Shxw'ow'hamel First Nation

Skawahlook First Nation

Cheam Band

Union Bar Indian Band

Chawathil Band

Hope — **118**

Silver Creek

Floods

Skagit Range

British Columbia / Washington

Canada / U.S.A.

Trans-Canada Highway

Fraser River

Harrison Lake

Chehalis Lake

Cultus Lake Provincial Park

RANGE — SKAGIT

This index is provided to help you locate a community in the atlas.

**BOLD TYPE** indicates an official municipal name. Blue type indicates a local community name.

**ABBOTSFORD, CITY OF** . . . . . . . . . . . . . . . . .
. . . . . . . . . . . . . . . . . .210, 230, 249-250, 270
Abbotsford (ABBOTSFORD) . . . . . . . . . . . .270
Agassiz (KENT) . . . . . . . . . . . . . . . . . . . . .175
Aldergrove (LANGLEY) . . . . . . . . . . . . . . . .248
**ANMORE, VILLAGE OF** . . . . . . .125-126, 145
Anniedale (SURREY) . . . . . . . . . . . . . . . . . .206
Bayshores (WHISTLER) . . . . . . . . . . . . . . . .401
**BELCARRA, VILLAGE OF** . . . . . . . .124-125
Brackendale (SQUAMISH) . . . . . . . . . . . . . .301
Bridgeport (RICHMOND) . . . . . . . . . . . . . . .182
Brio (WHISTLER) . . . . . . . . . . . . . . . . . . . .401
British Properties (W. VANCOUVER) . . . . . .122
Brookswood (LANGLEY) . . . . . . . . . . . . . . .247
Burkville (RICHMOND) . . . . . . . . . . . . . . . .182
**BURNABY, CITY OF** . . . . . . . . . . . . . . . . . .
. . . . . . . . . . . . . . .143-144, 163-164, 183-184
Burquitlam (COQUITLAM) . . . . . . . . . . . . . .165
Cheam (CHILLIWACK) . . . . . . . . . . . . . . . . .194
**CHILLIWACK, DISTRICT OF** . . . . . .193-194
Chilliwack (CHILLIWACK) . . . . . . . . . . . . . .213
Chinatown (VANCOUVER) . . . . . . . . . . . . . . .11
Clayburn Village (ABBOTSFORD) . . . . . . .250
Clearbrook (ABBOTSFORD) . . . . . . . . . . . .250
Cloverdale (SURREY) . . . . . . . . . . . . . . . . .226
**COQUITLAM, CITY OF** . . . . . . . . . . . . . . . .
. . . . . . . . . . . .125-126, 145-146, 165, 185
Crescent Beach (SURREY) . . . . . . . . . . . . .245
Cultus Lake Park Board . . . . . . . . . . . . . . . .253
Deep Cove (N. VANCOUVER) . . . . . . . . . . .124
**DELTA, CORPORATION OF** . . . . . . . . . . . . .
. . . . . . . . . .184, 203-204, 222-224, 242-244, 262
Dollarton (BURNABY) . . . . . . . . . . . . . . . . .144
Douglas (SURREY) . . . . . . . . . . . . . . . . . . .266
Downtown (VANCOUVER) . . . . . . . . . . . . . . .11
East Burnaby (BURNABY) . . . . . . . . . . . . . .164
Elgin (SURREY) . . . . . . . . . . . . . . . . . . . . .245
Emerald Estaes (WHISTLER) . . . . . . . . . . .401
English Bluff (DELTA) . . . . . . . . . . . . . . . . .262
Fishermans Cove (W. VANCOUVER) . . . .121
Forest Knolls (LANGLEY) . . . . . . . . . . . . . .207

Fort Langley (LANGLEY) . . . . . . . . . . . . . .207
**FRASER VALLEY REGIONAL DISTRICT**
**SUBDIVISION (F.V.R.D.S.)** . . . . . . .175, 193
Garibaldi Highlands (SQUAMISH) . . . . . . .301
Gastown (VANCOUVER) . . . . . . . . . . . . .11, 143
Guildford (SURREY) . . . . . . . . . . . . . . . . . .301
Haig (HOPE) . . . . . . . . . . . . . . . . . . . . . . . .118
Hamilton (RICHMOND) . . . . . . . . . . . . . . . .204
Haney (MAPLE RIDGE) . . . . . . . . . . . . . . . .187
**HARRISON HOT SPRINGS, VILLAGE OF** .
. . . . . . . . . . . . . . . . . . . . . . . . . . . . . . .155
Hatzic (MISSION) . . . . . . . . . . . . . . . . . . . .210
**HOPE, DISTRICT OF** . . . . . . . . . . . . . . . .118
Hope (HOPE) . . . . . . . . . . . . . . . . . . . . . . .118
Horseshoe Bay (W. VANCOUVER) . . . . . .101
Huntingdon (ABBOTSFORD) . . . . . . . . . . .270
Ioco (PORT MOODY) . . . . . . . . . . . . . . . . .145
Kensington (SURREY) . . . . . . . . . . . . . . . . .246
**KENT, DISTRICT OF** . . . . . . . . . . . .155, 175
Kitsilano (VANCOUVER) . . . . . . . . . . . . . . .162
Ladner (DELTA) . . . . . . . . . . . . . . . . .223, 243
**LANGLEY, CITY OF** . . . . . . . .187, 227, 247
**LANGLEY, TOWNSHIP OF** . . . . . . . . . . . . .
. . . . . . . . . . . . . . . . .207, 227, 247, 267
**LIONS BAY, VILLAGE OF** . . . . . . . . . . . .101
Lynn Valley (N. VANCOUVER) . . . . . . . . . .121
**MAPLE RIDGE, DISTRICT OF** . . . .167, 187
Matsqui Village (ABBOTSFORD) . . . . . . . .230
Middlegate (BURNABY) . . . . . . . . . . . . . . .184
Minoru Park (RICHMOND) . . . . . . . . . . . . .202
Minto Landing (CHILLIWACK) . . . . . . . . . .193
**MISSION, DISTRICT OF** . . . . . . . . .210, 230
Mission (MISSION) . . . . . . . . . . . . . . . . . . .230
Murrayville (LANGLEY) . . . . . . . . . . . . . . .227
**NEW WESTMINSTER, CITY OF** . . .164, 184
North Burnaby (BURNABY) . . . . . . . . . . . . .143
North Delta (DELTA) . . . . . . . . . . . . . . . . . .204
**NORTH VANCOUVER, CITY OF** . . .123, 143
**NORTH VANCOUVER, DISTRICT OF** . . . . .
. . . . . . . . . . . . . . . . . .103, 122-124, 143-144
Panorama Ridge (SURREY) . . . . . . . . . . .225

**PITT MEADOWS, CITY OF** . . . . . . . . . . . . .
. . . . . . . . . . . . . . . .146, 166-167, 186-187
Pitt Meadows (PITT MEADOWS) . . . .166, 186
**PORT COQUITLAM, CITY OF** .146, 165-166
Port Guichon (DELTA) . . . . . . . . . . . . . . . . .242
Port Hammond (MAPLE RIDGE) . . . . . . . .187
Port Kells (SURREY) . . . . . . . . . . . . . . . . . .206
**PORT MOODY, CITY OF** . . . . . . .125, 144-145
Promontory (CHILLIWACK) . . . . . . . . . . . . .233
**RICHMOND, CITY OF** . . . . . . . . . . . . . . . . .
. . . . . . . . . . . . .182-184, 202-204, 222-223
Queensborough (NEW WESTMINSTER) 184
Sapperton (NEW WESTMINSTER) . . . . .164
Sardis (CHILLIWACK) . . . . . . . . . . . . . . . . .233
Semiahmoo (SURREY) . . . . . . . . . . . . . . . .266
South Burnaby (BURNABY) . . . . . . . . . . . .163
**SQUAMISH, DISTRICT OF** . . . . . . . . . . .301
Squamish (SQUAMISH) . . . . . . . . . . . . . . .185
**SURREY, CITY OF** . . . . . . . . . . . . . . . . . . .
. . .184-186, 205-206, 225-226, 245-246, 265-266
Tsawwassen (DELTA) . . . . . . . . . . . . . . . . .263
Tynehead (SURREY) . . . . . . . . . . . . . . . . . .206
**UNIVERSITY ENDOWMENT LANDS**
**(U.E.L.)** . . . . . . . . . . . . . . . . . . . . . . .161-162
University Hill (U.E.L.) . . . . . . . . . . . . . . . . .161
Valleycliffe (SQUAMISH) . . . . . . . . . . . . . . .301
**VANCOUVER, CITY OF** . . . . . . . . . . . . . . . .
. . . . . . . . .10-11, 142-143, 162-163, 182-183
Vedder Crossing (CHILLIWACK) . . . . . . . .233
Walnut Grove (LANGLEY) . . . . . . . . . . . . .207
West Heights (MISSION) . . . . . . . . . . . . . .210
**WEST VANCOUVER, DISTRICT OF** . . . . . .
. . . . . . . . . . . . . . . . . .101-102, 121-122
**WHISTLER, RESORT MUN. OF** . . . . . . .401
Whistler Creek (WHISTLER) . . . . . . . . . . . .401
Whistler Highlands (WHISTLER) . . . . . . . .401
Whistler Village (WHISTLER) . . . . . . . . . . .401
**WHITE ROCK, CITY OF** . . . . . . . . . . . . . .265

## IMPORTANT! PLEASE READ! *The Page Numbering System*

**MapArt's** *Greater Vancouver & Fraser Valley Towns Street Atlas* has a new fixed-page numbering system. It will allow us to add pages in the future without changing page numbers.

This edition introduces *a new page numbering system.* The purpose of this system is to avoid constant change as the area grows. In our new system, the lower mainland has been sliced into strips of maps. Each strip can have up to 20 double pages. Numbering starts at the northwest edge of our coverage and increases towards the southeast:

- **100 to 119:**     From Horseshoe Bay eastward
- **120 to 139:**     From West Vancouver eastward
- **140 to 159:**     From English Bay eastward
- **160 to 179:**     From UBC eastward
- **180 to 199:**     From Vancouver International Airport eastward
- **200 to 219:**     From Richmond eastward
- **220 to 239:**     From Steveston eastward
- **240 to 259:**     From Westham Island eastward
- **260 to 279:**     From Tsawwassen eastward

Every inch of the Fraser Valley as far as Hope has been assigned a sequential page number, including sparsely developed areas that do not currently require street level maps. Until needed, those pages are not printed. For example, page 234 is reserved for Ryder Park in a future edition. (See the Key Map on page 2.)

On most of the pages the numbering is quite simple: **one number is assigned to the whole double page spread.** Occasionally each side of the spread will have a unique number.

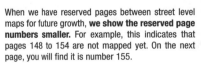

When we have reserved pages between street level maps for future growth, **we show the reserved page numbers smaller.** For example, this indicates that pages 148 to 154 are not mapped yet. On the next page, you will find it is number 155.

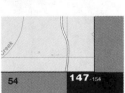

When you want an adjoining map, look for the black triangles in the coloured margin. **The triangles show the page number where coverage continues.**

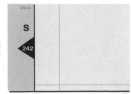

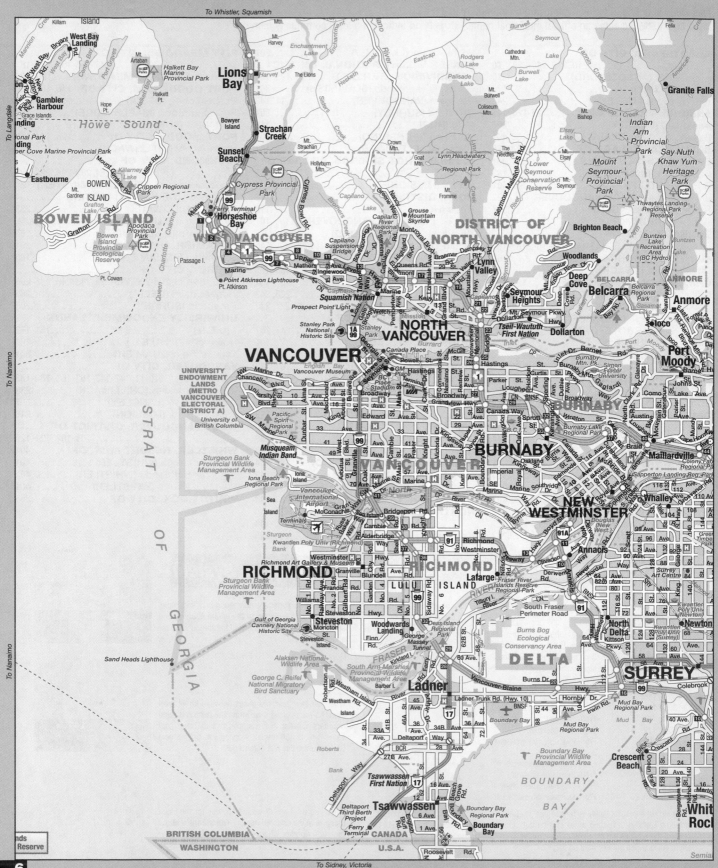

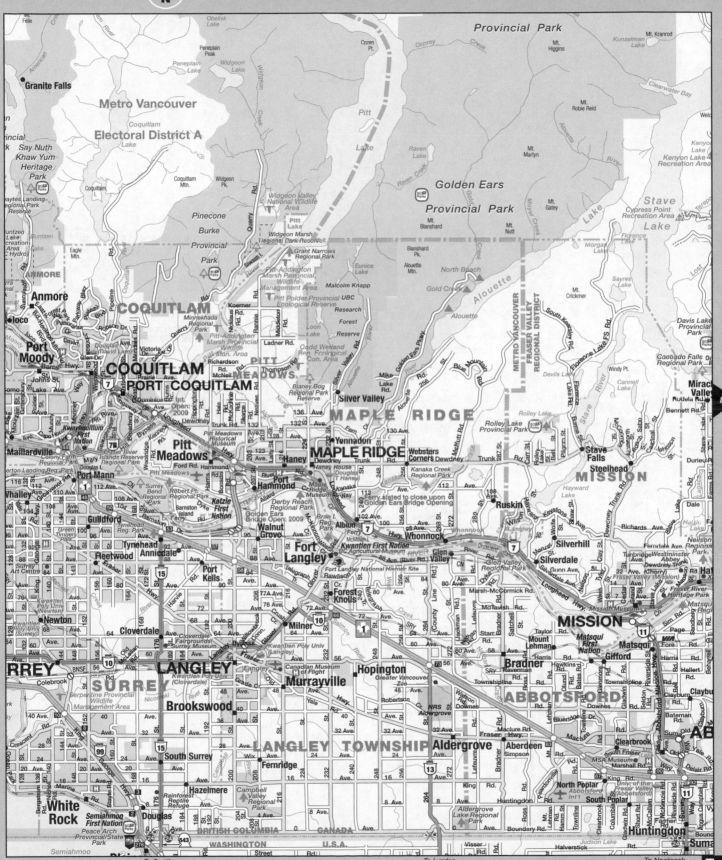

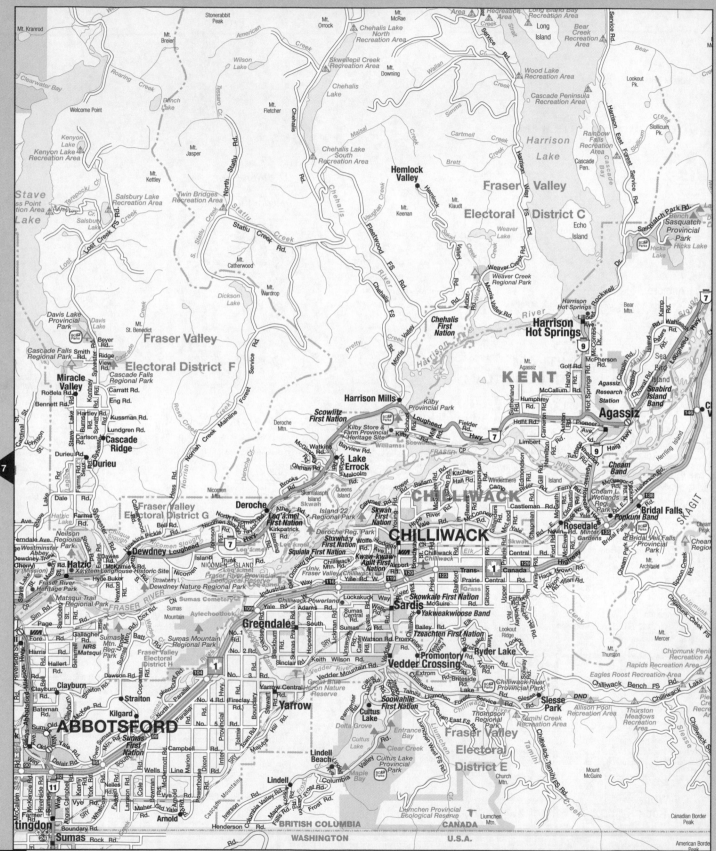

To Nooksack

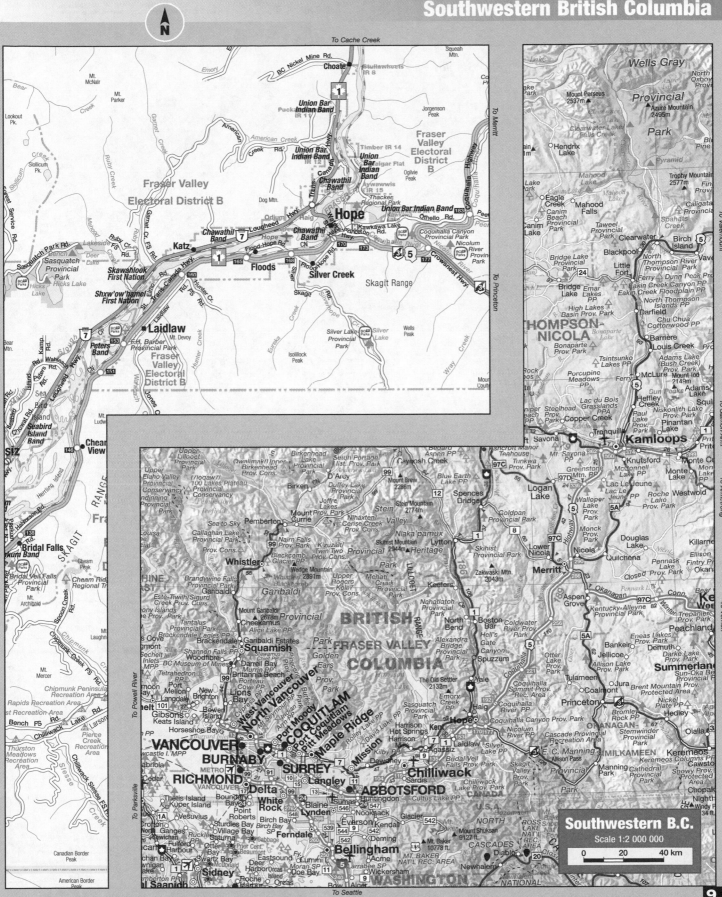

Southwestern B.C.

Scale 1:2 000 000

0    20    40 km

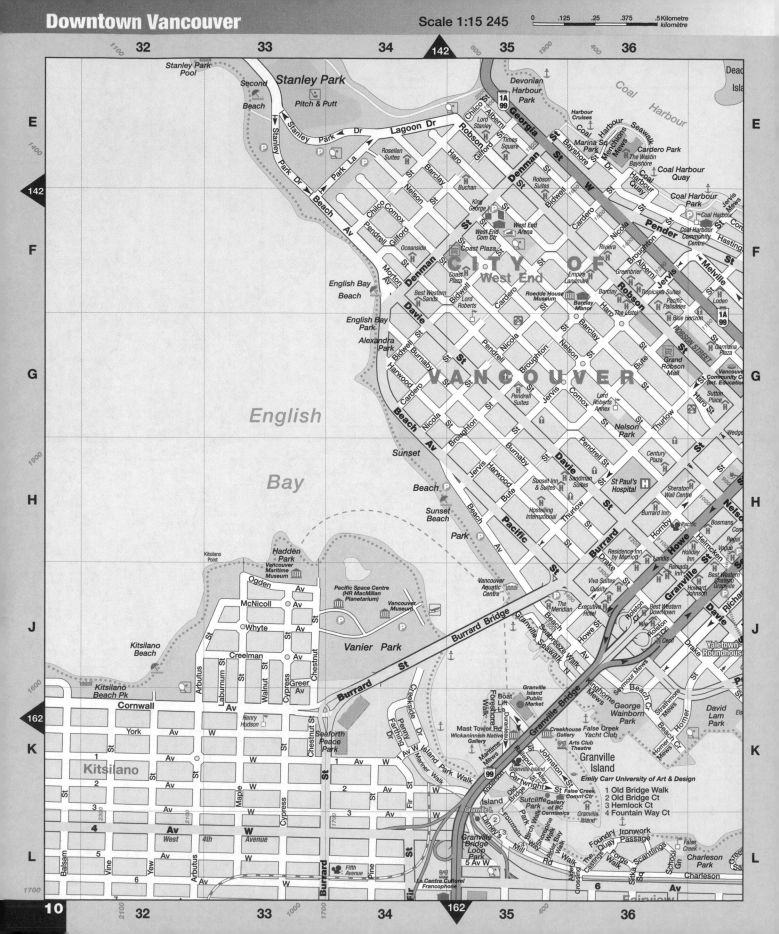

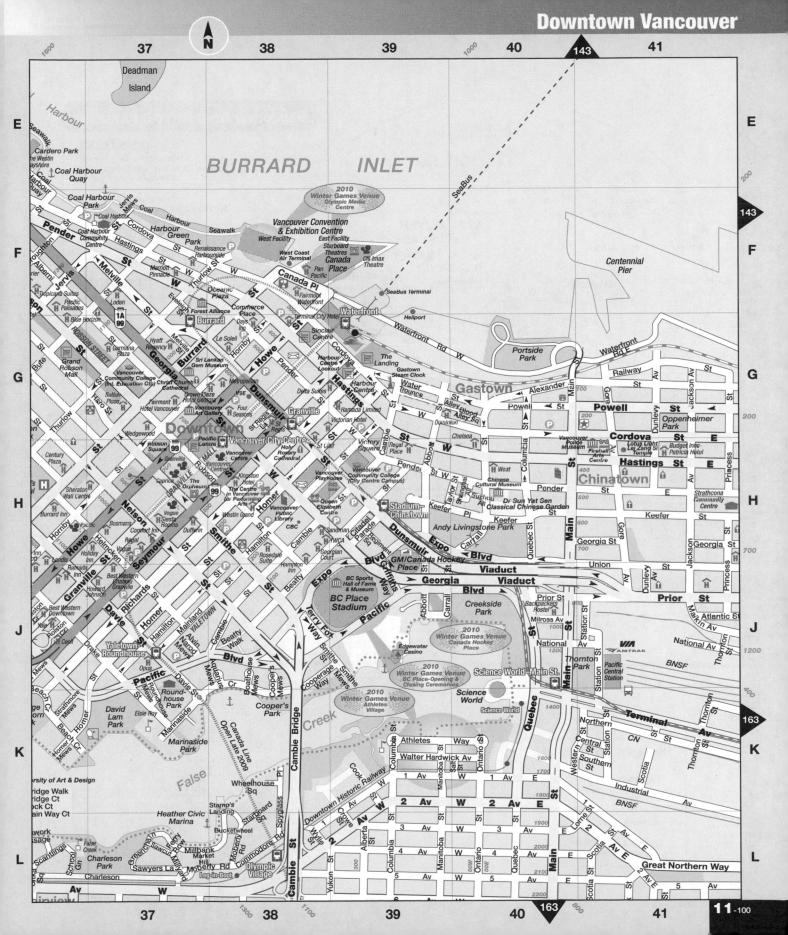

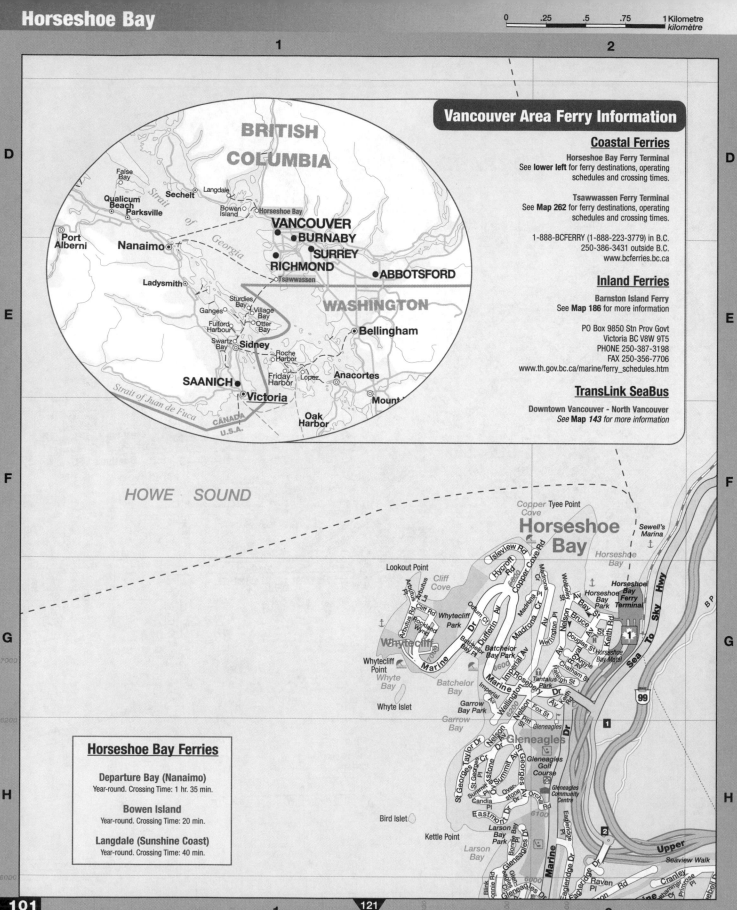

0 | .25 | .5 | .75 | 1 Kilometre
kilomètre

**BRITISH COLUMBIA**

False Bay
Sechelt • Langdale
Qualicum Beach
Parksville
Bowen Island • Horseshoe Bay
**VANCOUVER**
Strait of Georgia
Port Alberni
Nanaimo
• **BURNABY**
• **SURREY**
**RICHMOND**
Ladysmith
Tsawwassen
• **ABBOTSFORD**
Sturdies Bay
**WASHINGTON**
Ganges
Village Bay
Fulford Harbour
Otter Bay
Swartz Bay
Sidney
Roche Harbor
• **Bellingham**
**SAANICH**
Friday Harbor
Lopez
Anacortes
• **Victoria**
Mount
Strait of Juan de Fuca
CANADA
U.S.A.
Oak Harbor

## Vancouver Area Ferry Information

### Coastal Ferries

**Horseshoe Bay Ferry Terminal**
See **lower left** for ferry destinations, operating schedules and crossing times.

**Tsawwassen Ferry Terminal**
See **Map 262** for ferry destinations, operating schedules and crossing times.

1-888-BCFERRY (1-888-223-3779) in B.C.
250-386-3431 outside B.C.
www.bcferries.bc.ca

### Inland Ferries

**Barnston Island Ferry**
See **Map 186** for more information

PO Box 9850 Stn Prov Govt
Victoria BC V8W 9T5
PHONE 250-387-3198
FAX 250-356-7706
www.th.gov.bc.ca/marine/ferry_schedules.htm

### TransLink SeaBus

Downtown Vancouver - North Vancouver
See **Map 143** for more information

*HOWE SOUND*

Copper Cove • Tyee Point
**Horseshoe Bay**
Sewell's Marina
Lookout Point
Cliff Cove
Isleview Rd
Hygrott Rd
Copper Cove Rd
Horseshoe Bay
Horseshoe Bay Park
**Horseshoe Bay Ferry Terminal**
Madrona
Whytecliff Park
Arbutus Rd
Cliff Rd
Rockland Wynd
Dufferin Av
Odum Dr
Madrona Cr
Wellesley St
Nelson
Bruce Av
Keith Rd
Horseshoe Bay Motel
**Whytecliff**
Marine Dr
Batchelor Bay Park
Batchelor Bay Park
Imperial Av
Wellington
Douglas St
Argyle
Chatham St
Tantalus Park
Sea To Sky Hwy
Whytecliff Point
Rosebery
Fox St
Keith Rd
1
B P
*Whyte Bay*
Batchelor Bay
Whyte Islet
Garrow Bay Park
Imperial
Marine Dr
Nelson
Wallington
Gleneagles
*Garrow Bay*
Pitt
**99**
St Georges Taylor Dr
Nelson Dr
Summit Av
St Georges
**Gleneagles**
1
St Georges Pl
Firestone
St Georges
Summit Av
Overdale
Gleneagles Golf Course
Gleneagles Community Centre
Bird Islet
Summit Pl
Candia Pl
**Eastmon**
Larson Bay Park
Orchill Rd
Eagleridge Dr
Kettle Point
Larson Bay Dr
2
Marine
*Larson Bay*
Bonnie
Gleneagles
Blink Bonnie Rd
Gleneagles
Eagleridge Dr
**Upper**
Raven Pl
Cranley
Seaview Walk
Primrose

### Horseshoe Bay Ferries

**Departure Bay (Nanaimo)**
Year-round. Crossing Time: 1 hr. 35 min.

**Bowen Island**
Year-round. Crossing Time: 20 min.

**Langdale (Sunshine Coast)**
Year-round. Crossing Time: 40 min.

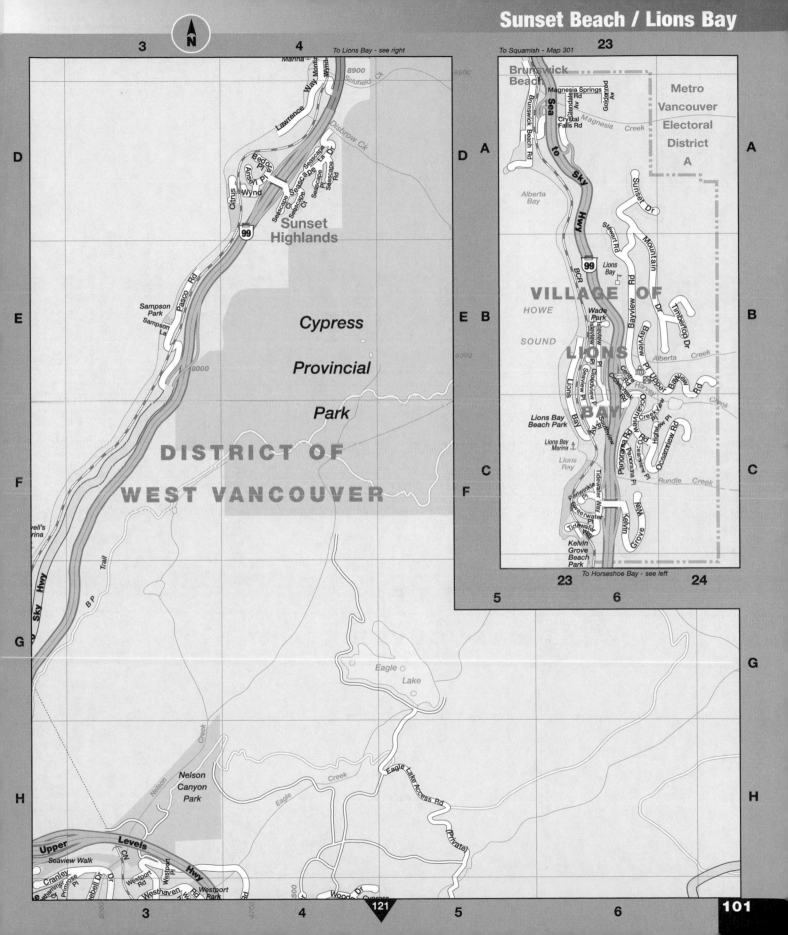

N

3    4    To Lions Bay - see right    To Squamish - Map 301    23

Marina
Way Montiz
Wynd
8900
Setofield Ck

Brunswick
Beach

Magnesia Springs
Rd
Glendale Av
Goldenrod Av

Metro
Vancouver
Electoral
District
A

Lawrence
Disbrow Ck

Brunswick Beach Rd
Sea
Crystal Falls Rd
Magnesia
Creek

D    A    A

Bedora Pl
Ansel Pl
Seascape Dr
Seascape La Dr
Seascape Rd

Alberta
Bay

Sunset Dr

Citrus
Wynd
Seascape Ct
Seascape Ch
Piscape Ct

to

Stewart Rd

Mountain

99

Sunset
Highlands

Sky

Bayview Rd

Timbertop Dr

Hwy

99
BCR
Lions
Bay

E    B

Sampson
Park
Sampson La

Pasco Rd

HOWE

SOUND

VILLAGE OF

Wade
Park
Iseaview
Iseaview Pl
Cloudview Pl

Bayview Dr

Alberta
Creek

B

8000

Cypress

LIONS

Centre
Rd
Upper Harvey
Crosscreek Rd

Bayview Rd

Provincial

Seaview Pl

Lions Bay

Oceanview Rd
Creekview Pl

Highview Pl
Oceanview Rd

Park

Lions Bay
Beach Park

BAY

Southview

Panorama Rd
Panorama Pl
seaview Pl

Rundle Creek    C

DISTRICT OF

Lions Bay
Marina

Lions
Ray

Kelvin
Grove

8000

WEST VANCOUVER

F

Partwinkle Way
Sweetwater Pl

Tidewater Way

Tidewater Way

Kelvin
Grove
Beach
Park

To Horseshoe Bay - see left

23    24

Lidwell's
Marina

Sky Hwy

BP Trail

E

F

5    6

G

Eagle
Lake

G

Nelson
Canyon
Park

Eagle Lake Access Rd

H    H

Nelson
Creek

Eagle
Creek

(Private)

Upper    Levels

Seaview Walk

CN

Cranley

Primrose Pl
rebell Dr
thanningrose Ct
Westport Pl
Westport Rd
Westhaven Rd
Hwy
Westport
Park
Woode Dr
Cypress

3    4    5    6

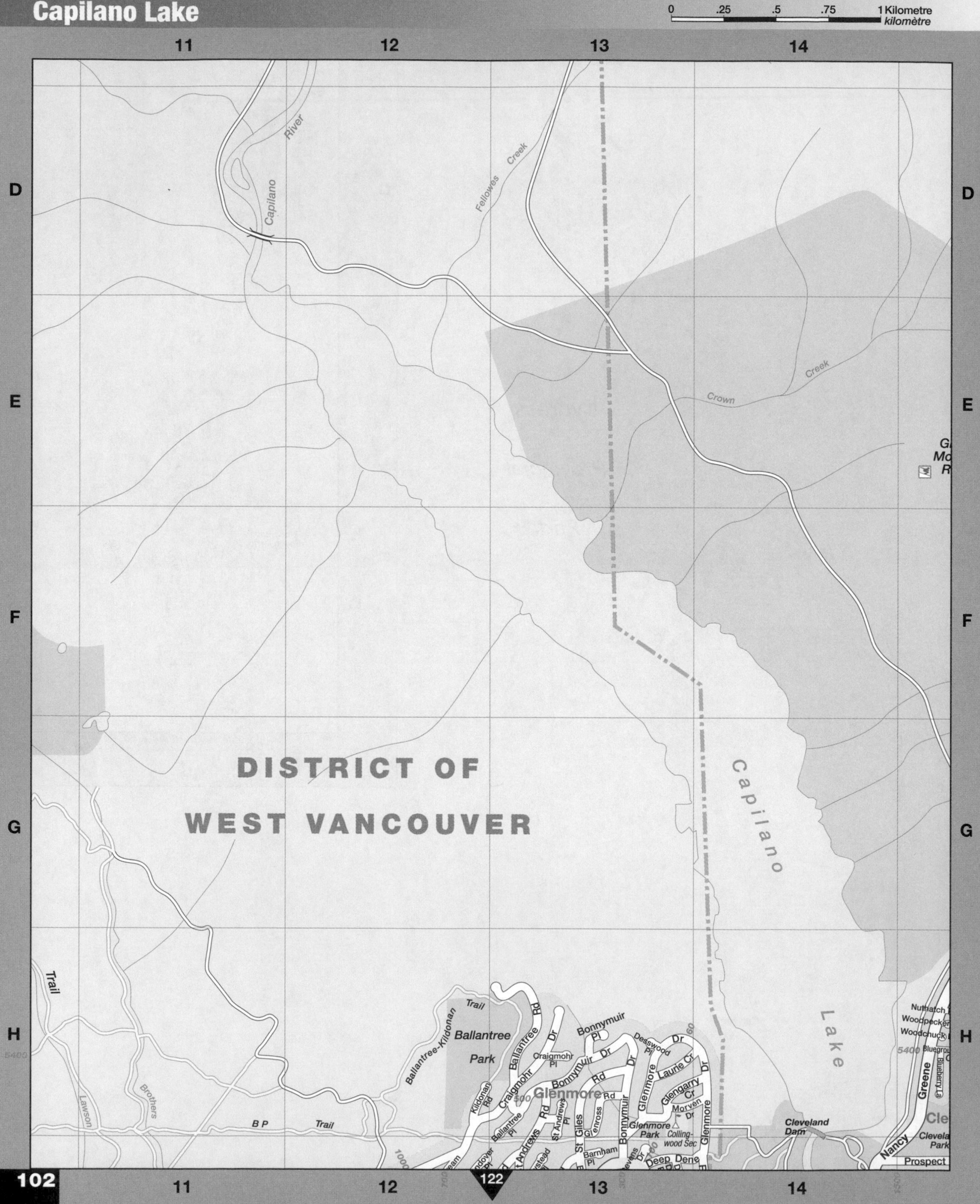

0  .25  .5  .75  1 Kilometre
*kilomètre*

**11**    **12**    **13**    **14**

D

*Capilano River*

*Fellowes Creek*

D

E

*Crown Creek*

E

Gl
Mo
R

F

F

# DISTRICT OF

## WEST VANCOUVER

*Capilano*

G

G

*Trail*

*Lake*

Nuthatch

Woodpecker

Woodchuck

H

*5480*

*Brothers*

*Ballantree-Kildonan Trail*

Ballantree
Park

Bonnymuir Pl

Craigmohr Pl

Desswood Dr

Laurie Cr

Greene

H

*5400*

Bluegro

*Lawson*

B P    Trail

Craigmohr Rd
Kildonan Rd

Ballantree Dr

Andover

Ballantree

Genross

St Andrews Rd

St Giles

Glenmore

Glenross

Bonnymuir Rd

Glenmore Rd

Glengarry Cr

Morven

Glenmore Dr

Cleveland Dam

Cleveland
Park

Nancy

Cle

Glenmore
Park

Collingwood Sec

*1000*

*700 Stream*

Barnham Pl

St Andrews

Deep Dene

Prospect

**11**    **12**    **122**    **13**    **14**

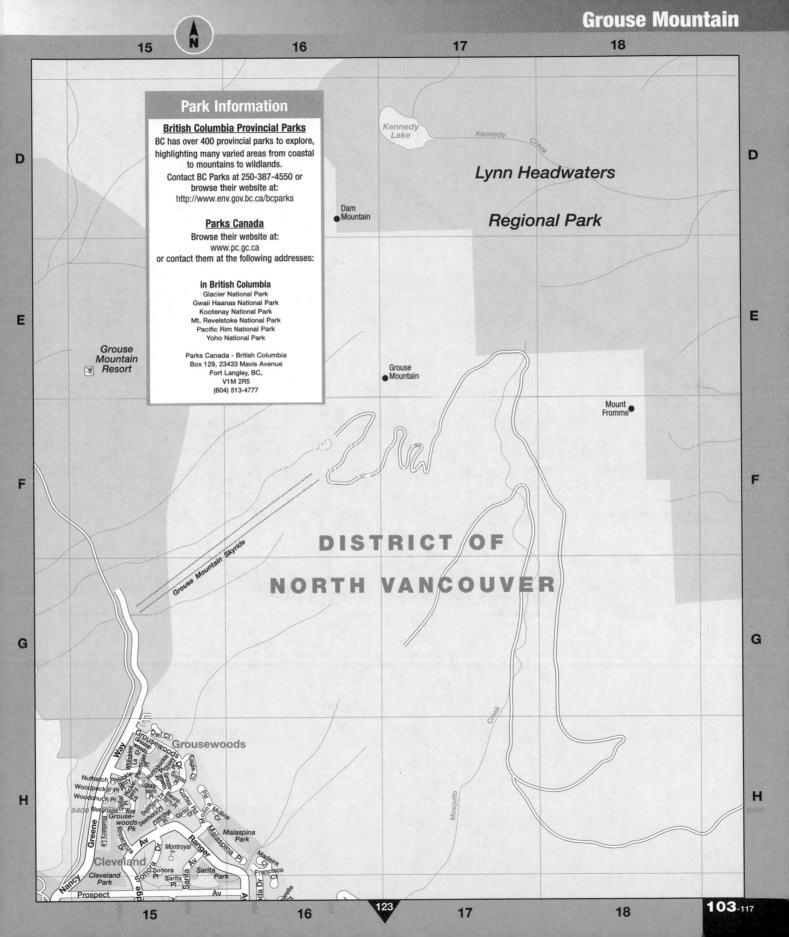

## Park Information

### British Columbia Provincial Parks

BC has over 400 provincial parks to explore, highlighting many varied areas from coastal to mountains to wildlands.

Contact BC Parks at 250-387-4550 or browse their website at: http://www.env.gov.bc.ca/bcparks

### Parks Canada

Browse their website at: www.pc.gc.ca or contact them at the following addresses:

**in British Columbia**
Glacier National Park
Gwaii Haanas National Park
Kootenay National Park
Mt. Revelstoke National Park
Pacific Rim National Park
Yoho National Park

Parks Canada - British Columbia
Box 129, 23433 Mavis Avenue
Fort Langley, BC,
V1M 2R5
(604) 513-4777

Kennedy Lake

Kennedy Creek

*Lynn Headwaters*

*Regional Park*

Dam Mountain

Grouse Mountain Resort

Grouse Mountain

Mount Fromme

Grouse Mountain Skyride

## DISTRICT OF

## NORTH VANCOUVER

Grousewoods

Cleveland

Cleveland Park

Malaspina Park

Sarita Park

Montroyal

Francisco

Mosquito Creek

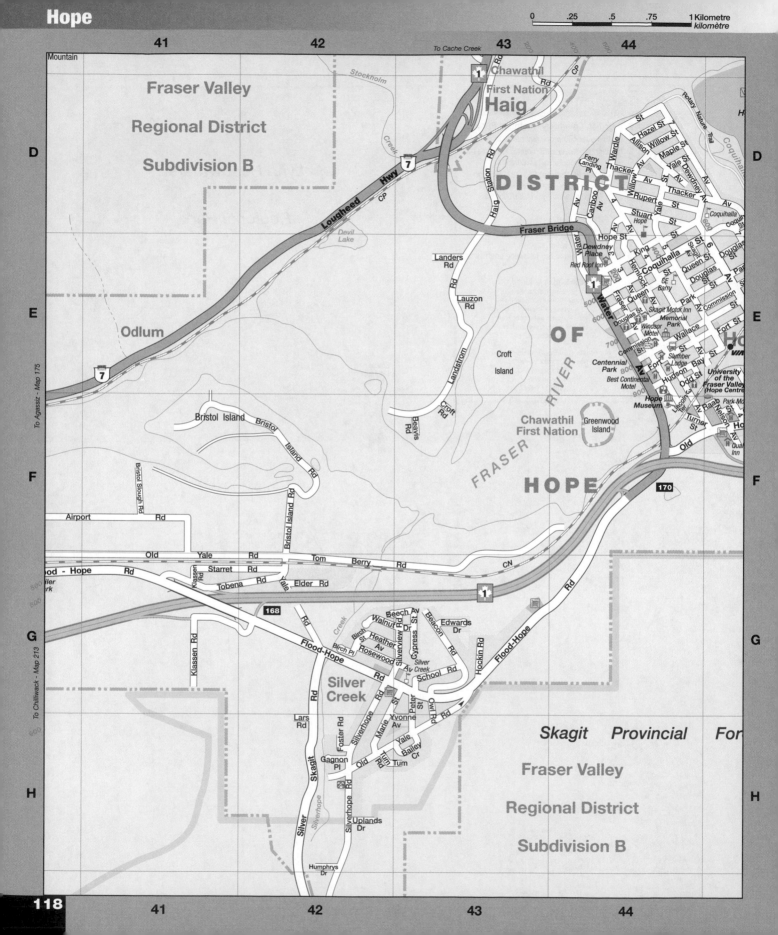

Mountain

Fraser Valley

Regional District

Subdivision B

Odlum

To Cache Creek

Chawathil
First Nation
Haig

DISTRICT

OF

RIVER

FRASER

HOPE

Chawathil
First Nation

Greenwood
Island

Croft
Island

Bristol Island

Landers
Rd

Lauzon
Rd

Landstrom

Croft
Rd

Beavis
Rd

Bristol Island Rd

Bristol Slough Rd

Airport        Rd

Old     Yale     Rd

Starret

Klassen Rd

Tobena     Rd

Elder   Rd

Tom     Berry      Rd

CN

Rd

Skagit Provincial For

Fraser Valley

Regional District

Subdivision B

Silver
Creek

Flood-Hope

Beech Av

Walnut

Heather

Rosewood

Birch Pl
Birch St

Cypress

Silverview

Silver
Creek
School Rd

Beacon

Edwards
Dr

Flood-Hope     Rd

Hockin Rd

Klassen Rd

Lars
Rd

Foster Rd

Silverhope

Marie

Gagnon
Pl

Old
Rd

Tum
Rd

Yale

Bailey
Cr

Tum

Peter
St

Owl Rd

Yvonne
Av

Silver

Skagit

Silverhope

Silverhope Dr

Uplands
Dr

Humphrys
Dr

Lougheed        Hwy

Stockholm

Creek

Devil
Lake

CP

Haig
Station
Rd

Fraser Bridge

Water

Coquihalla

Wardle

Thacker

Cariboo
Av

Hazel St
Allison
Willow St

Maple St

Yale
Dewdney Av

Rupert
St

Thacker
Av

Stuart
Hope

Yale
St

Coquihalla
Av

Hope St

King

Dewdney
Place

Queen
St

Douglas
St

Fraser

Queen

Douglas

Commission

Fort St

Skagit Motor Inn

Memorial
Park

Windsor
Motel

Wallace

Commission

Fort

Hudson

Slumber
Lodge

Odd St

Lincoln
St

Centennial
Park

Best Continental
Motel

Hope
Museum

Turner
St

Raab

Nelson

University
of the
Fraser Valley
(Hope Centre

Old

Red Roof Inn

Ferry
Landing
Pl

Rotary Nature Trail

Coquihalla

Quai
Inn

To Agassiz - Map 175

To Chilliwack - Map 213

0    .25    .5    .75    1 Kilometre
kilomètre

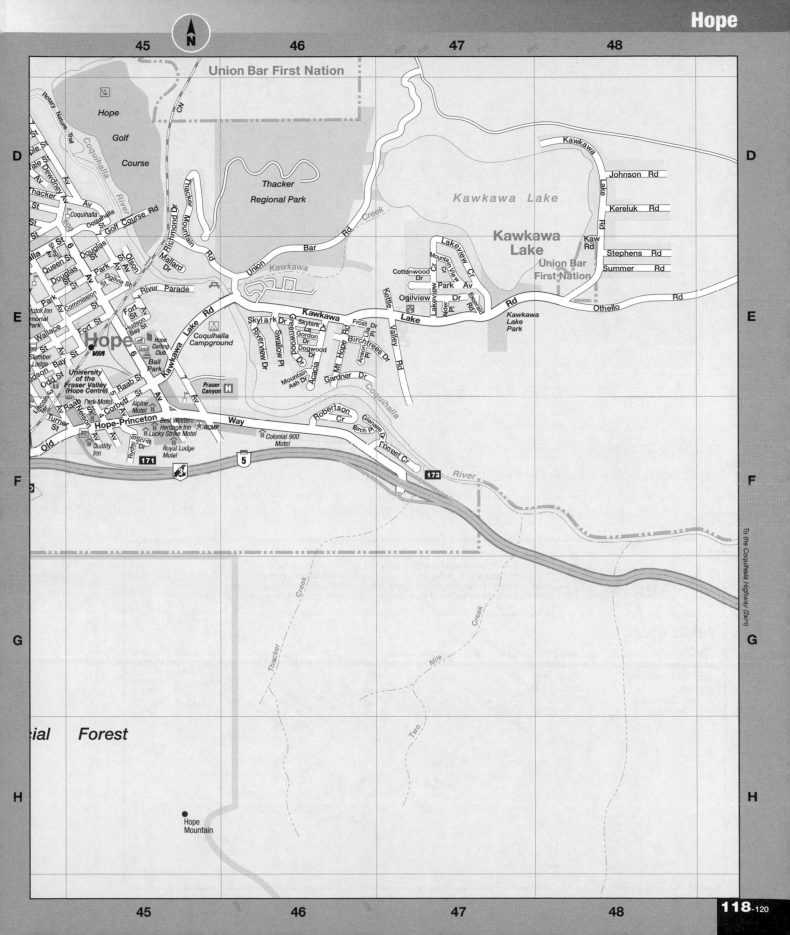

0    .25    .5    .75    1 Kilometre
                                  *kilomètre*

1          ▼ **101**          2

## J

Batchelor Point

Glenmore Rd · Blink · Bonnie Rd · Glenmore Pl · Glenmore · Glenwynn Dr · Glenwynn Pl · Glenmore Dr · Gleneagles Dr · Glenegal Pl · Eagleridge Dr · Eagleridge Pl · Eagleridge · Raven Rd · Falcon · Rothermere Ct · Condor Pl · **Fishermans Cove** · **Marine** Dr

Parry Island

Tall Trees Park

*Fishermans Cove*

Seaview Walk

Telegraph · Larson

Abode Island

Eagle Is

Eagle Is

Seaview · Eagle · Seaview Pl · Maple La

Seaview Harbour

Avalon Pl

**E** · Ea Ha

Eagle Creek Pl

Eagle Island

Eagle Harbour Park

Keith Rd

Gallagher Pl

Eagle Harbour

Parthenon Park

Parthenon Pl

Balmy Beach

Kew Cliff Rd

## HOWE SOUND

Kew Beach Park

Kew Cliff · Kew Cliff Ct · Greentree Rd · The Terrace

Erwin Point

Seaside Pl · Kew Rd

Gulf Beach Park

Kew Rd · Gulf Rd · Kew

Fri Par

Caulfe

## K

East Island
Grebe Islets

Pitcairn · Mariner · The La · Crestway

West Island

High Rock Passage

Klootchman Park

Keith Rd

M

Indian Bluff

Happy Valley La · Howe Sound La · BeaC

## L

Juniper Point

*Lighth*

Shore Pine Point

Atkinso Lighthou

Point Atkinson

---

## Public Transit Inset

**TRANS LINK**

**Public Transit**

*SkyTrain, SeaBus, and West Coast Express lines are shown on all maps. Bus lines are not shown.*

SkyTrain, SeaBus, and West Coast Express lines are depicted on all maps in this atlas. Bus lines are not depicted.
For information call Translink at 953-3333 or check out the website at www.translink.bc.ca

| |  |
|---|---|
| ▭▭▭ | West Coast Express |
| ▬▬ | Seabus |
| ▬▬ | SkyTrain Expo Line |
| ─── | Sky Train Millennium Line |
| ••• | Canada Line Opening August 2009 |

North Vancouver

SEABUS

Waterfront
Granville · Stadium–Chinatown
Burrard · Science World–Main Street
Vancouver City Centre
Yaletown–Roundhouse
Olympic Village
Broadway–City Hall
VCC/Clark · Commercial Dr · Renfrew · Rupert · Gilmore · Brentwood Town Centre · Holdom · Sperling–Burnaby Lake · Lake City Way · Production Way–University · Lougheed Town Centre · Port Moody · Coquitlam Central

Broadway
King Edward

**WEST COAST EXPRESS to Pitt Meadows Maple Meadows Port Haney Mission** →

Oakridge–41st Av
Langara–49th Av

Nanaimo
29th Av
Joyce–Collingwood

Marine Drive

Port Coquitlam

Patterson
Metrotown

Braid

Royal Oak

Sapperton

Edmonds

Columbia

New Westminster

22nd St

Scott Road

Gateway

Surrey Central

King George

YVR–Airport
Sea Island Centre
Templeton
Aberdeen
Bridgeport
Lansdowne
Richmond–Brighouse

© mapmobility

1                    2

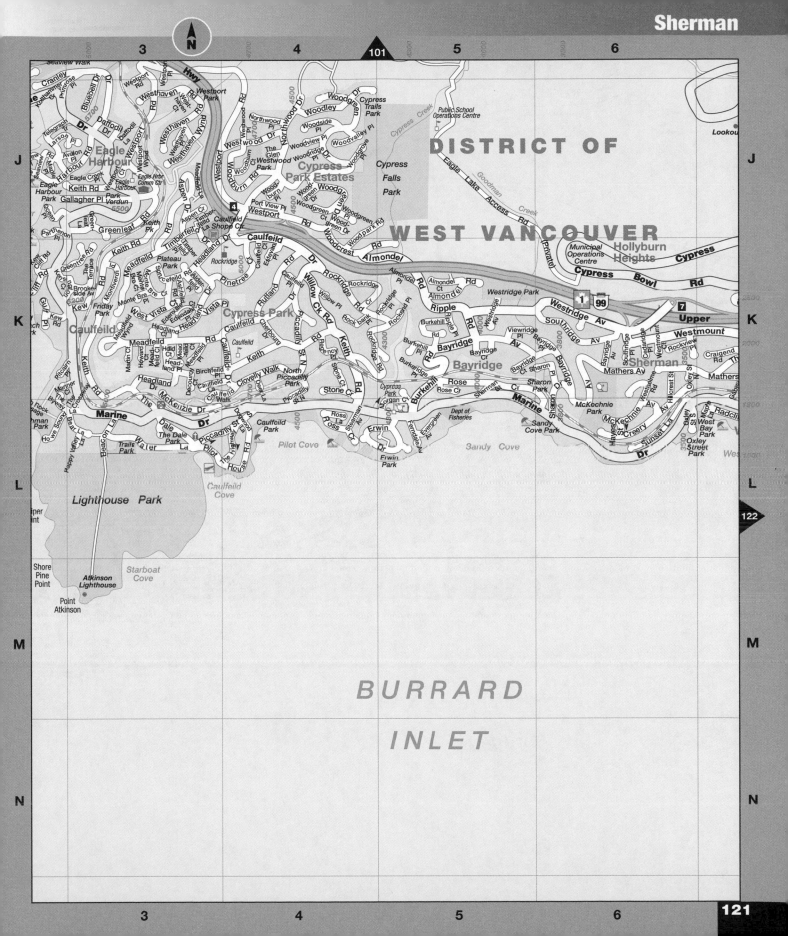

DISTRICT OF

WEST VANCOUVER

Eagle Harbour

Cypress Park Estates

Cypress Falls Park

Cypress Park

Caulfeild

Bayridge

Sherman

Lighthouse Park

Starboat Cove

Atkinson Lighthouse

Shore Pine Point

Point Atkinson

Sandy Cove

Pilot Cove

Caulfeild Cove

B U R R A R D

I N L E T

0  .25  .5  .75  1 Kilometre
kilomètre

7    8    9    10

To Cypress Provincial Park

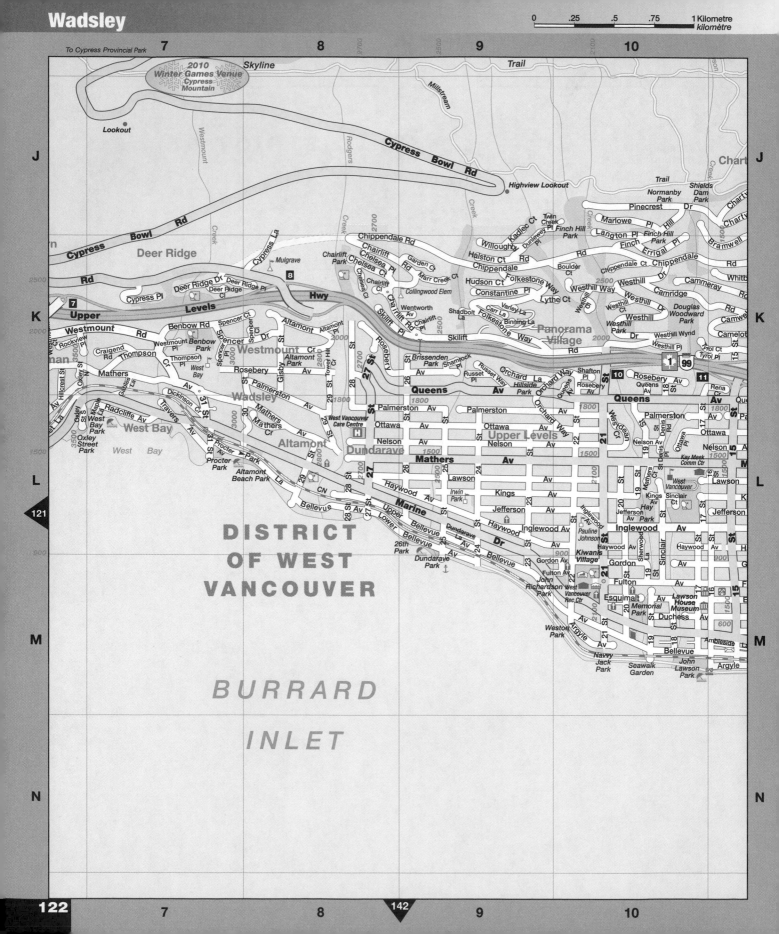

2010
Winter Games Venue
Cypress
Mountain

Skyline

Trail

Millstream

Lookout

Highview Lookout

Cypress Bowl Rd

J                                                                                                    J
Chart

Trail
Normanby
Park

Shields
Dam
Park

Pinecrest    Dr

Marlowe    Pl    Finch Hill
Langton  Pl  Finch Hill  Park

Cypress    Bowl    Rd
Deer Ridge

Chippendale Rd

Chairlift
Park

Willough by

Kadlec Ct
Dunlewey Pl

Finch

Errigal Pl
Bramwell

Chartw

Chartw

Cypress La
Mulgrave

Chairlift  Chelsea Ct
Chelsea Cl

Garden Ct
Marr Creek Ct

Halston Ct    Rd
Chippendale

Boulder
Ct

Chippendale Ct  Chippendale

Rd

Whitb

Cypress

Bowl

Rd

Deer Ridge    Deer Ridge Dr
Deer Ridge Pl
Deer Ridge

Chelsea Cl

Collingwood Elem

Hudson Ct
Constantine Pl
Folkestone Way
Varley La

Lythe Ct

Westhill    Dr
Westhill Way

Westhill

Camridge

Cammeray    Rd

Upper                                    Levels           Hwy

Wentworth
Av

Shadbolt
La

Carr La
Binning La

Folkestone

Way

Westhill
Ct

Westhill
Park    Dr

Douglas
Woodward
Park

Camwe

K    Cypress Pl                                                                                       K
Westmount    Rd

Benbow Rd    Spencer Ct
Altamont
Pl

Skilift
Rd    Skilift

Panorama
Village

Westhill

Westhill Wynd
Westhill Pl

Camelot

Upper

Rockview
Craigend    Rd
Thompson    Cr

Benbow
Park

Altamont
Park

Brissenden
Park    Shamrock
Pl

Orchard La

Shafton
Pl

Rd

Tyrol Ct
Tyrol Pl

15

Westmount    Rd

Spencer

Spencer
Dr

Altamont
Pl

Roseberry

St

Russet Way
Russet
Pl

Hillside
Park

Orchard Way

Queens
Av
Roseberry

St    10    Roseberry    Queens Av

11
Rena
Cr

Okley St
Hillcrest St

Mathers

Gisby    St

Thompson
Pl

West
Bay

Roseberry    Av
Tower Hill Rd

26

Queens    Av

Palmerston    Av

Queens

27 St

18 St

Av

Que

West
Bay
Park

Maple

Radcliffe Av

Palmerston

Av

Wadsley

Mathers
Mathers
Cr

27 St

West Vancouver
Care Centre

Palmerston    Av

Ottawa    Av
Nelson

Av

Upper Levels

Palmerston
Westdean

Nelson Av
Ottawa

15

L    Oxley                                                                                           L
West Bay    Park
Oxley Street
Park

West Bay

Travers
Av

Dickinson Ct
Procter
La

Altamont
Park

Dundarave
La Av

28 St

27 St

Mathers
Av

1500

Nelson
Av

1500

Av    Lawson

Av

St Denis Rd

21 St

19 St    Denis

Kay Meek
Comm Ctr

West Vancouver

Lawson

Jefferson

Altamont
Beach Park

CN

Haywood
Av

26 St

Upper    Bellevue

Lawson

Kings
Jefferson

24

23 St

Inglewood Av

Inglewood

Pauline
Johnson

Sherwood

Jefferson  Hay
Av  Kings
Sinclair
Ct

Haywood  Av

17 St

Jefferson

Bellevue

Lower    Bellevue
26th
Park

Dundarave
Park

Dundarave
Av

Bellevue

Haywood
Av

Gordon Av

Kiwanis
Village

Sherwood    Haywood  Av

900

M    **DISTRICT**                                                                                   M
**OF WEST**
**VANCOUVER**

Marine    Dr

Fulton Av

John
Richardson
Park

West
Vancouver
Rec Ctr

Gordon
Fulton

Esquimalt

Memorial
Park

Lawson
House
Museum

Duchess

21 St

19 St

18 St

17 St

600

Weston
Park

Argyle

Av

Bellevue

Ambleside

Navvy
Jack Park

Seawalk
Garden

John
Lawson
Park

Argyle

**BURRARD**

**INLET**

N                                                                                                    N

121

142

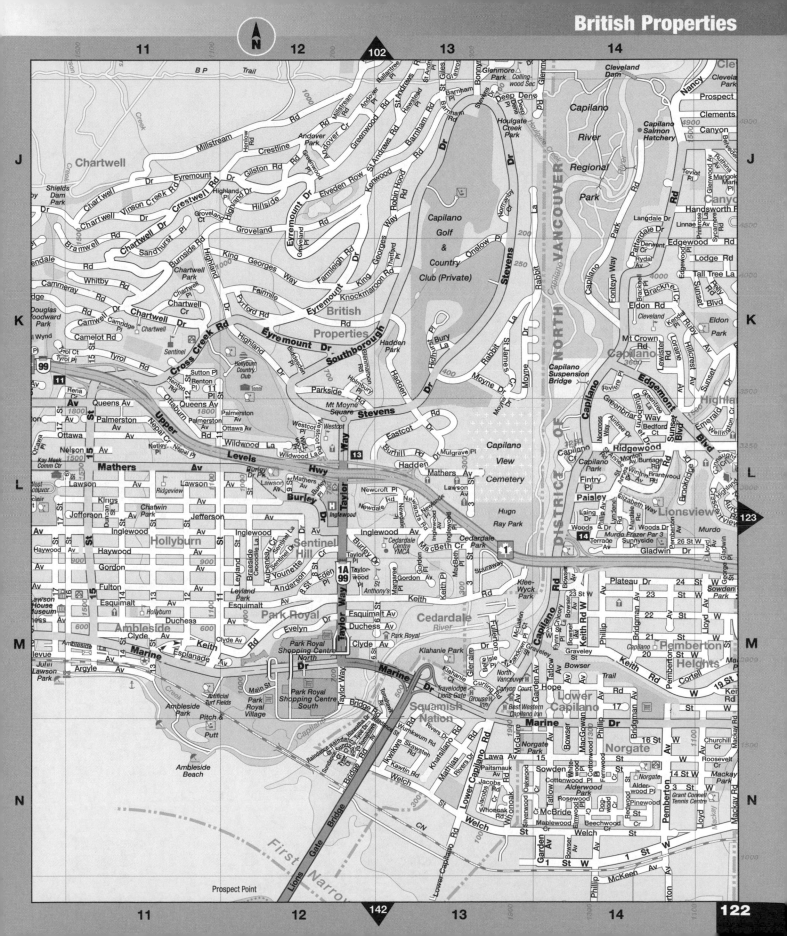

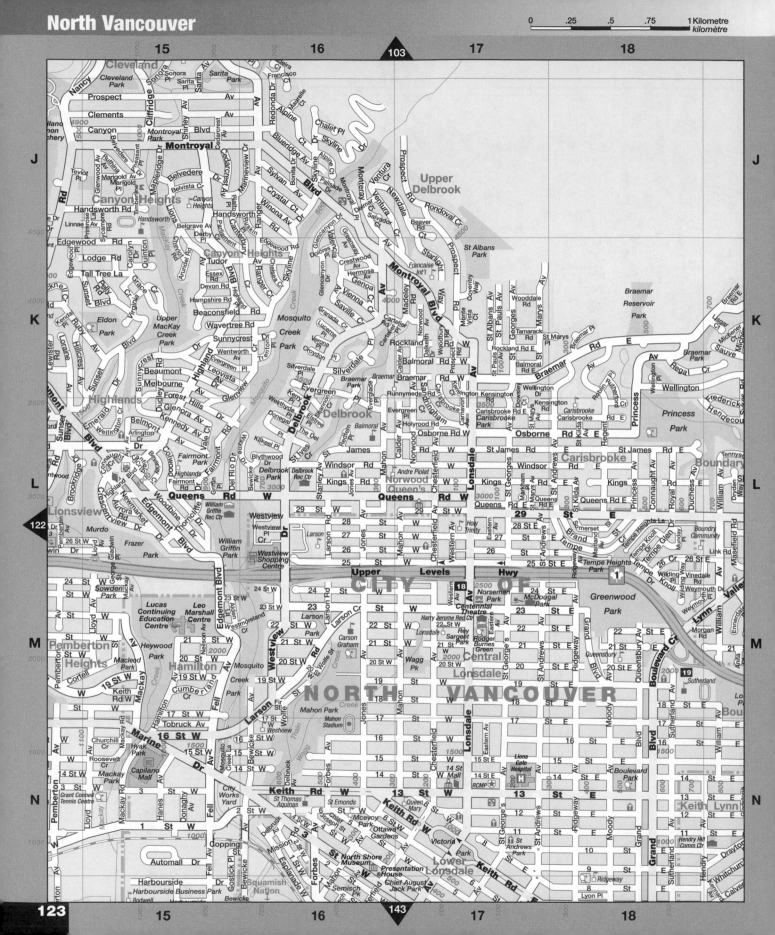

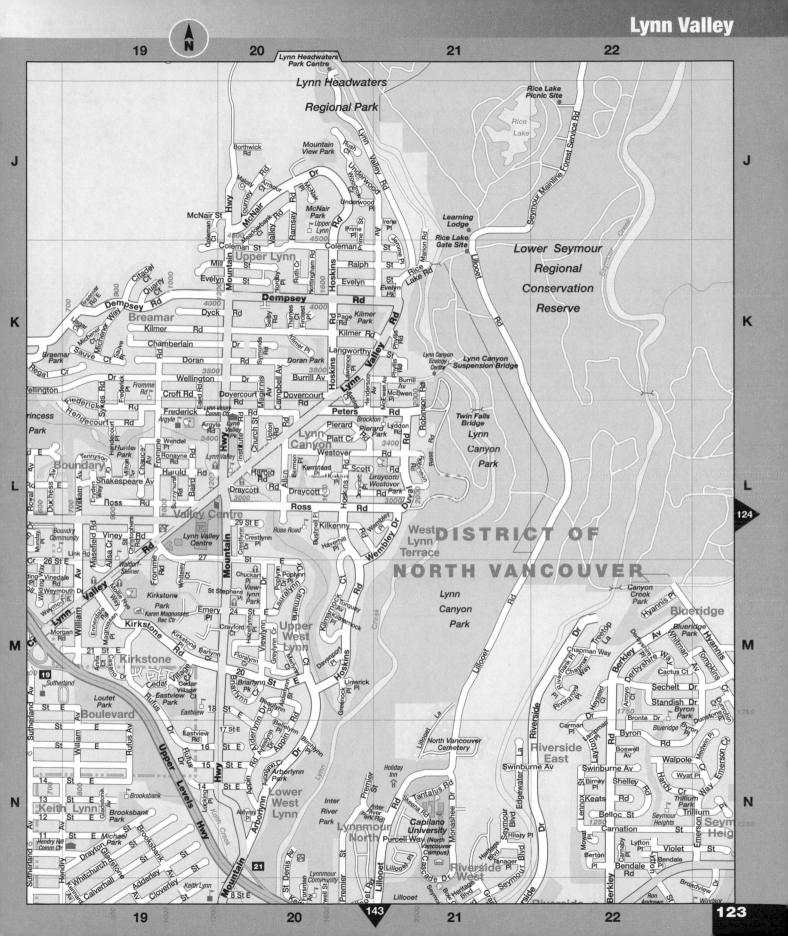

0   .25   .5   .75   1 Kilometre
kilomètre

**Tourism British Columbia**
For information call:
1-800-435-5622
Or on the internet:
www.hellobc.com

J

Seymour
Group Campsite

Deep Cove
Lookout

J

K

Lower  Seymour
Regional
Conservation
Reserve

Vancouver Picnic Area

K

L

123

Mount  Seymour
Provincial
Park

Mount Seymour Rd

Indian River Dr

L

## DISTRICT OF

## NORTH VANCOUVER

Deep
Cove

Deep
Cove

Panorama

M

Blueridge

Blueridge
Park

Whitman

Hyannis Pl

Hyannis

Hill

Mary
Kirk Pl

Blairview
Av

Dr

Way

Tompkins

Cactus Ct

Sechelt Dr

Dresden
Way

Standish Dr

Dunstone

Byron
Park

Blueridge

Byron

Cr

Medium Pl

Rd

Larkhall

Orkney Pl

Walpole

Wyat Pl

Emerson Cr

Emerson
Way

Hardy
Cr

Trillium
Park

McCartney
Creek Park

Trillium

Seymour
Heights
St

**Seymour
Heights**

Violet
St

Bendale
Pl

Northlands

Cr

**McCartney
Woods**

Northlands
Park

Strathaven

Northlands
Golf

Course

Gaspe Pl

Taylor
Creek Park

Anne  MacDonald  Way

**Northlands**

**Parkgate**

Parkgate
Park

Northlands

Parkgate

Parkgate
Comm Ctr

Parkgate
Village

Mount Seymour Rd

Banff Ct

Indian
Jubilee
Ct

Hamber Pl

Oriohma

Bishop
Pl

Indian
River
Park

Brockton
Pl

Norton

Lighthall

Cascade

Felix

Deane Pl

Ostler

Percy

Goldie

Brockton
Cr

Mystery
Cr

Frames
Ct

Frames

**Indian
River**

River
Dr

Cowdell Rd

Dorothy
Lynas

Violet
St

Beaufort Rd

Russell Av

Russell Rd

Lima Rd

Beaufort

Ct

Rhone
Ct

Indian River Cr

Hilon

Hixon
Ct

2000

Badger
Pl

1800

Badger
Rd

Caledonia Av

**Deep
Cove**

Panorama
Park

Gallant Av

*Deep Cove Lookout*

Naughton
La

Burns Av

Eastleigh La

Banbury

Panorama Dr

Caledonia Cove

Cliffwood

Cliffmont
Rd

1400

Caledonia
Cove

Deep Cove Rd

Deep Cove Rd

Deane

Seycove

Cliffwood
Rd

Eastleigh Rd

Raeburn

Cliffmont
Rd

Cove
Cliff
Rd

Deep
Cove
Park

Cove Cliff

Summerside La

**Cove Cliff**

Myrtle
Park

Deep
Cove

Rockcliff Rd

St

Parkside La

Lockehaven
Rd

Wicke

Eastri

Lockehaven
Pl

Wickenden Rd

Strathcona
Way

Strathcona
Park

Strathcona Rd

Epps Av

Stonehaven Av

Harris Pl

White Rock

**Strathcona**

M

N

Mount

**Seymour**

**Pkwy**

Gdon
Cr

Kinloch

Kinloch
Rd

Banbury Rd

Caledonia Av

Blvd

1000

Broadview

Windsor

Brixham
Rd

Plymouth
Pl

Tollcross Rd

Strathaven
La

Huntleigh Cr

Apex Av

Manning

Manning
Pl

Bowron

Garibaldi
Dr

Dr

144

3600

4000

N

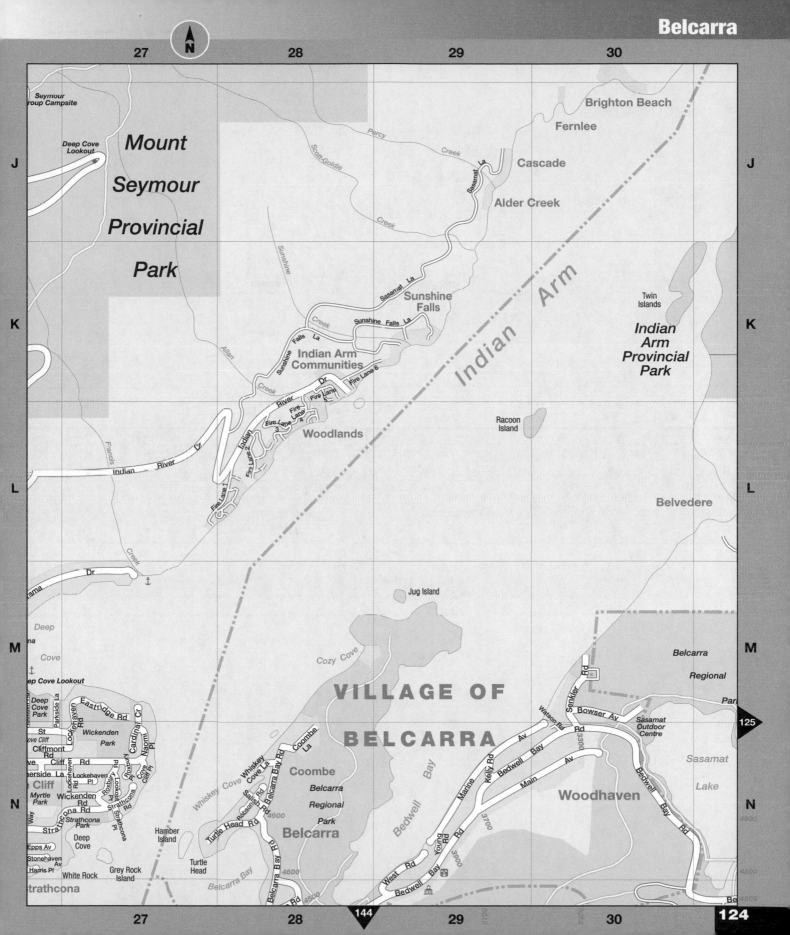

N

27    28    29    30

Seymour Group Campsite

Deep Cove Lookout

J

**Mount**

**Seymour**

**Provincial**

**Park**

Percy    Creek

Scott-Goldie

Creek

Brighton Beach

Fernlee

Sasamat La

Cascade

Alder Creek

K

Sunshine

Creek

Allan

Creek

Sunshine Falls La

Sunshine Falls La

Sasamat La

**Sunshine**

**Falls**

**Indian Arm**

**Communities**

Twin Islands

*Indian Arm Provincial Park*

Fire Lane 6

Dr

Fire Lane 5

River

Fire Lane 4

Fire Lane 3

Fire Lane 2

Indian

**Woodlands**

Racoon Island

Francis

Dr

Indian    River    Dr

Fire Lane 1

Creek

**Belvedere**

L

rama    Dr

⚓

Deep

na

Cove

⚓

Jug Island

Cozy Cove

Belcarra Regional

Par

125

M

ep Cove Lookout

Deep Cove Park

Parkside La

Eastridge Rd

Lockehaven

St

Wickenden Park

Cardinal Cr

Naomi    Pl

**VILLAGE OF**

**BELCARRA**

Senkler    Rd

Bowser Av

Watsop Rd

Rd    33000

Sasamat Outdoor Centre

ove Cliff

Cliffmont

Rd

ve    Cliff    Rd

Lockehaven    Rd

Cove    Cliff    Pl

Proxton    Pl

Lookout    Pl

Annorbog    Rd

Coombe La

Whiskey Cove La

Whiskey    Cove    Rd

Belcarra Bay Rd

**Coombe**

*Belcarra Regional Park*

Bedwell    Bay

Marine    Av

Kelly Rd

Bedwell    Bay

Main    Av

*Sasamat Lake*

**Woodhaven**

Bedwell    Bay    Rd

N

Myrtle Park

Wickenden    Rd

Strathcona    Rd

Strathcona    Rd

Strathcona    Pl

Strathcona    Park

**Deep Cove**

Turtle Head Rd

Robson Rd

Salish Rd

Rd    4900

**Belcarra**

Way

Epps Av

Stonehaven

Av

Harris Pl

Strathcona

White Rock

Grey Rock Island

Hamber Island

**Turtle**

**Head**

Belcarra    Bay    Rd    4600

Belcarra Bay

Rd    4500

West    Rd

Young    Rd

3900

Bedwell    Bay

Rd    3700

Be    4500

27    28    29    30

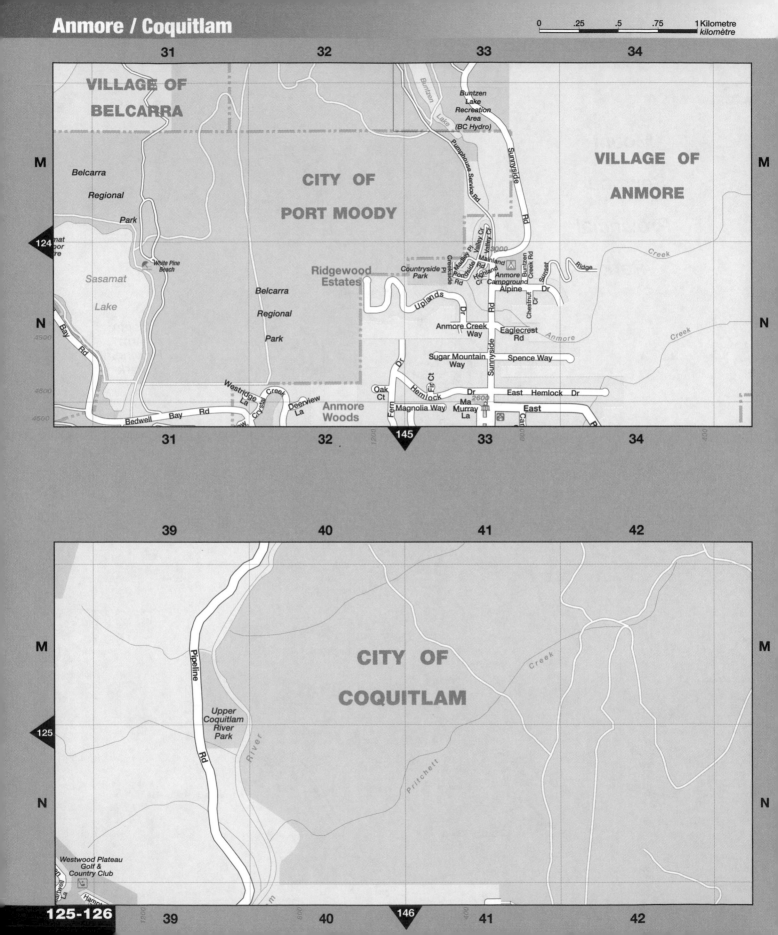

0   .25   .5   .75   1 Kilometre
                          *kilomètre*

**31**   **32**   **33**   **34**

M   M

**VILLAGE OF BELCARRA**

**CITY OF PORT MOODY**

Buntzen Lake Recreation Area (BC Hydro)

**VILLAGE OF ANMORE**

Sunnyside Rd

Pumphouse Service Rd

Belcarra Regional Park

124

White Pine Beach

Sasamat Lake

Ridgewood Estates

Countryside Park

Creek

Ridge

Creek

Creekside Rd

Oaside Rd

Manley Pl

Valley Cr

Valley Dr

Mainland

Highland

Buntzen Creek Rd

Sunset

Dr

Anmore Campground

Alpine

Chestnut Cr

N   N

Belcarra Regional Park

Anmore Creek Way

Uplands Dr

Sunnyside Rd

Eaglecrest Rd

Anmore Creek

Bay Rd

4500

4600

4500

Westridge La

Crystal Creek

Deerview La

Bedwell Bay Rd

Anmore Woods

Oak Ct

Fern Dr

Hemlock Dr

Fir Ct

Sugar Mountain Way

Magnolia Way

Ma Murray La

2600

Dr

East Hemlock Dr

Spence Way

East

1200

1200

**31**   **32**   ▼ **145**   **33**   **34**

---

**39**   **40**   **41**   **42**

M   M

**CITY OF COQUITLAM**

Pipeline Rd

Creek

125

Upper Coquitlam River Park

River

Pritchett

N   N

Westwood Plateau Golf & Country Club

1200

800

400

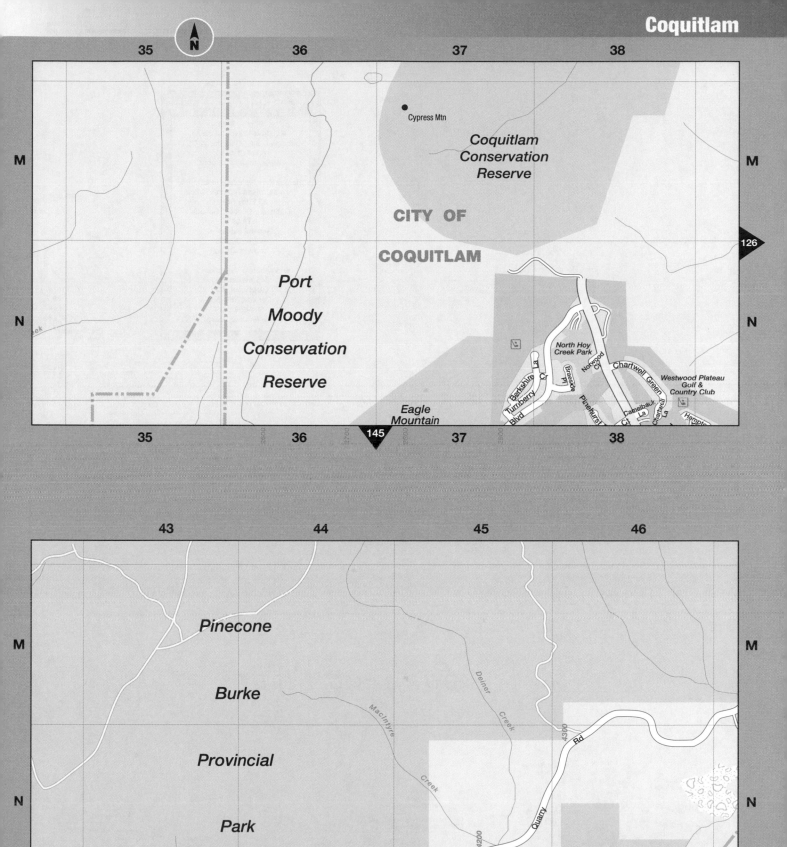

N

35  36  37  38

M

Cypress Mtn

Coquitlam
Conservation
Reserve

**CITY OF**

**COQUITLAM**

M

126

Port

Moody

Conservation

Reserve

North Hoy
Creek Park

N

Berkshire La

Turnberry

Cr

Braeside Pl

Norwood Ct

Chartwell Green

Westwood Plateau
Golf &
Country Club

N

Blvd

Pinehurst

Camelback La

Chartwell La

Hampto

Eagle
Mountain

Cr

35  36  145  37  38

43  44  45  46

M

Pinecone

M

Burke

Deiner

Creek

Provincial

Macintyre

4300 Rd

N

Park

Creek

4200

Quarry

N

43  44  146  45  46

0   .25   .5   .75   1 Kilometre
*kilomètre*

7     8     **122**     9     10

P

**Stanley Park**

Stanley Park
P.O. Box 1134, Station A
Vancouver, B.C., Canada, V6C 2T1
604-681-5115
www.stanleypark.com

Stanley Park National Historic Site
Parks Canada National Office
25 Eddy Street
Gatineau, Quebec, Canada
K1A 0M5
General Inquiries:
888-773-8888
www.pc.gc.ca

Vancouver Aquarium
845 Avison Way
Vancouver, B.C.
Canada, V6G 3E2
604-659-3474
www.vanaqua.org

P

*Siwash Rock*

*Promenade*

*Third Beach*

Q

*Seawall*

*Paulin Memo*

Q

*The Ferguson Point Tea House*

P

R     R

S     S

**BURRARD INLET**

SEE ENLARGEMENT PAGES 10-11

**161**

*Locarno Beach*

Jericho Sailing School

*Locarno Beach Park*

Trimble St

Hostelling Int'l

*Kitsilano Beach*

T     Simpson Av     *Jericho Beach Park*     Royal Vancouver Yacht Club     Pt Grey Rd     T

Belmont     Av     Jericho Beach     Cameron Av     Volunteer Park     Grey     Rd     **Cornwall**

Langara Av     Locarno Park     Old Hastings Mill Store     Hastings Mill Park     Point     Grey     Rd     York

Bellevue Dr     Sasamat St     Aberthau Cultural Centre at Aberthau     Point Grey     1     Av     Point     Grey     Rd     **Kitsilano**

Trimble St     Discovery St     2 Av     W     Jericho Park East     Wallace     Highbury St     Alma St     2     W     1700     Tatlow Park     2     1800     3

4     Av     W     4     3     Av     W     1900

N

P

**DISTRICT OF
NORTH
VANCOUVER**

Prospect Point

Siwash Rock

**CITY OF**

Lions Gate Bridge Rd

Seawall

Beaver Lake

**VANCOUVER**

Third Beach

Pauline Johnson Memorial

Stanley

Park

SS Empress of Japan Figurehead

Q

The Ferguson Point Tea House

Seawall

Stanley Park National Historic Site

1A 99

Miniature Railway

Zoo

Rose Garden

Malkin Bowl

Lumberman's Arch

Vancouver Aquarium

Brockton Oval

Brockton Point

Totem Poles

9 O'Clock Gun

Park Dr

Stanley

Lost Lagoon

Vancouver Rowing Club

Royal Vancouver Yacht Club

Coal Harbour

HMCS Discovery Naval Training Station

Deadmans Island

R

Stanley Park Pool

Pltch & Putt

Second Beach

Devonian Harbour Park

Harbour Cruises

Cardero Park Coal Harbour Quay

Winter Games Venue 2010 Olympic Media Centre

Lagoon Dr

Georgia

Hastings

Coal Harbour

Seawalk

Vancouver Convention & Exhibition Centre (West)

Starboard Theatres CN Imax Theatre

143

English Bay Beach

English Bay Park

Alexandra Park

Roselien Suites

Buchan Hotel

King George

West End Community Centre

Roedde House Museum

Pender

Robson

Cordova

St W

Canada Pl

Canada Place

Sea Bus Terminal

Portside Park

S

**English

Bay**

Denman

Davie

Beach

West End

Barclay Manor

Lord Roberts

Lord Roberts Annex

Vancouver Comm. College (Inter. Edu. Ctr.)

Robson

Robson Square Orpheum

Vancouver Art Gallery

Van City Ctr

**Downtown**

Burrard

Dunsmuir

VSE

Harbour Centre

Vancouver Comm. College (City Centre Campus)

The Centre

Queen Elizabeth Theatre

Waterfront

Gastown Steam Clock

Hastings St W

GASTOWN

Water St

Gastown

Stadium Chinatown

Dr Sun Yat Sen Classical Chinese Garden

T

Hadden Park

Kitsilano Point

Vancouver Maritime Museum & "St Roch"

Pacific Space Centre (HR MacMillan Planetarium)

Vancouver Museum

Sunset Beach

St Paul's Hospital

Pacific

Vancouver Aquatic Centre

Burrard

Hornby

Granville

Seymour

Richards

Homer

99

Smithe

Cambie

Beatty

Expo Blvd

BC Place Stadium

GM Place

Georgia Viaduct

Dunsmuir Viaduct

Expo Blvd

BC Sports Hall of Fame & Museum

Edgewater Casino

Creekside Park

Science World-Main St

Kitsilano Beach Park

Kitsilano Beach

Ogden

McNicoll

Whyte

Creelman

Cornwall

York

Arbutus

Laburnum

Walnut

Maple

Cypress

Vanier Park

Burrard Bridge

Granville Island Public Market

Boat Lift

Granville Bridge

False Creek Yacht Club

Art Club Theatre

Emily Carr University

Granville Island

George Wainborn Park

David Lam Park

Elsie Roy

Yaletown-Roundhouse

Roundhouse

Pacific

Pacific Blvd

Cambie Bridge

Science World

False Creek

Athletes Walter Hardwick

1 Av W

2 Av E

**142**

SEE ENLARGEMENT PAGES 10-11

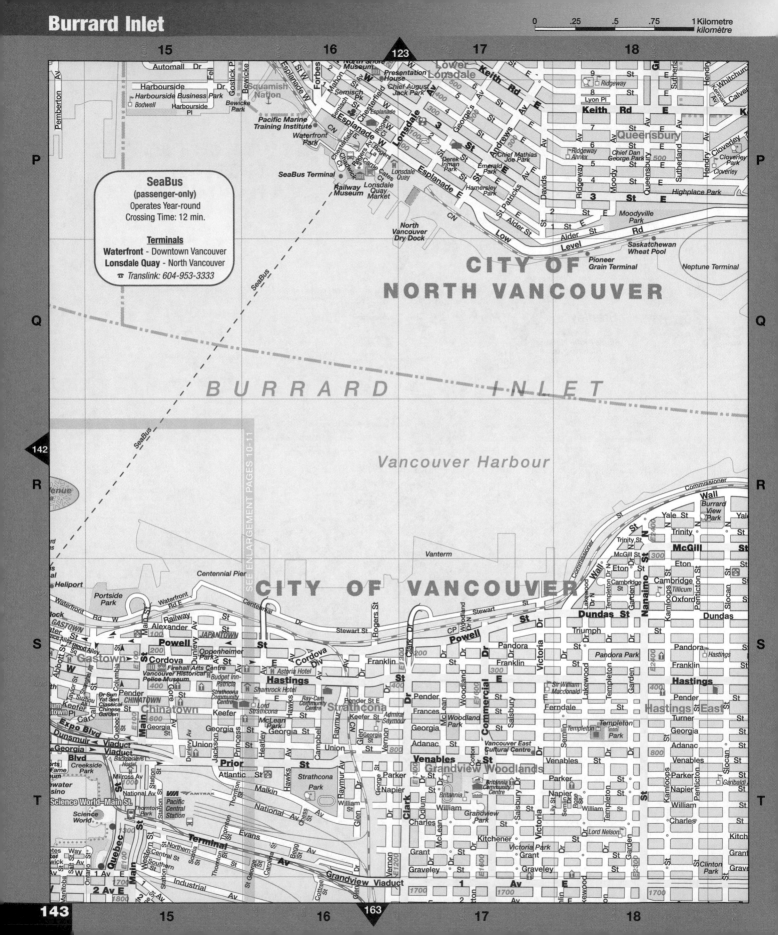

0   .25   .5   .75   1 Kilometre
*kilomètre*

15        16        123        17        18

**SeaBus**
**(passenger-only)**
Operates Year-round
Crossing Time: 12 min.

**Terminals**
**Waterfront** - Downtown Vancouver
**Lonsdale Quay** - North Vancouver
☎ Translink: 604-953-3333

**CITY OF
NORTH VANCOUVER**

B U R R A R D          I N L E T

*Vancouver Harbour*

**CITY OF VANCOUVER**

15        16        163        17        18

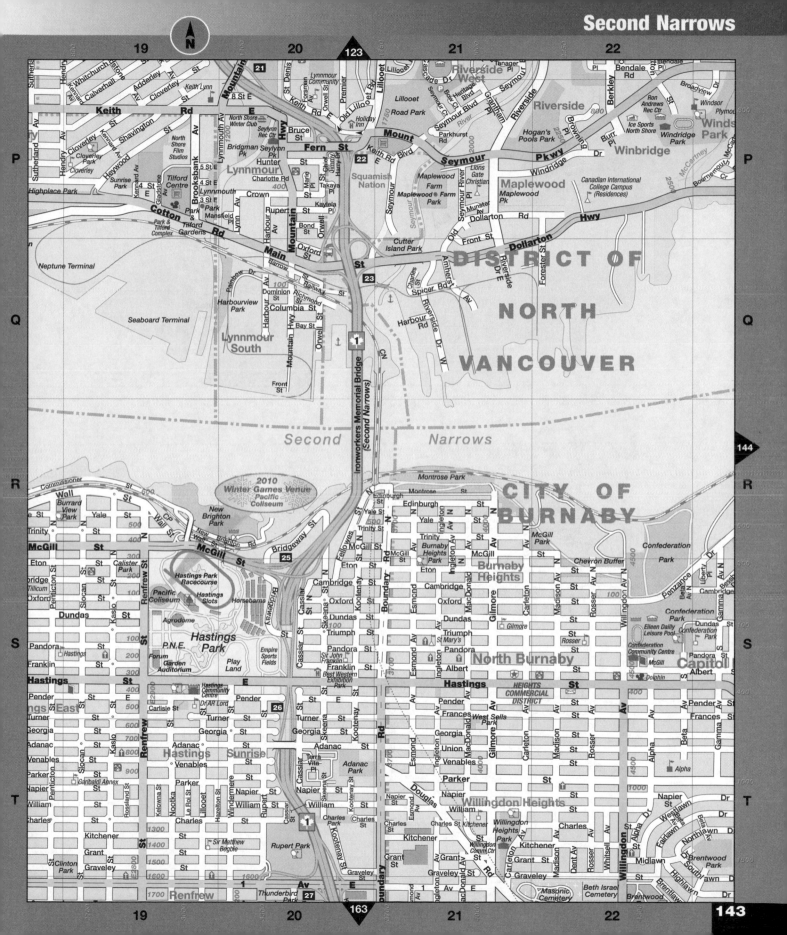

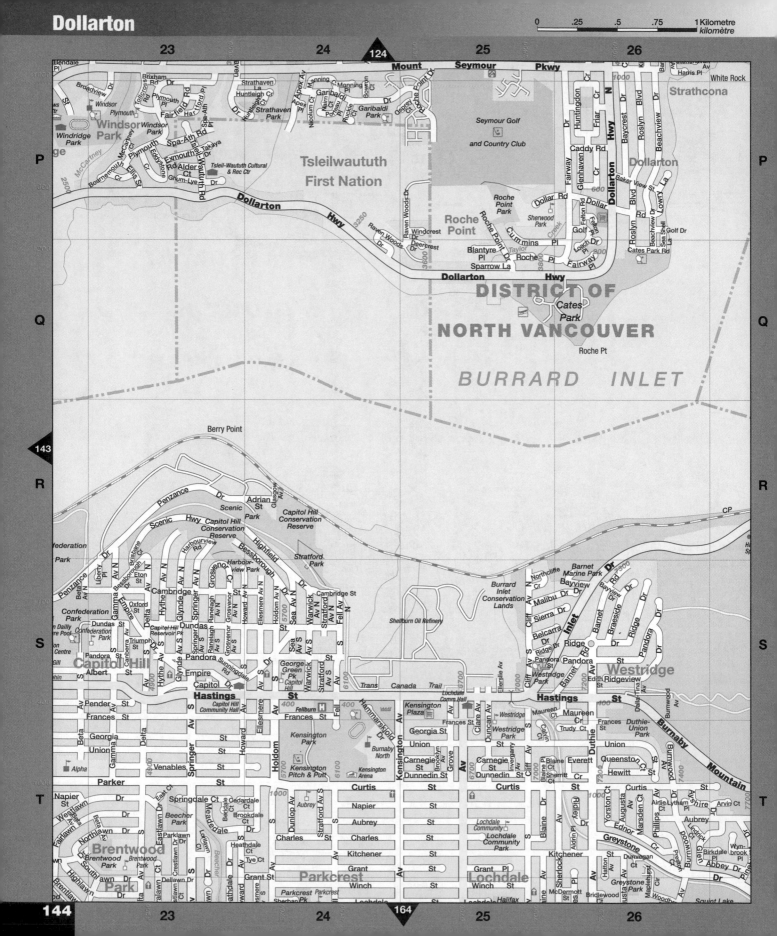

0   .25   .5   .75   1 Kilometre
*kilomètre*

**23**   **24**   **124**   **25**   **26**

Mount      Seymour      Pkwy

Tsleilwaututh
First Nation

Seymour Golf
and Country Club

Windsor Park

Windridge Park

Roche Point Park

Roche
Point

Dollarton

DISTRICT OF

NORTH VANCOUVER

Cates Park

Roche Pt

BURRARD INLET

Berry Point

**143**

Capitol Hill
Conservation Reserve

Capitol Hill
Conservation
Reserve

Stratford
Park

CP

Confederation
Park

Harbourview Park

Barnet
Marine Park

Burrard
Inlet
Conservation
Lands

Confederation
Park

Shellburn Oil Refinery

Capitol Hill

Westridge

Hastings      St

Hastings      St

Kensington
Park

Trans   Canada   Trail

Kensington
Plaza

Westridge
Park

Duthie-Union
Park

Kensington
Pitch & Putt

Burnaby
North

Kensington
Arena

Lochdale Comm Hall

Burnaby Mountain

Brentwood

Brentwood
Park

Parkcrest

Lochdale

Lochdale
Community
Park

Greystone
Park

Parkcrest
Park

Brentwood
Park

**23**   **24**   **164**   **25**   **26**

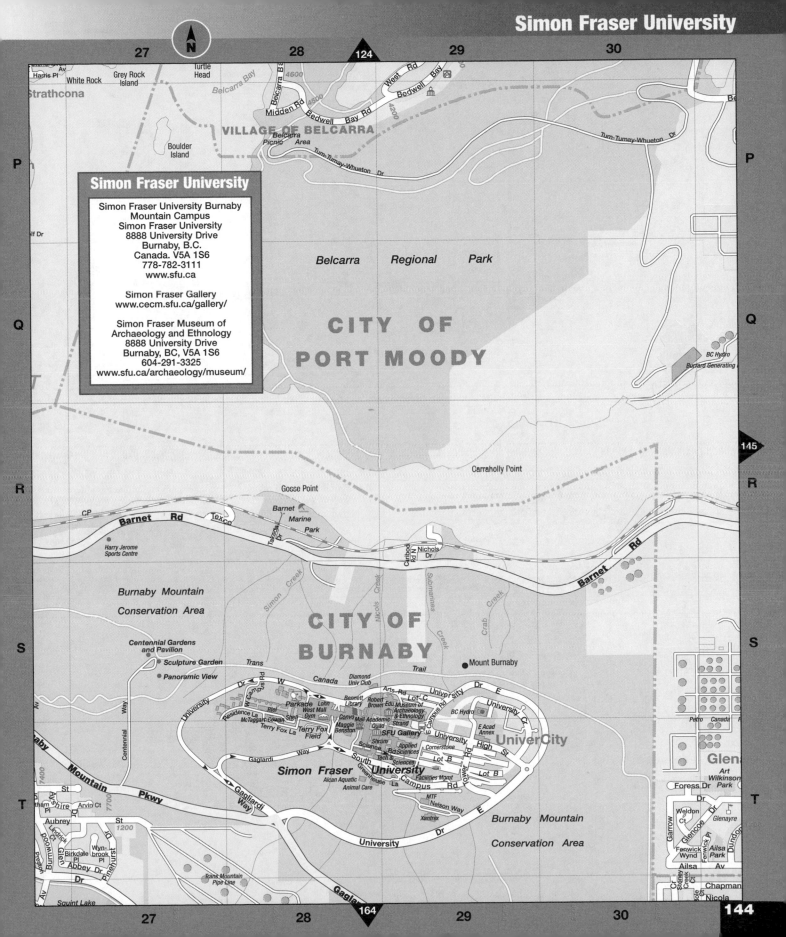

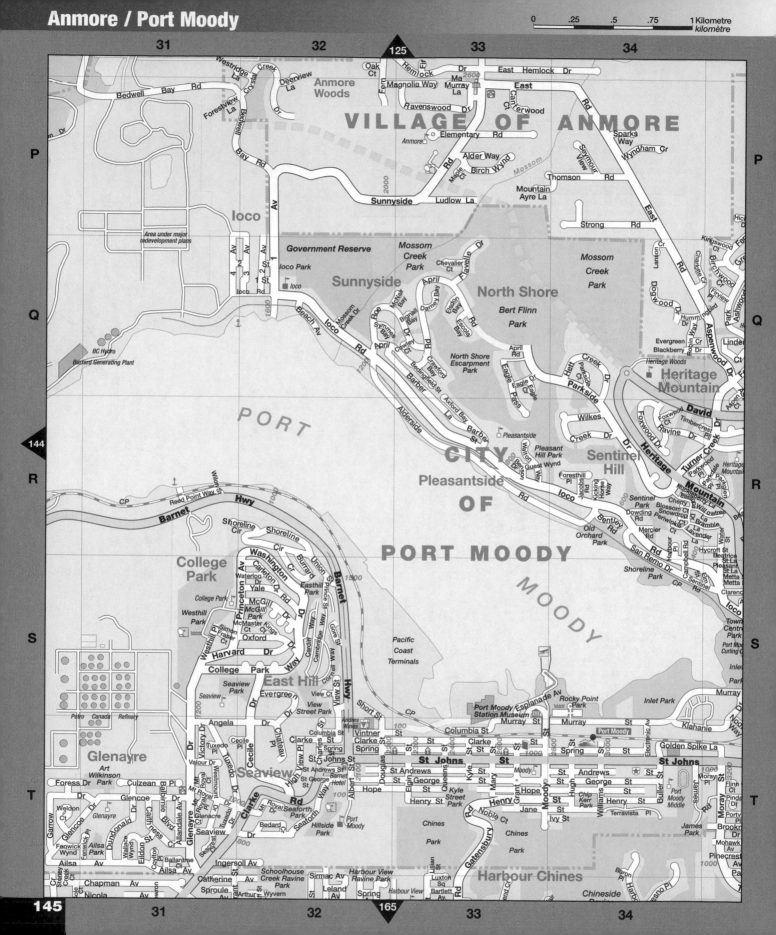

0   .25   .5   .75   1 Kilometre
*kilomètre*

**VILLAGE OF ANMORE**

Anmore Woods

Ioco

**CITY**

Pleasantside

**OF**

**PORT MOODY**

College Park

East Hill

Seaview

Glenayre

Harbour Chines

North Shore

Bert Flinn Park

Sentinel Hill

Heritage Mountain

144

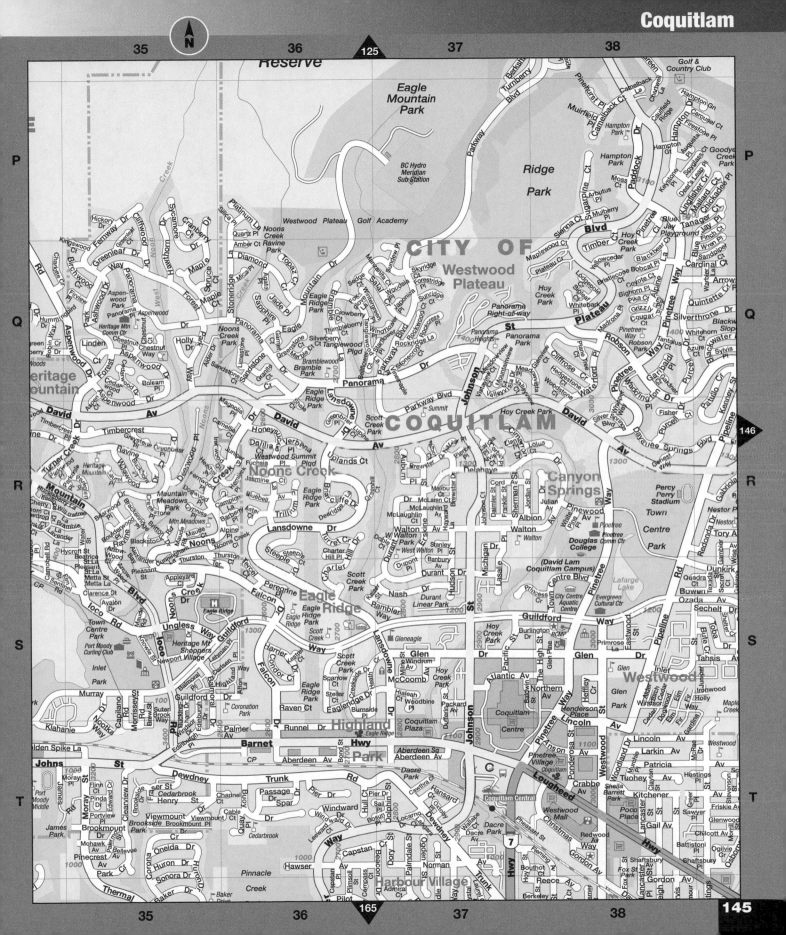

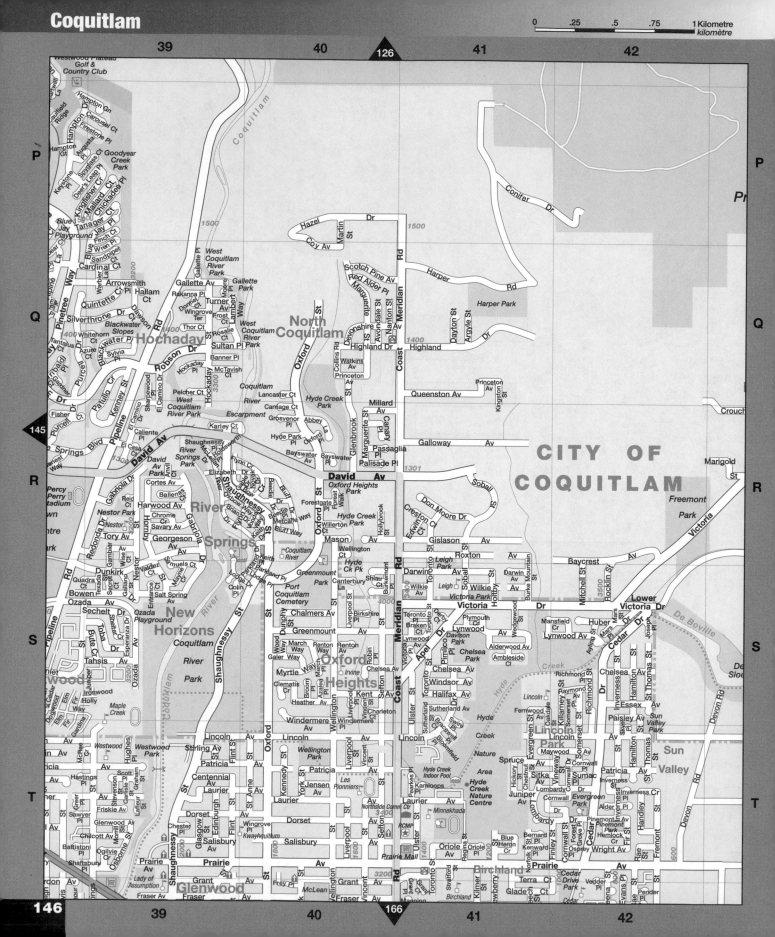

0   .25   .5   .75   1 Kilometre
*kilomètre*

39   40   ▼126   41   42

P   P

Westwood Plateau
Golf &
Country Club

Hampton Grn
Carousel Ct
Firestone Pl
Goodyear
Creek
Park

Coquitlam

Keystone
Spyglass Ct
Mallard Ct
Chickadee Pl
Augusta Ct
Hampton Gt
Deer's Leap Pl
Kingfisher
Tanager
Blue
Jay Playground
Wren Ct
Sandpiper
Cardinal Ct

1500

Hazel   Dr   1500
Coy Av   Martin   St

Conifer   Dr

*Pr*

Arrowsmith
Pl
Hallam
Ct
Silverthrone
Quintette   Dr

Gallette Av
Gallette Pl
Rakanna Pl
Turner
Av
Lambert
Wingrove Ter
Frost Ct
Thor Ct

West
Coquitlam
River
Park
Gallette
Park

Scotch Pine Av
Red Alder Pl
Marguerite

Meridian   Rd

Harper
Rd

Harper Park

Dayton St
Argyle St

Q   Q

1400
Whitehorn Ct
Tantalus Pl
Azute
Sylvia Pl

Blackwater
Slopes

Hochaday

Robson   Rd

1400
Hochaday

Sultan Pl
Banner Pl
McTavish Ct

West
Coquitlam
River
Park

North
Coquitlam

Oxford   St

Devonshire
Avondale St
Nanton St

Highland Dr

Collins Rd
Watkins   St
Princeton

Coast   Meridian   Rd

1400
Highland

Queenston Av

Princeton
Av
Kingston   St

Purcell
Pinetree   Way
Gardner
Dr

Pelcher Ct
El Camino
Sharewood
Hochaday

Coquitlam
River
West
Coquitlam
River Park

Lancaster Ct
Carriage Ct
Grosvenor

Hyde Creek
Park

Millard

Marguerite St
Canary

Galloway   Av

145

Fisher
Purcell
Springs   Blvd
Pipeline

El Camino
Caliente Pl
El Casa

David Av

Karley Ct
Escarpment
Abbey   La
Hyde Park
Pl
Oxford

Bayswater
Av   Bayswater

Glenbrook
Passaglia
Pl
Palisade Pl

1301

CITY   OF
COQUITLAM

Marigold
St

R   R

Percy
Perry
Stadium

David
Av
Park

Shaughnessy
River
Springs
Park

Cortes Av
Ballenas
Elizabeth
Beedie
Bluff
Beedie

David   Av

Oxford
St

Oxford Heights
Park
Forest
Walk
Forestgate

Hyde Creek
Park
Willerton   Ct
Mason

Sobali

Don Moore Dr
Creston
Edwin
Ct

Gislason   Av

Victoria   Dr

Freemont
Park

Priest
Way

Gabriola Dr
Reid
Nestor Pl
Chrome
Harwood Av
Cr
Savary Av
Gabriola

River
Springs

Bluff Way

Hyde Creek
Pk
Wellington
Ct
Hyde
Ck Pk

Roxton   Av

Leigh
Park
Darwin
Wilkie
Leigh

Darwin   St
Burke Mountain

Baycrest   Av
Mitchell St
Rocklin St

R

Redonda Dr
Nestor
Tory Av
Gambier
Georgeson
Av
Wise Ct
Valdez Ct
Samuels Ct
Keith

Coquitlam
River

Greenmount
Park
Canterbury
Birkshire

Shiau
Burkemont

Victoria Park
Wilkie

Victoria   Dr
Darwin

3500
Lower
Victoria   Dr
De Boville

S   S

Dunkirk
Quadra Ct
Bowen
Texada
Secord
Gliss
Ozada
Galiano

Salt Spring
Mayne
Entrance
Partland
Lodge Pl
Colin
Pl

New
Horizons

Coquitlam
River
Park

Shaughnessy   St

Port
Coquitlam
Cemetery

Greenmount

Chalmers Av

Dunphy
Liverpool

St
Birkshire
Liverpool St

4000

Toronto St
Braken Ct
Toronto St
Derby
Dr

Plymouth
Ct
Lynwood
Davison
Park
Alderwood Av
Ambleside
Cl

Mansfield
Cr
Huber

Lynwood Av

Mars
Cedar

Huber
St
Joseph
Pl

Creek
Hyde

Richmond
Pl

S

Pipeline   Rd
Sechelt
Bute Ct
Toba
Tahsis

Esperanza Dr
Ozada
Ozada
Playground

3200

Coquitlam
River
Park

Wood
Way
March
Way
Galer Way
Myrtle
Clematis
Cr
Heather
Broom
Azalea
Av

Renton
Way
Renton
Av
Robin
St
Irvine
Chelsea Av

Oxford
Heights

Vincent
Sefton
Charleton

Coast   Meridian   Rd

Victoria
Toronto St

Apel
Pimlico
Bancewell

Chelsea
Park

Chelsea Av
Windsor   Av
Halifax   Av
Sutherland Av

Lynwood Av

Richmond
Oakdale
Killarney
Somerset
Evergreen
Richmond

Chelsea Av
Inverness
Hamilton
Essex

Paisley   Av
Sun
Valley
Park

Sun
Valley

wood

Juniper
Ironwood
Holly
Dogwood
Elm
Fir
Way
Maple
Creek
Gladtris

Lincoln
Stirling Av
Centennial
Patricia

Westwood
Park

Oxford   St
Lincoln

Wellington
Park

Wellington
St
Liverpool
Vincent

Lincoln

Hyde
Creek
Nature
Area

Hyde Creek
Indoor Pool
Hyde Creek
Nature Centre

Spruce
Fernwood
Maywood

Lincoln
Park
Lincoln

Hickory
Sitka
Vineway
Lombardy
Cornwall St
Sumac
Cornwall

Patricia   Av
Inverness Cr

Patricia   Av

T   T

Hastings
Stevenson
Scott
Graham St
Lafleur
Sawyer
Greer
Friskie Av

Glenwood Av
Chilcott Av

Dorset
Laurier
Jensen
Av

Kennedy
York   St

Laurier
Patricia

Chester Pl
Glasgow
Edinburgh
Flint

Wingrove
Pl
Kwayhquitlam

Dorset

St. Anne
Laurier

Les
Pionniers
Northside Comm Ctr
RCMP

Pearkes
Kamloops

Minnekhada

Chestnut
Juniper
Tombardy

Cornwall St
Evergreen
Park
Alder
Pinemont Cr
Forest
Pinemont
Park

Hamilton
Thomas St
Inverness Cr
Handley

Devon Rd

Battistoni
Ogilvie Ct
Shaftsbury

Morrill
Glenwood   Glenwood
Salisbury
Salisbury
Av

Grant
Fraser

McLean
Av

Grant
Fraser

3200   Rd
Prairie Mall

Oriole
Oriole
Av
Regina St

Blue
Heron
Kenward

Bernard
Cornwall St
Finley Pl
Osprey

Cedar
Drive
Park
Vedder
Pi

Pender

146   39   40   ▼166   41   42

Prairie   Av
Birchland   Prairie   Av

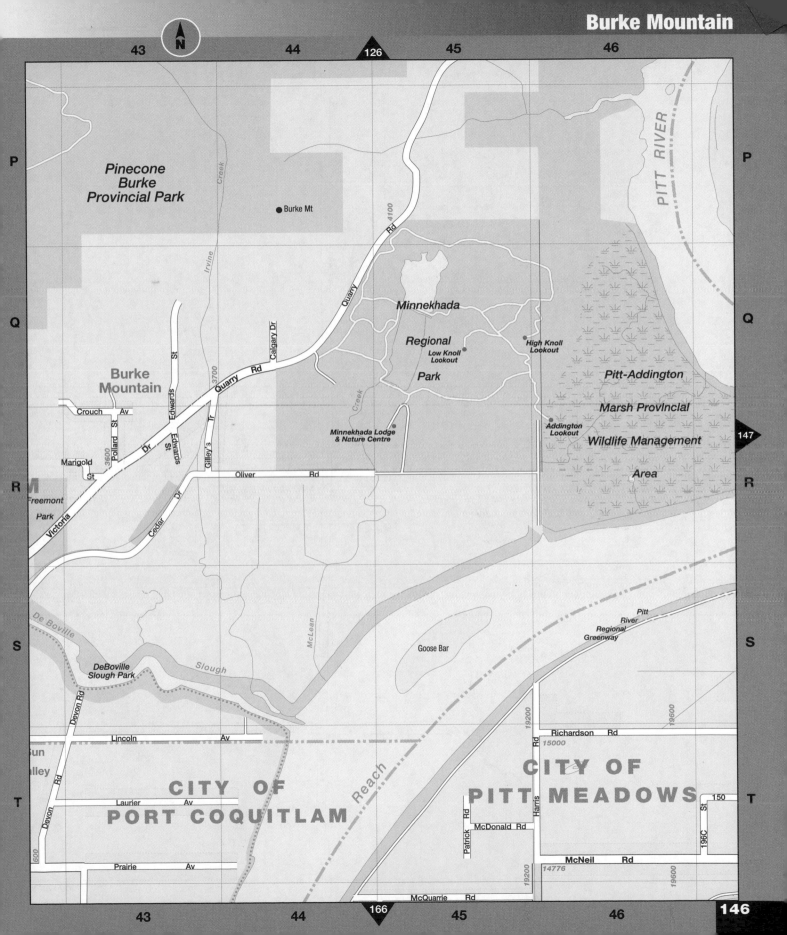

N

43 44 126 45 46

P

*Pinecone
Burke
Provincial Park*

• Burke Mt

Irvine Creek

Rd 4100

Quarry

Q

Calgary Dr

*Minnekhada*

*Regional*

Low Knoll
Lookout

High Knoll
Lookout

**Burke
Mountain**

Edwards St

*Park*

Pollard St

Crouch Av

3700

Quarry Rd

3600

Edwards Dr

Gilley's Tr

*Pitt-Addington*

*Marsh Provincial*

Addington
Lookout

*Wildlife Management*

Marigold
St

Creek

Minnekhada Lodge
& Nature Centre

*Area*

R

Victoria

Cedar Dr

Oliver Rd

Freemont
Park

M

De Boville

McLean

Goose Bar

S

*DeBoville
Slough Park*

Slough

Pitt
River
Regional
Greenway

19200

19600

Devon Rd

Lincoln Av

Richardson Rd

15000

Sun
Valley

Devon Rd

600

Laurier Av

**CITY OF
PORT COQUITLAM**

Reach

**CITY OF
PITT MEADOWS**

Patrick Rd

McDonald Rd

Harris Rd

150

196C St

Prairie Av

19200

14776

**McNeil Rd**

19600

McQuarrie Rd

147

PITT RIVER

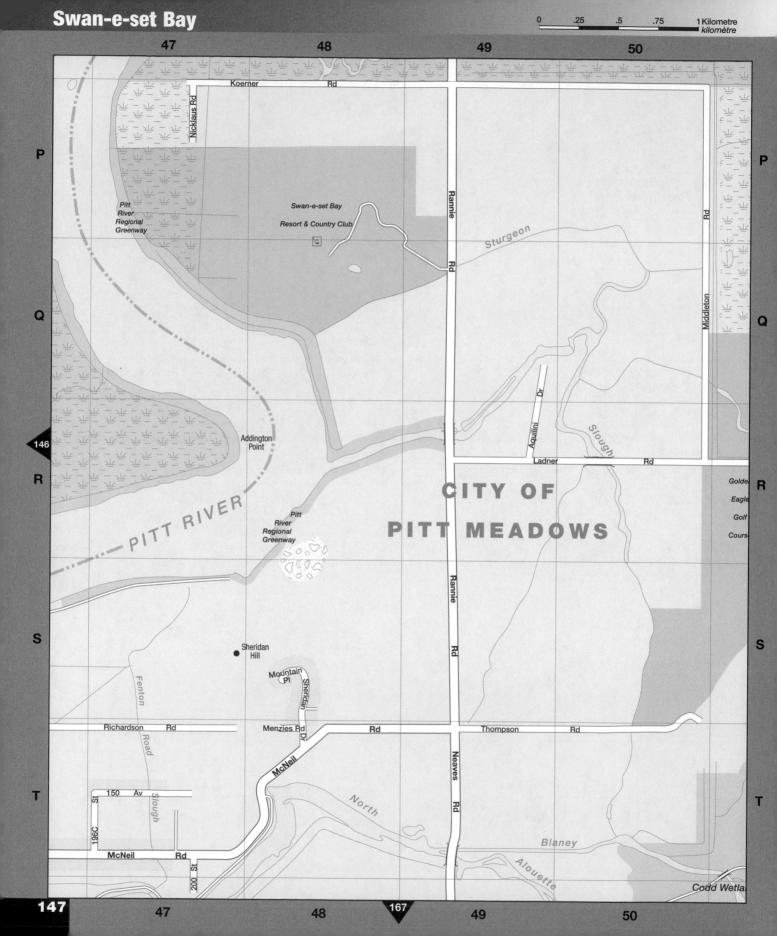

0   .25   .5   .75   1 Kilometre
*kilomètre*

47   48   49   50

P

Koerner   Rd

Nicklaus Rd

Pitt
River
Regional
Greenway

Swan-e-set Bay

Resort & Country Club

Rannie   Rd

Sturgeon

Middleton   Rd

P

Q

Aquilini   Dr

Slough

Q

146

Addington
Point

Ladner   Rd

Golde

R

PITT RIVER

Pitt
River
Regional
Greenway

# CITY OF

## PITT MEADOWS

Eagle

Golf

Cours

R

S

Sheridan
Hill

Fenton

Road

Rannie   Rd

S

Mountain
Pl

Sheridan Dr

Richardson   Rd

Menzies Rd   Rd

Thompson   Rd

McNeil

Neaves   Rd

T

196C St

150   Av

200 St

Slough

North

Blaney

Alouette

T

McNeil   Rd

Codd Wetla

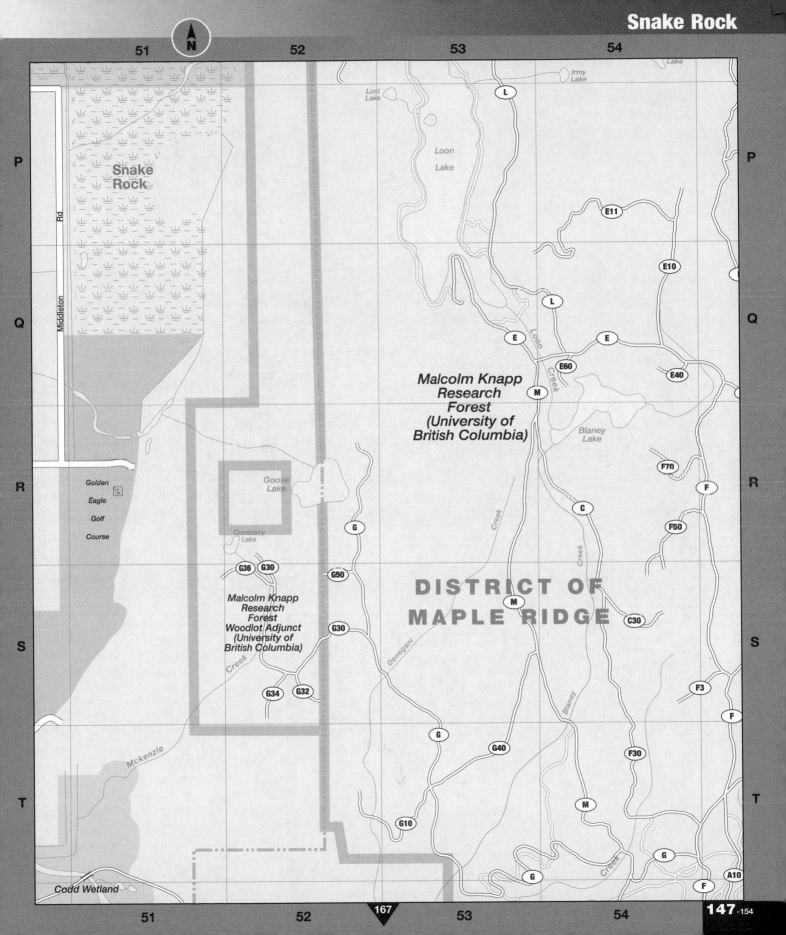

Snake Rock

Loon Lake

Lost Lake

Irmy Lake

Lake

L

E11

E10

L

E

E

E60

E40

Malcolm Knapp Research Forest (University of British Columbia)

M

Loon Creek

Blaney Lake

F70

F

Golden Eagle Golf Course

Goose Lake

Cranberry Lake

G

Creek

Creek

C

F50

G36 G30

G50

Malcolm Knapp Research Forest Woodlot Adjunct (University of British Columbia)

**DISTRICT OF MAPLE RIDGE**

M

C30

G30

Creek

Donegani

F3

G34 G32

Blaney

F

G

G40

F30

Mckenzie

M

G10

G

A10

G

F

**Codd Wetland**

Rd

Middleton

P

Q

R

S

T

51 52 53 54

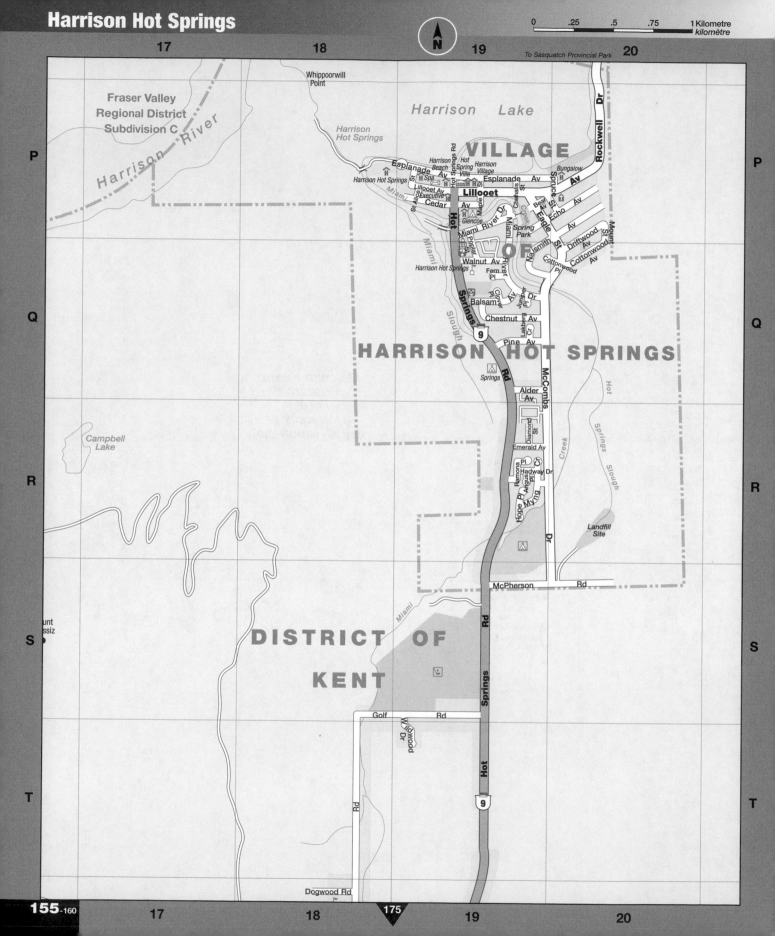

0    .25    .5    .75    1 Kilometre
kilomètre

N

To Sasquatch Provincial Park

17    18    19    20

P    P

Fraser Valley
Regional District
Subdivision C

Harrison River

Harrison Lake

Whippoorwill
Point

Harrison
Hot Springs

VILLAGE

Rockwell Dr

Esplanade Av

Harrison Hot Springs Spa

Harrison Beach St

Hot Spring Villa

Harrison Village

Esplanade Av

Bungalow

Av

Spruce St

Eagle St

Echo Av

Lillooet Av

Lillooet

Executive

Cedar

Av

Miami River Dr

Glencoe

Spring Park

Maple St

Chehalis St

Bear St

Naismith St

Driftwood Av

Cottonwood Pl

Cottonwood Av

Miami River

Poplar

Walnut Av

Harrison Hot Springs

Fern Pl

Q    Q

Balsam

Clover Pl

Juniper Dr

Chestnut Av

Lakberg Av

Pine Pl

Miami Slough

Springs Rd

9

HARRISON HOT SPRINGS

Hot

Springs Slough

Springs Rd

Alder Av

McCombs Dr

Diamond St

Emerald Av

Creek

Landfill
Site

R    R

Campbell
Lake

Ramona Pl

Hadway Pl

Airguard Pl

Hope Pl

Mxng

Dr

McPherson    Rd

Miami

Springs Rd

S    S

unt
ssiz

DISTRICT    OF

KENT

Golf    Rd

Wildwood Dr

Hot Springs Rd

9

T    T

Rd

Dogwood Rd

17    18    19    20

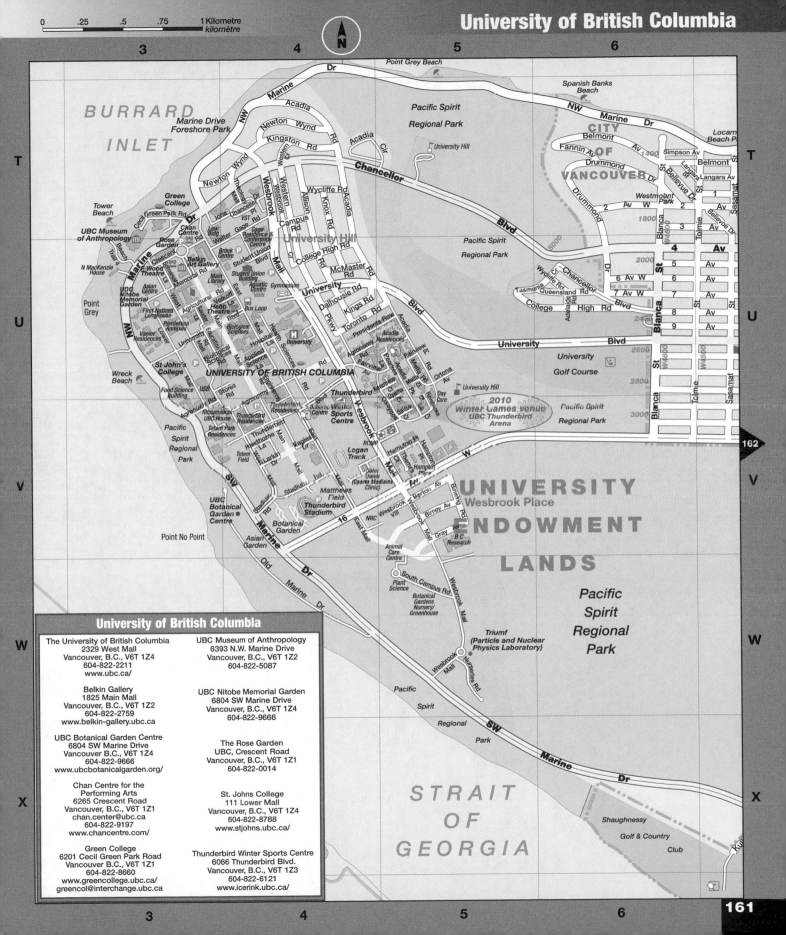

0 .25 .5 .75 1 Kilometre
*kilomètre*

**N**

**BURRARD**

**INLET**

Point Grey Beach

Spanish Banks Beach

Dr
NW Marine Dr
Marine
Acadia

Point Grey Beach

**CITY OF VANCOUVER**

Pacific Spirit Regional Park

University Hill

Belmont Av 1400
Fannin Av
Drummond
Dr
Simpson Av
Belmont
Langara St
Langara Av
1
Westmobnt Park
1800
Blanca 4600
2
3
Blanca St
4 Av
Tolmie St
Bellevue Dr
Sasamat

Marine Drive Foreshore Park

Newton Wynd
Kingston Rd
Western
Acadia
Cir

Chancellor
Blvd

Pacific Spirit Regional Park

5000

Marine Drive
Marine

Green College
Tower Beach
UBC Museum of Anthropology
Rose Garden
Chan Centre
Green Park Rd
Cecil Green Park Rd
Newton
Wynd
Western
Theology
Main
Chancellor
VST
Pl
Wycliffe Rd
Knox Rd
Acadia
Wesbrook
Allison Rd
Campus Rd
College High Rd
**University Hill**
McMaster Rd
Acadia St

Chancellor
Tasmania Rd
Wycliffe Rd
Queensland Rd
College
Adelaide Rd
High Rd

Pacific Spirit Regional Park

2000
6 Av W
7 Av W
Blanca St
5 Av
6 Av
7 Av

N MacKenzie House
F Wood Theatre
Law Bldg
Gage
Gage Residence & Conference Centre
Student Union Building
High Rd
McMaster Rd
University Blvd
Kings Rd
Dalhousie Rd

University Blvd

2400
8 Av
9 Av
Blanca St
W 4600
W 4500
Tolmie St
Sasamat St

Belkin Art Gallery
Brock Centre
Main Library
Student Union
Aquatic Centre
Gymnasium
University
Volkoff
Hebb Theatre
Bus Loop
Biological Sciences
Hospital
Health Sciences Rd
Applied Science
Biological Sciences Rd
Toronto Rd
Presidents Row
Acadia
Agronomy Rd
Fairview
Pl
Melfa Rd
Ortona Av

University Golf Course

2600

2800

University Hill

2010 **Winter Games venue** UBC Thunderbird Arena

Pacific Spirit Regional Park

Point Grey
Nund Nitobe Memorial Garden
Asian Centre
First Nations Longhouse
Ponderosa Annexes
Vanier Residences
Agricultural Rd
Main Mall
East Mall
Education Rd
Stores Rd
St John's College
USB
Food Science Building
Agronomy Rd
UBC House
Ritsumeikan UBC Residences
Thunderbird Residences
Totem Park Residences
Hawthorne La
Thunderbird
Westbrook
Thunderbird Blvd
Osoyoos Cr
Thunderbird Sports Centre
Day Care

3000

University Hill

**UNIVERSITY OF BRITISH COLUMBIA**

Wreck Beach

Pacific Spirit Regional Park

Totem Field
Stadium Rd
Logan Track
RCMP
John Owen (Sperm Medicine) Clinic

**UNIVERSITY ENDOWMENT LANDS**

Wesbrook Place

UBC Botanical Garden Centre
Botanical Garden
Asian Garden
Matthews Field
Thunderbird Stadium
16
East Mall
NRC
Wesbrook VIII
Wesbrook Mall
Birney Av
Gray
Berton Av
Binning Rd
Hampton Pl
B C Research

162

Point No Point

Old
Marine
Dr
SW
Marine Dr

Animal Care Centre
South Campus Rd
Plant Science
Botanical Gardens Nursery/ Greenhouse
Westbrook Mall
Nurseries Rd
Triumf (Particle and Nuclear Physics Laboratory)

**Pacific Spirit Regional Park**

**STRAIT OF GEORGIA**

Pacific Spirit Regional Park
SW Marine Dr

Shaughnessy Golf & Country Club

## University of British Columbia

The University of British Columbia
2329 West Mall
Vancouver, B.C., V6T 1Z4
604-822-2211
www.ubc.ca/

Belkin Gallery
1825 Main Mall
Vancouver, B.C., V6T 1Z2
604-822-2759
www.belkin-gallery.ubc.ca

UBC Botanical Garden Centre
6804 SW Marine Drive
Vancouver B.C., V6T 1Z4
604-822-9666
www.ubcbotanicalgarden.org/

Chan Centre for the Performing Arts
6265 Crescent Road
Vancouver, B.C., V6T 1Z1
chan.center@ubc.ca
604-822-9197
www.chancentre.com/

Green College
6201 Cecil Green Park Road
Vancouver B.C., V6T 1Z1
604-822-8660
www.greencollege.ubc.ca/
greencol@interchange.ubc.ca

UBC Museum of Anthropology
6393 N.W. Marine Drive
Vancouver, B.C., V6T 1Z2
604-822-5087

UBC Nitobe Memorial Garden
6804 SW Marine Drive
Vancouver, B.C., V6T 1Z4
604-822-9666

The Rose Garden
UBC, Crescent Road
Vancouver, B.C., V6T 1Z1
604-822-0014

St. Johns College
111 Lower Mall
Vancouver, B.C., V6T 1Z4
604-822-8788
www.stjohns.ubc.ca/

Thunderbird Winter Sports Centre
6066 Thunderbird Blvd.
Vancouver, B.C., V6T 1Z3
604-822-6121
www.icerink.ubc.ca/

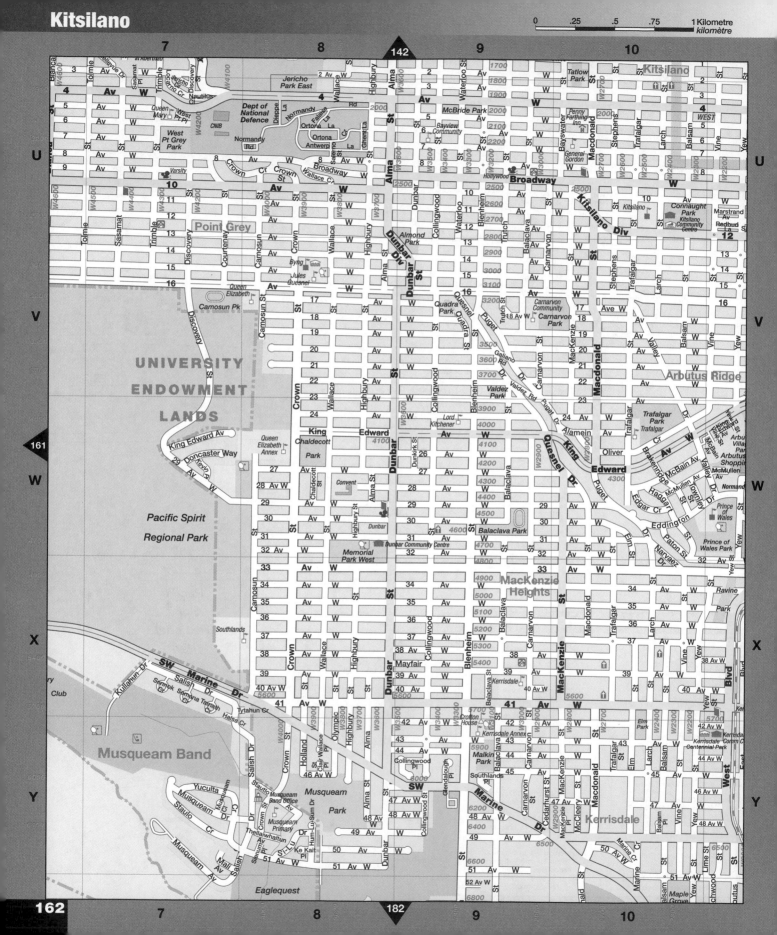

0  .25  .5  .75  1 Kilometre
kilomètre

7          8          142          9          10

Jericho Park East

Dept of National Defence

CNIB

West Pt Grey Park

West Pt Grey

Point Grey

UNIVERSITY ENDOWMENT LANDS

Pacific Spirit Regional Park

Musqueam Band

Musqueam Park

Eaglequest

McBride Park

Bayview Community

Penny Farthing Inn

General Gordon

Hollywood

Broadway

Kitsilano

Kitsilano Community Centre

Connaught Park

Kitsilano Div

Marstrand

Redbud

Almond Park

Byng

Jules Quesnel

Queen Elizabeth

Camosun Pk

Quadra Park

Carnarvon Community

Carnarvon Park

Arbutus Ridge

Valdez Park

Lord Kitchener

Trafalgar Park

King Edward

Queen Elizabeth Annex

Chaldecott Park

Convent

Alamein

Oliver

Edward

Prince of Wales

Prince of Wales Park

MacKenzie Heights

Dunbar

Balaclava Park

Memorial Park West

Dunbar Community Centre

Southlands

Ravine Park

Mayfair

Elm Park

Crofton House

Kerrisdale

Kerrisdale Annex

Malkin Park

Southlands Pl

Kerrisdale Centennial Park

Musqueam Band Office

Musqueam Primary

Kerrisdale

McCleery

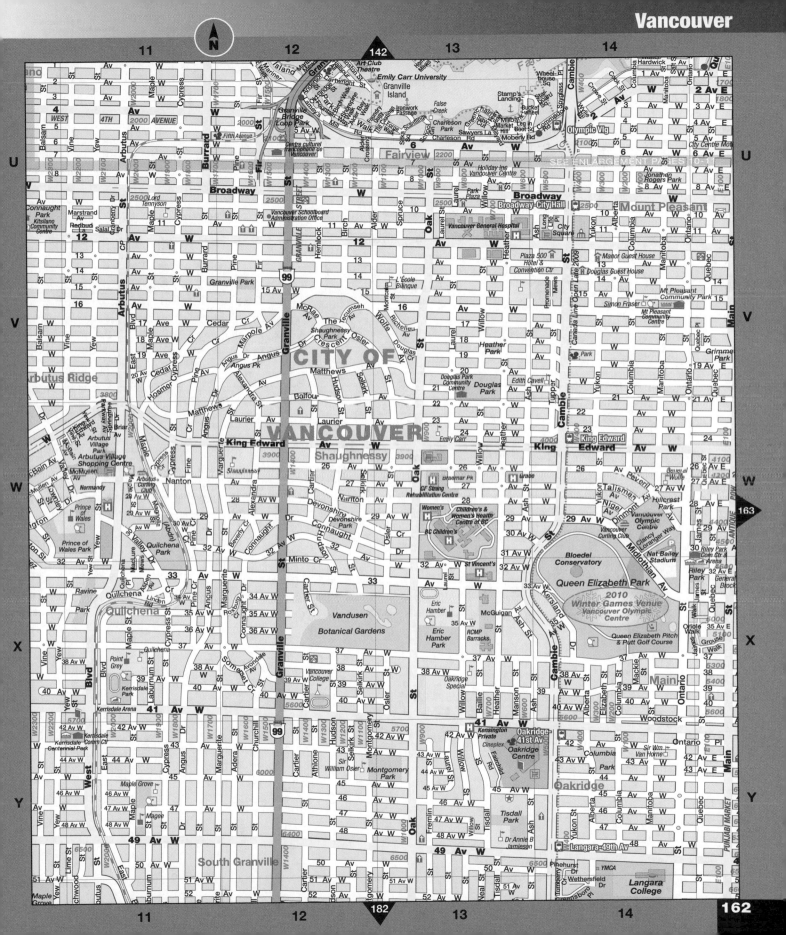

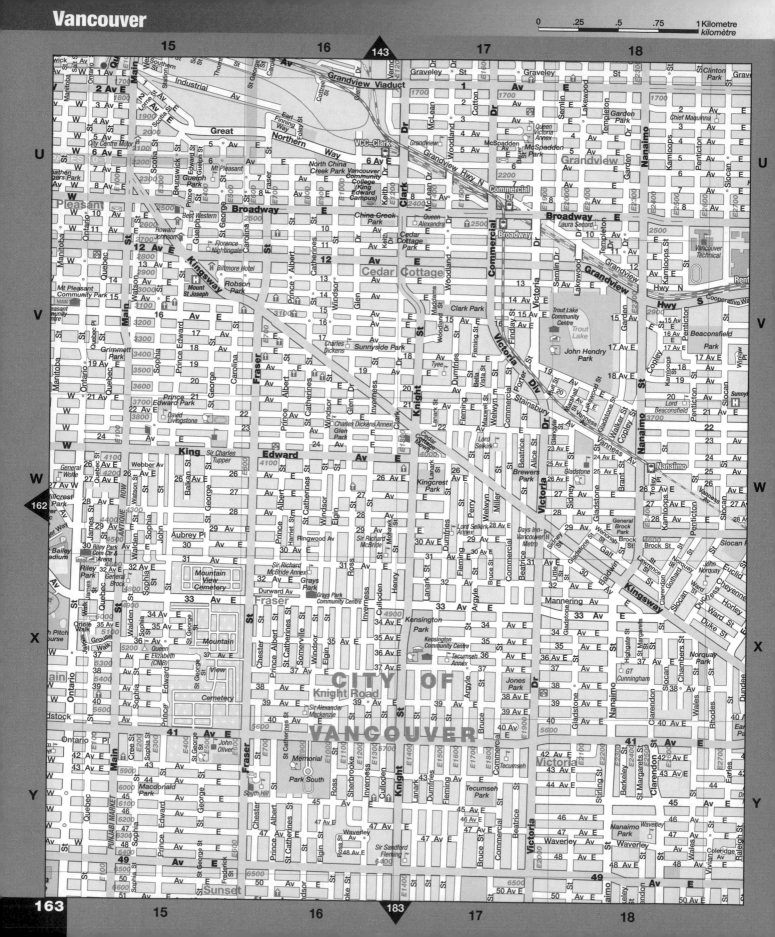

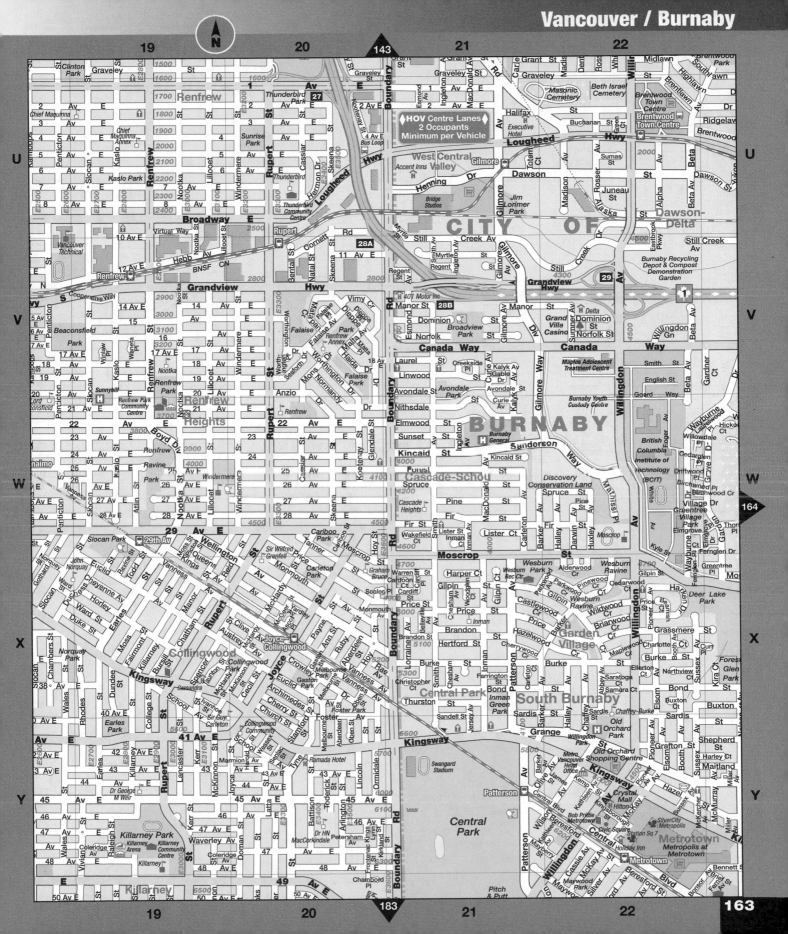

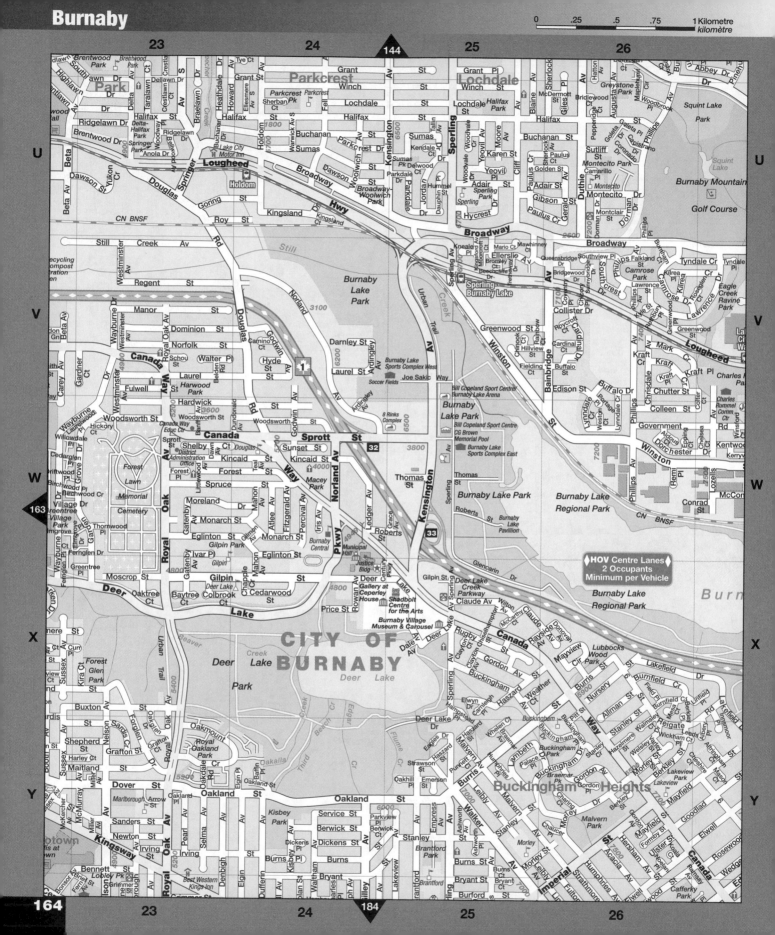

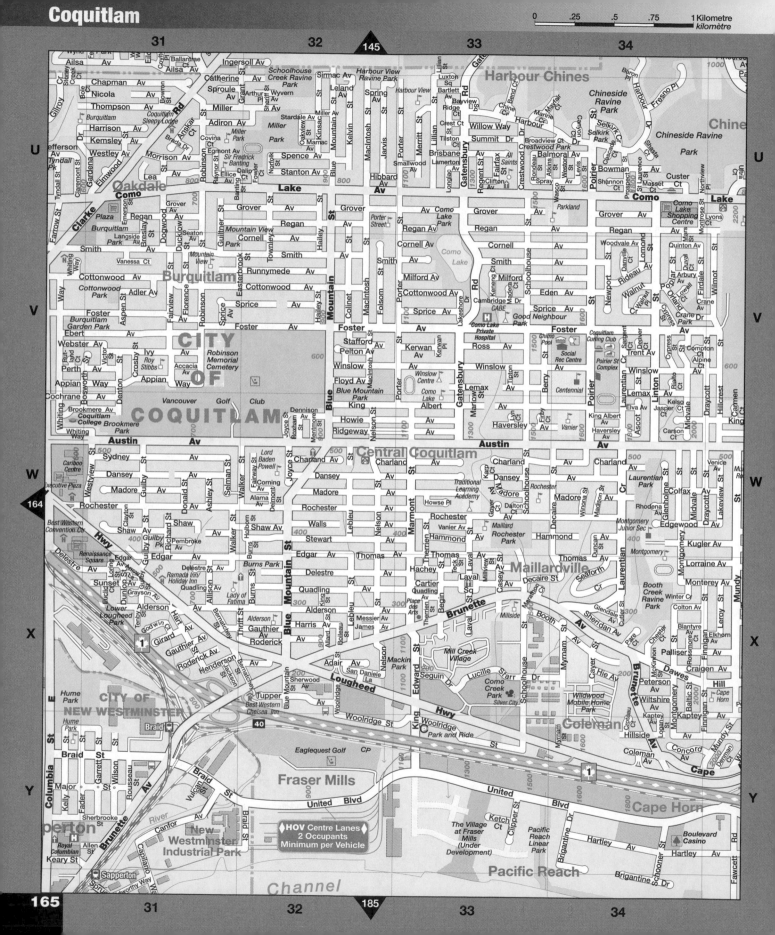

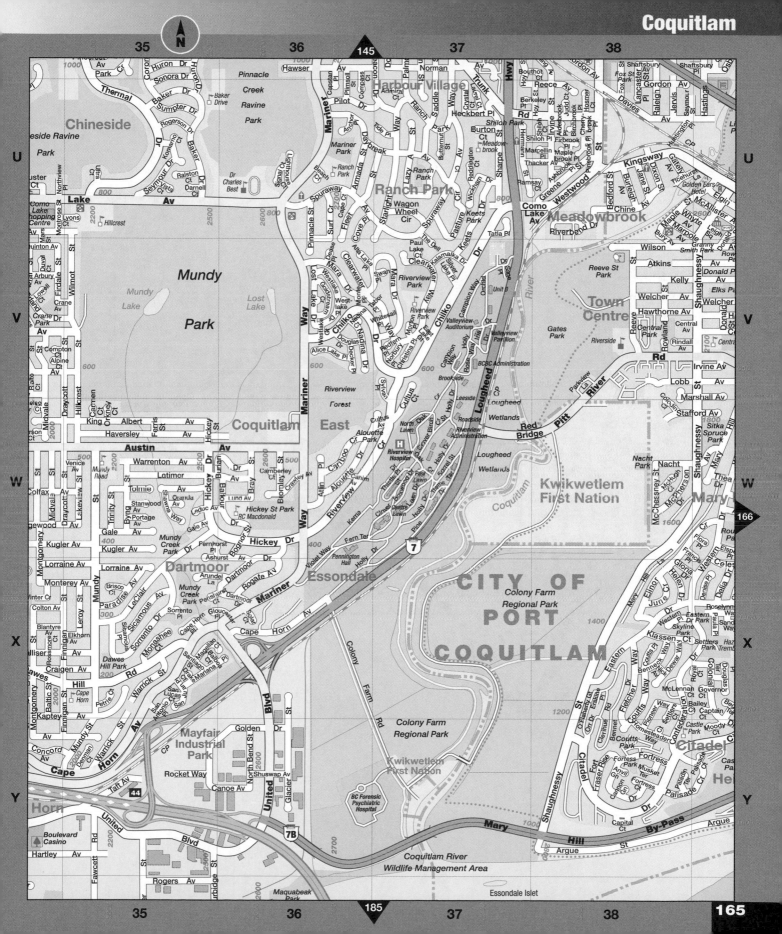

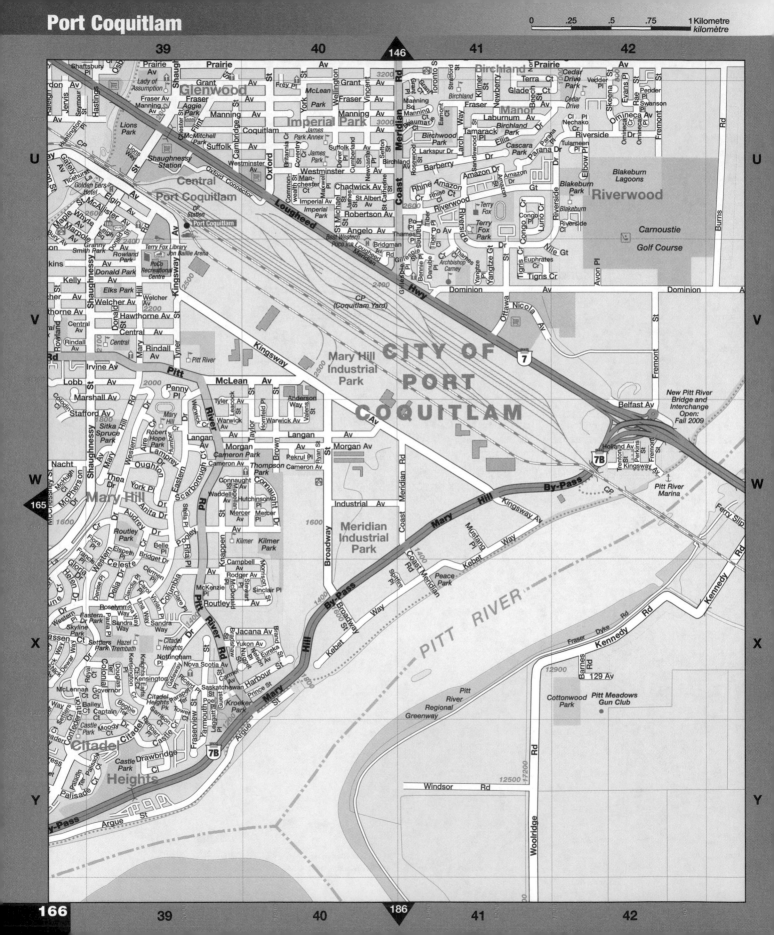

0   .25   .5   .75   1 Kilometre
kilomètre

**39**   **40**   **146**   **41**   **42**

## CITY OF PORT COQUITLAM

### Glenwood
### Imperial Park
### Central Port Coquitlam
### Riverwood
### Birchland Manor
### Mary Hill
### Mary Hill Industrial Park
### Meridian Industrial Park
### Citadel Heights

**PITT RIVER**

New Pitt River Bridge and Interchange Open: Fall 2009

Carnoustie Golf Course

Blakeburn Lagoons

Pitt River Regional Greenway

Cottonwood Park

Pitt Meadows Gun Club

43     44    146    45     46

N

U                 U

Prairie   Av

McNeil   Rd
14776     19600

McQuarrie   Rd

Charlier Rd

Fenton   Rd

Rd

Burns   Rd

Chatham

Pitt Meadows Marina

Alouette     River

Pitt River Regional Greenway

Fraser Dyke Rd

Rippington   Rd

14100     14100     14100   Rd

Hale   Rd

Harris   Rd

141   Av

Dominion   Av

V                 V

stie

urse

New Pitt River Bridge and Interchange Open: Fall 2009

Reichenbach   Rd

13500     13500     13500

Pitt Meadows Golf Club

# CITY OF PITT MEADOWS

Cranberry   Slough

Meadowlands

W                 W   167

River rina

Ferry Slip Rd

18400    18800    19200    19600

Old    Dewdney    Trunk     Rd

13000     13000

Old     Dewdney

Kennedy   Rd

Vancouver Intermodal Facility

Lougheed    Hwy

Slough

Katzie

X                 X

18400

CP

18800

Allen Way

Harris   Rd

Pitt Meadows Driving Range & Baseball Centre

7

Advent   Rd

19000     19200

Meadowvale Shopping Centre

Ramada Inn Hotel

McTavish   Rd

12500

Green   Rd

Cook   Slough

12500

Y                 Y

18800   St

124A Av

McMyn   Rd

190A St

191 St

191B St

Harris Road Park

19500

Meadow Gardens Way

124   Av

124 Av

Lehman

124 Av

193B St

194 St

Davison   Rd

194A St

194B St

Oak Ter

Bonson

Somerset Park

188 St

188A Av

188B Av

Highland Park

Nikola St

Doerksen Dr

Hoffman Museum

192A St

123   Av

123A St

McMyn St

Cypress

Tully   Slough

Advent Park

122B Av

**Pitt**

Pitt Meadows Museum

Hoffman Park Av

Cusick Cr

Park

Edith McDermott

122 Av

121B Av

Pitt

192B Rd

121B Av

Somerset Csc

0 | .25 | .5 | .75 | 1 Kilometre
kilomètre

47     48     147     49     50

Codd Wetlan
Regional Ecolog
Conservancy A

U

CITY OF
PITT MEADOWS

Alouette

River

Rd

Connecting Rd

14000

14000

McKechnie Rd

McKechnie

20000

20000

Sharpe Rd

20300

13200

Neaves Rd

20800

13200

Jerry Sulina
Municipal
Park

South

216 St

13200

132

Canoe
Park

V

166

W

Trunk Rd

132 Av

X

203 St

210 St

128 Av

21000

12800

South

Creek

21300

209 St

216 St

21600

12800

Abernethy Connector

(Open: August 2009)

Abernethy Connector

McKenny

Brooks Av

Powell Av

Powell Av

Meadow Gardens Way

7

Meadow
Gardens
Golf Course

11 Orchard La
12 Sunnyside Pl
13 Cherry La
14 Brighton Pl
15 Butternut La
16 Sunset La
17 Honeydew Dr
18 Blossom Bay

Davenport Dr

Allison St

McIvor St

202A St

201 St

125 Av

124 Av

202 St

204 St

203B St

Chatwin Av

123B Av

123 Av

Telep

124B St

205 St

124A Av

205A St

123B

12300

Brooks Av

125 Av

206 St

125

Av

124 Av

Knotts St

Krassen Pl

206B St

123B Av

206A St

125 Av

Skillen St

Blanshard St

Meadow
Pl

Chilcotin
Park

Skillen St

209 Cr

Laityview

12300

Volker
Park

Meadow Brook Pl

McCallum Ct

Dawson St

Douglas
Pl

Laity St

Hardy St

Thornton St

126

214 St

215 St

Exeter

124 Av

Cherry
Pl

124
Av

Carlton Av

214 St

123 Av

126

Thornton Av

Exeter Av

Spring Holly St

Hampton
Park

12400

Manor Av

124 Av

Stonehouse
Av

122B
Av

122 Av

Campbell Av

123

Ridge

122

216 St

Creston Av

Spring Cr

Evans

Cypress

Cinneplex

201A St

201B St

Makinson

Lindsay St

Lindsay

203 St

204 St

122

205B St

122B Av

121B Av

Fairview
Park

Fairview

123

122

123 Av

Tyner
Av

Wicklund

Westview

Stonehouse

211 St

McTavish

Forest Pl

Norfolk Pl

Campbell
Av

214 St

122 Av

Mountain

47     48     187     49     50

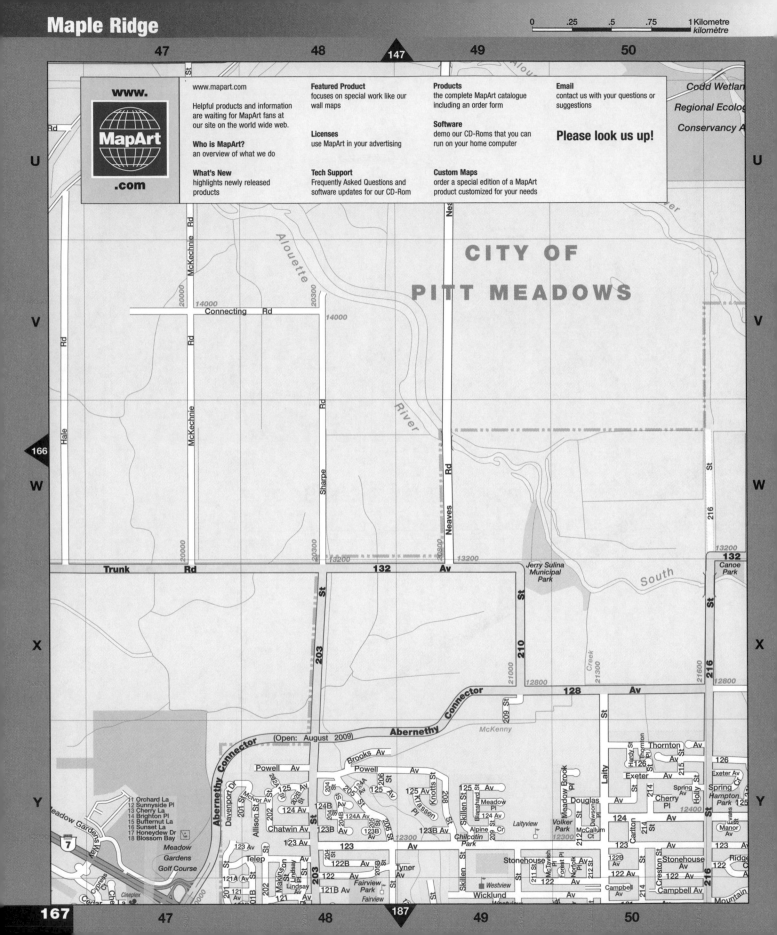

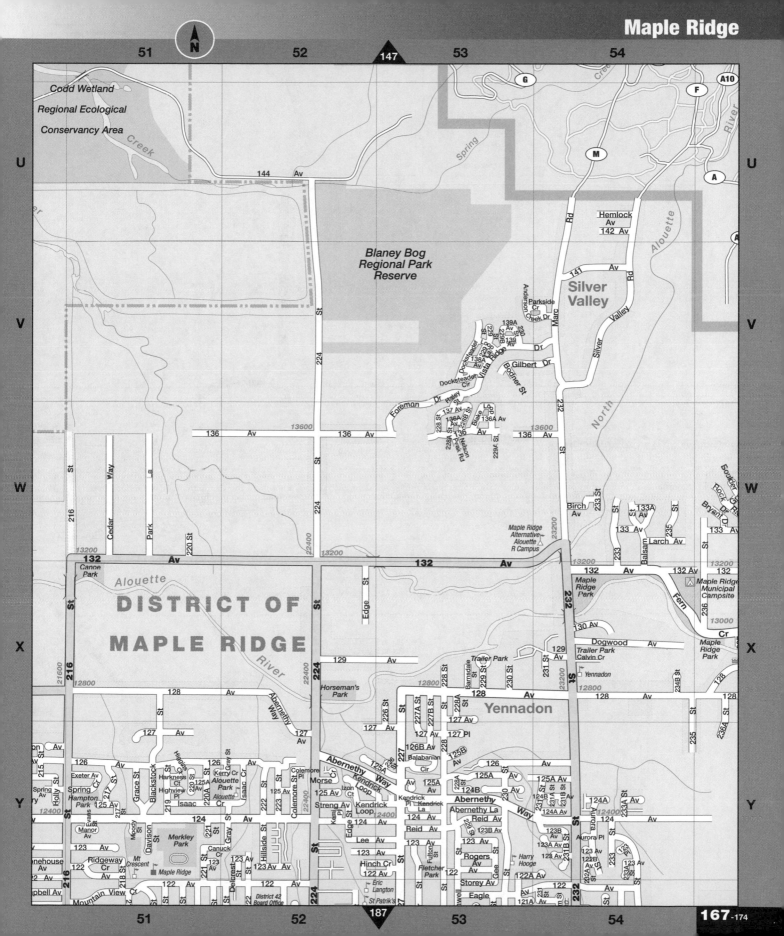

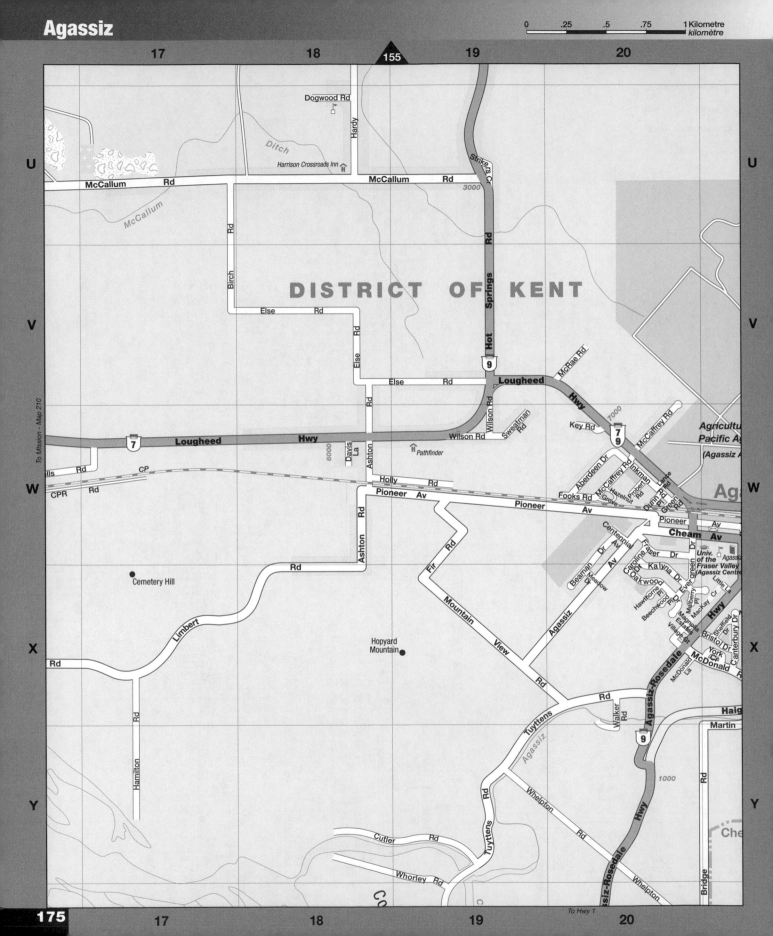

**District of Kent**

Scale: 0 .25 .5 .75 1 Kilometre / kilomètre

| | 17 | 18 | 155 | 19 | 20 | |
|---|---|---|---|---|---|---|

**U**

Dogwood Rd
Hardy
Ditch
Harrison Crossroads Inn
McCallum Rd
McCallum Rd 3000
McCallum
Strikers Cr

**V**

Birch Rd
Else Rd
Else Rd
Hot Springs Rd
**DISTRICT OF KENT**
9
Lougheed
McRae Rd

**W**

Wilson Rd
Sweatman Rd
Else Rd
Lougheed Hwy 7000
Key Rd
7 9
McCaffrey Rd
Agricultur
Pacific A
(Agassiz A
7 Lougheed Hwy 6000
Davis La
Ashton Rd
Pathfinder
Wilson Rd
To Mission - Map 210
CP
Aberdeen Dr
McCaffrey Rd
Inkman
Lance
CPR Rd
Holly Rd
Hazelnut Grove
Probert Rd
Quinn Rd
Green Rd
Ag
Pioneer Av
Fooks Rd
Pioneer Av
Pioneer Av
Pioneer Av
Cheam Av
Centennial Av
Fraser Dr
Univ. of the Fraser Valley (Agassiz Centre
Agassiz
Ashton Rd
Fir Rd
Caroline Dr
Kalyna Dr
Evergreen
Little La
Cemetery Hill
Rd
Beaman Meadow Pl
Oakwood
Hawthorne Pl
Mulberry Pl
MacKay Cr
Beechwood
Magnolia
Esplanade

**X**

Limbert
Hopyard Mountain
Mountain View Rd
Agassiz Rd
Village St
Bristol Dr
York Cr
Sheffield Dr
Canterbury Dr
McDonald
Agassiz-Rosedale Hwy
Rd
Haig
Martin

**Y**

Hamilton Rd
Tuyttens Rd
Walker Rd
9
Agassiz
Whelpton Rd
1000
Rd
Cutler Rd
Tuyttens Rd
Whorley Rd
Co
Agassiz-Rosedale Hwy
Whelpton
Bridge
Che
To Hwy 1

| | 17 | 18 | 19 | 20 | |
|---|---|---|---|---|---|

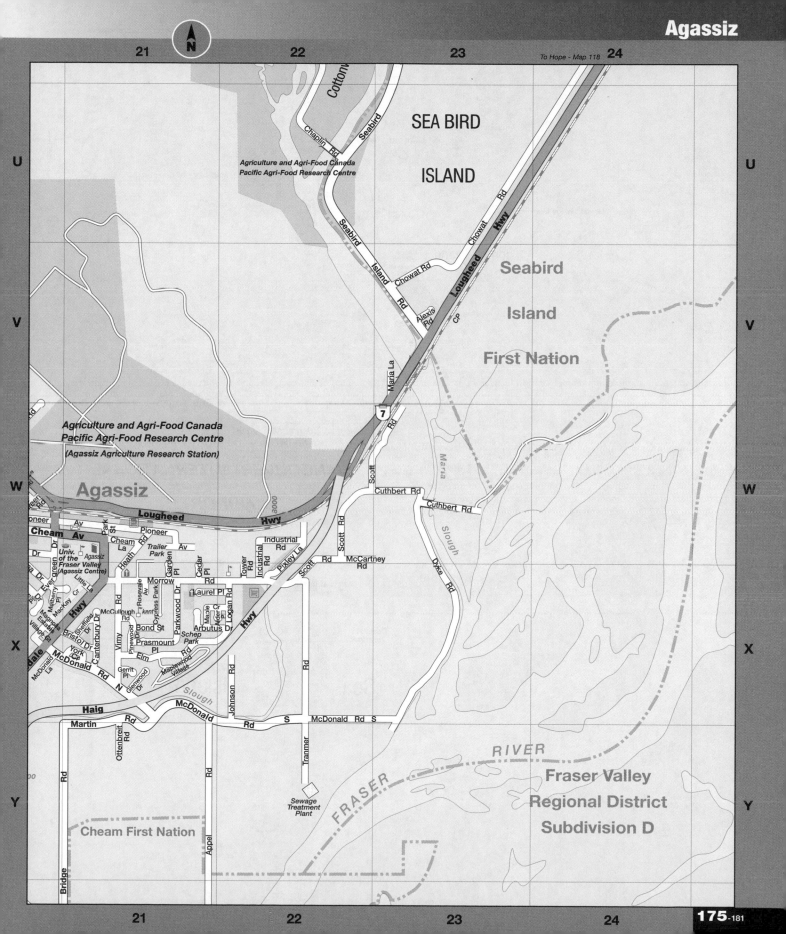

SEA BIRD

ISLAND

Seabird

Island

First Nation

Agriculture and Agri-Food Canada
Pacific Agri-Food Research Centre

Agriculture and Agri-Food Canada
Pacific Agri-Food Research Centre

(Agassiz Agriculture Research Station)

Agassiz

Lougheed Hwy

Cheam Av

Pioneer

Univ.
of the
Fraser Valley
(Agassiz Centre)

Agassiz
Centre

Trailer
Park

Cheam
La

Industrial
Rd

Tower
Rd

Scott Rd

Cuthbert Rd

Cuthbert Rd

Maria Slough

McCartney
Rd

Morrow
Av

Garden
Pl

Cedar
Pl

Pixley La

Industrial
Rd

Scott Rd

Logan Rd

Laurel Pl

Parkwood Dr

Rosevale

Cypress Park

McCullough
Rd

Pinewood Dr

Bond St

Vimy

Maple
Cr

Arbutus Dr

Schep
Park

Prasmount
Pl

Elm

Maplewood
Village

Gerrit
Pl

Glenwood
Dr

Canterbury Dr

York
Cr

McDonald La

Dale

McDonald Rd N

Haig

McDonald

Martin

Ottenbreit
Rd

Johnson Rd

McDonald Rd S

Tranmer Rd

Sewage
Treatment
Plant

Cheam First Nation

Bridge

Appel

FRASER

RIVER

Fraser Valley

Regional District

Subdivision D

Cottonw

Chaplin Rd

Seabird

Seabird Island Rd

Chowat Rd

Alexis Rd

Chowat Rd

Lougheed Hwy

CP

Maria La

7

Scott Rd

Dyke Rd

Maria Slough

Lougheed Hwy

Hwy

Hwy

Hwy

3000

Mulberry Pl

MacKay Pl

Magnolia

Evergreen
Village Cr

Sheffield Dr

Bristol

Heath

Park St

Evergreen Dr

Little
Cr

To Hope - Map 118

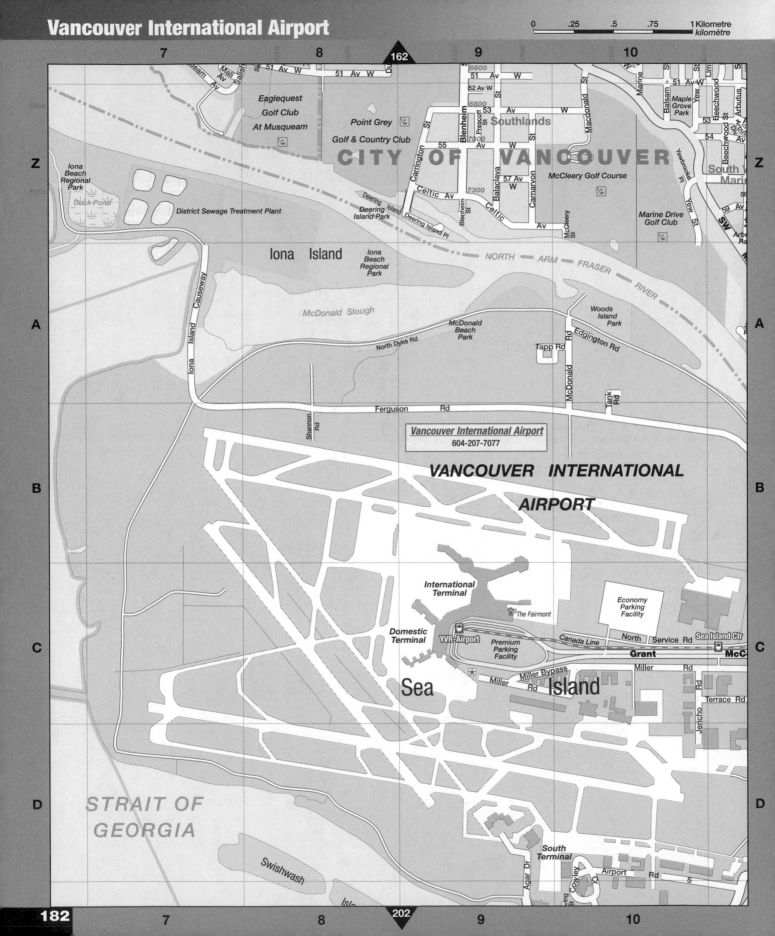

0    .25    .5    .75    1 Kilometre
*kilomètre*

**7**        **8**     ▼162    **9**        **10**

**Z**

Eaglequest
Golf Club
At Musqueam

Point Grey
Golf & Country Club

Southlands

# CITY OF VANCOUVER

Iona
Beach
Regional
Park

Duck Pond

District Sewage Treatment Plant

McCleery Golf Course

51 Av W
52 Av W

6600

6800
7000

53 Av

55

57 Av
W

7300

Carrington St
Blenheim St
Prescott St
Balaclava St
Carnarvon
Macdonald St
Yewbrooka Pl
Yew St
Balsam St
Beechwood St
Arbutus St

Celtic Av

Deering Island Av
Deering
Island Park
Deering Island Pl

Blenheim St
Celtic
McCleery St

Maple
Grove
Park

53
54
59

Marine Drive
Golf Club

South
Marin

**Z**

**A**

Iona Island

Iona
Beach
Regional
Park

McDonald  Slough

McDonald
Beach
Park

Woods
Island
Park

NORTH — ARM — FRASER — RIVER

North Dyke Rd

Tapp Rd

Edgington Rd

McDonald Rd

**A**

Iona Island Causeway

Iona

Ferguson          Rd

Tank
Rd

| Vancouver International Airport |
| 604-207-7077 |

## VANCOUVER  INTERNATIONAL

**B**

Shannon Rd

## AIRPORT

**B**

**C**

International
Terminal

The Fairmont

Economy
Parking
Facility

Domestic
Terminal

YVR-Airport

Premium
Parking
Facility

Canada Line

North    Service    Rd

Sea Island Ctr

Grant

McC

**C**

Sea

Miller    Rd

Miller Bypass

Island

Miller          Rd

Jericho Rd

Terrace Rd

**D**

# STRAIT OF
# GEORGIA

South
Terminal

Agar Dr

Cowley

Airport    Rd

**D**

Swishwash

Isl

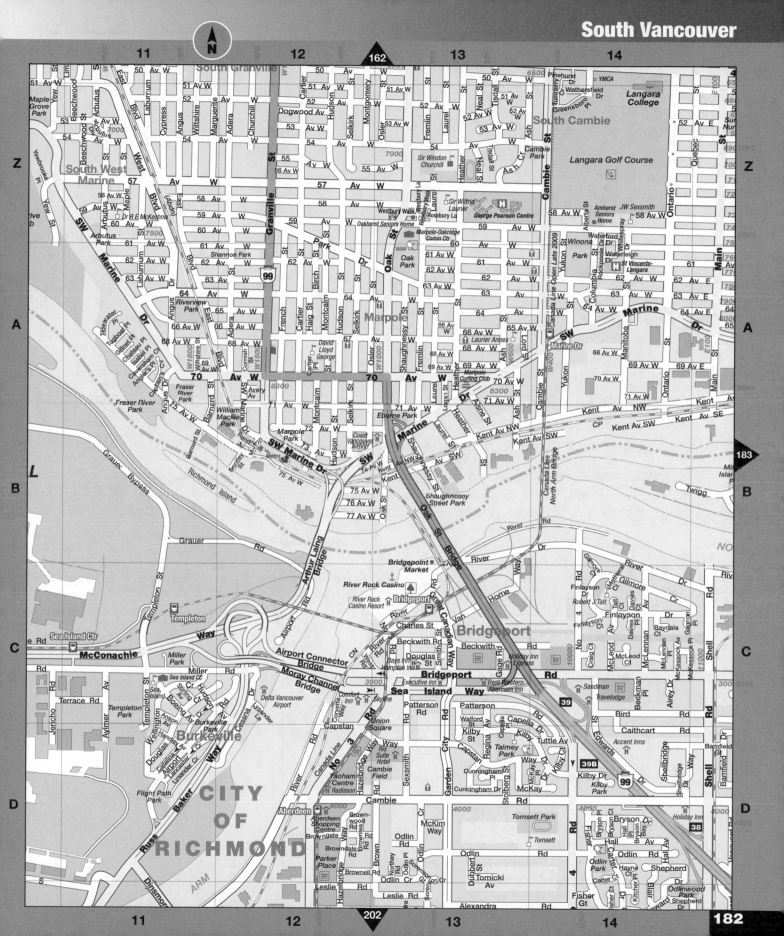

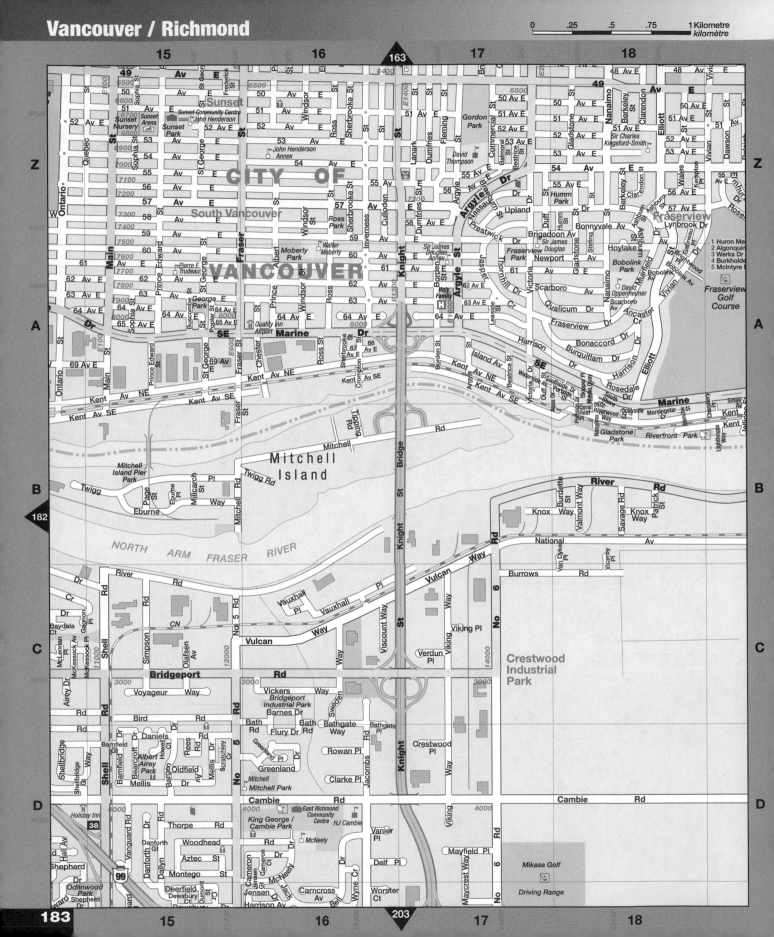

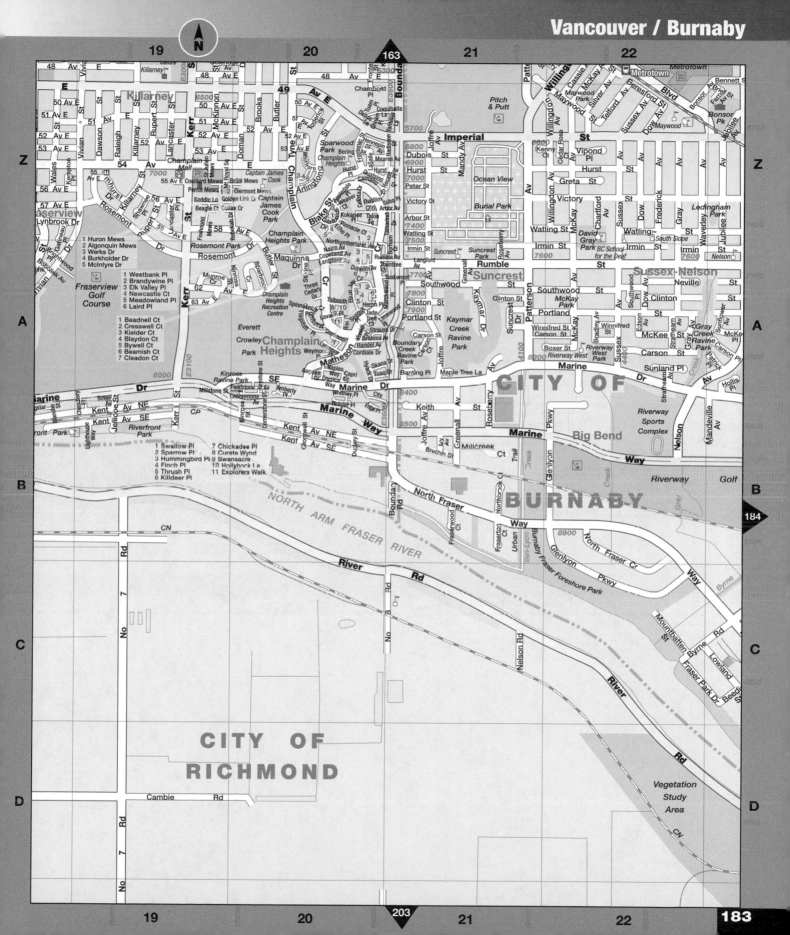

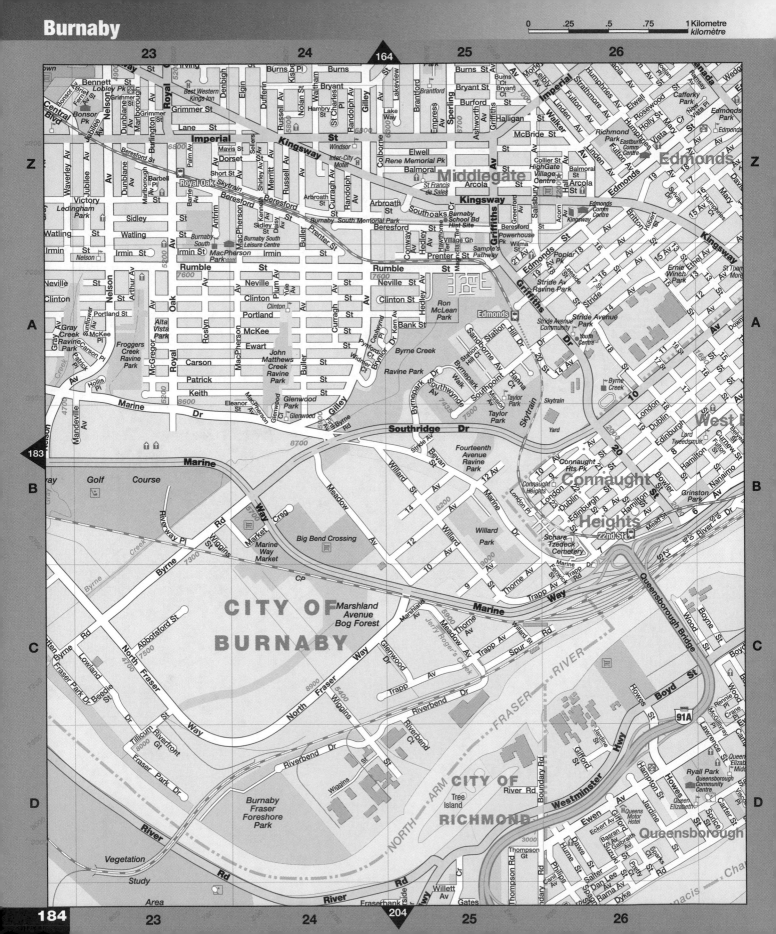

0 .25 .5 .75 1 Kilometre
kilomètre

CITY OF
BURNABY

CITY OF
RICHMOND

Middlegate

Edmonds

Connaught
Heights

West B

Queensborough

Golf Course

Marshland
Avenue
Bog Forest

Big Bend Crossing

Burnaby
Fraser
Foreshore
Park

Vegetation
Study
Area

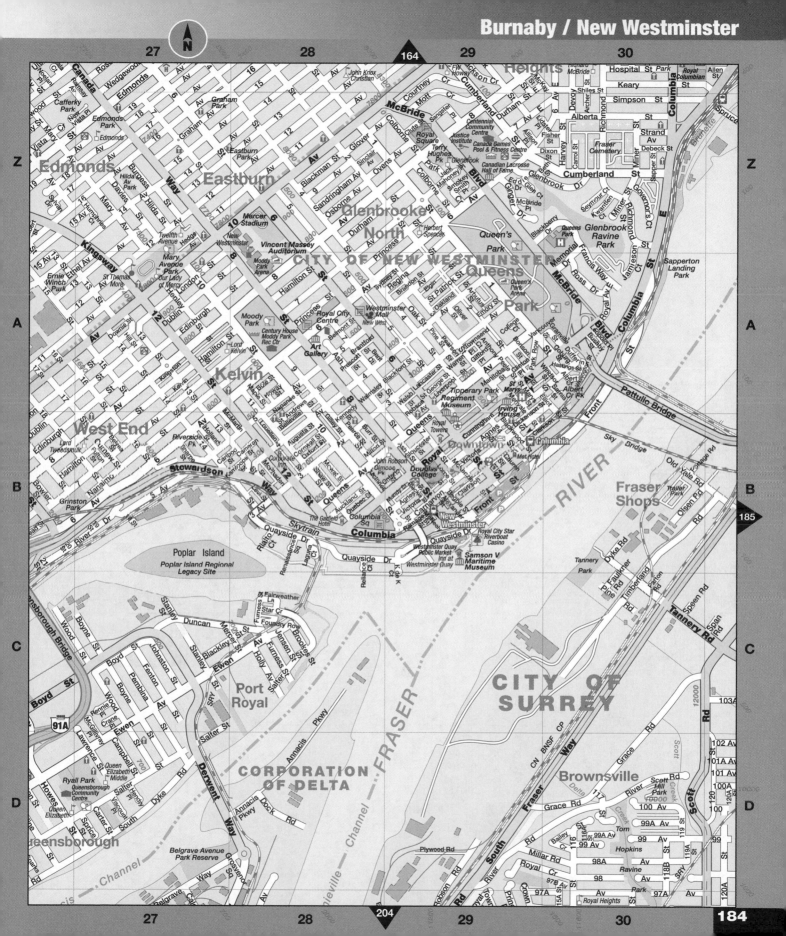

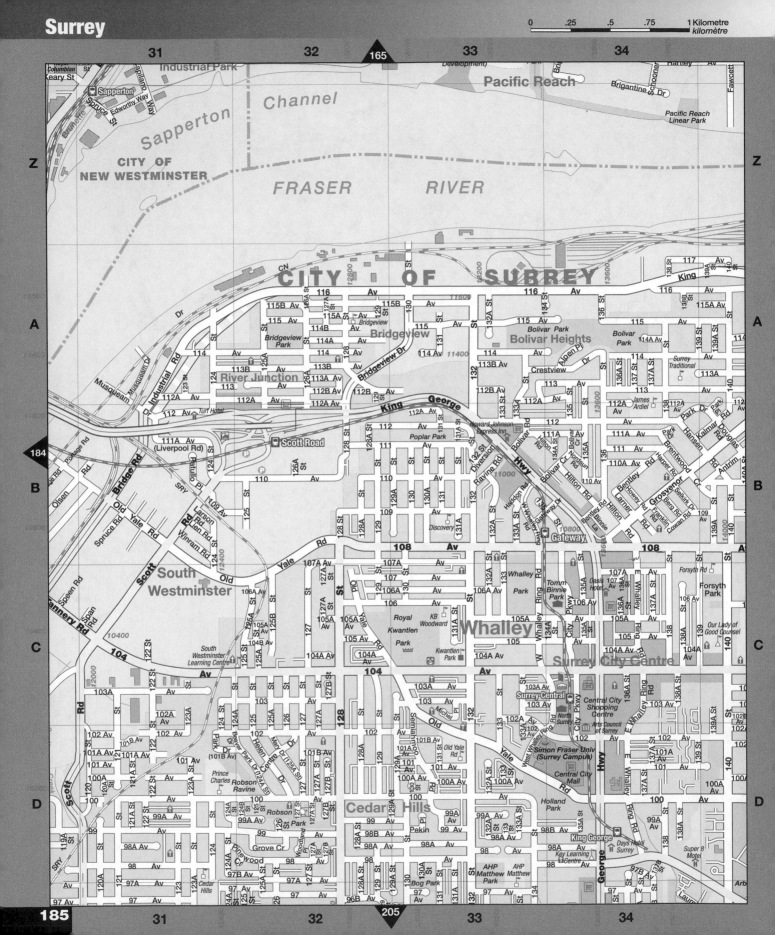

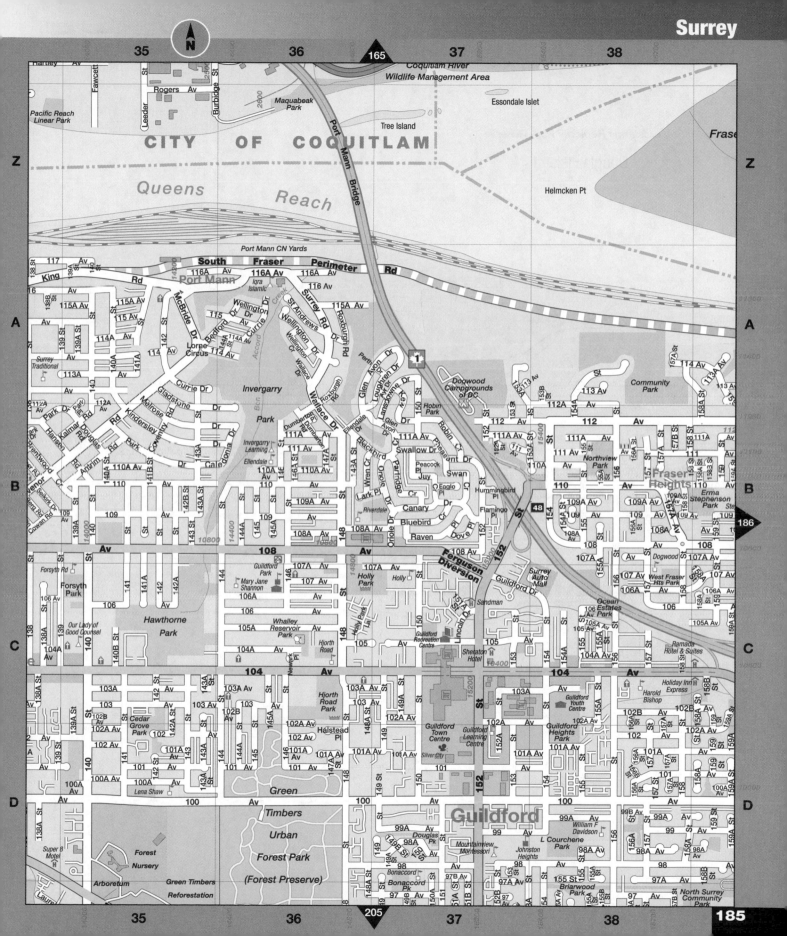

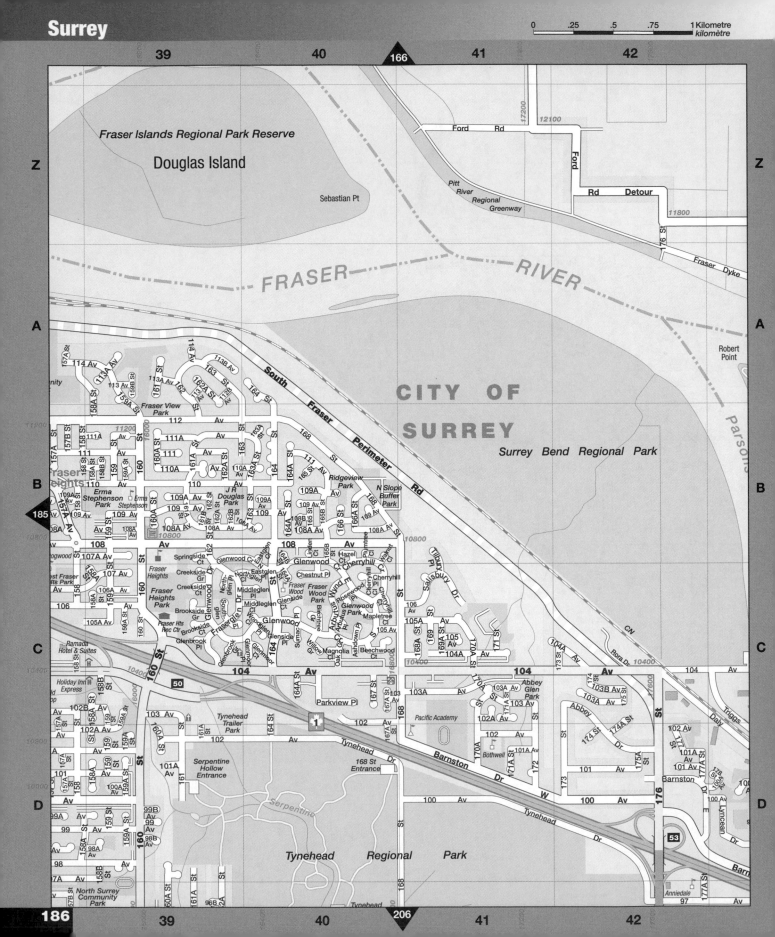

0 .25 .5 .75 1 Kilometre
kilomètre

39 40 166 41 42

Z

*Fraser Islands Regional Park Reserve*

## Douglas Island

Sebastian Pt

Ford Rd

17200

12100

Pitt River Regional Greenway

76 St

Fraser Dyke

11800

FRASER ———— RIVER

Robert Point

A

114 Av

157A St

113A

113B Av

163 St

162

162A St

112B

South Fraser Perimeter Rd

CITY OF

SURREY

Surrey Bend Regional Park

Parsons

114 Av

113A St

159B St

162A St

Fraser View Park

112 Av

164 St

168 St

163 St

158A St

159A St

11200

112 Av

111A St

163A St

111 Av

157A St

157B St

111A St

160A St

111 St

163 St

168 St

111 Av

16000

111A Av

164 Av

165 St

Ridgeview Park

N Slope Buffer Park

B

Fraser Heights

11200

157A St

158 St

158B St

159 St

110 St

161A St

162A St

164 St

165A St

168 St

185

Erma Stephenson Park

Erma Stephenson

109 Av

109A

162 St

163 St

109

109A Av

109 Av

165B St

166A St

168 St

109 Av

10800

157A Av

109 Av

160 St

108A Av

161A St

162A St

106A St

164A St

108B Av

166 St

108A St

108A Av

108 Av

108 Av

10800

107A Av

Fraser Heights

Springside

Glenwood Cr

Eastglen

Hazel

Chestnut Pl

Cherryhill

Plumtree

Walnut

Tilbury Dr

Salisbury Dr

Cogwood Ct

107 Av

158 St

160 St

Creekside Gr

Glenwood Dr

Northdale

Glenwood

Fraser Wood Park

Glenwood

Cherryhill

C

West Fraser Hts Park

106 Av

105A Av

158A St

160A St

160 St

Fraser Heights Park

Creekside Ct

Brookside

Middleglen Pl

Glenside Ct

Fraser Wood Park

Blichtree

Rosewood

Mapletree Ct

Cherry Pl

106 Av

Cherry

106 Av

169 St

105 Av

105 Av

171 St

104A Av

CN

Rora Dr

10400

104 Av

Fraser Hts Rec Ctr

Brookside Gr

Glenbrook

Glenmoor

Fraserglen Dr

Willow

Sumac Pl

Magnolia Ct

Ashdown Pl

Beechwood Ct

106 Av

168A St

169 St

104A

104A Av

120A St

104 Av

Av

Ramada Hotel & Suites

Glenbrook Pl

104 Av

164 St

164A Av

Parkview Pl

167 St

167A St

103

103A

168 St

Pacific Academy

170A St

103A Av

103 Av

Abbey Glen Park

174 St

103B Av

Abbey

75 St

176 St

102 Av

C

Holiday Inn Express

102B Av

157A St

158B St

102A Av

103 Av

160A St

161A St

102 Av

102 Av

164 St

102

167A St

167 St

Tynehead Trailer Park

102A Av

103A St

170A St

171A St

103 Av

102A Av

Bothwell

101A Av

174 St

174A St

175A St

101 Av

Barnston

177 St

101A Av

101 Av

D

101

159A St

101A Av

100A Av

Serpentine Hollow Entrance

168 St Entrance

168 St

Barnston Dr

100 Av

170A St

171A St

172 St

173 St

101 Av

175 St

Lyncean Dr

177A St

10000

99B Av

99A

99 Av

98A

98B Av

Serpentine

Tynehead Dr

100

100 Av

Tynehead Dr

53

Barn

98

98A Av

160 St

159A St

98B Av

## Tynehead Regional Park

168 St

97A Av

57B St

158 St

North Surrey Community Park

60A St

161A St

96B Av

Tynehead

Annedale

97 Av

177A St

39 40 206 41 42

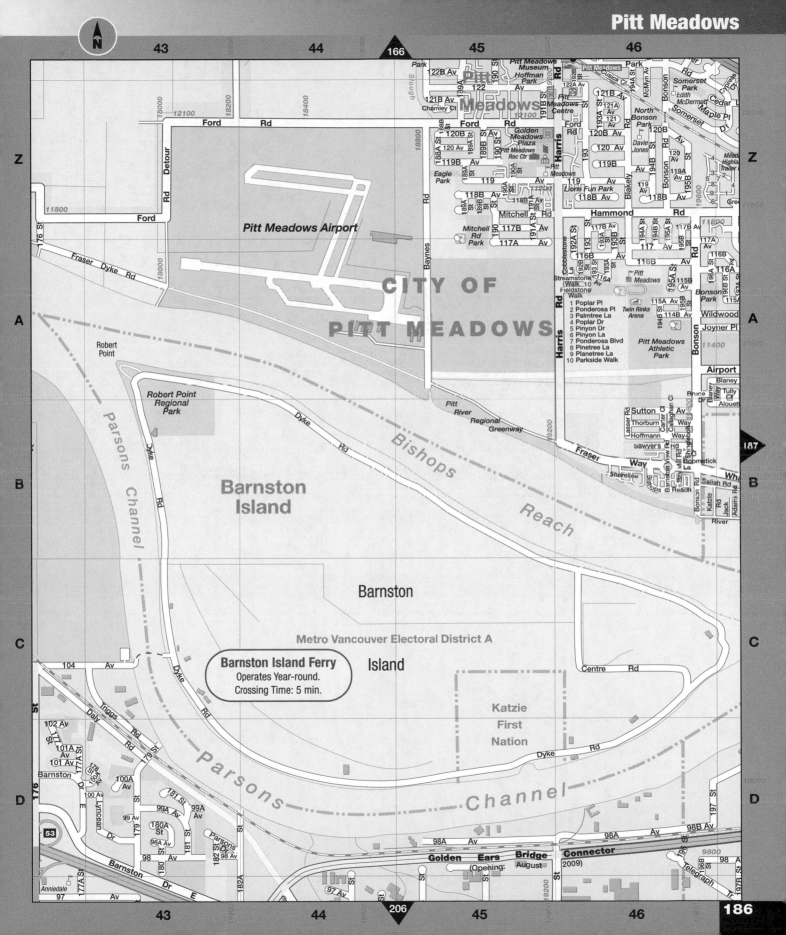

N

Park

122B Av

**Pitt Meadows**

Pitt Meadows Museum Hoffman Park

122

Cusick Gr

194 Av

McMyn Av

Somerset Park

Edith McDermott

Maple Pl

Cedar

Somerset Dr

Z

121B Av

Charnley Ct

121B Av

Pitt Meadows Centre

121A Av

120B Av

121

120B Av

North Bonson Park

Davie Jones

120 Av

Meadows Highland Trailer Ct

Ford        Rd

Ford    Rd

Harris

120B Av

119B

119B

Golden Meadows Plaza

120 Av

119B

Green

Eagle Park

Pitt Meadows Rec Ctr

Pitt Meadows

119

119B Av

119 Av

119A Av

118B Av

118B Av

Lions Fun Park

118B Av

Hammond        Rd

Rd

Mitchell Rd Park

Mitchell Rd

117B Av

117A

117

117 Av

117A Av

116B

116B Av

116A

**Pitt Meadows Airport**

Baynes

Harris Rd

Cobblestone La

Streamstone Walk

Fieldstone Walk

Pitt Meadows

115B Av

115A Av

Bonson Park

115B

115A

Rd

**CITY OF**

1 Poplar Pl
2 Ponderosa Pl
3 Palmtree La
4 Poplar Dr
5 Pinyon Dr
6 Pinyon La
7 Ponderosa Blvd
8 Pinetree La
9 Planetree La
10 Parkside Walk

Twin Rinks Arena

114B Av

Wildwood

A

**PITT  MEADOWS**

Pitt Meadows Athletic Park

Joyner Pl

Robert Point

Pitt River Regional Greenway

Airport

Blaney

Robert Point Regional Park

Blaney Way

Tully Ct

Alouet

Dyke

Rd

Bruce Dr

Lasser Rd

Sutton

Carter Ct

Callaghan Cl

Thorburn Way

Hoffmann

187

Fraser

Sawyers

Boomstick

**Bishops**

Way

Bansian View Rd

B

**Barnston Island**

**Reach**

Shoreline

Salish Rd

Wha

Bonson Rd

Katzie Rd

Jack Adams Rd

River

**Barnston**

C

Metro Vancouver Electoral District A

**Island**

Centre    Rd

104    Av

Katzie

**Barnston Island Ferry**
Operates Year-round.
Crossing Time: 5 min.

First

Triggs    Rd

181 St

Nation

Dyke    Rd

102 Av

181 St

101A Av

101 Av

99A Av

99A St

Barnston

100A Av

Lyncean Dr

179 St

99 Av

180A St

98A Av

182 Dr

98 Av

176

197 St

98B Av

D

53

98A    Av

98A

98

98B St

Barnston    Dr E

97 Av

**Golden    Ears    Bridge    Connector**
(Opening:    August    2009)

Telegraph Tr

Anniedale

177A St

97

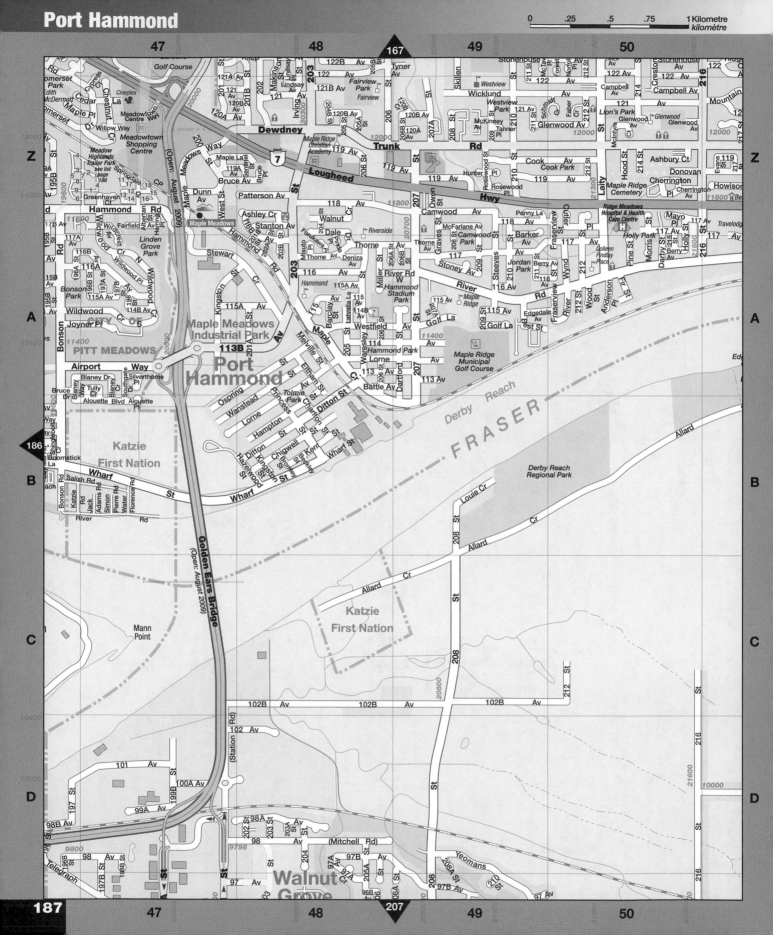

0   .25   .5   .75   1 Kilometre
                              *kilomètre*

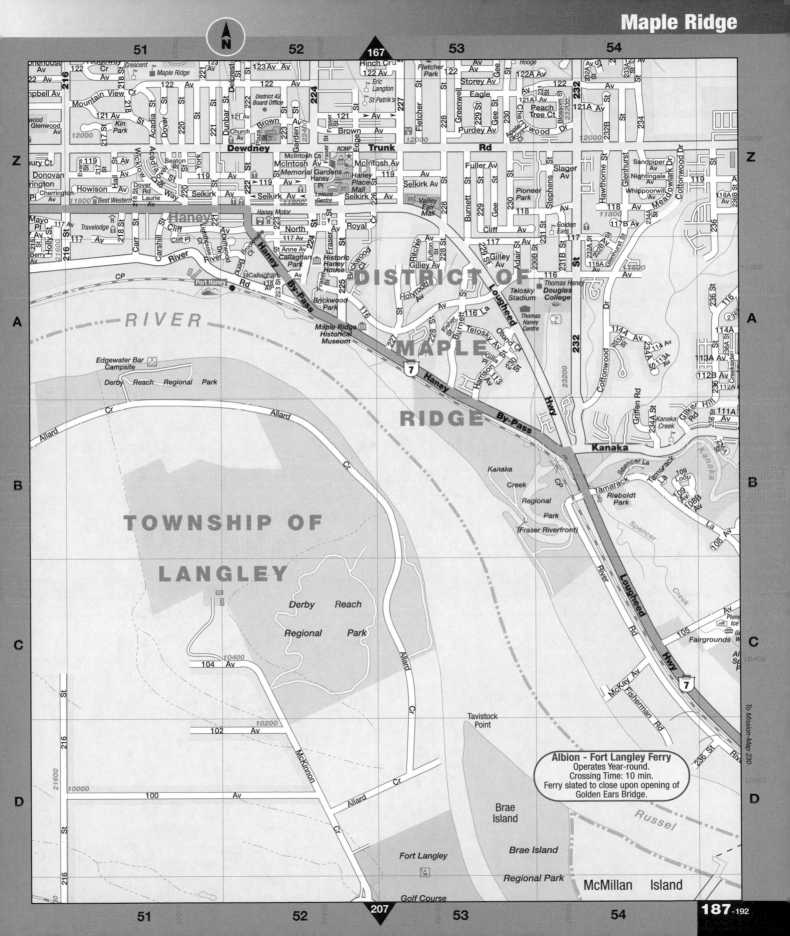

**Albion - Fort Langley Ferry**
Operates Year-round.
Crossing Time: 10 min.
Ferry slated to close upon opening of
Golden Ears Bridge.

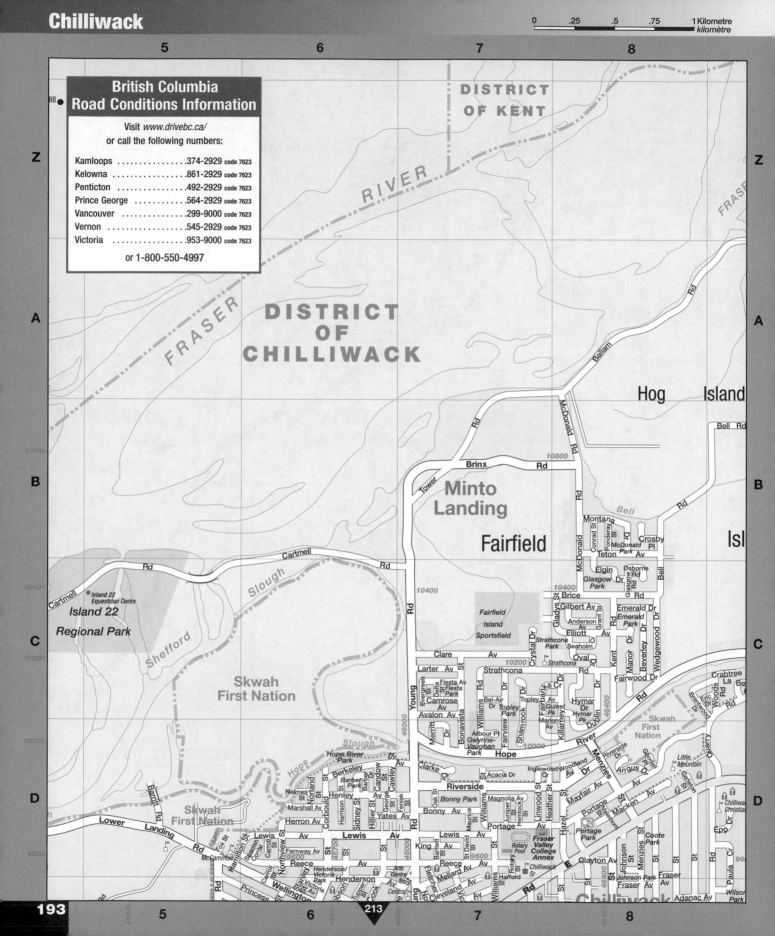

0    .25    .5    .75    1 Kilometre
kilomètre

**DISTRICT OF KENT**

**British Columbia Road Conditions Information**

Visit *www.drivebc.ca/*
or call the following numbers:

Kamloops ...............374-2929 code 7623
Kelowna ...............861-2929 code 7623
Penticton ..............492-2929 code 7623
Prince George .........564-2929 code 7623
Vancouver ..............299-9000 code 7623
Vernon ................545-2929 code 7623
Victoria ...............953-9000 code 7623

or 1-800-550-4997

RIVER

FRASER

FRASER

Z

A

**DISTRICT OF CHILLIWACK**

Hog    Island

Bell Rd

Isl

Ballam Rd

B

Minto Landing

McDonald Rd

Brinx    Rd

Tower

Bell

Montana

Conrad St
Ponderay St
Crosby Pl
McDonald Park Av
Teton

**Fairfield**

McDonald

Elgin
Glasgow Park
Osborne Rd
Glasgow Rd
Bell

10800

10400

Cartmell        Rd        Rd

Rd        Rd

Cartmell    Rd

Shefford    Slough

Island 22
Equestrian Centre

**Island 22 Regional Park**

10400

Brice

Gilbert Av
Gladys St
Anderson Av
Grant St
Seaholm
Elliott

Emerald Dr
Emerald Park
Kent
Manor

Fairfield Island Sportsfield

Crystal Dr

Strathcona Park
Oval
Strathcona

Beverley Dr
Wedgewood Dr

10400

10200

C

Clare        Av

Strathcona    Rd

Fairwood Dr

Crabtree La    Be

Eric Woods Rd
Brentwood Rd

**Skwah First Nation**

Larter Av

Young

Evergreen St
Delta St
Fiesta St
Fiesta Park

Strathcona Dr

Hymar Dr
Hymar Pk

Dublin

Skwah First Nation

Slough

Hope

Camrose Av

Williams

Bel-Air St
Topley Park

Topley Av
Guinet Pk
Fairbanks Cr
Marion Av

Killarney

River    Rd

Little Mountain

10000

Avalon Av
Merritt St

Bonavista St

Gwynne-Vaughan Park

Shamrock

**Hope**

Menzies

Riverside Dr

Angus

Goodall

10000

Hope River Park

Berkeley St

Barber Park

Clarke Dr

Acacia Dr

Riverside

Inglewood Cr
Woodland

Hazel St

Carleton

Chilliwack Christian

D

Lower    Landing    Rd

Barritt Rd

**Skwah First Nation**

Nelmes St
Norland St

Marshall Av

Herron Av

Corbould St

Henley
Harrison St
Sidney St
Hillier St
George St

Candow St
Cawley

Yates Av

Feniak St

Bonny Park

Oak St
Bonny Av

Maurice St

Magnolia Av
Williams

Juniper St
Hemlock St

Portage

Linwood St
Heather St

Portage Park

Mayfair Av
Portage

Macken St

Menzies St

Coote Park

Epp

9600

McCammon Rd
Hamilton St

Lewis Av
Fox St
Staplen St
Carroll St
Northview St

Fernway Av

Reece Av

Henderson/Victoria Park

Henderson

Wellington

Lewis    Av    St

King St

Bartlett St

St David St

Lewis    Av

Reece Av

Mellard St

Arts Centre

Central

Fraser Valley College Annex

Rotary Pool

Chilliwack Sr

Electrical St
Cleveland St
No

Williams St

Harford St

Clayton Av

E    Rd

Johnson St
Menzies St

Fraser St

Johnson Park
Fraser Av

Adanac Av

Paula Cr

96

Wilson Park

**Chilliwack**

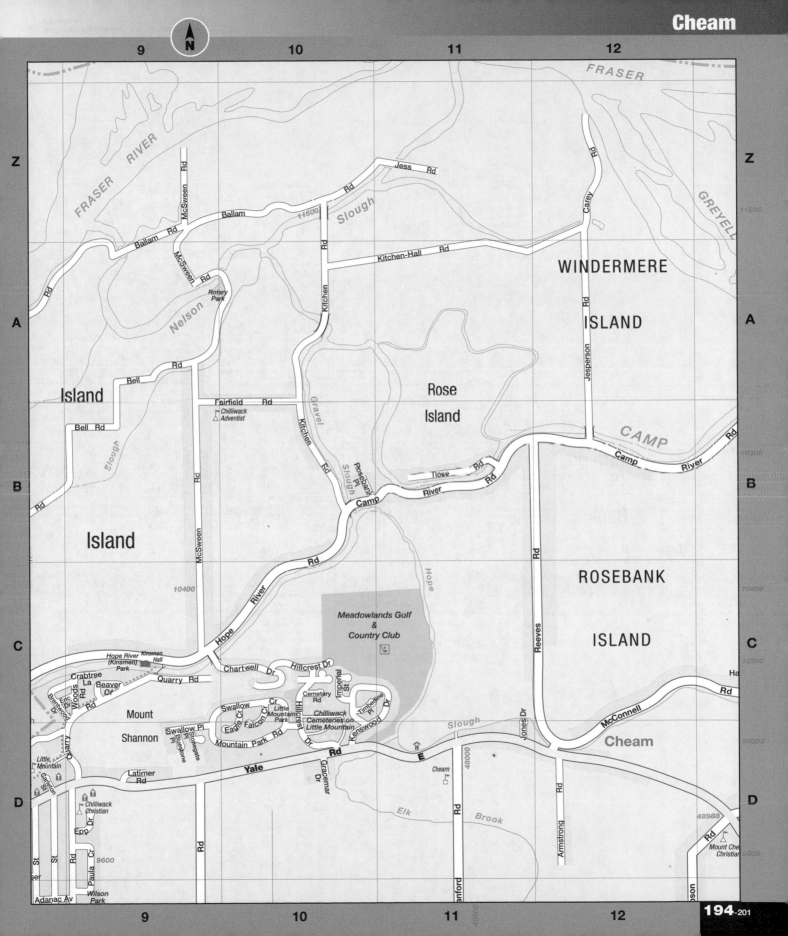

FRASER

9   10   11   12

N

Z

FRASER RIVER

McSween Rd

Ballam

11500

Slough

Jess   Rd

Carey   Rd

GREYELL

11500

WINDERMERE

Z

Ballam Rd

McSween Rd

Kitchen   Rd

Kitchen-Hall   Rd

ISLAND

A

Rd

Nelson

Rotary
Park

Kitchen   Rd

Jesperson   Rd

A

Island

Rd

Bell

Rose
Island

CAMP

Rd

Fairfield   Rd

Chilliwack
Adventist

Gravel

Camp   River

10300

Bell Rd

Slough

Kitchen   Rd

Rosebank Pl

Tioee   Rd

Rd

B

Rd

Island

McSween   Rd

Slough

Camp   River

Rd

ROSEBANK

B

10400

Hope

Reeves   Rd

ISLAND

10200

Meadowlands Golf
&
Country Club

10200

C

Hope   River   Rd

Hope River
(Kinsmen)
Park

Kinsmen
Hall

Chartwell   Dr

Hillcrest Dr

Imperial
St

Ha   Rd

C

Crabtree
La

Beaver
Cr

Quarry   Rd

Eric
Woods
Rd

Brentwood

Mount

Swallow
Cr

Eagle Cr   Falcon Ct

Cemetery
Rd

Little
Mountain
Park

Timberline
Pl

Kenswood Dr

McConnell   Rd

Slough

10000

Cheam

Shannon

Swallow Pl

Stonegate

Bluestone Pl

Mountain Park   Rd

Hillcrest Dr

Chilliwack
Cemeteries on
Little Mountain

Jones Dr

Little
Mountain

Quarry

Rd   Rd

Yale

Latimer
Rd

Rd

Rd

Gracemar
Dr

E

Cheam

48000

D

Carleton St

Chilliwack
Christian

Epp Dr

Rd

Paula Cr

9600

Elk

Brook

Rd

Armstrong   Rd

48988

Rd

Mount Che
Christian   9500

10000

Adanac Av

Wilson
Park

Fraser St

St

St

anford   Rd

son

D

9   10   11   12

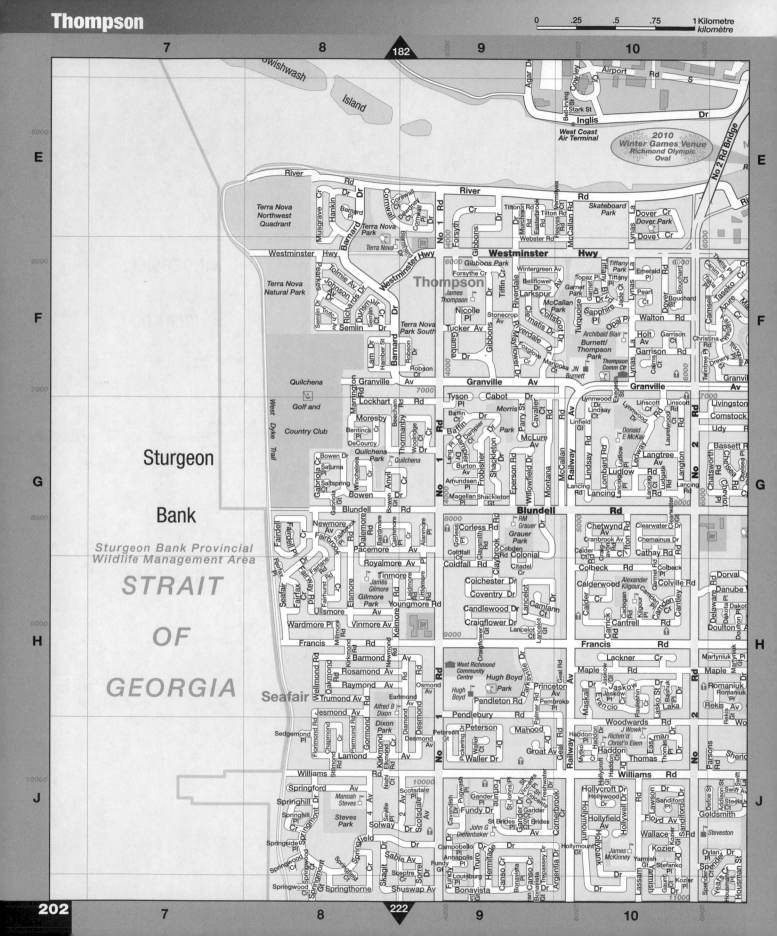

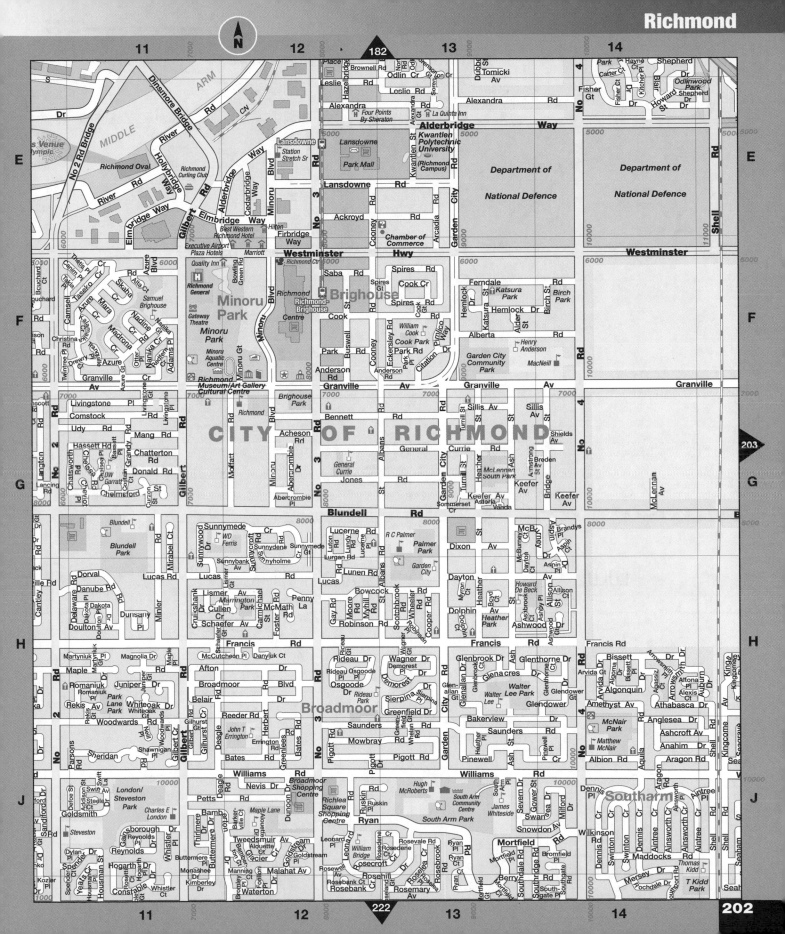

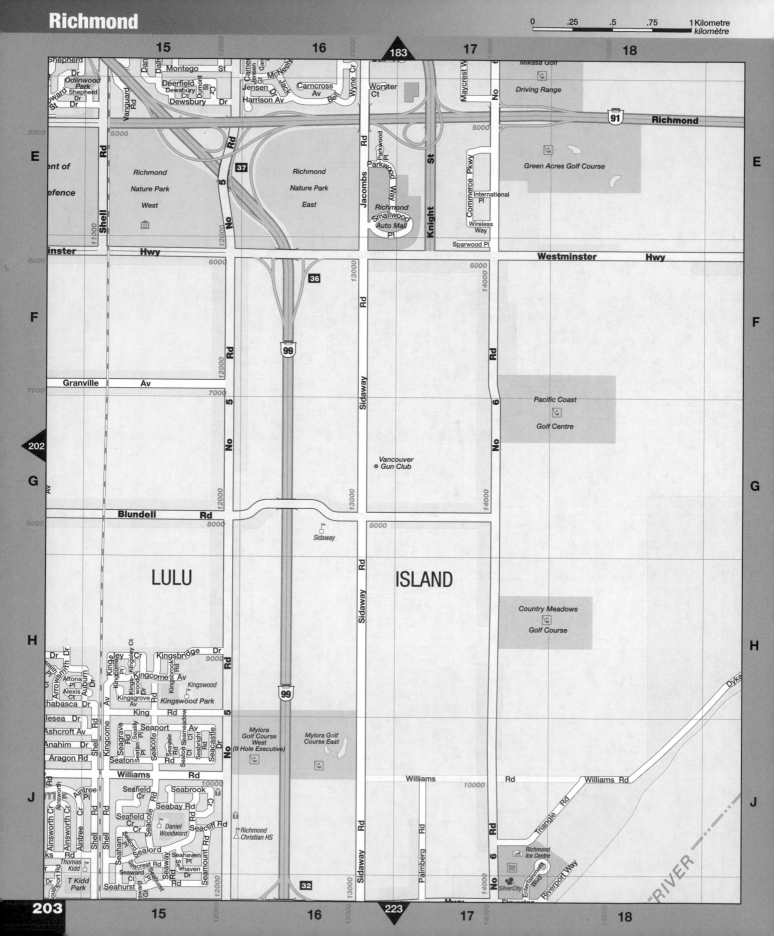

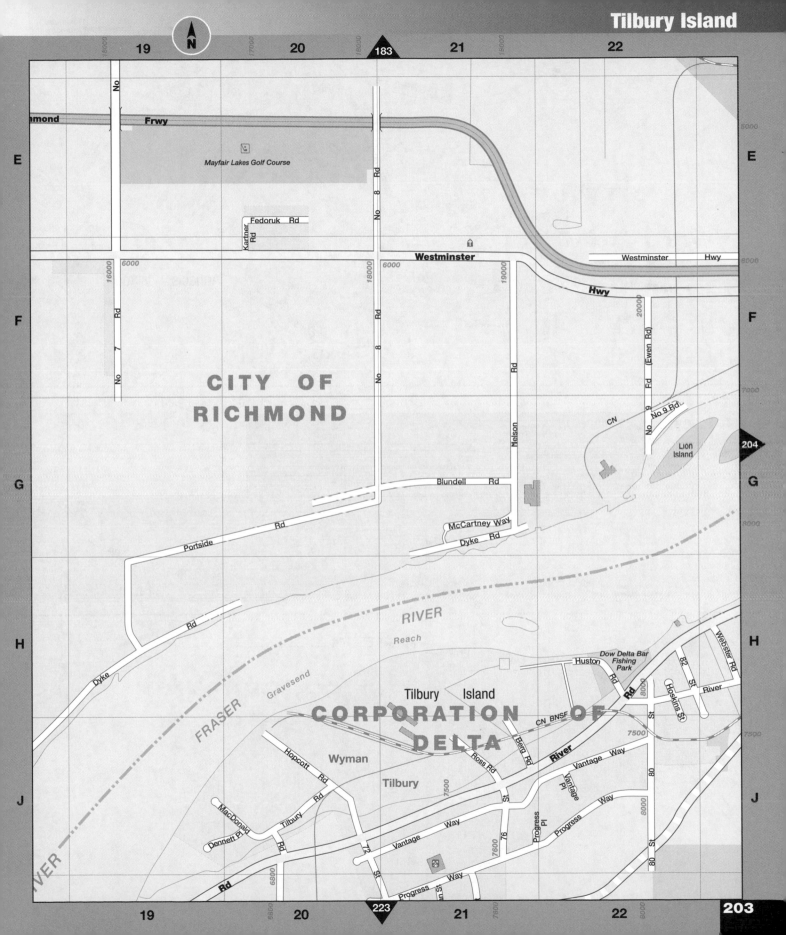

19    20    183    21    22

E

Mayfair Lakes Golf Course

Fedoruk   Rd

Kartner Rd

No   Rd

Frwy

Richmond

16000    6000    18000    6000    19000    20000    8000

Westminster

F

No   7   Rd

No   8   Rd

Westminster   Hwy

Hwy

No   9   Rd   (Ewen Rd)

**CITY   OF**
**RICHMOND**

7000

CN

Nelson   Rd

Lion
Island

204

G

Blundell   Rd

McCartney Way

Portside   Rd

Dyke   Rd

8000

RIVER

Reach

H

Dyke   Rd

Gravesend

FRASER

Dow Delta Bar
Fishing Park

Huston   Rd

Webster Rd

Hoskins St

82   St

River

7000

Tilbury   Island

**CORPORATION   OF**
**DELTA**

CN BNSF

River

7500

7500

Hopcott   Rd

Wyman

Tilbury

Ross Rd

Berg Rd

Vantage   Way

Vantage
Pl

80   St

80   St

MacDonald   Rd

Tilbury   Rd

7500

St

Progress   Pl

Progress

Way

7600    76

J

Dennett Pl

Vantage   Way

72   St

7600

Progress   Way

80   St

RIVER

6800

Rd

6800

Progress   Way

19    20    223    21    22    **203**

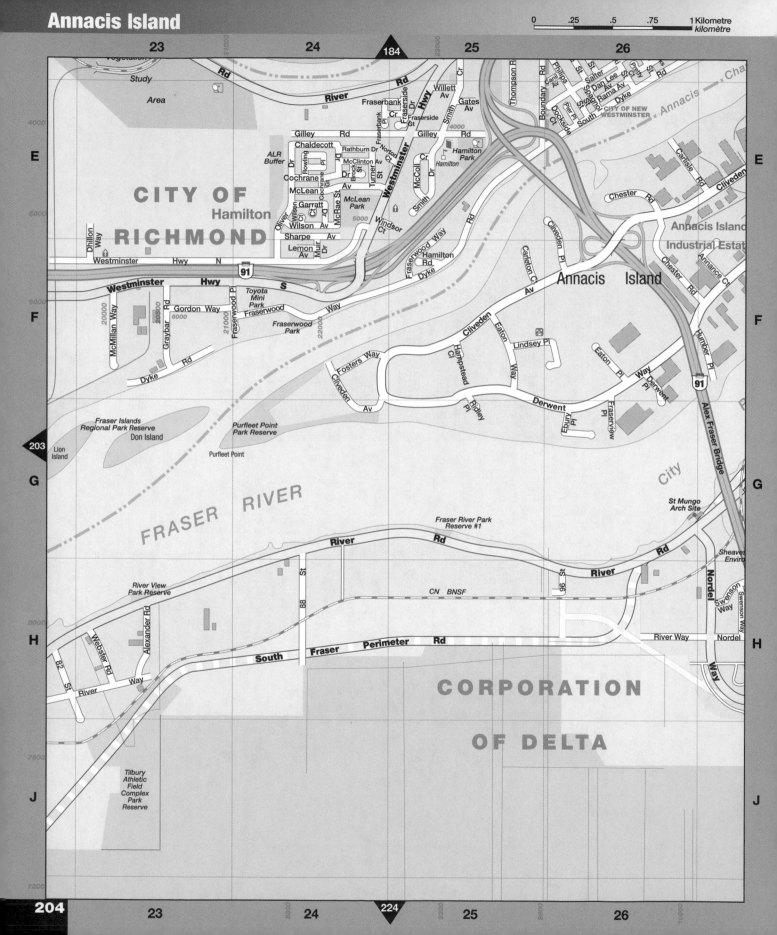

23   24   **184**   25   26

E

**CITY OF**

Study
Area

*Hamilton*

**RICHMOND**

River   Rd

Fraserbank

Willett
Av

Gates
Av

Fraserside
Gt

Gilley   Rd

ALR
Buffer

Chaldecott

Rathburn Dr

McClinton Av

Hamilton
Park

Rowling

McColl

Cochrane
Dr

Brock

Turner St

Gilley   Rd

Hamilton

Chester   Rd

McLean

Garratt

McLean
Park

5000

Windsor
Ct

Smith

Annacis Island
Industrial Estat

Sharpe   Av

Lemon
Av

Muir
Dr

Dillon
Way

Westminster   Hwy   N

**91**

Fraserwood   Way

Hamilton
Rd

Dyke

Annacis   Island

Carleton Ct

Cliveden
Pl

Chester   Rd

Annance Ct

Westminster   Hwy   S

McMillan Way

20000

20500

Graybar

Gordon Way
6000

Fraserwood

Toyota
Mini
Park

Fraserwood
Park

Way

22000

Cliveden
Av

Eaton
Way

Lindsey Pl

Eaton
Pl

Way

Derwent
Pl

Humber Pl

**91**

E

F

F

Dyke   Rd

Fosters Way

Hampstead
Cl

Ridley
Pl

Ebury
Pl

Derwent

Fraserview
Pl

Alex Fraser Bridge

203

Fraser Islands
Regional Park Reserve
Don Island

Lion
Island

Purfleet Point
Park Reserve

Purfleet Point

Cliveden
Av

City

St Mungo
Arch Site

G   G

**FRASER   RIVER**

Fraser River Park
Reserve #1

River   Rd

River   Rd

Sheaves
Enviro

River View
Park Reserve

St

88

CN   BNSF

99 St

River

Nordel

Swenson
Way

Swenson Way

8000

Webster Rd

Alexander Rd

River
Way

River Way

Nordel

H   H

82 St

**South   Fraser   Perimeter   Rd**

**CORPORATION**

Way

7800

Tilbury
Athletic
Field
Complex
Park
Reserve

**OF DELTA**

J   J

7200

23   24   **224**   25   26

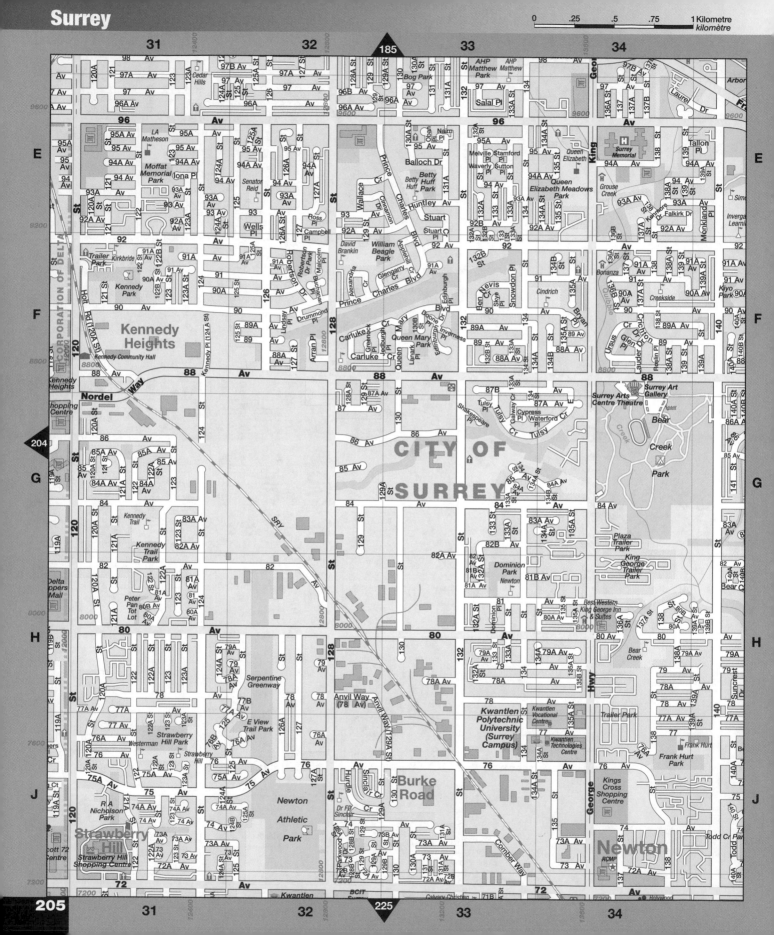

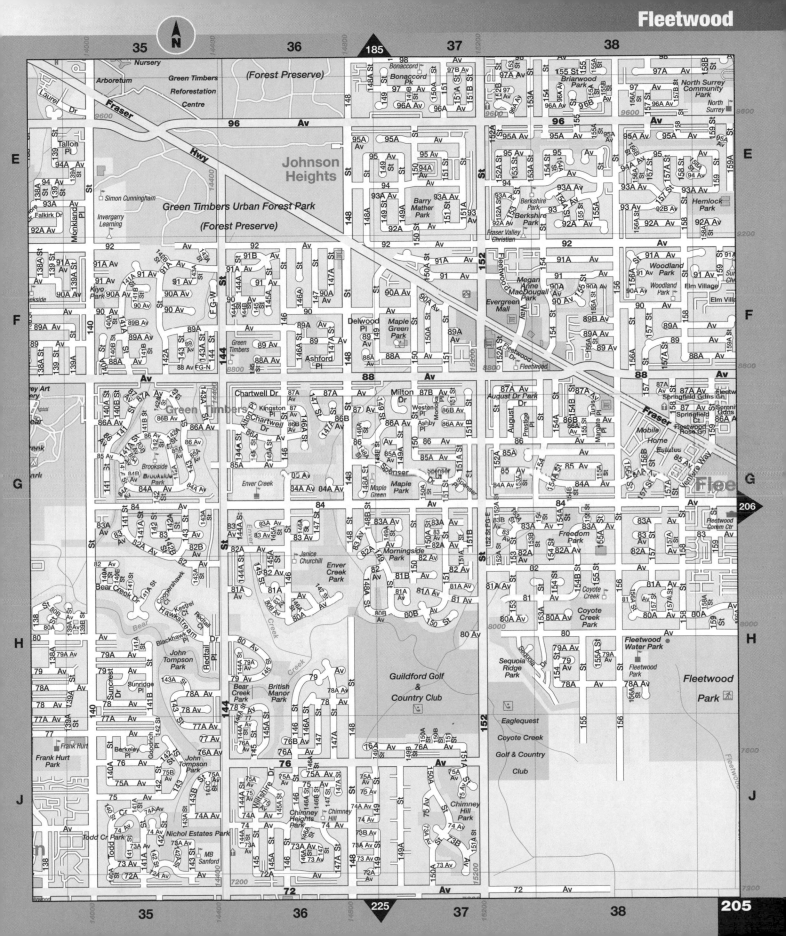

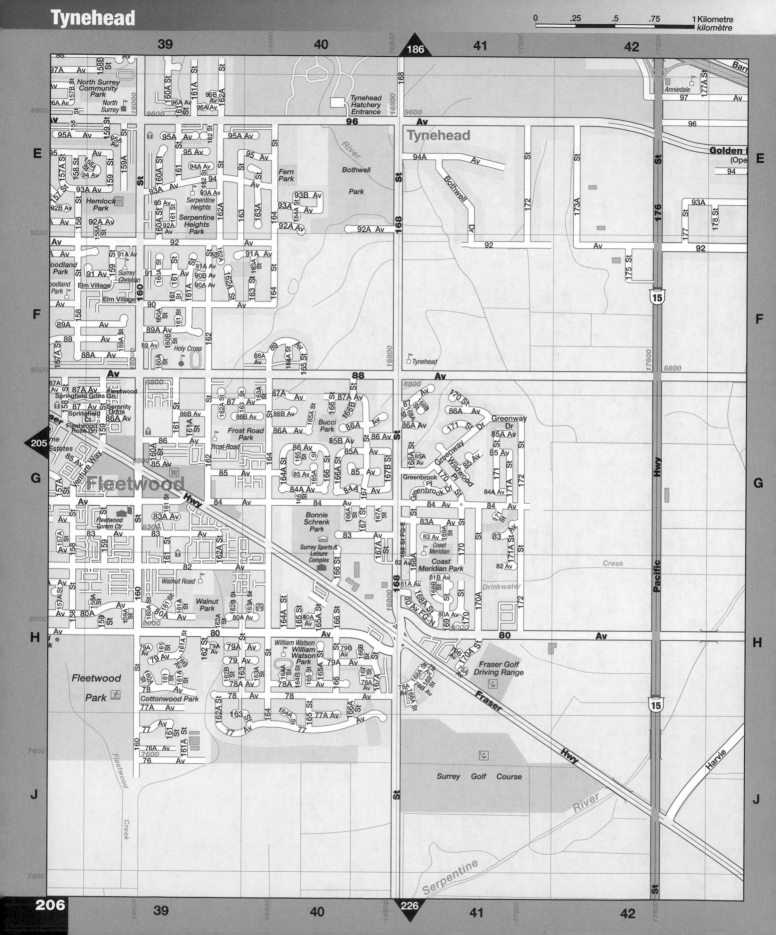

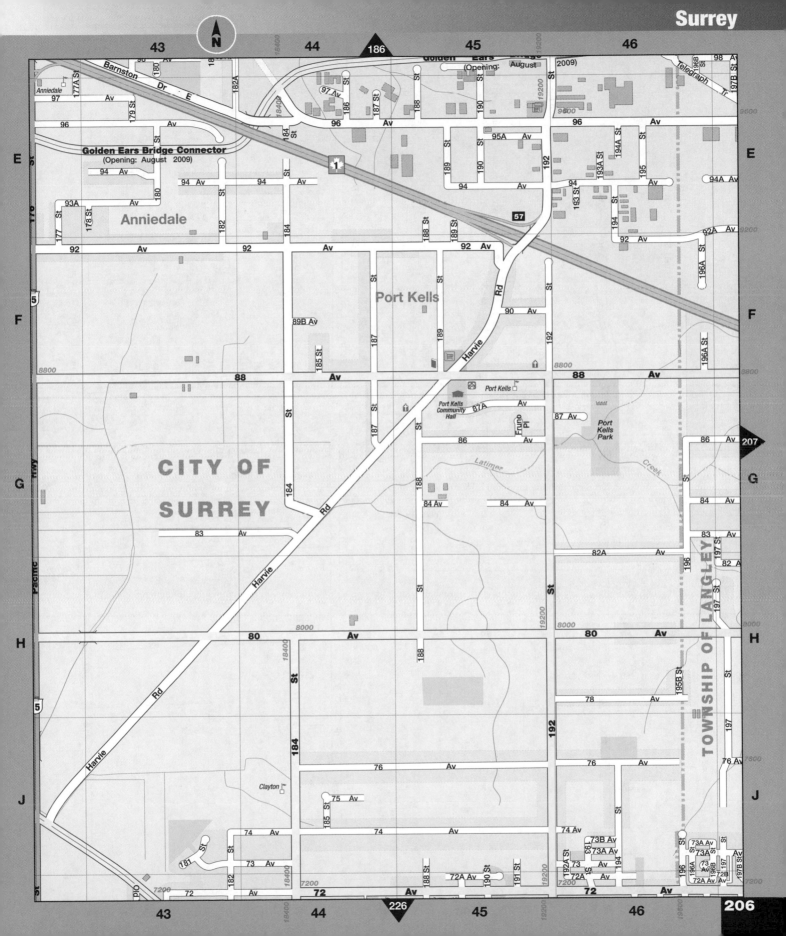

Anniedale

Golden Ears Bridge
(Opening: August 2009)

Golden Ears Bridge Connector
(Opening: August 2009)

Anniedale

Port Kells

CITY OF
SURREY

Port Kells
Community Hall

Port Kells Park

Clayton

TOWNSHIP OF LANGLEY

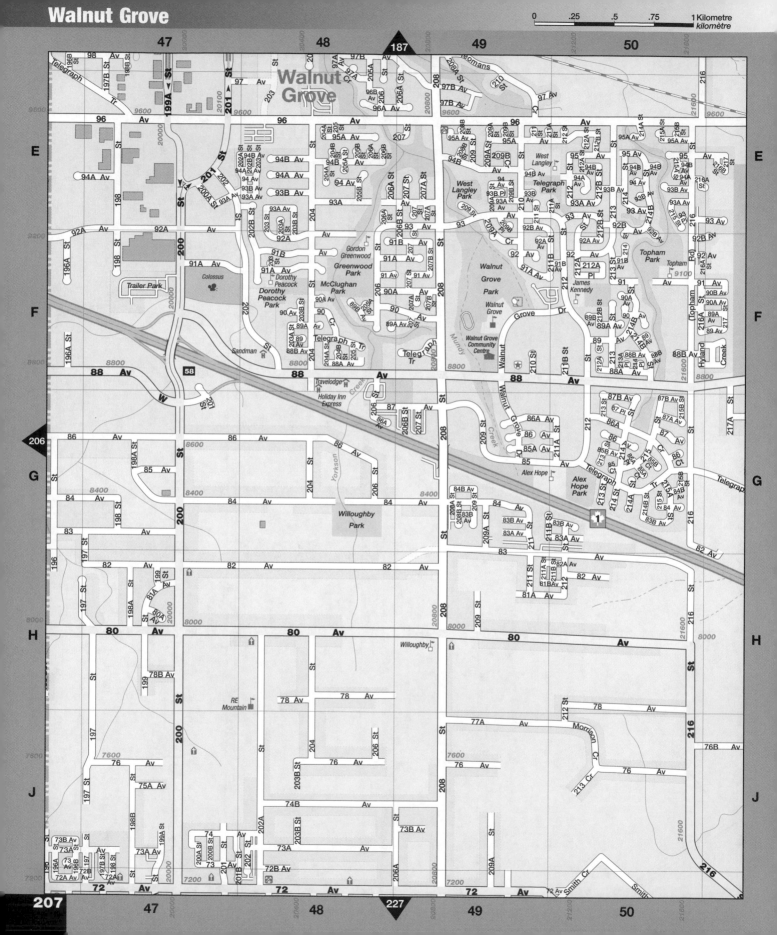

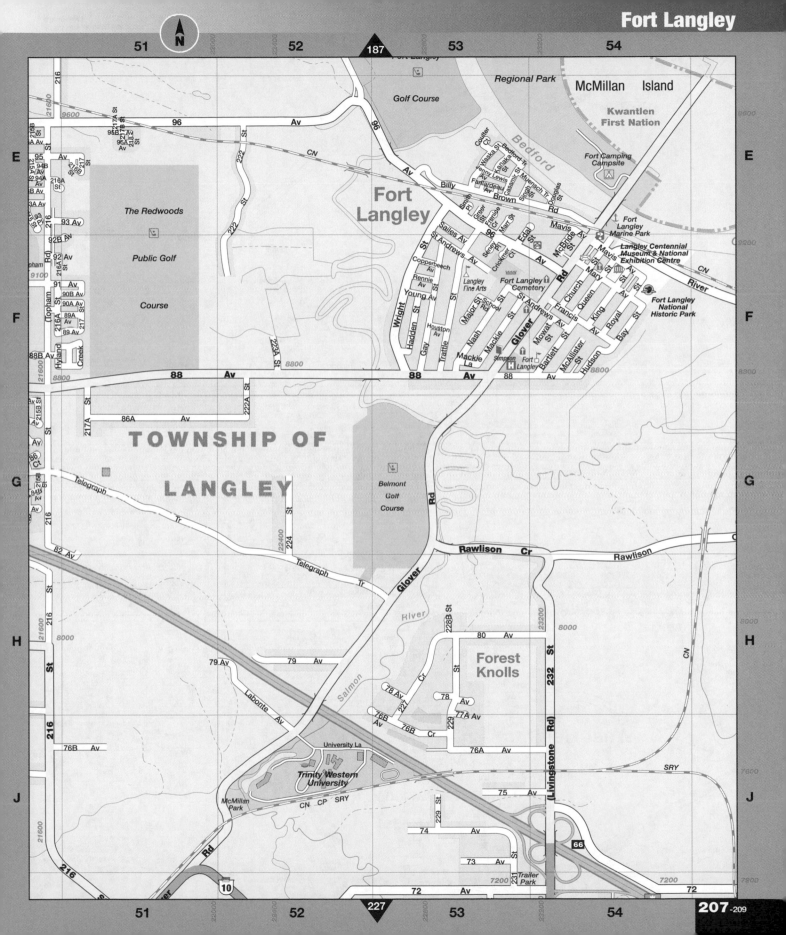

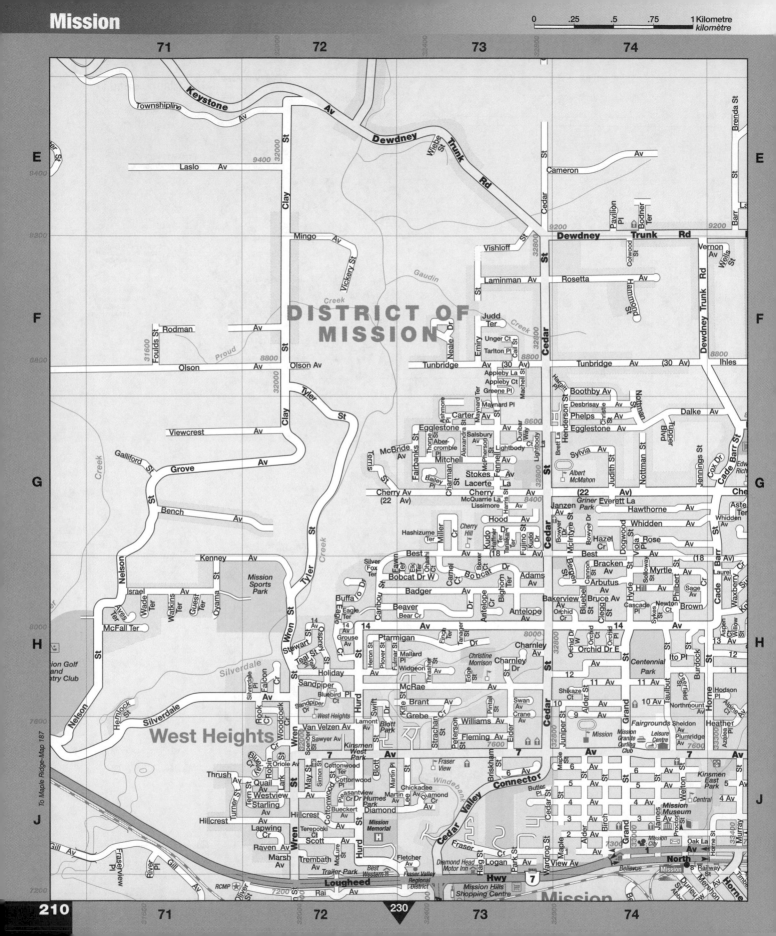

N

75　76　77　78

E

N Sward Rd　Sward

Brenda St　Barr St　Doyle St　Kirkpatrick　Av　9600

Vista St

Dawson Dr　Monte　Dlugosh　Av　Ferndale

Hartman　Av

Davidson St　Erickson St

Barr St　Larkspur　Av

9200　9200

Rd　**Ferndale**　**Av**　Ferndale　Av　Ferndale Av

Vernon Av　Wells St

Dewdney Trunk Rd

Laxton　Av

34000

Lake St

Stave St

F

Mission Medium Security Institution

Draper　Draper St　Taylor St

Creek

8800

Moss　Av　Wharton　Creek

8800

Ihles　Av　York Av　Goundrey St　Jones Ter

W Edwards　E Edwards St

Neilson Regional Park

Ferndale Minimum Security Institution

Hatzic Cemetery

Dalke　Av

Public Works

District of Mission Offices

8600　Dewdney　Trunk　Rd　Penner

Cemetery　Av

Draper

McEwen Ter　McEwen St

Edwards

Hatzic

G

Jennings St　Cade Barr St

Edwin S Richards

Bannister Dr

Doersen

Bowie Dr

Kimball Pl

Hollister

Araki Ct

8600　8600

Ireland Av　Penner

Penner St　Dunn St

Dewdney Trunk Rd

8600　Hatzic

Douglas Av

Weaver Cr

McEwen

Ewen Av

Fripp Ter

Av

Aster Ter　Cherry　Av　Graham Ct　Veres Ter

(22 Av)　Chorry Av　8400

Dunn St　Dunn St

8400

Dewdney　Trunk　Rd

Tingal

Fenmo Pl

Shimek

Mycon St

Henry

Dixon

Fisher Cr

Whidden Av　Blueberry　Casselman Cr　Hillside

Gale St　Mahoria

Wharton Pl

Herat

Parr　Av

Westminster Abbey (Benedictine Monastery)

Pfitzer Memorial Bell Tower

**Hatzic**

Cambridge　Pl

Fenmo Pl　Hatzic

Moffat

XÁ:YTEM Longhouse Interpretive Cen

Philbert St　Sage Av　Brown

(18　Av)

Blueberry Dr　Copper Pl

Peacock Pl　Appel Ct

Best

Barnett　Dorothea

Baynes　Rockridge Pl

Vosburgh Av

Manson St　Coleman St

Pakenham Pl

Brealey Ct

Brient　Dr

CP

H

To Pl　Burdock St

Cade Barr Av

Laurel St　Waxberry Cr　Knight

Sumac Pl

Forbes St

Crosby St

Broom St

Topper

Knight　St

Crewall St

Little Dr　Kettley

Bush St

Knight St

Willat　Pl　Jasper　Dann St　Ferguson　Av

Jasper St

Trailer Park

Lougheed　Hwy

RIVER

Aspen　Willow St

Balsam　Dunsmuir

Weatherhead

Hughes Ter　Clarion

Topper St

Melbon

Lake St

Catchpole Av　Norrish

Manson St

FRASER

Matsqui　Trail　Regional Park

13　Av

12

11

Peytavin　Traverner

Pine St　Fir St

Windebank

Prentis

University of the Fraser Valley (Mission Campus)

Heritage Park Centre (Clarke Theatre)

D'Herbomez Creek

**CITY OF ABBOTSFORD**

J

Horne St

Hodson Pl　Aldine St

10　Av

Stave St

Heritage Park

Heather St　Dunsmuir

9　Av

8

Sheldon Av　Plumridge Av

Azalea Pl

Columbia St

7600　7600

Fraser River Heritage Park

Mary St

CP

7600

7　Av

Kinsmen East Park

Dunsmuir St

Columbia St

Sharpe St

Ryan Av

4 Av　Central

6 Av　Northcote

Gilbard St

5 Av

Erskine St

Riverview St

Walters

Regional Park

Anderson　Av

Mission Museum

Proctor　Oak La

Av　North　ion

Railway　Railway

Home St　Murray St

Catherwood St

33400　7300

1　Av　Av

CP

7200

Kelleher St

7200

Sim　Rd

Behal

Dureau St　Mershon St

**Home**　St

Thompson St　Timberlake　Broadway

Timberwood St

230

75　76　77　78

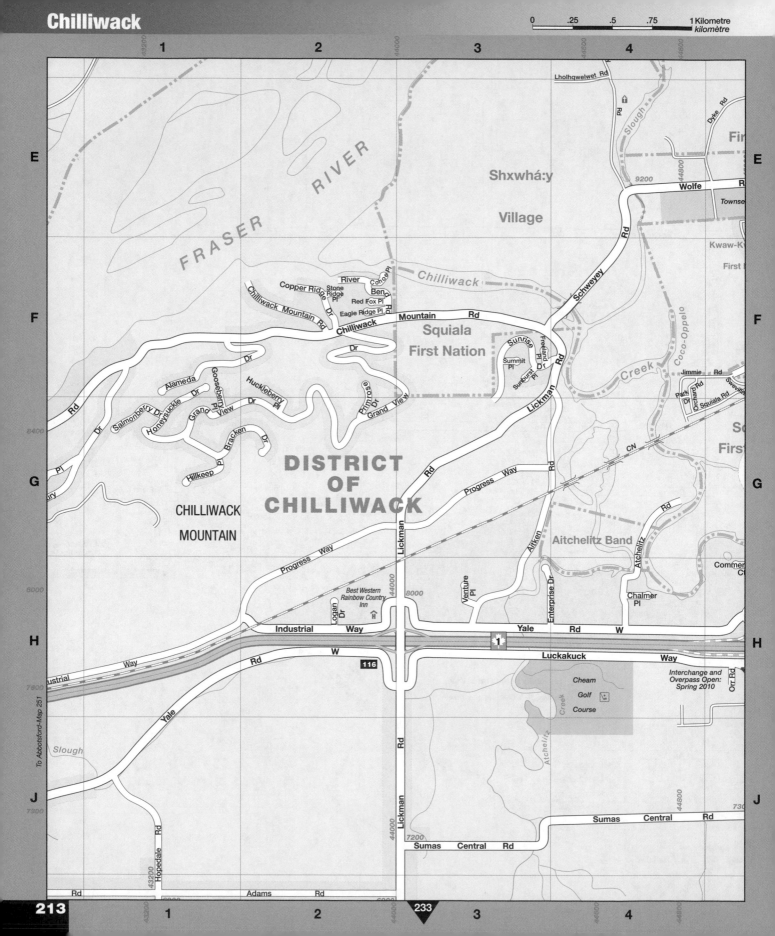

0    .25    .5    .75    1 Kilometre
*kilomètre*

**1    2    3    4**

Lholhqwelwet Rd

Dyke Rd

Slough

9200

44800

Wolfe

Fir

Townse

Kwaw-K

First

FRASER RIVER

Shxwhá:y

Village

Schweyey Rd

Coco-Oppelo Creek

River    Coho Pl

Copper Ridge Dr    Stone Ridge Pl    Ben

Chilliwack Mountain Rd    Red Fox Pl    Mountain    Rd

Eagle Ridge Pl    Chilliwack

Squiala

First Nation

Sunrise Pl    Freeland Dr

Summit Pl

Sunburst Pl    Lickman Rd

Jimmie    Rd

Park    Dr    Orchard Rd

Squiala Rd

Dr

Huckleberry Pl    Dr

Alameda    Dr

Gooseberry    Pl    View

Grand    Dr    Primrose    Dr

Salmonberry Dr    Honeysuckle    Dr

Grand    View

Rd    Dr

Pl    Bracken    Dr

Rd    Lickman    Rd

Hillkeep

**DISTRICT
OF
CHILLIWACK**

CHILLIWACK

MOUNTAIN

Progress    Way

Aitken    Rd

Aitchelitz    Rd

So

First

CN

Rd

Aitchelitz Band

Commer
C

Progress    Way

Venture    Pl

Enterprise Dr

Chalmer    Pl

6000

44000    8000

Best Western
Rainbow Country
Inn

Logan    Dr

Industrial    Way    Yale    Rd    W

**1**

Luckakuck    Way

W    **116**

Industrial    Way

Yale    Rd    W

Cheam

Golf

Course

Atchelitz    Creek

Interchange and
Overpass Open:
Spring 2010

Orr Rd

44800    730

7800

To Abbotsford–Map 251

Slough

Yale

Rd

7200

Hopedale    Rd

43200

Lickman    Rd

44000

7200    Sumas    Central    Rd

Sumas    Central    Rd

Rd    Adams    Rd

**1    2    233    3    4**

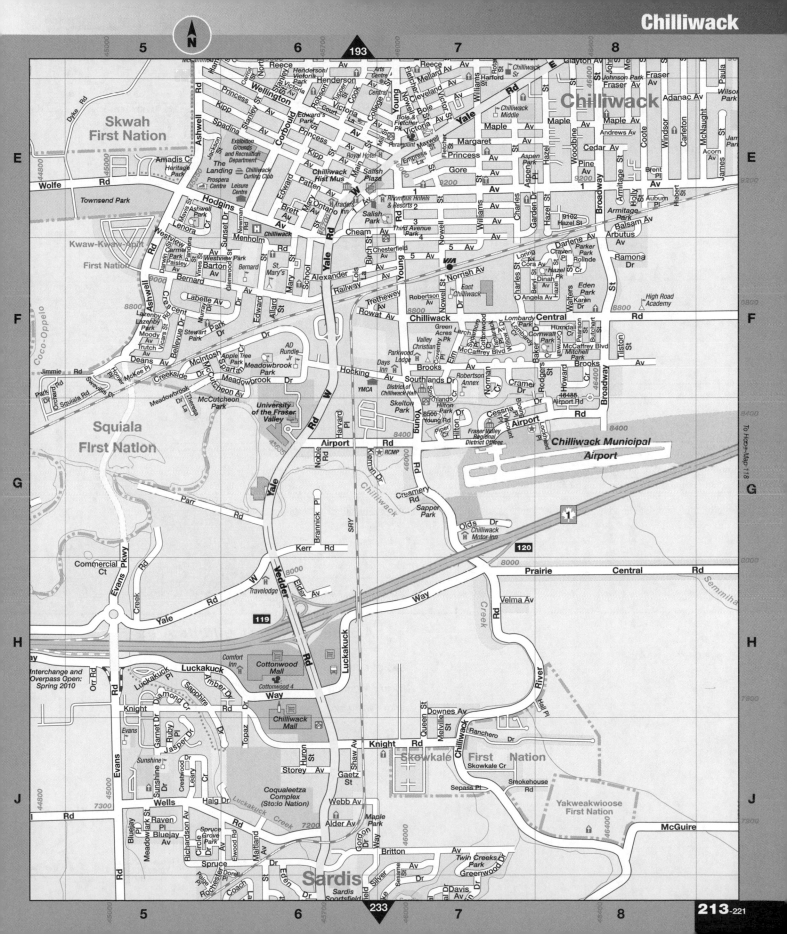

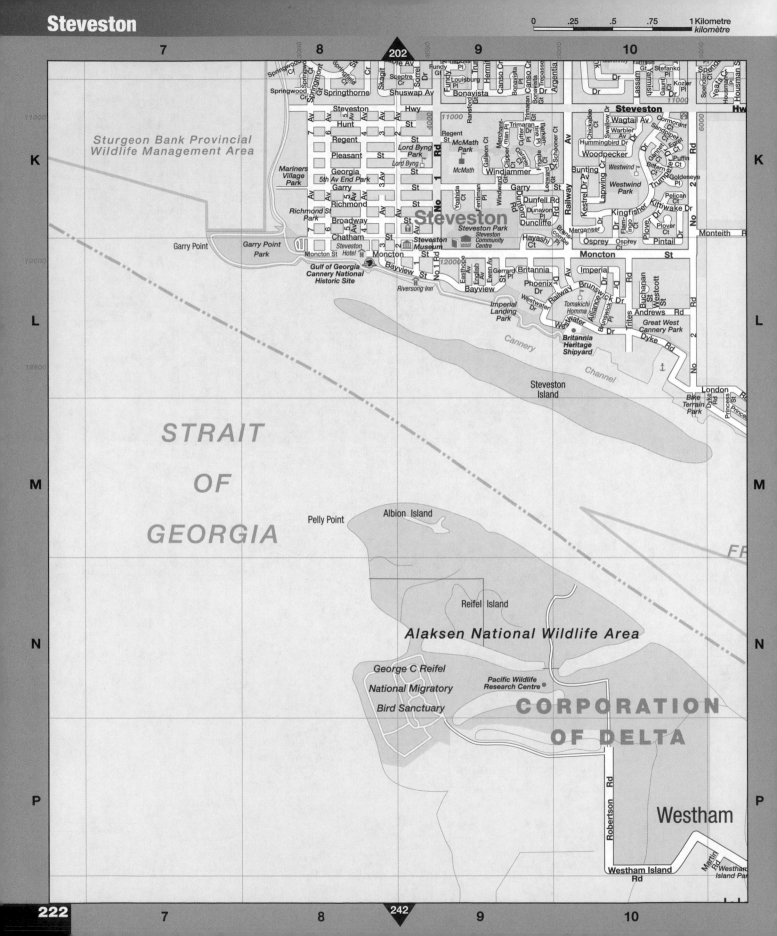

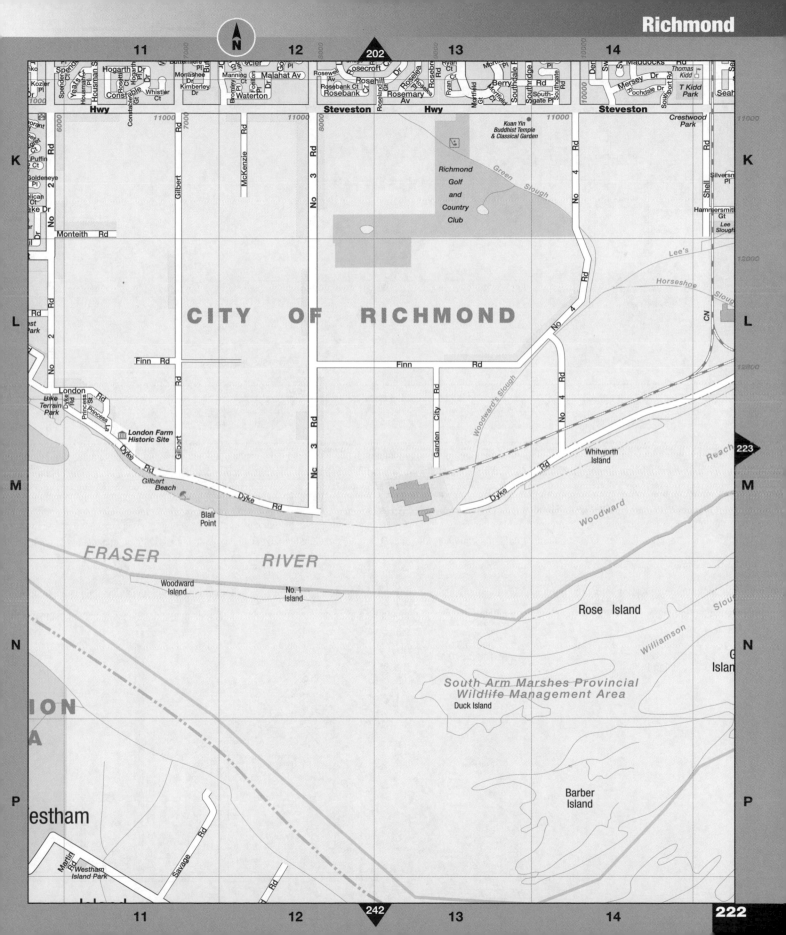

City of Richmond

K

L

M

N

P

11    12    202    13    14

Kozier
Pl
Spencer Pl
Housman St
Yeats Ct
Hogarth Dr
Constable
Rosetti
Whistler Ct
Hogarth Ct
Rosetti Ct
Butteriere Pl
Monashee Dr
Kimberley Dr
Manning Ct
Bromley Ct
Waterton Dr
Fallon Ct
Malahat Av
Rosewe Av
Rosecroft
Rosehill
Rosecroft Dr
Rosebank
Rosebank Ct
Roseland
Rosemary Av
Rosea
Rosea Ct
Rosebro Ct
Ryan Ct
Ryan Pl
Berryfield
Moffield Pl
Moffield Gt
Southridge Pl
Southridge Rd
Southgate Pl
South- gate Pl
Maddocks Rd
Mersey Dr
Rochdale Dr
Southport Rd
Thomas Kidd
T Kidd Park
Seah

**Hwy**

Cormorant
Egret Ct
Puffin Ct
Kozier Pl
Goldeneye Pl
Pelican Ct
Lake Dr

No 2 Rd

No 2 Rd

No 2 Rd

No 2 Rd

Constable Rd

Monteith Rd

Gilbert Rd

McKenzie Rd

No 3 Rd

No 3 Rd

No 3 Rd

No 3 Rd

**Steveston**    **Hwy**

Kuan Yin Buddhist Temple & Classical Garden

Richmond Golf and Country Club

Green Slough

No 4 Rd

No 4 Rd

No 4 Rd

No 4 Rd

Shell Rd

Crestwood Park

Silversm Pl

Hammersmith Gt

Lee Slough

**Steveston**

**CITY  OF  RICHMOND**

Finn Rd

Finn    Rd

Garden City Rd

Woodward's Slough

Lee's

Horseshoe Slough

CN

Reach

London
Bike Terrain Park
Dyke Rd
Princess La
Princess S Rd
London Farm Historic Site
Gilbert Rd
Dyke Rd
Gilbert Beach
Blair Point
Dyke Rd

Whitworth Island

Dyke Rd

Woodward

223

**FRASER     RIVER**

Woodward Island

No. 1 Island

Rose  Island

Williamson

G Islan

*South Arm Marshes Provincial*
*Wildlife Management Area*
Duck Island

Barber Island

estham

Martin Rd
Westham Island Park
Savage Rd

Rd

Island

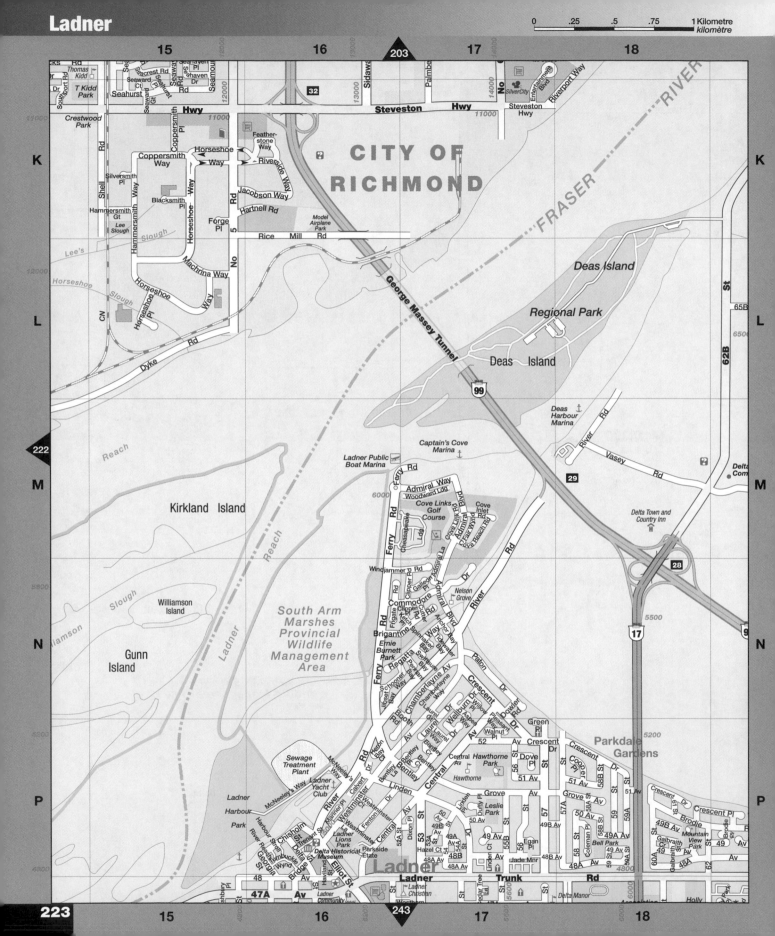

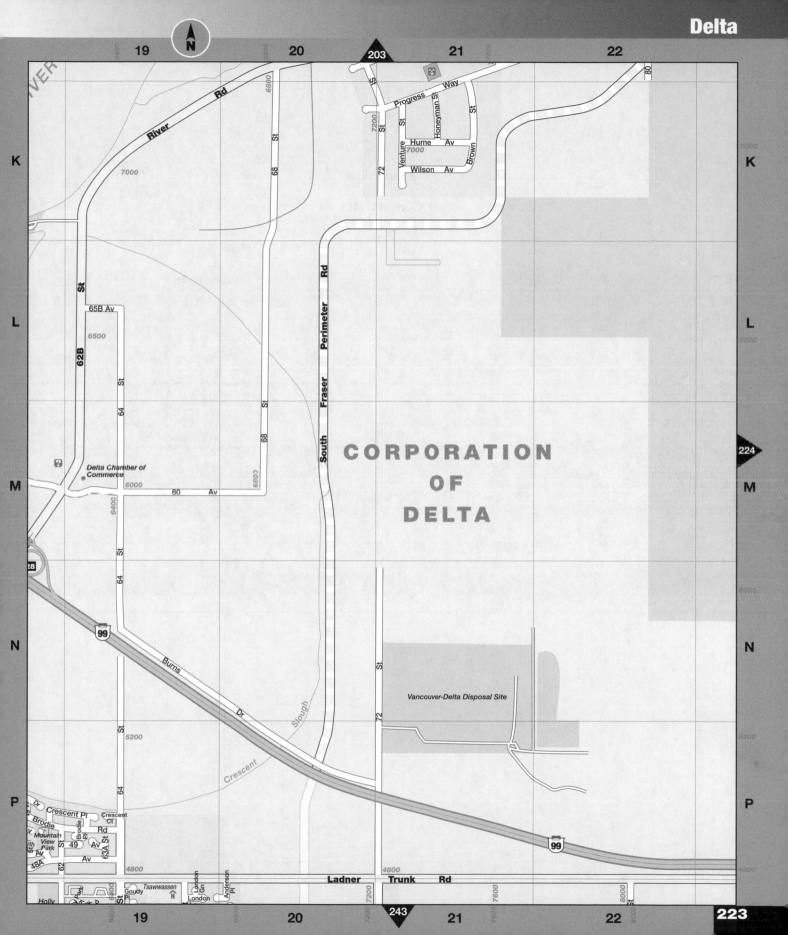

CORPORATION
OF
DELTA

Vancouver-Delta Disposal Site

Delta Chamber of Commerce

Ladner Trunk Rd

Tsawwassen

0    .25    .5    .75    1 Kilometre
*kilomètre*

**23**          **24**          ◆ **204**          **25**          **26**

K                                                                    K

*Burns Bog*

*Ecological*                                          Burns
                                                       Bog
*Conservancy*

*Area*

L                                                                    L

**CORPORATION**

◄ **223**

**OF DELTA**

M                                                                    M

N                                                                    N

St

96

P                                       9600                         P

88 St                    Ladner Private
                         Hospital H

Burns                                    Dr        **20**

**99**

**Ladner    Trunk      Rd**                        Hornby        Dr

6800  6800  *4800*        9200      6800   *4800*                  10000

**23**          **24**          ◆ **244**          **25**          **26**

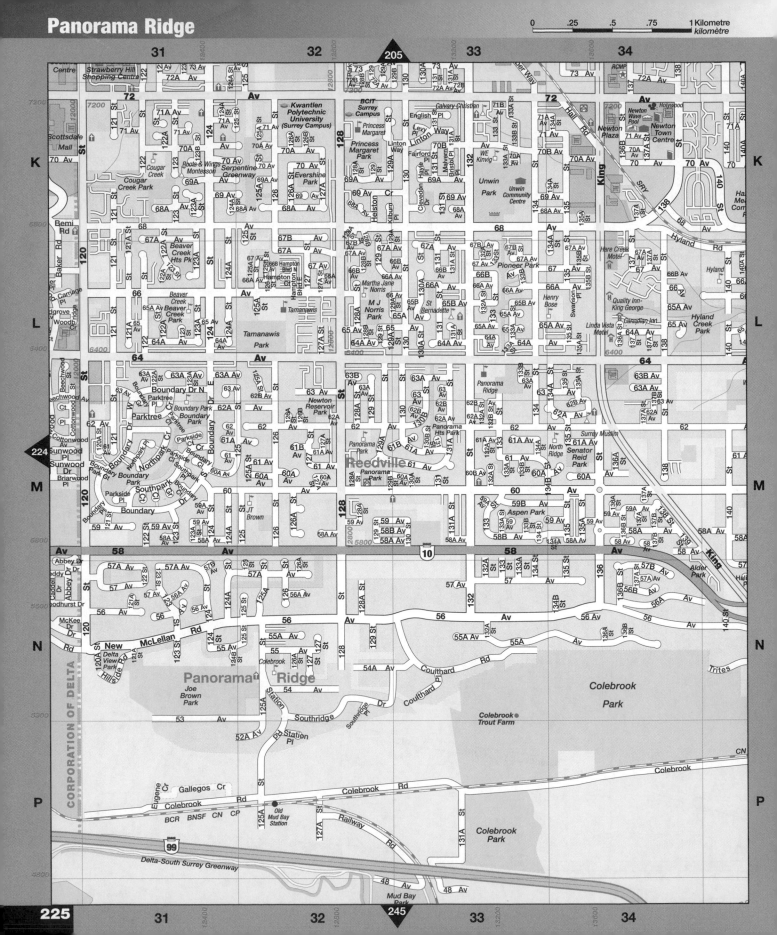

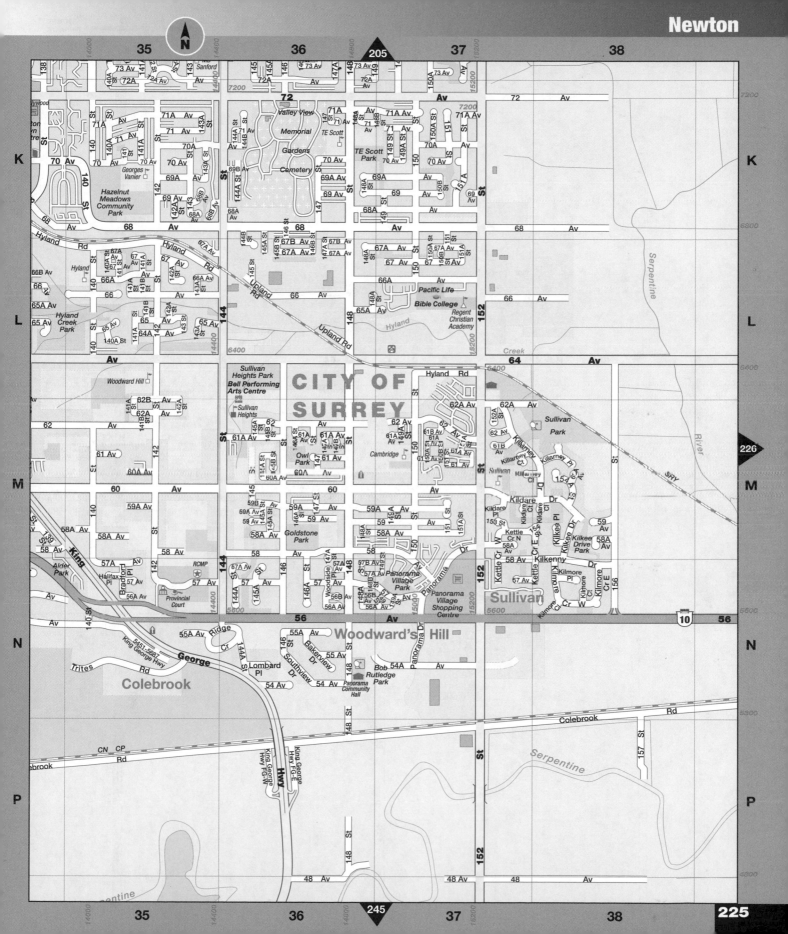

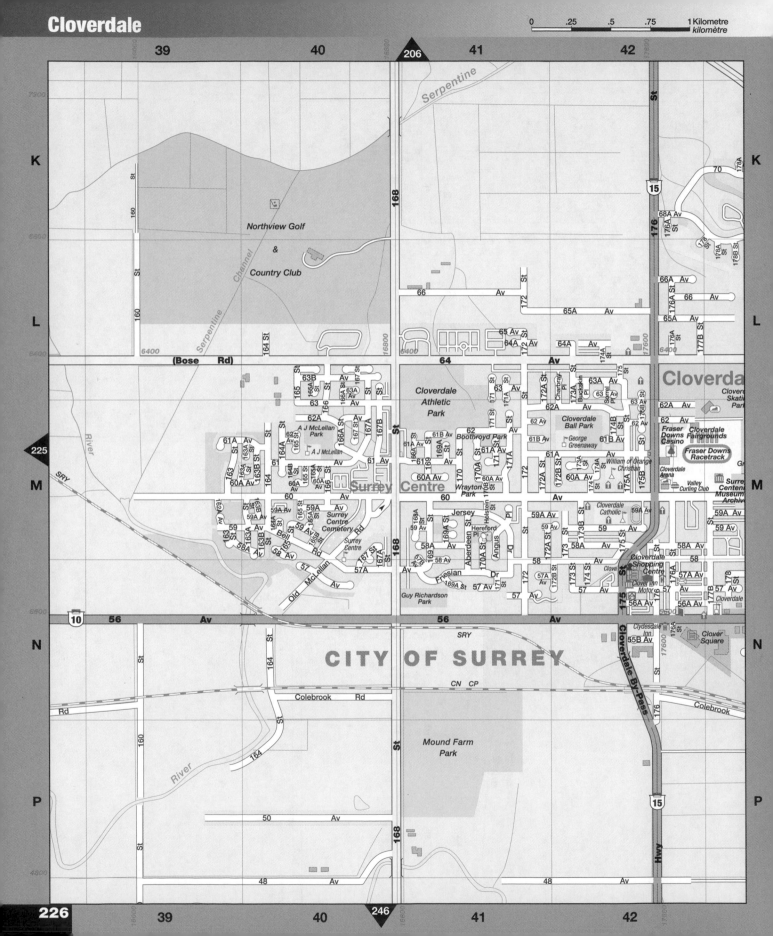

0   .25   .5   .75   1 Kilometre
kilomètre

**39**   **40**   **206**   **41**   **42**

K
Serpentine

Northview Golf
&
Country Club

Serpentine Channel

160 St
160 St
160 St
164 St

(Bose Rd)

L

168 St

66 Av
172 St
65A Av

65 Av
64A Av
172 Av
64A Av

66A Av
66 Av
176A St
65A Av
177B St
174A St

**Cloverdale**

70
178A St
68A Av
176A St
178 St
178A St
178B St

**15**
176 St

**225**

River
SRY

**Surrey Centre**

A J McLellan
Park
A J McLellan

63B Av
165 St
166A St
63A Av
187 St
63 Av
166 St
166A Av
62A Av
62A St
165 St
167A St
167B St
61A Av
61A St
163A St
163B St
164A Av
164B St
165A St
60A Av
61 Av
61
60A St
60A St
60
59A Av
165 St
165A St
59
59A Av
162A Av
59A St
163A St
163B St
164A St
Bell Rd
58A Av
58 Av
57
Old McLellan Av
167 St
167A St
57A Av

63 St
171 St
171A St
172 St
172A St
Charbray Pl
173A St
Bucksin
Sorrel St
63A Av
63 St
62 Av
61B Av
61B Av
62
Boothroyd Park
61A Av
171 St
170A St
171 St
171A St
172 St
172A St
60A Av
60
60A Av
59A Av
59 Av
59 Av
58
58A Av
57A Av
172B St
57

George
Greenaway
174B St
175 St
174A St
172B St
60A Av
173A St
175B St
59
173B St
58A
173 St
174A St
175 St
58
173 St
174A St

63A Av
63 St
175 St
62A Av
62 Av
Cloverdale
Catholic
59A Av

Cloverdale
Athletic
Park
64 Av
64A Av

Cloverdale
Ball Park
William of Orange
Christian
Wrayton Park
Jersey
Aberdeen Pl
Hereford
Angus
Holstein
170B St
169A St
168A St
Friesian
169A St
Guy Richardson
Park
58A
58 Av
57 Av
57A Av
169 St
170A St
171 St

**Cloverda**

Cloverdale
Skating
Park
62A Av
62 Av
Fraser
Downs
Casino
Cloverdale
Fairgrounds
Fraser Downs
Racetrack
Cloverdale
Arena
Valley
Curling Club
Surrey
Centre
Museum
Archives
59A Av
59 Av
58A Av
175 St
Cloverdale
Shopping
Centre
Clover Inn Motor
56A Av
57A Av
58
57
Cloverdale
176A St
177B St
57 Av
58 Av

**M**

**N**

**10**   **56 Av**   SRY   **56 Av**

## CITY OF SURREY

Colebrook Rd
164 St
160 St

CN   CP

Clydesdale Inn
55B Av
Cloverdale By-Pass
17600 St
176 St
Colebrook

Clover
Square

Mound Farm
Park

**P**

**15**

50 Av
164 St
160 St
168 St

48 Av   48 Av

Hwy

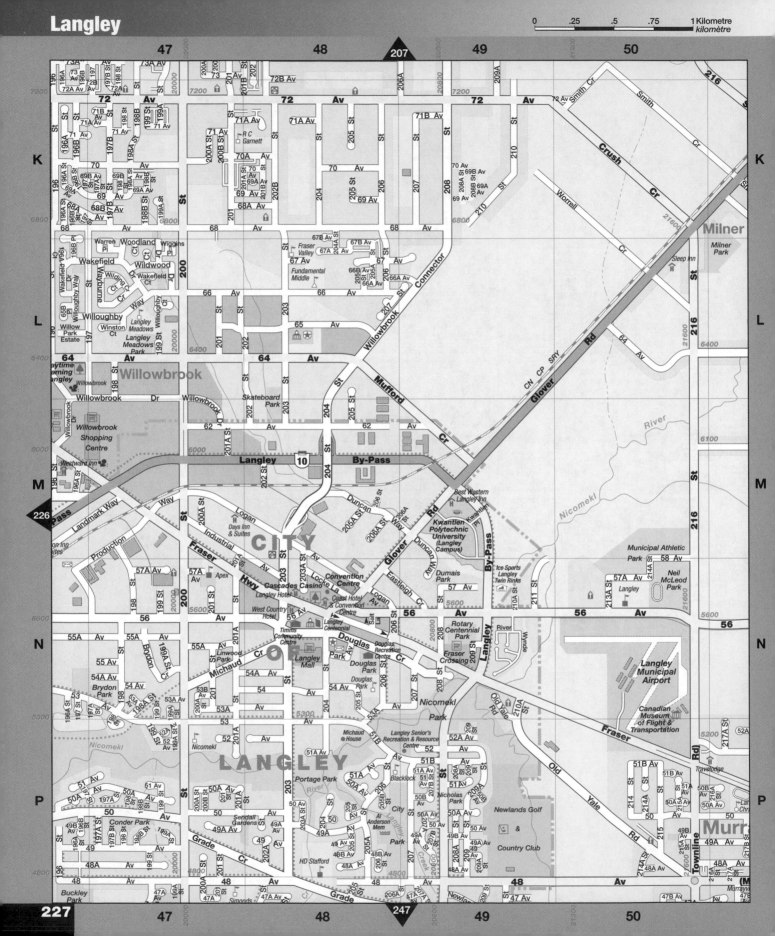

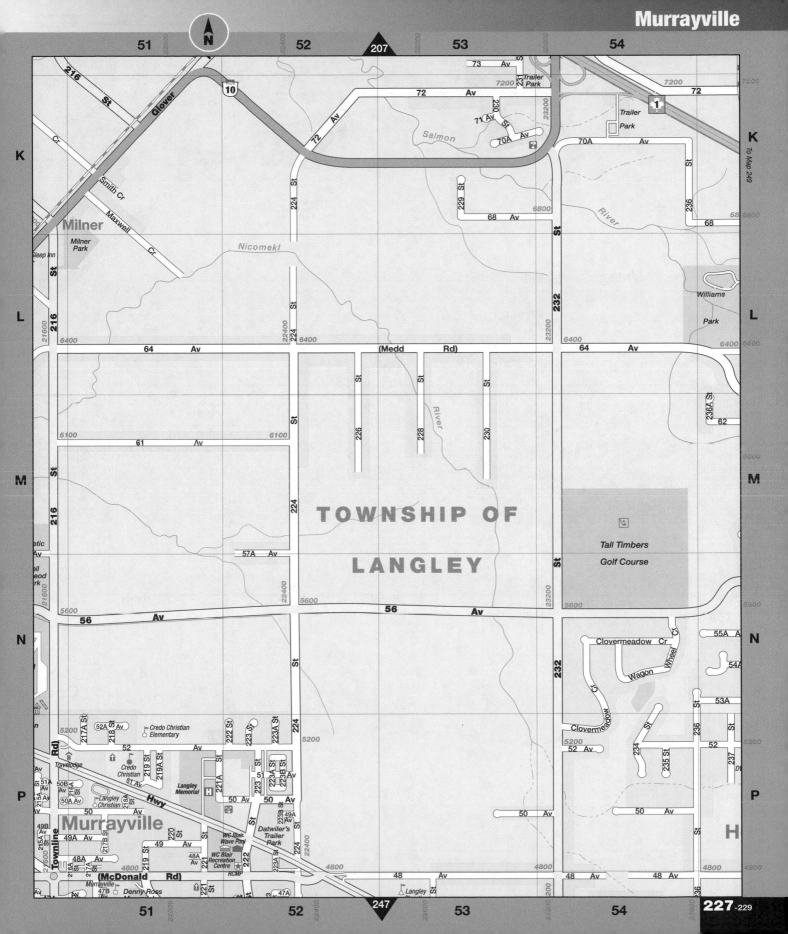

TOWNSHIP OF
LANGLEY

Milner

Milner Park

Sleep Inn

Nicomekl

Salmon

River

Williams Park

Trailer Park

Trailer Park

Tall Timbers Golf Course

Clovermeadow Cr

Credo Christian Elementary

Credo Christian St

Langley Memorial

Travelodge

Langley Christian

Murrayville

WC Blair Wave Pool

WC Blair Recreation Centre

Datwiler's Trailer Park

RCMP

Denny Ross

Langley

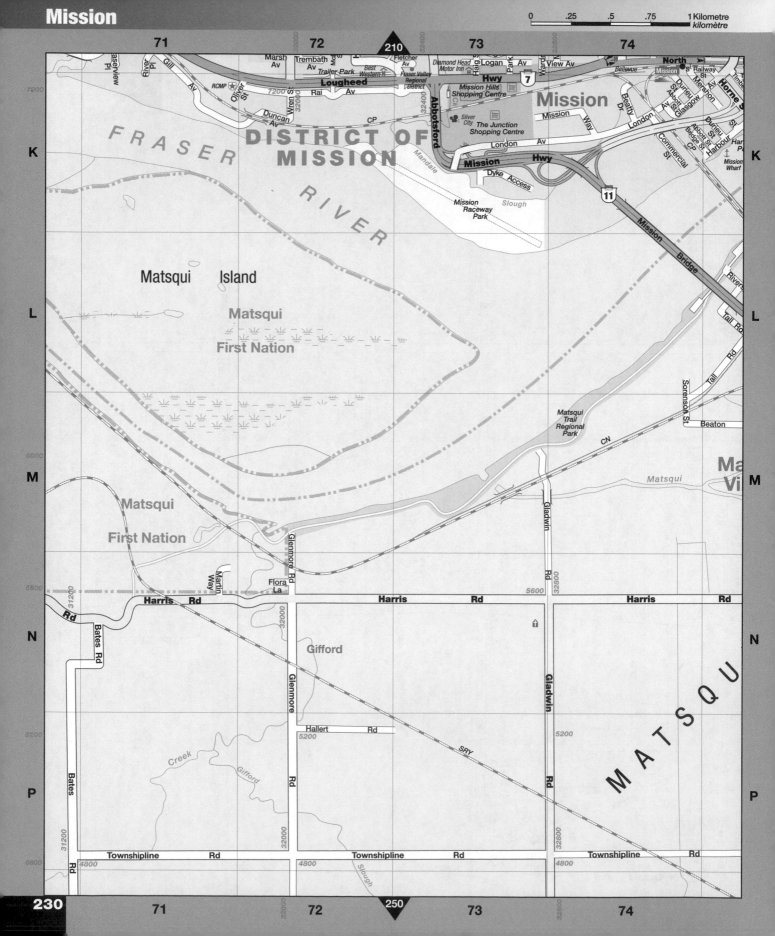

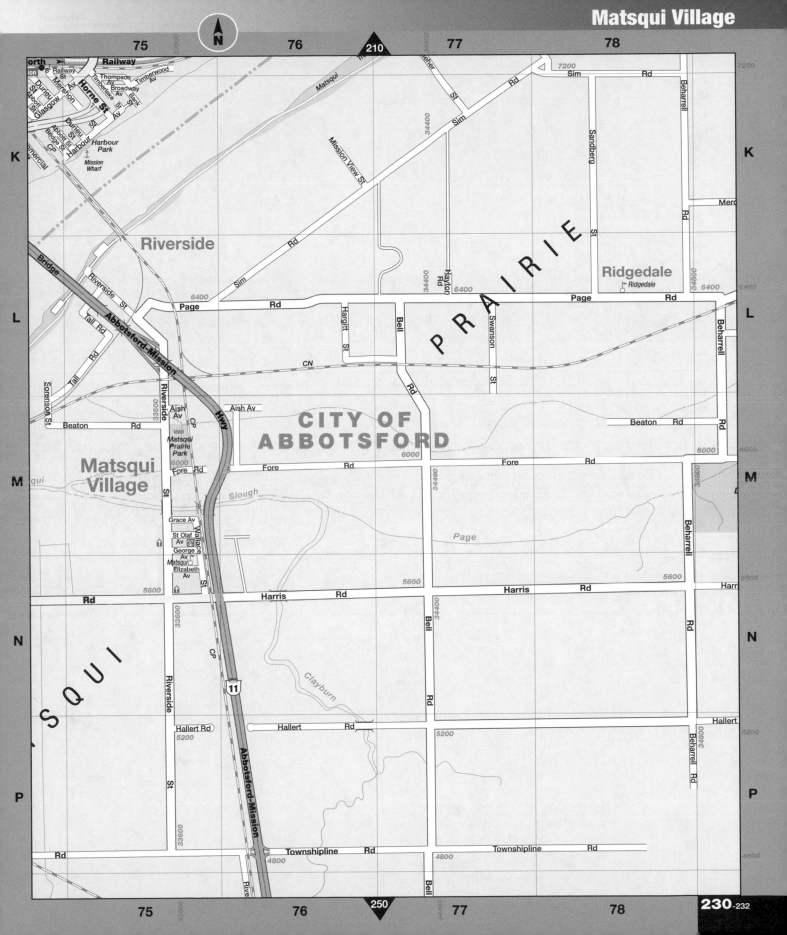

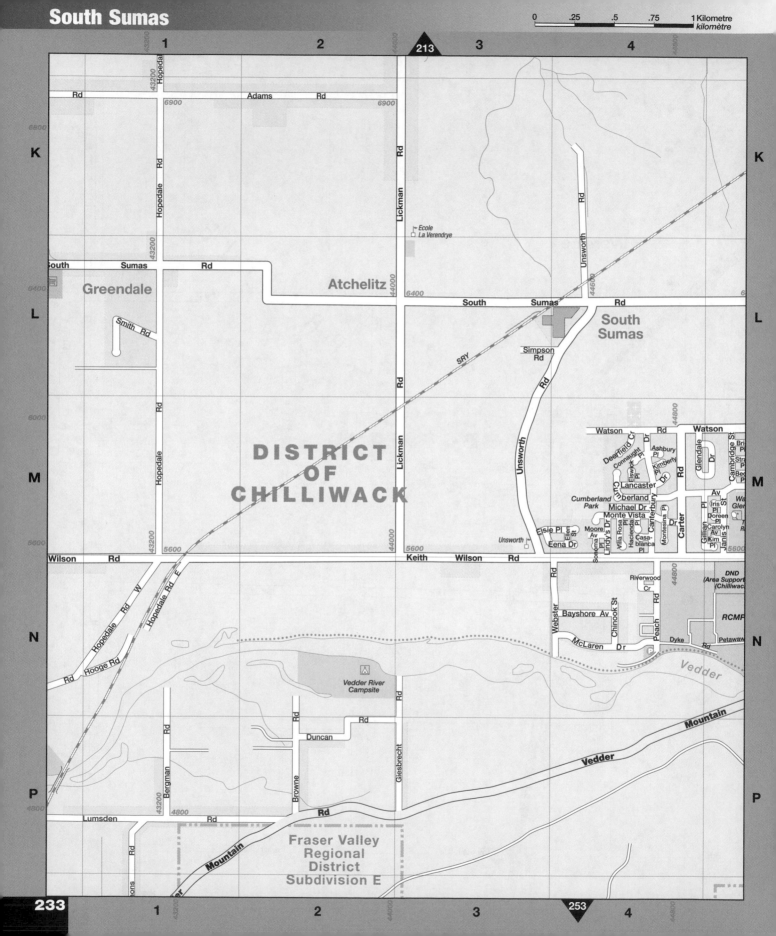

0   .25   .5   .75   1 Kilometre
*kilomètre*

**213**

**K** ... **K**

Rd
Hopeda

6900    Adams    Rd    6900

6800

Hopedale    Rd

43200

Lickman    Rd

Ecole
La Verendrye

South    Sumas    Rd

6400    **Greendale**    **Atchelitz**    6400

Smith Rd

**L**    South    Sumas    Rd    **L**

**South
Sumas**

SRY

Simpson
Rd

Unsworth Rd

6000

Hopedale    Rd

43200

Lickman    Rd

44000

Watson    Rd    Watson

Deerfield Cr
Connaught Pl
Ashbury Pl
Glendale Dr
Cambridge St

**DISTRICT
OF
CHILLIWACK**

Kimberly

Lancaster    Ellswick Pl    Pl

Cumberland
Park    Cumberland    Michael Dr    Canterbury    Montesina Pl    Carter Dr    Gillian Pl    Carolyn Av    Kim Pl    Janis Pl

Monte Vista

Elsie Pl    Moore Av    Lindy's Dr    Villa Rosa Pl    Casa-blanca Pl    Hacienda Pl    Sonoma    Av

Ellen St

Eena Dr

Unsworth

5600    5600

**M** ... **M**

5600    Wilson    Rd    Keith    Wilson    Rd    5600

Hopedale Rd W    Hopedale Rd E

Riverwood Cr

44800    **DND
(Area Support
(Chilliwac**

**RCMP**

Webster    Bayshore Av    Chinook St    Peach Rd    Dyke    Rd    Petawaw

**N**    Hopedale    Rd W    McLaren    Dr    Petawaw    **N**

Hooge Rd

Rd

*Vedder*

Vedder River
Campsite

Bergman Rd

Browne Rd

Duncan    Rd

Giesbrecht    Rd

**Mountain**

**Vedder**

**P**    6800    **P**

43200    4800

Lumsden    Rd

Mountain

**Fraser Valley
Regional
District
Subdivision E**

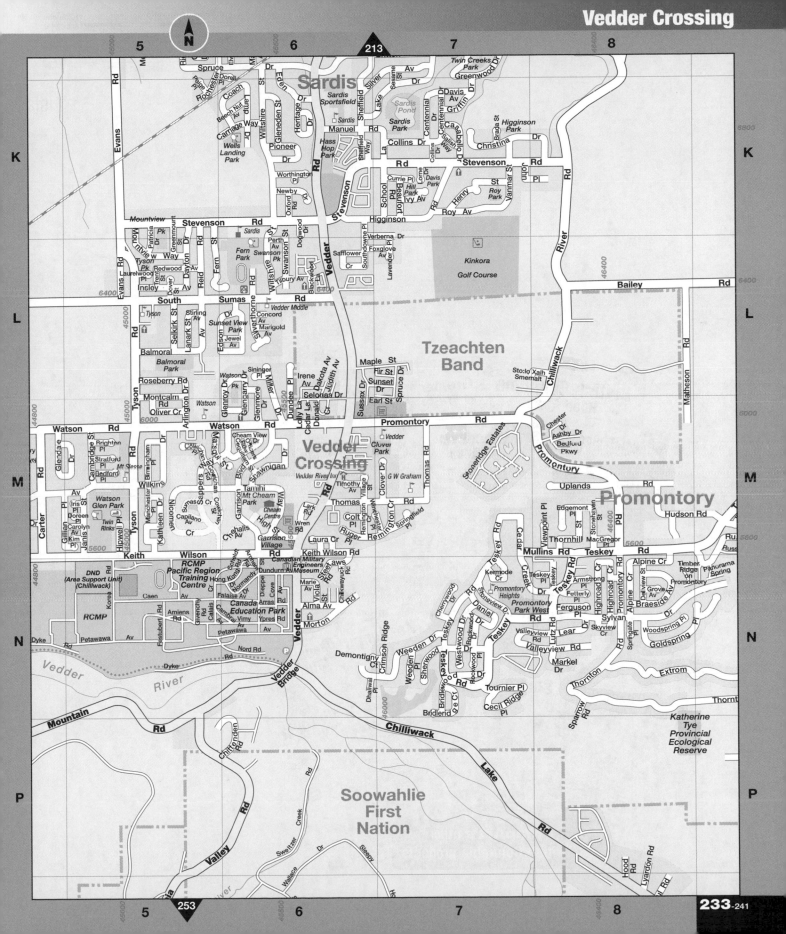

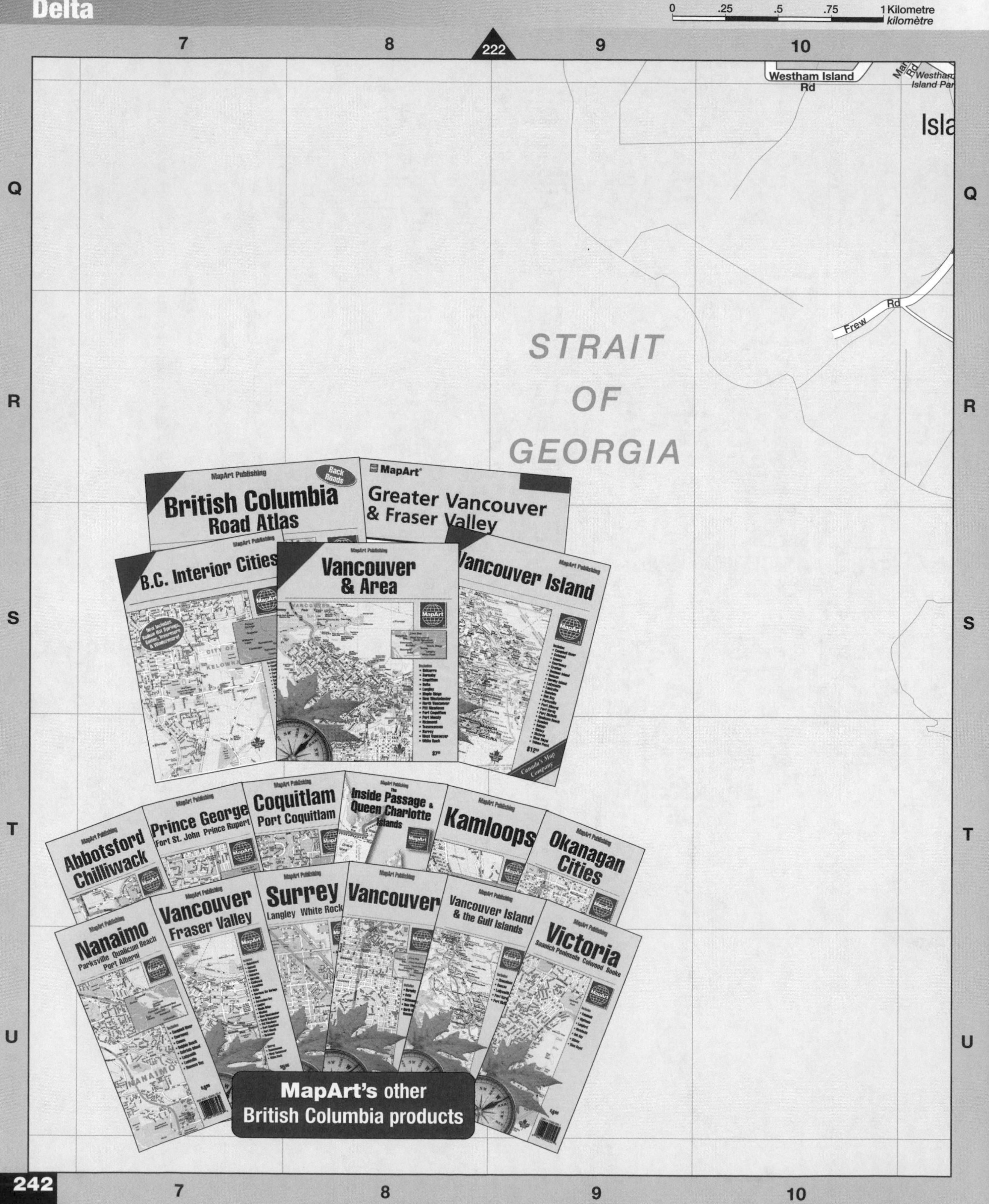

0   .25   .5   .75   1 Kilometre
*kilomètre*

7   8   ▲222   9   10

Q

R

**STRAIT**

**OF**

**GEORGIA**

S

T

U

Westham Island Rd

Isla

Frew Rd

7   8   9   10

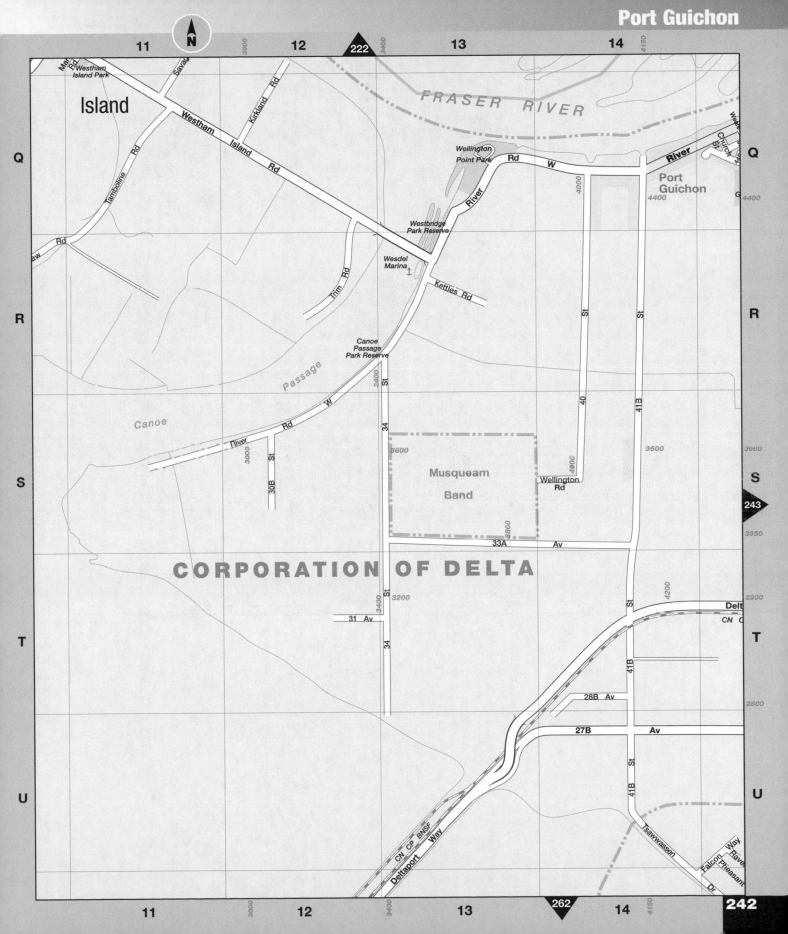

Island

FRASER RIVER

Westham Island Park

Westham Island Rd

Mar Rd

Savac

Kirkland Rd

Tamboline Rd

ew Rd

Trim Rd

Wellington Point Park

River Rd W

River

Westbridge Park Reserve

Wesdel Marina

Kettles Rd

River

Port Guichon

Church St

G

4400

4000

40 St

41B St

Canoe Passage Park Reserve

Passage

Canoe

River

Rd W

3400 St

3000

30B St

34 St

3600

Musqueam Band

3800

Wellington Rd

3600

4000

3600

3350

243

33A Av

CORPORATION OF DELTA

3400 St

3200

31 Av

34 St

41B St

Delt

4200

CN C

3200

2800

28B Av

27B Av

CN CP BNSF Deltaport Way

41B St

Tsawwassen Way Raven

Falcon Pheasant Dr

11  12  222  13  14

11  12  262  13  14

4150

4150

3000

3400

4400

Q  R  S  T  U

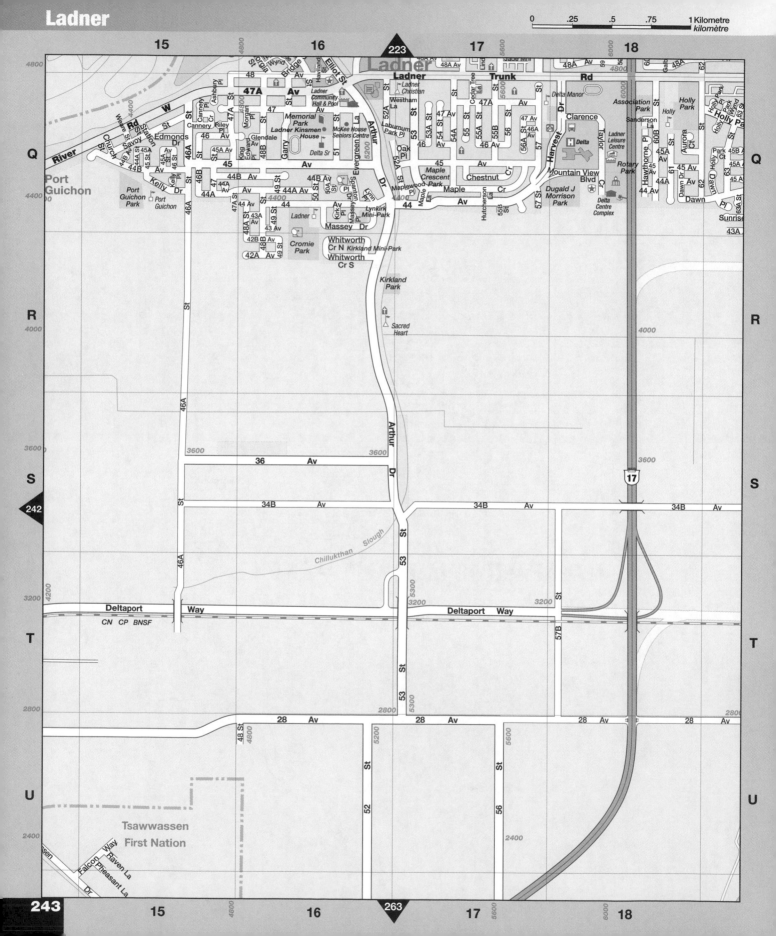

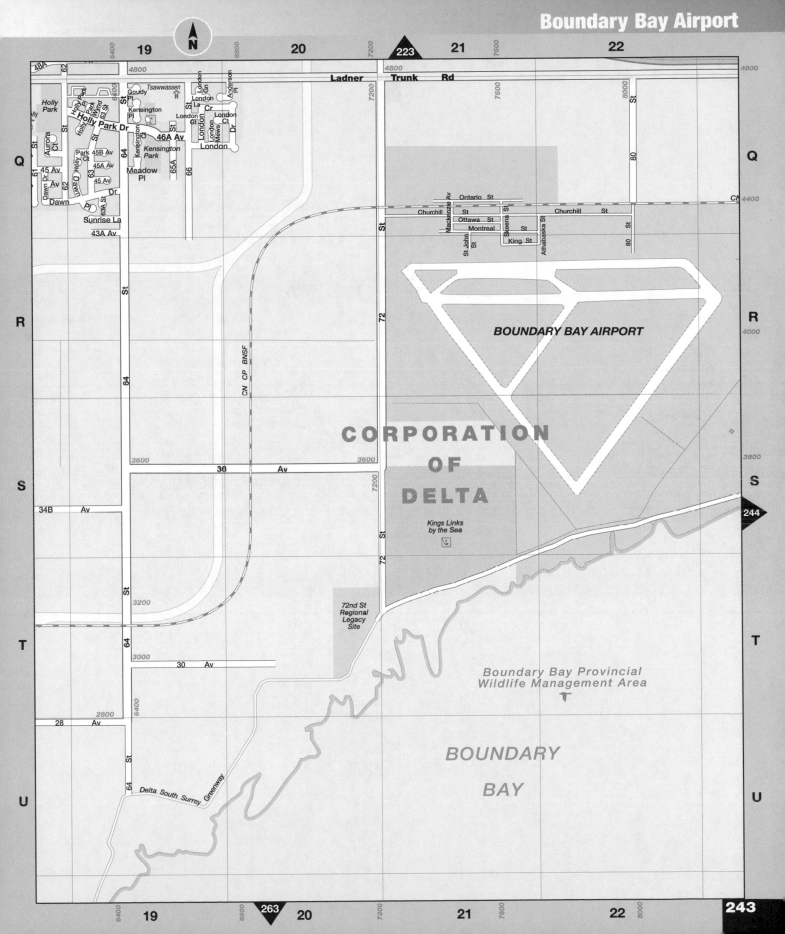

N

48A
62
4800
Ladner   Trunk   Rd
4800
4800

Holly
Park
Goudy
Pl
Tsawwassen
London
London
La
Anderson
Pl
76 00
80 00
St

Holly Park Dr
Kensington
Pl
London
Ct
London
Gt
London
Ct
London
Mews
Dr

Q
Aurora
Ct
Park
45B Av
46A Av
Kensington
Ct
Kensington
Park
65A
66
St
London
80
St
Q

Dawn Dr
62
45A Av
45A Av
Meadow
Pl
63
St
Mackenzie Av
Ontario St
Sheena St
Churchill St
80
St
CN 4400

45 Av
Dawn
63A St
Dr
Churchill
St
Athabaska St
CN

Dawn
Pl
Ottawa St
St

Sunrise La
Montreal
St John
St
King St

43A Av

R
St
BOUNDARY BAY AIRPORT
R
4000

64
CN CP BNSF
72
St

3600
3600
S
34B
Av
CORPORATION
3800
S

244

30
Av
7200
St
OF

St
3200
DELTA

Kings Links
by the Sea

64
3000
72
St

T
30
Av
72nd St
Regional
Legacy
Site
T

2800
6400
St

28
Av
Boundary Bay Provincial
Wildlife Management Area

64
St
BOUNDARY

U
Delta South Surrey
Greenway
BAY
U

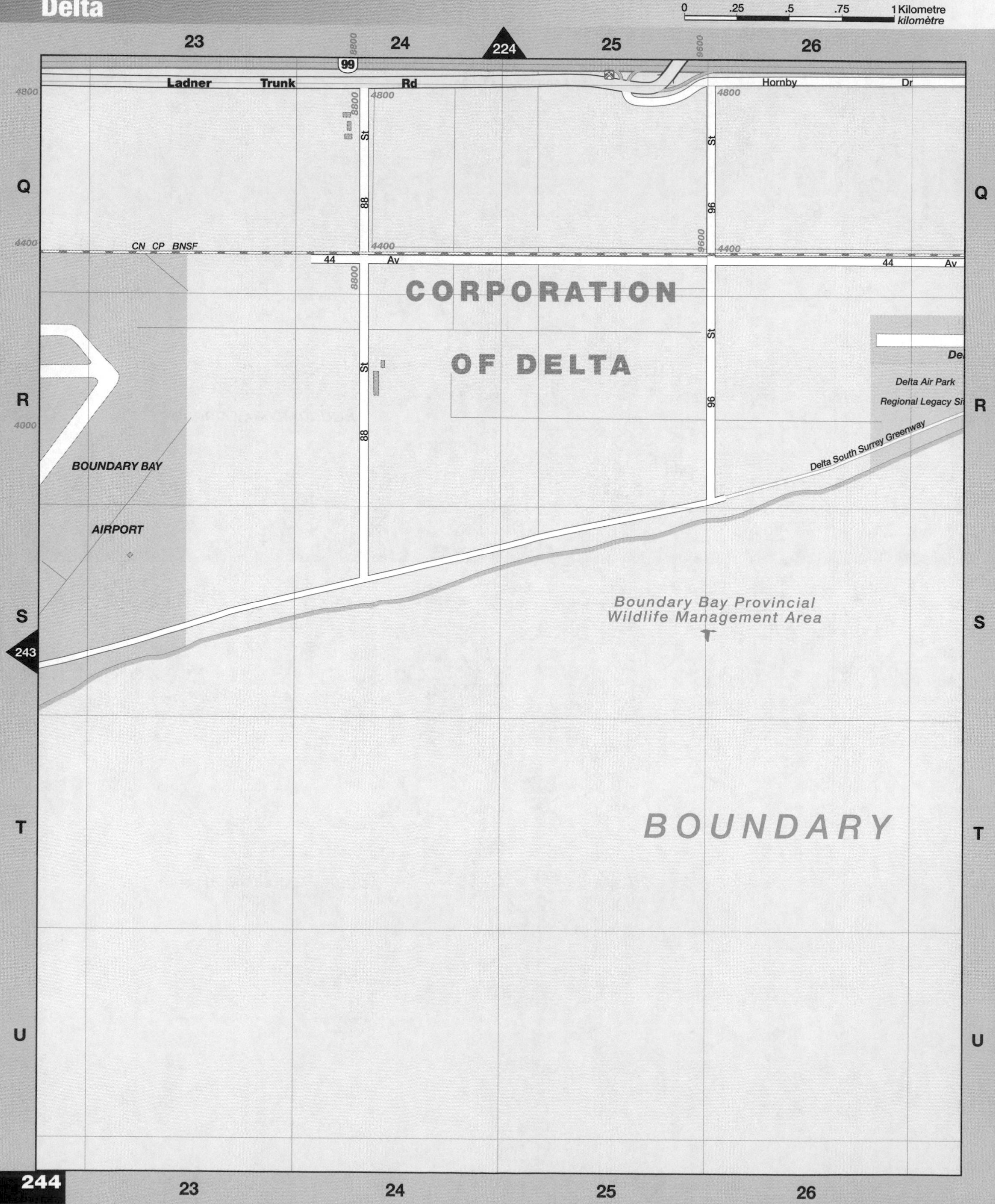

0   .25   .5   .75   1 Kilometre
*kilomètre*

23    24    ▲224    25    26

99

**Ladner    Trunk    Rd**    Hornby    Dr

4800    4800    4800

Q    Q

8800

CN CP BNSF    4400    4400    9600    4400

44    Av    44    Av

88 St    96 St    8800

# CORPORATION

# OF DELTA

St

**Delta Air Park**
**Regional Legacy Si**

R    88 St    St    96 St    R

4000

**BOUNDARY BAY**

Delta South Surrey Greenway

**AIRPORT**

*Boundary Bay Provincial*
*Wildlife Management Area*

S    S

◀243

T    *BOUNDARY*    T

U    U

23    24    25    26

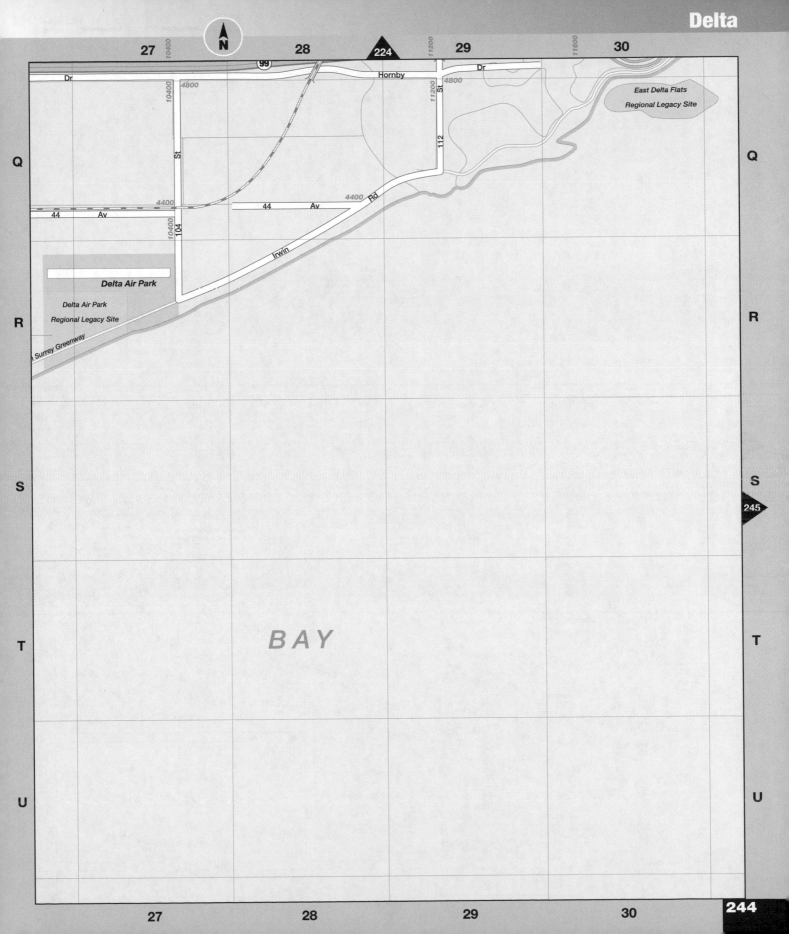

27      28      224      29      30

10400    11200    11600

Q      99      Hornby      Dr      Q

Dr    10400    4800    11200    St    4800

St    112

East Delta Flats
Regional Legacy Site

4400    44    Av    4400    Rd

44    Av    10400    104

Irwin

R      R

**Delta Air Park**

Delta Air Park
Regional Legacy Site

Surrey Greenway

S      S    245

*BAY*

T      T

U      U

27      28      29      30

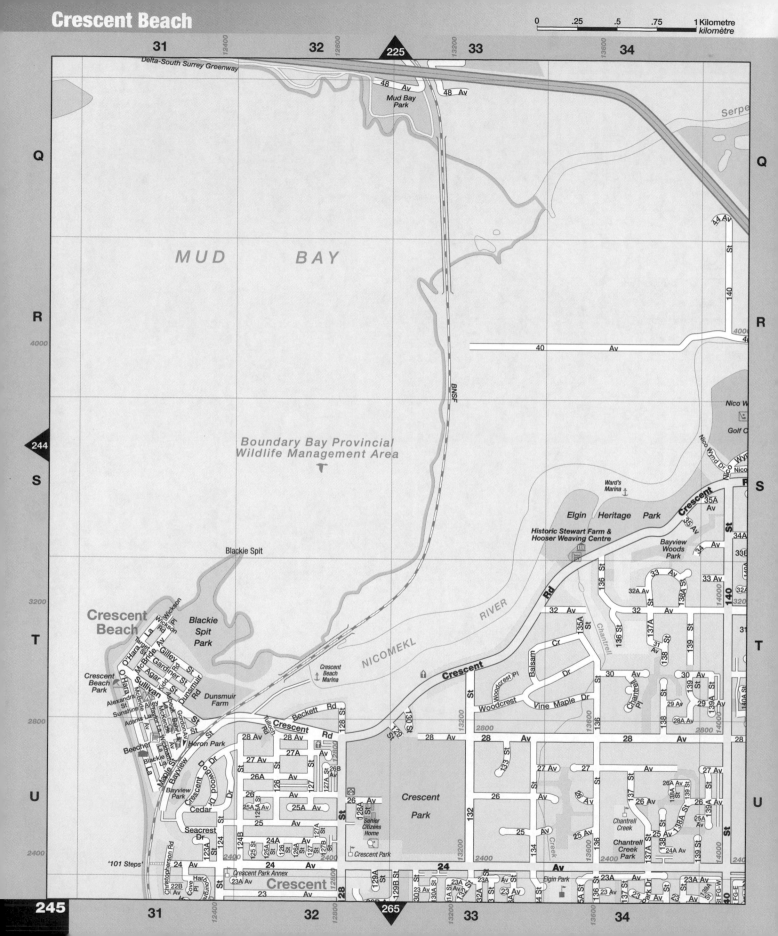

MUD BAY

Boundary Bay Provincial
Wildlife Management Area

Blackie Spit

Crescent
Beach

Blackie
Spit
Park

Crescent
Beach Park

Dunsmuir
Farm

Elgin Heritage Park

Historic Stewart Farm &
Hooser Weaving Centre

Bayview
Woods
Park

Ward's
Marina

Nico W

Golf C

NICOMEKL RIVER

Crescent
Beach
Marina

Crescent

Crescent
Park

Senior
Citizens
Home

Crescent Park

Chantrell
Creek
Park

Chantrell Creek

Elgin Park

Bayview
Park

Heron Park

Seacrest
Dr

Cedar

'101 Steps'

Crescent Park Annex

Crescent

Delta-South Surrey Greenway

Mud Bay
Park

48 Av

48 Av

40 Av

34 Av

35A Av

35A Av

34 Av

33 Av

33 Av

32A Av

32 Av

32 Av

31

30 Av

30 Av

29 Av

29 Av

28 Av

28 Av

28 Av

27 Av

27 Av

27 Av

26 Av

26A Av

26

26

25 Av

25A Av

24A Av

24 Av

24 Av

24 Av

23A Av

23A Av

23 Av

23 Av

23

BNSF

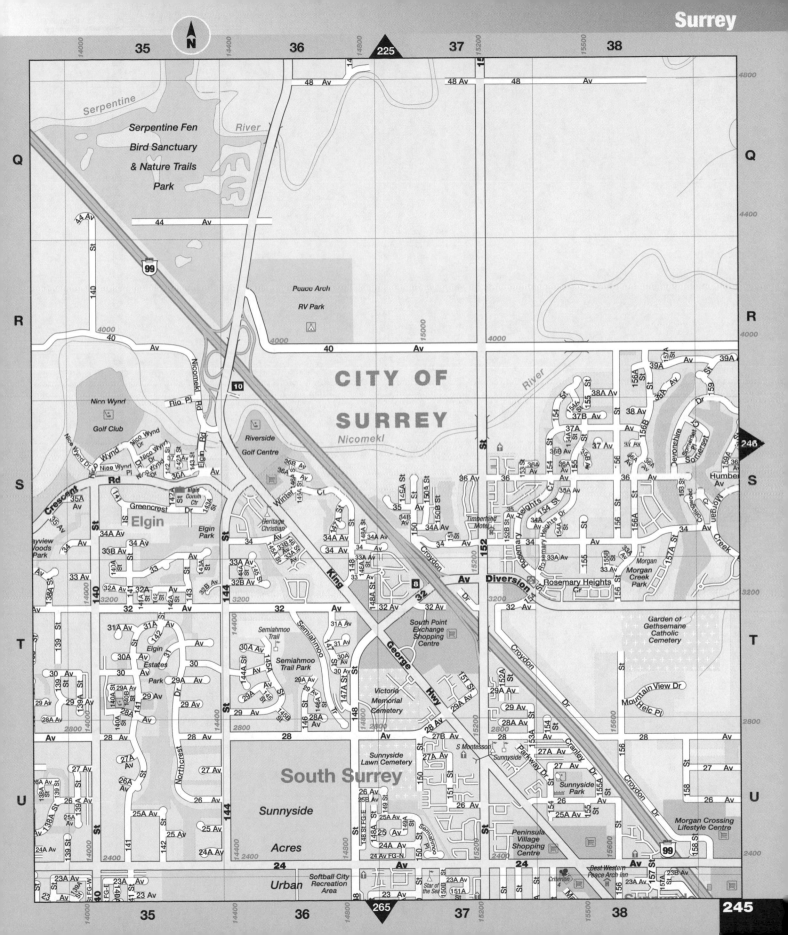

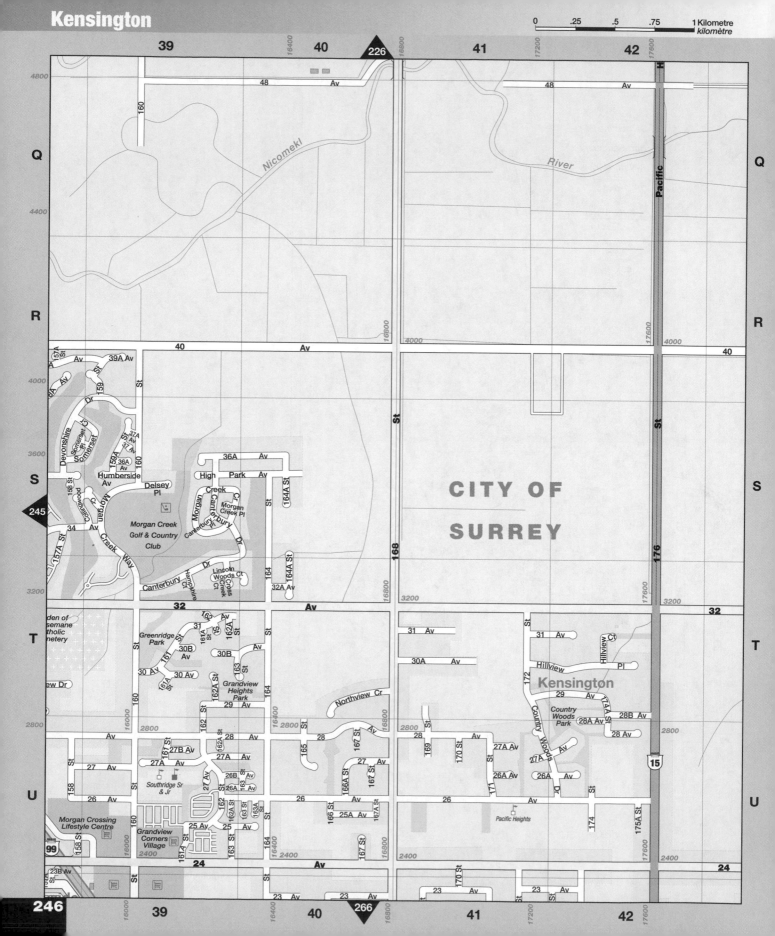

0 .25 .5 .75 1 Kilometre
*kilomètre*

**39** 40 ◣226 **41** **42**

4800

Q Q

Nicomekl River Pacific

4400

R R
4000 4000

**40** Av 168 St 176 St **40**

157A St 39A Av
160 St
159
Devonshire Dr
Somerset Pl
159A 37A Av
37A
36A Av
Humberside Av
Delsey Pl
158 St
Collingwood

**S** 36A Av High Park Av **S**
245◣ Morgan Creek Pl
Morgan Creek Golf & Country Club
Canterbury Cr
Morgan Creek
164A St
168 St
16800
34
157A St
Morgan Creek Way
Hampshire Dr
Canterbury Dr
Lincoln Woods Ct
Cross Creek Ct
164 St
164A St
32A Av

# CITY OF
# SURREY

**32** Av **32**

den of semane tholic netery
160 St
Greenridge Park
31
162 St
162A St
31 Av
31 Av
Hillview Ct

**T** 30B Av **T**
161 St
30B
163 St
30A Av
Kensington
172
Hillview
Hillview Pl
174A St
ew Dr 30 Av
161A St
Grandview Heights Park
162A St
164 St
Northview Cr
167 St
29 Av
Country Woods Park
28B Av
28A Av
2800 160 St 162 St 2800 16400 St 2800 168 St 2800 169 St 170 St 27A Av Country Woods 28A Av 28 Av 2800
28 Av
28 Av
27 Av
158 St
27B Av
162A St
27A Av
165 St
167 St
27 Av
26A Av
27A Av
26A Av

**U** 27A Av 26B Av **U**
163 St
163A St
26A Av
Southridge Sr & Jr
162 St
26 Av
166A St
167A St
26 Av
174 St
175A St
26 Av
26 Av 25A Av
Pacific Heights
Morgan Crossing Lifestyle Centre
158A St
Grandview Corners Village
160 St
25 Av
161A St
163 St
163A St
164 St
16400
167 St
16800
99
2400 2400 2400 2400

**24** Av **24**
23B Av
160 St
23 Av
23 Av
170 St
23 Av
23 St

**39** 40 ▼266 **41** **42**

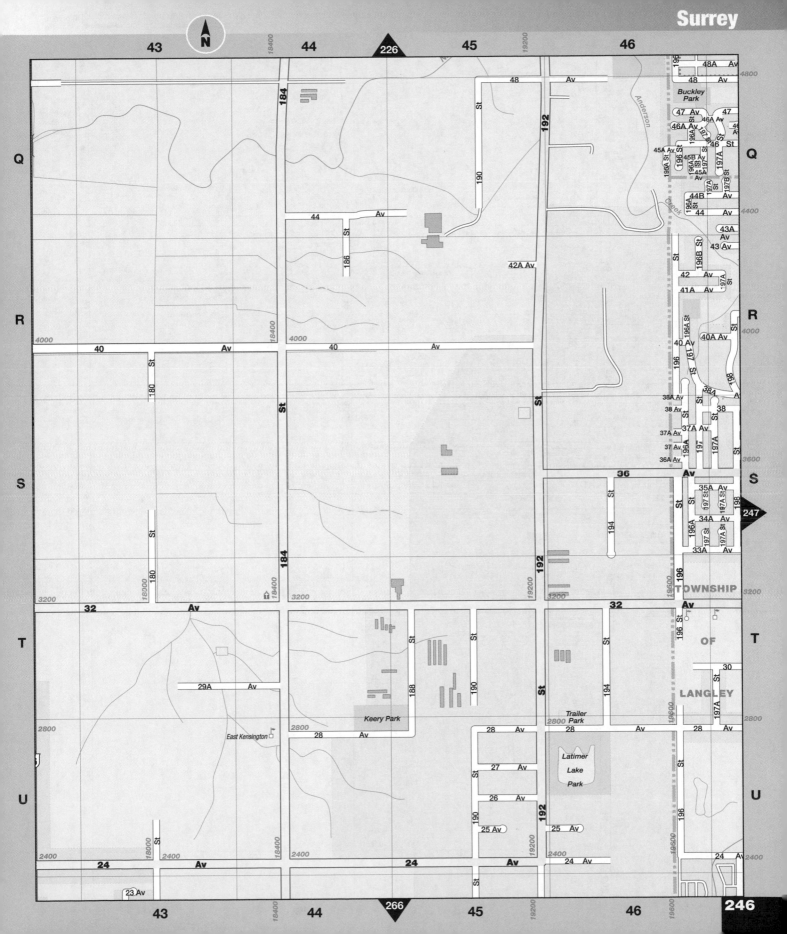

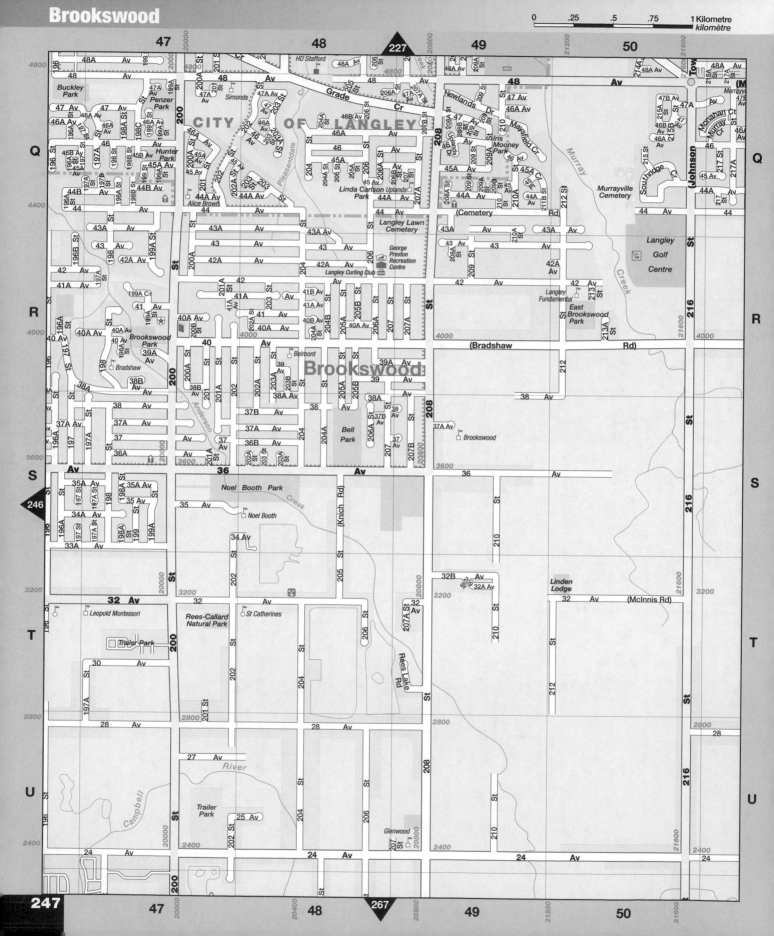

0   .25   .5   .75   1 Kilometre
*kilomètre*

Buckley Park
Penzer Park
Hunter Park
**CITY OF LANGLEY**
Simonds
Alice Brown
Linda Carlson Uplands Park
Langley Lawn Cemetery
George Preston Recreation Centre
Langley Curling Club
Newlands Dr
Iris Mooney Park
Mayfield Cr
(Cemetery)
Murrayville Cemetery
Southridge
Monahan Ct
Murray
Johnson St
Langley Golf Centre

Grade Cr

Pleasantdale
Anderson

Brookswood Park
Bradshaw
Belmont
**Brookswood**
Bell Park
Langley Fundamental
East Brookswood Park
(Bradshaw Rd)
Brookswood

Noel Booth Park
Noel Booth
(Knich Rd)
Rees Lake Rd
Creek
Linden Lodge
(McInnis Rd)

Leopold Montessori
Trailer Park
Rees-Callard Natural Park
St Catherines
Glenwood

Campbell
River
Trailer Park

227
246
267

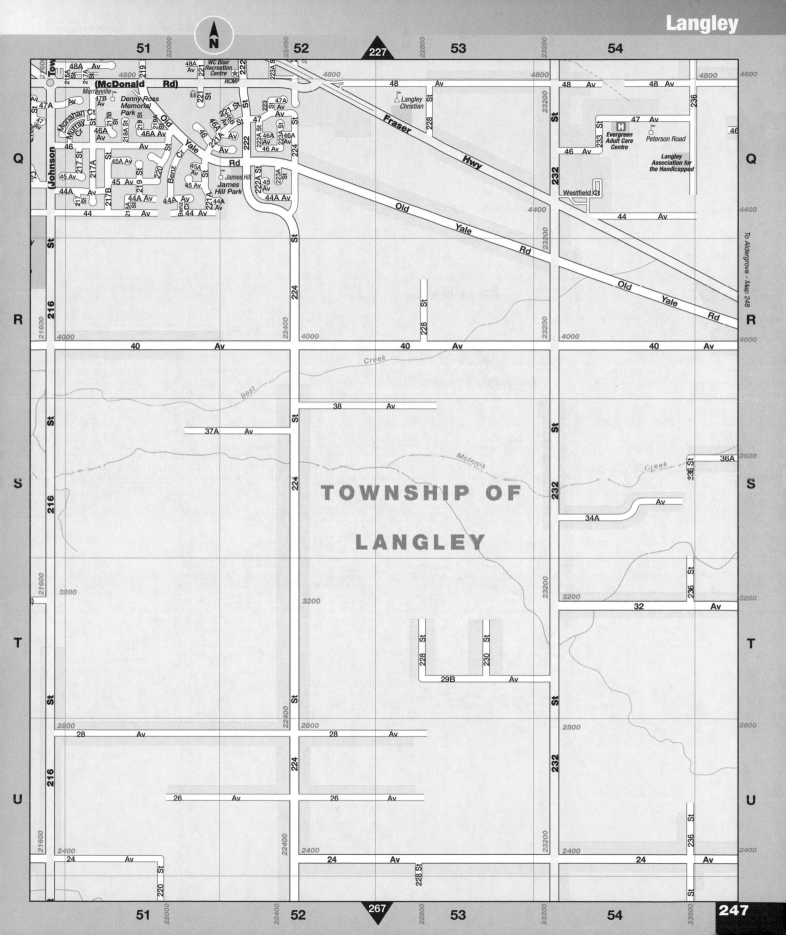

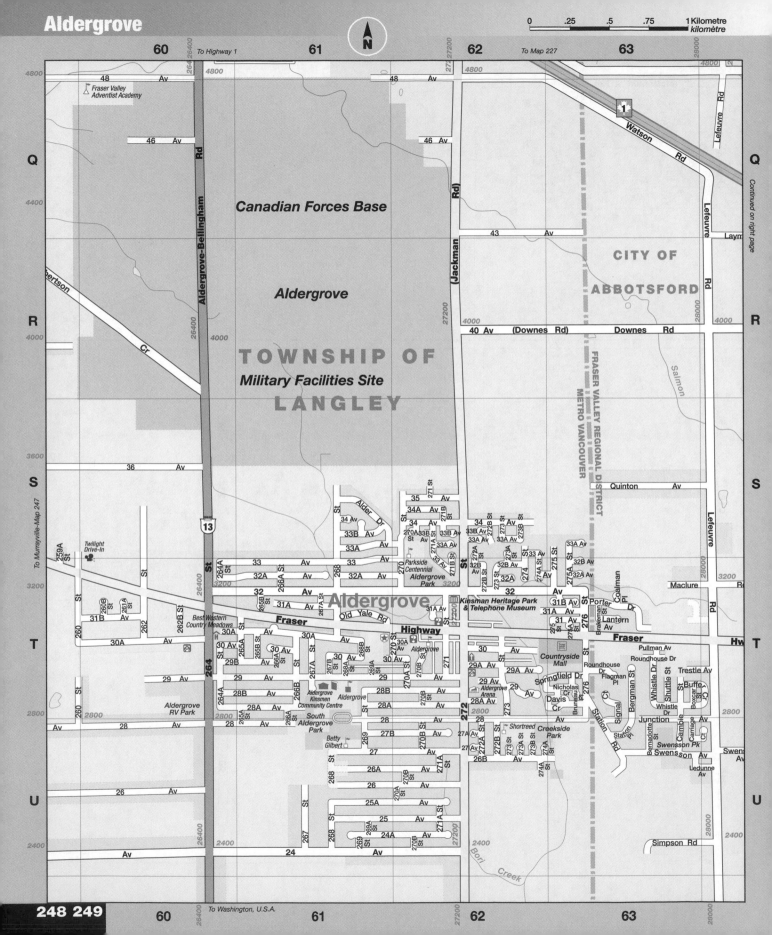

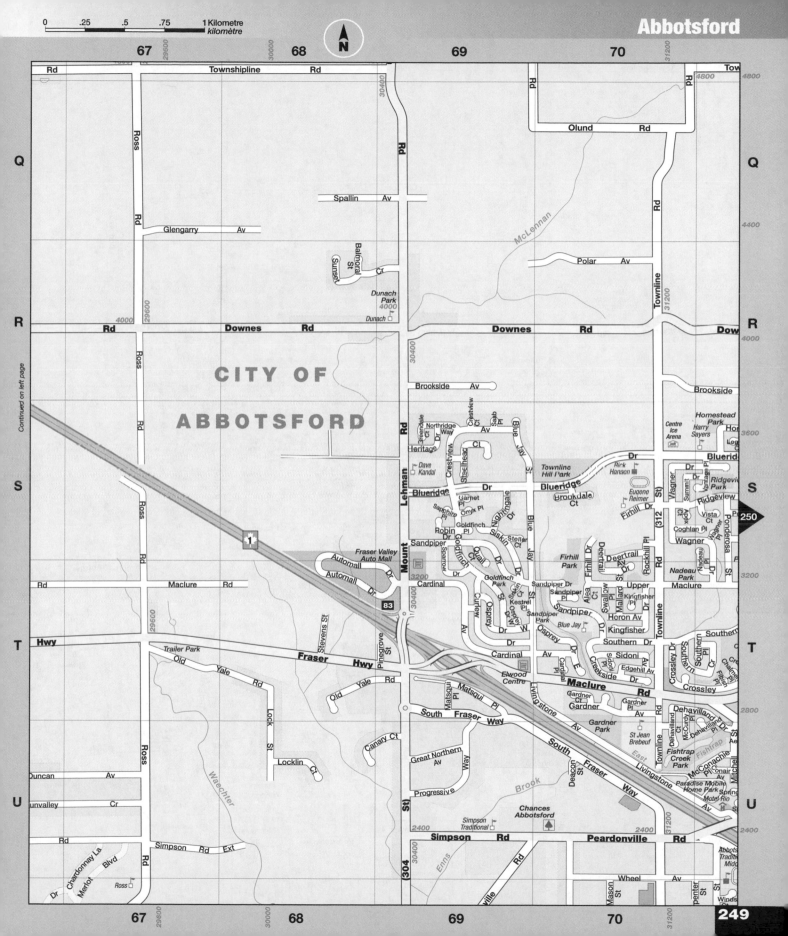

0  .25  .5  .75  1 Kilometre
*kilomètre*

N

67  68  69  70

Rd  Townshipline  Rd  Rd  4800  Tow  4800

Q  Q

Ross  Olund  Rd

Rd  Spallin  Av

McLennan  4400

Glengarry  Av  Polar  Av  Townline  31200

Balmoral  St  Sunset  Cr

Dunach Park  4000  Dunach  3200

R  Rd  Downes  Rd  Downes  Rd  Dow  R  4000

Ross  Rd  Brookside  Av  Brookside

CITY OF  Brookside  Av  Centre Ice Arena  Homestead Park  Harry Sayers  Hon  3600

ABBOTSFORD  Greendale Ct  Northridge Way  Crestview  Ct  Saab Av  Heritage  Dave Kandal  Townline Hill Park  Rirk Hansen  Blueridge

Lehman Rd  Steelhead  Dr  Blueridge  Dr  Blueridge  Brookdale Ct  Eugene Reimer  Ridgeview Park

S  Ross  Rd  Blueridge  Dr  Garnet  Onyx Pl  Nightingale Dr  Blue Jay Dr  Firhill  Wagner  Dr  Summit  Ridgeview  Vista Ct  S  250

Sapphire  Robin  Goldfinch Pl  Siskin  Stellar  Deertrail  Coghlan Pl  Ponderosa

1  Sandpiper  Sparrow  Dr  Quail Dr  Firhill Park  Deertrail  Wagner  Nadeau Park

Fraser Valley Auto Mall  Goldfinch Park  Sandpiper Dr  Rockhill  Nadeau  Maclure  3200

Rd  Maclure  Rd  Automall Dr  Cardinal  3200  Goldfinch Dr  Sandpiper Pl  Upper

83  Automall Dr  Mount St  Kestrel  Sandpiper Park  Mallow  Mallard  Kingfisher Pl

Stevens St  Cullen  Osprey  Sandpiper  Heron Av  Kingfisher

T  Hwy  Trailer Park  Pinegrove St  Cardinal  Blue Jay Dr  Osprey Dr  Southern Dr  Crossley Dr  Southern  T

Fraser  Hwy  Cardinal  Av  Sidoni  Sidoni  Crossley

Old  Yale  Rd  Matsqui Pl  Cardinal Pl  Creekside  Edgehill Av  Crossley

Lock St  Old  Yale  Rd  Maclure  Rd

Ross  Rd  Locklin  Ct  Livingstone  Gardner  Gardner  Dehavilland Dr

Canary Ct  South  Fraser  Way  Gardner Park  St Jean Brebeuf  McCurdy  Fishtrap  McConachie

Duncan  Av  Great Northern Av  Gardner Av  Fishtrap Creek Park  Paradise Mobile Home Park  Motel Rio

unvalley  Cr  Progressive  Way  South  Fraser  Way  Livingstone  Spring

U  Rd  Chances Abbotsford  Deacon St  Abbots  Tradit  Mid  U

Waechter  Simpson Traditional  2400  Brook  East  2400

Chardonnay La  Merlot Blvd  Ross  Simpson  Rd  Ext  2400  Simpson  Rd  Peardonville  Rd  Wheel  Av

Dr  304  30400  Enns  ville  Rd  Mason St  carpenter St  Winds

67  68  69  70

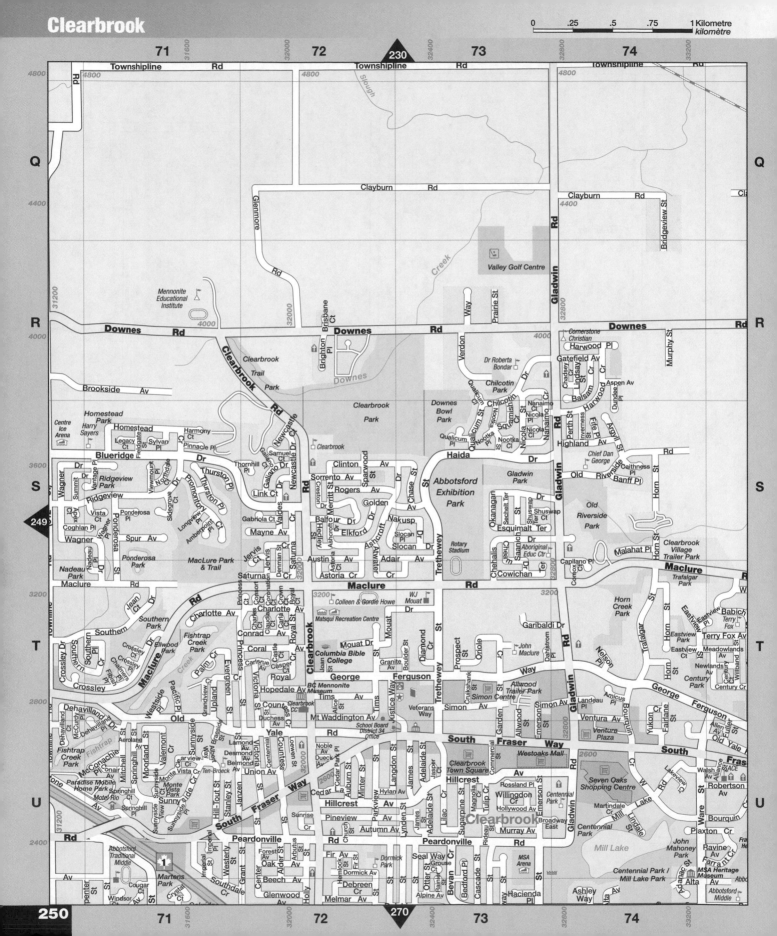

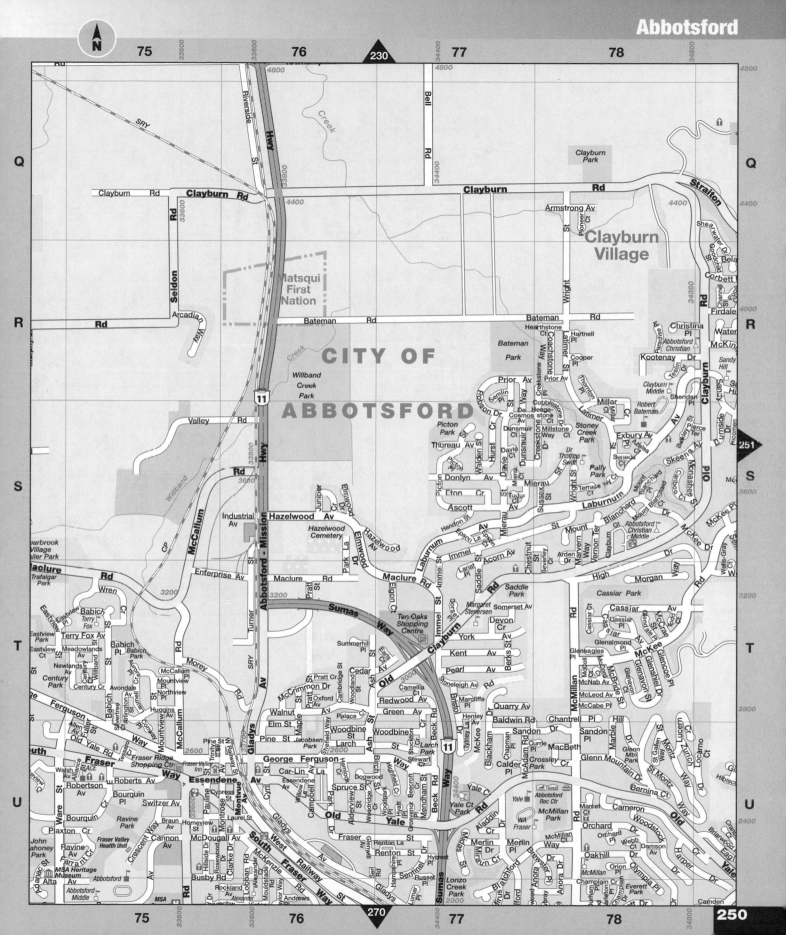

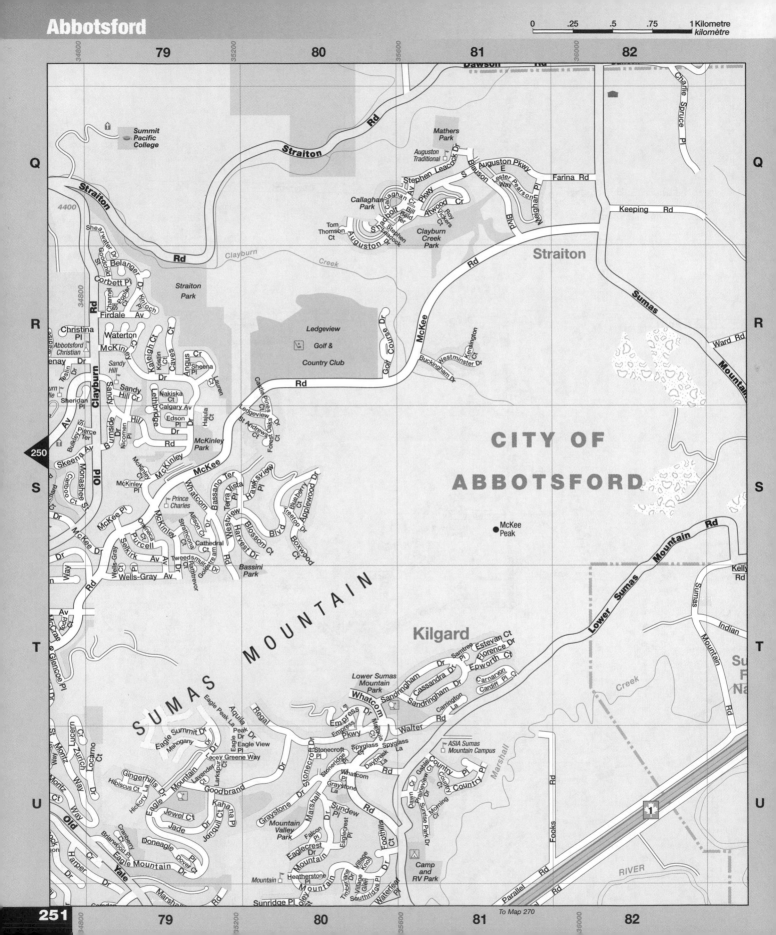

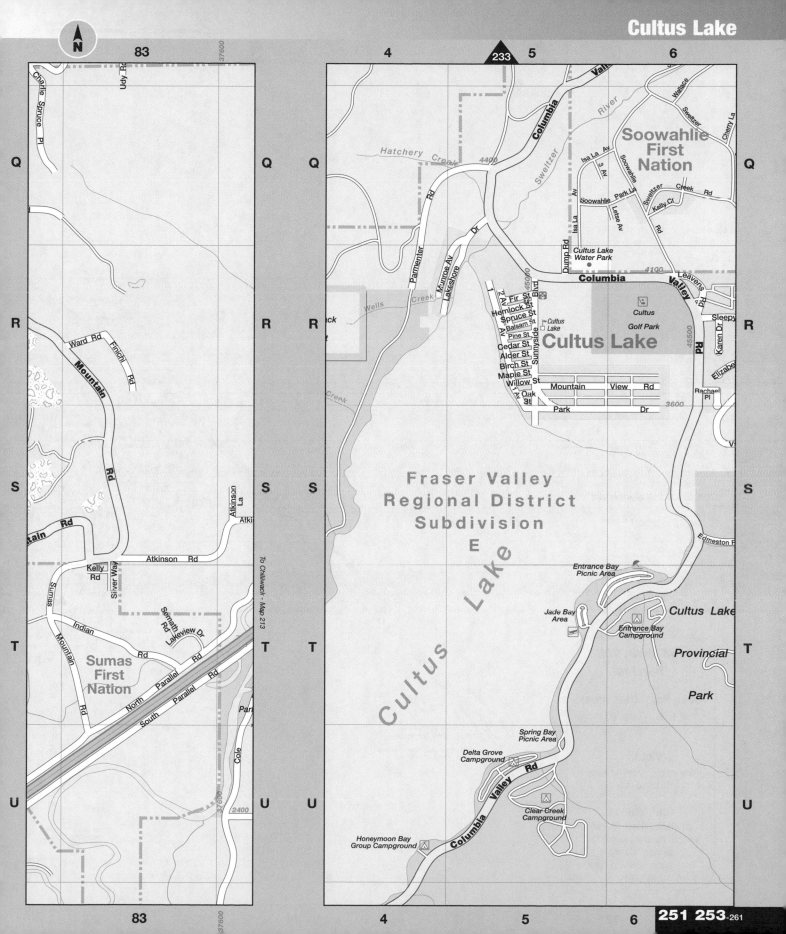

N

83

4 233 5 6

Q

Charlie Spruce Pl
Udy Rd
37600

**Soowahlie
First
Nation**

Columbia
Sweltzer
River
Wallace
Sweltzer
Cherry La

Hatchery Creek
4400

Isa La Av
3 Av
Soowahlie
Park La
Soowahlie
Sweltzer Creek Rd
Kelly Ct
Letse Av

Parmenter Rd
Munroe Av
Lakeshore Dr

Dump Rd
Cultus Lake
Water Park

4100

Columbia
Leavens Rd

R

Ward Rd
Finlcli Rd
Mountain
Rd

Wells Creek

1 Av
2 Av
Fir St
Hemlock St
Spruce St
Balsam St
Pine St
Cedar St
Alder St
Birch St
Maple St
Willow St
Oak St

Sunnyside Blvd
45600
45500

Cultus
Lake

Cultus
Golf Park

**Cultus Lake**

Sleepy
Karen Dr
Elizabe
Rachael Pl

Mountain View Rd
Park Dr
3600

S

Atkinson La
Atki
Atkinson Rd

tain Rd

Wells Creek

**Fraser Valley
Regional District
Subdivision
E**

Edmeston

T

Kelly Rd
Silver Way
Sumas
Indian Rd
Semath Rd
Lakeview Dr
Rd
Mountain Rd
North Parallel Rd
South Parallel Rd
Par

**Sumas
First
Nation**

To Chilliwack - Map 213

**Cultus Lake**

Entrance Bay
Picnic Area

Jade Bay
Area
Entrance Bay
Campground

**Cultus Lake**

**Provincial**

**Park**

Cole

Spring Bay
Picnic Area
Delta Grove
Campground
Columbia Valley Rd
Clear Creek
Campground

U

37600
2400

Honeymoon Bay
Group Campground
Columbia Valley Rd

83

4 5 6

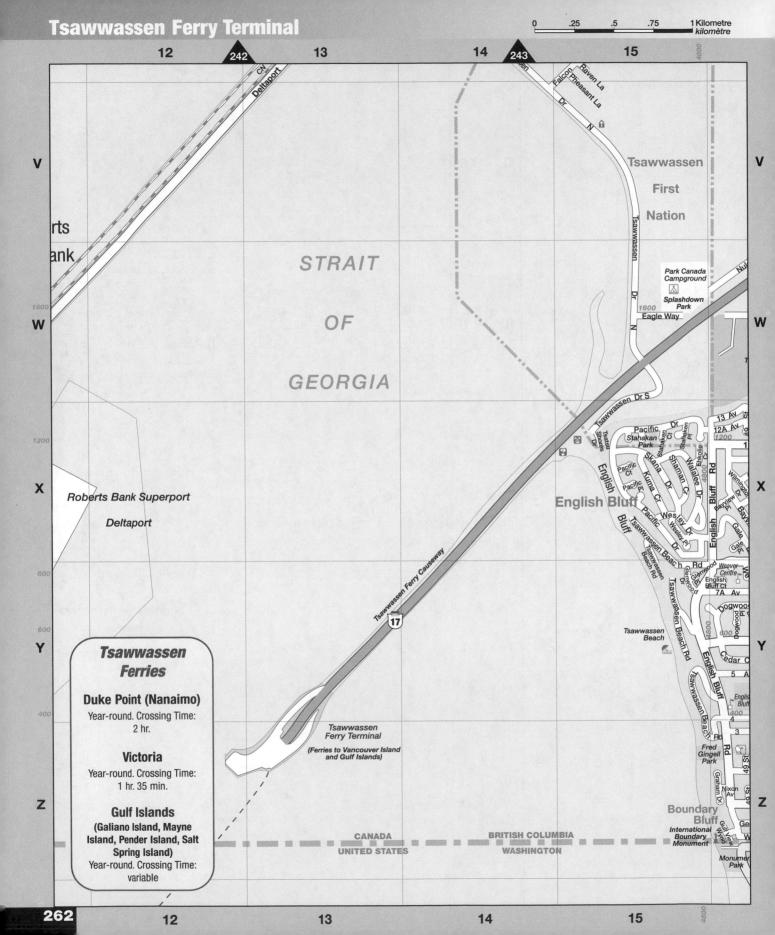

0 .25 .5 .75 1 Kilometre
*kilomètre*

12 **242** 13 14 **243** 15

CN
Deltaport

V
Tsawwassen
First
Nation

erts
ank

Raven La
Falcon  Pheasant La
Dr
N

Tsawwassen
Dr
N

Park Canada
Campground
Splashdown
Park

Nuk

*STRAIT*

*OF*

*GEORGIA*

W
1600
Eagle Way
1600

Tsawwassen Dr S

13 Av
12A Av
1200

Tsatsu
Shores

Pacific
Stahakan
Park

Pacific
Ct
Pacific

Stahaken Ct
Skana Dr
Kuma Cr
Shaman Cr
Stahaken Pl
Erkolie
Walalee Dr

English
Bluff
Rd
1

Wilmington

X
1200
**English Bluff**

Roberts Bank Superport

Deltaport

English
Bluff

Tsawwassen
Beach
Dr

Pacific
Wesley
Pl
Wesley Dr

Bayview Dr
Bayv

Gale
Gale
Av

800

Glenwood
Dr
Glenwood

Tsawwassen Beach Rd

Rd
Weaver
Centre
English
Bluff Ct
7A Av

Dogwood
Dr

600
**17**

Tsawwassen
Beach

Tsawwassen Beach Rd

Dogwood

400
1600

Y
Cedar C

Tsawwassen Ferry Causeway

English
Bluff

English
Bluff
400

5 A

4

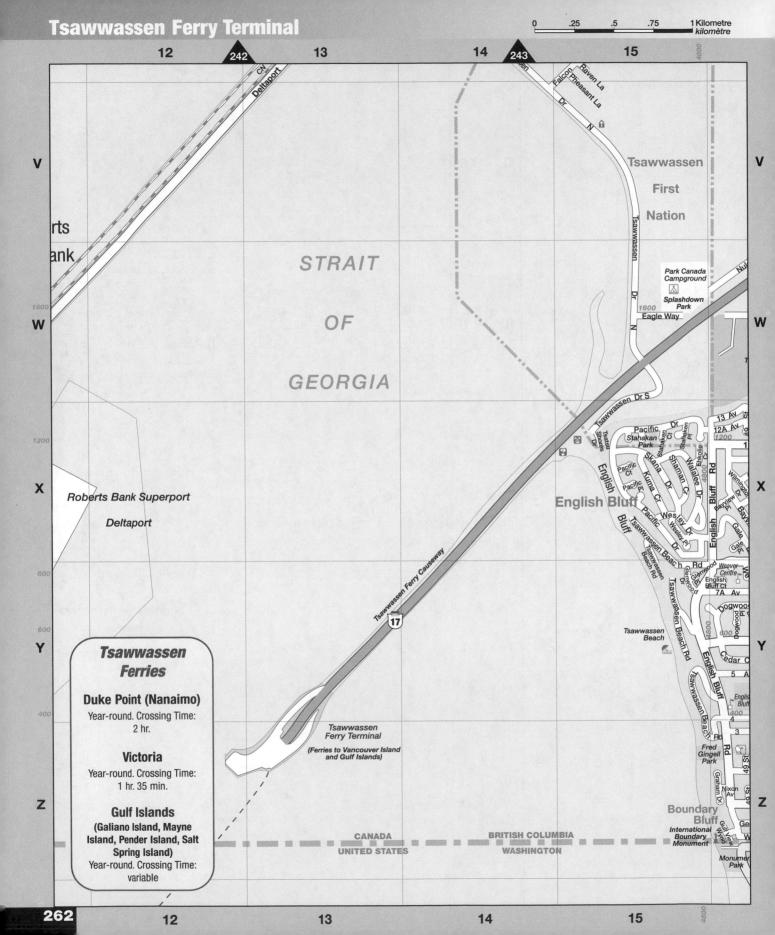

## Tsawwassen Ferries

### Duke Point (Nanaimo)
Year-round. Crossing Time:
2 hr.

### Victoria
Year-round. Crossing Time:
1 hr. 35 min.

### Gulf Islands
(Galiano Island, Mayne Island, Pender Island, Salt Spring Island)
Year-round. Crossing Time:
variable

Tsawwassen
Ferry Terminal

(Ferries to Vancouver Island
and Gulf Islands)

3

Fred Gingell
Park

Nixon
Dr

Graham Av

46 St

Z
**Boundary
Bluff**
*International
Boundary
Monument*

Gulf View
Wynd

Ge

Monumer
Park

CANADA
UNITED STATES

BRITISH COLUMBIA
WASHINGTON

12 13 14 15

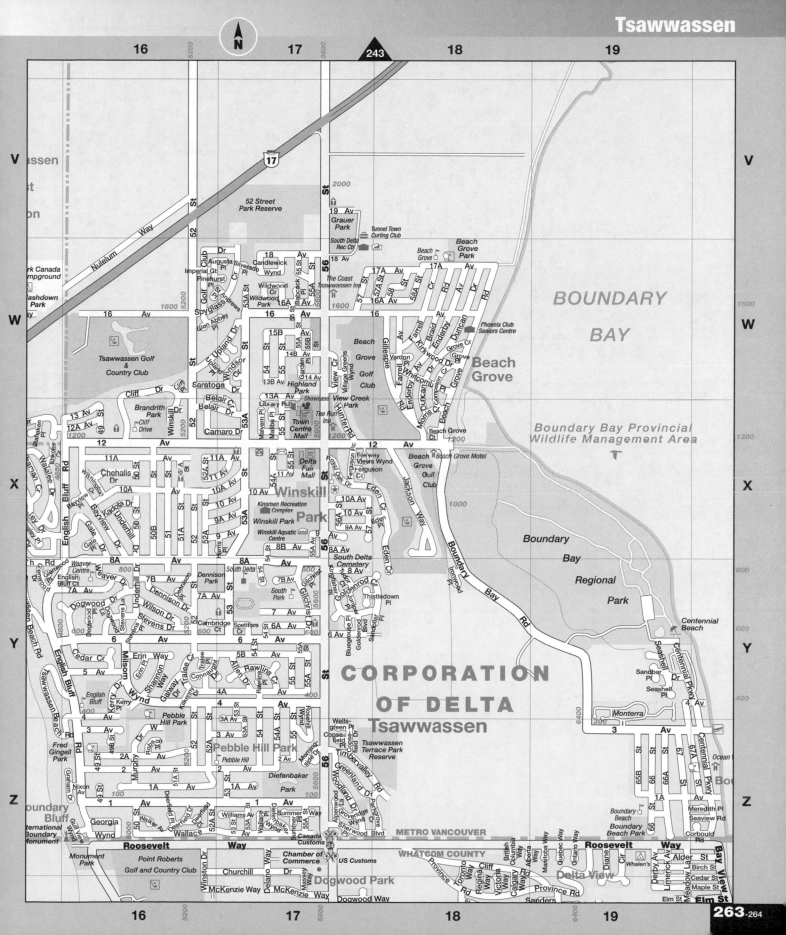

N

16     17     243     18     19

V

17

2000

52 Street
Park Reserve

19 Av

Grauer
Park

Tunnel Town
Curling Club

South Delta
Rec Ctr

The Coast
Tsawwassen Inn

18 Av

Beach
Grove

Beach
Grove
Park

17A Av

*BOUNDARY*
*BAY*

W

rk Canada
mpground

ashdown
Park

16 Av

Tsawwassen Golf
& Country Club

Spyglass

Glen Abbey

Augusta
Pl

Imperial Gt
Pinehurst
Pl

Andrews

Silverado
Pl

Candlewick
Wynd

Wildwood
Cr

Wildwood
Park

16A Av

16 Av

18 Av

15B

14B Av

13B Av

13A Av

14A Av

Garden
Pl

Highland
Park

Library Rd

Malibu

Malvern Pl

Showcase

View Creek
Park

The Run
Inn

Town Centre
Mall

Village Greens
Wynd

View Cr

Beach
Grove
Golf
Club

Gillespie

Farrell

Vardon

Whitcomb

Farrell

Kirkwood Dr

Enderby

Braid

Duncan

Grove

Grove Ct

Phoenix Club
Seniors Centre

**Beach
Grove**

Morris

Duncan

Beach

Beach Grove

1200

*Boundary Bay Provincial
Wildlife Management Area*

X

Stakaken

Walalee Dr

Eiholar

English Bluff Rd

13 Av

12A Av

1200

Brandrith
Park

Cliff
Drive

Winskill Dr

Belair Cr

Belair Dr

Cliff Dr

Saratoga

Upland Dr

Windsor

Upland

Camaro Dr

12 Av

11A

Chehalis
Dr

10A

Kadota Dr

Bayview

Gale Pl

Gale

Underhill

Willowdon

11A Av

10A Av

9A Av

52A St

52 St

51A

50B

51 St

11 Av

53A

54

Delta
Fair Mall

Harris

8B Av

**Winskill**

**Park**

Kinsmen Recreation
Complex

Winskill Park

Winskill Aquatic
Centre

Royal Oak Dr

Ferguson
Ct

Fairway
Views Wynd

Eden Dr

Eden

36A

Hunter Rd

12 Av

10A Av

10 Av

9A Av

8A Av

56 St

57

Beach
Grove
Gulf
Club

Beach Grove Motel

Jackson Way

Boundary

1000

*Boundary
Bay
Regional
Park*

Y

n Rd

Glenwood
Dr

Genwood
Ct

7A Av

Dogwood

Weaver Dr

Dennison Dr

Wilson Dr

Stevens Dr

Underhill

Stevens La

Cedar Cr

Milsom

Erin Way

Kerry

Kerry Pl

Shannon
Wynd

Galway
Dr

Tralee Cr

Kilkerby

Connaught

Allen Dr

Rawlins
Cr

Rawlins

Weaver
Centre

English
Bluff Ct

8A Av

7B Av

7A Av

Dennison
Park

South Delta

South
Park

6 Av

5 Av

English Bluff

Pebble
Hill Park

Pebble Hill

4A

4

Cambridge
Ct

Spetifore

7B Av

7 Av

6A Av

5B Av

5A St

3A Av

54

53A St

54A

55

Roosevelt
Wynd

Gilchrist

Gilchrist Dr

South Delta
Cemetery

Goldenrod

Thistledown
Pl

Bluegrouse Pl

Goldenrod

Goldenrod Blvd

Sandhill

8 Av

6A Av

Kingfisher

Knight Dr

Sandpiper

Eden Ct

Ironwood

*Boundary*

*Bay*

*Rd*

Centennial
Beach

Seashell Dr

Sandbar
Pl

Seashell
Pl

Centennial Pkwy

Monterra

3 Av

65B St

66 St

66A St

67A St

Centennial Pkwy

Z

oundary
Bluff

International
Boundary
Monument

Monument
Park

Gulf View Wynd

Graham Dr

Nixon Av

49 St

2A Av

1A

49A St

Murphy

Robson
Pl

Deerfield Dr

3A St

52A

3 Av

Williams Av

53A

52A St

54

55A

54A

Diefenbaker

Summer
Wynd

Diefenbaker
Wynd

Wallace
Wynd

**Pebble Hill Park**

Diefenbaker
Park

1A Av

Morningside Dr

56 St

Wells-
green Pl

Copse
field

Pl

Timbervalley Rd

Tsawwassen
Terrace Park
Reserve

Woodland La

Greenland Dr

Petrovenge
Wynd

Alpenrose

Grovenge
Wynd

Sherwood Blvd

**CORPORATION
OF DELTA
Tsawwassen**

Boundary

Boundary
Beach

Boundary
Beach Park

1A Av

Meredith Pl

Seaview Rd

Corbould
Rd

Ocean

Derby Av

Limerick Av

Bay View St

Georgia
Wynd

Point Roberts
Golf and Country Club

Winston Dr

Churchill
Dr

Delano
Dr

Massey
Dr

Williams Av

Wallace

Canada
Customs

US Customs

**METRO VANCOUVER**

**WHATCOM COUNTY**

Province

Toronto
Way

Regina
Way

Cliff
Way

Victoria
Way

Calgary
Way

British
Columbia
Way

Alberta
Way

Manitoba Way

Quebec
Way

Diane
Cir

Whalen's

*Delta
View*

Alder
St

Cedar
St

Maple St

Meadow La

Elm St

**Roosevelt**    **Way**

McKenzie Way

Chamber of
Commerce

Dogwood Park

Province Rd

Dogwood Way

Sanders

**Roosevelt**    **Way**

Meredith Pl

Elm St

16       17       18       19

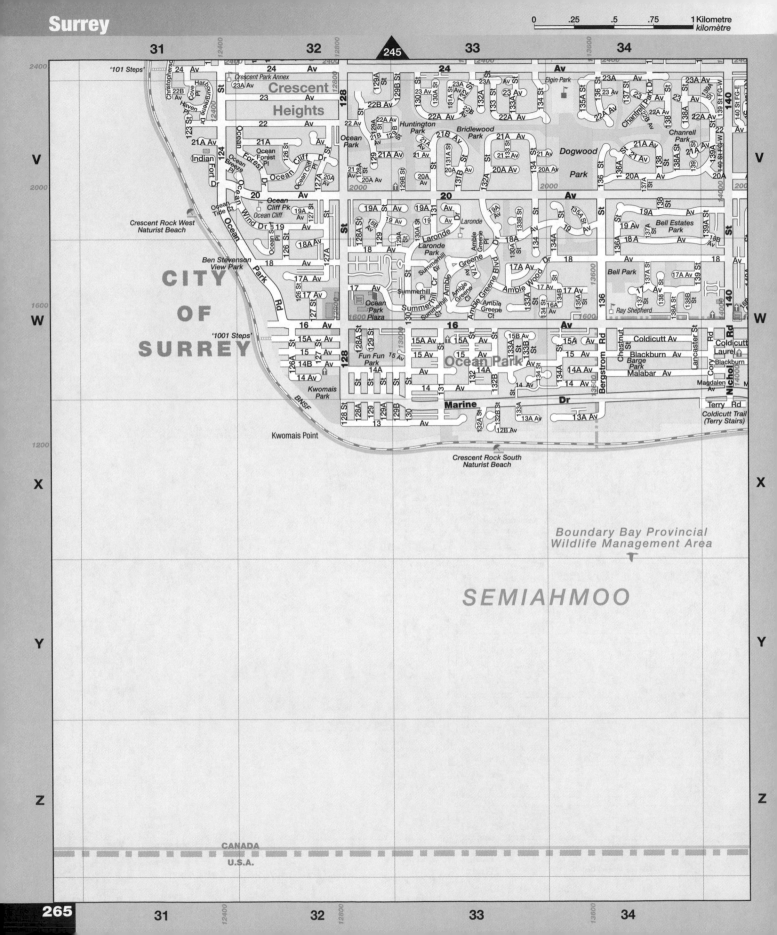

CITY

OF

SURREY

Crescent
Heights

Ocean Park

SEMIAHMOO

Boundary Bay Provincial
Wildlife Management Area

Crescent Rock West
Naturist Beach

Ben Stevenson
View Park

Kwomais Point

Crescent Rock South
Naturist Beach

CANADA
U.S.A.

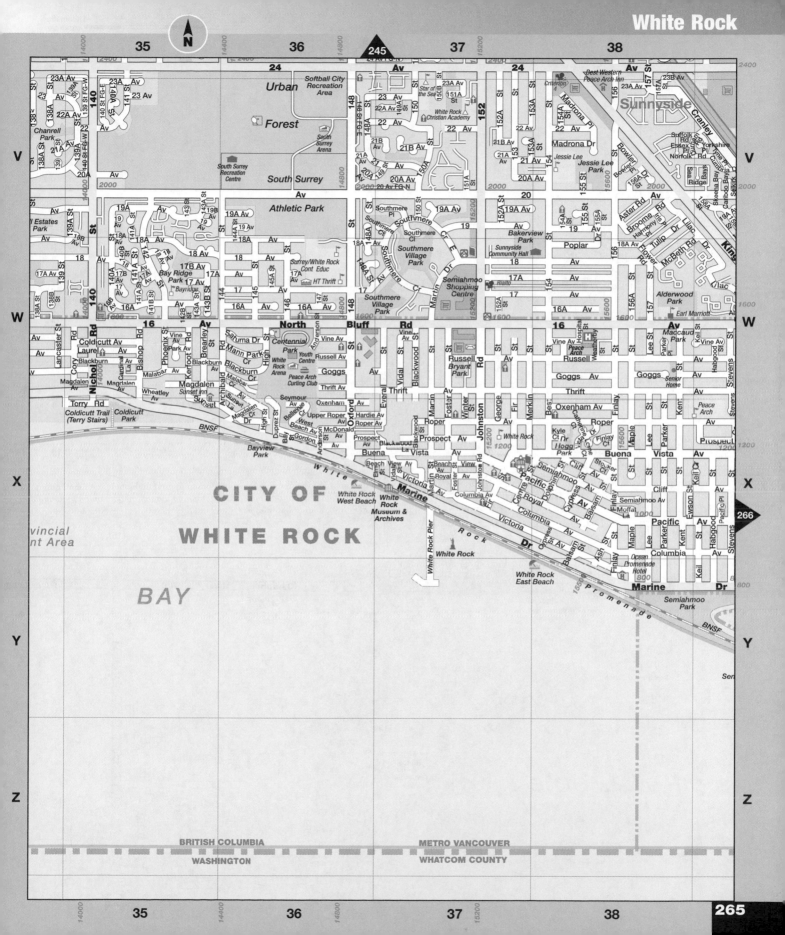

CITY OF

WHITE ROCK

BAY

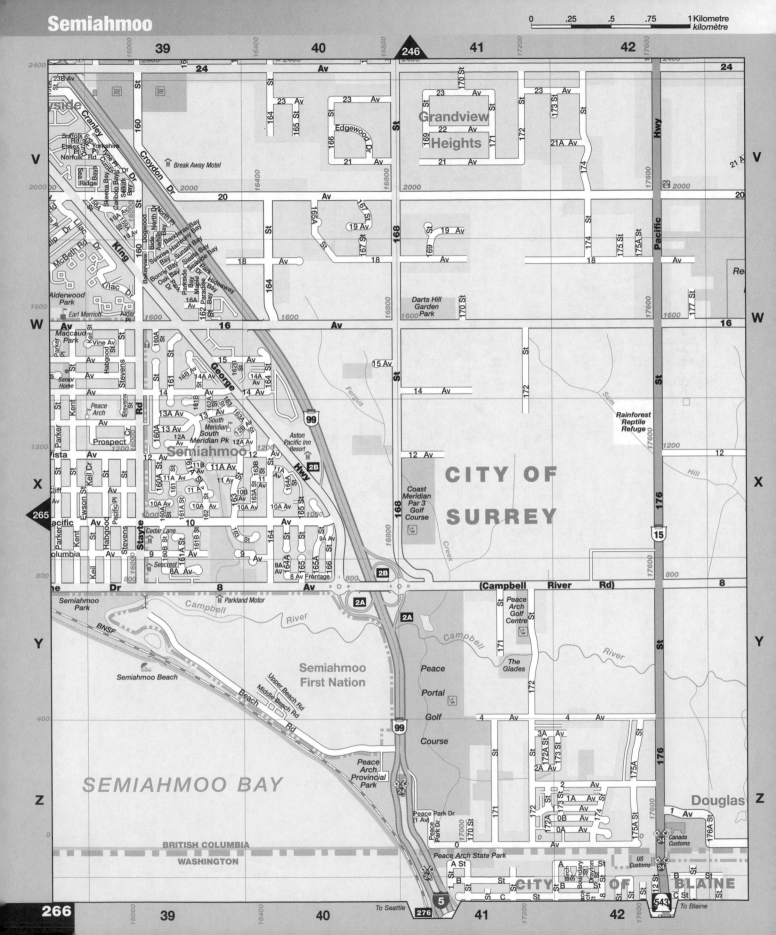

0  .25  .5  .75  1 Kilometre
*kilomètre*

39  40  **246**  41  42

**Grandview Heights**

Break Away Motel

Edgewood Dr

Alderwood Park

Earl Marriott

Maccaud Park

Senior Home

Peace Arch

Prospect

**Semiahmoo**

South Meridian

South Meridian Pk

Darts Hill Garden Park

Aston Pacific Inn Resort

**CITY OF SURREY**

Coast Meridian Par 3 Golf Course

Rainforest Reptile Refuge

Fergus Creek

Campbell Creek

Cedar Lane

Seacrest

8 Av Frontage

**2B**

**2A**

**(Campbell River Rd)**

Peace Arch Golf Centre

The Glades

Campbell River

**Semiahmoo Park**

Campbell River

BNSF

Parkland Motor

Semiahmoo Beach

Upper Beach Rd

Middle Beach Rd

Beach Rd

**Semiahmoo First Nation**

**Peace Portal Golf Course**

Peace Arch Provincial Park

**SEMIAHMOO BAY**

Peace Park Dr (1 Av)

Peace Park Dr

**Douglas**

Peace Arch State Park

Canada Customs

US Customs

**BRITISH COLUMBIA**

**WASHINGTON**

**CITY OF BLAINE**

**265**

To Seattle **5** **276**

**266** 39  40  41  42

To Blaine **543**

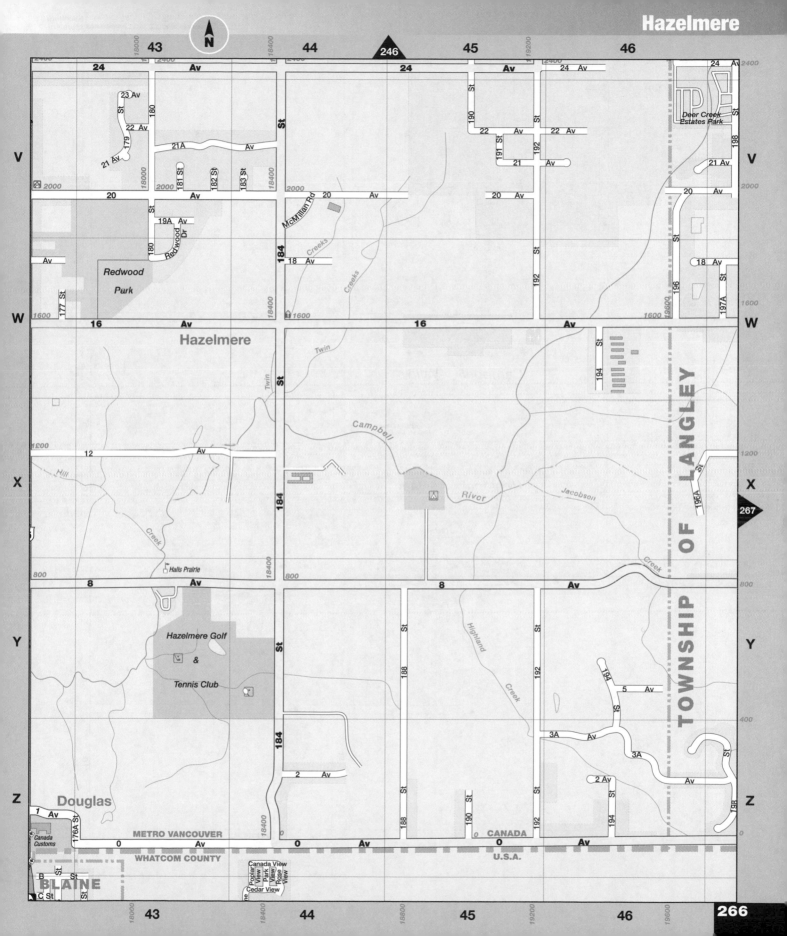

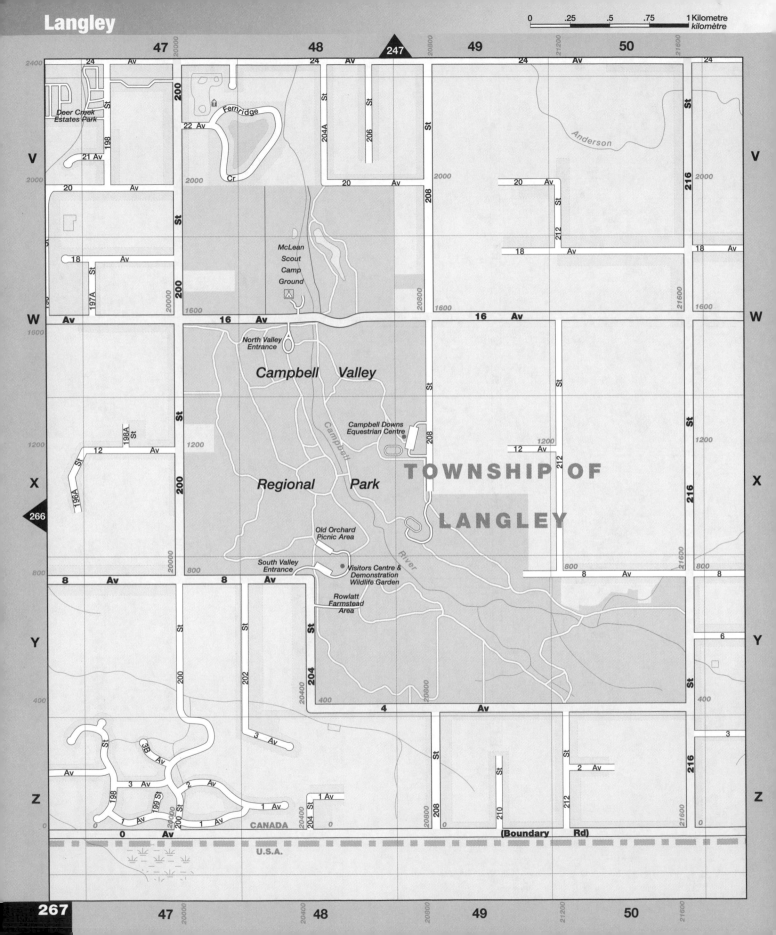

0    .25    .5    .75    1 Kilometre
                                *kilomètre*

**247**

47    48    49    50

Deer Creek
Estates Park

Fernridge

Cr

McLean
Scout
Camp
Ground

Anderson

North Valley
Entrance

Campbell     Valley

Campbell Downs
Equestrian Centre

Regional     Park

**TOWNSHIP OF**

**LANGLEY**

Old Orchard
Picnic Area

South Valley
Entrance

Visitors Centre &
Demonstration
Wildlife Garden

River

Rowlatt
Farmstead
Area

CANADA

(Boundary    Rd)

U.S.A.

47    48    49    50

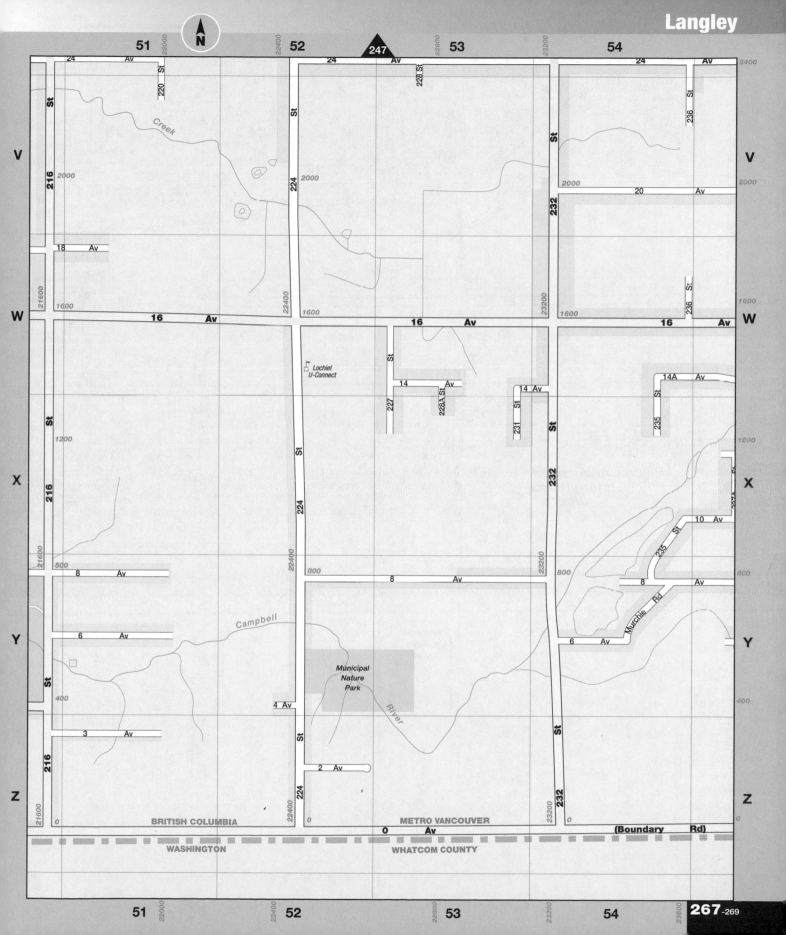

N

51  52  ▲247  53  54

24 Av  220 St  24 Av  228 St  24 Av  236 St  24 Av

V  216 St  2000  224 St  2000  2000  20 Av  232 St  V

18 Av  1600  1600  236 St  1600

W  216 St  16 Av  16 Av  16 Av  W

Lochiel U-Connect

227 St  14 Av  228A St  14 Av  231 St  14 Av  14A Av  235 St

X  216 St  1200  224 St  232 St  1200  X

10 Av  235 St

X  800  8 Av  800  8 Av  800  8 Av  8 Av

Campbell  6 Av  6 Av  Murchie Rd

Y  216 St  Municipal Nature Park  6 Av  Y

River  400  400  400

4 Av

224 St

3 Av

Z  216 St  2 Av  224 St  0  0 Av  232 St  0  Z

**BRITISH COLUMBIA**  **METRO VANCOUVER**  **(Boundary Rd)**

**WASHINGTON**  **WHATCOM COUNTY**

51  52  53  54

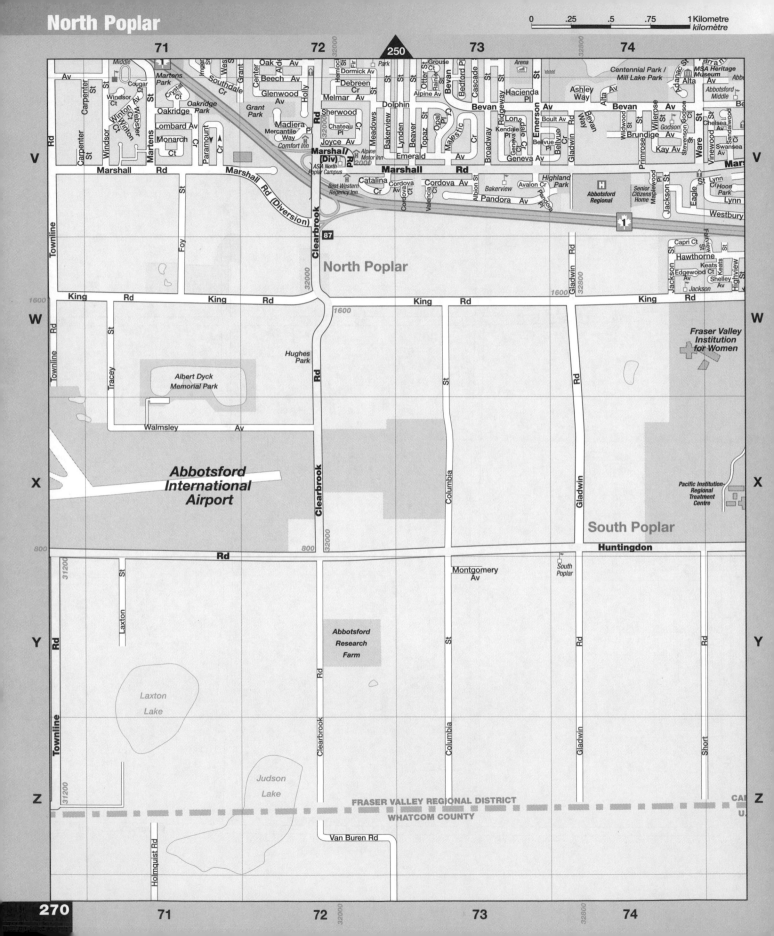

0   .25   .5   .75   1 Kilometre
kilomètre

71   72   250   73   74

North Poplar

South Poplar

Abbotsford International Airport

Albert Dyck Memorial Park

Laxton Lake

Judson Lake

Abbotsford Research Farm

Fraser Valley Institution for Women

Pacific Institution-Regional Treatment Centre

FRASER VALLEY REGIONAL DISTRICT
WHATCOM COUNTY

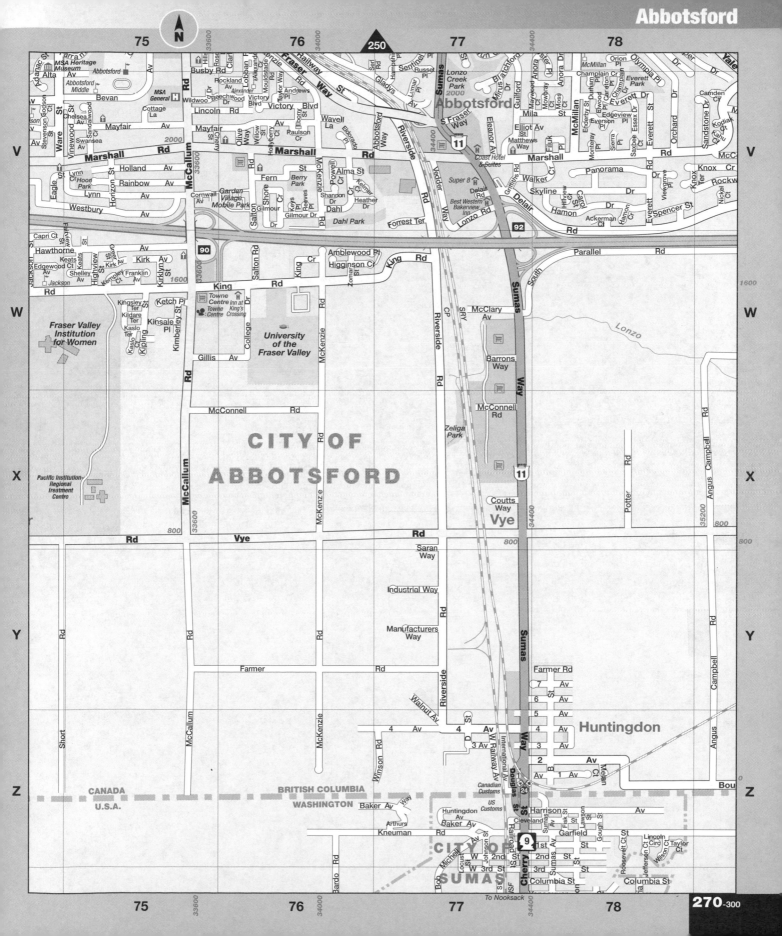

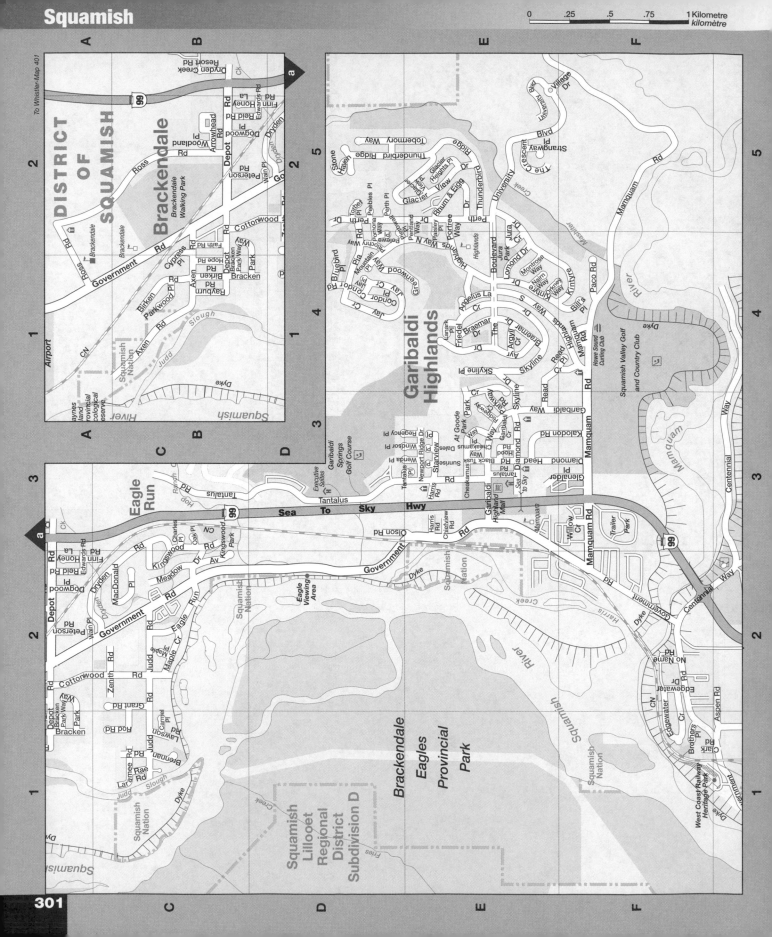

0   .25   .5   .75   1 Kilometre
*kilomètre*

**A**   **B**   **E**   **F**

To Whistler-Map 401

**DISTRICT OF SQUAMISH**

**Brackendale**

99

Dryden Creek Resort Rd

Honey La
Finn Rd
Reid Rd
Edwards Rd
Dryden Rd
Depot Rd

Arrowhead Pl
Woodland Pl
Dogwood Pl

Ross Rd

Peterson Rd
Main Rd

Brackendale Walking Park

Cottonwood Rd

Government Rd

Brackendale Rd

Faith Rd
Hope Rd
Cypress Pl
Birken Rd
Axen Rd
Rayburn Pl
Parkwood Pl

Depot Rd
Bracken Park Way
Bracken Park
Bracken

Airport

Squamish Nation

CN

Judd Slough

Dyke

Squamish River

**Garibaldi Highlands**

Village Dr

Tantalus Way
Stone Haven
Thunderbird Ridge
Tobermory Way
Glacier View Dr
Glacier Heights Pl
Rhum & Eigg Dr
Thunderbird Ridge

The Crescent
Strandway Pl
University Cr

Creek

Mashiter

Mamquam Rd

Torbet Dr
Pebbles Pl
Perth Pl
Perth Dr
Pomona Way
Pentland Dr
Paisley Way
Portree Way
Timothy Way
Bluebird Pl
Greenwood
Highlands Way N
Jura Cr
Jura Park
Boulevard
Lomond Dr
Montrose Way
Nairn Way
Kintyre Way
Kinmore Way
Paco Rd

Pia Pl
Mountain Way
Condor Pl
Jay Ct
Angelus La
Highlands Way S
Xintyre Way
Bill's
Lanark Pl
Friedel Cr
Braemar Dr
Argyll Cr
Braemar Dr
Read Pl
Mamquam Rd
Howe Sound Curling Club

Jay Cr
Condor Rd
Skyline Pl
Skyline Dr
Argyll Cr
Read Cr
Squamish Valley Golf and Country Club

Park Rd
At Goode Park
Ridgeway
Ridgeway Way
Park Way
Garibaldi Way
Read
Skyline Dr

Kaldoon Rd

River

Dyke

Garibaldi Springs Golf Course

Newport Ridge Dr
Windsor Pl
Wenda Pl
Tantalus Pl
Starview
Regency Pl
Sunrise Pl
Dales
Cheakamus Way
Hood Rd
Black Tusk Way
Diamond Rd
Sea to Sky
Diamond Head Rd

Glenalder Pl

Mamquam Rd

**Eagle Run**

Honey La
Finn Rd
Reid Rd
Edwards Rd
Depot Rd

Hop Rd
Ranph Rd
Tantalus Rd
Tantalus

Charles Rd
Kingswood Rd
Oak Pl
Kingswood Park
CN

Sea To Sky Hwy
99

MacDonald Pl
Meadow Dr

Dyke
Government Rd
Olson Rd

Harris Rd
Chiefview Rd

Garibaldi Highland Mall

Eagle Viewing Area

Squamish Nation

Willow Cr
Mamquam Rd
Trailer Park

99

No Name Rd

Dyke
Dryden Pl
Dogwood Pl
Wain Pl
Depot Rd
Peterson Rd
Government Rd

Cottonwood Rd
Judd Rd
Zenith Rd
Grant Rd
Maple Cr
Eagle Run
Rod Rd
Lawson Rd
Carmel Pl
Judd Rd
Brennan Rd
Lamee Rd
Rae Rd
Lara Rd

Depot Rd
Bracken Park Way
Bracken Park
Bracken

Judd Slough

Dyke

Squamish Nation

Creek

**Squamish Lillooet Regional District Subdivision D**

**Brackendale Eagles Provincial Park**

Squamish River

Squamish Nation

Harris Rd
Harris Creek

West Coast Railway Heritage Park

Edgewater Dr
Brothers Pl
Clark Rd
Edgewater Cr
CN
Aspen Rd
Government Rd
Centennial Way
Dyke

Centennial Way

Mamquam River

**A**   **B**   **C**   **D**   **E**   **F**

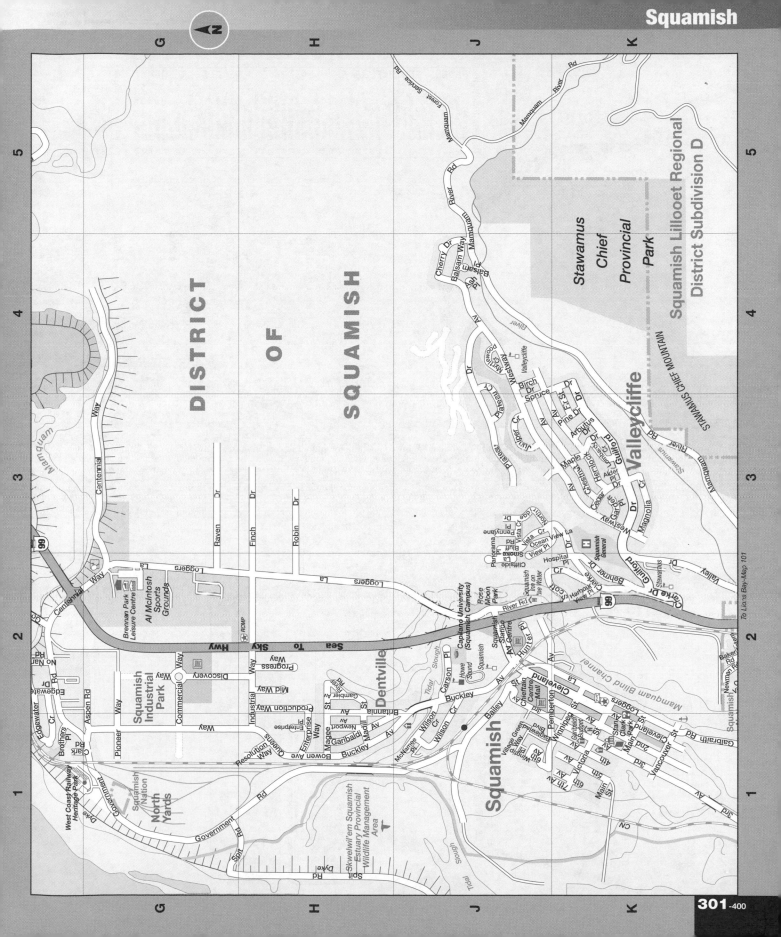

DISTRICT

OF

SQUAMISH

Stawamus
Chief
Provincial
Park

Squamish Lillooet Regional
District Subdivision D

Valleycliffe

Squamish Industrial Park

Brennan Park
Leisure Centre

Al McIntosh
Sports
Grounds

RCMP

Dentville

Squamish
North Yards

West Coast Railway
Heritage Park

Squamish Nation
North Yards

Skwelwil'em Squamish
Estuary Provincial
Wildlife Management
Area

Capilano University
(Squamish Campus)

Rose
Moon
Park

Squamish Inn on
the Water

Squamish
Station

Squamish

Cleveland

Chieftain
Centre Mall

Stan
Clark
Park

Squamish
General
Hospital

Mamquam Blind Channel

Howe
Sound

Sea To Sky Hwy

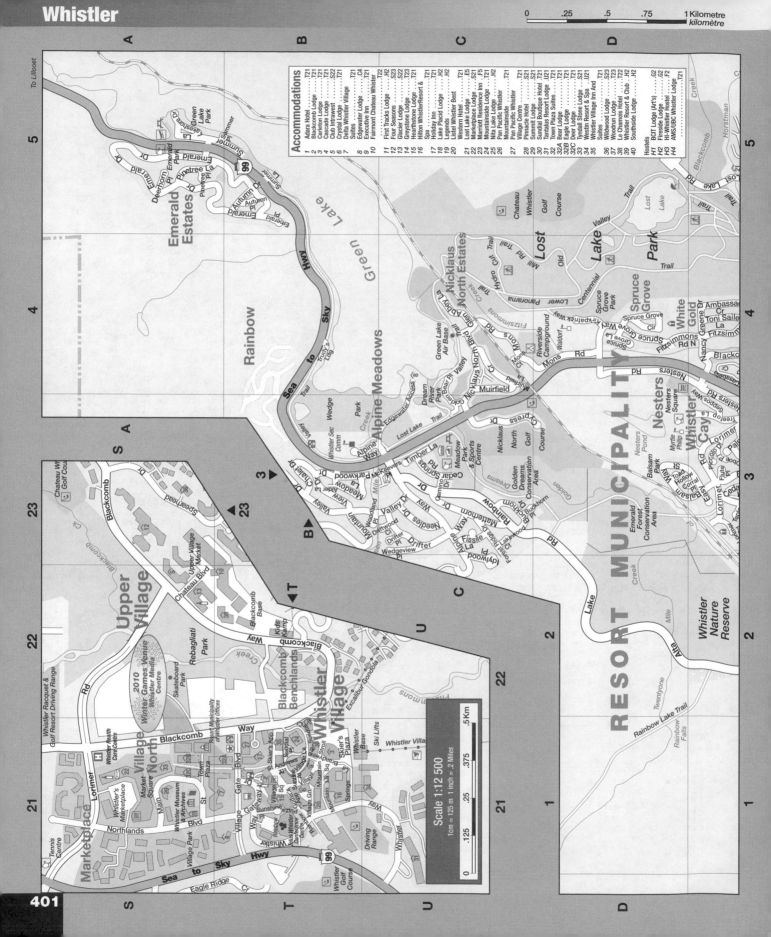

**RESORT MUNICIPALITY**

## Accommodations

| | | |
|---|---|---|
| 1 | Adara Hotel | T21 |
| 2 | Blackcomb Lodge | T21 |
| 3 | Carleton Lodge | T21 |
| 4 | Cascade Lodge | T21 |
| 5 | Club Intrawest | S22 |
| 6 | Crystal Lodge | T21 |
| 7 | Delta Whistler Village Suites | S22 |
| 8 | Edgewater Village | C4 |
| 9 | Executive Inn | T21 |
| 10 | Fairmont Chateau Whistler | T22 |
| 11 | First Tracks Lodge | H2 |
| 12 | Four Seasons | S23 |
| 13 | Glacier Lodge | S21 |
| 14 | Greystone Lodge | T23 |
| 15 | Hearthstone Lodge | T21 |
| 16 | Hilton WhistlerResort & Spa | H2 |
| 17 | Holiday Inn | T21 |
| 18 | Lake Placid Lodge | H2 |
| 19 | Legends | H2 |
| 20 | Listel Whistler Best Western Hotel | T21 |
| 21 | Lost Lake Lodge | E5 |
| 22 | Marketplace Lodge | S21 |
| 23 | Marriott Residence Inn | F5 |
| 24 | Mountainside Lodge | J21 |
| 25 | Nita Lake Lodge | H2 |
| 26 | Pan Pacific Whistler | H2 |
| 27 | Pan Pacific Whistler Village Centre | T21 |
| 28 | Pinnacle Hotel | S21 |
| 29 | Summit Lodge | S21 |
| 30 | Sundial Boutique Hotel | J21 |
| 31 | Tantalus Resort Lodge | J21 |
| 32 | Town Plaza Suites | T21 |
| 32A | Bear Lodge | T21 |
| 32B | Eagle Lodge | T21 |
| 32C | Deer Lodge | T21 |
| 33 | Tyndall Stone Lodge | S21 |
| 34 | Westin Resort & Spa | J21 |
| 35 | Whistler Village Inn And Suites | T21 |
| 36 | Wildwood Lodge | S23 |
| 37 | Woodrun Lodge | T21 |
| 38 | Le Chamois Hotel | T22 |
| 39 | Whistler Resort & Club | H2 |
| 40 | Southside Lodge | H2 |

**Hostels**
| | | |
|---|---|---|
| H1 | BGT Lodge (Art's) | G2 |
| H2 | Fireside Lodge | G2 |
| H3 | HI-Whistler Hostel | F2 |
| H4 | AMS/UBC Whistler Lodge | T21 |

### Scale 1:12 500
1cm = 125 m   1 inch = .2 Miles

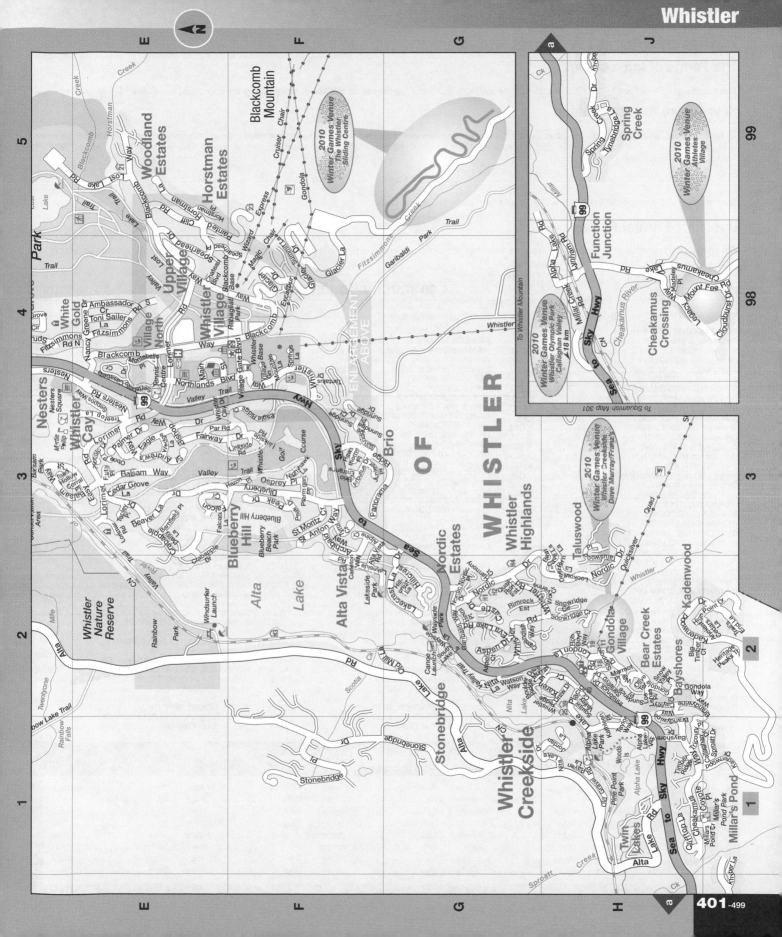

# Points of Interest & Street Index

## The Points of Interest Index

The Points of Interest are in the blue section of the index. It works the same way as the street index, using the municipal codes found in the table below.

## How to use the street index

To find a street, search through the alphabetically arranged columns. A three letter code beside the street name indicates which municipality the street is located in. Note the page number and the reference square to the right of the street name. For example, to find the location of Hajula Court in Abbotsford:

Hajula Ct *ABT* . . . . . . . **251** S79

Turn to map **251** and locate the square S79. Scan the square to find the street.

## Duplicated Street Names

When two or more streets in a municipality share the same name, an area name in brackets following the street name indicates in which part of the municipality the street is located.

# Community Codes

**BOLD TYPE** indicates an official municipal name.          Blue type indicates a local community name.

| | | |
|---|---|---|
| **ABBOTSFORD, CITY OF** . . . . . . . . . . . . . . . . . .*ABT* | Fort Langley (LANGLEY) . . . . . . . . . . . . . . . . . . .*LGT* | Peardonville (ABBOTSFORD) . . . . . . . . . . . . . . . .*ABT* |
| Abbotsford (ABBOTSFORD) . . . . . . . . . . . . . . . .*ABT* | **FRASER VALLEY REGIONAL DISTRICT** | **PITT MEADOWS, CITY OF** . . . . . . . . . . . . . . . . .*PTM* |
| Agassiz (KENT) . . . . . . . . . . . . . . . . . . . . . . . . . .*KNT* | **SUBDIVISION (F.V.R.D.S.)** . . . . . . . . . . . . . . .*FRA* | Pitt Meadows (PITT MEADOWS) . . . . . . . . . . . . .*PTM* |
| Aldergrove (LANGLEY) . . . . . . . . . . . . . . . . . . . . .*LGT* | Garibaldi Highlands (SQUAMISH) . . . . . . . . . . . .*SQM* | **POINT ROBERTS, WASHINGTON, U.S.A.** . . . .*PRB* |
| **ANMORE, VILLAGE OF** . . . . . . . . . . . . . . . . . . .*ANM* | Gastown (VANCOUVER) . . . . . . . . . . . . . . . . . . . .*VAN* | Popkum (F.V.R.D.S.) . . . . . . . . . . . . . . . . . . . . . .*FRA* |
| Anniedale (SURREY) . . . . . . . . . . . . . . . . . . . . . .*SUR* | Guildford (SURREY) . . . . . . . . . . . . . . . . . . . . . . .*SUR* | **PORT COQUITLAM, CITY OF** . . . . . . . . . . . . . .*PCQ* |
| Barnston Island (M.V.S.) . . . . . . . . . . . . . . . . . . . .*BTI* | Haig (HOPE) . . . . . . . . . . . . . . . . . . . . . . . . . . . .*HOP* | Port Guichon (DELTA) . . . . . . . . . . . . . . . . . . . . .*DEL* |
| Barrowtown (ABBOTSFORD) . . . . . . . . . . . . . . . .*ABT* | Hamilton (RICHMOND) . . . . . . . . . . . . . . . . . . . . .*RMD* | Port Hammond (MAPLE RIDGE) . . . . . . . . . . . . .*MAP* |
| Bayshores (WHISTLER) . . . . . . . . . . . . . . . . . . . .*WHS* | Haney (MAPLE RIDGE) . . . . . . . . . . . . . . . . . . . . .*MAP* | Port Kells (SURREY) . . . . . . . . . . . . . . . . . . . . . .*SUR* |
| **BELCARRA, VILLAGE OF** . . . . . . . . . . . . . . . . .*BEL* | **HARRISON HOT SPRINGS, VILLAGE OF** . . . . .*HHS* | **PORT MOODY, CITY OF** . . . . . . . . . . . . . . . . . .*PMD* |
| Brackendale (SQUAMISH) . . . . . . . . . . . . . . . . . .*SQM* | Hatzic (MISSION) . . . . . . . . . . . . . . . . . . . . . . . . .*MIS* | Promontory (CHILLIWACK) . . . . . . . . . . . . . . . . .*CHL* |
| Bradner (ABBOTSFORD) . . . . . . . . . . . . . . . . . . .*ABT* | **HOPE, DISTRICT OF** . . . . . . . . . . . . . . . . . . . .*HOP* | **RICHMOND, CITY OF** . . . . . . . . . . . . . . . . . . . .*RMD* |
| Bridal Falls (F.V.R.D.S.) . . . . . . . . . . . . . . . . . . . .*FRA* | Hope (HOPE) . . . . . . . . . . . . . . . . . . . . . . . . . . . .*HOP* | Rosedale (CHILLIWACK) . . . . . . . . . . . . . . . . . . .*CHL* |
| Bridgeport (RICHMOND) . . . . . . . . . . . . . . . . . . .*RMD* | Hopington (LANGLEY) . . . . . . . . . . . . . . . . . . . . .*LGT* | Ruskin (MAPLE RIDGE) . . . . . . . . . . . . . . . . . . . .*MAP* |
| Brio (WHISTLER) . . . . . . . . . . . . . . . . . . . . . . . . .*WHS* | Horseshoe Bay (W. VANCOUVER) . . . . . . . . . . . .*WVA* | Queensborough (NEW WESTMINSTER) . . . . . . . .*NEW* |
| British Properties (WEST VAN.) . . . . . . . . . . . . . .*WVA* | Huntingdon (ABBOTSFORD) . . . . . . . . . . . . . . . .*ABT* | Sapperton (NEW WESTMINSTER) . . . . . . . . . . . .*NEW* |
| Brookswood (LANGLEY) . . . . . . . . . . . . . . . . . . .*LGT* | Ioco (PORT MOODY) . . . . . . . . . . . . . . . . . . . . . .*PMD* | Sardis (CHILLIWACK) . . . . . . . . . . . . . . . . . . . . .*CHL* |
| Burkville (RICHMOND) . . . . . . . . . . . . . . . . . . . . .*RMD* | Kensington (SURREY) . . . . . . . . . . . . . . . . . . . . .*SUR* | Semiahmoo (SURREY) . . . . . . . . . . . . . . . . . . . . .*SUR* |
| **BURNABY, CITY OF** . . . . . . . . . . . . . . . . . . . . .*BUR* | **KENT, DISTRICT OF** . . . . . . . . . . . . . . . . . . . .*KNT* | Silverdale (MISSION) . . . . . . . . . . . . . . . . . . . . . .*MIS* |
| Burquitlam (COQUITLAM) . . . . . . . . . . . . . . . . . .*CQT* | Kitsilano (VANCOUVER) . . . . . . . . . . . . . . . . . . .*VAN* | South Burnaby (BURNABY) . . . . . . . . . . . . . . . . .*BUR* |
| Cheam (CHILLIWACK) . . . . . . . . . . . . . . . . . . . . .*CHL* | Ladner (DELTA) . . . . . . . . . . . . . . . . . . . . . . . . . .*DEL* | **SQUAMISH, DISTRICT OF** . . . . . . . . . . . . . . . .*SQM* |
| **CHILLIWACK, DISTRICT OF** . . . . . . . . . . . . . .*CHL* | Lake Errock (F.V.R.D.S.) . . . . . . . . . . . . . . . . . . .*FRA* | Squamish (SQUAMISH) . . . . . . . . . . . . . . . . . . . .*SQM* |
| Chilliwack (CHILLIWACK) . . . . . . . . . . . . . . . . . . .*CHL* | **LANGLEY, CITY OF** . . . . . . . . . . . . . . . . . . . . .*LGC* | Stave Falls (MISSION) . . . . . . . . . . . . . . . . . . . . .*MIS* |
| Chinatown (VANCOUVER) . . . . . . . . . . . . . . . . . .*VAN* | **LANGLEY, TOWNSHIP OF** . . . . . . . . . . . . . . . .*LGT* | Steelhead (MISSION) . . . . . . . . . . . . . . . . . . . . . .*MIS* |
| Clayburn Village (ABBOTSFORD) . . . . . . . . . . . .*ABT* | Lindell (F.V.R.D.S.) . . . . . . . . . . . . . . . . . . . . . . . .*FRA* | **SURREY, CITY OF** . . . . . . . . . . . . . . . . . . . . . .*SUR* |
| Clearbrook(F.V.R.D.S.) . . . . . . . . . . . . . . . . . . . . .*FRA* | **LIONS BAY, VILLAGE OF** . . . . . . . . . . . . . . . . .*LIO* | Tsawwassen (DELTA) . . . . . . . . . . . . . . . . . . . . .*DEL* |
| Cloverdale (SURREY) . . . . . . . . . . . . . . . . . . . . .*SUR* | Lynn Valley (N. VANCOUVER) . . . . . . . . . . . . . . .*DNV* | Tynehead (SURREY) . . . . . . . . . . . . . . . . . . . . . .*SUR* |
| **COQUITLAM, CITY OF** . . . . . . . . . . . . . . . . . . .*CQT* | **MAPLE RIDGE, DISTRICT OF** . . . . . . . . . . . . .*MAP* | **UNIVERSITY ENDOWMENT LANDS** (U.E.L.) . . .*UEL* |
| Crescent Beach (SURREY) . . . . . . . . . . . . . . . . .*SUR* | Matsqui Village (ABBOTSFORD) . . . . . . . . . . . . .*ABT* | University Hill (U.E.L.) . . . . . . . . . . . . . . . . . . . . .*UEL* |
| Cultus Lake Park Board (F.V.R.D.S.) . . . . . . . . . .*FRA* | Middlegate (BURNABY) . . . . . . . . . . . . . . . . . . . .*BUR* | Valleycliffe (SQUAMISH) . . . . . . . . . . . . . . . . . . .*SQM* |
| Deep Cove (N. VANCOUVER) . . . . . . . . . . . . . . .*DNV* | Minoru Park (RICHMOND) . . . . . . . . . . . . . . . . . .*RMD* | **VANCOUVER, CITY OF** . . . . . . . . . . . . . . . . . . .*VAN* |
| **DELTA, CORPORATION OF** . . . . . . . . . . . . . . .*DEL* | Minto Landing (CHILLIWACK) . . . . . . . . . . . . . . .*CHL* | Vedder Crossing (CHILLIWACK) . . . . . . . . . . . . .*CHL* |
| Dollarton (BURNABY) . . . . . . . . . . . . . . . . . . . . .*BUR* | **MISSION, DISTRICT OF** . . . . . . . . . . . . . . . . . .*MIS* | Walnut Grove (LANGLEY) . . . . . . . . . . . . . . . . . .*LGT* |
| Douglas (SURREY) . . . . . . . . . . . . . . . . . . . . . . .*SUR* | Mission (MISSION) . . . . . . . . . . . . . . . . . . . . . . . .*MIS* | Websters Corners (MAPLE RIDGE) . . . . . . . . . . .*MAP* |
| Downtown (VANCOUVER) . . . . . . . . . . . . . . . . . .*VAN* | Mount Lehman (ABBOTSFORD) . . . . . . . . . . . . . .*ABT* | West Heights (MISSION) . . . . . . . . . . . . . . . . . . .*MIS* |
| East Burnaby (BURNABY) . . . . . . . . . . . . . . . . . .*BUR* | Murrayville (LANGLEY) . . . . . . . . . . . . . . . . . . . .*LGT* | **WEST VANCOUVER, DISTRICT OF** . . . . . . . . .*WVA* |
| East Chilliwack (CHILLIWACK) . . . . . . . . . . . . . .*CHL* | **NEW WESTMINSTER, CITY OF** . . . . . . . . . . . .*NEW* | **WHISTLER, RESORT MUN. OF** . . . . . . . . . . . .*WHS* |
| Elgin (SURREY) . . . . . . . . . . . . . . . . . . . . . . . . . .*SUR* | Nordic Estates (WHISTLER) . . . . . . . . . . . . . . . .*WHS* | Whistler Creek (WHISTLER) . . . . . . . . . . . . . . . .*WHS* |
| Emerald Estaes (WHISTLER) . . . . . . . . . . . . . . .*WHS* | North Burnaby (BURNABY) . . . . . . . . . . . . . . . . .*BUR* | Whistler Highlands (WHISTLER) . . . . . . . . . . . . .*WHS* |
| English Bluff (DELTA) . . . . . . . . . . . . . . . . . . . . . .*DEL* | North Delta (DELTA) . . . . . . . . . . . . . . . . . . . . . .*DEL* | Whistler Village (WHISTLER) . . . . . . . . . . . . . . .*WHS* |
| Fishermans Cove (WEST VAN.) . . . . . . . . . . . . .*WVA* | **NORTH VANCOUVER, CITY OF** . . . . . . . . . . . .*CNV* | **WHITE ROCK, CITY OF** . . . . . . . . . . . . . . . . . .*WRK* |
| Forest Knolls (LANGLEY) . . . . . . . . . . . . . . . . . .*LGT* | **NORTH VANCOUVER, DISTRICT OF** . . . . . . . .*DNV* | Whonnock (MAPLE RIDGE) . . . . . . . . . . . . . . . . .*MAP* |
| | Panorama Ridge (SURREY) . . . . . . . . . . . . . . . . .*SUR* | Yarrow (CHILLIWACK) . . . . . . . . . . . . . . . . . . . . .*CHL* |

## Street Generics and Abbreviations

| | | | | | | | |
|---|---|---|---|---|---|---|---|
| Av . . . . . . . . . . . . .Avenue | Cv . . . . . . . . . . . . . . .Cove | Heath . . . . . . . . . . .Heath | Mnr . . . . . . . . . . . . .Manor | Sq . . . . . . . . . . . . . .Square |
| Bay . . . . . . . . . . . . . .Bay | Dr . . . . . . . . . . . . . . .Drive | Hill . . . . . . . . . . . . . .Hill | Path . . . . . . . . . . . . . .Path | St . . . . . . . . . . . . . .Street |
| Blvd . . . . . . . .Boulevard | Expwy . . . . .Expressway | Hts . . . . . . . . . . . .Heights | Pk . . . . . . . . . . . . . . .Park | Ter . . . . . . . . . . . .Terrace |
| Cir . . . . . . . . . . . . . .Circle | Frwy . . . . . . . . .Freeway | Hwy . . . . . . . . . . .Highway | Pkwy . . . . . . .Parkway | Tr . . . . . . . . . . . . . . .Trail |
| Cl . . . . . . . . . . . . . .Close | Gdns . . . . . . . . .Gardens | La . . . . . . . . . . . . . . .Lane | Pl . . . . . . . . . . . . . .Place | View . . . . . . . . . . . . .View |
| Cr . . . . . . . . . . .Crescent | Gn . . . . . . . . . . . . .Green | Ldg . . . . . . . . . .Landing | Pt . . . . . . . . . . . . . .Point | Vill . . . . . . . . . . . . .Villas |
| Crct . . . . . . . . . .Circuit | Gr . . . . . . . . . . . . . .Grove | Ln . . . . . . . . . . . . . . .Line | Rd . . . . . . . . . . . . . .Road | Walk . . . . . . . . . . . .Walk |
| Ct . . . . . . . . . . . . . .Court | Gt . . . . . . . . . . . . . . .Gate | Mews . . . . . . . . . .Mews | Rise . . . . . . . . . . . . .Rise | Way . . . . . . . . . . . . .Way |

## Points of Interest

Atkinson Lighthouse *WVA* . . . . . . .**121** M3
B.C. Place Stadium *VAN* . . . . . . . .**11** J38-39
Bentall Centre *VAN* . . . . . . . . . . . .**11** G37-38
Boulevard Casino *CQT* . . . . . .**165** Y34-35
Brockton Oval *VAN* . . . . . . . . . . . .**142** Q13
Burnaby Lake Nature House *BUR* . .**164** W27
Burnaby Sculpture Garden *BUR* . . .**144** S27
Burnaby Village Musuem & Carousel *BUR* . . . . . . . . . . . . . . . . . . . . .**164** X24-25
Canada Games Pool & Fitness Cen. *NEW* . . . . . . . . . . . . . . . . . . . . . . . .**184** Z29
Canadian Lacrosse Hall of Fame *NEW* . . . . . . . . . . . . . . . . . . . . . . . .**184** Z29
Canada Place *VAN* . . .**11** F39 **142** R14
Capilano Salmon Hatchery *DNV* . .**122** J14
Capilano Suspension Bridge *DNV* . .**122** K14
Cascades Casino *LGC* . . . . . . . . .**227** N48
Centennial Ecology Centre *DNV* . .**123** K21
Centennial Gardens & Pavillion *BUR* **144** S27
Chances Abbotsford *ABT* . . . .**249** U69-70
Chilliwack Exhibition Grounds *CHL* .**213** E5-6
Chinatown *VAN* . . . . . . . . . . . . . .**11** H41
Cleveland Dam *DNV* . . . . . . . . . .**122** J14
Cloverdale Fairgrounds *SUR* . . .**226** M42-43
Cultus Lake Water Park *FRA* . . . . . .**253** R5
Deep Cove Lookout *DNV* . . . . . . .**124** M26
Dr. Sun Yat Sen Classical Chinese Garden *VAN* . . . . . . . . . . . . . . . . . . . . . .**11** H40
Edgewater Casino *VAN* . . . . . . . . .**11** J39
Fraser Downs Racetrack & Casino *VAN* . . . . . . . . . . . . . . . . . . . .**226** M42-43
Gastown *VAN* . . . . . . . . . . . . . . . .**11** G40
Gastown Steam Clock *VAN* . . . . . .**11** G39
G.M. Place *VAN* . . . . . . . . . . . . . .**11** H39
Granville Island *VAN* . . . . . . . . . . .**10** K35
Grouse Mountain Skyride *DNV* . .**103** G15 F16
Harbour Centre *VAN* . . . . . . . . . . .**11** G39
Hastings Slots *VAN* . . . . . . . . . . .**143** S19
H.R. MacMillan Planetarium *VAN* . . .**10** J34
HMCS Discovery Naval Training Station *VAN* . . . . . . . . . . . . . . . . . . . . . . .**142** R13
Hyde Creek Nature Centre *CQT* . .**146** T41
International Boundary Monument *DEL* . . . . . . . . . . . . . . . . . . . . . . .**262** Z15-16
Lumbermans Arch *VAN* . . . . . . . . .**142** Q13
Lynn Canyon Suspension Bridge *DNV* . . . . . . . . . . . . . . . . . . . . . . . .**123** K21
Malkin Bowl *VAN* . . . . . . . . . .**142** Q12-13
Maplewood Farm *DNV* . . . . . . . . .**143** P21
Miniature Railway *VAN* . . . . . . . . .**142** Q12
Minnekhada Lodge & Nature Centre *CQT* . . . . . . . . . . . . . . . . . . . . . . .**146** R45
Nat Bailey Stadium *VAN* . . . . . . . .**162** X14
Nine O'Clock Gun *VAN* . . . . . . . . .**142** Q14
Old Hastings Mill Store *VAN* . . . . . .**142** T8
Pacific Nat'l Exhibition Grounds *VAN* . . . . . . . . . . . . . . . . . . . . .**143** S19-20
Pacific Space Centre *VAN* . . . . . . . .**10** J34
Pauline Johnson Memorial *VAN* . . . .**142** Q11
Pfitzer Bell Tower *PMD* . . . . . . . . .**210** G77
Playtime Gaming Langley *LGC* . . . .**226** L46
Provincial Court House *VAN* . . . . . . .**11** H37
Rainforest Reptile Refuge *SUR* . . .**266** X42
Richmond Oval *RMD* . . . . . . . . . .**202** E11
River Rock Casino *RMD* . . . . .**182** C12-13
Robson Square *VAN* . . . . . . . . . . .**11** H37
Royal City Star Riverboat Casino *NEW* . . . . . . . . . . . . . . . . . . . . . . . .**184** B29
S.S. Empress of Japan Figurehead *VAN* . . . . . . . . . . . . . . . . . . . . . . .**142** Q13
Science World *VAN* . . . . . . . . . . . .**11** J40
Scotia Tower *VAN* . . . . . . . . . . . . .**11** G37
Splashdown Park *DEL* . . . . . . . . .**262** W15
The Centre in Vancouver for Performing Arts *VAN* . . . . . . . . . . . . . . . . . . . . . . .**11** H38
Totem Poles *VAN* . . . . . . . . . . . . .**142** Q13
UBC Botanical Garden Centre *UEL* . .**161** V3-4
Vancouver Aquarium *VAN* . . . . . . .**142** Q13
Vancouver Aquatic Centre *VAN* . . . .**10** J35
Vancouver Convention & Exhibition Centre *VAN* . . . . . . . . . . . . . . . . . . . .**11** F38-39
West End *VAN* . . . . . . . . . . . . . . . .**10** F35

### Accommodations

401 Motor Inn Ltd *BUR* . . . . . . . .**163** V21
Accent Inns *RMD* . . . . . . . . . . . . .**182** D14
Accent Inns *BUR* . . . . . . . . . . . . .**163** U21
Alpine Motel *HOP* . . . . . . . . . . . .**118** F45
Alpine Motor Inn *ABT* . . . . . . . . .**270** V72
Aston Pacific Inn Resort & Conference Centre *SUR* . . . . . . . . . . . . . . . . .**266** X40
Astoria Hotel *VAN* . . . . . . . . . . . .**143** S16
Barnet Hotel *PMD* . . . . . . . . . . . .**145** T32
Beach Grove Motel *DEL* . . . . . . . .**263** X18
Bellevue Hotel Ltd. *MIS* . . . . . . . .**210** J74
Best  Continental Motel *HOP* . . . .**118** E44
Best Value Westward Inn *LGC* . . . . .**226** M46

Best Western *CQT* . . . . . . . . . . . .**164** W30
Best Western *VAN* . . . . . . . . . . . .**163** U15
Best Western Abercorn Inn *RMD* . .**182** C13
Best Western Bakerview *ABT* . . . .**270** V77
Best Western Capilano Inn & Suites *DNV* . . . . . . . . . . . . . . . . . . . . . . . .**122** M13
Best Western Chelsea Inn *CQT* . . . .**165** X32
Best Western Convention Ctr *CQT* . .**165** W30
Best Western Country Meadows *LGT* . . . . . . . . . . . . . . . . . . . . . . . . . .**248** T60
Best Western Exhibition Park *VAN* . .**143** S20
Best Western Heritage Inn *HOP* . . . .**118** F45
Best Western Heritage Inn *HOP* . . . .**118** F45
Best Western King George Inn & Suites *SUR* . . . . . . . . . . . . . . . . . . . . . .**205** H34
Best Western Kings Inn & Conference Centre *BUR* . . . . . . . . . . . . . . . .**184** Y-Z23
Best  Western Langley Inn *LGC* . . .**227** N48
  Best Western Maple Ridge *MAP* . .**187** Z51
Best Western Mission City Lodge *MIS* . . . . . . . . . . . . . . . . . . . . . .**230** J-K72
Best Western Peace Arch Inn *SUR* .**265** U-V38
Best Western Poco Inn & Suites *PCQ* . . . . . . . . . . . . . . . . . . . . . . .**166** U-V40
Best Western Rainbow Country Inn *CHL* . . . . . . . . . . . . . . . . . . . . . .**233** H2
Best Western Regency Inn *ABT* . . . .**270** V72
Best Western Richmond Hotel & Convention Centre *RMD* . . . . . .**202** E-F12
Biltmore Hotel *VAN* . . . . . . . . . . .**163** V15
Bonanza Motel *SUR* . . . . . . . . . .**205** F34
Break Away Motel *SUR* . . . . . . . .**266** V24
Canadian Inn *SUR* . . . . . . . . . . . .**225** L34
Canyon Court Inn & Suites *DNV* . .**122** M13
Carlson Hotel & Resorts *DNV* . . . .**122** M14
Cassandra Hotel *VAN* . . . . . . . . .**163** X19
Cedar Lane Motel *SUR* . . . . . . . .**266** X39
Chilliwack Motor Inn *CH* . . . . . . . .**213** G7
City Center Motor Hotel *VAN* . . . .**163** U15
Clover Inn Motor *SUR* . . . . . . . . .**226** N42
Clydesdale Inn *SUR* . . . . . . . . . .**226** N42
Coast Hotel & Suites *ABT* . . . . . .**270** V77
Coast-Vancouver Airport *VAN* . .**182** B12-13
Colonial 900 Motel *HOP* . . . . . . . .**118** F46
Comfort Inn *CHL* . . . . . . . . . . . . .**213** H6
Comfort Inn & Suites *DNV* . . . . . .**122** M13
Comfort Inn Airport *RMD* . . . . . . .**182** C12
Comfort Inn Airport *RMD* . . . . . . .**182** C12
Coquitlam Sleepy Lodge *CQT* . . . .**165** U31
Days Hotel *SUR* . . . . . . . . . . . . .**185** D34
Days Inn *CHI* . . . . . . . . . . . . . . . .**213** F7
Days Inn & Suites *LGC* . . . . . . . . .**227** M47
Days Inn Vancouver Airport *RMD* . .**182** C13
Days Inn-Vancouver Metro *VAN* . . .**163** W17
Delta Hotel *BUR* . . . . . . . . . . . . .**163** V22
Delta Vancouver Airport *RMD* . . . .**182** C12
Diamond Head Motor Inn *MIS* . . .**210** J-K73
Douglas Guest House *VAN* . . . . . .**162** V14
Executive Hotel *BUR* . . . . . . . . .**163** U21-22
Executive Airport Plaza Hotels & Conference Centre *RMD* . . . . . .**202** F12
Executive Inn Express Hotel *RMD* . .**182** C13
Executive Plaza *CQT* . . . . . . . . . .**164** W30
Flamingo Motor Hotel *SUR* . . . . . .**185** B34
Four Points By Sheraton Vancouver Airport *RMD* . . . . . . . . . . . . . . . . . . .**202** F12-13
Fraser Valley Inn *ABT* . . . . . . . . .**250** U75
Golden Ears Hotel *PCQ* . . . . . . . .**166** U39
Grand Villa Casino *BUR* . . . . . . . .**163** V22
Grouse Creek Motel *SUR* . . . . . . .**205** E34
Grouse Inn *DNV* . . . . . . . . . . . . .**122** M13
Hampton Inn & Suites *LGC* . . . . . .**226** M46
Hampton Inn-Vancouver Airport *RMD* **182** C13
Haney Motor Hotel Ltd *MAP* . . . . .**187** Z52
Happy Day Inn *BUR* . . . . . . . . . . .**164** Y27
Hare Creek Motel *SUR* . . . . . . . .**225** L34
Harrison Beach *HHS* . . . . . . . . . .**155** P19
Harrison Crossroads Inn *KNT* . . . . .**175** U18
Hilton Vancouver Airport *RMD* . . . .**202** E12
Hilton Vancouver Metrotown *BUR* . .**163** Y22
Holiday Inn Express *VAN* . . . . . . .**143** S19
Holiday Inn Express *ABT* . . . . . . .**270** V72
Holiday Inn Express Hotel & Suites *LGT* . . . . . . . . . . . . . . . . . . . . . . .**207** F-G48
Holiday Inn Express Metrotown *BUR* .**163** Y22
Holiday Inn Express Vancouver Airport *RMD* . . . . . . . . . . . . . . . . . . . . .**182** C13-14
Holiday Inn Hotel & Suites *VAN* . . .**143** P20
Holiday Inn Vancouver Airport *RMD* . . . . . . . . . . . . . . . . . . . . . . .**182** D14-15
Holiday Inn Vancouver Centre *VAN* . .**162** U13
Hope Windsor Motel *HOP* . . . . . . .**118** E44
Horseshoe Bay Motel *WVA* . . . . . .**101** G2
Hostelling International *VAN* . . . . . .**142** T7
Hot Spring Villa *HHS* . . . . . . . . . .**155** P19
Howard Johnson Express Inn *SUR* . .**185** B33
Howard Johnson Plaza Hotel *VAN* . .**163** U-V15
Inn at King's Crossing *ABT* . . . . . .**270** V77
Inn at Westminster Quay *NEW* . . . .**184** B29
Inn at Westminster Quay *NEW* . . . .**184** B29
Inn Corporate *NEW* . . . . . . . . . . .**184** B28
Inter-City Motel *BUR* . . . . . . . . . .**184** Z24

La Quinta Inn Vancouver Airport *RMD* . . . . . . . . . . . . . . . . . . . . . . . .**202** E13
Lake  City Motor Inn *BUR* . . . .**164** U23-24
Langley Hotel *LGC* . . . . . . . . . . . .**227** N48
Linda Vista Motel *SUR* . . . . . . . . .**225** L34
Lonsdale Quay *VAN* . . . . . . . . .**143** P16-17
Lucky Strike Motel *HOP* . . . . . . . .**118** F45
Manor Guest House *VAN* . . . . . . .**162** V14
Marriott  Hotels Resorts Suites *RMD* .**202** F12
Met Hotel *NEW* . . . . . . . . . . . . . .**184** B29
North Vancouver Hotel *DNV* . . . . .**122** M13
Oasis Hotel *SUR* . . . . . . . . . . . . .**185** C35
Ocean Promenade Hotel *WRK* . . .**265** X-Y38
Ocean View Lodging *DEL* . . . . . . .**263** Z19
Pakwood Lodge *CHL* . . . . . . . . . . .**213** F7
Park Plaza Hotel *VAN* . . . . . . . . .**162** U13
Parkland Motor *SUR* . . . . . . . .**266** Y39-40
Penny Farthing Inn *VAN* . . . . . . . .**162** U10
Plaza 500 Hotel & Convention Centre *VAN* . . . . . . . . . . . . . . . . . . . . . .**162** U13
Quality Inn *HOP* . . . . . . . . . . . . .**118** F45
Quality Inn Airport *VAN* . . . . . . . .**183** A16
Quality Inn Airport South *RMD* . .**202** F11-12
Queens Motor Hotel *NE* . . . . . . . .**184** D26
Radisson President Hotel & Suites *RMD* . . . . . . . . . . . . . . . . . . . . . . .**182** D12
Radisson Suites *RMD* . . . . . . . . .**182** D12
Rainbow Motor Inn *CH* . . . . . . . . .**213** G6
Ramada Hotel & Suites *SUR* . . .**185** C38-39
Ramada Inn *ABT* . . . . . . . . . . .**271** V80-81
Ramada Inn *CQT* . . . . . . . . . . . .**165** X31
Ramada Inn Hotel *PTM* . . . . . . . .**166** Y46
Ramada Inn *SUR* . . . . . . . . . . . .**226** N46
Ramada Limited *RMD* . . . . . . . . .**202** F12
Red Roof Inn *HOP* . . . . . . . . . . . .**118** E44
Rhombus Hotels & Resorts *CHL* . . .**213** E7
Rio Suite Hotel *RMD* . . . . . . . . . .**182** D13
River Rock Casino Resort Hotel *RMD* . . . . . . . . . . . . . . . . . . . . . .**182** C12-13
Riversong Inn Ltd *RMD* . . . . . . . . .**222** L9
Royal Hotel *CHL* . . . . . . . . . . . .**213** E6-7
Royal Lodge Motel *HOP* . . . . . . . .**118** F45
Royal Towers *NEW* . . . . . . . . . . .**184** B28
Sandman Hotel Vancouver Airport *RMD* . . . . . . . . . . . . . . . . . . . . . . .**182** C14
Sandman Hotels Inns & Suites *LGT* . . . . . . . . . . . . . . . . . . . . . . .**207** F47-48
Shamrock Hotel *VAN* . . . . . . . . . .**143** S16
Shaughnessy Village *VAN* . . . .**162** U-V13
Sheraton Vancouver Guildford Hotel *SUR* . . . . . . . . . . . . . . . . . . . . . .**185** C37
Skyline Airport Hotel *RMD* . . . .**182** C12-13
Sleep Inn *LGT* . . . . . . . . . . . . . . .**227** L50
Slumber Lodge *HOP* . . . . . . . . . .**118** E44
Steveston Hotel *RMD* . . . . . . . . . .**222** L8
Sunset Inn *WRK* . . . . . . . . . . .**265** W-X35
Super 8 *ABT* . . . . . . . . . . . . . . . .**270** V77
Super 8 Motel *LGT* . . . . . . . . . . .**228** N61
Super 8 Motel *SUR* . . . . . . . . .**185** D34-35
The Coast Hotel & Suites *ABT* . . . .**270** V77
The Coast Tsawwassen Inn *DEL* . . .**263** W17
The Fairmont Vancouver Airport *RMD* .**182** B9
The Garfield Hotel *NFW* . . . . . . . .**184** B28
The Run Inn *DEL* . . . . . . . . . . . . .**263** X17
Timberland Motel & Campground *SUR* . . . . . . . . . . . . . . . . . . . . . . .**245** S37
Traders Inn *CHL* . . . . . . . . . . . . .**213** E6
Travelodge Chilliwack *CHL* . . . . . .**213** H6
Travelodge Hotel *RMD* . . . . . . . .**182** C14
Travelodge *LGT* . . . . . . . . . . . .**227** P50-51
Travelodge *LGT* . . . . . . . . . . . . .**207** F48
Travelodge Lions Gate *VAN* . . . . .**122** M13
Travelodge Maple Ridge *MAP* . . . .**187** Z51
Turf Hotel *SUR* . . . . . . . . . . . . . .**185** B31
Vedder River Inn *CHL* . . . . . . . . . .**233** M6
West Country Hotel *LGC* . . . . . . . .**227** N48

### Downtown Accommodations

**Accommodation listing for Whistler on Map 401**

Austin Motor Hotel . . . . . . . . . . . . .**10** J36
Backpackers Hostel . . . . . . .**11** J40 **143** T15
Barclay Hotel . . . . . . . . . . . . . . . . .**11** F36
Best Western Chateau Granville . . . .**11** H-J37
Best Western Downtown . . . . . . . . .**10** J36
Best Western Sands Hotel . . . . . . . .**10** F34
Blue Horizon Hotel . . . . . . . . . . . .**10** G36-37
Bosman's Hotel . . . . . . . . . . . . . . .**11** H37
Buchan Hotel . . . . . . . . . . . . . . .**10** E34-35
Burrard Inn . . . . . . . . . . . . . . . . . .**10** H36
Budget Inn-Patricia Hotel . . . . . . . .**11** H41
Cecil Hotel . . . . . . . . . . . . . . . . . . .**10** J36
Century Plaza Hotel . . . . . . . . . . . .**10** H36
Chelsea Inn Inc. . . . . . . . . . . . . . .**11** G-H40
Coast Plaza Hotel & Suites . . . . . . .**10** E34-35
Comfort Inn . . . . . . . . . . . . . . . . . .**11** H37
Crowne Plaza-Hotel Georgia . . . . . .**11** G38
Days Inn Downtown . . . . . . . . . . . .**11** G38
Delta Vancouver Suites . . . . . . . .**11** G38-39

Dominion Hotel . . . . . . . . . . . . . .**11** G39-40
Dufferin Hotel . . . . . . . . . . . . . . . .**11** H37
Empire Landmark Hotel, The . . . . .**10** F35-36
Executive Hotel Vintage Park . . . . . .**10** J36
Fairmont Hotel Vancouver . . . . . . . .**11** G37
Fairmont Waterfront . . . . . . . . . . . .**11** F38
Four Seasons Hotel . . . . . . . . . . . .**11** G38
Georgian Court Hotel . . . . . . . .**11** H-J38-39
Granville Island Hotel . . . . . . . . . .**10** K-L36
Greenbrier Hotel . . . . . . . . . . . . . .**10** F36
Hampton Inn & Suites . . . . . . . . .**10** H36-37
Holiday Inn Express Hotel & Suites Downtown . . . . . . . . . . . . . . . .**10** H36-37
Hostelling International . . . . . . . . . .**10** H35
Howard Johnson Hotel . . . . . . . . .**11** J36-37
Hyatt Regency . . . . . . . . . . . . . . . .**11** G37
Kingston Hotel . . . . . . . . . . . . . . . .**11** H38
La Grande Residence . . . . . . . . . . .**11** G37
Landis Hotel & Suites . . . . . . . . . . .**10** H36
Le Soleil Hotel . . . . . . . . . . . . . . . .**11** G38
Listel Hotel . . . . . . . . . . . . . . . . .**10** F-G36
Lord Stanley . . . . . . . . . . . . . . . . .**10** E35
Marble Arch . . . . . . . . . . . . . . . .**11** G38-39
Marriott Pinnacle . . . . . . . . . . . . . .**11** F37
Meridian, The . . . . . . . . . . . . . . . . .**10** J35
Metropolitan Hotel . . . . . . . . . . . . .**11** G38
Oceanside Hotel . . . . . . . . . . . . . .**10** F34
Opus Hotel . . . . . . . . . . . . . . . . . .**11** J37
Pacific Palisades . . . . . . . . . . . . . .**10** F36
Pan Pacific Hotel . . . . . . . . . . . . . .**11** F38
Park Hill Hotel . . . . . . . . . . . . . . . .**10** H35
Quality Hotel Downtown . . . . . . . . .**10** J36
Ramada Hotel . . . . . . . . . . . . . . . .**11** G39
Regal Hotel . . . . . . . . . . . . . . . . . .**11** H37
Regal Place Hotel . . . . . . . . . . . . . .**11** H39
Renaissance Harbourside . . . . . . .**10** H35-36
Residence Inn by Marriott . . . . . . . .**10** J36
Riviera Hotel . . . . . . . . . . . . . . . . .**10** F36
Rosedale Suite Hotel . . . . . . . . . .**11** H-J38
Rosellen Suites . . . . . . . . . . . . . . .**10** E34
St. Regis Hotel . . . . . . . . . . . . . .**11** G-H38
Sandman Hotel . . . . . . . . . . . . . .**11** H38-39
Sandman Suites on Davie . . . . . . .**10** H35-36
Sheraton Wall Centre . . . . . . . . . .**10** H36-37
Siesta Rooms . . . . . . . . . . . . . . . .**11** H37
Sunset Inn & Suites . . . . . . . . . .**10** H35-36
Sutton Place Hotel . . . . . . . . . . . . .**11** G37
Sylvia Hotel & Spa . . . . . . . . . . . . .**10** F34
Terminal City Club Tower Hotel . . . .**10** F36
Tropicana Suite Hotel . . . . . . . . . . .**10** F36
Vancouver Centre Lodge . . . . . . . . .**10** J36
Victorian Hotel . . . . . . . . . . . . . .**11** G38-39
Viva Suites . . . . . . . . . . . . . . . . . .**10** J36
Vogue Hotel . . . . . . . . . . . . . . . . .**11** H37
Wedgewood Hotel . . . . . . . . . . . . .**11** G37
West Hotel . . . . . . . . . . . . . . . . . .**11** H40
Westin Bayshore . . . . . . . . . . . . . .**10** E36
Westin Grand . . . . . . . . . . . . . . . . .**11** H38
Yale Hotel . . . . . . . . . . . . . . . . . . .**10** J36
Y.W.C.A . . . . . . . . . . . . . . . . . . .**11** H38-39

## Art Galleries, Museums Historic Properties

B.C. Mennonite Museum *ABT* . . . . .**250** T72
B.C. Sports Hall of Fame & Mus. *VAN* .**10** J39
Britannia Heritage Shipyard *RMD* . .**222** L10
Burnaby School Board Hist. Site *BUR* . . . . . . . . . . . . . . . . . . . . . . . . . .**184** Z25
Canadian Museum of Flight & Transportation (Langley) *LGT* . . . .**227** N-P50
Canadian Military Engineers Mus. *CHL* . . . . . . . . . . . . . . . . . . . . . . . .**233** N6
Chilliwack Arts Centre *CHL* . . . . . .**193** D6-7
Chilliwack Historical Museum *CHL* . .**213** E6
Creekhouse Gallery *VAN* . . . . . . .**10** K35-36
Delta Historical Museum *DEL* . . . .**223** P16
Fort Langley National Hist. Park *LGT* **207** F54
Gallery of B.C. Ceramics *VAN* . . .**10** K35-36
Gulf of Georgia NHS *RMD* . . . . . . .**222** L8
Historic Haney House *MAP* . . . . . .**187** A52
Historic Stewart Farmhouse *SUR* **245** S34-35
Hope Museum *HOP* . . . . . . . . . . .**118** E44
Hooser Weaver Centre *SUR* . . . .**245** S33-34
Kinsmen Heritage Park & Telephone Museum . . . . . . . . . . . . .*LGT* **248** T62
Kinsmen House *DEL* . . . . . . . . . . .**243** Q16
London Farm NHS *RMD* . . . . . . . .**222** M11
Maple Ridge Historic Museum *MAP*  **187** A52
Maritime Museum *VAN* . . . . . . .**10** J33-34
Mission Museum *MIS* . . . . . . . . .**210** J74
MSA Heritage Museum *ABT* . . . .**250** U74-75
New Westminster Art Gallery *NEW* .**184** A28
New Westminster Regiment Mus. *NEW* . . . . . . . . . . . . . . . . . . . . . . . .**184** A29
North Shore Museum *CNV* . . . . . .**123** N16
Pitt Meadows Museum *PTM* . . . . .**166** Y46

Port Moody Station & Museum *PMD* . . . . .
. . . . . . . . . . . . . . . . . . . . . . **145 S-T33**
Presentation House *CNV* . . . . . . **123 N16-17**
Regiment Museum *NEW* . . . . . . . . .**184 A29**
Richmond Museum & Arts Ctr. *RMD* . . .
. . . . . . . . . . . . . . . . . . . . . . . **202 F11-12**
Roedde House Museum *VAN* . . . . .**10 F35-36**
Samson Maritime Museum *NEW* . . .**184 B-C29**
Sri Lankan Gem Museum *VAN* . . . .**11 G37-38**
Stanley Park National Hist. Site *VAN* . . .
. . . . . . . . . . . . . . . . . . . . . . . . **142 Q11-12**
Steveston Museum *RMD* . . . . . . . . .**222 L9**
Surrey Arts Gallery *SUR* . . . . . . **205 F-G34**
Surrey Centennial Museum *SUR* . **226 M42-43**
University of British Columbia Museum of
Anthropology *UEL* . . . . . . . . . .**161 T-U3**
Vancouver Art Gallery *VAN* . . . . .**11 G37-38**
Vancouver Maritime Museum & St. Roch
*VAN* . . . . . . . . . . . . . . . . . . . . . .**10 J33**
Vancouver Museum *VAN* . . . . . . . . .**10 J34**
Vancouver Police Hist. Society *VAN* **11 G-H41**
Vancouver Public Library *VAN* . . . . .**11 H38**
Whistler Historic Mus. & Archives *WHS* . .
. . . . . . . . . . . . . . . . . . . . . . . . . .**401 A1**
White Rock Mus. & Archives *WRK* **265 X36-37**
Wickaninnish Native Art Gallery *VAN* .**10 K35**
XÁ:YTEM Longhouse Interpretive Ctr. *MIS* . .
. . . . . . . . . . . . . . . . . . . . . . . . .**210 G78**

### Bridges & Tunnels

Airport Connector Bridge *RMD* . . . .**182 C12**
Alex Fraser Bridge *DEL* . . . . . . . .**204 G27**
Arthur Laing Bridge *RMD* . . . . . . **182 B-C12**
Burrard Bridge *VAN* . . . . . . . . . **10 J34-35**
Cambie Bridge *VAN* . . . . . . . . . . .**11 K38**
Dinsmore Bridge *RMD* . . . . . . . . .**202 E11**
Dunsmuir Viaduct *VAN* . . . . . . . **11 H39-40**
Fraser Bridge *HOP* . . . . . . . . . .**118 D43-44**
George Massey Tunnel *DEL* . . . . **223 L16-17**
Georgia Viaduct *VAN* . . . . . . . . **11 H39-40**
Golden Ears Bridge *MAP/LGT* . . . **187 B-C47**
Granville Bridge *VAN* . . . . . . . . **10 K35-36**
Ironworkers Memorial Bridge
(Second Narrows) *DNV* . . . . . . **143 Q-R20**
Knight Street Bridge *RMD* . . . . . .**183 B16-17**
Lions Gate Bridge *WVA* . . . . . . . .**122 N12**
Mission Bridge *ABT* . . . . . . . . . **230 K-L74**
Moray Channel Bridge *RMD* . . . . . .**182 C12**
Oak Street Bridge *RMD* . . . . . . . .**182 B-C13**
Pattullo Bridge *NEW* . . . . . . . . **184 A-B30**
Pitt River Bridge *PCQ/PTM* . . . . .**166 W42-43**
Port Mann Bridge *CQT* . . . . . . . . .**185 Z36**
Queensborough Bridge *NEW* . . . . . .**184 C26**
Vedder Bridge *CHL* . . . . . . . . . . . .**233 N6**

### Golf Courses

Beach Grove Golf Club *DEL* . . . .**263 W17-18**
Belmont G. C. *LGT* . . . . . . . . . . .**207 G53**
Burnaby Mountain G. C. *BUR* . . . . .**164 U27**
Capilano G. & C. C. *WVA* . . . . . . **122 J-K13**
Carnousite Golf Club *PCQ* . . . . . . **166 U-V42**
Chateau Whistler G. C. *WHS* . . .**401 A3, D-E5**
Coast Meridian Par 3 *SUR* . . . . . . .**266 X41**
Country Meadows G. C. *RMD* . . . .**203 H17-18**
Coyote Creek Golf Club *SUR* . . . . **205 H-J37**
Cultus Golf Park *FRA* . . . . . . . . . . .**253 R6**
Delta Public G. C. *DEL* . . . . . . . **224 N-P30**
Eaglequest at Musqueam Golf Club *DEL* . .
. . . . . . . . . . . . . . . . . . . . . . . **224 N-P30**
Fort Langley G. & C. C. *LGT* **187 D53 207 E53**
Fraser Golf Driving Range *SUR* . . . .**206 H41**
Fraserview G. C. *BUR* . . . . . . . . .**183 A19**
Gleneagles Golf Club *WVA* . . . . . . .**101 H1-2**
Green Acres G. C. *RMD* . . . . . . .**203 E17-18**
Guildford G. & C. C. *SUR* . . . . . . .**205 H37**
Hazelmere G. & C. C. *SUR* . . . . . . .**266 Y43**
Hollies G. C. *SUR* . . . . . . . . . . **226 L-M46**
Hollyburn Country Club *WVA* . . . . .**122 K12**
Hope G. C. *HOP* . . . . . . . . . . . . .**118 D45**
Kinkora G. C. *CHL* . . . . . . . . . . . .**233 L7**
Langara G. C. *VAN* . . . . . . . . . . .**182 Z14**
Langley Golf Centre *LGT* . . . . . . .**247 R50**
Ledgeview G. & C. C. *ABT* . . . . . . .**251 R80**
Maple Ridge Municipal G. C. *MAP* . **187 A49**
Marine Drive G. C. *VAN* . . . . . . . .**182 Z10**
Mayfair Lakes G. C. *RMD* . . . . . .**203 E19-20**
McCleery G. C. *VAN* . . . . . . . . . **182 Z9-10**
Meadow Gardens G. C. *PTM* . . . . . .**167 Y47**
Meadowlands G. & C. C. *CHL* . . **194 C10-11**
Mikasa Golf Driving Range *RMD* . .**183 D17-18**
Morgan Creek G. & C. C. *SUR* . . . . .**246 S39**
Mylora G. C. East *RMD* . . . . . . . . .**203 J16**
Mylora G. C. West *RMD* . . . . . . . . .**203 J16**
Newlands G. & C. C. *LGC* . . . . . . .**227 N49**
Nicklaus North G. C. *WHS* . . . . . . . .**401 C3**
Nico Wynd Golf Club *SUR* . . . . . .**245 R35-35**
Northview G. & C. C. *SUR* . . . . . .**226 K-L40**
Peace Arch Golf Centre *SUR* . . . . . .**266 Y41**
Peace Portal G. C. *SUR* . . . . . . . **266 Y-Z41**

Pitt Meadows Golf Club *PTM* . . . .**166 V-W45**
Point Grey G. & C. C. *VAN* . . . . . . .**182 Z5**
Quilchena G. & C. Club *RMD* . . . . **202 F-G8**
Redwoods Public G.C. *LGT* . . . . **207 E-F51**
Richmond G. & C. C. *RMD* . . . . . .**222 K13**
Riverside Golf Centre *SUR* . . . . . . .**245 S36**
Riverway G. C. *BUR* . . . . . . . **183 B22 184 B22**
Seymour G. & C. C. *DNV* . . . . . . . .**144 P25**
Shaughnessy G. & C. C. *VAN* . . . . . .**161 X6**
Squamish Valley G. & C. C. *SQM* . **301 D3-4**
Sunrise Golf & Racquet Club *SUR* . .**226 N45**
Sunshine Hills G. C. *DEL* . . . . . **224 L27-28**
Surrey G. C. *SUR* . . . . . . . . . . . .**206 J41**
Tall Timbers Golf Club *LGT* . . . . **227 M-N54**
Tsawwassen Golf Club *DEL* . . . . . .**263 W16**
University G. C. *UEL* . . . . . . . . . . .**161 U6**
Vancouver Golf Club *CQT* . . . . . **165 W31-32**
Westwood Plateau G. A. *CQT* . . . **145 P36-37**
Whistler G. C. *WHS* . . . . . . . . . . . .**401 F3**

### Higher Education

B.C. Institute of Technology *BUR* . .**163 W22**
Capilano University *DNV* . . . . . . . .**123 N21**
Douglas College *MAP* . . . . . . . . . .**187 A54**
Kwantlen University College (Langley) *LGC* .
. . . . . . . . . . . . . . . . . . . . . . . . .**227 M49**
Kwantlen University College *SUR* . .**225 K32**
Pacific Life Bible College *SUR* . . . .**225 L37**
Simon Fraser University *BUR* . . . **144 T28-29**
Summit Pacific College *ABT* . . . . . .**251 Q79**
Trinity Western University *LGT* . . . .**207 J52**
Vancouver Community College *VAN* . .**11 H38**
University College of the Fraser Valley *ABT* .
. . . . . . . . . . . . . . . . . . . . . . . . .**270 W76**
University of British Columbia *UEL* . .**161 U4**
University of the Fraser Valley *CHL* .**213 G6**
University of the Fraser Valley Annex *CHL* . .
. . . . . . . . . . . . . . . . . . . . . . . . . .**193 D7-8**

### Hospitals

Abbotsford Reg'l *ABT* . . . . . . . . . .**270 V74**
B.C. Children's *VAN* . . . . . . . . . . .**162 W13**
B.C. Forensic Psychiatric *CQT* . . .**165 Y36-37**
Burnaby General *BUR* . . . . . . . . . .**163 W21**
Chilliwack (General) *CHL* . . . . . . .**213 E-F6**
Delta *DEL* . . . . . . . . . . . . . . . . . .**243 Q18**
Eagle Ridge *PMD* . . . . . . . . . . . . .**145 S36**
Fraser Canyon *HOP* . . . . . . . . . **118 E45-46**
George Derby Long Term Care Centre *BUR* .
. . . . . . . . . . . . . . . . . . . . . . . . . .**164 X28**
George Pearson Centre *VAN* . . . . . .**182 Z13**
Grace *VAN* . . . . . . . . . . . . . . . . .**162 W13**
Inglewood *WVA* . . . . . . . . . . . . . .**122 L12**
Ladner *DEL* . . . . . . . . . . . . . . . . .**224 P25**
Langley Memorial *LGT* . . . . . . . . .**227 P51**
Lions Gate *CNV* . . . . . . . . . . . . .**123 N17**
Maple Ridge *MAP* . . . . . . . . . . . . .**187 Z50**
Mission General *MIS* . . . . . . . . . . .**210 J72**
Mount St. Joseph *VAN* . . . . . . . . .**163 V15**
MSA General *ABT* . . . . . . . . . . . . .**270 V75**
Peace Arch *WRK* . . . . . . . . . . . . . .**265 W38**
Queens Park *NEW* . . . . . . . . . . . . .**184 Z30**
Richmond General *RMD* . . . . . . . . .**202 F11**
Ridge Meadows *MAP* . . . . . . . . . . .**187 Z50**
Riverview Psychiatric *CQT* . . . . . . .**165 W37**
Royal Columbian *NEW* . . . . . . . . . .**164 Y30**
Saint Mary's *NEW* . . . . . . . . . . . . .**184 A29**
Saint Pauls *VAN* . . . . . . . . . . . . . .**10 H36**
Squamish *SQM* . . . . . . . . . . . . . . .**301 H2-3**
Surrey Memorial *SUR* . . . . . . . . . .**205 E34**
Vancouver General *VAN* . . . . . . . . .**162 U13**
Whistler Health Care Centre *WHS* . . .**401 A1**

### Major Parks

Alaksen National Wildlife Area *DEL* . .**222 N9**
Alpha Lake *WHS* . . . . . . . . . . . . . . .**401 H1**
Ambleside *WVA* . . . . . . . . . . . .**122 M-N11**
Barnet Marine *BUR* . . . . . . . . . . . .**144 R28**
Bear Creek *SUR* . . . . . . . . . . . . . .**205 G34**
Belcarra Regional *BEL* . . . . . . . . . .**124 N28**
Blackie Spit *SUR* . . . . . . . . . . . . .**245 T31**
Blueberry Beach *WHS* . . . . . . . . . **401 F2-3**
Boundary Bay Regional *DEL* . . . . .**263 X-Y19**
Brackendale Eagles Provincial *SQM* . . .
. . . . . . . . . . . . . . . . . . . . . . . . .**301 D1-2**
Burnaby Lake Nature *BUR* . . . . . **164 W25-26**
Burnaby Mountain *BUR* . . . . . . . . .**144 S29**
Burnaby Mountain Cons. Area *BUR* . . . .
. . . . . . . . . . . . . . . . . . . . . . . . **144 S26-30**
Campbell Valley Regional *LGT* . . **267 W-X48**
Capilano River Regional *DNV* . . . . .**122 J14**
Castle Fun *ABT* . . . . . . . . . . . **271 V80-81**
Cates *VAN* . . . . . . . . . . . . . . . . . .**144 Q26**
Central Park Pitch & Putt *BUR* . . . . .**164 X24**
Chineside Ravine *CQT* . . . . . . . .**165 U34-35**
Colony Farm Reg'l *CQT/PCQ* .**165 X37-38 Y37**
Coquitlam River *CQT* . . . . . . . . . . .**146 S39**

Cultus Lake Provincial *FRA* . . . . . . .**253 T3-6**
Cypress Provincial *WVA* . . . . . . . . .**101 D-E4**
Deas Island Regional *DEL* . . . . . **223 L17-18**
Derby Reach Regional *LGT* . . . **187 A51, C52**
Dream River *WHS* . . . . . . . . . . . . .**401 C3-4**
Elgin Heritage *SUR* . . . . . . . . . . . .**245 S34**
English Bay Beach *VAN* . . . . . . . . . .**10 G34**
Fort Langley National Historic Site *LGT* . . .
. . . . . . . . . . . . . . . . . . . . . . . . . .**207 F54**
Fraser River Heritage *MIS* . . . . . . . .**210 J76**
George C. Reifel Nat'l Migratory Bird
Sanctuary *DEL* . . . . . . . . . . . . . .**222 N9**
Hastings *VAN* . . . . . . . . . . . . . .**143 S19-20**
International Ridge Prov. Rec. *FRA* . . .**253 U6**
Invergarry *SUR* . . . . . . . . . . . . **185 A-B36**
Jericho Beach *VAN* . . . . . . . . . . . .**142 T7-8**
Kawkawa Lake *HOP* . . . . . . . . . **118 E47-48**
Lighthouse *WVA* . . . . . . . . . . . . . . .**121 L3**
Lost Lake *WHS* . . . . . . . . . . . . . . .**401 D4**
Lower Seymour Reg'l Conservation Reserve
*DNV* . . . . . . . . . . **123 K21-22 124 K24**
Lynn Canyon *DNV* . . . . . . . . . . .**123 K-L21**
Lynn Headwaters Reg. *DNV* . . . . . . . . . .
. . . . . . . . . . **103 D17-18 123 J20-21**
Mahon *CNV* . . . . . . . . . . . . . . **123 M-N16**
Matsqui Trail Regional *ABT* . . . . **210 J77-78**
Meadow *WHS* . . . . . . . . . . . . . . . . .**401 C3**
Minnekhada Regional *CQT* . . . . . . .**146 Q45**
Minoru *RMD* . . . . . . . . . . . . . . **202 F11-12**
Mount Seymour Provincial *DNV* . .**124 J-K26**
Mundy *CQT* . . . . . . . . . . . . . . . . .**165 V35**
Pacific Spirit Regional *UEL* .**161 T5 W6 162 W7**
Peace Arch Provincial *SUR* . . . . . . .**266 Z40**
Pinecone Burke Provincial *CQT* . . . .**146 P43**
Queen Elizabeth *VAN* . . . . . . . . . .**162 X14**
Queen's *NEW* . . . . . . . . . . . . . . . .**184 Z29**
Rainbow *WHS* . . . . . . . . . . . . . . . .**401 E2**
Robert Burnaby *BUR* . . . . . . . . . .**164 X-Y27**
Serpentine Fen Bird Sanctuary *SUR* .**245 Q35**
Stanley *VAN* . . . . . . . . . . . . . . .**142 Q11-12**
Town Centre *CQT* . . . . . . . . . . . . .**145 R38**
Tynehead Regional *SUR* . . . . . . .**186 D40-41**
Vanier *VAN* . . . . . . . . . . . . . . . . . .**10 J34**
Wayside *WHS* . . . . . . . . . . . . . . . .**401 G2**
Wedge *WHS* . . . . . . . . . . . . . . . . .**401 B3**
Whytecliff *WVA* . . . . . . . . . . . . . . .**101 G1**

### Municipal Halls

Abbotsford *ABT* . . . . . . . . . . . . . .**250 U73**
Anmore *ANM* . . . . . . . . . . . . . . . .**145 P33**
Belcarra *BEL* . . . . . . . . . . . . . . . .**144 P29**
Burnaby *BUR* . . . . . . . . . . . . . . **164 W-X24**
Chilliwack *CHL* . . . . . . . . . . . . . . . .**213 F7**
Coquitlam *CQT* . . . . . . . . . . . . . . .**145 S38**
Delta *DEL* . . . . . . . . . . . . . . . . . .**243 Q18**
Fraser Valley *FRA* . . . . . . . . . . . . .**213 G7**
Hope *HOP* . . . . . . . . . . . . . . . . . .**118 E44**
Langley City *LGC* . . . . . . . . . . . . .**227 N48**
Langley Township *LGT* . . . . . . . . . .**227 P51**
Lions Bay *LIO* . . . . . . . . . . . . . . . .**101 B24**
Maple Ridge *MAP* . . . . . . . . . . . . .**187 Z52**
Metro Vancouver Head Office *BUR* . .**163 Y22**
Mission *MIS* . . . . . . . . . . . . . . . . .**210 G76**
New Westminster *NEW* . . . . . . . . . .**184 B29**
North Vancouver City *CNV* . . . . . . .**123 N17**
North Vancouver District *DNV* . . . . .**123 L17**
Pitt Meadows *PTM* . . . . . . . . . . . . .**186 Z45**
Port Coquitlam *PCQ* . . . . . . . . . . . .**166 U39**
Port Moody *PMD* . . . . . . . . . . . . . .**145 S35**
Richmond *RMD* . . . . . . . . . . . . . . .**202 F12**
Surrey *SUR* . . . . . . . . . . . . . . . . .**225 M35**
Vancouver *VAN* . . . . . . . . . . . . . . .**162 U14**
West Vancouver *WVA* . . . . . . . . . . .**122 M10**
Whistler *WHS* . . . . . . . . . . . . . . . . .**401 A1**
White Rock *WRK* . . . . . . . . . . . . . .**265 X37**

### Performing Arts

Arts Club Theatre *VAN* . . . . . . . . . .**10 K35**
Burnaby Art Centre *BUR* . . . . . . . . .**164 X24**
Centennial Theatre *CNV* . . . . . . . . .**123 M17**
Firehall Arts Centre *VAN* . . . . . . . . .**11 H41**
Ford Centre *VAN* . . . . . . . . . . . . . .**11 H38**
North Shore Film Studios *CNV* . . . . .**143 P19**
Orpheum, The *VAN* . . . . . . . . . . . . .**11 H37**
Queen Elizabeth Centre *VAN* . . . . . .**11 H38**
Starboard Theatres *VAN* . . . . . . . . .**11 F39**
Surrey Arts Centre Theatre *SUR* . . . .**205 G34**
Vancouver Playhouse *VAN* . . . . . . . .**11 H39**

### Shopping Centres

Aberdeen Shopping Centre *RMD* . . .**182 D12**
Arbutus Village Shopping Centre *VAN* . . . .
. . . . . . . . . . . . . . . . . . . . . . . . . .**162 W11**
Brentwood Mall *BUR* . . . . . . . . . . .**163 U22**
Bridgepoint Market *RMD* . . . . . . . .**182 B-C13**
Capilano Mall *CNV* . . . . . . . . . . . .**123 N15**
Cariboo Centre *CQT* . . . . . . . . . . . .**164 W30**

Chieftain Centre Mall *SQM* . . . . . . .**301 G1-2**
Chilliwack Mall *CHL* . . . . . . . . . . **213 H-J6**
Clearbrook Town Square *ABT* . . . . .**250 U73**
Clover Square *VAN* . . . . . . . . . . . . .**226 N42**
Cloverdale Shopping Centre *SUR* . **226 M-N42**
Columbia Square *NEW* . . . . . . . . . .**184 B28**
Coquitlam Centre *CQT* . . . . . . . . **145 S-T37**
Coquitlam Plaza *CQT* . . . . . . . . . . .**145 T37**
Cottonwood Mall *CHL* . . . . . . . . . . **213 H-J6**
Countryside Mall *LGT* . . . . . . . . . . .**249 T63**
Crystal Mall *BUR* . . . . . . . . . . . . . .**163 Y22**
Delta Fair Mall *DEL* . . . . . . . . . . . .**263 X17**
Delta Shoppers Mall *DEL* . . . . . . . .**204 H30**
Eaton Centre *VAN* . . . . . . . . . . . . .**163 Y22**
Elwood Centre *ABT* . . . . . . . . . . . .**249 T69**
Evergreen Mall *SUR* . . . . . . . . . . .**205 F37**
Fraser Ridge Shopping Centre *ABT* . .**250 T77**
Grand Robson Mall *VAN* . . . . . . . . .**10 G36**
Grandview Corners Village *SUR* . . . .**246 U39**
Granville Island Public Market *VAN* . .**10 J35**
Granville Mall *VAN* . . . . . . . . . . . **11 37-38**
Guildford Town Centre *SUR* . . . . . .**185 D37**
Haney Place Mall *MAP* . . . . . . . . . .**187 Z52**
Harbour Centre *VAN* . . . . . . . . . . . .**11 G39**
Heritage Mountain Shoppers Vill. *PMD* . . .
. . . . . . . . . . . . . . . . . . . . . . . . . .**145 S35**
Highgate Village Centre *BUR* . . . .**184 Z25-26**
Landing, The *VAN* . . . . . . . . . . . . . .**11 G39**
Langley Mall *LGC* . . . . . . . . . . . . .**227 N48**
Lansdowne Park *RMD* . . . . . . . . .**202 E12-13**
Lonsdale Quay Market *CNV* . . . . . . .**143 P16**
Lougheed Mall *BUR* . . . . . . . . . . . .**164 W30**
Lynn Valley Mall *DNV* . . . . . . . . . .**123 L19**
Metropolis at Metrotown *BUR* . . . . .**163 Y22**
Morgan Crossing Lifestyle Ctr. *SUR* . . . .
. . . . . . . . . . . . . . . . . . . . . . . . **245 U38-39**
Newton Plaza *SUR* . . . . . . . . . . . .**225 K34**
Newton Town Centre *SUR* . . . . . . . .**225 K34**
Ocean Park Plaza *SUR* . . . . . . . . . .**265 W32**
Park Royal *WVA* . . . . . . . . . . . . . .**122 M12**
Peninsula Shopping Centre *SUR* . . . .**245 U37**
Pinetree Village *CQT* . . . . . . . . . . .**145 T38**
Plaza International *WVA* . . . . . . . . .**122 N13**
Poco Plaza *PCQ* . . . . . . . . . . . . . .**166 U39**
Prairie Mall *PCQ* . . . . . . . . . . . **146 T40-41**
Renaissance Square *CQT* . . . . . . . .**165 X31**
Richmond Centre *RMD* . . . . . . . . . .**202 F12**
Richmond Square *RMD* . . . . . . . . . .**202 F12**
Royal Square *NEW* . . . . . . . . . . . . .**184 Z27**
Salish Plaza *CHL* . . . . . . . . . . . . . .**213 E6-7**
Scottsdale Mall *DEL* . . . . . . . . . . . .**224 K30**
Semiahmoo *SUR* . . . . . . . . . . . . . .**265 W37**
Seven Oaks Shopping Centre *ABT* . . .**250 U74**
Simon Centre *ABT* . . . . . . . . . . . . .**250 T73**
Sinclair Centre *VAN* . . . . . . . . . . . .**11 G38**
Strawberry Hill Shopping Centre *SUR* . . . .
. . . . . . . . . . . . . . . . . . . . . . . . . . .**205 J31**
Surrey Place *SUR* . . . . . . . . . . . **185 D33-34**
Ten Oaks Shopping Centre *ABT* . . . .**250 T77**
Tilford Centre *CNV* . . . . . . . . . . . .**143 P19**
Town Centre Mall *DEL* . . . . . . . . . .**263 X17**
Valley Fair Mall *MAP* . . . . . . . . . . .**187 Z53**
Ventura Plaza *ABT* . . . . . . . . . . . . .**250 U74**
West Oaks Mall *ABT* . . . . . . . . . . .**250 U73**
Westminster Mall *NEW* . . . . . . . . . .**184 A28**
Westminster Quay Public Market *NEW* . . . .
. . . . . . . . . . . . . . . . . . . . . . . . . .**184 B29**
Westview *CNV* . . . . . . . . . . . . . **123 L-M16**
Westwood Mall *CQT* . . . . . . . . . . . .**145 T38**
Willowbrook Shopping Centre *LGT* . .**227 M47**
Woodwards *SUR* . . . . . . . . . . . . . .**185 C34**

### Transportation

Abbotsford International Airport *ABT* **270 X71**
BC Rail North Vancouver *DNV* . . . . .**122 N14**
BC Rail Squamish *SQM* . . . . . . . . . .**301 G1**
BC Rail Whistler *WHS* . . . . . . . . . . .**401 H1**
Boundary Bay Airport *DEL* . . . . . **243 R21-22**
Chilliwack Municipal Airport *CHL* . .**213 G7-8**
Delta Air Park *DEL* . . . . . . . . . . . .**244 R27**
Deltaport *DEL* . . . . . . . . . . . . . . . .**262 U13**
Granville Island Ferries *VAN* . . . . .**10 H34 J35**
Heliport *VAN* . . . . . . . . . . . . . . . .**11 F-G39**
Horseshoe Bay Ferry Terminal *WVA* . .**101 G2**
Langley Airport *LGT* . . . . . . . . . . . .**227 N50**
Pitt Meadows Airport *PTM* . . . . . . . .**186 Z44**
Roberts Bank Superport *DEL* . . . . . .**262 W12**
SeaBus Terminal North Shore *CNV* . .**143 P16**
SeaBus Terminal Vancouver *VAN* . . . .**11 F39**
Squamish Airport *SQM* . . . . . . . . . . .**301 A4**
Tsawwassen Ferry Terminal *DEL* . . . .**262 Z13**
Vancouver International Airport *RMD* . . . .
. . . . . . . . . . . . . . . . . . . . . . . . . .**182 B9-10**
VIA Rail Chilliwack *CHL* . . . . . . . . . .**213 F7**
VIA Rail Vancouver (Pacific Central Station)
*VAN* . . . . . . . . . . . . . . . . . . . . . .**11 J41**
West Coast Air Terminal *VAN* . . . . . .**11 F37**

# Highways

**1**
ABT . . . . . . . . . . . . .249 S68 270 V74
BUR . . . . . . . .163 V22 164 V24 W29 X27
CHL . . . . . . . . . . . . . .213 G8 H3
CNV . . . . . . . . . . . . . . .123 M18
CQT . . . . . . . . . . . . .165 X31 Y34
DNV . . . . . . . . . . . . . .143 Q20
HOP . . . . . . . . . . . . .118 E44 H43
LGT . . . . . . . . . . . . . .207 G50
SUR . . . .185 A37 C38 186 C-D40 206 E44
WVA . . . . .101 G2 121 K6 122 K10 L13

**1A**
VAN . . . . . . . . . . . . . . .142 Q12
WVA . . . . . . . . . . . . . .122 M12

**3**
HOP . . . . . . . . . . . . . . .118 F45

**5**
HOP . . . . . . . . . . . . . . .118 F46

**7**
CQT . . . . . . . . . .145 T37 165 W37 Y33
HOP . . . . . . . . . . . . . . .118 D43
KNT . . . . . . . . .175 W17 W20 W23
MAP . . . . . . . . . . . . .187 Z48 Z53
MIS . . . . . . . .210 H-J77 J73 230 K73
PCQ . . . . . . . . . . . . . . .166 V41

**7B**
PCQ . . . . . . . . . . . . .166 W42 Y39

**9**
KNT . . . . . . . . . . . . . . .175 X21

**10**
DEL . . . . . . . . . . . . . . .224 N30
LGT . . . . . . . . . . . . . .227 K52
SUR . . . . . .225 M32 N38 226 N46

**11**
ABT .230 N76 250 R-S76 T-U77 270 V77 X77
MIS . . . . . . . . . . . . . . .230 K74

**13**
LGT . . . . . . . . . . . . . .248 S60

**15**
SUR . . . . . . . . . . . .206 F42 H42
. . . . . . .226 K42 M42 P42 246 U42 266 X42

**17**
DEL . . . .223 N18 243 S18 262 Y13 263 V17

**91**
DEL . . . . . . .204 F26-27 224 L28 N30
RMD . . . . . . . .203 E18 204 F24

**91A**
NEW . . . . . . . . . . . .184 C26-27 C-D27

**99**
DEL . . . . . .223 L17 N19 P22 224 P24 P28
LIO . . . . . . . . . . . . . . .101 B23
RMD . . . . . . .182 D14 203 F16 H16
SQM . . . . . . .301 B2 C-D3 F3 J2
SUR .225 P31 245 R35 U38 266 X40 Z40-41
VAN . . . . . . . . .142 Q12 S-T13 T13
. . . . . . . . .162 V12 Y12 182 A12
WHS . . . . . . . . . .401 B5 E3-4 H1 T21
WVA . . . . .101 D4 G2 121 K6 122 K10 M12

# Numbered Streets

0 Av SUR . . . . . . . . .266 Z41-42 Z43-46
0 Av (Boundary Rd) LGT 267 Z47 Z49-50 Z53-54
0A Av SUR . . . . . . . . . . . . .266 Z42
0B Av SUR . . . . . . . . . . . . .266 Z42

1 Av LGT . . . . . . . . . . .267 Z47 Z48
1 Av MIS . . . . . . . . . . . .210 J74-76
1 Av PMD . . . . . . . . . . .145 P-Q32
1 Av RMD . . . . . . . . . . . .222 K-L9
1 Av SUR . . . . . . . .266 Z41-42 Z42
1 Av VAN . . . . . . . . . . . . . .11 K41
1 Av E BUR . . . . . . . . . . . . .163 U21
1 Av E VAN. 11 K40 K41 143 T15 163 U15 U17-20
1 Av W VAN . . . . . . . . . . . . . . . . .
. . . . . .10 K32-34 11 K39-40 142 T10-12 T14 T7 T9
1 St BUR . . . . . . . . . . . . .164 Y28
1 St NEW . . . . . . . .184 A29-30 Z28-29
1 St PMD . . . . . . . . . . . . .145 Q32
1 St E CNV . . . . . . . . . . .143 P17-18
1 St W CNV . . . . .123 N15 N16 143 P16 P16
1 St W DNV . . . . . . . . . . . . .122 N14
1A Av DEL . . . . . .263 Z16 Z17 Z19-20
1A Av SUR . . . . . . . . . . . . .266 Z42

2 Av DEL . . . . . . . . . . . .263 Z16-17
2 Av LGT . . . . . . .267 Z47 Z50 Z52
2 Av MIS . . . . . . . . . . . .210 J74-75
2 Av PMD . . . . . . . . . . . . .145 Q32
2 Av RMD . . . . . . . .222 K8-9 L8-9
2 Av SUR . . . . . . . .266 Z42 Z44 Z46
2 Av E BUR . . . . . . . . . . . . .163 U21
2 Av E VAN . . . . . .11 K40 163 U15 U17-20
2 Av W VAN . . . . . . . .10 K32-33 11 K39-40
. . . . . .142 T10 T7 T8 T9 161 T6 162 U10 U11 U14
2 St BUR . . . . . . . . . .164 Y28 184 Z28
2 St NEW . . . . . . . . .184 A29 Z28
2 St PMD . . . . . . . . . . . . .145 Q32
2 St E CNV . . . . . . . . . . .143 P17-18
2 St W CNV . . . .123 N15-16 N16 143 P16
2A Av DEL . . . . . . . . . . . . .263 Z16
2A Av SUR . . . . . . . . . . .266 Z41-42
2nd Av SQM . . . . . . . . . . . . .301 K1

3 Av DEL . . . . . . .263 Z16 Z17 Z19
3 Av LGT . . . . . . .267 Z47 Z48 Z51
3 Av MIS . . . . . . . .210 J74-75 J75-76
3 Av NEW . . . . . . . .184 A28-29 B28
3 Av PMD . . . . . . . . . . . . .145 Q32
3 Av RMD . . . . . . . . . .222 K8 K-L8
3 Av E VAN . . . . . . . .163 U15 U17-20
3 Av W VAN . . . . . . . . . . . . . . . . .
. . . . . .10 K32 K33 142 T7 161 T6 162 U14 U9-1
3 St NEW . . . . . . . . . . . . .184 A29
3 St WVA . . . . . . . . . .122 L13 L-M13
3 St E CNV . . . . . . . . . .143 P17-18 P19
3 St W CNV . . . . .123 N15 N16 143 P16
3 St W DNV . . . . . .122 N14 123 N15
3A Av DEL . . . . . . . . . . . .263 Y-Z17
3A Av SUR . . . . . . . .266 Z41-42 Z47
3B Av LGT . . . . . . . . . . . . .267 Z47
3rd Av SQM . . . . . . . . . . . . .301 K1

4 Av DEL . . . . . . .263 Y17 Y19-20 Y-Z16
4 Av LGT . . . . . . . .267 Y48-49 Y52
4 Av MIS . . . . . . . . . . .210 J74 J75
4 Av NEW . . . . . . . .184 A28-29 B29
4 Av PMD . . . . . . . . . . . . .145 Q31
4 Av RMD . . . . . . . . . . . .222 K8
4 Av SUR . . . . . . . . . . . .266 Y-Z42
4 Av E VAN . . . . . .163 U15 U17 U18-19 U20
4 Av W VAN . . . .161 U6 162 U14 U7-12
4 St BUR . . . . . . . . .164 Y27 184 Z28
4 St NEW . . . . . . .184 A28-29 B29 Z28
4 St E CNV . . . . . . . . . .143 P17-18 P19

4 St W CNV . . . . . . . . . . .123 N16
4A Av DEL . . . . . . . . . . . .263 Y17
4th Av SQM . . . . . . . . . . . .301 K1

5 Av DEL . . . . . . . . . . . .263 Y16
5 Av MIS . . . . . . . . . .210 J74 J75
5 Av NEW . . . . . .184 A28-29 B27-28
5 Av RMD . . . . . . . . . . . .222 K8
5 Av SUR . . . . . . . . . . . .266 Y46
5 Av E VAN . .163 U15 U15-16 U17 U18-20
5 Av W VAN . . . . . . . . . . . . . . . . .
. . . . . .161 U6 162 U7 163 U15-16 U17 U18-20
5 St NEW . . . . . . .184 A28-29 Z28
5 St E CNV . . . . . . . . . .143 P17-18 P19
5 St W CNV . . . . . . . . .123 N16-17
5A Av MIS . . . . . . . . . . . .210 J75
5B Av DEL . . . . . . . . . . . .263 Y17
5th Av SQM . . . . . . . . . . . .301 K1

6 Av DEL . . . . . . . . . . . .263 Y16-17
6 Av LGT . . . . . . . . . .267 Y51 Y54
6 Av MIS . . . . . . . . .210 J73-74 J75
6 Av NEW . . . . . . .184 A28-29 B27
6 Av RMD . . . . . . . . . . . .222 K8
6 Av E NEW . . . . . .164 Y30 184 Z30
6 Av E VAN . . .163 U15 U15-16 U16 U17-20
6 Av W VAN.. 161 U6 162 U12-14 U14 U7 U9-12
6 St BUR . . . . . . . .164 X26 Y27 184 Z27
6 St NEW . . . . . . .184 A28-29 B29 Z28
6 St WVA . . . . . . . . . .122 M12-13 M13
6 St E CNV . . . . . . . . . . .143 P17-18
6 St W CNV . . . . . . . . .123 N16 N16-17
6A Av DEL . . . . . . . . . . . .263 Y17
6th Av SQM . . . . . . . . . . . .301 K1

7 Av DEL . . . . . . . . . . . .263 Y17
7 Av MIS . . . . . . . . .210 J72-75 J75
7 Av NEW . . . .184 A28 B26-27 Z28-29
7 Av RMD . . . . . . . . . . . .222 K8
7 Av E NEW . . . . . . . . . .184 Z29-30
7 Av E VAN . . .163 U15 U16 U17-18 U18-20
7 Av W VAN . .161 U6 162 U14 U7 U9-13
7 St BUR . . . . . . . .164 Y26 184 Z27
7 St NEW . . . . . . . .184 A28 A-B29
7 St E CNV . . . . . . . . . . . .143 P18
7A Av DEL . . . . . . . . .263 Y16 Y16-17
7B Av DEL . . . . . . . . . .263 Y16 Y17
7th Av SQM . . . . . . . . . . . .301 K1

8 Av DEL . . . . . . . . . . . .263 Y17
8 Av LGT . . . . . . .267 Y50-51 Y53 Y54
8 Av MIS . . . . . . . . . . . . .210 J75
8 Av NEW . . . . . .184 A27-28 B26-27 Z28
8 Av (Campbell River Rd) SUR . .266 Y39-46
8 Av (Campbell River Rd) LGT. . . . . . . .
. . . . . . . . .266 Y46 267 Y47-48
8 Av E NEW . . . . . .164 Y29 Y30 184 Z29
8 Av E VAN . . . . . .163 U16 U17 U17-20
8 Av Frontage SUR . . . . . . .266 Y40
8 Av W VAN . . . . . .161 U6 162 U7-14
8 St DNV . . . . . . . . . . . . .143 P20
8 St NEW . . . . . . .184 A-B28 B29
8 St WVA . . . . . . . . . . . . .122 M12
8 St E CNV . . . . . .123 N17 143 P17 P18
8 St W CNV . . . . . . . . . . .123 N17
8A Av DEL . . . . . . . . .263 X17 Y16-17
8A Av SUR . . . . . . . . . . .266 Y39 Y40
8B Av DEL . . . . . . . . . . . .263 X17

9 Av BUR . . . . . . . . . . . .184 C25
9 Av DEL . . . . . . . . .263 X16-17 X17
9 Av MIS . . . . . . . . .210 H74 J75
9 Av NEW . . . . . . . . .184 B26 Z28
9 Av SUR . . . . . . . . . . . .266 X39
9 Av W VAN . . . . . .161 U6 162 U7
9 St NEW . . . . . . . . . .184 A-B28
9 St WVA . . . . . . . . . . . . .122 L12

9 St E CNV . . . . . . .123 N18 143 P18
9A Av DEL . . . . . . . . .263 X16-17 X17

10 Av BUR . . . . . . . . . . .184 B-C25
10 Av DEL . . . . . . . . . . .263 X16-17
10 Av MIS . . . . . . . . .210 H74 H75
10 Av NEW . . . .184 A26-27 B25-26 Z27-28
10 Av SUR . . . . . . . . . . . .266 X39
10 Av E NEW . . . . . . . . . .164 Y29-30
10 Av E VAN . . . .163 U16-17 V-V18 U-V19
10 Av W VAN . . . . . .162 U7-8 U9-13
10 St NEW . . . . . . . .184 A27-28 B28-29
10 St E CNV . . . . . . . . . . . .123 N18
10A Av DEL . . . . . . . . .263 X16-17 X17
10A Av SUR . . . . . .266 X39 X39-40 X40
10B Av SUR . . . . . . . .266 X39-40 X40

11 Av BUR . . . . . . .164 Y29 184 A26-27 Z27-28
11 Av DEL . . . . . . . . . .263 X16-17 X17
11 Av MIS . . . . . . . .210 H74 H74-75
11 Av SUR . . . . . . . . . .266 X39 X40
11 Av E VAN . . . .163 U15 V16-17 V18 V20
11 Av W VAN . . . .162 U11-13 U14 U7-10
11 Pl WVA . . . . . . . . . .122 K-L11
11 St NEW . . . . . . . . .184 A B28
11 St WVA . . . . . .122 K11-12 L11-12 M11-12
11 St E CNV . . . . . . . . . .123 N17-18
11 St E DNV . . . . . . . . . .123 N18-19
11A Av DEL . . . . . . . . .263 X16 X16-17
11A Av SUR . . . . . . . .266 X39 X40
11B Av SUR . . . . . . . . . . . .266 X39

12 Av BUR . .164 Y28 Y29 184 A27 B25 Z27-28
12 Av DEL . . . . . . . . . . .263 X16-18
12 Av LGT . . . . . . . .266 X46 267 X49
12 Av MIS . . . . . . . . .210 H74 H75
12 Av SUR . . .266 X39 X40 X41 X43
12 Av (Kyle Rd) LGT . . . . . . . .267 X47
12 Av E VAN . . . . .163 V15-17 V18 V19
12 Av W VAN . . . .162 U11 U7-10 U-V12 V13
12 St NEW . . . . . . . . . .184 A27 B28
12 St WVA . . . . . . . .122 K-L11 L-M11
12 St E CNV . . . . . . . . . .123 N17-18
12 St E DNV . . . . . . . . . .123 N18-19
12A Av DEL . . . . . . . . . . . .263 X16
12A Av SUR . . . . . . . .266 X39 X39-40
12B Av SUR . . . . .265 X33 266 X39-40

13 Av BUR . . . . . . .164 Y28 184 A26-27 Z27-28
13 Av DEL . . . . . . . . . . .263 X16
13 Av MIS . . . . . . . . . . . .210 H75
13 Av SUR . . . . . . . . . . . .266 X39
13 Av (Ocean Park) SUR . . . . .265 X32-33
13 Av E VAN . . . . .163 V15 V16-18
13 Av W VAN . . . . .162 U7-8 V8 V9-14
13 St BUR . . . . . . . . . . .184 A26-27
13 St NEW . . . . . . . .184 A-B27 B28
13 St WVA . . . . . . . . . . . .122 L-M11
13 St E CNV . . . . . . . . . .123 N17-18
13 St E DNV . . . . . . . . . .123 N18-19
13 St W CNV . . . . . . . . . .123 N16-17
13A Av DEL . . . . . . . . . . .263 W-X17
13A Av SUR . . . .265 X33 X34 266 X39
13B Av DEL . . . . . . . . . . . .263 W17

14 Av BUR. . . . . . . . . . . . . . . . . . .
. . . . .164 Y28 Y28 184 A26 B25 Z27 Z27-28 Z28
14 Av DEL . . . . . . . . . . . .263 W17
14 Av LGT . . . . . . . .267 W53 W53-54
14 Av MIS . . . . . . . . . . .210 H72-74
14 Av SUR . . . . . . . .266 W39-40 W41
14 Av (Ocean Park) SUR . .265 W32 W33 W34
14 Av E VAN . . . .163 V15 V16-17 V19-20
14 Av W VAN . . . . . . . . . . .162 V7-14
14 St NEW . . . . . . . . .184 A-B27 B28
14 St WVA . . . . . . . . . . . .122 L-M11
14 St E CNV . . . . . . . . . .123 N17 N18

14 St E DNV . . . . . . . . . .123 N18-19
14 St W CNV . . . . . .123 N15-16 N16-17
14 St W DNV . . . . . .122 N14 123 N15
14A Av LGT . . . . . . . . . . . .267 W54
14A Av SUR . . .265 W32 W33 W34 266 W39 W40
14B Av DEL . . . . . . . . . . . .263 W17
14B Av SUR . . . . .265 W32 266 W39

15 Av BUR . . . .164 X29 Y28 184 A25 Z26-27 Z27
15 Av SUR . . . . . . . .266 W39-40 W40
15 Av (Ocean Park) SUR . . . .265 W32 W33 W34
15 Av E VAN . . . .163 V15-17 V17 V18 V19-20
15 Av W VAN . . . .162 V12-13 V14 V7-8 V8-11
15 St BUR . . . . . . . . . . . .184 A26
15 St NEW . . . . . . . . . . . .184 A27
15 St WVA . . . . . . . .122 K11 L-M11
15 St E CNV . . . . . . . . . .123 N17-19
15 St E DNV . . . . . . . . . .123 N19-20
15 St W CNV . . . .123 N15 N15-16 N16-17
15 St W DNV . . . . . . . . . . . .122 N14
15A Av SUR . . . . . .265 W32 W33 W34
15A Av DEL . . . . . . . . . . . .263 W17
15B Av SUR . . . . . . . . . . . .265 W33

16 Av BUR . . . .164 X29 Y28 184 A26 Z27
16 Av DEL . . . . .262 W15 263 W16 W17-18
16 Av SUR . . . . . . . . . . .266 W39-46
16 Av (North Bluff Rd) LGT . . . . . . . . .
. . . . .266 W46 267 W47 W49 W51-52 W54
16 Av (Ocean Park) SUR . . . . .265 W32-34
16 Av E VAN . . . .163 V15-17 V18 V19-20
16 Av W UEL . . . . . . . . . . .161 V4-5
16 Av W VAN . . . . . . . . . . .162 V13 V7-11
16 St BUR . . . . . . . . . . .184 A26 Z26
16 St NEW . . . . . . . . . .184 A-B27
16 St WVA . . . . . . . . . . . .122 L-M11
16 St E CNV . . . . . . . . .123 N17-18 N18-19
16 St E DNV . . . . . . . . . .123 N19-20
16 St W CNV . . . .123 N15 N16 N16-17
16 St W DNV . . . . . . . . . . . .122 N14
16A Av DEL . . . . . . . . .263 W17 W17-18
16A Av SUR .265 W33-34 W35 W36 266 W39
16B Av SUR . . . . . . . . . . . .265 W35

17 Av BUR . . . .164 Y27-28 184 A26 Z26 Z26-27
17 Av SUR . . . . . . . . . . . . . . . . . . .
. . . . .265 W32 W33-34 W34 W35 W36-37 W37-38
17 Av E VAN . . . .163 V15-16 V16-17 V18 V19-20
17 Av W VAN. . . . .162 V13-14 V8-11
17 St BUR . . . . . . . . . . . .184 A26
17 St NEW . . . . . . . . . . . .184 A26
17 St WVA . . . . . . . . . .122 L10 L-M10
17 St E CNV . . . . . . . . . .123 N17-19
17 St E DNV . . . . . . . . . . . .123 N20
17 St W CNV . . . .123 N15 N16 M-N16 M-N17
17 St W DNV . . . .122 M14 M14 123 M15
17A Av DEL . . . . . . . . . .263 W17-18
17A Av SUR .265 W32 W33 W34 W35 W36 W37-38
17B Av SUR . . . . . . . . . . . .265 W35

18 Av BUR . .164 Y27 Y27-28 184 A26 Z26-27 Z27
18 Av DEL . . . . . . . . . . . .263 W17
18 Av LGT . . . . . . .266 W46 267 W47 W49-51
. . . . .265 W32 W32-33 W34-35 W35 W35-36 W37-38
. . . . .266 W39-40 W40-41 W41 W42 W44
18 Av (Best Av) MIS . . .210 G73-74 G-H75
18 Av E VAN. . . . . . . . . . . . . . . . . . .
. . . . .163 V15-16 V17 V18-19 V19-20 V20
18 Av W VAN. . . . . .162 V13-14 V8-11
18 St BUR . . . . . . . . . . . .184 A26
18 St NEW . . . . . . . .184 A-B26 B27
18 St WVA . . . . . . . . . .122 K10 M10
18 St E CNV . . . . . .123 M17-18 M18-19
18 St E DNV . . . . . . . . . .123 M19-20
18 St W CNV . . . . . . . . . .123 M16-17

18A Av *SUR*
. . . . . . . 265 V-W33 V-W35 V-W36 W32 W36-37 W38
18A Av *SUR* . . . . . . . . . . . . . . . . . . . . 265 W34
18B Av *SUR* . . . . . . . . . . . . . . . 265 V32 V-W35

19 Av *BUR.*
. . . . . . . 164 Y27 Y27-28 184 A25-26 Z26-27 Z27
19 Av *DEL* . . . . . . . . . . . . . . . . . . . . 263 V17
19 Av *SUR.* . 265 V32 V32-33 V33 V34 V35 V36 V37
. . . . . . . . . . . . . . . . . . V38 266 V39 V40 V41
19 Av E *VAN.*
. 163 V15 V15-16 V16-17 V17-18 V18-19 V19 V19-20
19 Av W *VAN.* . . . . . . . . 162 V13-14 V8-11
19 St *DNV* . . . . . . . . . . . . . . . . . . 123 M15
19 St *NEW.* . . . . . . . . . . . . . 184 B26 B27
19 St *WVA.* . . . . . . . . . . . . . 122 L10 M10
19 St E *CNV* . . . . . . . . . . . . . . . 123 M17-18
19 St W *CNV* . . . . . . . . 123 M15 M16 M16-17
19A Av *SUR*
. . . . . . 265 V32 V33 V34 V35 V36 V37 266 V39 V43
19B Av *SUR.* . . . . . . . . . . . . . . . . . 265 V35

20 Av *LGT.*
. . 266 V46 V46 267 V47 V48-49 V49-50 V50-51 V54
20 Av *SUR.* . . . . . . . . . . . 265 V32-38 266 V39-45
20 Av E *VAN.*
. . . . . 163 V15-16 V17 V18 V18-19 V19 V19-20 W18
20 Av FG-N *SUR* . . . . . . . . . . . . . . 265 V37
20 Av W *VAN.* . . . . . . . 162 V10 V13-14 V8-9
20 St *BUR.* . . . . . . . . . . . . . . 184 A25-26
20 St *NEW.* . . . . . . . . . . . . . . . . . 184 B26
20 St *WVA.* . . . . . . . . . . . . . 122 L10 M10
20 St E *DNV.* . . . . . . . . . . . 123 M17-18 M18
20 St E *DNV.* . . . . . . . . . . . . . . . . 123 M20
20 St W *CNV.* . . . 123 M15 M16 M16-17 M17
20 St W *DNV.* . . . . . . . . 122 M14 123 M15
20A Av *SUR*
. . . . . 265 V32 V33 V33-34 V34 V35 V36 V37 V37-38

21 Av *BUR.* . . . . . . . . . . . . . . . . 184 A25
21 Av *LGT.* . . . . . . . . . 266 V46 V46 267 V47
21 Av *SUR.*
. . . . . . 265 V31 V32 V33 V33-34 V34 V36-37 V37-38
. . . . . . . . . . 266 V40 V41 V43 V45-46
21 Av E *VAN.* 163 V-W15 W16-17 W18-19 W19-20
21 Av W *VAN* 162 V10 V11 V13 V13-14 V8-9 V-W14
21 St *NEW.* . . . . . . . . . . . . . . . . . 184 B26
21 St *WVA.* . . . . . . . . . . . . . . 122 K-M10
21 St E *CNV.* . . . . . . . . . . . 123 M17-18 M18
21 St E *DNV.* . . . . . . . . . . . . . . . . 123 M19
21 St W *CNV.* . . . . . . . 123 M15 M16 M16-17
21 St W *DNV.* . . . . 122 M14 M14 123 M15
21A Av *SUR*
. . . . . 265 V31 V32 V32-33 V33 V34 V34-35 V37
. . . . . . . . . . . . . . . . . . 266 V41-42 V43
21B Av *SUR.* . . . 265 V32 V33 V36-37 V37

22 Av *LGT.* . . . . . . . . . . . . . . . . . 267 V47
22 Av *SUR.*
. 265 V32 V35 V37 V37-38 V38 266 V41 V43 V45 V46
22 Av (Cherry Av) *MIS* . . . . . . . . . 210 G72-76
22 Av E *VAN.* . . . . . . . 163 W15-16 W18-20
22 Av W *VAN* . . . . . . . 162 V8-10 V9 W13
22 St *NEW.* . . . . . . . . . . . . . . . . . 184 B26
22 St *WVA.* . . . . . . . . . . . . . . 122 L-M10
22 St E *CNV.* . . . . . . . . . . . 123 M17-18 M18
22 St W *CNV.* . . . . . . . 123 M16 M16-17 M17
22 St W *DNV.* . . . 122 M14 123 M15
22A Av *SUR*
. . . . . 265 V32-33 V33 V33-34 V34 V34-35 V37
22B Av *SUR.* . . . 265 V31 V32-33 V33 V34

23 Av *SUR.* . . . . 265 V32 V33 V34 V34-35 V35 V37
. . . . . . . . . . . 266 V40 V41 V41-42 V43
23 Av E *VAN.* . . . . 163 W15-16 W16 W18-20
23 Av W *VAN.* . . . . . . 162 V-W10 V-W8 W13-14
23 St *NEW.* . . . . . . . . . . . . . . . . . 184 B26
23 St *WVA.* . . . . . . . . . . . . . . . . 122 L9
23 St E *CNV.* . . . . . . . . . . . . . . 123 M17-18
23 St W *CNV.* . . . . . . . . . . . . . 123 M16-17
23 St W *DNV.* . . . 122 M14 M14 123 M15
23A Av *SUR*
. . . . . 245 U33 U34 U35 265 V31-32 V33 V34 V35 V37

24 Av *LGT.*
. . 246 U46 U46 247 U47-51 U52-54 248 U60-62
24 Av *SUR.* . . . . . . . 245 U31-38 246 U39-45 U46
24 Av E *VAN.* . . 163 W15 W16 W18 W18-19 W20
24 Av FG-N *SUR* . . . . . . . . . . 246 U36-37
24 Av W *VAN* . . . . . . . . . . . . 162 W13 W8-10
24 St *WVA.* . . . . . . . . . . . . . . . . 122 L9
24 St E *CNV.* . . . . . . . . . . . . . . 123 M17-18
24 St E *DNV.* . . . . . . . . . . . . . . . . 123 M20
24 St W *CNV.* . . . . . . . . . . . . . . . . 122 L7
24 St W *DNV.* . . . 122 M14 M14 123 M15
24A Av *LGT.* . . . . . . . . . . . . 248 U61-62
24A Av *SUR.* . . . 245 U32 U34 U35-36 U36-37

25 Av *LGT.* . . . . . . . . 247 U48 248 U61-62
25 Av *SUR.* . . 245 U32 U33-34 U34 U35 U35-36
. . . . . . . . . . . U36-37 246 U40-41 U45 U46

25 Av E *VAN.* . 163 W17-18 W18 W18-19 W19 W20
25 St *WVA.* . . . . . . . . . . . . . . . . . 122 L9
25 St E *CNV.* . . . . . . . . . . . . . . 123 M17-18
25 St W *CNV.* . . . . . . . . . . . . . . 123 M16-17
25A Av *LGT.* . . . . . . . . . . . . 248 U61-62
25A Av *SUR.*
. . . . . . . . 245 U32 U34-35 U35 U36-37 U38 246 U40
25B Av *SUR.* . . . . . . . . . . . . . . . . 245 U36

26 Av *LGT.* . . . . . . 247 U51-53 248 U60 U61-62
26 Av *SUR.*
. . . . . 245 U32 U33-34 U34 U35 U35-36 U36-37 U38
. . . . . . . . . . 246 U39 U40-41 U45
26 Av E *VAN.*
. . . . . . . . 163 W15 W15-16 W16-17 W17 W17-18
. . . . . . . . . . . . W18 W18-19 W19 W20
26 Av W *VAN.* . . . . . . . . . 162 W12-14 W9
26 Cr *CNV.* . . . . . . . . . . . . . . . . . 123 M18
26 St *WVA.* . . . . . . . . . . . . . . . 122 K-L9
26 St E *CNV.* . . . . . . . . . . . . . . 123 L17-18
26 St E *CNV.* . . . . . . . 123 L-M18 L-M19
26 St W *CNV.* . . . . . . . . . . . . . 123 L16-17
26 St W *DNV.* . . . . . . . . 122 L14 123 L15
26A Av *LGT.* . . . . . . . . . . . . 248 U61-62
26A Av *SUR.* . . 245 U32 U34 U35 246 U40-41 U41
26B Av *LGT.* . . . . . . . . . . . . . . . . 248 U62
26B Av *SUR.* . . . 245 U32 246 U40-41

27 Av *LGT.* . . . . . . . . . 247 U47 248 U61-62
27 Av *SUR.* . 245 U32 U33-34 U34 U34-35 U35 U38
. . . . . . . . . . . 246 U39 U40 U45
27 Av E *VAN.*
. . . . . . . . 163 W15 W15-16 W16-17 W18 W19 W20
27 Av W *VAN.* . . . . 162 W12-13 W13-14 W4 W9
27 St *WVA.* . . . . . . . . . . . . . . . 122 K-L8
27 St E *CNV.* . . . . . . . . . . . . . . 123 L17-18
27 St E *DNV.* . . . . . . . . . . . 123 L19 L-M20
27 St W *CNV.* . . . . . . . . . . . . . 123 L16-17
27A Av *LGT.* . . . . . . . . . . . . . . . . 248 U62
27A Av *SUR.* . . 245 U32 U35 U37 U37-38
. . . . . . . . . . 246 U40 U41 U41-42
27B Av *DEL.* . . . . . . . . . . . . . . . . 242 U14
27B Av *LGT.* . . . . . . . . . . . . 248 U61-62
27B Av *SUR.* . . . 245 U37 246 U39

28 Av *DEL.* . . . . . . . . . . . . . . . 243 U16-19
28 Av *LGT.* . . . . 246 U46 247 U47-48 U51-53
. . . . . . 248 T-U61 T-U62 T-U63 U60-61
28 Av *SUR .* . . 245 U32 U33-35 U35-37 U37-38 U38
. . . . . . . . . 246 U39 U39-41 U42 U44 U46
28 Av E *VAN.*
. . 162 W14 163 W15 W15-17 W18 W18-19 W19-20
28 Av W *VAN.* . . . 162 W11 W12 W13-14 W8 W9
28 St *WVA.* . . . . . . . . . . . . . . . 122 K8 L8
28 St E *CNV.* . . . . . . . . . . . . . . . 123 L17
28 St W *CNV.* . . . . . . . . . . . . . 123 L16-17
28A Av *LGT.* . . . . . . . . . 248 T61 T61-62 T62
28A Av *SUR* 245 T34-35 T-U35 T-U36 U37 246 T42
28B Av *DEL.* . . . . . . . . . . . . . . . . 242 T14
28B Av *LGT.* . . . . . . . . . . . 248 T60-61 T61-62
28B Av *SUR.* . . . . . . . . . . . . . . . . 246 T42

29 Av *LGT.* . . . . 248 T60 T60-61 T61-62 T62
29 Av *SUR .* . 245 T34 T35 T36 T37 246 T39-40 T42
29 Av E *VAN.*
. . . . . . . 163 W15-16 W16-17 W17 W18 W18-20
29 Av W *VAN.*
. . . . . . . . 162 W11 W11-12 W12-13 W13-14 W7-10
29 St *WVA.* . . . . . . . . . . . . . . . 122 K-L8 L8
29 St E *CNV.* . . . . . . . . . . . . . . 123 L17-18
29 St E *DNV.* . . . . . . . . . . . . . . . . 123 L20
29 St W *CNV.* . . . . . . . . . . . . . 123 L16 L17
29A Av *LGT.* . . . . . . . . . . . . . . . . 248 T62
29A Av *SUR.* . . 245 T35 T36 T37 246 T43
29B Av *LGT.* . . . . . . . . . 247 T53 248 T60-61

30 Av *DEL.* . . . . . . . . . . . . . . . . 243 T19
30 Av *LGT.*
. . . . . 246 T46 247 T47 248 T60 T61 T61-62 T62
30 Av *SUR.* . . 245 T34 T34-35 T35 T36 246 T39
30 Av E *VAN.* . . 163 W15 W15-16 W16 W17 X18
30 Av W *VAN.* 162 W11 W13 W13-14 W8-9 W9-10
30 St *WVA.* . . . . . . . . . . . . . . . 122 K-L8
30A Av *LGT.* . . . . . . . 248 T60 T60-61 T61 T62
30A Av *SUR.* . . . . . . . . 245 T35 T36 246 T41
30B Av *SUR.* . . . . . . . . . . 246 T39 T39-40
30B St *DEL.* . . . . . . . . . . . . . . . . 242 S12

31 Av *DEL.* . . . . . . . . . . . . . . 242 T12-13
31 Av *LGT.* . . . . . . . . . . . . 248 T62-63
31 Av *SUR.* . . . 245 T34 T35 T36 246 T41 T41-42
31 Av E *VAN.* . . 163 W-X17 X15-16 X17-18
31 Av W *VAN.* . . . . . . . . 162 W13-14 W8-10
31 St *WVA.* . . . . . . . . . . . . . . . . . 122 L7
31A Av *LGT.* . . . . . . . . . 248 T61 T62 T62-63
31A Av *SUR.* . . . . . . . . . 245 T35 T36
31B Av *SUR.* . . . . . . . . . . . . . 248 T60 T63

32 Av *LGT* 247 T47-48 T49 T50 T54 248 T61 T62-63
32 Av *SUR.* . . . . . 245 T34-36 246 T39-46
32 Av (McInnis Rd) *LGT* . 246 T46 T46 247 T47

32 Av Diversion *SUR* . . . . . . . . . . . . 245 T37
32 Av E *VAN.* . . . . 163 X15 X16 X17-18
32 Av W *VAN.* . . 162 W11-12 W8 W9-10 W-X10
. . . . . . . . . . W-X11 X12-13 X13
32A Av *LGT.* . . . . . . 247 T49 248 T61 T62 T63
32A Av *SUR.* . . . . . . . . . . . . . . . . 245 T34
32B Av *LGT.* . . . . . . 247 T49 248 T62 T63
32B Av *SUR.* . . . . . . . . . . . . 245 T35 T36

33 Av *LGT.* . . . . . . 248 S62-63 S-T62 T61
33 Av *SUR.* . . . 245 T34 T35 T36-37 T38
33 Av E *VAN.* . . . . . . . . . . . . . 163 X15-18
33 Av W *VAN.* . . . . . . . . . . . . 162 X8-13
33A Av *DEL.* . . . . . . . . . . . . . . 242 S13-14
33A Av *LGT.* . . . 246 S-T46 T46 247 T47
. . . . . . . . 248 S61 S62 S63
33A Av *SUR.* . . . 245 S-T36 S-T38 T36
33B Av *LGT.* . . . . . . . . . . . . 248 S61 S62
33B Av *SUR.* . . . . . . . . . . . . 245 S35 S36

34 Av *LGT.* . . . . . . 247 S47-48 248 S61 S62
34 Av *SUR.* . . 245 S34-35 S36 S36-37 S37 S37-38
34 Av E *VAN.* . . 163 X15 X16-17 X17 X18
34 Av W *VAN.* . . . . . . . . . . . . 162 X8-12
34 St *DEL.* . . . . . . . . . . . . . . 242 R-T13
34A Av *LGT.* . 246 S46 S46 247 S47 S54 248 S62
. . . . . . . . . . 245 S35 S36-37 S37-38
34B Av *DEL.* . . . . . . . 243 S16 S17-19
34B Av *SUR.* . . . . . . . . . . . . . . . . 245 S37

35 Av *LGT.* . . . . . . . . 247 S47 248 S62
35 Av *SUR.* . . . . . . . . 245 S34-35 S37
35 Av E *VAN .* . 163 X15 X16 X16-17 X17 X18
35 Av W *VAN .* . 162 X11-12 X12 X13 X14 X8-10
35A Av *LGT.* . . 246 S46 S46 247 S47 S47
35A Av *SUR.* . . . . . . . . . . . . 245 S35 S38

36 Av *DEL.* . . . . . . . . . . . . 243 S16 S19-20
36 Av *LGT.* . . . . . . . . . . . 247 S47 S49
36 Av *SUR.* . . . 245 S37 S38 246 S46
36 Av E *VAN.* . . . 163 X15 X16-17 X17-18
36 Av W *VAN.* . . . . . . 162 X11-12 X8-10
36A Av *LGT.* . . . . . . 246 S46 247 S47
36A Av *SUR*
. . . . . 245 S35 S36 S37-38 S38 246 S39 S39-40
36B Av *LGT.* . . . . . . . . . . . . . . . . 247 S48
36B Av *SUR.* . . . . . . . . . . . . 245 S36 S38

37 Av *LGT.* . . . . . . 246 S46 247 S47 S48-49
37 Av *SUR.* . . . . . . . . . . . . 245 S35 S38
37 Av E *VAN* . . . 163 X15 X16 X16-17 X18
37 Av W *VAN.* . . . . . . . . . . . . 162 X8-14
37A Av *LGT.*
. . . . . 246 S46 S46 247 S47 S47 S48 S49 S51-52
37A Av *SUR.* . . . . . . . . . . . . . . . . 245 S38
37B Av *LGT.* . . . . . . . . . . . . . . . . 247 S48

38 Av *LGT.*
. . . . . . 246 S46 247 S47 S48 S48-49 S49-50 S52
38 Av *SUR.* . . . . . . . . . . . . . . . . 245 S38
38 Av E *VAN.* . . . 163 X15 X16 X17 X18-19
38 Av W *VAN.*
. . . . 162 X10-11 X11 X12-13 X13 X14 X8 X9 X9-10
38A Av *LGT.* . . 246 R-S46 247 R-S47 R-S48 S48
38A Av *SUR.* . . . . . . . . . . . . . . . 245 R-S38
38B Av *LGT.* . . . . . . . . . 247 R47 R-S47

39 Av *LGT.* . . . . . . . . . . . . . . . . 247 R48
39 Av E *VAN.* . . . 163 X15 X16-17 X17 X18
39 Av W *VAN.*
. . . 162 X11 X12 X12-13 X13-14 X8-9 X9-10
39A Av *LGT.* . . . . . . . 247 R47 R48-49
39A Av *SUR.* . . . . . . . . . 245 R38 246 R39

40 Av *LGT.* . . . . 246 R46 247 R47 R51 R54 248 R62
40 Av *SUR.* . . . 245 R33-35 R35-38 246 R39-45
40 Av (Bradshaw Rd) *LGT* . 247 R47-50 R51-53
40 Av (Downes Rd) *LGT.* . . . . . . . 248 R62-63
40 Av E *VAN.* . 163 X15 X19 X-Y17 X-Y18 Y16 Y17
40 Av W *VAN.*
. . . . . . 162 X10-11 X11-12 X12 X12-13 X14 X8 X9
40 St *DEL.* . . . . . . . . . . . . . . . . 242 R-S14
40A Av *LGT.* . . . 246 R46 247 R47 R47 R48
40B Av *LGT.* . . . . . . . . . . . . . . . . 247 R48

41 Av *LGT.* . . . . . . . . . . . . 247 R47 R48
41 Av E *VAN.* . . . . . . . . . . . . . 163 Y15-19
41 Av W *VAN.* . . 162 X8 X9-11 X-Y12 X-Y13
41A Av *LGT.* . 246 R46 R46 247 R47 R47 R48
41B Av *LGT.* . . . . . . . . . . . . . . . . 247 R48
41B St *DEL.* . . . . . . . . . . . . 242 R-T14 U14

42 Av *LGT.* . . . 246 R46 R46 247 R47 R47 R48-49 R49
42 Av E *VAN.* . . 162 Y14 163 Y15 Y17-18 Y18 Y19
42 Av W *VAN.*
. . . . . . . 162 Y10-11 Y11 Y12-13 Y13 Y14 Y9 Y9-10
42A Av *DEL.* . . . . . . . . . . . . . . . . 243 R16
42A Av *LGT.* . . . . . . . 247 R47 R49-50
42A Av *SUR.* . . . . . . . . . . . . . . . . 246 R45
42B Av *DEL.* . . . . . . . . . . . . . . . . 243 R16

43 Av *DEL.* . . . . . . . . . . . . . . 243 Q-R16
43 Av *LGT.* . . . . . . 247 R47 R49 248 Q62-63
43 Av E *VAN.*
. . 162 Y14 163 Y15 Y15 Y17 Y17-18 Y18 Y19-20 Y20
43 Av W *VAN.* . . . . . . 162 Y11-13 Y14 Y9 Y9-10
43A Av *DEL.* . . . . . . . . . . . . . . 243 Q16 Q19
43A Av *LGT.* . 246 Q-R46 247 Q49 Q49-50 Q-R47

44 Av *DEL.* . . . . 243 Q16-17 Q18 244 Q28
44 Av *LGC.* . . . . . . . 247 Q47-48 Q48-49
44 Av *LGT.* . . . 246 Q46 247 Q50 Q51-52 Q54
44 Av *SUR.* . . . . . . . . 245 Q35 246 Q44
44 Av (Cemetery Rd) *LGT* . . . . . . 247 Q48-50
44 Av E *VAN.* . . 163 Y15 Y17-18 Y19 Y9
44 Av W *VAN.* . 162 Y10-11 Y11 Y13 Y14 Y9 Y9-10
44A Av *DEL.* . . . . . . . . . . 243 Q15-16 Q18
44A Av *LGC.* . . . . . 247 Q47 Q47-48 Q48-49
44A Av *LGT.* . . 247 Q49 Q50-51 Q51 Q51-52 Q52
44A St *DEL.* . . . . . . . . . . . . . . . . 243 Q15
44B Av *DEL.* . . . . . . . . 243 Q15 Q15-16 Q16
44B Av *LGT.* . . . 246 Q46 247 Q47 Q47

45 Av *DEL.* . . . . . . . 243 Q15-16 Q17 Q18 Q19
45 Av *LGC.* . . . . . . 247 Q47 Q47-48 Q48 Q49
45 Av *LGT.* . . . 247 Q49 Q50 Q50-51 Q51 Q52
45 Av E *VAN.* . . . . . . . . . . 163 Y15-17 Y18-20
45 Av W *VAN.* . . . . . . 162 Y13 Y13-14 Y9-13
45 St *DEL.* . . . . . . . . . . . . . . . . . 243 Q15
45A Av *DEL.* . . . . . . . . . . 243 Q15 Q18 Q19
45A Av *LGC.* . 246 Q46 247 Q47 Q48 Q48-49 Q49
45A Cr *LGT.* . . . . . . . . . . . . . . . . 247 Q51
45B Av *DEL.* . . . . . . . . . . . . . . . . 243 Q19
45B Av *LGC.* . . 246 Q46 Q46 247 Q47 Q47

46 Av *DEL.* . . . . . . . . . . . . 243 Q15 Q17
46 Av *LGC.* . . 246 Q46 247 Q47 Q48 Q48-49 Q49
46 Av *LGT.*
. . . . 247 Q49 Q50-51 Q51 Q52 Q54 248 Q60 Q62
46 Av E *VAN.* . . 163 Y15 Y17 Y18-19 Y19-20 Y20
46 Av W *VAN.* . . 162 Y10-11 Y11 Y12-13 Y14 Y8
46 St *DEL.* . . . . . . . . . . . . . . . . . 243 Q15
46A Av *DEL.* . . . . . . . . . . . . . . . . 243 Q17 Q19
46A Av *LGC.* . 246 Q46 Q46 247 Q47 Q48 Q48-49 Q49
46A Av *LGT.* . . . . . . 247 Q49 Q50 Q51 Q52
46A St *DEL.* . . . . . . . . . . . . . . 243 Q-T15
46B Av *LGC.* . . . . . . . . . . . . . . . . 247 Q48
46B Av *LGT.* . . . . . . . . . . . . . . . . 247 Q52
46B St *DEL.* . . . . . . . . . . . . . . . . 243 Q15

47 Av *DEL.* . . . . . . . . . . . . 243 Q16 Q17
47 Av *LGC.* . . 246 Q46 247 Q47 Q48 Q49
47 Av *LGT.* . . . . . . 247 Q49 Q50 Q52 Q54
47 Av E *VAN.*
. . 163 Y15-16 Y16-17 Y17 Y17-18 Y18-19 Y19-20 Y20
47 Av W *VAN.*
. . . . . . 162 Y10 Y10-11 Y11 Y11-13 Y13 Y14 Y8-9
47 St *DEL.* . . . . . . . . . . . . . . . . . 243 Q15
47A Av *DEL.* . . . . . . . . . . . . . . . . 243 Q16 Q17
47A Av *LGC.* . . . . . . 247 Q47 Q48 Q49
47A Av *LGT.* . . . . . . . . . . . . . . 247 Q50 Q52
47B Av *DEL.* . . . . . . . . . . . . . . . . 243 Q15
47B Av *LGT.* . . . . . . . . . . . 247 Q50 Q51

48 Av *DEL.* . . . . . . . . . 223 P16 243 Q16
48 Av *LGC.* . . 226 P46 246 Q46 247 Q47-48 Q48-49
48 Av *LGT.* . . . . . . 247 Q53 Q54 248 Q62
48 Av *SUR .* 225 P33 P36-37 245 Q33 Q36 Q37-38
. . . . . . . . 246 Q39-40 Q41-42 Q45-46
48 Av (McDonald Rd) *LGT.* . . . . 247 Q49-51
48 Av E *VAN* 163 Y15 Y16 Y18 Y18-19 Y19-20 Y20
48 Av W *VAN*
. . . . . . 162 Y10-11 Y11 Y12-13 Y13 Y14 Y8-9 Y9
48 St *DEL.* . . . . . . . . . . . . . . . . . 243 U16
48A Av *DEL.* . . . . . . . . . 223 P17 P18 P19
48A Av *LGC.* . . 226 P46 P46 227 P47 P48 P49
48A Av *LGT.* . . . . . . . . . . . . 227 P50 P51
48A St *DEL.* . . . . . . . . . . . . . . 243 Q-R16
48B Av *DEL.* . . . . . . . . . . . . 223 P17 P17-18
48B Av *LGC.* . . . . . . . . . . . . . . . . 227 P48
48B St *DEL.* . . . . . . . . . 243 Q16 Q-R16

49 Av *DEL.* . . . . . . . . . 223 P17 P18 P19
49 Av *LGC.* . . 226 P46 P46 227 P47 P48 P49
49 Av *LGT.* . . . . . . . . . . . . . . . . 227 P51
49 Av W *VAN.* . . . 163 Y15-17 Y18 183 Z18 Z18-20
49 Av W *VAN.* . . . . . . . 162 Y10-14 Y8-9 Y9
49 St *DEL.* . . . . 243 Q16 R16 263 X16 Z16
49A Av *DEL.* . . . . . . . . . . . . 223 P17 P18
49A Av *LGC.* . . . . . . . . . . . . 227 P47 P48 P49
49A Av *LGT.* . . . . . . . . . . . . 227 P50-51 P51
49B Av *DEL.* . . . . . . . . 223 P17 P17-18 P18
49B Av *LGC.* . . 226 P46 P46 227 P47 P49
49B Av *LGT.* . . . . . . . . . . . . . . . . 227 P50
49B St *DEL.* . . . . . . . . . . . . . . . . 263 Z16

50 Av *DEL.* . . . . . . . . . . . . 223 P17 P18
50 Av *LGC.* . . 226 P46 227 P47-48 P48 P49
50 Av *LGT.* . . . 227 P50 P51 P52 P53-54 P54
50 Av *SUR.* . . . . . . . . . . . . . . . . 226 P40

50 Av E VAN.
...... 183 Z15-16 Z17 Z17-18 Z18-19 Z19-20 Z20
50 Av W VAN...... 162 Y10 Y11 Y12 Y13 Y8
50 St DEL............ 243 Q16 263 X16 Z16
50A Av LGC........ 226 P46 227 P47 P48 P49
50A Av LGT........... 227 P50 P50-51
50A St DEL............ 243 Q16
50B Av LGC........... 227 P49
50B Av LGT........... 227 P50
50B St DEL........... 263 X16

51 Av DEL............. 223 P17 P18
51 Av LGC...... 226 P46 P46 227 P47 P47 P49
51 Av LGT............ 227 P51 P52
51 Av E VAN 183 Z15-17 Z17 Z18 Z19 Z19-20 Z20
51 Av W VAN
...... 162 Y10 Y11 Y12 Y8 Y9 182 Z10 Z11 Z12 Z13
51 St DEL............ 243 Q16 263 X16
51A Av LGC............ 227 P48 P49
51A Av LGT............ 227 P50
51A St DEL............ 263 X16 Z16
51B Av LGC............ 227 P48-49
51B Av LGT............ 227 P50
51B Av SUR............ 226 P45

52 Av DEL............. 223 P17
52 Av LGC............ 227 P47 P49
52 Av LGT............ 227 P51 P54
52 Av SUR............ 226 P45
52 Av E VAN.
.... 182 Z14 183 Z15-17 Z17 Z18 Z19 Z19-20 Z20
52A Av W VAN...... 182 Z11-13 Z13 Z9
52 St DEL.... 243 U16 263 V-X16 X-Y16 Y-Z16
52A Av LGC............ 227 P47
52A Av LGT............ 227 P51
52A Av SUR............ 225 P31-32
52A St DEL...
... 223 P16 243 Q16-17 263 X16 Y-Z16 Z16

53 Av LGC.... 226 N46 227 N47 P47-48
53 Av SUR.... 225 N-P31 226 N44
53 Av E VAN.. 183 Z15-17 Z18 Z19-20 Z20
53 Av W VAN.... 182 Z10-11 Z12 Z13 Z9
53 St DEL.
... 223 P17 243 Q17 S-T17 263 Y17 Y-Z17 Z17
53A Av LGC.... 227 N47 N47-48 N-P48
53A Av SUR............ 226 N45
63A St DEL 223 P17 243 Q17 263 W-X17 Y-Z17 Z17
53B Av LGC............ 227 N47
53B Av SUR............ 226 N45

54 Av LGC.... 226 N46 227 N47 N48
54 Av SUR.. 225 N32 N36 226 N44 N44-45 N46
54 Av F VAN...... 183 715 716 718-20
54 Av W VAN...... 182 Z10-11 Z11-13
54 St DEL.
... 223 P17 243 Q17 263 W17 X-Y17 Y17 Y-Z17
54A Av LGC.... 226 N46 227 N47 N47-48
54A St DEL..... 223 P17 243 Q17 263 X17 Y-Z17

55 Av LGC............ 226 N46 227 N47
55 Av SUR............ 225 N31-32 N32 N36
...... 226 N43 N43-44 N44 N45 N46
55 Av E VAN.. 183 Z15-16 Z16-17 Z17 Z18 Z19
55 Av W VAN...... 182 Z12 Z12-13 Z9
55 St DEL.... 243 Q17 263 W17 X17 Y17 Y-Z17
55A Av DEL............ 263 X-Y17
55A Av LGC.... 226 N46 N46 227 N47 N47
55A Av SUR
...... 225 N32 N33-34 N35 N36 226 N44 N45 N46
55A St DEL..... 243 Q17 263 W17 Y17 Y-Z17
55B Av SUR............ 226 N42 N44
55B St DEL.... 223 P17 243 Q17 263 W17

56 Av LGC............ 226 N46 227 N49
56 Av LGT............ 227 N51 N53
56 Av SUR.... 224 N30 225 N31 N32-34 N34-35
...... N36-38 226 N39-45 N46
56 Av E VAN...... 183 Z15-16 Z17 Z18 Z19
56 Av FG-N SUR............ 226 N44-45
56 Av W VAN............ 182 Z12
56 St DEL.... 223 P17 243 Q17 U17 263 V-Z17
56A Av SUR.... 225 N31 N32 N34 N35 N36-37
...... 226 N42 N42-43 N43 N44
56A St DEL............ 243 Q17 263 X17
56B Av SUR.... 225 N34 N36-37 226 N44 N45

57 Av LGC............ 227 N49
57 Av SUR.. 225 N31 N33 N33-34 N35
...... N35-36 N36-37 N37 226 N40 N41
...... N42-43 N43 N44 N44-45 N45
57 Av E VAN............ 183 Z15-17 Z18
57 Av W VAN............ 182 Z11-13 Z9
57 St DEL.. 223 P17 243 Q17 263 W17 X17-18
57A Av LGC............ 227 N47
57A Av LGT............ 227 M-N52 N50
57A Av SUR
... 224 N30 225 M-N35 N31 N32 N34 N36 N36-37
...... 226 N40-41 N41 N42-43 N43 N43-44 N44
57A St DEL............ 223 P18 263 W17-18

57B Av SUR.... 225 N31 N34 N36-37 226 M-N41
57B St DEL............ 243 T18

58 Av DEL............ 224 M30
58 Av LGT............ 227 M-N50
58 Av SUR............ 224 M29 M30
...... 225 M31-34 M34-35 M35 M36 M36-37 N37
...... 226 M40 M45 M-N41 M-N42 M-N43 M-N44 M-N45
58 Av E VAN............ 183 Z15-16 Z17 Z19-20
58 Av W VAN............ 182 Z11 Z11-13 Z14
58 St DEL............ 223 P18 263 W18
58A Av SUR.. 225 M31 M32 M33 M34 M35 M37
...... M38 226 M39-40 M41 M42 M42-43 M43
...... M43-44 M44 M45
58A St DEL............ 223 P18 263 W18
58B Av SUR............ 225 M33 226 M43-44
58B St DEL............ 223 P18

59 Av DEL............ 224 M27
59 Av SUR.. 224 M30 225 M31 M32 M33 M33-34
...... M34 M37 M38
...... 226 M40 M41 M42 M43 M44 M45 M46
59 Av E VAN............ 183 Z15-17 Z19
59 Av W VAN............ 182 Z11 Z11-12 Z12-14
59 St DEL............ 223 P18
59A Av SUR.. 225 M31 M33 M34 M35 M36 M36-37
...... 226 M40 M41-42 M42 M43 M43-44 M45 M45-46
59A St DEL............ 223 P18
59B Av SUR............ 225 M33 M36

60 Av DEL............ 223 M19-20
60 Av SUR.... 225 M31-37 M37-38 226 M40-46
60 Av E VAN............ 183 A15-16 A16-17
60 Av W VAN............ 182 A13 Z11 Z11-12 Z13
60A Av SUR
... 225 M31 M32 M33 M33-34 M35 M36 M38
...... 226 M39-40 M40 M41 M42 M43-44 M45 M46
60A St DEL............ 223 P18
60B Av SUR............ 225 M33 226 M45
60B St DEL............ 243 Q18

61 Av LGT............ 227 M51
61 Av SUR............ 224 M30
...... 225 M31 M31-32 M32 M33 M35 M36 M37
...... 226 M40-41 M43 M46
61 Av E VAN............ 182 A14 183 A15-18
61 Av W VAN............ 182 A11-12 A13 Z11
61 St DEL............ 223 P18 243 Q18
61A Av SUR... 225 M31 M32 M33 M34 M36 M37
...... 226 M39-40 M41 M41-42 M43 M44
61B Av SUR............ 225 M32-33 M37
...... 226 M41-42 M42 M43

62 Av SUR............ 224 M30
...... 225 M31 M32 M32-33 M33-34 M36 M37
...... 226 M40 M41 M42 M43 M44 M45 M46
62 Av (Sheridan Rd.) LGC...... 227 M47-48
62 Av E VAN.. 182 A14 183 A15-17 A17-20
62 Av W VAN...... 182 A11 A11-12 A13 A13-14
62 St DEL............ 223 P18-19 243 Q18-19
62A Av SUR
... 225 M31 M32 M33 M33-34 M34 M35 M37-38
...... 226 L-M46 M40 M41-42 M42 M44-45 M46
62B Av SUR 225 L32 L-M33 L-M34 L-M35 226 M45
62B St DEL............ 223 L19

63 Av DEL............ 224 L28
63 Av SUR.... 225 L31 L31-32 L33 L33-34 L-M34
...... 226 L41 L42 L46 L-M42 L-M43 L-M44 L-M45 M40
63 Av E VAN.. 182 A14 183 A15 A15-17 A17 A19
63 Av W VAN...... 182 A11 A11-12 A13 A13-14 A14
63 St DEL............ 243 Q19
63A Av DEL............ 224 L28
63A Av SUR............ 225 L31 L32 L33 L34
...... 226 L40 L42 L43 L44 L45 L46
63A St DEL............ 223 P19 243 Q19
63B Av SUR............ 225 L32 L34 226 L43 L45

64 Av DEL............ 224 L27-28 L29 L30
64 Av LGT............ 226 L46 227 L50 L51 L54
64 Av SUR.... 225 L31-32 L34-38 226 L39-46
64 Av (Bose Rd) SUR............ 226 L39
64 Av (Matheson Rd) LGT.. 226 L46 227 L47-48
64 Av (Medd Rd) LGT............ 227 L51-53
64 Av E VAN............ 182 A14
...... 183 A15 A15 A15-16 A16 A17
64 Av FG-N SUR
...... 182 A11-12 A12-13 A13-14 A14
64 St DEL............ 223 L-N19 N-P19 243 Q-T19
64A Av DEL............ 224 L28 L28-29 L30
64A Av SUR............ 225 L31 L32 L33 L35
...... 226 L42 L43 L44 L46
64B Av DEL............ 224 L30
64B Av SUR............ 226 L44

65 Av LGT............ 227 L48
65 Av SUR.. 225 L31 L32 L32-33 L33 L34 L36
...... 226 L44 L45 L46
65 Av E VAN............ 183 A15 A15-16
65 Av W VAN............ 182 A11-12 A13-14
65A Av SUR.... 225 L31 L33 L33-34 L34 L36-37
...... 226 L42 L43 L44 L44-45
65A St DEL............ 243 Q19

65B Av DEL............ 223 L19
65B Av SUR............ 225 L33
65B Pl LGT............ 226 L46
65B St DEL............ 263 Z19

66 Av DEL............ 227 L47-48
66 Av SUR 225 L31-32 L32-33 L34 L35 L36 L37-38
...... 226 L41 L42-43 L43-44 L44 L44-45 L46
66 Av E (Anderson Rd) LGT...... 227 L47-48
66 Av W VAN...... 182 A11 A11-12 A13
66 St DEL............ 243 Q19 263 Z19
66A Av LGT............ 227 L48
66A Av SUR.. 225 L32-33 L33 L33-34 L35 L37
...... 226 L42 L43 L44 L46
66A St DEL............ 263 Z19
66B Av LGT............ 227 L48
66B Av SUR.. 225 L32 L32-33 L33 L34

67 Av LGT............ 227 L48 L48-49
67 Av SUR............ 225 L32 L33 L34 L35 L37
...... 226 L43-44 L45 L46
67 Av E VAN............ 183 A16
67 Av W VAN............ 182 A12-13
67A Av LGT............ 227 L48
67A Av SUR.. 225 K-L31 L32 L33 L34 L35 L36 L37
...... 226 L44 L45
67A St DEL............ 263 Z19-20
67B Av LGT............ 227 K-L40 L40
67B Av SUR.. 225 K-L32 L33 L36

68 Av LGT............ 226 K46 K46
...... 227 K47 K47-48 K48-49 K53
68 Av SUR.. 225 K31-34 K34-38 226 K43-44 K45
68 Av W VAN............ 182 A11 A12 A13 A14
68 St DEL............ 263 K-M20
68A Av LGT.. 226 K46 227 K47 K47-48
68A Av SUR
... 225 K31 K31-32 K32 K33 K33-34 K35 K36 K36-37
...... 226 K42 K43 K44 K45 K46
68B Av LGT............ 227 K47
68B Av SUR............ 225 K35 226 K45

69 Av LGT............ 227 K47 K48 K49
69 Av SUR.. 225 K31-32 K32 K33 K33-34 K35 K36
...... 226 K43 K44 K45-46
69 Av E VAN............ 182 A14 183 A15-15
69 Av W VAN............ 182 A11-12 A13 A14
69A Av LGT.. 226 K46 227 K47 K49
69A Av SUR.. 226 K31 K32 K33 K35 K36 K36-37
...... 226 K45
69B Av LGT.. 225 K46 227 K47 K47 K49
69B Av SUR............ 225 K36

70 Av DEL............ 224 K30
70 Av LGT............ 226 K46 227 K47 K48 K49
70 Av SUR.. 225 K31-32 K32 K34-35 K35 K36 K37
...... 226 K43 K44 K45-46
70 Av E VAN............ 182 A11-13 A13 A14
70A Av LGT............ 227 K53-54 K54
70A Av SUR.. 225 K31 K32 K33 K34 K35 K37
...... 226 K43 K45 K46
70B Av SUR............ 225 K33 226 K45

71 Av DEL............ 224 K29 K30
71 Av LGT............ 227 K53
71 Av SUR. 225 K31 K32 K33-34 K34 K35 K36 K37
...... 226 K43 K44 K45 K46
71 Av W VAN...... 182 A13 A14 A-B12 A-B13
71A Av DEL............ 224 K30
71A Av LGT............ 227 K47-48
71A Av SUR............ 225 K31 K35 K36 K37
...... 226 K43 K45 K46
71B Av LGT............ 227 K47 K49
71B Av SUR............ 225 K33

72 Av DEL............ 224 K28-30
72 Av LGT............ 227 K49 K52 K53 K54
72 Av SUR............ 225 K31-38 K44-46
72 Av (Jericho Rd) LGT.. 226 K46 227 K47-48
72 Av W VAN............ 182 B12
72 St DEL.... 223 K21 N-P21 243 Q-T21
72A Av DEL.... 204 J29 J30 224 K29 K30
72A Av LGT............ 226 K46 227 K47
72A Av SUR.. 205 J31 J32 J34 J35 J36
...... 225 K31 K32 K33 K34 K35 K36 226 K46
72B Av LGT.. 207 J48 226 K46 227 K47 K48
72B Av SUR............ 205 J32 225 K32 K33

73 Av DEL............ 204 J29 J30
73 Av LGT............ 207 J47 J53
73 Av SUR. 205 J31 J32-33 J33 J34 J35 J36 J37
...... 206 J44 J46 226 K44
73 Av W VAN............ 182 B12
73A Av DEL............ 204 J30
73A Av LGT............ 207 J53
73A Av SUR. 205 J31 J31-32 J33 J34 J35 J36 J37
...... 206 J46
73B Av LGT.. 206 J46 207 J49
73B Av SUR............ 205 J32 J37 206 J46

74 Av DEL............ 204 J29 J30
74 Av LGT............ 207 J47-48 J53
74 Av SUR.. 205 J31 J32-33 J34-35 J35 J36 J37
...... 206 J44-45
74 Av W VAN............ 182 B12-13
74A Av DEL............ 204 J29 J30
74A Av SUR.. 205 J31 J31-32 J35 J35-36 J36
74B Av DEL............ 204 J30
74B Av LGT............ 207 J48

75 Av DEL............ 204 J29
75 Av LGT............ 207 J53-54
75 Av SUR.. 205 J31-32 J35 J36 J37 206 J44
75 Av W VAN............ 182 A-B11 B12 B12-13
75A Av DEL............ 204 J29-30
75A Av LGT............ 207 J47
75A Av SUR.. 204 J30 205 J31 J35 J36 J37
75B Av DEL............ 204 J29
75B Av SUR............ 205 J35

76 Av DEL............ 204 J30
76 Av LGT.. 206 J46 207 J47 J48 J49 J50
76 Av SUR.. 204 J30 205 J31 J31-34 J35 J36-37
...... 206 J39 J44-46
76 Av W VAN............ 182 B12-13
76 St DEL............ 203 J21
76A Av DEL............ 204 J29 J30
76A Av LGT............ 207 J53
76A Av SUR............ 204 J30
...... 205 J31 J32 J33-34 J35 J36 J36-37 J37
...... 206 J39
76B Av LGT............ 207 H-J53 J50-51
76B Av SUR............ 205 J31 J36
76B Cr LGT............ 207 J53

77 Av DEL............ 204 J29 J30
77 Av SUR.. 205 J31 J34 J34-35 J35 J36
...... 206 J39 J39-40
77 Av W VAN............ 182 B12-13
77A Av DEL............ 204 H29 H30
77A Av LGT............ 207 H-J53 J49
77A Av SUR
...... 205 H31-32 H-J31 H-J35 J32 J34 J35-36 J36
...... 206 H-J39 H-J40
77B Av DEL............ 204 H30
77B Av SUR............ 205 H32

78 Av DEL............ 204 H28-29 H29 H29-30 H30
78 Av LGT............ 207 H48 H50 H53
78 Av SUR.. 205 H31 H32 H33-34 H34 H35 H36
...... 206 J39 J39-40 H46
78A Av DEL............ 204 H28 H29 H30
78A Av SUR 205 H31-32 H33 H34-35 H35 H36 H38
...... 206 H39-40 H41
78B Av DEL............ 204 H29 H30
78B Av LGT............ 207 H47
78B Av SUR............ 206 H39 H41

79 Av DEL............ 204 H28 H29 H30
79 Av LGT............ 207 H51-52 H52
79 Av SUR. 205 H32 H33-34 H34-35 H35 H36 H38
...... 206 H39 H39-40 H41
79A Av DEL............ 204 H28 H29 H30
79A Av SUR
...... 205 H31-32 H33 H34 H34-35 H35 H36 H38
...... 206 H39-40 H40 H41
79B Av SUR............ 206 H40 H41

80 Av DEL............ 204 H28-30
80 Av LGT............ 207 H49 H53
80 Av SUR.. 205 H31-34 H34-35 H36 H37 H38
...... 206 H39-40 H41-46
80 Av (McLarty Rd) LGT.. 206 H46 207 H47-48
80 Av FG-N SUR............ 206 H41
80 St DEL............ 203 H-J22 243 Q22
80A Av DEL............ 204 H29 H30
80A Av LGT............ 207 H47
80A Av SUR.. 205 H31 H34 H36 H37 H38 H38
...... 206 H39 H39 H39-40 H40
80B Av SUR.. 205 H31 H34 H36 H36-37 H37

81 Av DEL............ 204 H29 H30
81 Av SUR.. 205 H31 H33-34 H37-38 H38
81A Av DEL.. 204 H28-29 H29 H29-30 H30
81A Av LGT............ 207 H49-50
81A Av SUR. 205 H31 H33 H36 H37 H38 206 H41
81B Av LGT............ 207 H48-49
81B Av SUR.. 205 H33 H33-34 H37 206 H41

82 Av DEL............ 204 H28-30
82 Av LGT.
.. 206 H46 207 G-H50 H47 H47-48 H48-49 H50 H51
82 Av SUR.
.... 205 H31-32 H33 H35 H36 H36-37 H37 H37-38
...... 206 H39-40 H41
82 St DEL............ 203 H22 204 H23
82A Av DEL............ 204 G-H29 H30
82A Av LGT............ 207 H49
82A Av SUR
.. 205 G31 G36 G37 G-H33 G-H35 G-H37 G-H38 H-39
...... 206 G-H46

82B Av *DEL* . . . . . . . . . . . . . . . . . . . 204 G30
82B Av *SUR* . . . . . . . . . . . . . . . . 205 G33 G35

83 Av *DEL* . . . . . . . 204 G28 G29 G29-30 G30
83 Av *LGT* . . . . . . 206 G46 G46 207 G47 G-H49
83 Av *SUR* . . . . . . . 205 G35 G36 G37 G38 G38
. . . . . . . . . . . . 206 G39 G39 G40 G41 G43-44
83A Av *DEL* . . . . . . . . 204 G28-29 G29-30 G30
83A Av *LGT* . . . . . . . . . . . . . . . 207 G48 G49
83A Av *SUR*
. 205 G31 G33-34 G35 G36 G36-37 G37 G37-38 G38
. . . . . . . . . . . . . . . . . . . . . 206 G39 G41
83B Av *LGT* . . . . . . . . . . . . . . 207 G48 G49 G50
83B Av *SUR* . . . . . . . . . . . . . . . . . . 205 G37

84 Av *DEL* . . . . . . . . . . . . . . . 204 G28-30
84 Av *LGT* . . 206 G46 207 G47 G47-48 G48-49 G50
84 Av *SUR* . . . . . 205 G31 G32-34 G35 G36-38
. . . . . . . . . . . . . . . 206 G39-40 G41 G45
84A Av *DEL* . . . . . . . . . . . . . . . 204 G29 G30
84A Av *SUR* . . . . . . .
. . . . . . . 205 G31 G33 G35 G36 G37 G38 206 G40 G41
84B Av *DEL* . . . . . . . . . . . . . . . 204 G29 G30
84B Av *LGT* . . . . . . . . . . . . . 207 G48 G50
84B Av *SUR* . . . . . . . . . . . . . . . . 205 G35

85 Av *DEL* . . . . . . . . . . . . . . . . . . 204 G29
85 Av *LGT* . . . . . . . . . 207 G47 G49-50 G50
85 Av *SUR* . . . . . . . . . . . . . . . . . . . 204 G30
. . . . . 205 G31 G32 G33-34 G35 G36 G37 G38
. . . . . . . . . 206 G39 G39-40 G40 G41 G45
85 Ct *LGT* . . . . . . . . . . . . . . . . . . 207 G50
85A Av *DEL* . . . . . . . . . 204 G28 G29 G30
85A Av *LGT* . . . . . . . . . . . . . . . . 207 G49
85A Av *SUR* . . . . 204 G30 205 G31 G35 G36 G37
. . . . . . . . . . . . . . . . . . . 206 G40 G41
85A Ct *LGT* . . . . . . . . . . . . . . . . 207 G50
85A Pl *LGT* . . . . . . . . . . . . . . . . 207 G50
85B Av *DEL* . . . . . . . . . 204 G28 G29 G30
85B Av *LGT* . . . . . . . . . . . . . . . . 207 G50
85B Av *SUR* . . . . . . . . . . . . 205 G35 206 G40
85B Ct *LGT* . . . . . . . . . . . . . . . . 207 G50

86 Av *DEL* . . . . . . . . . . . . . . . 204 G28-30
86 Av *LGT* . . . . . . 207 G47 G47-48 G49 G50
86 Av *SUR* . . 205 G31 G33 G35 G36-37 G37-38
. . . . . . . . . . . . 206 G39 G40 G45
86 Ct *LGT* . . . . . . . . . . . . . . . . 207 G50
86A Av *DEL* . . . . . . . . . 204 G28 G29 G30
86A Av *LGT* . . . . . . . . . 207 G48 G49-50 G51
86A Av *SUR* . . . . . . 205 G35 G36 G37 G38
. . . . . . . . . . . . . 206 G39 G40 G40-41
86A Cr *LGT* . . . . . . . . . . . . . . . . 207 G50
86B Av *SUR* . . . . . . 205 G35 G36 G37 G38
. . . . . . . . . . . . . . . 206 G39 G39-40

87 Av *DEL* . . . . . . . . . . . . . . . 204 G29 G30
87 Av *LGT* . . . . . . . . . 207 G48-49 G50
87 Av *SUR* . . . . . 205 F-G35 G32 G36 G38
. . . . . . . . . . . 206 F-G41 G39 G39-40 G46
87 Pl *LGT* . . . . . . . . . . . . . . . . 207 G50
87A Av *DEL* . . . . . . . . . . . 204 F29-30 F30
87A Av *LGT* . . . . . . . . . . . . . . . . 207 G50
87A Av *SUR*
. . . 205 F37 F38 F-G32 F-G35 F-G36 F-G38 G33-34
. . . . . . . . . . . . 206 F39 G40 G45
87B Av *LGT* . . . . . . . . . . . 207 F-G50 G50
87B Av *SUR* . . . . . . . . . . . 205 F33-34 F37

88 Av *DEL* . . . . . . . . . . . . . . . 204 F29 F30
88 Av *LGT* . . . . . . . . . 207 F47 F48 F51 F53-54
88 Av *SUR* . . . . . . 205 F31-38 206 F39-46
88 Av (McClughan Rd) *LGT* . . . . 207 F48-50
88 Av (Sellers Rd) *LGT* . . . . . 207 F51-53
88 Av *FG-N* *SUR* . . . . . . . . . . . . 205 F35
88 St *DEL* . . . . 204 H24 224 P24 244 Q-R24
88A Av *DEL* . . . . . . . . . . . . . . . 204 F29 F30
88A Av *LGT* . . . . . . . . . . . . . 207 F48 F50
88A Av *SUR* . . 205 F32 F33 F34 F35 F36 F37 F38
. . . . . . . . . . . . . . . . 206 F39 F44
88B Av *LGT* . . . . . . . . . . . . . . 207 F48 F50

89 Av *DEL* . . . . . . . . . . . . . . . 204 F29 F30
89 Av *LGT* . . . . . . . . . . . . . 207 F48 F50
89 Av *SUR* . . . . 205 F32 F33 F34-35 F35 F36-38
. . . . . . . . . . . . 206 F39 F39 F40
89A Av *DEL* . . . . . . . . . . . . . . 204 F29 F30
89A Av *LGT* . . . . . . . . . 207 F48 F48-49 F50
89A Av *SUR*
. . . . 205 F32 F33 F34 F35 F35-36 F36 F37 F38
. . . . . . . . . . . . . . . . 206 F39 F39
89B Av *LGT* . . . . . . . . . . . . . 207 F48 F50
89B Av *SUR* . . . . . . . 205 F35 F38 206 F44

90 Av *DEL* . . . . . . . . . . . . 204 F29 F29-30
90 Av *LGT* . . . . . . . . . 207 F48 F48-49 F50
90 Av *SUR* . . . . . . . . . . . . . . . . . 204 F30
. . . 205 F31-32 F33-34 F34 F35 F36-37 F38
. . . . . . . . . . . . 206 F39-40 F40 F45
90A Av *DEL* . . . . . . . . . . . . . . . . . 204 F30
90A Av *LGT* . . . . . . . 207 F48 F48-49 F50 F51

90A Av *SUR* . . . . . . . . . . . . . . . . . 204 F30
. . . 205 F31 F34 F34-35 F35 F36 F37 F38 206 F39
90B Av *LGT* . . . . . . . . . . . . . . . . 207 F51
90B Av *SUR* . . . . . . . . . . . . . . . . 206 F39

91 Av *DEL* . . . . . . . . . . . . . . . . . 204 F29 F30
91 Av *LGT* . . . . . 207 F48-49 F49 F50 F50-51
91 Av *SUR* . .
. . 205 F31 F31-32 F33-34 F34 F35 F36 F37 F38 F38
. . . . . . . . . . . . . . . . 206 F39 F39
91A Av *DEL* . . . . . . . . . . . . . . . . . 204 F29 F30
91A Av *LGT* . . . . . 207 F47 F48 F48-49 F49
91A Av *SUR*
. . . 205 F31 F32 F33 F34 F34-35 F35 F36 F37 F38
. . . . . . . . . . . . . . . . 206 F39 F40
91B Av *LGT* . . . . . . 207 F48 F48-49 F50
91B Av *SUR* . . . . . . . . . . . . . . . . 205 F36

92 Av *DEL* . . . . . . . . . . . . . . . . . . 204 F29
92 Av *LGT* . . . . . . 206 F46 207 E-F47 F49 F50
92 Av *SUR* . . . . . . 205 F31-32 F33-35 F35-38
. . . . . . . 206 F39-40 F41 F42-45 F46
92A Av *DEL* . . . . . . . 204 E29-30 E30 E-F29
92A Av *LGT* . . . . . . 207 E-F47 F49 F50
92A Av *SUR* . . . . . . . . . . . . . . 204 E30
. 205 E31 E32 E33-34 E37 E38 E-F31 206 E39 E-F40
92B Av *LGT* . . . . . . 207 E49 E-F50 F50-51
92B Av *SUR* . . . . . . . . . . . . . 205 E33 E38

93 Av *DEL* . . . . . . . . . . . . . 204 E29-30 E30
93 Av *LGT* . . . . . . . . . 207 E49 E50 E51
93 Av *SUR* . . . . 205 E31 E32 E37 E38 206 E39
93 Pl *LGT* . . . . . . . . . . . . . . . . 207 E50
93A Av *DEL* . . . . . . . . . . . . . 204 E29-30
93A Av *LGT* . . . . . . 207 E47-48 E48 E49 E50
93A Av *SUR*
. 205 E31 E32 E33 E34 E34-35 E36-37 E37 E38 E38
. . . . . . . . . 206 E39 E40 E42-43
93B Av *LGT* . . . . . . . . 207 E48 E49 E50
93B Av *SUR* . . . . . . . . . . . . . . . 206 E40
93B Pl *LGT* . . . . . . . . . . . . . . . . 207 E49

94 Av *DEL* . . . . . . . . . . . . . 204 E29-30 E30
94 Av *LGT* . . . . . . 207 E47-48 E48 E49 E50
94 Av *SUR* . . . . . . . . . . . . . . . . . . 204 E30
. . . 205 E31 E31-32 E32 E33 E34-35 E37 E37-38 E38
. . . . 206 E39 E39-40 E43 E43-44 E45 E46
94A Av *DEL* . . . . . . . . . . . . . 204 E29-30 E30
94A Av *LGT* . . . . 206 E46 E46 207 E47 E48 E50
94A Av *SUR*
. . . . 205 E31 E32 E33-34 E34 E34-35 E37 E38
. . . . . . . . . . . . . . . 206 E39 E41
94B Av *LGT* . . . . . . . . . . 207 E48 E49 E50

95 Av *DEL* . . . . . . . 204 E29 E29-30 E30
95 Av *LGT* . . . . . . . . . . . . . . 207 E50-51
95 Av *SUR* . . . . . . . . . . . . . . . . . . 204 E30
. . . 205 E31 E32 E33 E33-34 E36-37 E37 E38 E38
. . . . . . . . . . . . 206 E39 E39 E40
95A Av *DEL* . . . . . . . . . . . . . 204 E29-30 E30
95A Av *LGT* . . . . 207 E48 E49 E49-50 E50 E51
95A Av *SUR* . . . 205 E31 E33 E36 E37 E37-38 E38
. . . . . . . . . . . . 206 E39 E39-40 E45
95B Av *LGT* . . . . . . . . . . . . . . . . 207 E51

96 Av *DEL* . . . . . 206 E46 207 E47 E49-50 E52-53
96 Av *SUR* 204 E29 205 E31-38 206 E39-43 E44-46
96 Av (Wilson Cr) *LGT* . . . . . . . 207 E-F53 F54
96 Av (Wilson Townline Rd) *LGT* . . . . 206 E46
. . . . . . . . . . . . 207 E47-48 E49-52
96 St *DEL* . 204 H26 224 N25-26 P25-26 244 Q-R26
96A Av *LGT* . . . . . . . . . . . . . 207 E48-49
96A Av *SUR* . . . 204 E30 205 E31 E32 E33 E37 E38
. . . . . . . . . . . . . . . . . . . 206 E39
96B Av *LGT* . . . . . . . . . . . . . . . . 207 E48
96B Av *SUR* . . . . . . . 205 E32 E38 206 E39

97 Av *LGT* . . . . . 207 E47-48 E49 E49-50
97 Av *SUR* . . . . . . . . . . . . . 204 E30 E30
. . . . . . 205 E31 E31-32 E32 E33 E34 E37 E38
. . . . . . . . . . . . 206 E42-43 E44
97A Av *LGT* . . . . . . . . . . . . . . . . 207 D48
97A Av *SUR* . . 184 D30 185 D31 D32 D37 D38 D38
. . . . . . . 186 D39 204 E29-30 205 E31 E32 E37 E38
97A Cr *LGT* . . . . . . . . . . . . 187 D48 207 E49
97B Av *LGT* . . . . . . . . . . . . 187 D48 207 E49
97B Av *SUR*
. . . . . . 184 D29-30 185 D31-32 D37 205 E34

98 Av *LGT* . . . . 186 D46 D46 187 D47 D47 D48
98 Av *SUR* . . . . . . . . . . . . . . . . . . 184 D30
. . . 185 D31 D32 D32-33 D33 D34 D37 D38 186 D43
98 Av (Mitchell Rd) *LGT* . . . . . . . 187 D48 D48
98A Av *LGT* . . . . . . . . . . . . . . . . 187 D48
98A Av *SUR* . . . . . . . . . . . . . . . . 184 D30
. . . . 185 D31 D32-33 D33 D34 D37 D38
. . . . . . . . . . . . 186 D39 D43 D45 D46
98B Av *LGT* . . . . . . . . . . . . . . . . 186 D46
98B Av *SUR* . . . . . 185 D32-33 D33-34 186 D39

99 Av *SUR* . . . . . . . . . . . . . . . . 184 D30
. . . 185 D31-32 D32-33 D33 D34 D37-38 D38
. . . . . . . . . . . . . . 186 D39 D39
99A Av *LGT* . . . . . . . . . . . . . . . . 187 D47
99A Av *SUR* . . . . . . . . . . . . . . . . 184 D30
. . . 185 D31 D32 D32-33 D33 D34 D37 D38 186 D43
99B Av *SUR* . . . . . . . . . . . . 185 D38 186 D39

100 Av *LGT* . . . . . . . . . . . . . . 187 D51-52
100 Av *SUR* . . . 184 D30 185 D31 D31-33 D34-38
. . . . . . . . . . . . . . 186 D41 D42
100A Av *LGT* . . . . . . . . . . . . . . . . 187 D47
100A Av *SUR* . . . . . 184 D30 185 D31 D33 D35
. . . . . . . . . . . . . . 186 D39 D43

101 Av *LGT* . . . . . . . . . . . . . . . . 187 D47
101 Av *SUR* . . . . . . . . . . . . . . . . 184 D30
. . . 185 D31 D33 D34 D35 D36 D37-38 D38
. . . . . . . . . . . . . . 186 D39 D42
101A Av *LGT* . . . . . . . . . . . . . . . . 187 D47
101A Av *SUR*
185 D31 D33 D34 D35 D36 D36-37 D37-38 D38 D38
. . . . . . . . . . . 86 D39 D39 D41 D42
101B Av *SUR* . . . . 184 D30 185 D31 D32 D33

102 Av *LGT* . . . . . . . . 187 D47-48 D51-52
102 Av *SUR* . . . . . . . . . . . . . . . . 184 D30
. . . 185 D31 D32-33 D34 D35 D36 D38
. . . . . . 186 C40 D39-40 D41 D42
102A Av *SUR* . . . . . . . . . . . . . . . . 184 D30
. . . . 185 C31 C33 C37 C37-38 C-D36 D35 D38
. . . . . . . . . . . . . . 186 C41 D39
102B Av *LGT* . . . . . . . . . . . . 187 C48 C49
102B Av *SUR* . . . 185 C35 C36 C38 C38 186 C39
102B Av (White Rd) *LGT* . . . . . . 187 C48-49

103 Av *SUR*
. . . . . 185 C32 C33 C33-34 C34 C35 C36 C36-37
. . . . . . . . . . . . 186 C39 C40-41 C41
103A Av *SUR* . . . . . . . . . . . . . . . . 184 C30
. . . 185 C31 C33 C33-34 C35 C36 C36-37 C37-38
. . . . . . . . . . . . . . 186 C41 C42
103B Av *SUR* . . . . . . . . . . . . . . . 186 C42

104 Av *LGT* . . . . . . . . . . . . . . 187 C51-52
104 Av *SUR* . . . . . . 185 C31-38 186 C39-43
104 St *DEL* . . . . 204 G-H27 224 L-P27 244 Q-R27
104A Av *SUR* . . . . 185 C32 C33 C34 C36 C38
. . . . . . . . . . . . . . 186 C41 C42
104B Av *SUR* . . . . . . . . . . . . . . . 185 C32

105 Av *MAP* . . . . . . . . . . . . . . . 187 C54
105 Av *SUR* 185 C32 C33-34 C34 C36 C37 C37-38
. . . . . . . . . . . . 186 C40-41 C41
105A Av *SUR* . . . . . . . . . . . . . . .
. . . . . 185 C32 C33-34 C34 C36 C38 186 C39 C41

106 Av *SUR* . . . . 185 C32-33 C34 C35 C36 C38 C38
. . . . . . . . . . . . . . 186 C39 C41
106A Av *SUR* . . . . . . . . . . . . . . . .
. . . . . . 185 C32 C32-33 C33 C36 C38 186 C39

107 Av *SUR* . . . 185 C32-33 C34 C36 C38 186 C39
107A Av *SUR* . . . . . . . . . . . . . . . .
. . . 185 B38 B38 B-C32 B-C33 B-C36 B-C37 C34 C38
. . . . . . . . . . . . . . . 186 B39 C39

108 Av *SUR* . . . 185 B33 B34-35 B36-37 B37 B38
. . . . . . . . . . . . . . . B39 B40
108 St *DEL* . . . . . . . . . . . . . . . 204 G-H28
108A Av *SUR* . . . . . . 185 B36 B36-37 B38
. . . . . . . . . . . 186 B39 B39-40 B40
108A St *DEL* . . . . . . . . . . . . . . 224 L28 M28
108B Av *MAP* . . . . . . . . . . . . . . . 187 B54
108B Av *SUR* . . . . . . . . . . . . . . . 186 B40
108B St *DEL* . . . . . . . . . . . . . . . 204 H28

109 Av *MAP* . . . . . . . . . . . . . . . 187 B54
109 Av *SUR* . . . . . . . . . . . . . . . .
185 B31 B32-33 B34-35 B35 B36 B38 186 B39 B40
109 St *DEL* . . . . . . . . . . . . . . . . 224 L28
109A Av *SUR* . . . . . . 185 B36 B38 186 B39 B40
109A St *DEL* . . . . . . . . . . . 204 H28 224 L28
109B St *DEL* . . . . . . . . . . . 204 G28 G-H28

110 Av *SUR*. . . . . . . . . . . . . . . .
. . . 185 B32 B32-33 B34 B35 B36 B37-38 B38
. . . . . . . . . . . . . 186 B39 B39-40
110 St *DEL* . . . . . . . . . . . 204 H28 H28-29
110A Av *SUR* . . . . . . 185 B34 B36 B37-38
. . . . . . . . . . . 186 B39 B39-40
110A St *DEL* . . . . . 204 F-G29 G28-29 H28 H28-29

111 Av *SUR* . . . 185 B32-33 B34 B36 B37 B38
. . . . . . . . . . . . . 186 B39 B39 B40
111 St *DEL* . . . . . . . . . . . . . 204 G29 H29
111A Av *SUR*
. . . . . 185 B31 B33-34 B34 B36 B37 B38 186 B39

111A St *DEL* . . . . . . . . . . 204 G29 J29
111B St *DEL* . . . . . . . . . . 204 G29 G-H29

112 Av *SUR*. . . . . . . . . . . . . . . .
. . . 185 B31 B32-33 B34 B37-38 B38 186 B39
112 St *DEL* . . . . 204 F-J29 224 N-P29 244 Q29
112A Av *SUR* . 185 A31 A-B31 A-B32 A-B33 A-B34
. . . . . . . . . . . A-B35 A-B38 B33
112A St *DEL* . . . 204 F29 G29 G-H29 H29 J29
112B Av *SUR* . . . . . . . 185 A32 A33 186 A-B39
112B St *DEL* . . . . . . . . . . . . . 204 H29

113 Av *MAP* . . . . . . . 187 A48-49 A53
113 Av *SUR*. . . . . . . . . . . . . . . .
. . . 185 A31 A33-34 A34-35 A37-38 186 A39
113 St *DEL* . . . . . . . . . . . . . 204 F29 J29
113A Av *MAP* . . . . . . . . . . . . . . . 187 A54
113A Av *SUR* . . . . . . 185 A32 A35 186 A39
113A St *DEL* . . . . 204 E29 F29 G29 H29 J29
113B Av *MAP* . . . . . . . . . . . . . 187 A47-48
113B Av *SUR* . . . 185 A31-32 A32 A33 186 A39
113B St *DEL* . . . . . . . . . . 204 E29 G29 H29

114 Av *MAP* . . . . . . . 187 A48-49 A54
114 Av *SUR*. . . . . . . . . . . . . . . .
. 185 A31-32 A32 A33 A34-35 A35 A38 186 A39 A39
114 St *DEL* . . . . . . . 204 E-F29 G-H29 J29
114A Av *MAP* . . . . . . . . . . . . . . . 187 A54
114A Av *SUR* . . . . . 185 A32 A34 A35 A36
114A St *DEL*
. . . . . . 204 E29 F29 G29 H29 H-J29 J29 224 K29
114B Av *MAP* . . . . . . . . . . . . . 187 A48
114B Av *PTM* . . . . . . . . . . . . . 186 A46
114B Av *SUR* . . . . . . . . . . . . . 185 A32

115 Av *MAP* . . . . . . . . . . . 187 A48 A49
115 Av *SUR* . . . . . 185 A32 A34 A35 A35-36
115 St *DEL*
. . . . . 204 E29 E-F29 G29-30 H-J29 224 K29-30
115A Av *MAP* . . . . . . . . . . . 187 A47-48 A48
115A Av *PTM* . . . . . . . . . . . . . 186 A46
115A Av *SUR* . . 185 A32 A33 A34-35 A35 A36
115A St *DEL*. 204 E30 F30 G30 H-J30 J30 224 K30
115A St *SUR* . . . . . . . . . . 184 D30 204 E30
115B Av *PTM* . . . . . . . . . . . . . 186 A46
115B Av *SUR* . . . . . . . . . . 185 A32 A32-33

116 Av *MAP* . . . 187 A48 A49 A49-50 A52 A52-54
116 Av *SUR* . . . . 185 A32 A33-34 A34-35 A36
116 St *DEL* . . . . . . . 204 H-J30 224 K30 L30
116 St *SUR* . . . . . . . . . 184 D30 204 E30
116A Av *MAP* . . . . . . . . . . . . . . . 187 A54
116A Av *PTM* . . . 186 A46 A46 187 A47
116A Av *SUR* . . . . . . . . . . . . . 185 A36
116A St *DEL*
. . . . . . 204 E30 F30 G30 H30 H-J30 J30 224 L30
116A St *SUR* . . . . . . . . . . . . . 184 D30
116B Av *MAP* . . . . . . . . . . . 187 A48 Z48
116B Av *PTM* . . . 186 A46 A46 187 A47
116B St *DEL* . . . . . . . . . . . . . 204 F30 G30

117 Av *MAP*. . . . . . . . . . . . . . . .
. . . 187 A49-50 A51 A52 A53 A54 Z50 Z51 Z52 Z54
117 Av *PTM* . . . . . . . . . . . . . 186 A46
117 Av *SUR* . . . . . . . . . . . . . 185 A34-35
117 St *DEL* . . . . 204 E30 E-F30 F30 H30 H-J30
117 St *SUR* . . . . . . . . . . . . . 184 D30
117A Av *PTM* . . . . . . . . . . . . . 186 A45 A46
117A St *DEL* . . 204 E30 F30 G30 H30 J30 224 L30
117B Av *MAP* . . . . . . . . . . . . . 187 Z54
117B Av *PTM* . . . . . . . . . . . . . 186 Z45 Z46
117B St *DEL* . . . . . . . . . . . . . 204 G30
117B St *SUR* . . . . . . . . . . . . . 204 G30

118 Av *MAP* . . . . . . . 187 Z48 Z49 Z53-54 Z54
118 St *DEL* 204 E30 F30 G-H30 H-J30 J30 224 K30
118A St *DEL* . . . . . 204 F30 G30 H30 J30
118A Av *PTM* . . . . . . . . . . . . 186 Z45 Z46
118B St *DEL* . . . . . . . . . . . . . 204 E30
118B St *SUR* . . . . . . . . . . . . . 184 D30

119 Av *MAP* . . . 187 Z48 Z48-49 Z49 Z49-50 Z51
. . . . . . . . . . . Z51-52 Z52 Z53 Z54
119 Av *PTM* . . . . . . . . . . . . 186 Z45 Z46
119 St *DEL* . . . . . . . 204 E30 F30 G30 H30
119 St *SUR* . . . . . . . . . . . . . 184 D30
119A Av *MAP* . . . . . . . . . . . . . 187 Z47-48
119A Av *PTM* . . . . . . . . . . . . . 186 Z46
119A St *DEL* . 204 E30 F30 G30 G-H30 H-J30 J30
119A St *SUR* . . . . . . . . . . . . . 184 D30
119B Av *PTM* . . . . . . . . . . . . 186 Z45 Z46
119B St *DEL* . . . . . . . . . . . . . 204 H30

120 Av *PTM* . . . . . . . . . . . . 186 Z45 Z46
120 St *SUR* . . . . . . 185 D31 204 H30 J30
. . . . . . 205 E-G31 H31 J31 225 K-N31
120A Av *MAP* . . . . . . . . . . . . . 187 Z47-48 Z49
120A St *SUR* . . . . . . . . . . . . . 185 D31 D31
. . . 205 E31 E31 G31 G-H31 H31 J31 225 M31 N31
120B Av *MAP* . . . . . . . 187 Z47-48 Z48 Z49
120B Av *PTM* . . . . . . . . . . . . 186 Z45 Z46

121 Av MAP
.... 187 Z47-48 Z48 Z49 Z50 Z51 Z52 Z52-53
121 Av PTM......... 186 Z46
121 St SUR........ 185 C-D31 D31
.. 205 E31 E31 E-F31 F31 G31 225 K31 L-M31 M31
121A Av MAP... 167 Y47-48 187 Z47-48 Z53 Z54
121A Av PTM......... 186 Z46
121A St SUR..... 185 D31 C31 G31 H31 J31
........... 225 K-L31 L31 N31
121B Av MAP........... 187 Z48
121B Av PTM......... 186 Z45 Z46
122 Av MAP...... 167 Y48 Y50 Y50 Y52-53 Y53
.... 187 Z48 Z49-50 Z50 Z51-52 Z54
122 Av PTM......... 186 Z45
122 St SUR........ 185 C31 C-D31 D31
.. 205 E31 F31 G31 H-J31 J31 225 K31 L31 M31 N31
122A Av MAP........... 167 Y53-54
122A Av PTM......... 186 Z46
122A St SUR..... 205 G31 H31 J31 225 K31 L31
122B Av MAP........... 167 Y48 Y50 Y54
122B Av PTM...... 166 Y45 186 Z45
122B St SUR........... 205 F31

123 Av MAP
.... 167 Y47-48 Y48-51 Y51 Y52 Y52-53 Y53 Y54
123 Av PTM........... 166 Y46
123 PI MAP........... 167 Y54
123 St SUR........ 185 A31 D31
.. 205 E31 E31 F31 F-G31 G31 H31 H-J31 J31
........... 225 K31 L31 M31 N31 265 V31
123A Av MAP........... 167 Y54
123A Av PTM........... 166 Y45
123A St SUR..... 185 C31 C-D31 D31 D31
.. 205 E31 E31 F31 H31 H-J31 J31
.. 225 K31 K-L31 L31 M31 245 U31
123A Av MAP........... 167 Y48 Y54
123A Av PTM........... 166 Y45
123B Av MAP........... 167 Y48 Y49 Y53 Y54
123B Av PTM........... 166 Y45
123B St SUR........... 225 K31

124 Av MAP...... 167 Y48 Y49 Y50-53 Y53 Y54
124 Av PTM........... 166 Y45
124 St SUR...... 185 A31 B31 B-C31 C-D31 D31
.. 205 E-F31 F-G31 G-J31 225 K-L31 M31 N31
........... 245 U31 265 V31
124A Av MAP........... 167 Y48 Y54
124A Av PTM........... 166 Y45
124A St SUR........ 185 C-D31 D31 D31-32
.. 206 E31 E-F31 H31 J31 J31
.. 225 K31 K31 L31 M31 N31
124B Av MAP........... 167 Y48 Y53 Y53-54
124B St SUR
...... 185 D32 205 J32 225 N31-32 245 U32

125 Av MAP........... 167 Y48 Y49 Y51 Y52
125 St SUR........ 185 B32 C-D32 D32
.. 205 E32 F32 H32 J31-32 J32
125A Av MAP...... 167 Y52 Y52-53 Y53 Y54
125A St SUR..... 185 A32 C32 C-D32 D32
.. 205 E32 E32 F32 H32
.. 225 K32 L32 M32 N32 P32 245 U32
125B Av MAP........... 167 Y53
125B St SUR........... 185 C32 225 J32

126 Av MAP...... 167 Y50 Y50-52 Y53-54
126 St SUR..... 185 C-D32 D32 D32 205 E-F32
........... 225 K32 L-M32 M-N32
126 St (Crescent Heights) SUR
........... 225 L32 245 U32 265 V32 V-W32 W32
126A St SUR... 185 A32 B32 205 E32 E-F32 J32
.. 206 K32 M32 M-N32 N32 245 U32 265 W32
126B Av MAP........... 167 Y53
126B St SUR........... 225 K32 M32

127 Av MAP...... 167 Y53 Y51 Y52 Y52-53
127 PI MAP........... 167 Y53
127 St SUR........ 185 C32 C-D32 D32
.. 205 E32 E-F32 F32 H-J32 225 L32 M32 N32
127 St (Crescent Heights) SUR
........... 245 U32 265 V32 W32
127A St SUR 185 A32 C32 C-D32 D32 205 E32 J32
.. 225 K32 L32 M32 P32 245 U32 265 V32 W32
127B St SUR........... 185 C32 D32 245 U32

128 Av MAP...... 167 Y50 Y51-52 Y53-54
128 St SUR..... 185 A32 B32 C-D32 205 E-J32
........... 225 K-M32 M-N32
128 St (Crescent Heights) SUR ... 167 W52
........... 265 V-W32 X32
128A St SUR..... 185 B32 C-D32 D32 D32
.. 205 E32 F-G32 G32
.. 225 K32 K-L32 L32 L-M32 M32 N32
........... 245 U32 265 V32 V-W32 W32 X32
128B St SUR ..... 205 J32 225 K-L32 L32
129 Av MAP........... 167 Y52-53 X54
129 Av PTM........... 166 X42
129 St SUR.... 185 A32-33 B32 C32 C-D32 D32
.. 205 E32 E-F32 F-G32 G32 J32
........... 225 K32 K-L32 L32 L-M32 N32

129 St (Crescent Heights) SUR..........
........... 265 V32 V-W32 W32 X32
129A St SUR . 185 B32-33 C-D33 D32 D32-33 D33
........... 205 E32 E33 G32-33 J32 J32-33
........... 225 K32-33 L32-33 M32 245 U32
........... 265 V32 V-W32 W32 X32
129B St SUR........... 185 J33 225 K33 M32-33
........... 245 U33 265 V32-33 V33 V33 X32-33

130 Av MAP........... 167 X54
130 St SUR........ 185 D33 B33 C33 D33
.. 205 E33 F-G33 H33 J33 J33 225 K-L33 L-M33
130 St (Crescent Heights) SUR..........
........... 245 T-U33 U33 W-X33
130A St SUR........ 185 B33 D33 205 E33 J33
.. 225 L33 M33 245 U33 265 V33 V-W33
130B St SUR........... 205 F33 225 M33

131 St SUR... 185 A33 B33 D33 D33 205 E33 J33
........... 225 K33 K33 K-L33 L33 M33
131 St (Crescent Heights) SUR 265 V33 W-X33
131A St SUR
........ 185 B33 C33 D33 205 E33 E33 J33 J33
.. 225 K33 K33 L33 L-M33 M33 P33 265 V33
131B St SUR........... 265 V33

132 Av MAP .. 167 W-X51 W-X53 X48-49 X54 X54
132 St SUR
...... 185 A33 B33 C-D33 205 E-J33 225 K-N33
132 St (Crescent Heights) SUR..........
........... 245 T-U33 265 V33 W33
132 St Diversion SUR........... 185 B33
132A St SUR
.. 185 A33 B33 B-C33 C33 D33 205 E33 E-F33 H33
........... 225 L33 M33 M-N33 N33 265 V33 X33
132B St SUR..... 205 E-F33 F33 265 W33 X33

133 St SUR.... 185 A-A33 A-B33 B-C33 C-D33 D33
.. 205 E33 E-F33 H33 225 K33 L33 M33 M-N33
133 St (Crescent Heights) SUR..........
........... 245 U33 265 V33
133A Av MAP........... 167 W54
133A St SUR........ 185 A33 B33 C-D33 D33
.. 205 E33 E-F33 F33 G33 H33
.. 225 K33 L33 M33 M-N33 265 V33 X33
133B St SUR..... 225 K L33 L33 M33 265 V33 W33

134 St SUR........ 185 A34 D33 205 E-F33 F-G33 G33 H33 H-J33
........... 225 K-M33 M33 M-N33
134 St (Crescent Heights) SUR..........
........... 245 U33 265 V33 V-W33 W33
134A St SUR........ 185 B34 C33-34
.. 205 E33-34 E34 F33-34 G33-34 G34 H33-34
.. J33-34 J34 225 K34 K-L34 L-M34 M33 M33-34
........... 265 V-W34 W34
134B St SUR
...... 205 F34 G34 225 M33-34 N34 265 W34

135 St SUR... 185 A-B34 C-D34 205 E34 H34 J34
........... 225 K-L34 L34 M34 M-N34
135A St SUR........ 185 A-B34 C34 D34
.. 205 F34 G34 H34 H-J34 225 K34 L34 M34
........... 245 T34 265 V34 W34
135B St SUR........... 205 H34 225 L34

136 Av MAP........... 167 W52 W53-54
136 St SUR........ 185 A34 A-B34 225 M-N34
........... 245 S-T34 T-U34 265 V34 V-W34
136A Av MAP........... 167 W53
136A St SUR..... 185 A34 C34 205 E34 F34 H34
........... 225 L34 M34 N34 265 V34 V-W34
136B St SUR..... 205 E-F34 F34 225 K34 M34 N34

137 Av MAP........... 167 W53
137 St SUR..... 185 A34 D34 205 E34 F34 J34
........... 225 K34 K-L34 245 U34 265 V34 W34
137A St SUR........ 185 A34 C34 D34
.. 205 E34 E-F34 F34 H34 225 K34 L34 M34 N34
........... 245 T34 U34 265 V34 W34
137B St SUR..... 205 E34 225 L-M34 M34

138 St SUR........ 185 A34 A-B34 B-C34 D34
.. 205 E34 E-F34 F34 H34 H-J34 J34
.. 225 K34 L34 L-M34 M34
........... 245 T34 T-U34 U34 U34 265 V34 V34 W34
138A Av MAP........... 167 V53
138A St SUR..... 185 C34 D34 205 F34 H34
........... 245 T34 U34 265 V34 V34 W34
138B St SUR........... 185 A34 265 W34

139 Av MAP........... 167 V53
139 St SUR..... 185 A34-35 B34-35 C34-35 D34
.. 205 E34 F34 225 M34 245 T34 U34 U34-35
........... 265 V34 W34-35
139 St FG-W SUR........... 265 V35
139A Av MAP........... 167 V53
139A St SUR..... 185 A35 B35 C-D35
.. 205 E35 F35 H35 H-J35 245 T35 U35
........... 265 V34-35 V35
139B St SUR........... 205 H35

140 St SUR....... 185 A35 B-D35 205 E-J35
.. 225 K35 K35 L35 M35 N35 245 R35 S-U35
........... 265 V-W35
140 St FG-E SUR........... 185 V35
140 St FG-W SUR........... 245 U35 265 V35
140A St SUR........... 185 A35 B35
.. 205 F35 F-G35 H35 J35 J35 225 K35 K35 L35
.. 245 T35 T-U35 265 V35 W35
140B St SUR..... 185 C35 205 F35 F-G35 H35
........... 245 T35 265 W35

141 Av MAP........... 167 V54
141 Av PTM........... 166 V44
141 St SUR........ 185 B-C35 C35 C-D35
.. 205 G35 H35 J35 225 K35 L35
........... 245 S35 T-U35 265 W35
141A St SUR . 185 A35 C35 205 F35 G35 H35 J35
.. 225 K35 L35 M35 245 T35 265 V-W35 W35
141B St SUR
.. 185 B35 205 F35 G35 225 L35 M35 265 W35

142 Av MAP........... 167 U54
142 St SUR...... 185 A35 B-C35 C35 D35
.. 205 G35 H-J35 J35 225 K35 L35 L-N35
........... 245 S35 T35 U35 265 W35
142A St SUR..... 185 C35 C-D35 205 H35 J35
.. 225 K35 L35 M35 245 S35 T35
142B St SUR..... 185 B35 205 F35 G35 265 W35

143 St SUR........ 185 B35 C-D35
.. 205 F35 G35 H-J35 J35 225 L35
........... 245 S35 T35 265 V35
143A St SUR....... 185 B35 C35 C-D35 D35
.. 205 F35 G35 H-J35 J35
........... 225 K35 L35 245 S35 265 V35 W35
143B St SUR........... 205 J35 265 W35
143C St SUR........... 205 J35

144 Av MAP........... 167 U52
144 St SUR........ 185 B-C36 C-D36 205 F-J36
.. 225 K-N36 245 S-U36 265 V35-36 W35-36
144 St FG-W SUR........... 205 F35
144A St SUR........ 185 A36 B36 C D36
.. 205 F36 G36 G-H36 225 K36 N36
........... 245 T36 265 V-W36
144B St SUR........... 205 F36

145 St SUR. 185 B36 C-D36 205 F36 G36 H36 J36
........... 225 L36 M36 T36 265 W36
145A St SUR........ 185 B36 C-D36
.. 205 F36 G36 G-H36 H-J36 J36 225 N36
........... 245 S-T36 T36 265 W36
145B St SUR..... 225 K-L36 M36 245 T36 T-U36

146 St SUR........ 185 B36 B-C36 C-D36
.. 205 F36 G36 H36 H-J36 J36 J36
.. 225 L36 M-N36 N36 245 S36 T36 265 W36
146A St SUR 185 B36 205 F36 G36 H36 H-J36 J36
.. 225 M36 M-N36 245 S36 T36
........... 245 S36 T36 T36-37 U36 265 V36 V-W36 W36
146B St SUR........... 205 J36 225 K-L36

147 St SUR...... 205 F36 F-G36 H-J36 J36
........... 225 K36 M36 245 T36 265 W36
147A St SUR..... 185 B36 205 F36 G36 J36
........... 225 K-L36 M36 245 S36 T36
147B St SUR........... 225 M36

148 St SUR. 185 B36 C-D36 205 E36 E-G36 H-J36
.. 225 K-N36 P36 245 S-T36 T-U36 U36 265 V36
148 St FG-E SUR........... 245 U36 265 V36
148A St SUR..... 185 C36 C-D36 D36
.. 205 E36 E36 G36 H36 225 K36 L36-37 M36 N36
........... 245 S36 T36 T36-37 U36 265 V36 V-W36 W36
148B St SUR 205 G36 G36-37 L36-37 N36-37

149 St SUR........ 185 C-D37 D37 D37
.. 205 E37 E37 F36-37 G37 G-H37 J36
.. 225 K37 M-N37 N37 245 U37 265 V37
149A St SUR....... 185 C37 D37 205 E37 J37
.. 225 K37 M37 N37 245 S37 265 V37
149B St SUR........... 185 D37 205 E37 J37

150 Av PTM........... 147 T47
150 St SUR........ 185 A-B37 C-D37 D37
.. 205 E37 E-F37 F-G37 G-H37 H37
.. 225 K37 L37 L-M37 M37 M37 245 S37 265 V37
150A St SUR..... 185 D37 205 E37 G37 J37 J37
.. 225 K37 L37 M37 245 S37 265 V37
150B St SUR . 205 J37 225 K37 L37 M37 265 V37

151 St SUR . 185 D37 205 E37 E37 F37 G-H37 J37
.. 225 K37 K-L37 M37 245 S37 T37 U37
151A St SUR........... 185 C37 D37
.. 205 E37 E37 F37 G37
........... 225 K37 M37 265 V37
151B St SUR........... 185 D37 205 E37 F-G37
.. 225 K37 L-M37 M37 247 U37 265 V37 W37
152 St SUR........ 185 B37 C-D37 205 E-J37
.. 225 K-P37 245 Q-U37 265 V-W37
152 St FG-E SUR........... 205 G37
152A St SUR........... 185 B37 C-D37
.. 205 E37 F37 G37 G-H37 225 M37
........... 245 T37 265 V37 W37 W37

152B St SUR....... 185 D37 205 E37 245 S37

153 St SUR........ 185 A-B37 C37 D37 D37
.. 205 E37 E37 G-H37 H37 265 V37
153A St SUR........ 185 A37 B37-38 D37 D37
.. 205 E37 E37-38 E38 G37 H37
........... 245 T-U37 265 V37-38
153B St SUR........... 185 A38 205 G37-38

154 St SUR........ 185 B38 C-D38 D38
.. 205 E38 E38 E-F38 G38 G-H38 H38
........... 245 S38 U38 265 V-W38
154A St SUR..... 185 A-B38 B38 C38 205 E38 G38
........... 225 M38 245 S38 265 V38
154B St SUR........... 205 F-G38 G38 H38

155 St SUR........... 185 B38 C38 D38
.. 205 E38 F38 G38 H38 H-J38
........... 245 R-S38 S38 S-T38 U38 265 V38
155A St SUR........... 185 B38 B-C38 C38 D38
.. 205 E38 F38 G38 H38 J38 225 M38
155B St SUR........... 205 E38 245 S-T38

156 St SUR..... 185 B38 B-C38 C-D38 205 E-J38
.. 225 M-N38 245 S-T38 T-U38 265 V-W38
156A St SUR
.. 185 B38 C-D38 205 E38 E-F38 F38 G38 H38
........... 245 R38 265 V38 266 V39
156B St SUR..... 185 D38 205 E38 G38 245 R-S38

157 St SUR..... 185 B38 B-C38 C38 C-D38 D38
.. 205 E38 F38 F-G38 G38 G-H38 H38
........... 225 P38 245 U38 265 V38 W38
157A St SUR........... 185 A37 B38 C38 D38
.. 205 E38 G38 G38 H38 245 R38
157B St SUR........... 185 B38 205 E38

158 St SUR........ 185 B38 B-C38 C38 C-D38
.. 205 E38 E-F38 F-G38 G38 H38 245 S38 U38
158A St SUR
.. 185 D38 186 A-B39 B39 C39 C-D39 D39
.. 205 E38 206 E39 E-F39 H39 265 V38 266 V39
158B St SUR........... 186 B39 C39 D39

159 St SUR........... 186 B39 B-C39 C39 D39
.. 206 E39 F39 G39 G-H39 H39 246 R39
159A St SUR..... 186 A-B39 B39 C39 C-D39 D39
........... 206 E39 F39 H39 266 V39
159D St SUR........... 186 A39

160 St SUR........... 186 B39 B-C39 C-D39
.. 206 E-F39 G-J39 220 L39 N-P39
.. 246 U39 R-S39 T-U39 266 V39 V-W39
160A St SUR........... 186 B39 C-D39
.. 206 E39 E-F39 F39 G39 H39 266 W39 X39
160B St SUR........... 206 F39 266 X-Y39

161 St SUR........... 186 A39 C-D39
.. 206 E39 F39 G39 G-H39 H39 246 R39
.. 246 T39 U39 266 V39 W39 X39
161A St SUR........... 186 B39 D39
.. 206 E39 F39 G39 H39 J39
.. 246 T39 U39 266 X39 X-Y39
161B St SUR........... 186 B39 266 W-X39 X39

162 St SUR.. 186 A-B39 206 E39 G39 H39
........... 246 T-U39 266 W39 X39
162A St SUR........... 186 A39 B39 D39
.. 206 E39 E39 F39 G39 H39 J-39
.. 226 M39 246 U40 266 W-X39
162B St SUR... 186 B39 206 H39 266 W39-40

163 St SUR........ 186 A-B39 B39-40 B40
.. 206 E39 F40 G40 H39-40 H-J39 H-J40
.. 226 M39 246 T39-40 U39 U40 U41 266 W-X39 X39
163A St SUR. 186 B39-40 206 E40 F40 F-G40 H40
........... 226 M39-40 246 U41 266 X39-40 X40
163B St SUR........... 226 M40 266 X40

164 St SUR . 186 A-C40 C-D40 206 E40 F40 G-J40
.. 226 M40 N-P40 246 S-U40 266 V40 V-W40 W40
164A St SUR........... 186 B40 C40
.. 206 E40 F40 G40 H40 H-J40
.. 226 M40 246 S40 266 X40 X-Y40
164B St SUR........... 206 H40 226 M40

165 St SUR........ 186 B40 206 F40 G40 H40 H-J40
........... 226 M40 246 U40 266 V40 X40 Y40
165A St SUR . 206 G40 H40 226 M40
165B St SUR........... 186 B40 C40 226 M40

166 St SUR........ 186 B40 206 F-G40 G40 H40
........... 246 U40 266 V40 X-Y40
166A St SUR
........... 186 B40 206 G40 H-J40 226 M40 246
166B St SUR........... 206 F-G40 H40

167 St SUR........ 186 B40 206 G40 H40
.. 226 M40 M-N40 246 U40 266 V40 W40
167A St SUR...... 186 C40 D40 206 G-H40 H40
........... 226 M40 M-N40 246 U40
167B St SUR........... 206 G40 226 L-M40

168 St *SUR* . . . . . . . . 186 B40 C40-41 D40-41
. . . 206 E40-41 J40-41 226 K40-41 M40-41 P40-41
. . . 246 S40-41 266 V40-41 W40-41 X40-41
168 St FG-E *SUR* . . . . . . . . . . . . . . . . 206 G41
168A St *SUR* . 186 C41 206 G41 H41 226 M41 N44
168B St *SUR* . . . . . . . . . . . . . . . . 206 G41 H41

169 St *SUR* . . . 186 C41 206 H41 226 M41 M-N41
. . . . . . . . . 246 T-U41 266 V41 V-W41
169A St *SUR* . . . 186 C41 206 G41 226 M41 N41

170 St *SUR* . . . . . 206 G41 226 M41 246 U41 U41
. . . . . . . . . . . . . . . . 266 V41 W41 Z41
170A St *SUR* . . . . . . . . . . . . . . . . . . . . . .
. . . . . 186 C41 C-D41 206 H41 226 M41 M-N41
170B St *SUR* . . . . . . . . . . . . . . . . . . 226 M41

171 St *SUR* 186 C41 206 G41 226 L-M41 M41 N41
. . . . . . . . . 246 U41 266 V41 Y41 Z41
171A St *SUR* . . . . . . . . . . . . . . . . . . . . . .
. . . . . 186 C41 D41 206 G-H41 226 L-M41 M41

172 St *SUR* 186 C-D41 206 E41 G41 226 L41 L-N41
. . . . . . . . . 246 T41 266 V41 W41 Y-Z41
172A St *SUR* . . 226 L-M41 M41 M41-42 266 Z41
172B St *SUR* . . . . . . . . . 226 M42 N41-42

173 St *SUR* . . . . . . . . . . . . . . . . . . . . . .
. . . . 186 C42 D42 226 M42 N42 266 V42 Z42
173A St *SUR* . . . 206 E42 226 L-M42 M42 N42
173B St *SUR* . . . . . . . . . . . . . . . . 226 M42

174 St *SUR* . . . . . . . . . . . . . . . . . . . . . .
186 C42 C-D42 226 M42 N42 246 U42 266 V42 Z42
174A St *SUR* . 186 C-D42 226 L42 M42 246 T-U42
174B St *SUR* . . . . . . . . . . . . . . . . 226 M42

175 St *SUR* . . 186 C42 206 F42 226 L42 M42 N42
. . . . . . . . . . . . . . . . . . . . 266 V-W42
175A St *SUR* . . . . . . . . . . . . . . . . . . . . . .
. . . . . 186 D42 226 M42 246 U42 266 V-W42 Z42
175B St *SUR* . . . . . . . . . . . . . . . . 226 M42

176 St *PTM* . . . . . . . . . . . . . . 186 A42 Z42
176 St *SUR* . . 186 C-D42 206 E-J42 226 K-P42
. . . . . . . . . . . . 246 Q-U42 266 V-Z42
176A St *SUR* . . . 226 K42 L42 N42 266 Z42

177 St *SUR* . . . 186 D42 206 E-F42 266 W42
177A St *SUR* . . . 186 D42 206 D42 266 E42
177B St *SUR*. . . . . . . . . . . . 226 L42-43 N43

178 St *SUR* . . . 186 D43 206 E43 226 L42-43 L43
178A St *SUR* . . . . . . . . . . . 226 K43 L43
178B St *SUR* . . . . . . . . . . . . . . . 226 L43

179 St *SUR*. . . . . . . . . . . . . . . . . . . . . .
. . . . . 186 D43 206 E43 226 K43 L43 M43 266 V43
179A St *SUR* . . . . . . . 226 K43 L43 M43 N43

180 St *SUR* . 186 D43 206 E43 226 K43 L43 L-N43
. . . . . . . . . 246 R43 S-T43 U43 266 V-W43
180A St *SUR* . . . . . . . . . . . 186 D43 226 M43

181 St *SUR*. . . . . . . . . . . . . . . . . . . . . .
. . . . . 186 D43 206 J43 226 K43 L43 M43 266 V43
181A St *SUR* . . . . . . . . . . . . . . 226 M43 N43
181B St *SUR* . . . . . . . . . . . . . . . . 226 K43

182 St *SUR* . . . . . . . . 186 D43 206 E43 J43
. . . . 226 K43 K43 M-N43 N43-44 266 V43
182A St *SUR*. . . . 186 D43 D44 206 E43 E44
. . . . . . . . . 226 K44 L44 M43-44 N43-44
182B St *SUR*. . . . . . . . . . . . . 226 K44 N44

183 St *SUR* . . . . . . . . 226 L44 M44 266 V44
183A St *SUR* . . . . . . . . . . 226 L44 M44 N44

184 St *SUR* . . . 206 E-F44 G44 H-J44 226 L44 N44
. . . . . . . . 246 Q44 S-T44 266 W44 X44 Z44
184A St *SUR* . . . . . . . 226 K44 L44 M44 N44
184B St *SUR* . . . . . . . . . . 226 K46 M44 N44

185 St *SUR*. . 206 F44 J44 226 K46 L44 M44 N44
185A St *SUR*. . . . . . . . . . . . . . . . . . . . . .
. . . . . 226 K44 K46 L44 L-M44 M44 N44 P44
185B St *SUR* . . . . . . . . . . . . . . . . 226 M44

186 St *SUR*. . . . . . . . . . . . . . . . . . . . . .
. . . . . 186 D44 206 E44 226 L44 M44 N44 246 Q-R44
186A St *SUR*. . . . . . . 226 L44 L-M44 M44 N44

187 St *SUR*. . . . . . . . . . . . . . . . . . . . . .
. . 206 E44 F44 226 L44-45 L-M44 M44-45 N44-45
187A St *SUR* . . . 226 L45 L-M45 M45 N44-45
187B St *SUR*. . . . . . . . . . . . . . . . . 226 M45

188 St *PTM* . . . . . . . . . . . . . . . . 166 Y45
188 St *SUR* . 186 D45 206 E45 E-F45 G45 H45 J45
. 226 K45 L45 M45 N45 N-P45 246 T45 266 Y45 Z45
188A St *PTM* . . . . . . . . . . . 166 Y45 186 Z45
188A St *SUR* . . . . . . . . . . 226 L45 M45 N-P45
188B St *PTM*. . . . . . . . . . . . . . . . 186 Z45

189 St *SUR* . 206 E45 E-F45 F45 226 K45 M45 N45
189A St *PTM*. . . . . . . . . . . . . . . . . 186 Z45
189A St *SUR* . . . . . . . 226 L45 M45 M-N45 N45
189B St *SUR* . . . . . . . . . . . . . . . . . 186 Z45

190 St *PTM* . . . . . . . . 166 Y45 186 Z45 Z45
190 St *SUR* 186 D45 206 E45 226 K45 M45 M-N45
. . . . . . . . . 246 Q45 T45 U45 266 V45
190A St *PTM* . . . . . . . . . . . 166 Y45 186 Z45
190A St *SUR*. . . . . . . . . . . . . . . . 226 M45
190B St *SUR*. . . . . . . . . . . . . . . . 226 M45

191 St *PTM* . . . . . . . . . . . . . . . . . 166 Y45
191 St *SUR*. . . . 206 J45 226 K45 M45 266 V-W45
191A St *PTM*. . . . . . . . . . . . . . . . . 186 Z45
191A St *SUR* . . . . . . . 226 K-L45 M45 M-N45
191B St *PTM* . . . . . . . . . . . 166 Y45 186 Z45

192 St *SUR* . . . . . . . . 206 E45-46 F45-46 H-J45
. . . . . 226 L45-46 N45-46 246 Q45-46 T45 U45
. . . . . . . . . . . . . . . . 266 V45 Y45 Z45
192 St Diversion *SUR* . . . . . . . . . . 226 L45
192A St *PTM* . . . . . . . . . . . . . . . . . 186 Z46
192A St *SUR*. . . . . . . . 206 J46 226 K46 L46
192B St *PTM*. . . . . . . . 166 Y46 186 A46 Z46

193 St *PTM* . . . . . . . . 166 Y46 186 A46 Z46
193 St *SUR* . . . . . . . . . 206 E46 226 K46
193A St *PTM* . . . . . . . . . . . . . 186 A46 Z46
193A St *SUR*. . . . 206 E46 226 K-L46 L46
193B St *PTM* . . . . . . . . 166 Y46 186 A46 Z46
193B St *SUR* . . . . . . . . . . . . . . . . 226 L46

194 St *PTM* . . . . . . . . . . . . . . . . . 166 Y46
194 St *SUR* . . . . 206 E-F46 J46 226 L46 M46
. . . . 246 S46 T46 266 W46 W46 Z46 Z46
194A St *PTM* . . . 166 Y46 Y46 186 A46 Z46 Z46
194A St *SUR* . . . . . . . 206 E46 226 K46 M46
194B St *PTM* . . . . . . . . 166 Y46 186 A46 Z46
194B St *SUR*. . . . . . . . . . . . . . . 226 L-M46

195 St *SUR* . . . . 206 E46 226 L46 L-M46 M46
195A St *PTM*. . . . . . . . . . . . . 186 A46 Z46
195A St *SUR* . . . . . . . . 226 M46 246 Q46
195B St *PTM*. . . . . . . . . . . . . 186 A46 Z46
195B St *SUR* . . . . . . . . . 206 H46 226 L-M46

196 St *LGC* . . . . . . . 226 M46 P46 246 Q46 Q46
196 St *LGT*. . . 206 G-H46 J46 226 K46 K-L46 M46
. . . . . . . . . 246 R46 S-T46 U46 266 V-W46
196 St *SUR* . . . . . . . . 186 D46 206 J46 226 K46
196A Ct *LGT* . . . . . . . . . . . . . . . . . 226 L46
196A St *LGC* . . . . 226 M46 N-P46 P46 246 Q46
196A St *LGT*. . . 226 K46 L46 K-L46 M46 M46
. . . . . 246 Q46 R46 S46 266 X46 267 X47
196A St *SUR* . . . . . . . . . . . . . . . . . 186 A46
196B Pl *LGT* . . . . . . . . . . . . . . . 226 K-L46
196B St *LGC* . . . . . . . . . . . . . . . . 226 P46
196B St *LGT* . . . . . . . 186 D46 246 R46 246
196B St *PTM* . . . . . . . . . . . . . . . . . 187 A47
196C *PTM* . . . . . . . . . . . . . . . . . 147 T47

197 St *LGC* . . . . . . . . . . . . . . . . . . . . . .
. . 226 N-P46 P46 227 P47 246 Q46 Q46 247 Q47
197 St *LGT* . . . . . . . . 186 D46 206 G-H46 H46
. . . . . 207 G-H47 H47 J47 226 K46 L46
. . . . . . . . . 227 K47 L47 246 R46 S46
197A St *LGC* . . . 226 N46 227 N47 P47 247 Q47
197A St *LGT* . . . . 227 K47 246 Q46 T-U46
. . . . . . 247 Q47 R47 S47 T-U47 267 W47
197A St *PTM* . . . . . . . . . . . . . . . . . 187 A47
197B St *LGC* . . . . . . . . . . . . . . . . 227 P47
197B St *LGT* . . . . . . . . . . . . . . . . . . . . . .
. . . . . 187 D47 207 E47 J47 227 K47 K47 247 Q47
197B St *PTM* . . . . . . . . . . . . . . . . . 187 A47

198 St *LGC* . . . . . . . 227 N47 P47 247 Q47
198 St *LGT* 207 E47 F47 G47 J47 227 K47 K47 L47
. . . . . 247 Q-R47 R47 S47 267 V47 Z47
198 St *PTM* . . . . . . . . . . . . . . . . . 187 A47
198A St *LGC* . . . . . . . . . . . 227 N47 247 Q47
198A St *LGT* . . . . . . . . . . . . . . . . . . . . . .
. . 207 G47 H47 227 K47 247 Q47 R47 S47 267 X47
198B St *LGC* . . . . . . . . . . . 227 P47 247 Q47
198B St *LGT* . . . 187 D47 207 E47 J47 247 Q47
198C St *LGC* . . . . . . . . . . . . . . . . 247 Q47

199 St *LGC* . . . . . . . 227 N47 P47 247 Q47
199 St *LGT* 207 H47 227 K47 L47 247 S47 267 Z47
199A Cr *LGT* . . . . . . . . . . . . . . . . 247 R47
199A St *LGT* . . . . . . . 227 N47 N-P47 247 Q47
199A St *LGT* . . . . . . . . . . . . . . . . . . . . . .
. . . . . 187 D47 207 E47 J47 227 K47 247 Q-R47 S47
199B St *LGT* . . . . . . . . . . . . . . . . 187 D47

200 St *LGC* . . . . . . . . . . 227 M-P47 247 Q47
200 St *MAP* . . . . . . . . . . . . . . . . . . 187 A47
200 St *PTM* . . . . . . . . 147 T47 167 U47
200 St (Carvolth Rd) *LGT* . 207 E-J47 227 K-L47
. . . . . 247 R-U47 267 V-Y47 Z47
200A St *LGC* . 227 M47 N47 P47 P47 247 Q47 R47

200A St *LGT* . . . . . . . . 207 E47 J47 247 R47
200B St *LGC* . . . . . . . . . . . . . . . . 227 P47
200B St *LGT* . . . . . . . 207 J47 247 R47 R47

201 St *LGC* . . . . . . . 227 N47 P47 247 Q47
201 St *LGT* . . . . . . . 207 E47 E47 J47 Q47
. . . . . 227 K47 L47 247 R-S47 T-U47
201 St *MAP* . . . . . . . . . . 167 Y47 187 Z47
201 St (Station Rd) *LGT* . . 187 D47 207 E47
201A St *LGC* . . . . 227 M47 N47-48 N-P47 P47
201A St *LGT* . . . . . . . 247 R47 R-S47 S47
201A St *MAP* . . . . . . . . . . . . . . . . . 187 A48
201B St *LGT* . . . . . . . . 207 J47 228 Z47 K48
201B St *MAP* . . . . . . . . . . . . 187 A47-48 Z48

202 St *LGC* . . . . . . . 227 M48 247 Q47-48
202 St *LGT* . . 187 D48 207 E47 F48 J48 227 M48
. . . . . 247 R-S47 S-T47 T47 U47 247 Q47
202 St *MAP* . . . . . . . 167 Y48 Y48 187 Z48
202A St *LGC* . . . . . . . . . . 227 P48 247 Q47
202A St *LGT* . 207 E47-48 J48 247 R48 R-S48 S48
202A St *MAP* . . . . . . . 167 Y48 187 A48 Z48
202B St *LGT* . . . . . . . . . . . 207 E-F48 247 Q47
202B St *MAP* . . . . . . . 167 Y48 187 A48 Z48

203 St *LGC* . . . . . . . . . . 227 N-P48 247 Q48
203 St *LGT*. . 187 D48 D48 207 E48 E48 E-F48 F48
. . . . . 227 L48 L-M48 247 R48 S48
203 St *MAP* . . . . . . . 167 X-Y48 187 A48 Z48
203A St *LGC* . . . . 227 M-N48 P48 247 Q48
203A St *LGT* 187 D48 208 E-F48 F48 247 R48 S48
203B St *LGT* . . . 207 E-F48 F48 J48 247 R48

204 St *LGC* . . . . . 227 M48 N48 P48 247 Q48
204 St *LGT* . . . . 187 D48 207 E48 G48 H-J48
. . 227 K48 M48 247 R48 S48 T48 U48 267 Y48 Z48
204 St *MAP* . . . . . . . 167 Y48 187 A48 Z48
204A St *LGT* . . . . . . . . . . . . . . . . 247 Q48
204A St *LGT* . . . . . . . . . . . . . . . . . . . . . .
. . 207 E48 F48 227 K-L48 247 R48 S48 267 V48
204B St *LGT* . . . . . . . 207 E48 248 F48 R48
204B St *MAP* . . . . . . . 167 Y48 187 Z48

205 St *LGC* . . . . . 227 N48 P48 247 Q48
205 St *LGT* . . . . . . . . . . . . . . . . . . . . . .
. . 207 E48 F48 227 K48 L48 L-M48 247 S-T48
205 St *MAP* . . . . . . . 167 Y48 187 A48 Z48
205 St (Knich Rd) *LGT* . . . . . . . 247 S-T48
205A St *LGC* . . . . . . . 227 M48 P48 247 Q48
205A St *LGT* . . . . . . . . . . . . . . . . . . . . . .
. . 187 D48 207 E48 E48 F48 227 L48 247 R48 R-S48
205A St *MAP* . . . . . . . . . . . . . . . . . 187 Z48
205B St *LGC* . . . . . . . . . . . . . . . . 227 P48
205B St *LGT* . . . . . . . 207 E48 247 R-S48
205B St *MAP* . . . . . . . . . . . . . . . . . 167 Y48

206 St *LGC* . . . 227 M48 N48 P48 247 Q48
206 St *LGT* . . . 207 E48 F48 F-G48 G48 J48
. . 227 K48 L48 247 R48 T48 U48 267 V48
206 St *MAP* . . . . . . . 167 Y48 187 A48 Z48
206A St *LGC* . . 227 M48 M48-49 247 Q48
206A St *LGT* . . . . . . . . . . . . . . . . . . . . . .
. . 207 E48 E48-49 J49 227 K49 247 R48 S48
206A St *MAP* . . . . . . . . . . . . . . . . 187 A48-49
206B St *LGC* . . . . . . . . . . . . . . . 247 Q48-49
206B St *LGT* . . . . . . . 207 E48 E-F48 G48-49
206B St *MAP* . . . . . . . . . . . . . . . . 187 A49 Z49

207 St *LGC* . . . . . . . 227 N49 P49 247 Q49
207 St *LGT* . . 207 E48-49 E49 F49 G49 227 K49
. . . . . . . . . 247 R49 S49 U48-49
207 St *MAP* . . . . . . . . . . . . 187 A49 Z49
207A St *LGC* . . . . . . . . . . 227 P49 247 Q49
207A St *LGT* . . . 207 E49 F49 247 R49 T49
207B St *LGC* . . . . . . . 227 P49 247 Q49
207B St *LGT* . . . . . . . . . . . 207 F49 247 S49

208 St *LGC* . . . . . . . 227 N49 P49 247 Q49
208 St *LGT* . . . . . . . . . . . 187 C-D49 207 E-G49
208 St *MAP* . . . . . . . 167 Y49 187 A49 Z49
208 St (Alexander Rd) *LGT* . 207 H-J49 227 K49
208 St (Berry Rd) *LGT* 247 R-U49 267 V-X49 Z49
208A St *LGC* . . . . . . . . . . 227 P49 247 Q49
208A St *LGT* . . . . . . . . . . . . . . . . . . . . . .
. . . 187 D49 207 E49 G48 227 K49 247 Q49 R49
208B St *LGC* . . . . . . . . . . . . . . . . 247 Q49
208B St *LGT* . . . . . . . 207 E49 247 Q49 K49

209 Cr *LGT* . . . . . . . . . . . . . . . . . 207 E-F49
209 St *LGC* . . . . . . . 227 N49 P49 247 Q49
209 St *LGT* . . 207 E49 G49 H48 247 R49 S49
209 St *MAP* . . . . . . . 167 X49 Y49 187 A49 Z49
209A St *LGC* . . . . . . . . . . 227 P49 247 Q49
209A St *LGT* . . . 207 E49 G49 J49 227 K49 247 R49
209B St *LGT* . . . . . . . 207 E49 E-F49 247 Q49

210 St *LGC* . . . . . . . . . . . . . . . . 247 Q49
210 St *LGT* . . . . . . . . 207 E49 F49 227 K49
. . . . . 207 Q49 S49 T49 U49 267 Z49
210 St *MAP* . . . 167 X49 Y49 187 A49 Z49 Z49
210A St *LGC* . . . . . . . . . . . . . . . . 227 N-P49
210A St *LGT* . . . 227 N49 P49 247 Q49 Q-R49

211 St *LGT* . . . . . . . 207 E49 G48 H48 227 N49
211 St *MAP*. . . . . . . 167 Y49 187 A49 Z49 Z49
211A St *LGT* . . . . . . . . . . 207 E49-50 G50 H48
211B St *LGT*. . . . . 207 F49-50 F50 H49 247 Q49

212 St *LGT* . . . . . . . . . . . . . . . . . . . . . .
. . . . . 187 C50 207 E50 E-F50 F-G50 H50 H-J50
. . . . . 247 Q50 R50 T50 267 V-W50 W-X50 Z50
212 St *MAP*. . . . . . . . 167 Y50 187 A50 Z50
212A St *LGT* . . . . . . . . . . . . . . . . 207 E50 F50
212B St *LGT* . . . . . . . . . . 207 E50 E-F50 F50

213 St *LGT* . . . 207 E-F50 F50 G50 J50 247 R50
213A Pl *LGT* . . . . . . . . . . . . . . . . . 207 F50
213A St *LGT* . . . . . . . . . . . 227 N50 247 R50

214 Pl *LGT* . . . . . . . . . . . . . . . . . 207 F50
214 St *LGT*. . . 207 E50 E-F50 F50 G50 247 Q50
214 St *MAP* . . . 167 Y50 Y50 187 Z50 Z50
214A St *LGT* . . . . . . . . . . . . . . . . . . . . . .
. . . . . 207 E50 G50 227 M-N50 P50 247 Q50
214B St *LGT* . . . . . . . . . . . . . . . 207 F50 G50

215 St *LGT* . . . 207 E50 G50 227 P50 247 Q50
215 St *MAP*. . . . . . . . . . . . 167 Y50 187 A50
215A St *LGT* . . . 207 E50 G50 227 P50 247 Q50
215B St *LGT* . . . . . . . . . . 207 E50 G50 247 Q50

216 St *LGT* . . . . . . . . . . . 207 H-J50 227 K51
216 St *MAP* . . . 167 W51 X50-51 Y50 Y51
. . . . . 187 A50-51 Z50 Z50-51 Z51
216 St (Johnston Townline Rd) *LGT* . . . . . . .
. . . . . 227 L-P50 207 Q-U50 267 V-Z50
216 St (Topham Rd) *LGT* . 187 C-D50 207 E-G50
216A St *LGT* . . . 227 P50 P50-51 P51 247 Q50 Q51
216B St *LGT* . . . . . . . . . . . . . . . . 207 E51

217 St *LGT* . . . . . . . . . . . 207 E51 247 Q51
217 St *MAP* . . . . . . . . . . . 167 Y51 187 Z51
217A St *LGT* . . . . . . . . . . . . . . . . . . . . . .
. . . . . 207 E51 G51 227 N-P51 P51 247 Q51 Q51
217B St *LGT* . . . 207 E51 227 P51 247 Q51

218 St *LGT* . . . . . . . . . . . 207 E51 227 P51
218 St *MAP* . . . . . . . . . . . . . . . . . 187 Z51
218A St *LGT* . . . . . . . . . . . 227 P51 247 Q51

219 St *LGT* . . . . . . . . . . . 227 P51 247 Q51
219 St *MAP* . . . . . . . . . . . . . . . . . 167 Y51
219A St *LGT* . . . . . . . . . . . 227 P51 247 Q51

220 St *LGT* 207 E51 227 P51 247 Q51 U51 267 V51
220 St *MAP* . . . . . . . 167 W51 Y51 187 Z51
220A St *MAP* . . . . . . . . . . . . . . . . . 167 Y51

221 St *LGT* . . . . . . . 227 P51 247 Q51-52
221 St *MAP* . . . . . . . 167 Y51 187 Z51
221A St *LGT* . . . 227 P51 247 Q51 Q51-52

222 St *LGT* . . . 207 E-F52 227 P52 247 Q52
222 St *MAP* . . . 167 Y52 Y52 187 Z52 Z52
222A St *LGT*. . . . . . . . 207 F-G52 247 Q52

223 St *LGT* . . . . . . . 227 P52 247 Q52
223 St *MAP* . . . . . . . 167 Y52 187 A52 Z52
223A St *LGT* . 207 F52 227 P52 P52 247 Q52 Q52
223B St *LGT* . . . . . . . . . . . . . . . . 227 P52

224 St *LGT* . . . . . . . 207 G52 227 K52 L52 M52
. . . . . 247 R52 S52 U52 267 V52 Z52
224 St *MAP* 167 V52 W52 X52 Y52 187 A52 Z52 Z52
224 St (Biggar Rd) *LGT* . . . 227 P52 247 Q-R52
. . . . . . . . . . . . . . . . 267 W-Z52

225 St *MAP* . . . . . . . . . . . . . . . . . 187 A52

226 St *LGT* . . . . . . . . . . . . . . . 227 L-M52
226 St *MAP* . . . 167 X-Y53 Y53 187 Z52-53

227 Cr *LGT* . . . . . . . . . . . . . . . . . 207 H53
227 St *LGT* . . . . . . . . . . . . . . . . 267 W-X53
227 St *MAP* . . . 167 X-Y53 Y53 187 A53 Z53
227A St *MAP* . . . . . . . . . . . . . . . . 167 X-Y53
227B St *MAP* . . . . . . . . . . . . . . . . 167 X-Y53

228 St *LGT* . . . 227 L-M53 247 Q53 R53 T53
228 St *MAP* . . . 167 W53 X53 X-Y53 187 A53 Z53
228A St *LGT* . . . . . . . . . . . . . . . . 267 W-X53
228A St *MAP* . . . . . . . 167 W53 X53 Y53
228B St *LGT* . . . . . . . . . . . . . . . . . 207 H53
228B St *MAP* . . . . . . . . . . . . . . . . . 167 W53

229 La *MAP* . . . . . . . . . . . . . . . . . 167 V53
229 St *LGT* . . . . . . . . 207 J53 227 K53
229 St *MAP* . 167 V53 X53 Y53 187 A53 Z53
229A St *MAP* . . . . . . . . . . . . . . . . . 167 W53
229B St *MAP* . . . . . . . . . . . . . . . . . 167 V53

230 St *LGT*. . . . . . . 227 K53 L-M53 247 T53
230 St *MAP* 167 V53 X53 Y53 Y53 187 A53 Z53 Z53
230B St *MAP* . . . . . . . . . . . . . . 187 A53-54

Street Index
231 St / Appleby


231 St *LGT* . . . . . . . . . **207** J53 **227** K53 **267** X53
231 St *MAP* . . . . . . . . . **167** X54 Y54 **187** A54 Z54
231A St *MAP* . . . . . . . . . . . . . . . . . . . . **167** Y54
231B St *MAP* . . . . . . . . . . . . . **167** Y54 **187** A54

232 St *LGT* **227** L54 N54 **247** Q54 S54 U54 **267** V54
232 St *MAP* . . . . . . . . . **167** X54 Y54 **187** A54 Z54
232 St (Livingstone Rd) *LGT* . . . . . . . . . . . . . . . . . . . . . . . . . . . . . . . . **207** H-J54 **227** K-L54
232A St *MAP* . . . . . . . . . . . **167** Y54 **187** A54 Z54
232B St *MAP* . . . . . . . . . . . . . . . . **187** A54 Z54

233 St *LGT* . . . . . . . . . . . . . . . . . . . . . . **247** Q54
233 St *MAP* . . . . . . . . . . . . . **167** W54 W-X54 Y54
233A St *MAP* . . . . . . . . . . . . . . **167** Y54 **187** A54

234 St *LGT* . . . . . . . . . . . . . . . . . . . . . . **227** P54
234 St *MAP* . . . . . . . . . . . . . . . . . . . . . . **187** Z54
234A St *MAP* . . . . . . . . . . . . . . . . . . **187** B54 Z54
234B St *MAP* . . . . . . . . . . . . . . . . . . . . . . **167** X54
235 St *LGT* . . . . . . . . . **227** P54 **267** W-X54 X-Y54
235 St *MAP* . . . . . . . . . . . . . . . . . . . . . **167** X-Y54

236 St *LGT* . . . . . . . . . . . . . . . . . . . . . . . . . . . . . . **227** K54 P54 **247** Q54 S54 T54 U54 **267** W54
236 St *MAP* . . . . . . . . . . . . . **167** W-X54 **187** D54

260 St *LGT* . . . . . . . . . . . . . . . . . . . . . . **248** T60
260B St *LGT* . . . . . . . . . . . . . . . . . . . . . **248** T60

261A St *LGT* . . . . . . . . . . . . . . . . . . . . . **248** T60

262 St *LGT* . . . . . . . . . . . . . . . . . . . . . . **248** T60
262B St *LGT* . . . . . . . . . . . . . . . . . . . . . **248** T60

264 St *LGT* . . . . . . . . . . . . . . . . . . . . **248** S-T60
264A St *LGT* . . . . . . . . . . . . . . . . . . . . . **248** T60

265A St *LGT* . . . . . . . . . . . . . . . . **248** T61 T-U61
265B St *LGT* . . . . . . . . . . . . . . . . . . . . . **248** T61
266A St *LGT* . . . . . . . . . . . . . . . . **248** T61 T-U61
266B St *LGT* . . . . . . . . . . . . . . . . . . . . . **248** T61

267 St *LGT* . . . . . . . . . . . . . . . . . . . . . . **248** U61
267A St *LGT* . . . . . . . . . . . . . . . . . . . . . **248** T61
267B St *LGT* . . . . . . . . . . . . . . . . . . . . . **248** T61

268 St *LGT* . . . . . . . . . . . . . . . . . **248** S-T61 U61
268A St *LGT* . . . . . . . . . . . . . . . . . . . . . **248** T61
268B St *LGT* . . . . . . . . . . . . . . . . . . . . . **248** T61

269 St *LGT* . . . . . . . . . . . . . . . . . **248** T-U61 U61
269A St *LGT* . . . . . . . . . . . . . . . . . . **248** T61 U61

270 St *LGT* . . . . . . . . . . . . . . . **248** S-T62 T61-62
270A St *LGT* . . . . . . . . . . . . . . . . **248** S62 T62 U62
270B St *LGT* . . . . . . . . . . . . . **248** T62 T-U62 U62

271 St *LGT* . . . . . . . . . . . . . . . . . . . **248** S62 T62
271A St *LGT* . . . . . . . . . . . . . . . . . . **248** S62 U62
271B St *LGT* . . . . . . . . . . . . . . . . . **248** S62 S-T62
272 St *LGT* . . . . . . . . . . . . . . . . . . . . . **248** S-U62
272 St (Jackman Rd) *LGT* . . . . . **248** Q-R62 T62
272A St *LGT* . . . . . . . . . . . . . . . . . **248** S-T62 U62
272B St *LGT* . . . . . . . . . . . . . . . . . . **248** T62 U62

273 St *LGT* . . . . . . . . . . . . . . . . . . . **248** T62 U62
273A St *LGT* . . . . . . . . . . . . . . . . . . **248** S62 U62
273B St *LGT* . . . . . . . . . . . . . . . . . . **248** S62 U62

274 St *LGT* . . . . . . . . . . . . . . . . . . . . **248** S-T62
274A St *LGT* . . . . . . . . . . . . . . **248** S-T62 U62-63

275 St *LGT* . . . . . . . . . . . . . . . . . . **248** S-T63 T63
275A St *LGT* . . . . . . . . . . . . . . . . **248** S-T63 T63

276 St *LGT* . . . . . . . . . . . . . . . . . . . . . . **248** T63
276 St (Station Rd) *LGT* . . . . . . . . . . . **248** T63


## A


Abbey Av *BUR* . . . . . . . . . . . **163** X22
Abbey Dr *DEL* . . . . . . **224** M-N30 N30
Abbey Dr *SUR* . . . . . . . . . . . **186** C-D42
Abbey La *CQT* . . . . . . . . . . . . **146** R40
Abbotsford St *BUR* . . . . . . . **184** C23
Abbotsford Way *ABT* . . . **270** V76-77
Abbotsford-Mission Hwy *ABT* . . . . . . . . . . . . . . . . **230** L75 P76 **250** Q-T76
Abbotsford Mission Hwy *MIS* . . . . . . . . . . . . . . . . . . . . . . . . . . . **230** K73
Abbott St *MIS* . . . . . . . . . **230** K74-75
Abbott St *VAN* . . . . **11** G-H39 **142** S14
Abercrombie Dr *RMD* . . . . . **202** G12
Abercrombie Pl *MIS* . . . . . . **210** G73
Abercrombie Pl *RMD* . . . . . **202** G12
Aberdeen Av *CQT* . . . . . **145** T36 T37
Aberdeen Dr *KNT* . . . . . . . . **175** W20
Aberdeen St *SUR* . . . . . . **226** M-N41
Aberdeen St *VAN* . . . . **163** X20 X-Y20
Abernethy Connector *MAP* . . . . . . . . . . . . . . . . . . . **167** X-Y49 Y47-48
Abernethy La *MAP* . . . . . . . **167** Y53
Abernethy Way *MAP* . . . . . . . . . . . . . . . . . . . . . . . . **167** X-Y52 Y52-53 Y53
Acacia Av *BUR* . . . . **164** Y26 **184** Z26
Acacia Dr *CHL* . . . . . . . . . . . **193** D7
Acacia Dr *HOP* . . . . . . . . . . **118** E46
Acadia Cir *UEL* . . . . . . . . . . **161** T4-5
Acadia Rd *UEL* . . . . . . . . . **161** T4 U5
Acadia St *MAP* . . . . . . . . . . **187** Z51
Acadia Park La *UEL* . . . . . . . . **161** U-V5
Accacia Av *CQT* . . . . . . . . . **165** V31
Acheson Rd *RMD* . . . . . . . . **202** G12
Ackerman Ct *ABT* . . . . . . . . **270** V78
Ackroyd Rd *RMD* . . . . . . **202** E12-13
Acorn Av *ABT* . . . . . . . . . . **250** S-T77
Acorn Av *BUR* . . . . . . . . . . . **184** Z26
Adair Av *ABT* . . . . **250** S72-73 T72-73
Adair Av *CQT* . . . . . . . . . . . . **165** X32
Adair St *BUR* . . . . . . **164** U25 U25-26
Adair St *MAP* . . . . . . . . . . . . **187** A53
Adams Av *MIS* . . . . . . . . . . . **210** H73
Adams La *SUR* . . . . . . . . . . . **245** U31
Adams Pl *RMD* . . . . . . . . . . . **202** F11
Adams Rd *CHL* . . . . . . . . . . . . **233** K1
Adanac Av *CHL* . . . . . . . . . . . . **213** E8
Adanac St *ABT* . . . . **250** U74 **270** V74
Adanac St *VAN* . . . . . . . . **143** T17-20
Adderley St *DNV* . . . **123** N19 **143** P19
Addison St *RMD* . . . . . . . . . . **202** J11
Adelaide Rd *UEL* . . . . . . . . . . **161** U6
Adelaide St *ABT* . . . . . . . . . **250** U73
Adera St *VAN* . . **162** Y12 **182** A12 Z12
Adiron Av *CQT* . . . . . . . . **165** U31-32
Adler Av *CQT* . . . . . . . . . . . . **165** V31
Admiral Blvd *DEL* . . . . . . **223** M-N17
Admiral Ct *CQT* . . . . . . . . . . **165** U37
Admiral La *DEL* . . . . . . . . **223** M-N17
Admiral Way *DEL* . . . . . . . . **223** M17
Adrian St *BUR* . . . . . . . . . . . **144** R24
Advent Rd *PTM* . . . . . **166** Y44-45 Y45
Aegean Cr *VAN* . . . . . . . . . . **183** A20
Aerolane Av *ABT* . . . . . . . . . **250** U71
Afton Dr *RMD* . . . . . . . . . **202** H11-12
Afton La *PMD* . . . . . . . . . . . . **145** S36
Agar Dr *RMD* . . . . . . . **182** D9 **202** E9
Agar St *SUR* . . . . . . . . . . . . . **245** T31
Agassiz Av *KNT* . . . . . . . **175** W-X20
Agassiz Ct *RMD* . . . . . . . . . **202** H14
Agassiz-Rosedale Hwy *KNT* . . . . . . . . . . . . . . . . . . . . . . . **175** X20-21 Y20
Agate Pl *CQT* . . . . . . . . . . . . **145** Q36
Agnes St *NEW* . . . **184** A30 A-B29 B29
Agricultural Rd *UEL* . . . . . . **161** U3-4
Agronomy Rd *UEL* . . . . . . . **161** U-V4 V3
Ailsa Av *PMD* . . . . . . **144** T30 **145** T31
Ailsa Cr *DNV* . . . . . . . . . . **123** L-M19
Ainsworth Cr *RMD* . . . . . . . . **202** J14
Ainsworth Pl *RMD* . . . . . . . . **202** J14
Aintree Cr *RMD* . . . . **202** J14 **203** J15
Aintree Dr *DNV* . . . . . . . . . . . **122** L14
Aintree Pl *RMD* . . . . **202** J14 **203** J15
Aire Cr *PCQ* . . . . . . . . . . . . . **166** W39
Airey Dr *RMD* . . . . . **182** C14 **183** C15
Airlie Ct *BUR* . . . . . . . . . . . . **144** T26
Airlynn Pl *DNV* . . . . . . . . . . . **123** N20
Airport Rd *CHL* . . . . . . . . . . **213** G6-8
Airport Rd *HOP* . . . . . . . . . . . **118** F41
Airport Rd *RMD* . . . . . . . . . . **182** C12
Airport Rd *RMD* . . . . . . . . . . **182** D11
Airport Rd S *RMD* . . . . . . . . . . . . . . . . . . . . . . . . . . **182** D10 **202** F10 F11
Aish Av *ABT* . . . . . . . . . **230** M75 M76
Aisne St *VAN* . . . . . . . . . . **182** A-B13
Aitken Rd *CHL* . . . . . . . . . . . . **213** G3
Aladdin Cr *ABT* . . . . . . . . . . **250** U77
Alama Av *CQT* . . . . . . . . . . . **165** W32
Alameda Dr *CHL* . . . . . . . . . **213** F1-2
Alamein Av *VAN* . . . . . . . . . . **162** W10
Alanmore Pl *RMD* . . . . . . . . . . **202** G9
Alaska St *BUR* . . . . . . . . . . . **163** U22
Alaska Way *DEL* . . . . . . . . . . **204** E28
Alberni St *VAN* . . . . . . . . . . . . . . . . . . . . . . . . . **10** E35 F36 **142** R12-13 S13
Albert Cr *NEW* . . . . . . . . . . . **184** A30
Albert St *BUR* . . . . **143** S21-22 **144** S23
Albert St *PMD* . . . . . . . . . . . . **145** T32
Albert Way *ABT* . . . . . . . . . . . **250** U71
Alberta Rd *RMD* . . . . . . . **202** F13-14
Alberta St *NEW* . . . . . . . . . . . **184** Z30
Alberta St *VAN* . . . . . . . . . . . . . . . . . . . . . . . . **162** U-V14 X-Y14 **182** Z14
Albertan St *PTM* . . . . . . . . . . **187** Z47
Albery Pl *BUR* . . . . . . . . . . . . **164** Y27
Albion Dr *CQT* . . . . . . . . . **145** R37-38
Albion Rd *RMD* . . . . . . . . . . . **202** J14
Albion St *ABT* . . . . . . . . . . . . **270** V73
Albion Way *DEL* . . . . . . . . . . . **224** L28
Alden La *CNV* . . . . . . . . . . . . **123** M15
Alder *CQT* . . . . . . . . . . . . . . . **145** S38
Alder Av *CHL* . . . . . . . . . . . . . **213** J6
Alder Av *HHS* . . . . . . . . . . **155** Q-R19
Alder Crsg *VAN* . . . . . . . . . . **162** U12
Alder Ct *DNV* . . . . . . . . . . . . . **144** P23
Alder Dr *LGT* . . . . . . . . . . . . . **248** S61
Alder Dr *PMD* . . . . . . . . . . . . **145** Q35
Alder La *WHS* . . . . . . . . . . . . **401** B3
Alder Pl *HOP* . . . . . . . . . . . . . **118** E47
Alder Pl *KNT* . . . . . . . . . **175** X21-22
Alder Pl *PCQ* . . . . . . . . . . . . . **146** T42
Alder Pl *SQM* . . . . . . . . . . . . . **301** K3
Alder Pl *SUR* . . . . . . . . . . . . **266** W39
Alder St *ABT* . . . . . . . . . . . . **250** U72
Alder St *CNV* . . . . . . . . **143** P17 Q18
Alder St *FRA* . . . . . . . . . . . . . . **253** R5
Alder St *MIS* . . . . . . . . . . . . . **210** J74
Alder St *VAN* . . . . . . . . . . **162** U12-13
Alder Way *ANM* . . . . . . . . . . . **145** P33
Alder Bay Walk *VAN* . . . . **162** U12-13
Alderbridge Way *RMD* . . **202** E11-14
Alderbrook Pl *CQT* . . . . . . . . **165** U38
Alderfeild Pl *WVA* . . . . . . . . . . **121** K3
Aldergrove-Bellingham Rd *LGT* . . . . . . . . . . . . . . . . . . . . . . . . . . **248** Q-R60
Alderlynn Dr *DNV* . . . . . . **123** M-N20
Alderlynn St *DNV* . . . . . . . . . **123** M20
Alderside Rd *PMD* . . . . . **145** R32-33
Alderson Av *CQT* . . . . . . **165** X31-33
Alderview St *ABT* . . . . . . . . . **250** U76
Alderwood Av *PCQ* . . . . . . . . **146** S41
Alderwood Cr *BUR* . . . . . . . . **163** X22
Alderwood Cr *DEL* . . . . . . . . . **224** L30
Alderwood La *DEL* . . . . . . . **224** L-M30
Alderwood Pl *DNV* . . . . . . . . **122** N14
Aldford Av *DEL* . . . . . . . . . . . **204** E28
Aldous Ct *BUR* . . . . . . . . . . . **164** W26
Aldrin Pl *BUR* . . . . . . . . . . . . **144** T26
Alea Ct *ABT* . . . . . . . . . . . . . **249** T70
Alexander Av *CHL* . . . . . . . . **213** F6-7
Alexander Bay *PMD* . . . . . . . **145** S35
Alexander Cr *ABT* . . . . . . . . . **250** U76
Alexander Rd *DEL* . . . . . . . . . **204** H23
Alexander St *NEW* . . . . . . . . . **184** B29
Alexander St *VAN* . . . **11** G41 **143** S15
Alexandra Gt *RMD* . . . . . . . . **202** E13
Alexandra Rd *RMD* . . . . . **202** E12-14
Alexandra St *MIS* . . . . . . . . . **210** G73
Alexandra St *SUR* . . . . . . . . . **245** T31
Alexandra St *VAN* . . . **162** V-W12 W12
Alexandria Cr *SUR* . . . . . . . . **205** F32
Alexis Ct *RMD* . . . . . . . . . . . **202** H14
Alexis Rd *KNT* . . . . . . . . . . . **175** V23
Algoma Dr *RMD* . . . . . . . . . . **202** H14
Algonquin Dr *RMD* . . . . . . . . **202** H14
Algonquin Mews *VAN* **183** A19 Z19-20
Alice St *ABT* . . . . . . . . . . . . . **250** T72
Alice St *NEW* . . . . . . . . . . . . . **184** A30
Alice St *VAN* . . . . . . . . . . . . . **163** W17
Alice Lake Pl *CQT* . . . . . . . . . **165** V36
Allan Rd *DNV* . . . . . . . . . . . . **123** L20
Allandale Av *PMD* . . . . . . . . . **145** T31
Allard Cr *LGT* . . . . . . . . . . . . . . . . . . **187** B49-50 B52 C48-49 C53 D52-53
Allard St *CHL* . . . . . . . . . . . . . **213** F6
Allard St *CQT* . . . . . . . . . . . . **165** X32
Allen Av *ABT* . . . . . . . . . . . **250** T-U75
Allen Dr *DEL* . . . . . . . . . . . . . **263** Y17
Allen St *NEW* . . . . . . . . . . . . . **165** Y31
Allen Way *PTM* . . . . . . . . . . **166** X-Y45
Alliance Dr *RMD* . . . . . . . . . . **222** L10
Alliance St *ABT* . . . . . . . . . . . **250** U75
Allison Av *HOP* . . . . . . . . . . . **118** D44
Allison Ct *ABT* . . . . . . . . . . . . **251** S79
Allison Ct *RMD* . . . . . . . . . . . **202** H14
Allison Pl *NEW* . . . . . . . . . . . . **184** Z29
Allison Rd *UEL* . . . . . . . . . . . **161** T-U4
Allison St *CQT* . . . . . . . . . . . . **165** X31
Allison St *MAP* . . . . . . . . . . . **167** Y48
Allison St *RMD* . . . . . . . . . . . **202** H14
Allman St *BUR* . . . . . . . . . . **164** X-Y26
Allwood St *ABT* . . . . . . . . . . **250** T-U73
Alma Av *CHL* . . . . . . . . . . . . . . **233** N6
Alma St *ABT* . . . . . . . . . . . . . **270** V76
Alma St *VAN* **142** T8 **162** U8 V8 W8 X-Y8
Almond Pl *BUR* . . . . . . . . . . . **164** X29
Almondel Ct *WVA* . . . . . . . . . . **121** K5
Almondel Pl *WVA* . . . . . . . . . . **121** K5
Almondel Rd *WVA* . . . . . . . . **121** K4-5
Alouette Blvd *PTM* . . . . . . . . **187** B47
Alouette Ct *RMD* . . . . . . . . . . **202** J12
Alouette Dr *CQT* . . . . . . . . . . **165** W36
Alouette Dr *RMD* . . . . . . . . . . **202** J12
Alouette Pl *PTM* . . . . . . . . . . **187** B47
Alpen Pl *SUR* . . . . . . . . . . . . **185** A34
Alpenwood La *DEL* . . . . . . . . **263** Z17
Alpha Av *BUR* . . . . **143** S-T22 **163** U22
Alpha Dr *BUR* . . . . . . . . . . . . **143** T22
Alpha Lake Rd *WHS* . . . . . . . **401** H98
Alpha Lake Vlg *WHS* . . . . . . . **401** H1
Alpine Av *ABT* . . . . . . . . . . . . **270** V73
Alpine Cr *CHL* . . . . . . . . . . . . **233** N8
Alpine Cr *MAP* . . . . . . . . . . . **167** Y49
Alpine Cr *WHS* . . . . . . . . . . . . **401** F3
Alpine Ct *CQT* . . . . . . . . . **165** V34-35
Alpine Ct *DNV* . . . . . . . . . . . . **123** J16
Alpine Ct *MIS* . . . . . . . . . . . . **210** H75
Alpine Dr *ANM* . . . . . . . . . . . **125** N33
Alpine La *CQT* . . . . . . . . . . . . **145** Q38
Alpine Pl *DEL* . . . . . . . . . . . . **224** K30
Alpine Pl *PMD* . . . . . . . . . . . . **145** R36
Alpine Way *WHS* . . . . . . . . **401** B-C3
Alta Av *ABT* . . . . . . . . . . **270** V74-75
Alta Ct *RMD* . . . . . . . . . . . . . **202** F11
Alta Lake Pl *CQT* . . . . . . . . . **165** V36
Alta Lake Rd *WHS* . . . . . . . . . . . . . . . . . . . . . . . . **401** D2-3 F2 G1-2 H1
Alta Vista Rd *WHS* . . . . . . . **401** F2-3
Altair Pl *BUR* . . . . . . . . . . . . . **164** V29
Altamont Cr *WVA* . . . . . . . . . . **122** K8
Altamont Pl *WVA* . . . . . . . . . . **122** K8
Alton Pl *SUR* . . . . . . . . . . . . **205** G36
Altona Pl *RMD* . . . . . . . . . . . **202** H14
Altringham Ct *BUR* . . . . . **164** Y26-27
Alvin Narod Mews *VAN* . . . . **142** T13
Alvis Ct *CQT* . . . . . . . . . . . . . **145** R37
Amadis Cr *CHL* . . . . . . . . . . . **213** E5
Amazon Ct *PCQ* . . . . . . . . . . **166** U41
Amazon St *PCQ* . . . . . . . . . . **166** U41
Ambassador Cr *WHS* . . . . . . **401** E4
Amber Ct *CQT* . . . . . . . . . . . **145** Q36
Amber Dr *CHL* . . . . . . . . . . **213** H5-6
Amberly Pl *VAN* . . . . . . . . . . **183** A20
Amberpoint Pl *ABT* . . . . . . . . **250** S71
Amberwood Pl *BUR* . . . . . . . **164** U28
Amble Greene Blvd *SUR* . . . . **265** W33
Amble Greene Cl *SUR* . . . . . **265** W33
Amble Greene Ct *SUR* . . . . . **265** W33
Amble Greene Dr *SUR* . . . **265** V-W33
Amble Greene Pl *SUR* . . . **265** V-W33
Amble Wood Dr *SUR* . . . **265** W33-34
Ambleside Cl *PCQ* . . . . . . . . **146** S41
Ambleside La *WVA* . . . . . **122** M10-11
Amblewood Pl *ABT* . . . . **270** W76-77
Amess St *NEW* . . . . . . . . . **164** X-Y30
Amethyst Av *RMD* . . . . . . . . **202** H14
Amherst Av *DNV* . . . . . . . . . . **143** Q21
Amicus Pl *ABT* . . . . . . . . . . . **250** T74
Amiens Rd *CHL* . . . . . . . . . . . **233** N5
Amundsen Pl *RMD* . . . . . . . . **202** G9
Anahim Dr *RMD* . . . . **202** J14 **203** J15
Ancaster Cr *VAN* . . . . . . . . . . **183** A18
Anchor Bay *DEL* . . . . . . . . . . **223** N17
Anchor Pl *CQT* . . . . . . . . . . . **165** U36
Ancient Cedars La *WHS* . . . **401** H-J2
Anderson Av *ABT* . . . . . . . . . **210** J78
Anderson Av *CHL* . . . . . . . . . . **193** C8
Anderson Cr *WVA* . . . . . . . . **122** L-M12
Anderson Pl *DEL* . . . **223** P20 **243** Q20
Anderson Pl *MAP* . . . . . . . . . **187** A50
Anderson Rd *RMD* . . . . . **202** F12-13
Anderson St *VAN* . . . **10** K35 **162** U12
Anderson St *WRK* . . . . . . . . **265** W-X36
Anderson Way *PCQ* . . . . . . **166** V-W40
Anderson Creek Dr *MAP* **167** V53-54
Andover Cr *WVA* . . . . . . . . . . **122** J12
Andover Pl *WVA* . . . . . . . . **122** J12-13
Andrews Av *CHL* . . . . . . . . . . . **213** E8
Andrews Pl *ABT* . . . . . . . . . . **270** V76
Andrews Rd *RMD* . . . . . . . . . **222** L10
Angela Av *CHL* . . . . . . . . . . **213** F7-8
Angela Dr *PMD* . . . . . . . . **145** T31-32
Angelo Av *PCQ* . . . . . . . . . . **166** U40
Angelus La *SQM* . . . . . . . . . . . **301** E4
Anglers Pl *VAN* . . . . . . . . . . . **182** A11
Anglesea Dr *RMD* . . . . . . . . **202** J14
Angus Cr *ABT* . . . . . . . . . . . . **251** R79
Angus Dr *CHL* . . . . . . . . . . . . **193** D8
Angus Dr *VAN* . . . . . . . . . . . . . . . . . . . . . . . . **162** V12 V-Y11 **182** A-B11 Z11
Angus Pl *HHS* . . . . . . . . . . . . **155** R19
Angus Pl *SUR* . . . . . . . . . . . . **226** M41
Anita Ct *CNV* . . . . . . . . . . . . **123** M19
Anita Dr *PCQ* . . . . . . . . . . . . **166** W39
Ann St *VAN* . . . . . . . . . . . . . . **163** X20
Annacis Hwy *DEL* . . . . . . . . . . . . . . . . . **204** J27 **224** K28 M28-29 P30
Annacis Pkwy *DEL* . . . . . . **184** C-D28
Annance Ct *DEL* . . . . . . . **204** F26-27
Annapolis Pl *RMD* . . . . . . . . . **202** J9
Anne Macdonald Way *DNV* . . . . . . . . . . . . . . . . . . . . . . . . . . . . **124** N24-25
Annieville Pl *DEL* . . . . . . . . . **204** F29
Anola Dr *BUR* . . . . . . . . . . . **164** U23
Anora Dr *ABT* . . . . . **250** U78 **270** V78
Ansell Pl *WVA* . . . . . . . . . . . . **101** D4
Anskar Ct *CQT* . . . . . . . . . . . **165** U31
Anson Av *CQT* . . . . . . . . . . . . **145** T38
Anson Av *RMD* . . . . . . . . . . **182** C-D11
Anson Pl *HOP* . . . . . . . . . . . . **118** E46
Antelope Av *MIS* . . . . . . . . . **210** H73
Antelope Cr *MIS* . . . . . . . . . **210** H73
Anthony Ct *NEW* . . . . . . . . . **184** A29
Antrim Av *BUR* . . . . . . . . . . . **184** Z23
Antrim Rd *SUR* . . . . . . . . . . . **185** B35
Antwerp La *VAN* . . . . . . . . . . . **162** U8
Anvil Cr *RMD* . . . . . . . . . . . **202** G8-9
Anvil Ct *CQT* . . . . . . . . . . . . **146** R39
Anvil Gn *PCQ* . . . . . . . . . . . . **165** Y38
Anvil Way *SUR* . . . **205** H32-33 J32-33
Anvil Way (129A St) *SUR* . . . **205** J33
Anvil Way (78 Av) *SUR* . . . . **205** H32
Anzio Dr *VAN* . . . . . . . . . . **163** V-W20
Apaloosa Pl *SUR* . . . . . . . . **226** M44
Apel Dr *PCQ* . . . . . . . . . . . . **146** S41
Apex Av *DNV* . . . . . **124** N24 **144** P24
Apex Ct *ABT* . . . . . . . . . . . . **249** S70
Apex Pl *DNV* . . . . . . . . . . . . **144** P24
Appel Rd *KNT* . . . . . . . . . . . **175** Y21
Appian Way *CQT* . . . **164** V30 **165** V31
Appin Rd *DNV* . . . . . . . . . **123** M-N20
Apple Grove Cl *MAP* . . . . . . **187** Z53
Appleby Ct *MIS* . . . . . . . . . . **210** G73

Appleby La *MIS* . . . . . . . 210 F73
Appledale Pl *VAN* . . . . . . 183 Z20
Applehill Cr *SUR* . . . . . . . 205 F33
Applewood Dr *ABT* . . . . . 251 S80
Appleyard Ct *PMD* . . . . . 145 S35
Appliance Science La *UEL* . . 161 U4
Apps Ct *MIS* . . . . . . . . . . 210 G75
April Rd *PMD* . . . . . . . 145 Q32-33
Aqua Dr *VAN* . . . 183 A17-18 B17-18
Aquarius Dr *BUR* . . . . . . 164 V29
Aquarius Mews *VAN* . . . . . . . . .
. . . . . . . . 11 J37-38 142 T13-14
Aquila Dr *ABT* . . . 251 T79-80 U80
Aquila Pl *RMD* . . . . . . . 202 H-J14
Aquilini Dr *PTM* . . . . . 147 Q-R49
Aragon Rd *RMD* . . . 202 J14 203 J15
Araki Gt *MIS* . . . . . . . . . 210 G76
Arbor Av *VAN* . . . . . . 183 Z20-21
Arbor St *BUR* . . . . . . . . 183 Z21
Arborlynn Dr *DNV* . . . . . 123 N20
Arbour Pl *CHL* . . . . . . . . 193 D7
Arbour Pl *DEL* . . . . . . . . 204 G27
Arbroath St *BUR* . . 184 Z24 Z24-25
Arbury Av *CQT* . . . . . . . 165 V34
Arbutus Av *CHL* . . . . . . 213 E-F8
Arbutus Av *MIS* . . . . . . . 210 H74
Arbutus Div *VAN* . . . . . . 182 Z11
Arbutus Dr *KNT* . . . . 175 X21-22
Arbutus Dr *SQM* . . . . . . . 301 K3
Arbutus Dr *WHS* . . . . . . . 401 F3
Arbutus La *WVA* . . . . . . . 101 G1
Arbutus Pl *CQT* . . . . . . . 145 P38
Arbutus Pl *SUR* . . . . . . . 186 C40
Arbutus Pl *WVA* . . . . . . . 101 G1
Arbutus Rd *WVA* . . . . . . . 101 G1
Arbutus St *ABT* . . . . . . . 250 U72
Arbutus St *NEW* . . . . . . 184 A29
Arbutus St *VAN* . . 10 J-K32 142 T11
. . . 162 U11 U-V11 Y11 182 Z11 Z11
Arbutus Wynd *SUR* . . . . . 186 C40
Arcadia Rd *RMD* . . . . 202 E-F13
Arcadian Way *ABT* . . . . . 250 R75
Archer St *NEW* . . . 164 Y30 184 Z30
Archibald Rd *WRK* . . . 265 W-X36
Archibald Way *WHS* . . . . . 401 F3
Archimedes St *VAN* . . . . 163 X-Y20
Arcola St *BUR* . . . . 184 Z25 Z26
Arden Av *BUR* . . . . . . . . 164 U27
Arden Dr *ABT* . . . . . . . 250 S-T78
Ardingley Av *BUR* . . 164 V24 V-W24
Argentia Dr *RMD* . . 202 J10 222 K10
Argo Pl *BUR* . . . . . . . . . 164 V29
Argue St *PCQ* . . 165 Y38 166 Y39-40
Argyle Av (Ambleside) *WVA* . . . .
. . . . . . . . . . . 122 M10 M11
Argyle Av (Horseshoe Bay) *WVA* . .
. . . . . . . . . . . . . . . . 101 G2
Argyle Dr *VAN* . . . . . . . . . . .
. . . 163 X17 X-Y17 183 A17 Z17
Argyle Rd *DNV* . . . . . . 123 L19-20
Argyle St *CQT* . . . . . . . 146 Q41
Argyll Cr *SQM* . . . . . . . . 301 E4
Argyll St *ABT* . . . . . . . . 250 S74
Aries Dr *BUR* . . . . . . . . 164 V29
Arlington Cr *DNV* . . . . . . 123 L15
Arlington Dr *CHL* . . . . . 233 L-M5
Arlington St *ABT* . . . . . 250 T-U75
Arlington St *VAN* . . 163 Y20 183 Z20
Armada St *CQT* . . . . . . . 165 U36
Armitage St *CHL* . . . . . . 213 E8
Armour Ct *DNV* . . . . . . . 123 J20
Armstrong Av *ABT* . . . . . 250 Q78
Armstrong Av *BUR* . . . 164 X-Y29
Armstrong Pl *CHL* . . . . . 233 N8
Armstrong Rd *CHL* . . . . . 194 D12
Armstrong St *RMD* . . 202 G13-14
Arnhem Rd *CHL* . . . . . 233 M-N6
Arpe Ct *DEL* . . . . . . . . 204 G27
Arpe Rd *DEL* . . . . . . . . 204 G27
Arran Pl *SUR* . . . . . . . . 205 F32
Arras Rd *CHL* . . . . . . . . 233 N6
Arrow La *CQT* . . . . . . . . 165 X31
Arrow St *BUR* . . . . . . . . 164 Y23
Arrow-Wood Cl *PMD* . . 145 R-S35
Arrow-Wood Pl *PMD* . . . 145 S35
Arrowhead Rd *SQM* . . . . 301 B2
Arrowsmith Dr *RMD* . . . . 202 H14
Arrowsmith Pl *CQT* . . . . 146 Q39
Arrowsmith Pl *RMD* . . . . 202 H14
Arroyo Ct *DNV* . . . . . . . 123 M22
Arthur Av *BUR* . . . . . . . 184 A23
Arthur Dr *DEL* . . . 243 Q16 S16-17
Arthur Pl *CQT* . . . . . . . 165 U32
Arts Rd *MIS* . . . . . . . . . 144 S29
Arundel La *CQT* . . . . 165 X35-36
Arundel Rd *DNV* . . . . . . 123 K15

Arvida Dr *RMD* . . . . . . . 202 H14
Arvida Gt *RMD* . . . . . . . 202 H14
Arvin Ct *BUR* . . . . . . . . 144 T27
Asbeck La *SUR* . . . . . . . 245 T31
Ascot Pl *VAN* . . . . . . . . 163 X20
Ascot St *CQT* . . . . . . 165 V-W34
Ascott Av *ABT* . . . . . . . 250 S77
Ash Cr *VAN* . . . . . . . . . 182 Z13
Ash Pl *SQM* . . . . . . . . . 301 J4
Ash St *ABT* . . . . . . . . 250 T-U76
Ash St *NEW* . . . . . 184 A28 B29
Ash St *RMD* . . . . . . . . 202 G-J13
Ash St *VAN* . . . . . . . . . . . . . .
. . . 162 U-V14 V13-14 W13 X13-14 Y13
. . . . . . 182 A13 A-B13 Z13
Ash St *WRK* . . . . . . . 265 X-Y38
Ash Grove Cr *BUR* . . . . . 164 U29
Ashbrook Ct *RMD* . . . . 202 H13-14
Ashbrook Pl *CQT* . . . . . 165 U38
Ashburn St *VAN* . . 183 A18 Z18
Ashbury Ct *MAP* . . . . . . 187 Z50
Ashbury Pl *CHL* . . . . . . 233 M4
Ashbury Pl *DEL* . . . . . . 243 Q15
Ashby Dr *CHL* . . . . . . . 233 M8
Ashby Pl *RMD* . . . . . . . 202 H14
Ashby St *CQT* . . . . . . . 165 W31
Ashby Way *ABT* . . . . . . 270 V74
Ashcroft Av *RMD* . . 202 J14 203 J15
Ashcroft Dr *ABT* . . . 250 S72-73
Ashdown Pl *SUR* . . . . . 186 C40
Ashfeild Rd *WVA* . . . . . . 121 K3
Ashford Rd *SUR* . . . . . . 205 F36
Ashley Cl *DNV* . . . . . . 123 K-L20
Ashley Cr *MAP* . . . . . . . 187 Z48
Ashley St *CQT* . . . . . . . 165 W31
Ashley Way *ABT* . . . . . . 270 V74
Ashley Grove Ct *BUR* . . . . 164 U29
Ashmore Pl *MIS* . . . . . . 210 G73
Ashton Rd *KNT* . . . . . . 175 V-W18
Ashurst Av *CQT* . 165 W35-36 X35-36
Ashwell Rd *CHL* . . . . . 213 E-F5
Ashwood Dr *PMD* . . . . . 145 Q35
Ashwood Dr *RMD* . . 202 H13-14
Ashwood Gt *RMD* . . . . . 202 H14
Ashworth Av *BUR* . 164 Y25 184 Z25
Ashworth Pl *BUR* . . . . . 164 Y25
Aspen Av *ABT* . . . . . . . 250 R74
Aspen Av *VAN* . . . . . . . 162 X11
Aspen Cr *WVA* . . . . . . . 121 J3
Aspen Ct *MIS* . . . . . . . 210 H75
Aspen Ct *PMD* . . . . . . . 145 R35
Aspen Ct *WHS* . . . . . . . 401 G2
Aspen Dr *WHS* . . . . . . . 401 G2
Aspen Dr *WVA* . . . . . . . 121 J3
Aspen Pl *BUR* . . . . . . . 164 X30
Aspen Pl *CHL* . . . . . . . 213 E7-8
Aspen Rd *SQM* . . . . . . . 301 F1-2
Aspen St *CQT* . . . . . . . 165 V31
Aspen Way *DEL* . . . . . . 223 N-P17
Aspenwood Dr *PMD* . . 145 Q-R35
Aspenwood Pl *BUR* . . . . 164 U28
Aspin Ct *RMD* . . . . . . . 202 G-H14
Aspin Dr *RMD* . . . . . . . 202 G-H14
Aspin Pl *RMD* . . . . . . . 202 H14
Aster Ct *CQT* . . . . . . . 145 R36
Aster Rd *SUR* . . . . . . . 265 V38
Aster Ter *MIS* . . . . . . . 210 G75
Astor Dr *BUR* . . . . . . . 164 V30
Astoria *RMD* . . . . . . . . 202 G13
Astoria Cr *ABT* . . . . . . 250 T72
Astoria Ct *ABT* . . . . . 250 S-T72
Atchelitz Rd *CHL* . . . . . 213 G-H4
Athabasca Dr *RMD* . 202 H14 203 H15
Athabaska St *DEL* . . . . 243 Q-R22
Athlone St *VAN* . . . . . . 162 Y12
Athletes Way *VAN* 11 K39-40 142 T14
Atkins Av *PCQ* . . 165 V38 166 V39
Atkins Ct *CQT* . . . . . 165 U33-34
Atkinson Rd *ABT* . . . . . 251 S83
Atlantic Av *CQT* . . . . . . 145 S37
Atlantic St *VAN* . . 11 J41 143 T15-16
Atlee Av *BUR* . . . . . . . 164 W24
Atlin Pl *CQT* . . . . . . . . 165 W36
Atlin St *VAN* . . . . . . . . 163 W19
Atwater Cr *ABT* . . . . . 250 S-T72
Atwood Ct *ABT* . . . . . . 251 Q81
Aubeneau Cr *WVA* . . . . 122 L-M12
Aubrey Pl *VAN* . . . . . . 163 W24
Aubrey St *BUR* . . . 144 T24-25 T26-27
Auburn Dr *RMD* . . 202 H14 203 H15
Auburn Pl *CHL* . . . . . . 213 E8
Auburn Pl *CQT* . . . . . . 145 R37
Auburn Pl *DEL* . . . . . . 224 K30
Auburn St *ABT* . . . . . . 250 U72
Auckland St *NEW* . . . . . 184 B28
Audley Blvd *DEL* . . . . . 204 E27
Audrey Dr *PCQ* . . . . . . 166 W39

August Dr *SUR* . . . . . . . 205 G37
Augusta Av *BUR* 144 T26 T26 164 U26
Augusta Pl *CQT* . . . 145 P38 146 P39
Augusta Pl *DEL* . . . . . . 263 W16
Augusta St *NEW* . . . . . . 184 B28
Auguston Pkwy E *ABT* . . . 251 Q81
Auguston Pkwy S *ABT* . 251 Q80-81
Aurora Ct *DEL* . . . . . . . 243 Q18
Aurora Pl *ABT* . . . . . . . 250 T75
Aurora Pl *MAP* . . . . . . . 167 Y54
Aurora Rd *DNV* . . . . . . . 123 L15
Aurora St *MAP* . . . . . . . 167 Y54
Austin Av *ABT* . . . . . . . 250 S-T72
Austin Av *CQT* . . . . . 165 W31-36
Austin Rd *BUR* . . . . . . . 164 W30
Austin Rd *CQT* . . . . . . . 165 W31
Austrey Av *VAN* . . . . . . 163 X19-20
Automall Dr *ABT* . . . . 249 S-T68
Automall Dr *CNV* . . . . . . 123 N15
Autumn Av *ABT* . . . . . . 250 U72-73
Autumn Dr *WHS* . . . . . . . 401 B5
Autumn Pl *WHS* . . . . . . . 401 B5
Avalon Av *BUR* . . . . . . . 164 X28
Avalon Av *CHL* . . . . . . . 193 C7
Avalon Cr *ABT* . . . . . . . 270 V73
Avalon Dr *PMD* . . . . . . . 145 S35
Avalon Pl *WVA* . . . . . . 121 J2-3
Avery Av *VAN* . . . . . . . 182 A12
Aves Ter *MIS* . . . . . . . . 210 H71
Avison Way *VAN* . . . . . . 142 Q13
Avon Pl *PCQ* . . . . . . . . 166 V42
Avondale Av *ABT* . . . . . . 250 T75
Avondale Av *VAN* . . . . . . 162 X12
Avondale St *BUR* . . . . . . 163 V21
Avondale St *CQT* . . . . . . 146 Q40
Avonlynn Cr *DNV* . . . . . . 123 N20
Axen Rd *SQM* . . . . . . . 301 B1-2
Axford Bay *PMD* . . . . . . 145 R33
Ayleslynn Dr *DNV* . . . . . 123 N20
Ayling St *PCQ* . . . . . . . 146 S42
Aylmer Av *RMD* . . . . . . 182 C-D11
Ayr Av *DNV* . . . . . . . . . 123 L15
Ayr Dr *SQM* . . . . . . . . . 301 E4
Ayr Dr *SUR* . . . . . . . . . 185 A37
Ayshire Dr *BUR* . . . . 144 T26-27
Azalea Cl *ABT* . . . . . . . 250 S78
Azalea Pl *MIS* . . . . . . . 210 J75
Azalea Pl *PCQ* . . . . . . . 146 S40
Aztec St *RMD* . . . . . . . 183 D15
Azure Blvd *RMD* . . . . . . 202 F11
Azure Ct *CQT* . . . 145 Q38 146 Q39
Azure Gt *RMD* . . . . . . . 202 F11
Azure Rd *RMD* . . . . . . . 202 F11

## B

B St *ABT* . . . . . . . . . 270 Y-Z78
Babcock Pl *DEL* . . . . . . 263 W17
Babich Pl *ABT* . . . . . . . 250 T75
Babich St *ABT* . . . . . . . 250 T75
Badger Av *MIS* . . . . . . . 210 H73
Badger Pl *DNV* . . . . . . . 124 M26
Badger Rd *DNV* . . . . . . 124 M26
Baffin Ct *RMD* . . . . . . . 202 G9
Baffin Dr *RMD* . . . . . . . 202 G9
Baffin Pl *BUR* . . . . . . . 164 Y24
Bahr La *SUR* . . . . . . . 245 T-U31
Bailey Cr *HOP* . . . . . . . 118 H43
Bailey Cr *SUR* . . . . . . . 184 D30
Bailey Ct *PCQ* . . 165 X38 166 X39
Bailey Pl *MIS* . . . . . . . . 210 G73
Bailey Rd *CHL* . . . . . . . 233 L8
Bailey St *SQM* . . . . . . . 301 J1-2
Baillie St *VAN* . . . . . . . 162 X13
Bainbridge Av *BUR* . . . . 164 V26
Baird Rd *DNV* . . . 123 K-L19 L19
Bairdmore Cr *RMD* . . . 202 G8-9
Baker Dr *CHL* . . . . . . . 213 F7-8
Baker Dr *CQT* . . . . . . . 165 U35
Baker Pl *DEL* . . . . . . . 224 L30
Baker Rd *DEL* . . . . . . 224 K-L30
Baker Rd *SQM* . . . . . . . 301 K2
Baker View St *DNV* . . . . 144 P26
Bakerview *SUR* . . . . . . 266 W39
Bakerview Av *MIS* . . . 210 H73-74
Bakerview Dr *RMD* . . . 202 J13-14
Bakerview Dr *SUR* . . . . 225 N36
Bakerview St *ABT* . 250 U72 270 V72
Balabanian Cir *MAP* . . . 167 Y53
Balaclava St *VAN* . . . . . . . . . .
. . . 162 U-V9 W9 W-X9 X9 X-Y9 182 Z9
Balbirnie Blvd *PMD* . . . . 145 T31
Balboa Ct *CQT* . . . . . . . 165 X35
Baldwin Rd *ABT* . . . . . 250 T-U77

Baldwin St *CQT* . . . . 145 S37-38
Baldwin St *VAN* . . . . . 163 W-X18
Balfour Av *VAN* . . 162 V-W12 V-W13
Balfour Dr *ABT* . . . . . . . 250 S72
Balfour Dr *CQT* . . 165 W35-36
Balkan St *VAN* . . . . . . . 163 W15
Ballam Rd *CHL* . . . . . . . 193 A8
Ballantrae Ct *PMD* . . . . 145 T31
Ballantree Pl *WVA* . 102 H13 122 J13
Ballantree Rd *WVA* . . . . 102 H13
Ballenas Ct *CQT* . . . . . . 146 R39
Balloch Dr *SUR* . . . . 205 E33
Balmoral Av *CHL* . . . . . . 233 L5
Balmoral Av *CQT* . . . 165 U33-34
Balmoral Dr *CQT* . . . 145 S-T35
Balmoral Pl *PMD* . . . . . 145 S35
Balmoral Rd E *DNV* . . . 123 K17
Balmoral Rd W *DNV* . . . 123 K17
Balmoral St *ABT* . . . . . 249 R68
Balmoral St *BUR* . . 184 Z25 Z26
Balmoral St *VAN* . . . . . 183 Z17
Balsam Av *CHL* . . . . . . 213 E8
Balsam Av *HHS* . . . . . 155 Q19
Balsam Av *MIS* . . . . . . 210 H75
Balsam Cr *ABT* . . . . . . 250 R74
Balsam Cr *SUR* . . . . . . 245 T33
Balsam Pl *PMD* . . . . . . 145 Q35
Balsam Pl *SQM* . . . . . . 301 J4
Balsam Pl *VAN* . . . . . . 162 Y10
Balsam St *FRA* . . . . . . 253 R5
Balsam St *MAP* . . . . . 167 W-X54
Balsam St *VAN* . . . . . . . . . .
. . 10 K32 162 U10 V10 X-Y10 Y10 182 Z10
Balsam Way *SQM* . . . . . 301 J4-5
Balsam Way *WHS* . . . . . 401 D-E3
Baltic St *CQT* . . . . . . . 165 X34
Bamberton Ct *RMD* . . 202 J11-12
Bamberton Dr *RMD* . . . 202 J11-12
Bamfield Dr *RMD* . . . . . 183 D15
Bamfield Gt *RMD* . . . . . 183 D15
Banbury Av *CQT* . . . . 145 R-S37
Banbury Rd *DNV* . 124 M-N26 N26
Banderas Bay *SUR* . . 266 V-W39
Banff Av *BUR* . . . . . . . 164 W23
Banff Ct *DNV* . . . . . . . 124 N25
Banff Pl *ABT* . . . . . . . 250 S74
Banford Rd *CHL* . . . . . . 194 D11
Bank St *BUR* . . . . . . . . 184 A25
Bank St *MIS* . . . . . . . . 230 K75
Banner Pl *CQT* . . . . . . 146 Q39
Bannister Dr *MIS* . . . . . 210 G75
Banting Pl *BUR* . . . . . . 183 A21
Banting St *CQT* . . . . 165 U31-32
Barbell Pl *BUR* . . . . . . 184 Z23
Barber Dr *CHL* . . . . . . . 193 D6
Barber La *PMD* . . . . . 145 Q-R33
Barber St *PMD* . . . . . . 145 R33
Barberry Dr *PCQ* . . . . . 166 U41
Barberry Pl *PMD* . . . 145 R35-36
Barclay St *MAP* . . . . . . 187 A48
Barclay St *VAN* . . . . . . . . . .
. . . 10 F35 G36 142 R-S12 S13
Bargen Dr *RMD* . . . . . 183 C-D15
Barkentine Rd *RMD* . . . 222 K9
Barker Av *BUR* . . . . . . . . . .
. . . . . 163 W21 X22 Y21 Y21-22
Barker Av *MAP* . . 187 A49 Z49
Barker Cr *BUR* . . . . . 163 X21-22
Barkerville Ct *RMD* . . . 202 J12
Barkley Dr *DEL* . . . . . . 224 K30
Barkley Pl *DEL* . . . . . . 224 K30
Barlynn Cr *DNV* . . . . . . 123 M19
Barmond Av *RMD* . . 202 H8-9
Barnard Dr *RMD* . . . 202 E-F8
Barnard Pl *RMD* . . . . . 202 E8
Barnard St *VAN* . . . . . 182 A-B11
Barnes Dr *RMD* . . . . . . 183 C16
Barnes Rd *DEL* . . . . . 204 E-F29
Barnes Rd *PTM* . . . . . . 166 X42
Barnet Hwy *CQT* . . . . 145 T36
Barnet Hwy *PMD* . . . . 145 S32
Barnet Rd *BUR* . . 144 R27 R-S30 S26
Barnett St *MIS* . . . . . 210 H75-76
Barnfield Pl *WHS* . . . . . 401 E3
Barnham Pl *WVA* . . . . . 122 J13
Barnham Rd *WVA* . . . . 122 J13
Barnsdale St *MAP* . . . . 167 X53
Barnston Dr E *SUR* 186 D43 206 E43
Barnston Dr W *SUR* . . 186 D41
Barnston View Rd *PTM* . 186 B46
Baron Pl *CQT* . 145 T34 165 U34
Barr St *MIS* . . . . . . . . 210 E75
Barrie Av *BUR* . . . . . . 184 Z23
Barritt Rd *CHL* . . . . . . 193 D5

Barrons Way *ABT* . . . . . 270 W77
Barrow St *DNV* . . . . . . 143 Q20
Barrymore Dr *DEL* . . . . 204 J28
Bartlett Av *CQT* . . . . . . 165 U33
Bartlett Ct *BUR* . . . . . . 164 W30
Bartlett St *CHL* . . . . . . 193 D7-8
Bartlett St *LGT* . . . . . . 207 F54
Barton Av *CHL* . . . . . . 213 F5-6
Bashuk Pl *RMD* . . . . . . 202 H10
Basran Av *NEW* . . . . . . 184 D26
Bassani Av *ABT* . . . . . . 251 S79
Bassano Ter *ABT* . . . . . 251 S79
Bassett Pl *RMD* . . . . . . 202 G11
Bassett Rd *RMD* . . . . . 202 G11
Batchelor Bay Pl *WVA* . . 101 G1
Bateman Rd *ABT* . . . 250 R76-78
Bates Rd *ABT* . . . . 230 N71 249 Q70
Bates Rd *DEL* . . . . . . . 204 J28
Bates Rd *RMD* . . . . . . . 202 J12
Bath Rd *RMD* . . . . . . . 183 C-D16
Bathgate Pl *RMD* . . . . 183 C-D16
Bathgate Way *RMD* . . 183 C-D16
Battison St *VAN* . . . . . . 163 Y20
Battistoni Pl *PCQ* . 145 T38 146 T39
Battle Av *MAP* . . . . . . . 187 A48
Bauer St *VAN* . . . . . . . 163 U17
Baxter Pl *BUR* . . . . . . . 164 V29
Bay St *DNV* . . . . . . . . 143 Q20
Bay St *LGT* . . . . . . . . 207 F54
Bay St *WRK* . . . . . . . . 265 X36
Bay St *WVA* . . . . . . . . 101 G2
Bay Mill Rd *PTM* . . . . . 186 B46
Bayard Pl *SUR* . . . . . . 226 M44
Baycrest Av *CQT* . . . . 146 R-S42
Baycrest Dr *DNV* . . . . . 144 P26
Baydala Ct *RMD* . . . . . 182 C14
Baynes St *MIS* . . . . . . 210 H77
Bayridge Av *WVA* . . 121 K5-6 K6
Bayridge Cr *WVA* . . . . . 121 K5
Bayridge Ct *WVA* . . . 121 K5-6
Bayridge Pl *WVA* . . . 121 K5-6
Bayshore Av *CHL* . . . . 233 N4
Bayshore Dr *VAN* . . . . . . . .
. . . . . . . 10 E35-36 142 R12-13
Bayshore Dr *WHS* . . . . . 401 H1
Bayswater Av *CQT* . . . . 146 R40
Bayswater Pl *CQT* . . . . 146 R40
Bayswater St *VAN* . 142 T10 162 U10
Baytree Ct *BUR* . . . . . . 164 X23
Bayview Dr *BUR* . . . . . 144 S26
Bayview Dr *DEL* . . . . . 263 X16
Bayview Pl *DEL* . . . . . 263 X16
Bayview Pl *LIO* . . . . . . 101 B23
Bayview Pl *LIO* . . . . . . 101 B23
Bayview Sq *CQT* . . . . . 165 U33
Bayview St *RMD* . . . . . 222 L18-9
Bayview St *SUR* . . . . . 245 U31
Beach Av *PMD* . . . . . . 145 Q32
Beach Av *VAN* . . . . . . . . . .
. . . . 10 F33-34 G-H34 H35 J35-36
. . . 142 R11-12 S12-13 S-T12 T12 T13
Beach Cr *VAN* . . 10 J-K36 142 T13
Beach Ct *CQT* . . . . . . . 165 U36
Beach Rd *SUR* . . . 266 Y39-40 Z40
Beach Grove Ct *DEL* . . . 263 X18
Beach Grove Rd *DEL* . . 263 W-X18
Beach View Av *WRK* . . 265 X36-37
Beachview Dr *DNV* . . . 144 P-Q26
Beacon Dr *CQT* . . . . . 145 T36-37
Beacon La *WVA* . . . . . . 121 L3
Beacon Rd *HOP* . . . . . . 118 G43
Beaconsfield Rd *DNV* . . 123 K15-16
Beadnell Ct *VAN* . 183 A19 A20 Z20
Beagle Ct *VAN* . . . . . . 183 Z19
Beaman Dr *KNT* . . . . 175 W-X20
Beamish Ct *BUR* . . . . . 163 X22
Beamish Ct *VAN* . . . . 183 A19-20
Bear Av *HHS* . . . . . 155 P19-20
Bear Cr *MIS* . . . . . . . . 210 H73
Bear La *WVA* . . . . . . . 121 L3
Bear Cave La *WHS* . . 401 G-H2
Bear Creek Dr *SUR* . . . 205 H35
Bearcroft Dr *RMD* . . . . 183 D15
Beaton Rd *ABT* . . . 230 M74-75 M78
Beatrice St *VAN* . . . . . . . . . .
. . . 163 W-X17 Y17 183 A17 Z17
Beatrice St La *PMD* . . 145 R-S35
Beatty Dr *MIS* . . . . . . . 230 K74
Beatty St *VAN* . . 11 J38 142 S-T14
Beatty Walk *VAN* . 11 J38 142 T13-14
Beaufort Pl *DNV* . . . . . 124 N26
Beaufort Rd *CHL* . . . . . 233 K7
Beaufort Rd *DNV* . . . 124 N25-26
Beaulynn Pl *DNV* . . . 123 M-N20
Beaumaris Cl *PCQ* . . . 166 U41

Beaumont Dr DNV . . . . . . . 123 K15
Beaver Cr CHL . . . . . . . . . . 194 C9
Beaver Dr MIS . . . . . . . . 210 H72-73
Beaver Dr SUR . . . . . . . 185 D31-32
Beaver La WHS . . . . . . . . . . 401 E3
Beaver Rd DNV . . . . . . . . . 123 J17
Beaver St ABT . . . . 250 U73 270 V73
Beaverbrook Cr BUR . . . 164 V29-30
Beaverbrook Dr BUR . . . . . 164 V29
Beavis St HOP . . . . . . . . . . 118 F43
Beck Rd ABT . . . . . . . . . 250 T-U77
Beckett Rd SUR . . . . . . . . 245 T32
Beckley St MAP . . . . . . . . 187 A48
Beckman Pl RMD . . . . . . . 182 C14
Beckwith Rd RMD . . . . . . 182 C13
Bedard Cr PMD . . . . . . . . 145 T32
Bedford Ct DNV . . . . . . . . 122 L14
Bedford Dr SUR . . . . . . 185 A35-36
Bedford Pl ABT . . . 250 U73 270 V73
Bedford Pl CHL . . . . . . . . 233 M5
Bedford St PCQ . . . . . . . . 165 U38
Bedford Tr LGT . . . . . . . . 207 E53
Bedingfield St PMD . . . . . 145 Q33
Bedora Pl WVA . . . . . . . . 101 D4
Bedwell Bay Rd ANM . . 145 P31-32
Bedwell Bay Rd BEL . . . . . . . . . .
. . . . . . . . 124 N29-30 144 P28-29
Bedwell Bay Rd PMD . . . . 145 P31
Beech Av ABT . . . . 250 U72 270 V72
Beech Av HOP . . . . . . . 118 G42-43
Beech St PCQ . . . . . . . . . 166 U41
Beech Nut Av CHL . . . . . . 233 K5-6
Becham Rd RMD . . . . . . . 202 F-G8
Beechcliffe Dr BUR . . . . 164 V25
Beecher St SUR . . . . . . . . 245 U31
Beechwood Av DEL . . . . 224 L-M30
Beechwood Cr DNV . . . . . 122 N14
Beechwood Ct SUR . . . 106 C40-41
Beechwood Dr ABT . . . 270 V75-76
Beechwood Dr KNT . . . . 175 X20
Beechwood St DEL . . . . . 224 L30
Beechwood St VAN . . . . . . . . . . .
. . . . . . . . 162 Y11 182 Z11 Z11
Beecroft Cr ABT . . . . . . . 250 U77
Deedie Ct CQT . . . . . . . . 146 R40
Beedie Pl CQT . . . . . . . . 146 R40
Beedie St BUR . . . . . . . . 184 C23
Begbie St NEW . . . . . . . . 184 B29
Begg St VAN . . . . . . . . . . 143 T16
Begin St CQT . . . . . . . . . 165 X33
Beharrell Rd ABT . . . . 230 K78 M-P78
Behrner Dr SQM . . . . . . . 301 K2
Belair Cr DEL . . . . . . . 263 X16-17
Belair Dr CHL . . . . . . . . . 193 C7
Belair Dr DEL . . . . . . . 263 X16-17
Belair Dr RMD . . . . . . . 202 H11-12
Belanger Dr ABT . . . . . . . 251 R79
Belcarra Cr DNV . . . . . 144 S25-26
Belcarra Bay Rd BEL . . . . . . . . .
. . . . . . . . 124 N28 144 P28
Belden Rd BUR . . . . . . . . 164 V23
Belfast Av PCQ . . . . . . . . 166 W42
Belfriar Dr BUR . . . . . . . 164 W30
Belgrave Av DNV . . . . . . 123 J15
Belgrave Way DEL . 184 D27 204 E27
Bell Av BUR . . . . . . . . . . 164 V23
Bell Rd ABT . . . . . . 230 L-P77 250 Q77
Bell Rd CHL . . . . . 193 B-C8 194 A-B9
Bell Rd SUR . . . . . . . . . 226 M-N40
Bell-Irving St RMD . . . . . 202 E10
Bella Vista St VAN . . . . . 163 V17
Belle Pl PCQ . . . . . . . . . 166 W39
Belle Isle Pl DNV . . . . . . 122 M13
Bellelynn Pl DNV . . . . . . 123 N20
Belleville Av BUR . . . . . . 163 X21
Belleville St NEW . . . . 184 A-B28
Bellevue Av CQT . . . . . . 145 T35
Bellevue Cr WRK . . . . . . 265 X36
Bellevue Cr WVA 122 L8 L-M9 M10-11
Bellevue Dr CHL . . . . . . 213 F5
Bellevue Dr VAN . . . . 142 T7 161 T6
Bellflower Ct CQT . . . 145 Q36-37
Bellflower Dr RMD . . . . . 202 F9
Belloc St DNV . . . . . . . . 123 N22
Bellvue Cr ABT . . . . . . . 270 V74
Bellvue Pl ABT . . . . . . 270 V73-74
Bellwood Av BUR . . . . . 164 U23
Belmond Av ABT . . . . . 250 U71-72
Belmont Av DNV . . . . . . 123 L15
Belmont Av VAN . . . . 142 T7 161 T6
Belmont St NEW . . . . . . 184 A28
Belvedere Dr DNV . . . . . 123 J15
Belvista Cr DNV . . . . . . 123 J15
Belyea St NEW . . . . . . . 184 B27

Bemi Rd DEL . . . . . . . . . 224 K30
Ben Nevis Cr SUR . . . . . 205 F33
Benbow Rd WVA . . . . . . 122 K7
Bench Av MIS . . . . . . . 210 G71-72
Bend Ct CQT . . . . . . . . . 165 U33
Bendale Pl DNV . . . . . . . 123 N22
Bendale Rd DNV . . . . . . 123 N20
Benneck Way PCQ . . . . 165 X38
Bennet Dr PCQ . . . . . . 165 X-Y38
Bennett Rd RMD . . . . 202 G12-13
Bennett St BUR . . . 164 Y23 184 Z23
Bennie Pl PCQ . . . . . . . . 166 V41
Benson Dr PMD . . . . . . . 145 R33
Bent Ct NEW . . . . . . . . . 184 A28
Bentall St VAN . . . . . . . 163 V20
Bentinck Pl RMD . . . . . . 202 G8
Bentley Cr DEL . . . . . . . 223 P17
Bentley Ct DEL . . . . . . . 223 P17
Bentley Dr DEL . . . . . 223 P16-17
Bentley La DEL . . . . . . . 223 P16
Bentley Pl DEL . . . . . 223 P16-17
Bentley Rd PMD . . . . . . . 145 R34
Bentley Rd SUR . . . . . . . 185 B34
Bentley St VAN . . . . . . . 182 B12
Benz Cr LGT . . . . . . . . . 247 Q51
Beresford St BUR . . . . . . . . . . .
. . . . . . 163 Y22 Y22 183 Z22
. . 184 723 723-24 Z24 Z25 Z25-26
Berg Rd DEL . . . . . . . . . 203 J21
Berg Rd SUR . . . . . . . . . 185 B34
Bergen St MIS . . . . . . . . 210 H74
Bergman Cr CHL . . . . . . 233 P71
Bergman St ABT . . . . . . 249 T63
Bergstrom Rd WRK . . . . 265 W34
Beridale Ct BUR . . . . . . 144 T23
Bering Av VAN . . . . . . . 183 Z20
Berkeley Av CHL . . . . 193 D6-7
Berkeley Pl CQT . . . . 165 U37-38
Berkeley Pl SUR . . . . . . 205 J35
Berkeley St VAN . 163 Y18 183 Z18
Berkley Av DNV . . . . . . 123 M22
Berkley Pl BUR . . . . . 164 X-Y26
Berkley Rd DNV . . 123 N22 143 P22
Berkley St BUR . . . . . . . 164 Y26
Berks St ABT . . . . . . . . 250 T77
Berkshire Cr CQT . . . 125 N37-38
Bermon Pl DNV . . . . . . . 123 L20
Bernadotte St ABT . . . . 249 U63
Bernard Av CHL . . . . . . 213 F5-6
Bernard Pl PCQ . . . . . . 146 T41
Bornatchey St CQT . . 165 X31-32
Bernina Ct ABT . . . . . . . 250 U78
Berry Av MAP . . . 187 A49-50 A50
Berry Rd RMD . . . . . 222 K13-14
Berry St CQT . . . . . . . . 165 V33
Berton Av UEL . . . . . . . 161 V5
Berton Pl DNV . . . . . . . 123 N22
Berwick Ct BUR . . . . 164 Y24-25
Berwick St BUR . . . . . . 164 Y24
Beryl St CHL . . . . . . . . 213 F7-8
Bessborough Dr BUR . . . . . . . . .
. . . . 144 R23-24 R-S23 S24
Best Av MIS . . . . . . . . 210 G74 G-H75
Best Ct DNV . . . . . . . . . 124 N26
Best St MAP . . . . . . . . . 187 A49
Best St WRK . . . . . . . 265 W-X38
Beta Av BUR . . . . . . . . . . . . . .
. . . . 144 T23 163 U22 V22 164 U23
Beta Av N BUR . . . 143 S22 144 S23
Beta Av S BUR . . . . . 143 S-T22
Beth St NEW . . . . . . . . 184 Z29-30
Bevan Av ABT . . . . . . . 270 V73-75
Bevan Cr ABT . . . 250 U73 270 V73
Bevan St BUR . . . . . . . 184 B25
Bevan Way ABT . . . . . . 270 V74
Beverley Cr ABT . . . . . 250 S-T78
Beverley Cr DNV . . . . . 123 L15
Beverley Dr CHL . . . . . 193 C8
Beverly Cr VAN . . . . . . 162 W12
Beverly Rd DEL . . . . . . 204 F29
Bewicke Av CNV . 123 M-N16 143 P16
Bewicke Av DNV . . . . . 123 L16
Biddesden Pl WVA . . . . 122 K12
Bide Awhile Bay SUR . 266 V-W39
Bidwell St VAN . . . . . . . . . . . . .
. . . . . 10 F35 G34 142 R-S12 S12
Big Timber Ct WHS . . . 401 H-J2
Bighorn Pl CQT . . . . . . 145 Q38
Bighorn Ter MIS . . . . . . 210 H73
Bigleaf Ct CQT . . . . . . 145 Q38
Bignall Bay PMD . . . . . 145 Q33
Bill's Pl SQM . . . . . . . . 301 F4
Bill Reid Ter ABT . . . . . 251 Q81
Billy Brown Rd LGT . . . 207 E53-54
Binnie La SUR . . . . . . . 185 B34
Binning Av UEL . . . . . . 161 V5

Binning La WVA . . . . . . 122 K9
Biological Sciences Rd UEL . . . . .
. . . . . . . . . . . . . . . 161 U3-4
Birch Av MAP . . . . . . . 167 W54
Birch Cr CQT . . . . . . . . 145 S38
Birch Dr SQM . . . . . . . . 301 J4
Birch Pl DEL . . . . . . . . 204 F30
Birch Pl (Hop) HOP . . . . 118 G43
Birch Pl (Silver Creek) HOP 118 G42
Birch Rd KNT . . . . . . . 175 U-V17
Birch St ABT . . . . . . . . 250 U77
Birch St CHL . . . . . . . . 213 E-F6
Birch St FRA . . . . . . . . . 253 R5
Birch St HOP . . . . . . . . 118 G42
Birch St MIS . . . . . . . . . 210 J74
Birch St VAN . . . . 162 U-V12 182 A12
Birch Walk VAN . . . 10 K35 162 U12
Birch Wynd ANM . . . . . 145 P33
Birch Grove Pl BUR . . . . 164 U29
Birchbrook Pl CQT . . . . 165 U38
Birchfeild Pl WVA . . . . . 121 K3-4
Birchland Av PCQ . . . 166 U40-41
Birchlynn Pl DNV . . . . . 123 N20
Birchtree Gr SUR . . . . . 186 C40
Birchtrees Dr HOP . . 118 E46-47
Birchwood Cr BUR 163 W22 164 W23
Birchwood Cr PMD . . . . 145 Q35
Birchwood Pl BUR 163 W22 164 W23
Bird Rd RMD . . . . 182 C14 183 C15
Birkdale Pl BUR . . . . 144 T26-27
Birken Rd SQM . . . . . . 301 B1
Birkshire Pl PCQ . . . . . 146 S40
Birmingham Pl CHL . . . 233 M5
Birney Av UEL . . . . . . . 161 V5
Birney Pl DNV . . . . . . . 123 N22
Bishop Dr DNV . . . . . . 124 N25
Bishop Rd WRK . . . . . . 265 W35
Bishop Way WHS . . . . . 401 E3
Bishops Reach PTM . . . 186 B46
Bison Pl DEL . . . . . . . . 224 K30
Bissett Dr RMD . . . . . . 202 H14
Bissett Rd RMD . . . . . . 202 H14
Bittern Ct RMD . . . . . . 222 K10
Black Tusk Way SQM . . 301 E3
Blackbear Ct CQT . . . . 145 Q30
Blackberry Dr ANM . . . 145 U34
Blackberry Dr NEW . . 184 Z29-30
Blackbird Cr SUR . . . 185 B36-37
Blackburn Av WRK . . 265 W34-35
Blackburn Cr WRK . . . . 265 W36
Blackcomb Way WHS . . . . . . . . .
. . . 401 E5 E-F4 S23 S-T21 T22
Blackford St NEW . . . 184 A28-29
Blackham Dr ABT . . . 250 T-U77
Blackhawk Pl SUR . . . 205 H35
Blackie La SUR . . . . . . 245 U31
Blackie St NEW . . . . . . 184 B29
Blackley St NEW . . . . 184 C-D27
Blackman St NEW . . . . 184 Z28
Blacksmith Pl RMD . . . 223 K15
Blackstock Pl PMD . . . 145 R35
Blackstock St MAP . . . 167 X-Y51
Blackstone St MAP . . . 167 X-Y51
Blackwater Pl CQT . . . 146 Q39
Blackwood La CHL . . . 233 L6
Blackwood La WRK . . . 265 X37
Blackwood St NEW . . 184 B29
Blackwood St WRK . 265 W37 X37
Blaine Av BUR . . . . 144 T25 164 U25
Blaine Ct BUR . . . . . 144 T25-26
Blaine Dr BUR . . . . . . 144 T25
Blaine Pl BUR . . . . . . . 144 T25
Blair Av NEW . . . . . . . . 184 Z28
Blair Dr RMD . . . 182 D14 202 E14
Blairview Av DNV . . . . 124 M23
Blake Dr DEL 204 J28 224 K28 K28-29
Blake Loop MAP . . . . . 167 W53
Blake Pl DEL . . . . . . . 204 J28-29
Blake St VAN . . . 163 Y20 183 Z20
Blakely Rd PTM . . . . . 186 Z46
Blanca St VAN . . . . . . 161 T-V6
Blanche St VAN . . . . . 183 B18
Blaney Cr PTM . . . . . . 187 A-B47
Blaney Dr PTM . . 186 A46 187 A47
Blaney Way PTM . . . . 186 A-B46
Blanshard Dr RMD . . . 202 E-F9
Blanshard St MAP . . . . 167 Y49
Blantyre Av CQT . . . . . 165 X34
Blantyre Pl CQT . . . . . 144 Q25
Blatchford Way ABT 250 U77 270 V77
Blauson Blvd ABT . . . . 251 Q81
Blaydon Ct VAN . . . 183 A19-20
Blenheim St VAN . . 162 U-Y9 182 Z9
Blink Bonnie Rd WVA. 101 H1 121 J1
Blood Alley Sq VAN . . . . . . . . . .
. . . . . 11 G40 142 S14 143 S15

Bloomfield Pl PCQ . . . . 146 T41
Blossom Bay PTM . . . 187 Z47
Blossom Ct ABT . . . . 251 S-T80
Blossom St MAP . . . . . 187 Z54
Blott St MIS . . . . . . . . . 210 J72
Blue Heron Cr PCQ . . . 146 T41
Blue Jay Cr VAN . . . . . 183 A20
Blue Jay Pl CQT . . . . 146 P-Q39
Blue Jay St ABT . . . 249 S-T69
Blue Mountain St CQT 165 U-X32
Bluebell Av CQT . . . . . 145 R36
Bluebell Dr WVA . . 101 H3 121 J3
Bluebell St MIS . . . . . . 210 H74
Blueberry Ct ABT . . . . 251 S80
Blueberry Dr MIS . . . 210 G75-76
Blueberry Dr WHS . . . 401 E-F3
Blueberry La DNV . . . . 103 H15
Bluebird Cr SUR . . . . . 185 B37
Bluebird Ct MIS . . . . . 210 H72
Bluebird Pl NEW . . . . . 301 E4
Bluebonnet Dr DNV . . 122 K-L14
Bluegrouse Pl DEL . . . 263 Y17
Bluegrouse Way DNV . 103 H15
Bluejay Av CHL . . . . . . 213 J5
Bluejay Cr MIS . . . . . . 210 J72
Bluejay Pl CHL . . . . . . 213 J5
Blueridge Av DNV . . . 123 J16
Blueridge Dr ABT 249 S69-70 250 S71
Bluestone Pl CHL . . . . 194 D9
Bluff Dr CQT . . . . . . . 146 R40
Bluff Way CQT . . . . . . 146 R40
Blundell Rd RMD . . . . . . . . . . .
. . . . 202 G8-14 203 G15 G21
Blythwood Dr DNV . . 123 L16
Boat Lift La VAN . . . 10 K35 142 T12
Boathouse Mews VAN . . . . . . . . .
. . . . 11 J-K38 142 T14
Bobcat Dr MIS . . . . . . 210 H73
Bobcat Dr W MIS . . 210 H72-73
Bobcat Pl CQT . . . . . 145 Q38
Bobolink Av VAN . . . . 183 A18
Bodner St MAP . . . . . . 167 V53
Boeing Av RMD . . . . 182 C-D11
Boeing Pl CHL . . . . . . 213 F-G7
Bognor St CQT . . . . 165 W-X36
Boileau St CQT . . . . . 165 X32
Bole Av CHL . . . . . . . . 213 E7
Bole Ct CQT . . . . 164 U30 165 U31
Bole St NEW . . . . . . . 184 A28
Bolivar Cr SUR . . . 185 B33-34 B34
Bolivar Rd SUR . . . . . 185 B33
Bonaccord Dr VAN . . 103 A18
Bonavista Dr RMD . . 222 K9
Bonavista Gt RMD . . 202 J9 222 K9
Bonavista Pl RMD . . . 202 J9 222 K9
Bonavista St CHL . . 193 C-D7
Bond Blvd DEL . . . . . 224 L29
Bond St BUR 163 X21-22 X22 164 X23
Bond St CQT . . . . . . . 145 T36
Bond St DNV . . . . . . 143 P-Q20
Bond St KNT . . . . . . . 175 X21
Bonita Dr DNV . . . . . 123 N22
Bonneville Pl BUR . . 164 V-W29
Bonnie Bay Pl WVA . . . 101 H1
Bonny Av CHL . . . . . . 193 D7
Bonny Bay SUR . . . . 266 W39
Bonnymuir Av WVA . 102 H13 122 J13
Bonnymuir Pl WVA . . 102 H13
Bonnyvale Av VAN . . 183 Z18
Bonson Rd PTM . . 186 A46 Z46
Bonson St NEW . . . . 184 A29
Bonsor Av BUR . . 163 Y22 184 Z23
Booth Av BUR . . . 163 X22 Y22
Booth Av CQT . . . . 165 X33-34
Booth Rd DEL . . . 223 N16-17 P16-17
Boothby Av MIS . . . . 210 F74
Borden St VAN . . . . . 183 A17
Borham Cr VAN . . . . 183 A21
Borthwick Rd DNV . . 123 J20
Bosun Pl CQT . . . . 145 T36-37
Boswell Av DNV . . . . 123 N22
Bosworth St CQT . . . . . . . . . . .
. . . . 164 V-W30 165 V-W31
Bothwell Dr SUR . . 206 E41
Bouchard Ct RMD . . 202 F10
Bouchard Gt RMD . . 202 F10
Boulder Ct WVA . . . 122 K10
Boulder Ridge WHS . 401 G-H2
Boulder St ABT . . . . 250 T73
Boulderwood Pl PMD . 145 R35
Boulevard, The SQM . . 301 E4-5
Boulevard Cr CNV . . 123 M18
Boult Av ABT . . . . 270 V73-74
Boundary Cl SUR . . . 225 M31
Boundary Ct SUR . . . 225 M31
Boundary Dr E SUR . 225 L-M31

Boundary Dr N SUR . . . . 225 L31
Boundary Dr S SUR . . . 225 M31
Boundary Dr W SUR . . . 225 M31
Boundary Gr SUR . . . 225 L-M31
Boundary Pl SUR . . . . . 225 M31
Boundary Rd RMD . 184 D25 204 E25
Boundary Rd VAN . . . . . . . . . . . .
. . . . . 143 T21 163 U-Y21 183 Z21
Boundary Rd N VAN . . 143 R-S21
Boundary Bay Rd DEL . 263 X-Y18
Boundary Park Gt SUR . 225 M31
Bournemouth Cr DNV . . 144 P23
Bourquin Cr E ABT . . . 250 U75
Bourquin Cr W ABT . . 250 T-U74
Bourquin Pl ABT . . . . 250 U75
Bouthot Ct CQT . . . . 145 T37-38
Bow Ct WVA . . . . . . . 143 P21
Bow Dr CQT . . . . . . 146 R39-40
Bowcock Rd RMD . . 202 H12-13
Bowen Ave SQM . . . . . . 301 H1
Bowen Dr CQT . . 145 S38 146 S39
Bowen Dr RMD . . . . 202 G8-9
Bowen Gt RMD . . . . . 202 G8
Bower Ct DEL . . . . . 224 K30
Bowie Dr MIS . . . . . 210 G75
Bowler Dr SUR . . . . 265 V38
Bowler Pl SUR . . . . 265 V38
Bowling Green Rd RMD . 202 F12
Bowman Av CQT . . . . 165 U34
Bowron Ct DNV . . 124 N24 144 P24
Bowron St CQT . . . . 165 U31
Bowser Av BEL . . . . 124 M30
Bowser Dr MIS . . . . 210 G74
Boxcar St ABT . . . . . 249 T63
Boxer Ct MIS . . . . 210 G-H73
Boxer St BUR . . . . 183 A21-22
Boxwood Cr ABT . . . 251 S80
Boxwood Ct ABT . . . 251 S80
Boxwood Dr CQT . . . 165 W37
Boyd Ct RMD . . . . . 202 H13
Boyd Div VAN . . . . 163 W19
Boyd St NEW . . 184 C27 C-D26
Boyne St NEW . . . 184 C-D27
Boynton Pl DEL . . 204 H-J28
Bracewell Ct PCQ . . 146 S-T41
Bracewell Pl PCQ . . 146 S-T41
Bracken Av MIS . . . 210 H74
Bracken Dr CHL . . . 213 G1-2
Bracken Park Way SQM . 301 B1
Brackonridge Pl PMD . 145 R35
Bracknell Cr DNV . . 122 K14
Bracknell Pl DNV . . 122 K14
Brada Dr CQT . . . . . 165 U31
Brada St CHL . . . . . 233 K7
Bradford Pl DEL . . . 224 L29
Bradford Pl SUR . . . 225 N35
Bradley Av BUR . . . 183 A22
Bradshaw St PCQ . . 166 X39
Braeburn St VAN . . 183 Z17
Braelawn Dr BUR . 144 T23 164 U23
Braemar Av BUR . . 164 Y25
Braemar Dr SQM . . . 301 E4
Braemar Pl DNV . . . 123 K18
Braemar Rd E DNV . 123 K17-18
Braemar Rd W DNV . 123 K16-17
Braemoor Pl BUR . 164 U29-30
Braeside Av CHL . . . 233 N8
Braeside Dr BUR . . 144 S26
Braeside Pl CQT . . . 125 N38
Braeside St ABT . . . 250 U71
Braeside St WVA . . 122 L-M12
Brahms Av VAN . . . 183 A20
Braid Rd DEL . . . . . 263 W18
Braid St NEW164 Y30 165 Y31 Y31 Y32
Brakeman St ABT . . 249 T63
Braken Ct PCQ . . . . 146 S41
Brakenridge St VAN . 162 W10
Bramble La CQT . . . 145 Q36
Bramble La PMD . . . 145 R34
Bramwell Rd WVA . 122 J-K11
Brand St CNV . . . . . 123 L18
Brand St PCQ . . . . 166 X40
Brandon St BUR . . . 163 X21
Brandon St NEW . . . 184 Z28
Brandy Dr DEL . 204 G28 G-H28
Brandy Pl DEL . . . . 204 G28
Brandys Pl RMD . . . 202 G14
Brandywine Al WHS . 401 T21
Brandywine Pl VAN 183 A19 Z20
Brandywine Way WHS . 401 H-J2
Brannick Pl CHL . . . 213 G6
Branscombe Pl RMD . 222 K-L10
Brant Av MIS . . . . . 210 H73
Brant St VAN . . . . . 163 W18

Brantford Av *BUR* . . 164 Y25 184 Z25
Brantford St *NEW* . . . . . . 184 A28
Brantwood Rd *DNV* . . . . 122 L14
Braun Av *ABT* . . . . . . . . . 250 U75
Bray St *CQT* . . . . . . . . . . 165 W36
Brealey St *MIS* . . . . . 210 H77-78
Brearley St *WRK* . . . . . . 265 W35
Brechin St *BUR* . . . . . . . 183 B21
Breden Av *RMD* . . . . . 202 G13-14
Bremridge Dr *DEL* . . . . 204 H-J29
Brenda St *MIS* . . . . . . . . 210 E75
Brennan Rd *SQM* . . . . . . . 301 C1
Brent Pl *CHL* . . . . . . . . . 213 E8
Brentlawn Dr *BUR* . 163 U22 164 U23
Brentwood Cr *SUR* . . . . . 185 B34
Brentwood Dr *BUR*. 163 U22 164 U23
Brentwood Dr *CHL* . . . . 193 C-D8
Breslay St *CQT* . . . . . . 165 U-V31
Breton Rd *BUR* . . . . . . . 183 C22
Brett Av *CHL* . . . . . . . . . 213 E6
Brett La *MIS* . . . . . . . . . 210 G74
Brew St *PMD* . . . . . . . . 145 S-T35
Brewster Dr *CQT* . . . . . . 145 R37
Brewster Dr E *DEL* . . . . 224 K30
Brewster Dr W *DEL* . . . . 224 K30
Brewster Pl *ABT* . . 250 U78 270 V78
Brian Dr *CQT* . . . . . . . . 146 R39-40
Briar Av *VAN* . . . . . . . . . 162 W11
Briar Rd *BUR* . . . . . . . 164 X29-30
Briarcliffe Dr *CQT* . . . . . 145 R36
Briarlynn Cr *DNV* . . . . . . 123 M20
Briarwood Cr *BUR* . . . . . . 163 X22
Briarwood Cr *DEL* . . . . . . 224 M30
Briarwood Pl *ABT* . . 250 U78 261 Y19
Briarwood Pl *DEL* . . . . . . 224 M30
Briarwood Pl *PMD* . . . . . . 145 R35
Brice Rd *CHL* . . . . . . . . . 193 C8
Brickwood Cl *MAP* . . . . . 187 A52
Bridge Rd *KNT* . . . . . . . . 175 Y21
Bridge Rd *SUR* . . . . . . . . 185 B31
Bridge Rd *WVA* . . . . 122 M12-13 N12
Bridge St *DEL* . . . . 223 P16 243 Q16
Bridge St *MIS* . . . . . . . . 230 K74
Bridge St *RMD* . . . . . . . . 202 G14
Bridge Way *VAN* . . . . . 143 R20-21
Bridgeport Rd *RMD* . . . . .
. . . . . . 182 C13-14 183 C15-16
Bridget Dr *PCQ* . . . . . . 166 W-X39
Bridgeview Dr *SUR* . . . . . 185 A32-33
Bridgeview St *ABT* . . . . . 250 Q-R74
Bridgewater Cr *BUR* . . . . 164 W30
Bridgeway St *VAN* . . . . . . 143 R20
Bridgewood Dr *BUR* . . . . 164 U26
Bridgman Av *DNV* . . 122 M14 M-N14
Bridgman Av *PCQ* . . . . . 166 V40-41
Bridleridge Cr *CHL* . . . . 233 N-P7
Bridlewood Ct *BUR* . . . . . 164 U26
Bridlewood Dr *CHL* . . . . 233 N-P7
Bridlington Dr *DEL* . . . . . 224 H-J29
Brief St *BUR* . . . . 164 Y23 184 Z23
Brient Dr *MIS* . . . . . . . . 210 H78
Brigadoon Av *VAN* . . . . . 183 Z17-18
Brigantine Rd *DEL* . . . . 223 N16-17
Brighton Av *BUR* . . . . . 164 V-W28
Brighton Pl *ABT* . . . . . . . 250 R72
Brighton Pl *CHL* . . . . . . . 233 M5
Brighton Pl *PTM* . . . . . . 187 Z47
Brightwood Pl *VAN* . . . . . 183 A18
Brinx Rd *CHL* . . . . . . . . 193 B7
Brio Entrance *WHS* . . . . . 401 F3
Brisbane Av *CQT* . . . . . . 165 U33
Brisbane Cr *BUR* . . . . . 144 R-S23
Brisbane Ct *ABT* . . . . . . 250 R72
Brisco Ct *CQT* . . . . . . . 165 X35
Briskham St *MIS* . . . . . . 210 J73
Bristlecone Ct *CQT* . . . . 145 Q38
Bristol Dr *ABT* . . . . . . . 250 T-U77
Bristol Dr *KNT* . . . . . . . 175 X20-21
Bristol Pl *SUR* . . . . . . . 225 K33
Bristol Island Rd *HOP* . . . 118 F42
Bristol Slough Rd *HOP* . . . 118 F41
Britannia Av *SQM* . . . . . 301 H1-2
Britannia Cr *PCQ* . . . . . 166 U40
Britannia Dr *RMD* . . . . . 222 L9-10
Britton Av *CHL* . . . . . . . 213 J7
Britton Dr *PMD* . . . . . . 145 R35
Britton St *BUR* . . . . 184 A26 Z26
Brixham Rd *DNV* . . . 124 N23 144 P23
Broadmoor Blvd *RMD* . . 202 H11-12
Broadview Ct *CQT* . . . . 165 U33-34
Broadview Dr *DNV* . . 143 P22 144 P23
Broadway *BUR* . . . . .
. . . . . . 164 U24-25 U30 V26-27 V29
Broadway E *VAN* . . . . . 163 U15-20
Broadway W *VAN* . . . . . 162 U8-14

Broadway Av *MIS* . . . . . . 230 K75
Broadway E *ABT* . . . . . 250 U73-74
Broadway St *ABT* . . . 250 U73 270 V73
Broadway St *CHL* . . 193 D8 213 E-G8
Broadway St *PCQ* . . . . . 166 W-X40
Broadway St *RMD* . . . . . 222 K8-9
Broadway St *VAN* . . . . .
. . . . . . . . . 265 X36-38 266 X39
Brock St *RMD* . . . . . . . . 204 E24
Brock St *VAN* . . . . . . . . 163 W18
Brockton Cr *DNV* . . . . . . 124 N25
Brockton Pl *DNV* . . . . . . 124 N25
Brodie Pl *DEL* . . . . . . . . 223 P19
Brodie Rd *DEL* . . . . . 223 P18-19
Bromfield Pl *RMD* . . . . . 202 J14
Bromley Ct *BUR* . . . . . . 164 V25
Bromley Pl *RMD* . . . . . . 222 K12
Bromley St *CQT* . . . . . . 165 W36
Bromley St *MAP* . . . . . . 187 B48
Bronte Dr *DNV* . . . . . . 123 M-N22
Brookdale Ct *ABT* . . . . . 249 S70
Brookdale Ct *BUR* . . . 144 T23-24
Brookdale Pl *DEL* . . . . . 224 K29
Brooke Pl *DEL* . . . . . . . 204 F28
Brooke Rd *DEL* . . . . . . 204 F-G28
Brookes St *NEW* . . . . . . 184 C28
Brookeside Av *WVA* . . . . 121 K3
Brooklyn Av *BUR* . . . . . . 144 T25
Brookmere Av *CQT* 164 W30 165 W31
Brookmere Ct *MAP* . . . . . 187 A52
Brookmount Dr *PMD* . . . . 145 T35
Brookridge Dr *DNV* . . . . 122 L14
Brooks Av *CHL* . . . . . . . 213 F7-8
Brooks Av *MAP* . . . . . . . 167 Y48
Brooks Cr *SUR* . . . . . . . 226 M46
Brooks St *VAN* . . . . 163 Y20 183 Z20
Brooksbank Av *CNV* . . . . 143 P19
Brooksbank Av *DNV* 123 N19 143 P19
Brookside Av *ABT* . . . . .
. . . . . . 249 R69 R70 250 R71
Brookside Dr *PMD* . . . . . 145 T35
Brookside Gr *SUR* . . . . . 186 C39
Broom Pl *PCQ* . . . . . . . 146 S40
Broom St *MIS* . . . . . . . 210 H75
Broome Rd *SUR* . . . . . . 265 V38
Brothers Pl *SQM* . . . . . . 301 F1
Broughton St *VAN* 10 G35 142 S12-13
Brown Av *MAP* . . . . 187 Z52 Z52-53
Brown Cr *MIS* . . . . . . . . 210 H74
Brown Rd *MIS* . . . . . . . 182 D13
Brown Rd *DEL* . . . . . . . 223 K21
Brown St *PCQ* . . . . . . . 166 V-W40
Browndale Rd *RMD* . . . . 182 D12
Browne Rd *CHL* . . . . . . 233 N-P2
Brownell Rd *RMD* . . . . 182 D12-13
Browngate Rd *RMD* . . . 182 D12-13
Browning Pl *DNV* . . . . . . 143 P22
Brownlea Rd *RMD* . . . . 182 D12
Brownwood Rd *RMD* . . . 182 D12
Bruce Av *MAP* . . . . . 187 Z47-48
Bruce Av *MIS* . . . . . . . 210 H74
Bruce Dr *PTM* . . . . . . . 186 A46
Bruce Pl *MAP* . . . . . . . 187 Z48
Bruce St *DNV* . . . . . . . 143 P20
Bruce St *VAN* . . . 163 X17 X-Y17 Y17
Bruce St *WVA* . . . . . . . 101 G2
Brûlé Mews *VAN* . . . . . 183 Z19-20
Brundige Av *ABT* . . . . . 270 V74
Bruneau Pl *LGT* . . . . . . . 248 T63
Brunette Av *CQT* . . 165 X32-33 X-Y34
Brunette Av *NEW* . . . . . . 165 Y31
Brunswick Dr *RMD* . . . . 222 L10
Brunswick Pl *RMD* . . . . . 222 L10
Brunswick St *VAN* . . . . . 163 U15
Brunswick Beach Rd *LIO* . . 101 A23
Bryan Pl *SUR* . . . . . . . . 205 F34
Bryant St *BUR* . . . . . . . . 184 Z25
Bryant St *BUR* . . 164 Y24 184 Z24 Z25
Brydon Cr *LGC* . . . . . . . 227 N47
Brynlor Dr *BUR* . . . . 184 A24-25
Bryson Bay *RMD* . . . . . 182 D14
Bryson Ct *RMD* . . . . . . . 182 D14
Bryson Dr *RMD* . . . . . . . 182 D14
Bryson Pl *RMD* . . . . . . . 182 D14
Buchanan Av *NEW* . . . . 164 X25
Buchanan Pl *SUR* . . . . . 205 F32
Buchanan St *BUR* . . . . .
. . . . . 163 U22 164 U23 U24 U25-26
Buchanan St *RMD* . . . . . 222 L10
Bucketwheel *VAN* . . . . . 162 U13-14
Buckhorn Dr *WHS* . . . . . 401 C3
Buckhorn Pl *PMD* . . . . . 145 R35
Buckhorn Pl *WHS* . . . . . 401 C-D3
Buckingham Av *BUR* . . . . 164 X25
Buckingham Dr *ABT* . . . . 251 R81
Buckingham Dr *BUR* 164 Y25-26 Y26
Buckingham Dr *PMD* . . . 145 S-T35
Buckingham Pl *BUR* . . . . 164 X-Y26

Buckley Av *SQM* . . . . . 301 H1 J2
Buckskin Pl *SUR* . . . . 226 L-M42
Bueckert Av *MIS* . . . . . 210 J72
Buena Vista Av *BUR* . . . 164 X29
Buena Vista Av *WRK* . . . .
. . . . . . 265 X36-38 266 X39
Buffalo Dr *BUR* . . . . . . 164 V26
Buffalo Dr *MIS* . . . . . . . 210 H72
Buffalo St *BUR* . . . . . . . 164 V26
Buffer Cr *ABT* . . . . . . . 249 T63
Bulkley St *ABT* . . . . . 250 R-S78
Buller Av *BUR* . . 184 A24 B24 Z24
Buller St *PMD* . . . . . . . 145 T34
Bunting Av *RMD* . . . . . . 222 K10
Buntzen Creek Rd *ANM* . . 125 N33
Buoy St *PMD* . . . . . . . 145 T36
Burbank Dr *DEL* . . . . . . 144 P26
Burbidge St *CQT* . . . 165 Y35 185 Z35
Burdette St *RMD* . . . . . . 183 B18
Burdock St *MIS* . . . . . . 210 H74
Burford St *BUR* . . . . . . 184 Z25
Burgess St *BUR* . . . . . . 184 Z27
Burhill Rd *WVA* . . . . . . 122 L13
Burian Dr *CQT* . . . . . . . 165 W36
Burke St *BUR* . . . 163 X21-22 X22
Burke Mountain St *CQT* . . 146 R-S41
Burkehill Pl *WVA* . . . . . 121 K5
Burkehill Rd *WVA* . . . . 121 K5 K-L5
Burkemont Pl *CQT* . . . . 146 S41
Burkholder Dr *VAN* . . . . 183 Z20
Burleigh Av *PCQ* . . . . . 165 U38
Burley Dr *WVA* . . . . 122 L12 L-M12
Burley Pl *WVA* . . . . . . . 122 L12
Burlington Av *BUR* . . . . 184 Z23
Burlington Dr *CQT* . . . 145 S37-38
Burnaby St *NEW* . . . . . 164 Y30
Burnaby St *VAN* . . 10 G34-35 142 S12
Burnaby Mountain Pkwy *BUR* . . . .
. . . . . 144 S-T26 T27 U27
Burnage Rd *DNV* . . . . . . 122 L14
Burnett St *MAP* . . . 187 A53 Z53
Burnfield Cr *BUR* . . . . . . 164 X26
Burnlake Dr *BUR* . . . 164 W27-28
Burns Av *DNV* . . . . . 124 M-N26
Burns Ct *BUR* . . . . 164 Y25 184 Z25
Burns Dr *DEL* . 223 N19-20 224 P24-25
Burns Pl *BUR* . . . . . . . 164 Y24
Burns Rd *PCQ* . . . . . . . 166 U43
Burns St *BUR* . . . . . . . 164 Y25
Burns St *CQT* . . . . . . . 165 W-X32
Burnside Dr *ABT* . . . . . 251 S79
Burnside Pl *CQT* . . . . . 145 S36-37
Burnside Rd *WVA* . . . . . 122 K11
Burnwood Av *BUR* . . . . 144 S26
Burnwood Av *BUR* . . . . 144 T26
Burnwood Dr *BUR* . . . . . 144 T26
Burquitlam Dr *VAN* . . . . 183 A18
Burr Pl *DEL* . . . . . . . . 204 J29
Burr Pl *DNV* . . . . . . . . 143 P22
Burr St *NEW* . . . . . . . . 184 A30
Burrard Cr *PMD* . . . . . 145 R-S32
Burrard Pl *VAN* . . . . . . 11 F38
Burrard St *VAN* . . . . . .
. . 10 H36 K33 142 S13-14 T11 T12-13
. . . . . . . . . . 162 U-V11
Burrill Av *DNV* . . . . 123 K20 K21
Burris St *BUR* . . . . 164 X26 Y25
Burrows Rd *RMD* . . . . . 183 C17-18
Bursill St *VAN* . . . . . . . 163 X19
Burton Av *RMD* . . . . . . 202 G9
Burton Ct *CQT* . . . . . . . 165 W36
Bury Av *PCQ* . . . . . . . 165 U-V38
Bury La *WVA* . . . . . . . 122 K13
Busby Rd *ABT* . . . . 250 U75 270 V75
Buscombe St *VAN* . . . . 183 A15
Bush Ct *MIS* . . . . . . . 210 G-H76
Bushby St *NEW* . . . . . . 184 A30
Bushnell Pl *DNV* . . . . . 123 L20
Buswell St *RMD* . . . . . . 202 F12
Butchart St *CHL* . . . . . 213 F8
Bute Cr *CQT* . . . . . . . 146 S39
Bute St *VAN* . 10 G36 H35 142 S12 S13
Butler Pl *MIS* . . . . . . . 210 J73
Butler St *VAN* . . 163 Y20 183 A20 Z20
Buttermere Dr *RMD* . . . 202 J12
Buttermere Pl *RMD* . . . . 202 J11
Butternut La *PTM* . . . . 187 Z47
Butternut St *CQT* . . . . 165 U37
Buxton Ct *BUR* . . . . . . 163 X22
Buxton St *BUR* . . . . . . 163 X23
Byng St *CQT* . . . . . . . 165 W35
Byrne Rd *BUR* . . . . . . . 184 B-C23
Byrne Rd *BUR* . . . . . . . 184 B24
Byrnepark Walk *BUR* . . . 184 A-B25

Byrnepark Walk *BUR* . . . 184 A25
Byron Pl *DNV* . . . . . . . 123 N22
Byron Rd *DEL* . . . . . . . 204 G28
Byron Rd *DNV* . . . . . . 123 N22
Byway *WVA* . . . . . . . . 121 K-L2
Bywell Ct *VAN* . . . . . . . 183 A19-21

## C

Cabeldu Cr *DEL* . . . . . . 224 L29
Cable Ct *CQT* . . . . . . . 145 T36
Cabot Dr *RMD* . . . . . . . 202 F-G9
Cactus Ct *DNV* . . . . . . 123 M22
Caddell Dr *DEL* . . . . . . 224 N30
Caddy Rd *DNV* . . . . . . 144 P26
Cade Barr St *MIS* . . . . 210 G-H75
Cadogan Rd *RMD* . . . . 202 H10
Caen Av *CHL* . . . . . . . 233 N5
Cail St *MIS* . . . . . . . . . 210 F73
Cairnmore Pl *RMD* . . . . 202 G8-9
Cairns Ct *RMD* . . . . . . . 202 F10
Caithcart Rd *RMD* . 182 D14 183 D15
Caithness Cr *PMD* . . . . . 145 T31
Caithness Rd *ABT* . . . . 250 S74
Calais Cr *CHL* . . . . . . . 233 N5
Calder Av *DNV* . . . 123 K17 L17
Calder Cr *RMD* . . . . . . . 202 G-H10
Calder Pl *ABT* . . . . . . . 250 U77
Calder Rd *RMD* . . . . . . 202 G-H10
Calderwood Cr *RMD* . . . 202 H10
Caldew St *DEL* . . . . . . 204 E27
Caledonia Av *DNV* . . . .
. . . . 124 M26 M-N26 N26
Caledonia Dr *SUR* . . . . 185 B36
Calgary Av *ABT* . . . . . 251 S79
Calgary Dr *CQT* . . . . . . 146 Q44
Caliente Pl *CQT* . . . . . 146 R39
Callaghan Av *MAP* . . . . 187 A52
Callaghan Cl *PTM* . . . . 186 B46
Callaghan Ct *ABT* . . . . 251 Q80-81
Callaghan Dr *WHS* . . . . 401 H-J1
Calverhall St *DNV* . . 123 N19 143 P19
Calvert Dr *DEL* . . . . . . 223 P16
Calvin Ct *MAP* . . . . . . 167 X54
Calvin Ct *BUR* . . . . . . 144 T25
Camano St *VAN* . . . . . . 183 Z20
Camarillo Pl *BUR* . . . . 164 U26
Camaro Dr *DEL* . . . 263 X16-17
Camberley Ct *CQT* . . . . 165 W36
Cambie Ct *MIS* . . . . . . 210 G78
Cambie Rd *RMD* . . . . .
. . . . . 182 D12-14 183 D15-19
Cambie St *ABT* . . . . . . 249 T-U63
Cambie St *VAN* . . . . .
. . 11 G-H39 H38 142 S14 S-T14 T14
162 U-W14 X13-14 X-Y14 182 A-B14 Z14
Cambrai Av *CHL* . . . . . 233 N5-6
Cambridge Ct *DEL* . . . . 263 Y16-17
Cambridge Dr *CQT* . . . 165 V33
Cambridge Pl *MIS* . . . . 210 G-H77
Cambridge St *ABT* . . . . 250 T76
Cambridge St *BUR* . . . . 144 S23 S24
Cambridge St *CHL* . . . . 233 M5
Cambridge St *PCQ* . . . . 166 U39
Cambridge St *VAN* . . . . .
. . . . . . 143 S18 S18-19 S20
Cambridge Way *PMD* . . . 145 S32
Camden Ct *RMD* . . . . . . 202 H10
Camden Pl *RMD* . . . . . . 202 H10
Camel Ct *MIS* . . . . . . . 210 H73
Camelback Ct *CQT* . . . . 145 P38
Camelback La *CQT* . . . . 145 P38
Camellia Ct *ABT* . . . . . 250 T77
Camellia Ct *CQT* . . . . 145 R35-36
Camelot Rd *WVA* . . . . . 122 K11
Cameron Av *MIS* . . . . . 210 E73-74
Cameron Av *PCQ* . . . . . 166 W39-40
Cameron Av *VAN* . . . . 142 T8-9
Cameron Cr *ABT* . . . 250 U78 251 U79
Cameron Ct *RMD* . . . . . 183 D16
Cameron Dr *RMD* . 183 D16 203 E16
Cameron St *BUR* . . . . . 164 V30
Cameron St *NEW* . . . . 184 B28
Camino Ct *BUR* . . . . . . 164 V24
Camino Dr *WHS* . . . . . . 401 C3
Camlann Ct *RMD* . . . . . 202 H9-10
Cammeray Rd *WVA* . . . 122 K10-11
Camosun St *VAN* . . 162 U-V8 W-X8
Camp River Rd *CHL* . . . 194 B10-12
Campbell Av *ABT* . . . . . 270 V75
Campbell Av *DNV* . . . . . 123 K-L20
Campbell Av *MAP* . . . . 187 Z50
Campbell Av *PCQ* . . . . . 166 X39-40
Campbell Av *VAN* . . . . . 143 S-T16

Campbell Pl *SUR* . . . . . 205 E-F32
Campbell Rd *PMD* . . . . 145 R-S34
Campbell St *NEW* . . . . 184 D27
Campion La *PMD* . . . . . 145 R35-36
Campion Way *CQT* . . . . 165 V37
Campobello Pl *RMD* . . . 202 J9
Campus Rd *UEL* . . . . . 161 T-U4
Camridge Pl *WVA* . . . . 122 K11
Camridge Rd *WVA* . . . . 122 K10
Camrose Av *CHL* . . . . . 193 C7
Camrose Dr *BUR* . . . . . 164 V26
Camsell Cr *RMD* . . . . 202 F10-11
Camwell Dr *WVA* . . . . . 122 K11
Camwood Av *MAP* . . . . 187 Z49
Canada Pl *VAN* . . 11 F38 142 R-S14
Canada Way *BUR* . . . . 163 V22
164 V23 W23-24 X25-26 Y26-27 184 Z27
Canadore Ct *ABT* . . . . 249 U68-69
Canary Ct *CQT* . . . . . . 165 W36
Canary Dr *SUR* . . . . . . 185 B37
Canberra Av *BUR* . . . . 144 S23
Candia Pl *WVA* . . . . . . 101 H1
Candlelick Wynd *DEL* . . . 263 W17
Candlewood Dr *RMD* . . . 202 H9
Candow St *CHL* . . . . . . 193 D6
Canfield Cr *DNV* . . . . . 123 L15
Canfor Av *NEW* . . . . . . 165 Y31
Canil Av *NEW* . . . . 184 D26 204 E26
Canim Av *CQT* . . . . . . 165 W36
Canim Pl *RMD* . . . . . . . 202 F10-11
Cannery Cr *DEL* . . . . . 243 Q15
Cannery Pl *DEL* . . . . . . 243 Q15-16
Cannon Av *ABT* . . . . . . 250 U75
Cannon Gn *PCQ* . . . . . 165 Y38
Cannon St *MIS* . . . . . . 210 H74
Canoe Av *CQT* . . . . . 165 Y35-36
Canso Cr *RMD* . . . . 202 J9 222 K9
Canterbury Cr *DNV* . . 123 J15-16 K16
Canterbury Dr *CHL* . . . . 233 M4
Canterbury Dr *KNT* . . . . 175 X21
Canterbury Dr *SUR* . . 246 S39 T39
Canterbury La *CQT* . . . 146 S39
Canterbury Pl *SUR* . . . 246 S39
Canterwood Ct *ANM* . . . 145 P33
Cantley Rd *RMD* . . . . . 202 G-H10
Cantrell Rd *RMD* . . . . . 202 H10
Canuck Cr *MAP* . . . 167 Y51-52
Canyon Blvd *DNV* . . . . 123 J15
Canyon Cr *DEL* . . . . . . 224 K29
Canyon Ct *CQT* . . . . . . 165 U34
Canyon Ct *DEL* . . . . . . 224 K29
Cape Ct *CQT* . . . . . . . 165 U36
Cape Horn Av *CQT* . 165 X36 Y34-35
Cape Horn Pl *CQT* . . . . 165 X35
Capella Dr *BUR* . . . . 164 U-V29
Capella Pl *RMD* . . . . 182 C13 D14
Capella Pl *RMD* . . . . . 182 C-D13
Capilano Av *CHL* . . . . . 233 M5
Capilano Cr *DNV* . . . . . 122 L14
Capilano Pl *ABT* . . . . 250 S-T74
Capilano Rd *DNV* . 122 J-L14 M13-14
Capilano Rd *PMD* . . . . . 145 S-T35
Capilano Way *NEW* . 165 Y31 185 Z31
Capistrano Dr *BUR* . . . . 164 U26
Capital Ct *PCQ* . . . . . . 165 Y38
Capitol Dr *BUR* . . . . . 144 S23-24
Capri Cr *VAN* . . . . . . . 183 A20
Capri Ct *ABT* . . . . . . . 270 W74
Capstan Cr *CQT* . . . . . 145 T36-37
Capstan Pl *CQT* . . . 145 T36 165 U36
Capstan Way *RMD* . . . . 182 D12-13
Captain Ct *PCQ* . . . . . 166 X-Y39
Captains Cv *VAN* . . . . . 182 A11
Car-Lin La *ABT* . . . . . . 250 U76
Caravel Ct *RMD* . . . . . 222 K9
Caraway Ct *BUR* . . . . . 164 U29
Cardero St *VAN* . . . . .
. . 10 F35-36 G34 142 R12-13 R-S12 S12
Cardiff Pl *ABT* . . . . . . . 251 T81
Cardiff Pl *BUR* . . . . . . 163 X21
Cardiff St *BUR* . . . . . . 163 X21
Cardiff Way *PMD* . . . . . 145 S32
Cardinal Av *ABT* . . . 249 T69-70
Cardinal Cr *DNV* . . . 124 M-N27
Cardinal Ct *BUR* . . . . . 164 V26
Cardinal Dr *BUR* . . . . . 164 V26
Cardinal Dr *CQT* . 145 Q38 146 Q39
Cardinal La *WRK* . . . . . 265 W35
Cardinal Pl *ABT* . . . . . 249 T70
Cardoon Ct *BUR* . . . . . 163 X21
Cardston Ct *BUR* . . . . . 164 W30
Carey Rd *CHL* . . . . . . 194 Z12
Cariboo Av *HOP* . . . . . 118 D44
Cariboo Bay *SUR* . . . . 266 V39
Cariboo Cr *CQT* . . . . . 165 W36

Cariboo Ct ABT . . . . . . . . . 250 S78
Cariboo Dr BUR . . . . . . 164 X29
Cariboo Pl BUR . . . . . . . 164 W29
Cariboo Rd BUR . . . . . . . . . . .
. . . . . . . . . 164 W-X29 X29-30 Y30
Cariboo Rd N BUR . . . . 144 R-S29
Cariboo St NEW . . . . . 184 B27-28
Cariboo St VAN . . . . . . . . 163 W29
Cariboo Pl DEL . . . . . . . 224 K30
Caribou Rd DEL . . . . . . . 224 K30
Caribou St MIS . . . . . . . 210 H72
Carina Pl BUR . . . . . . . 164 V29
Carion Ct MIS . . . . . . . . 210 H75
Carisbrooke Cr DNV . . . . 123 K-L17
Carisbrooke Rd E DNV . 123 L17 L18
Carla Ct ABT . . . . . . . . . 250 T72
Carleton Av BUR . . . . . . . . . . .
. . . . . . . 143 R-T21 163 U21 W21
Carleton Av N BUR . . . . 143 R-S21
Carleton Ct BUR . . . . . . . 163 X21
Carleton Ct DEL . . . . 204 E-F25 F26
Carleton Dr PMD . . . . . . 145 S32
Carleton Pl ABT . . . . 250 U78 270 V78
Carleton St CHL . . . . 193 D8 213 E8
Carleton Way WHS . . . . . . 401 F2
Carley Pl DEL . . . . . . . . . 224 K30
Carlisle Rd DEL . . . . . . 204 E26-27
Carlisle St PCQ . . . . . . . . 146 T39
Carlisle St VAN . . . . . . . 143 S19
Carlsen Pl PMD . . . . . 145 S35-36
Carlsrue Av ABT . . . . . . . 250 T72
Carlton St MAP . . . . . . . 167 Y50
Carluke Cr SUR . . . . . 205 F32-33
Carman Pl DNV . . . . . . . 123 N22
Carmaria Ct DNV . . . . . . 123 M20
Carmel Av PCQ . . . . . . . 166 X39
Carmel Pl SQM . . . . . . . 301 C1-2
Carmel Rd PMD . . . . . . . 202 H10
Carmen Ct CQT . . . . . 165 V-W35
Carmen Pl PCQ . . . . . . . 166 X39
Carmichael St RMD . . . . . 202 H12
Carnaby Pl DEL . . . . . . . 204 J29
Carnaby Pl DNV . . . . . . . 123 N22
Carnarvon Ct ABT . . . . . . 251 T81
Carnarvon St NEW . . . . . 184 B29
Carnarvon St VAN . . . . . . . . . . .
. . . . . . . 162 U-V9 V9 Y9 182 Z9
Carnation St DNV . . . . . . 123 N22
Carnavon Av DNV . . . . . . 123 L17
Carncross Av RMD . . . . . . 203 E16
Carncross Cr DEL . . . . . 224 K-L29
Carnegie St BUR . . . . . . . 144 T25
Carnegie St NEW . . . . . . 164 Y30
Carnleigh Pl BUR . . . . . 164 X-Y25
Carol Pl PCQ . . . . . . . . . 166 X39
Carol St ABT . . . . . . . . . 270 V78
Carolina St VAN . . . . . . . . . . .
. . . . . . 143 T16 163 U16 U-V16 V15
Caroline Dr KNT . . . . . 175 W-X20
Carolyn Av CHL . . . . . . 233 M4-5
Carolyn Dr DNV . . . . . . . 123 K15
Carousel Ct CQT . . . 145 P38 146 P39
Carpenter St ABT . . . . . . 270 V71
Carr La WVA . . . . . . . . . 122 K9
Carr St MAP . . . . . . 187 A51 Z51
Carrall St VAN . . . . . . . . . . . . .
. . . . . 11 H40 142 T14 143 S15 T15
Carriage Ct ABT . . . . . . . 249 U63
Carriage Ct CQT . . . . . . . 146 R40
Carriage Pl DEL . . . . . . . 224 L30
Carriage Way CHL . . . . . 233 K5-6
Carrick Rd RMD . . . . . . . 202 H10
Carrie Cates Ct CNV . . . . . 143 P16
Carrigan Ct BUR . . . . . . . 164 W30
Carrington La ABT . . . . . . 251 T81
Carrington St VAN . . . . . . 182 Z9
Carrol St NEW . . . . . . . . 184 Z30
Carroll St CHL . . . . . . 193 D6 213 E6
Carshill St MAP . . . . 187 A51 Z51
Carson Ct BUR . . . . . . . . 183 A21
Carson Ct CQT . . . . . . . 165 W34
Carson Pl BUR . . . . . . . . 184 A23
Carson Pl SQM . . . . . . . . 301 J2
Carson St BUR . . . . . . . . . . . .
. . . 183 A21 A21-22 A22 184 A23-24
Carstone Cr DEL . . . . . . . 224 L29
Cartelier Pl DNV . . . . . 123 K16-17
Cartelier Rd DNV . . . . . 123 K16-17
Carter Av MIS . . . . . . . . 210 G73
Carter Cl PTM . . . . . . . . 186 B46
Carter Ct RMD . . . . . . . . 182 D14
Carter Dr RMD . . . . 182 D14 202 E14
Carter Rd CHL . . . . . . . . 233 M4
Carter St NEW . . . . . . . . 184 D27
Cartier Av CQT . . . . . . . 165 X33
Cartier Pl VAN . . . . . . . . 182 A12
Cartier St VAN . . . . . . . . . . . . .
. 162 W12 X12 Y12 Y12 182 A-B12 Z12
Cartmell Rd CHL . . . . . 193 B-C6 C5
Cartwright St VAN . . . . . . . . . . . .
. . . . . . 10 K35 142 T12 162 U12
Carver Cr DEL . . . . . . . . 204 F30
Casabella Dr WHS . . . . . . 401 E4
Casabello Dr CHL . . . . . . 233 K7
Casablanca Pl CHL . . . . . . 233 M4
Casamir St LGT . . . . . . 207 E53
Casano Dr CNV . . . . . . . 123 M19
Cascade Ct CQT . . . . . . 165 U34
Cascade Dr DNV . . . . . . . 124 N25
Cascade Dr DEL . . . . . . . 224 K30
Cascade Dr DNV . . . . . . . 123 N21
Cascade Pl MIS . . . . . . . 210 H74
Cascade St ABT . . . . 250 U73 270 V73
Cascade St BUR . . . . . . . 164 X29
Casewell St BUR . . . . . . . 164 V30
Casey St CQT . . . . . 165 W-X33
Casper Ct ABT . . . . . . . . 250 T72
Cassandra Dr ABT . . . . . . 251 T81
Casselman Cr MIS . . . . . . 210 G75
Cassiar Av ABT . . . . . . . 250 T78
Cassiar Ct ABT . . . . . . . 250 T78
Cassiar Pl ABT . . . . . . . 250 T78
Cassiar St VAN . . . . . . . . . . . .
. . . . . . 143 S-T20 163 U20 W20
Cassiar St N VAN . . . . . . 143 S20
Cassie Av BUR . . . 163 Y22 183 Z22
Castings VAN . . . . . . . . . 162 U13
Castle Cr PCQ . . . . . . 166 X-Y39
Castle Ct ABT . . . . . . . . 250 T72
Castle Dr WHS . . . . . . . . 401 G2
Castle Pines Ct ABT . . . . 251 R-S80
Castlewood Cr BUR . . . . 163 X21-22
Catalina Cr ABT . . . . . . . 270 V72
Catalina Cr RMD . . . . . . 182 C-D11
Catchpole Av MIS . . . . . . 210 H77
Cates Park Rd DNV . . . . . 144 Q26
Cathay Rd RMD . . . . . . . 202 G10
Cathedral Ct ABT . . . . . . 251 S79
Cathedral Ct ABT . . . . . . 251 S79
Catherine Av CQT . . . . . 165 U31-32
Catherine Ct WRK . . . . . . 265 X38
Catherine Ct PCQ . . . . . . 166 U40
Catherwood St MIS . . . . . 210 J75
Caulfeild Ct WVA . . . . . . 121 K4
Caulfeild Dr WVA . . . 121 J-K4 K4
Caulfeild Pl WVA . . . . . . 121 K4
Caulfeild La WVA . . . . 121 K3-4
Caulfeild Ridge CQT . . . . 145 P38
Cavalier Ct RMD . . . . . 202 F-G9
Cavendish Dr RMD . . . . . 202 J9
Cavendish Way WHS . . . . 401 G2
Caversham Ct VAN . . . . . 182 A11
Caves Ct ABT . . . . . . . . 251 R79
Cawley St CHL . . . . . . . . 193 D6
Cawthra Ct CQT . . . . . . . 145 T37
Cayer St CQT . . . . . . . . 165 X34
Cayley St WHS . . . . . . . . 401 H2
Cayton Pl DEL . . . . . . . . 204 J29
Cecil St VAN . . . . . . . . . 163 X20
Cecil Green Park Rd UEL . . . 161 T3
Cecil Ridge Pl CHL . . . . . 233 N-P7
Cecile Dr PMD . . . . . 145 S-T32
Cecile Pl PMD . . . . . . 145 T31-32
Cedar CQT . . . . . . . . . 145 S-T38
Cedar Av ABT . . . . . . 250 T76-77
Cedar Av CHL . . . . . . . . 213 E8
Cedar Av HHS . . . . . . . . 155 P19
Cedar Cr DEL . . . . . . . . 224 K30
Cedar Cr VAN . . . . 162 V11 V11-12
Cedar Dr CQT . . . . . . . . 146 R43
Cedar Dr PCQ . . . . . . 146 S-T42
Cedar Dr SQM . . . . . . . . 301 K3
Cedar Dr SUR . . . . . . . . 245 U31
Cedar La ABT . . . . . . . . 250 U72
Cedar La CHL . . . . . . . . 233 M6
Cedar La PTM . . . . . . . . 187 Z47
Cedar Pl KNT . . . . . . 175 W-X21
Cedar St FRA . . . . . . . . 253 R5
Cedar St MIS . . . . . . . 210 E-J73
Cedar St NEW . . . . . . . . 164 Y30
Cedar St VAN . . . . . . . . 143 T16
Cedar Way MAP . . . . . . . 167 W51
Cedar Cottage Mews VAN . . 163 W17
Cedar Creek Dr CHL . . . 233 M-N7 N8
Cedar Grove La WHS . . . . . 401 E3
Cedar Park Pl ABT . . . . . 250 U72
Cedar Rose Ct BUR . . . . . 183 Z22
Cedar Springs Rd WHS . . . 401 G3
Cedar Tree La DEL . . 223 P17 243 Q17
Cedar Valley Connector MIS . . . . .
. . . . . . . . . 210 J73 230 K73
Cedar Village Cl CNV . . . . 123 M19
Cedar Village Cr CNV . . . . 123 M19
Cedarbridge Way RMD . . . 202 E12
Cedarbrook Pl DEL . . . . . 224 K30
Cedarcrest Av DNV . . . . . 123 J15
Cedardale Ct BUR . . . . . 144 T23-24
Cedarglen Pl BUR . 163 W22 164 W23
Cedarhurst St VAN . . . . . 162 Y9
Cedaridge Pl WVA . . . . . . 121 K6
Cedarwood Ct BUR . . . . . 163 X22
Cedarwood Dr PMD . . . . 145 Q-R35
Cedarwood St BUR . . . . . 164 X24
Celeste Cr PCQ . . . . . 166 W-X39
Celista Dr VAN . . . . . . . 183 Z20
Celtic Av VAN . . . . . . . . 182 Z9
Cemetery Av MIS . . . . . 210 G77-78
Cemetery Rd CHL . . . . . . 194 C10
Centaurus Ct BUR . . . . . 164 V29
Centaurus Dr BUR . . . . . 164 V29
Centennial Av KNT . . . . . 175 W20
Centennial Av PCQ . . . . . 146 T39
Centennial Dr CHL . . . . . 233 K7
Centennial Pkwy DEL 263 Y19-20 Z20
Centennial Rd VAN . . . . . 143 S16
Centennial St ABT . . . . 250 T-U72
Centennial Way BUR . . . . 144 S-T22
Centennial Way SQM . . 301 F-G2 G2-3
Center St ABT . . . . 250 U72 270 V72
Central Av DEL . . . . . . 223 P16-17
Central Av PCQ . . . . 165 V38 166 V39
Central Blvd BUR . . . . . . . . . . .
. . . . . . 163 Y22 183 Z22 Z22 Z22
Central St VAN . . . . 11 K41 143 T15
Centre Dr SUR . . . . . . . . 185 D32
Centre Rd BTI . . . . . . . . 186 C46
Centre Rd LIO . . . . . . . . 101 B23
Centre St DEL . . . . . . . . 204 G27
Centre St WRK . . . . . . 265 X37-38
Century Cr ABT . . . . . . . 250 T75
Century Ct ABT . . . . . . . 250 T75
Century Pkwy BUR . . . . . 164 X25
Cessna Dr CHL . . . . . . . 213 G7-8
Cessna Dr RMD . . . . . . 182 C-D12
Chadsey Cr ABT . . . . . . . 250 R74
Chadwick Av PCQ . . . . . . 166 U40
Chadwick St CNV . . . . . . 143 P16
Chaffey Av BUR . . . . . . 163 X-Y22
Chairlift Ct WVA . . . . . . 122 K8
Chairlift Pl WVA . . . . . . 122 K9
Chairlift Rd WVA . . . 122 J-K8 K8-9
Chaldecott Dr RMD . . . . . 204 E24
Chaldecott St VAN . . . . . 162 W8
Chalet Ct DEL . . . . . . . . 224 K30
Chalet Dr WHS . . . . . . . . 401 B3
Chalet Pl DNV . . . . . . . . 123 J16
Chalmer Pl CHL . . . . . . . 213 H4
Chalmers Av PCQ . . . . . . 146 S40
Chalmers Pl ABT . . . . . . 250 T71
Chalmers Pl DEL . . . . . . 204 J30
Chamberlain Dr DNV . . . 123 K19-20
Chamberlayne Av DEL . . . 223 N17
Chamberlayne Way DEL . . . 223 N17
Chambers St VAN . . . . . . 163 X18
Chambord Pl VAN . . . . . . 183 Z20
Champlain Cr ABT . . . . . 250 U78
Champlain Cr VAN . . . 183 A20 Z20
Champlain Dr ABT . 250 U78 270 V78
Chancellor Blvd UEL . . 161 T4-5 U6
Chancellor Pl UEL . . . . . . 161 T4
Chandlery Pl VAN . . . . 183 A-B19
Channel Ct CQT . . . . . 145 T35-36
Channel St ABT . . . . . . . 251 R79
Chantrell Pl ABT . . . . . 250 T-U78
Chantrell Pl SUR . . . . . . 245 T34
Chantrell Park Dr SUR . . . . . . .
. . . . . . . 245 U34 265 V34
Chapin Rd KNT . . . . . . . 175 U22
Chapman Av CQT . . . . . . 165 U31
Chapman Pl ABT . . . . . . 250 U77
Chapman Way DNV . . . . . 123 M22
Chapmond Cr RMD . . . . . 202 J8
Chapple Cr BUR . . . . . . . 164 X24
Charbray Pl SUR . . . . . 226 L-M42
Chardonnay La ABT . . . . . 249 U67
Charing Ct BUR . . . . . . . 164 Y26
Charland Av CQT . . . . 165 W32-34
Charles Ct ABT . . . . . . . 250 T72
Charles Pl SQM . . . . . . . 301 C3
Charles St BUR . . . . . . . . . . . .
. . 143 T21 T21-22 144 T24 T24-25
Charles St CHL . . . . . . 213 E7 F7
Charles St DNV . . . . . . . 143 Q20
Charles St PMD . . . . . . . 145 T32
Charles St RMD . . . . . . . 182 C13
Charles St VAN . . . . . . 143 T17-20
Charleson Rd VAN . . . . . 162 U13
Cedar Village Cl CNV . . . . 123 M19

Charleton Ct PCQ . . . . . 146 S-T40
Charlford Av BUR . . . . . . 183 Z22
Charlie Spruce Pl ABT . . . 251 Q82
Charlier Rd PTM . . . . . . 166 U45
Charlotte Av ABT . . . . 250 T71-72
Charlotte Cr ANM . . . . 145 P-Q34
Charlotte Ct BUR . . . . . . 163 X22
Charlotte Rd DNV . . . . . . 143 P20
Charlton St MAP . . . . . . 187 B48
Charnley Av MIS . . . . . . 210 H73
Charnley Ct PTM . . . . . . 186 Z45
Charnley Dr MIS . . . . . . 210 H73
Charter Hill Dr CQT . . . 145 R-S36
Charter Hill Pl CQT . . . 145 R-S36
Chartwell Av WVA . . . . . 122 K11
Chartwell Dr CHL . . . . . . 194 C10
Chartwell Dr SUR . . . 205 F-G36 G36
Chartwell Dr WVA . 122 J11 J-K11 K11
Chartwell Gn CQT . . . . . 125 N38
Chartwell La CQT . . 125 N38 145 P38
Chartwell Pl WVA . . . . . . 122 K11
Chase St ABT . . . . . . . . 250 S73
Chateau Blvd WHS . . . 401 E4 S22
Chateau Ct DEL . . . . . . . 224 K30
Chateau Pl ABT . . . . . . . 270 V72
Chateau Pl PMD . . . . . . . 145 T32
Chateau Pl VAN . . . . . . . 182 A11
Chateau Wynd DEL . . . . . 224 K30
Chatham St RMD . . . . . 222 K-L8
Chatham St VAN . . . . . . . 163 X19
Chatham St WVA . . . . . . 101 G2
Chatsworth Rd RMD . . . . 202 G10-11
Chatterton Rd RMD . . . . . 202 G11
Chatwin Av MAP . . . . . . 167 Y48
Chaucer Av DNV . . . . . . . 123 L19
Chaucer Pl BUR . . . . . 164 Y25-26
Cheakamus Pl SQM . . . . . 301 E3
Cheakamus Way WHS . . . . 401 H1
Cheakamus Lake Rd WHS . 401 J98
Cheam Av CHL . . . . . . . 213 E6-7
Cheam Av KNT . . . . . 175 W20-21
Cheam Dr ABT . . . . . . 250 S-T73
Cheam La KNT . . . . . . . 175 W21
Cheam Pl VAN . . . . . . . . 183 Z20
Cheam View Cr CHL . . . . 233 M5-6
Chehalis Av CHL . . . . . . . 233 M6
Chehalis Dr ABT . . . . . 250 S-T73
Chehalis Dr DEL . . . . . . . 263 X16
Chehalis Pl VAN . . . . . . . 183 Z20
Chehalis St HHS . . . . . . 155 P19
Chelmsford St RMD . . . . . 202 G11
Chelsea Av ABT . . . . . 270 V74-75
Chelsea Av PCQ . . . 146 S40-41 S42
Chelsea Cl WVA . . . . . . 122 K8
Chelsea Cr DNV . . . . . . 123 K1G
Chelsea Ct BUR . . . . . . . 164 W27
Chelsea Ct WVA . . . . . . 122 K8
Chelsea Pl RMD . . . . . . . 202 G11
Chelsea Pl WVA . . . . . . . 122 K8
Chelsea Rd RMD . . . . . . . 202 G11
Chemainus Dr RMD . . . . . 202 G10
Cherbourg Dr WVA . . . . . 121 K4
Cherrington Av MAP . . . 187 Z50-51
Cherrington Pl MAP . . . . . 187 Z50
Cherry Av MIS . . . . . . 210 G72-76
Cherry Dr SQM . . . . . . . 301 J4
Cherry La DEL . . . . . . . . 224 L28
Cherry La PTM . . . . . . . 187 Z47
Cherry Pl MAP . . . . . . . . 167 Y50
Cherry St ABT . . . . . . . . 270 V75
Cherry St NEW . . . . . . . . 164 Y30
Cherry St VAN . . . . . . . 163 X-Y20
Cherry Blossom Cl PMD . . 145 R34
Cherrybrook Pl CQT . . . . 165 U38
Cherryhill Cl SUR . . . . . 186 C40
Cherryhill Cr SUR . . . . 186 B-C40
Cherryhill Cr SUR . . . . . 186 C40
Cherryhill Pl SUR . . . . . 186 C40-41
Cherrywood Cr BUR . . . . 163 X21
Cherrywood Dr CHL . . . . 233 N7
Cherrywood Dr MAP . . . 187 Z53-54
Chesapeake Ldg DEL . . . 223 M17
Chesham Av BUR . . . . . . 163 X21
Cheshire Ct BUR . . . . . 164 Y26-27
Chess St VAN . . . . . . . . 143 T16
Chester Ct CQT . . . . . . . 165 X34
Chester Dr CHL . . . . . . . 233 M8
Chester Pl PCQ . . . . . . . 146 T39
Chester Rd DEL . . . . . 204 E-F26
Chester St PCQ . . . . . . . 146 T39
Chester St VAN . 163 X16 Y16 183 A16
Chesterfield Av CHL . . . . 213 F6-7
Chesterfield Av CNV . . . . . . . . .
. . 123 L-N17 N16 N16-17 143 P16
Chesterfield Av DNV . . . . 123 L17
Chesterfield Pl CNV . . . . 143 P16
Chestnut Av HHS . . . . . . 155 Q19

Chestnut Av SQM . . . . . 301 J-K3
Chestnut Cr ANM . . . . . 125 N33
Chestnut Cr DEL . . . . . . 243 Q17
Chestnut Cr PTM . . . . . . 187 Z47
Chestnut Ct PMD . . . . . . 145 Q35
Chestnut Dr PMD . . . . . . 145 Q35
Chestnut Pl SUR . . . . . . 186 C40
Chestnut St ABT . . . . . . 250 S-T77
Chestnut St NEW . . . . . 164 Y29-30
Chestnut St PCQ . . . . . . 146 T41
Chestnut St VAN . . . 10 J33 142 T11
Chestnut St WRK . . . . . . 265 W34
Chestnut Way PMD . . . . . 145 Q35
Chetwynd Av RMD . . . . . 202 G10
Chevalier Ct PMD . . . . . . 145 Q33
Cheviot Pl RMD . . . . . . . 202 G11
Cheviot Rd DNV . . . . . 123 J-K15
Cheyenne Av VAN . . . . . . 163 X19
Chickadee Av MIS . . . . . 210 J72-73
Chickadee Ct RMD . . . . . 222 K10
Chickadee Pl CQT . . . . . . 146 P39
Chickadee Pl VAN 183 A20-21 B19-20
Chicory La DNV . . . . . . . 122 M14
Chicory Pl BUR . . . . . . . 164 V26
Chief Billy Dr SQM . . . . . 301 K2
Chief Harry Rd SQM . . . . 301 K2
Chief Jimmy Harry Dr DNV . 143 P20
Chief Joseph St CNV . . . . 123 N16
Chief View Rd SQM . . . . . 301 K2
Chiefview Rd SQM . . . . . . 301 E3
Chigwell St MAP . . . . . . . 187 B48
Chilco St VAN . . 10 E35 F34 142 R12
Chilcotin Dr ABT . . . . . 250 R-S73
Chilcott Av PCQ . . . . . . . 146 T39
Chilko Dr CQT . . . . . . 165 V36-37
Chilkwayuck Rd CHL . . . . 233 N6
Chilliwack Central Rd CHL 213 F7-8
Chilliwack Lake Rd CHL . . 233 P7-8
Chilliwack Mountain Rd CHL . . . . .
. . . . . . . . . . . . . . 213 F2-3
Chilliwack River Rd CHL . . . . . . .
. . . . . . 213 H7-8 J7 233 K-L8
Chine Av PCQ . . . . . . . . 165 U38
Chine Cr CQT . . . . . . . . 165 U33
Chinook Ct BUR . . . . . . . 164 V25
Chinook St CHL . . . . . . . 233 N4
Chippendale Ct WVA . . . . 122 K10
Chippendale Rd WVA . . 122 K10 11
Chiselhampton St BUR . . . 164 X25
Chisholm St DEL . . . . . . 223 P16
Chittenden Rd CHL . . . . . 233 P5-6
Chowat Rd KNT . . . . . . 175 U-V23
Chrisdale Av BUR . . . . . 164 W26
Christina Dr CHL . . . . . . 233 K7-8
Christina Pl ABT . . . 250 R78 251 R79
Christina Pl CQT . . . . . . 165 V37
Christmas Way CQT . . . . 145 T38
Christopher Ct BUR . . . . . 163 X21
Christopherson Rd SUR . . . . . . . .
. . . . . . . . 245 U31 265 V31
Chrome Ct CQT . . . . . . . 146 R39
Chrstle St MIS . . . . . . . 210 G74
Chuckart Pl DNV . . . . . . 123 M20
Church Av MAP . . . . . . . 187 Z52
Church St ABT . . . . . . . . 250 U72
Church St DEL . . . . . . . . 243 Q15
Church St DNV . . . . . . . 123 L20
Church St LGT . . . . . . . 207 F54
Church St NEW . . . . . . . 184 B29
Church St VAN . . . . . . . 163 X-Y20
Churchill Av NEW . . . . 164 Y29-30
Churchill Cr DNV . . . . . . 123 N15
Churchill St DEL . . . . . 243 Q21-22
Churchill St VAN . 162 X-Y12 182 Z12
Chutter St BUR . . . . . . . 164 V26
Cimarron Dr CQT . . . . . . 145 R37
Cinnamon Dr BUR . . . . 164 U28-29
Cinnamon Dr SUR . . . . . 205 E32
Circle Dr CHL . . . . . . . . 213 J5
Citadel Cr RMD . . . . . . . 202 H9
Citadel Dr CNV . . . . . . . 123 K19
Citadel Dr PCQ . . . 165 Y38 166 X39
Citadel Parade VAN 11 H39 142 S-T14
Citation Dr RMD . . . . . . 202 F13
Citrus Wynd WVA . . . . . . 101 D4
City Edge Pl VAN . . . . . 183 A-B20
City Pkwy SUR . . . . . . 185 C-D34
Claire Pl PCQ . . . . . . . . 166 X39
Clancy Loranger Way VAN . 162 W14
Clare Av BUR . . . . . . . 144 S-T25
Clare Av CHL . . . . . . . . 193 C-E2
Claremont Pl BUR . . . . . 164 V27
Claremont St CQT . . . . . 164 U30
Clarence St PMD . . . . . . 145 S35
Clarence Taylor Cr DEL . . . 243 Q18

Clarendon St VAN.
. . . . . . 163 X-Y18 Y18 183 Z18 Z18
Claridge Ct BUR . . . . . . . 164 V27
Clark Dr DEL . . . . . . . . . . 224 N30
Clark Dr VAN. . . . . . . . . . . . . . .
. . . . . 143 S-T17 163 U17 V16-17 W16-17
Clarke Dr ABT . . . . . . . . . 250 U76
Clarke Dr CHL . . . . . . . . . . 193 D7
Clarke Dr SQM . . . . . . . 301 J3 K2-3
Clarke Pl RMD . . . . . . . . . 183 D16
Clarke Rd CQT . . . . 164 U30 165 U31
Clarke Rd PMD . . . . . . . . . 145 T32
Clarke St PMD . . . . . . . . 145 T32-33
Clarkson St NEW . . 184 A30 B29-30
Claude Av BUR . . . . . . . . 164 X25
Claudia Ct ABT . . . . . . . . 250 T72
Claudia Pl PCQ . . . . . . . . 166 X39
Clay St MIS. . . . . . . . . . 210 E-G72
Claybrook Rd RMD . . . . . 202 G-H9
Clayburn Gt ABT . . . . . . . 250 S78
Clayburn Rd ABT . . . 250 Q74 Q75-78
Claymore Pl BUR. . . . . . . 164 V30
Claysmith Rd RMD . . . . . 202 G-H9
Clayton Av CHL. . . . . . . . . 193 D8
Clayton Ct BUR . . . . . . . . 164 X25
Clayton St CQT. . . . . . . . . 165 W31
Clayton St PCQ . . . . . . . . 145 T38
Claytonhill Dr SUR . . . . 226 L43-44
Claytonhill Gr SUR . . . . 226 L43-44
Claytonhill Pl SUR . . . . . 226 L44
Claytonwood Cr SUR . 226 L43 L44
Claytonwood Ct SUR . . . 226 L43
Claytonwood Dr SUR . . . 226 L43
Claytonwood Gr SUR . . 226 L43-44
Claytonwood Pl SUR . . 226 L43-44
Cleadon Ct VAN. . . . . . . 183 A19-20
Clearbrook Rd ABT. . . . . . . . . . .
. . . . . . . . . . 250 S-U72 270 V-Z72
Clearview Cr ABT . . . . . . . 250 U71
Clearview Dr PMD . . . . . . 145 T35
Clearwater Dr RMD . . . . . 202 G10
Clearwater Gt RMD . . . . . 202 G10
Clearwater Way CQT . . . 165 V36-37
Clegg Pl DNV. . . . . . . . . . . 124 N25
Clegg St MIS. . . . . . . . . . 210 H74
Clematis Cr PCQ . . . . . . . 146 S40
Clematis Dr RMD. . . . . . . 202 F9
Clements Av DNV . . . . . . . 123 J15
Clerihue Ct MIS . . . . . 210 G75-76
Clerihue Rd PCQ . . . . . . 165 X-Y38
Clermont Mews VAN. . . . . 183 Z20
Clevedon Dr SUR . . . . . . 225 K33
Cleveland Av CHL . . . . . . . 213 E7
Cleveland Av SQM . . . . . . 301 J-K2
Cliff Av MAP . . . . 187 Z51-52 Z53
Cliff Av WRK . . . . . 265 X38 266 X39
Cliff Av N BUR . . . . . . . . 144 S25
Cliff Av S BUR . 144 S25 T25 164 U25
Cliff Dr DEL . . . . . . . . . . . 263 W16
Cliff Pl DEL . . . . . . . . . . . 263 W16
Cliff Pl MAP . . . . . . . . 187 A51 Z51
Cliff Rd WVA . . . . . . . . . . . 101 G1
Cliffmont Rd DNV. . 124 N26 N26-27
Cliffridge Av DNV . . 103 H15 123 J15
Cliffridge Pl DNV. . . . . . . . 103 H15
Cliffrose Cr CQT . . . . . . . . 145 Q38
Cliffside La SQM . . . . . . . . 301 J2
Clifftop La WHS . . . . . . . . . 401 H1
Cliffwood Dr PMD . . . . 145 P-Q35
Cliffwood La DNV . . . . . . . 124 M26
Cliffwood Rd DNV. . . . . 124 M-N26
Clifton Av CQT . . . . . . . . 165 U33
Clifton Rd RMD . . . . . . . . 202 G10
Clinton Av ABT . . . . . . . . 250 S72
Clinton Pl NEW . . . . . . . . 184 A29
Clinton St BUR . . . . . . . . . . . . . . .
. . . . 183 A21 A22 184 A23 A24 A24-25
Clipper Ct RMD . . . . . . . . 222 K9
Clipper Pl DEL . . . . . . 223 N16-17
Clipper Rd DEL . . . . . . . . 223 N17
Clipper St CQT . . . . . . . . 165 Y33
Clive Av VAN . . . . . . . . . . 163 X20
Cliveden Av DEL. . 204 E27 F25 F-G24
Cliveden Pl DEL. . . . . . 204 E-F26
Cloudburst Dr WHS . . . . . 401 J98
Cloudview Pl LIO . . . . . . 101 B-C23
Clovelly Walk WVA. . . . . . 121 K3-4
Clover Dr CHL . . . . . . . . . 233 M7
Clover Pl HHS . . . . . . . . . 155 Q19
Clover St CQT. . . . . . . . . 165 W37
Cloverdale By-Pass SUR . 226 N42
Cloverlake Ct BUR. . . . 164 W27-28
Cloverley St CNV. . . . . . . 143 P19
Cloverley St DNV . . 123 N19 143 P19
Clovermeadow Cr LGT . . . 227 N54

Clute St NEW . . . . . . . . . . 184 Z29
Clyde Av WVA. . . . . . . . . . . . . . . . .
. . . . . . 122 M11 M11-12 M12-13
Coach Lamp Dr CHL. . . . . 233 K6
Coachstone Way ABT. . . 250 R78
Coal Harbour Quay VAN. . . . . . . . .
. . . . . . . . . . . . . 10 E-F36 142 R13
Coal Harbour Seawalk VAN. . . . . . .
. . . . . . 10 E36 11 F37-38 142 R13
Coalman Pl ABT . . . . . . . 249 T63
Coast Meridian Rd CQT . 146 Q-R41
Coast Meridian Rd PCQ. . . . . . . . .
. . . . . . . . . 146 T41 166 U41 W41
Cobblestone Av VAN. . . 183 A-B20
Cobblestone Dr ABT . . 250 R-S78
Cobblestone La PTM . . . . 186 A46
Coburg St NEW. . . . . . . . 184 A30
Cochrane Av CQT. 164 W30 165 W31
Cochrane Dr RMD. . . . . . 204 E24
Cochrane Gt RMD. . . . . . 204 E24
Coghlan Pl ABT. . . . 249 S70 250 S71
Cohoe Pl CHL . . . . . . . . . . 213 F2
Colbeck Pl RMD . . . . . . . 202 H10
Colbeck Rd RMD . . . . . . . 202 H10
Colborne Av BUR . 164 Y24 184 Z24
Colborne St NEW . . . . . . 184 Z29
Colbrook Ct BUR . . . . . 164 X23-24
Colby St NEW . . . . . . . . 164 X30
Colchester Dr RMD. . . . . 202 H9
Coldfall Ct RMD. . . . . . 202 G-H9
Coldfall Rd RMD. . . . . . 202 G-H9
Coldicutt Av WRK . . 265 W34 W35
Coldicutt St BUR . . . . . 164 X-Y29
Coldwell Rd DNV. . . . . . 124 N25
Colebrook Rd SUR. . . . . . . . . . . . .
. . . . 225 N-P38 P31-32 P32-33 P34-35
. . . . 226 N40 N42-43 P43 P46
Coleman Av CQT. . . . . . . 165 Y34
Coleman Cl DNV. . . . . . 123 J-K19
Coleman Pl DEL . . . . . . . 223 P18
Coleman St DNV. . . . . 123 K20-21
Coleman St MIS. . . . . . . 210 G-H77
Colemore Pl MAP. . . . . . 167 Y52
Colemore St MAP. . . . . . 167 Y52
Coleridge Av VAN . 163 Y19 Y19-20
Colfax Av CQT . . . . . . 165 W34-35
Colfax Cr VAN. . . . . . . . 183 Z19-20
Colin Pl CQT . . . . . . 146 S39-40
Colinet St CQT . . . . . . . . 165 V32
Colleen St BUR. . . . . . . . 164 W26
College Av NEW. . . . . . . . 184 A29
College Dr ABT . . . . . . . . 270 W76
College St CHL . . . . . . 213 E6-7
College St VAN. . . . . . . 163 X-Y19
College High Rd UEL . . 161 U4 U5-6
College Park Way PMD . 145 S31-32
Collier St BUR. . . . . . . . 184 Z25-26
Collings Pl DEL . . . . . . . 204 F28
Collings Way DEL . . . . . . 204 F28
Collingwood Cr SUR245 S38 246 S39
Collingwood Pl VAN. . . . . 162 Y9
Collingwood St VAN . 162 U-Y9 Y9
Collins Dr CHL. . . . . . . . . 233 K7
Collins Rd CQT . . . . . . . 146 Q40
Collister Dr BUR . . . . . . 164 V26
Colodin Cl PCQ. . . . . . . 165 V-W38
Colonial Dr PCQ . . . . . 166 X-Y39
Colonial Dr RMD. . . . . . . 202 G9
Colony Farm Rd CQT . . 165 X36-37
Colt Pl CHL . . . . . . . . . . 233 M6
Colter Ct BUR . . . . . . . 164 V-W27
Colton Av CQT. . . . . . . . 165 X34
Coltsfoot Dr RMD. . . . . 202 F19-10
Columbia Av PCQ . . . . . 166 X39
Columbia Av WRK . . . . . . . . . . . .
. . . . . . 265 X37-38 266 X39
Columbia St ABT. . . . . . 270 W-Z73
Columbia St DNV . . . . . 143 Q20
Columbia St MIS . . . . . 210 J75
Columbia St NEW. . . . 184 B28-29
Columbia St PMD . . . 145 T32 T33
Columbia St VAN. . . . . . . . . . . . . .
. . . . 11 G-H40 K39 142 T14 143 S15
. . . . 162 U14 U-W14 X-Y14 182 A14
Columbia St E NEW. . . . . . . . . . . . .
. . . . . . . . 164 Y30 184 A30 Z30
Columbia Valley Hwy CHL . 233 P6
Columbia Valley Hwy FRA. . . . . . . .
. . . . . . . . . 253 R5-6 T-U5
Colville Rd RMD . . . . . . . 202 H10
Colwood Dr DNV. . . . . . . 123 L15
Colwood Pl CHL. . . . . . . 233 M7
Colwood St MIS. . . . . . . 210 F74
Comber Way SUR. 205 J33 225 K33
Commerce Ct BUR. . . 164 V28-29
Commerce Pkwy RMD . . 203 E17

Commercial Ct CHL . . . . . 213 H5
Commercial Dr VAN. . . . . . . . . . . .
. . . . . . . 143 S-T17 163 U-V17
Commercial St ABT. . . . . 250 U73
Commercial St MIS. . . . . 230 K74
Commercial St VAN. . . . . . . . . . . . .
. . . . 163 V-X17 X-Y17 Y17 183 Z17
Commercial Way SQM . . 301 G1-2
Commission St HOP . 118 E44 E45
Commissioner St VAN. . 143 R18-19
Commodore Dr DEL. . 223 N16-17
Commodore Rd VAN. . . . 162 U14
Commonwealth Cr DEL . 224 K29-30
Commonwealth St PCQ . 166 U40
Como Lake Av CQT. . . . . . . . . . . . .
. . . . . . . 165 U31-35 U37-38
Comox Ct ABT. . . . . . . . . 250 T74
Comox St VAN. . . . . . . . . . . . . . . . .
. . . . 10 K32-33 142 T10-11
Compass Ct CQT . 145 T36 165 U36
Compston Cr DEL . . . . 263 W-X18
Compton Ct CQT . . . . 165 V34-35
Comstock Rd RMD. . . . . 202 G11
Conair Av ABT. . . . . . . . . 250 U71
Concord Av CHL . . . . . . . 233 L6
Concord Av CQT. . . . . 165 Y34-35
Condor SQM . . . . . . . . . . . 301 D4
Condor Cr CQT . . . . . . . 145 S36
Condor Pl WVA . . . . . . . . 121 J2
Condor Rd SQM . . . . . . . . 301 D4
Confederation Dr PCQ . 165 X-Y38
Congo Cr PCQ . . . . . . . 166 U41
Congo Pl PCQ . . . . . . . 166 U41
Conifer Dr CQT . . . . . . . 146 P41
Connaught Av DNV . . . . . 123 L18
Connaught Av PCQ . . . . 166 W39-40
Connaught Cr DNV . . . . . 123 L15
Connaught Dr DEL. . . . . . 263 Y16
Connaught Dr PCQ . . . . . 166 W40
Connaught Dr VAN. . . . 162 W-X12
Connaught Pl CHL. . . . . . 233 M4
Connecting Rd PTM. . . . 167 V47-48
Conrad Av ABT. . . . . . . 250 T71-72
Conrad St BUR . . . . . . 164 W26-27
Conrad St CHL . . . . . . . . 193 B8
Consort Ct ABT . . . . . . . . 250 T72
Constable Dr RMD. . . . . . 222 K11
Constable Gt RMD . . . . . 222 K11
Constantine Pl WVA. . . . . 122 K9
Conway Av BUR . . 184 A25 Z25
Conway Pl ABT . . . . . . 250 T-U75
Cook Av MAP . . . . . . . 187 Z49-50
Cook Cr RMD. . . . . . . . . 202 F13
Cook Gt RMD . . . . . . . . 202 F13
Cook Rd RMD. . . . . . . 202 F12-13
Cook St CHL . . . . . . 193 D6 213 E6
Cook St VAN. 11 K39 142 T14 162 U14
Coombe La BEL . . . . . 124 M-N28
Cooney Rd RMD. . . . . . 202 E-F12
Cooper Pl ABT . . . . . . . . 250 R78
Cooper Pl DEL . . . . . . . . 223 P18
Cooper Rd RMD . . . . . . . 202 H13
Cooper's Mews VAN. . . . . . . . . . . . . .
. . . . . . . . . 11 J-K38 142 T14
Cooperage Way VAN. . . . . . . . . . . . . .
. . . . . . . . . 11 J38-39 142 T14
Cooperative Way VAN . 163 V18-19
Coopershawk Ct SUR. . 205 H35
Coote St CHL . . . . . 193 D8 213 E8
Copeland Av VAN . . . . . 183 A20
Copley St VAN . . . 163 V18 V-W18
Copper Pl MIS . . . . . . . . 210 G75
Copper Cove Rd WVA . 101 F2 G1
Copper Ridge Dr CHL. . . 213 F2
Copperbeech Av LGT. . . . 207 F53
Coppersmith Pl RMD. . . 223 K15
Coppersmith Way RMD . 223 K15
Copping St CNV . . . . . . . 123 N15
Copsefield Dr DEL. . . . . . 263 Z17
Copsefield Pl DEL. . . . . . 263 Z17
Coquihalla La VAN . 183 Z20-21
Coquihalla St HOP . 118 D45 E44
Coquitlam Av PCQ . . . . . 166 U40
Coquitlam St BUR . . . . . 164 Y29
Coquitlam St CHL . . . . . 233 M6
Cora Av CHL. . . . . . . . 213 F7-8
Coral Av CHL. . . . . . . . . 250 T72
Coral Reef Pl VAN . . . . . 183 B18
Corbett Pl ABT . . . . . . . 251 R79
Corbett St HOP. . . . . 118 E-F45
Corbin Pl CQT . . . . . . 145 R37
Corbould Rd DEL . . . . 263 Z19-20
Corbould St CHL . . 193 D6 213 E6
Cord Av CQT . . . . . . . . 145 R37
Cordiale Dr VAN . . . . . . 183 A20
Cordova Ct ABT. . . . . . 270 V72-73

Cordova Ct ABT . . . . . . . 270 V73
Cordova Div VAN. . . . . . . 143 S16
Cordova St E VAN11 G41 143 S15-16
Cordova St W VAN. . . . . . . . . . . . . .
. . . . 11 F37-38 G39 142 R13-14 S14
Corless Pl RMD. . . . . . . . 202 G9
Corless Rd RMD. . . . . . . 202 G9
Cornell Av CQT. . . . . 165 V32-34
Cornell Way PMD . . . . . . 145 S32
Cornerbrook Cr RMD. . . 202 J9-10
Cornerstone St VAN. . 183 A-B20
Cornett Rd VAN. . . . . . 163 U-V20
Corning Av CQT. . . . . 165 W32
Cornwall Av ABT . . . . . . 270 V75
Cornwall Av VAN. . . . . . . . . . . . . . . .
. . . . . . 10 K32-33 142 T10-11
Cornwall Cr CHL . . . . . . . 213 F8
Cornwall Ct RMD . . . . . 202 E8-9
Cornwall Dr PCQ . . . . . . 146 T42
Cornwall Dr RMD. . . . . . 202 E8-9
Cornwall Pl PCQ . . . . . . 146 T42
Cornwall Pl RMD. . . . . . . 202 E9
Cornwall St NEW. . . . . . . 184 B28
Cornwall St PCQ . . . . . . 146 T42
Corona Cr CQT . . 145 T35 165 U35
Corona Pl BUR . . . . . . . 164 V29
Coronado Dr BUR . . . . . 164 U26
Coronation Ct ABT . . . . . 250 T72
Corral Pl WHS . . . . . . . 401 D-E3
Corsica Way VAN . . . . . . 183 A20
Cortell St DNV . . . 122 M14 123 M15
Cortes Av CQT . . . . . . . 146 R39
Cortez Cr DNV. . . . . . . . 103 H15
Corvette Way RMD . . . . 182 C12
Cory Dr DEL . . . . . . . . . 224 K30
Cory Rd WRK. . . . . . . . 265 W35
Costain Ct RMD . . . . . . . 202 G11
Cottage La ABT . . . . . . . 270 V75
Cotton Dr VAN. . . . . . . . 143 T17
Cotton Dr VAN. . 143 T17 163 U17
Cotton Rd CNV. . . . . . . . 143 P19
Cottonwood Av CQT. . . . . . . . . . . . . .
. . . . 164 V30 165 V31-32 V33
Cottonwood Av DEL. . . 224 M30
Cottonwood Av HHS . . . 155 Q20
Cottonwood Ct CHL . . . . 213 F7
Cottonwood Dr HOP . . . 118 E47
Cottonwood Dr MAP. . 187 A54 Z54
Cottonwood Pl DNV. . . . 122 N14
Cottonwood Pl HHS . . 155 Q19-20
Cottonwood Pl MIS . . . 210 J72
Cottonwood Rd SQM . . 301 B-C2
Cottonwood St DEL. . . . 224 L-M30
Cottonwood St MIS. . . . 210 J72
Cottonwood Ter MIS . . . 210 J72
Cottrell St VAN . . . . 143 T16 163 U16
Cougar Ct ABT . . 250 U71 270 V71
Cougar Ct CQT . . . . . . . 145 Q38
Cougar Dr DEL . . . . . . . 224 L30
Couillard Mews VAN . . . 183 Z19
Coulter Ct DEL . . . . . . . 204 H29
Coulter Pl LGT . . . . . . . . 207 E53
Coulthard Ct VAN . . . . . 225 N33
Coulthard Rd SUR. . . . . 225 N33
Countess Cr ABT . . . . . . 250 T-U72
Country Ct ABT . . . . . . . 251 U81
Country Pl ABT . . . . . . . 251 U81
Country Woods Dr SUR. . . . . . . . . . .
. . . . . . 246 T-U41 U42
Court La CHL . . . . . . . . 213 E6
Courtenay St VAN . . . . . 162 U-V7
Courtney Cr NEW . 164 Y29 184 Z29
Coutts Pl PCQ . . . . . . . 165 X38
Coutts Way ABT . . . . . . 270 X77
Coutts Way PCQ . . . . . . 165 X38
Cove Av CHL. . . . . . . . . 233 N6
Cove Pl CQT . . . . . 165 U-V36
Cove Pl SUR . . . . . . . . 265 V31
Cove Cliff Pl DNV . . . . . 124 N27
Cove Cliff Rd DNV . . . 124 N26-27
Cove Inlet Rd DEL . . . . 223 M17
Cove Link Rd DEL . . . . 223 M17
Cove Reach Rd DEL . . 223 M17
Coventry Cr PCQ . . . . . 166 U40
Coventry Dr RMD . . . . . 202 H9
Coventry Pl BUR . . . . . 164 V26
Coventry Pl CHL . . . . . . 213 F7
Coventry Rd SUR . . . . 185 B35
Coventry Way DNV . . . . 123 K17
Covey Pl DNV . . . . . . . . 103 H15
Covina Ct CQT . . . . . . 165 U31
Cowan Rd SUR . . . . . . 185 B34
Cowichan Pl CHL . . . . . 233 M5

Cowichan Rd CHL . . . . . 233 M5
Cowichan St CHL . . . . . 233 M5-6
Cowichan Ter ABT . . . . 250 S-T73
Cowley Cr RMD . . 182 D10 202 E10
Cowley Ct PMD . . . . . 145 Q32-33
Cowley Dr N DEL . . . . 224 K30
Cowley Dr S DEL . . . . 224 K30
Cox Dr MIS . . . . . . . . . 210 G75
Coy Av CQT . . . . . . . . 146 P-Q40
Coylton Pl PMD . . . . . . 145 T31
Coyote Ct CQT . . . . . . 145 Q38
Coyote Pl WHS . . . . . . 401 H-J1
CPR Rd KNT. . . . . . . . . 175 W17
Crabapple Dr WHS. . . . . 401 E2-3
Crabbe Av CQT . . . . . . 145 T38
Crabtree La CHL . . . . . . 194 C9
Craig Av BUR. . . . . . . . 164 X30
Craig Rd ABT . . . . . . . 182 C14
Craigavon Rd RMD . . . . 202 G10
Craigen Av CQT . . . . . 165 X34-35
Craigend Rd WVA . . . . . 122 K7
Craigflower Dr RMD . . . 202 H9
Craigflower Pl RMD . . . 202 H9
Craigmohr Dr WVA . . . . 102 H13
Craigmohr Pl WVA . . . . 102 H13
Cramer Dr CHL . . . . . . . 213 F7
Cranberry Ct ABT . . . . . 251 U79
Cranberry Ct PMD . . . . 145 P35
Cranberry Dr VAN . . . . 162 U11
Cranbrook Av RMD . . . . 202 G10
Crane Av CQT . . . . . 165 V34-35
Crane Av MIS . . . . . . . 210 H73
Crane Pl NEW . . . . . . 184 C-D27
Cranley Dr SUR . . 245 T38 266 V39
Cranley Dr WVA. 101 H2 H3 121 J2 J3
Craven Pl CHL . . . . . . . 213 F8
Crawford Bay PMD . . . . 145 Q33
Crawford Dr DEL . . . . 204 J28-29
Crawley Av CQT . . . . . 165 W36
Crayford Cl DNV . . . . . 123 M20
Creamery Rd CHL . . . . . 213 G7
Cree St VAN. . . . . . . . 163 Y15
Creek Pl BUR. . . . . . . . 164 U30
Creek Rd CHL . . . . . . . 213 H5
Creekside Ct SUR . . . . 186 C39
Creekside Dr ABT . . . . 249 T70
Creekside Dr CHL . . . . 213 F5
Creekside Dr CQT. . . . 145 S36
Creekside Dr VAN . 10 J-K34 142 T12
Creekside Gr SUR. . . . 186 C39
Creekside Pl ANM. . . . 125 N33
Creekside Pl BUR . . . . 163 V21
Creekstone Dr ABT. . . 250 S77-78
Creekstone Pl ABT . . . 250 R78
Creekstone Pl PMD . . . 145 R35
Creekview Pl LIO. . . . 101 C23-24
Creelman Av VAN . . 10 J33 142 T11
Creery Av WVA . . . . . . . 121 L6
Crescent VAN . . . . . . . 162 V12
Crescent, The SQM. . . . . 301 F5
Crescent Ct DEL . . . . . . 223 P19
Crescent Dr CHL . . . . . 213 F5-6
Crescent Dr DEL. . . . . . . . . . . . . . . .
. . . . . . 223 N-P17 P17-18 P18
Crescent Dr SUR. . . . . . 245 U31
Crescent Pl DEL . . . . . 223 P18-19
Crescent Rd SUR. . . . . . . . . . . . . . . .
. . . . 245 S34-35 T33 T-U32
Crescent Rd UEL . . . . . . 161 U3
Crescent Way ABT . . . . 250 U75
Crescentview Dr DNV . . 123 L15
Cresswell Av VAN. 183 A19-21 Z20-21
Crest Ct CQT. . . . . . . . 165 U33
Crest Dr BUR. . . . . . . . 164 Y29
Crestlawn Ct BUR . . . . 164 U23
Crestlawn Dr BUR. . . . 144 T23
Crestline Rd WVA . . . . 122 J12
Crestlynn Dr DNV . . . . 123 L20
Crestlynn Pl DNV. . . . . 123 L20
Creston Cl CQT . . . . . . 146 R41
Creston Dr ABT . . . . . . 250 S72
Creston St MAP. . . 167 Y50 187 Z50
Crestview Av ABT . . . . 249 S69
Crestview Dr DEL. . . . . 224 L30
Crestview Dr SUR. . . . 185 A33-34
Crestwell Rd WVA . . . . 122 J11
Crestwood Av DNV . . . 123 K16
Crestwood Dr CHL . . . . 213 J5
Crestwood Dr CQT . . . 165 U33
Crestwood Pl RMD . . . 183 D17
Crichton Dr SUR . . . . . 205 F34
Crickmer Ct LGT . . . . . 207 F53
Crimson Ridge CHL . . . 233 N3
Croft Rd DNV . . . . . . . 123 K19
Croft Rd HOP. . . . . . . . 118 F43

Crompton St VAN . . . . . . . 183 A16
Cromwell St VAN . . . . . 183 A-B20
Crosby Pl CHL . . . . . . . . . . 193 B8
Crosby St CQT . . . . . . . . . 165 V31
Crosby St MIS . . . . . . . . . . 210 H75
Cross Creek Ct SUR . . . . . 246 T39
Cross Creek Rd WVA . . . . 122 K11-12
Crosscreek Rd LIO . . . . . . 101 B-C23
Crossley Ct ABT . . . . . . . . 250 T71
Crossley Dr ABT . . . 249 T70 250 T71
Crossley Pl ABT . . . . . . . . 250 T71
Crossway WVA . . . . . . . . . 121 K-L3
Croteau Ct VAN . . . . . . . 165 X-Y34
Crouch Av CQT . . . . . . . . 146 R43
Crowberry Ct CQT . . . . . . 145 Q36
Crowe St VAN . . . . . . 11 K39 162 U14
Crowley Dr VAN . . . . . . . . 163 X20
Crown Cr SUR . . . . . 184 D29 204 E29
Crown Cr VAN . . . . . . . . 162 U7-8
Crown Ct ABT . . . . . . . . . 250 T72
Crown St DNV . . . . . . . . . 143 P20
Crown St VAN . . . . . 162 U-V8 V-Y8
Croydon Dr SUR . . . . . . . . . . . . . . .
. . . . . 245 S-T37 T37-38 U38 266 V39
Croydon Pl DNV . . . . . . . . 123 K16
Cruikshank Dr RMD . . . . . 202 H11
Cruikshank St ABT . . . . . . 250 T73
Crush Cr LGT . . . . . . . . . 227 K50
Crystal Ct ABT . . . . . . . . . 270 V71
Crystal Ct CQT . . . . . . . . . 165 U37
Crystal Ct DNV . . . . . . . . 123 J16
Crystal Dr CHL . . . . . . . . . 193 C7
Crystal Creek Dr ANM . . . . . . . . . .
. . . . . . . . . . . 125 N32 145 P32
Crystal Falls Rd LIO . . . . . 101 A23
Cullen Cr RMD . . . . . 202 H11-12
Culloden St VAN . . . . . . . . . . . . . . .
. . . . . 163 W-X16 X-Y16 183 Z16
Cultus Av CQT . . . . . 165 W36-37
Cultus Ct CQT . . . . . . . 165 V-W37
Cultus Lake Rd CHL . . . . . 233 N5-6
Culzean Pl PMD . . . . . . . . 145 T31
Cumberland Av CHL . . . . . 233 M4
Cumberland Cr CNV . . . . . 123 M15
Cumberland Pl DUR . . . 164 X Y28
Cumberland St BUR . . . 164 Y28-29
Cumberland St NEW . . . . . . . . . . .
. . . . . 164 Y29 184 Z29 Z30
Cumberland St PCQ . . . . . 166 U40
Cumbria Dr SUR . . . . . . . . 266 V39
Cummins Pl DNV . . . . 144 P-Q25 Q26
Cundy Av DEL . . . . . 204 E27-28
Cunningham Dr RMD . . . . . 202 H11
Cunningham La PMD . . . . 145 R-S35
Cunningham Pl RMD . . . . . 182 D13
Cunningham St NEW . . . . 184 A-B29
Curate Wynd VAN . . 183 A20 B19-20
Curie Av BUR . . . . . . . . 163 V-W21
Curlew Dr ABT . . . . . . . . 249 T69
Curling Rd DNV . . . . . . . . 122 M13
Curnew St NEW . . . . . . . . 184 B27
Curr Pl BUR . . . . . 163 X22 164 X23
Curragh Av BUR . . . . 184 A24 Z24
Currie Dr SUR . . . . . 185 A35-36 A36
Currie Pl ABT . . . . . 250 U77-78
Currie Pl CHL . . . . . . . . . . 233 K7
Curtis St BUR . . . . . . . 144 T24-26
Curzon St ABT . . . . . . . . . 202 G11
Cusick Cr PTM . . . . 166 Y46 186 Z46
Custer Ct CQT . . . . . . . . . 165 U34
Cuthbert Rd KNT . . . . . . . 175 W23
Cutler Pl MAP . . . . . . . . . 187 Z50
Cutler Rd KNT . . . . . 175 Y18-19
Cutler St CQT . . . . . . . . . 165 X34
Cutter Pl RMD . . . . . . . . . 222 K9
Cutter Rd DEL . . . . . . . . . 223 N17
Cypress Cr VAN . . . . . . . . 162 W11
Cypress Ct PTM . . . . . . . . 187 Z47
Cypress Dr WHS . . . . . . . 401 C-D3
Cypress La WVA . . . . . . . 122 J-K8
Cypress Pk KNT . . . . . . . . 175 X21
Cypress Pl PMD . . . . . . . . 145 R35
Cypress Pl SQM . . . . . . . . 301 B1-2
Cypress Pl SUR . . . . . . . . 205 G33
Cypress Pl WVA . . . . . . . . 122 K7
Cypress St ABT . . . . . 250 U75-76
Cypress St CQT . . . . . . . . 165 V34
Cypress St HOP . . . . . . . . 118 G43
Cypress St VAN . . . . 10 K33 142 T11
. . . . . 162 U-V11 X11 X-Y11 182 Z11
Cypress St WRK . . . . . . . . 265 X38
Cypress Bowl Rd WVA . . . . . . . . . . .
. . . . . . . . . . . 121 K6 122 J8-9 K7
Cyril St ABT . . . . . . . . . . . 250 U76

## D

D St ABT . . . . . . . . . . . . . 270 Z77
D'Herbomez Dr MIS . . . . . 210 H75
Dacre Av CQT . . . . . . . . . 145 T37
Daffodil Dr WVA . . . . . . . . 121 J3
Daffodil La WVA . . . . . . . . 121 J3
Dahl Cr ABT . . . . . . . . . . 270 V76
Dahlia Ct CQT . . . . . . . . . 145 R36
Dahlstrom Pl ABT . . . . . 250 T73-74
Daimler St CQT . . . . . . . . 145 R37
Daisy Av BUR . . . . . . . . . 184 Z24
Daisy La WHS . . . . . . . . . . 401 E3
Dakota Av CHL . . . . . . . . . 233 L6
Dakota Dr RMD . . . . . . . . 202 H11
Dakota Pl RMD . . . . . . . . 202 H11
Dale WVA . . . . . . . . . . . 121 K-L3
Dale Av BUR . . . . . . . . . . 164 X25
Dale Dr MAP . . . . . 187 A48 Z48
Dalebright Dr BUR . . . . . . 164 U26
Dalemore Rd RMD . . . . . . 202 G8
Dales Pl SQM . . . . . . . . . . 301 E3
Dalhousie Rd UEL . . . . . . 161 U4
Dalip Ct CQT . . . . . . . 165 U31-32
Dalke Av MIS . . . . . 210 U74-75
Dalkeith Dr DNV . . . . . . . 123 K17
Dalla-Tina Av BUR . . . . . . 144 S26
Dallyn Rd RMD . . . . . . . . 183 D15
Dalton Ct CQT . . . . . . . . . 165 W33
Daly Pl DEL . . . . . . . . . 204 H-J29
Daly Rd SUR . . . . . . . . 186 C-D43
Dampier Ct RMD . . . . . . . 202 G9
Dampier Dr RMD . . . . . . . 202 G9
Damson Av ABT . . . . . . . . 250 U78
Dan Lee Av NEW . . . . . . . 204 E26
Danforth Ct RMD . . . . . . . 183 D15
Danforth Gt RMD . . . . . . . 183 D15
Daniel Dr CHL . . . . . . . . . 233 N7
Daniels Rd RMD . . . . . . . . 183 D15
Dann Av MIS . . . . . . . . . . 210 H77
Dansey Av CQT . . . . . 165 W31-34
Danube Pl PCQ . . . . . . . . 166 V41
Danube Rd RMD . . . . . . . 202 H11
Danville Ct CQT . . . . . . . . 165 V34
Darwin Av BUR . . . . . . . . 163 W22
Darwin Av CQT . . . . 146 S40 S41
Darwin St CHL . . . . . . . . . 213 F5
Dauphin Pl BUR . . . . . . . . 164 U25
Dave Murray Pl WHS . . . . 401 G-H2
Davenport Dr MAP . . . . . . 167 Y47
Davenport Pl DNV . . . . . . 123 M20
David Av PMD . . . . 145 R34-35
David Dr BUR . . . . . . . . . 164 V30
Davidson St MIS . . . . . . . 210 E77
Davie Ct ABT . . . . . . . . . 250 S77
Davie St ABT . . . . . . . . . 250 S77
Davie St VAN . . . . . . . . . . . . . . . . . .
. . . . . 10 G35 11 J37 142 S12-13
Davie Way DEL . . . . . . . . 204 J28
Davies Av PCQ . . . . . . . . 165 U38
Davies Ct RMD . . . . . . . . 182 C14
Davies Pl RMD . . . . . . . . 182 C14
Davies St BUR . . . . . . . . . 184 Z27
Davis Av CHL . . . . . . . . . 233 K7
Davis Cr LGT . . . . . . 248 T62-63
Davis St NEW . . . . . . . . . 175 W18
Davis Ct CQT . . . . . . . . . . 203 C7
Davison Rd PTM . . . . . . . 166 Y46
Davison St MAP . . . . . . . . 167 Y51
Dawe St NEW . . . . . . . . . 184 D26
Dawes Hill Rd CQT . . . . 165 X34-35
Dawn Av BUR . . . . . . . . . 164 W23
Dawn Ct ABT . . . . . . . . . . 251 U81
Dawn Dr DEL . . . . . . . 243 Q18-19
Dawn Pl DEL . . . . . . . . . 243 Q19
Dawson Cr DEL . . . . . . . . 204 E29
Dawson Ct CQT . . . . . . . . 146 Q39
Dawson Dr MIS . . . . . . . . 210 E75
Dawson Pl DEL . . . . . . . . 204 E29
Dawson Pl MAP . . . . . . . . 167 Y50
Dawson St BUR . . . . . . . . . . . . . . . . .
. . . . . 163 U21-22 U22 164 U23 U24
Dawson St VAN . . . . . . . . 183 Z19
Daybreak Av CQT . . . . 165 U36-37
Daybreak La ABT . . . . . . . 251 U80
Dayton Av RMD . . . . . 202 H13-14
Dayton Ct RMD . . . . . . . 202 G-H13

Dayton Dr CHL . . . . . . . 233 K-L5
Dayton St CQT . . . . . . . . 146 Q41
Deacon St ABT . . . . . . . . 249 U70
Deagle Rd RMD . . . . . . . 202 H-J11
Deane Pl DNV . . . . . . . . . 124 N26
Deans Av CHL . . . . . . . . . 213 F5
Dease La VAN . . . . . . . . . 183 Z20
Dease Pl CQT . . . . . . . . . 165 V36
Debeck St NEW . . . . . . . . 184 Z30
Debreen Cr ABT . . . . . . . . 270 V72
Decaire St CQT . . . . . 165 W-X34
Decker Ct CQT . . . . . . . . 165 V36
DeCosmos Av ABT . . . . . . 250 S77
DeCourcy Cr RMD . . . . . . 202 G8
Decourcy St WVA . . . . . . . 121 K3
Deep Cove Cr DNV . . . . . 124 N26
Deep Cove Pl DNV . . . . . . 124 N26
Deep Cove Rd DNV . . . . . 124 N26
Deep Dene Pl WVA . . . . . 122 J13
Deep Dene Rd WVA . . . . . 122 J13
Deer La WVA . . . . . . . . . . 121 K4
Deer Lake Av BUR . . . . 164 X24-25
Deer Lake Ct BUR . . . . 164 Y24-25
Deer Lake Pkwy BUR . . . . . . . . . . . .
. . . . . . . . 164 W24 X23-24
Deer Lake Pl BUR . . . . 164 W24
Deer Ridge Cl WVA . . . . . 122 K7
Deer Ridge Dr WVA . . . . . 122 K7
Deer Ridge Pl WVA . . . . 122 K7-8
Deercrest Dr DNV . . . . . . 144 Q25
Deerfern La WHS . . . . . . . 401 H2-3
Deerfield Cr CHL . . . . . . . 233 M4
Deerfield Cr RMD . . . . . . 203 E15
Deerfield Ct DEL . . . . 263 Z16-17
Deerfield Dr DEL . . . . . . . 263 Z16
Deerfield Pl DEL . . . . . . . 263 Z16
Deerfield St MIS . . . . . . . 210 H74
Deerhorn La DNV . . . . . . 103 H15
Deerhorn Pl DNV . . . . . . . 103 H15
Deerhorn Pl WHS . . . . . . . 401 A5
Deeridge La CQT . . . . . . . 145 R36
Deering Island Pl VAN . . . . . . 182 Z9
Deers Leap Pl CQT . 145 P38 146 P39
Deertrail Av ABT . . . . . 249 S-T70
Deertrail Dr ABT . . . . . 249 S-T70
Deerview La ANM . . 126 N32 146 P32
Deerwood Pl PMD . . . . . . 145 R35
Defoe St RMD . . . . . . 202 J10-11
Dehavilland Ct ABT . . . 249 T-U70
Dehavilland Dr ABT . 249 T70 250 T71
Dehavilland Pl ABT . 249 U70 250 U71
Del DNV . . . . . . . . . . . . . 123 L10
Del Rio Dr DNV . . . . . 123 L15-16
Delahaye Dr CQT . . . . 145 R37-38
Delair Rd ABT . . . . . . . 270 V77-78
Delaware Rd RMD . . . . . . 202 H11
Delbrook Av DNV . . . . 123 K-L16
Delbruck Av CNV . . . . . . . 123 N16
Delcourt Ct DEL . . . . . . . 204 G28
Delcrest Dr DEL . . . . . . . 204 G28
Delcrest St MAP . . . 167 Y52 187 Z52
Delestre Av CQT . 164 X30 165 X31-32
Delf Pl RMD . . . . . . . 183 D16-17
Delia Dr PCQ . . . . . . . . . 166 X39
Dell, The CQT . . . . . . . 165 U-V37
Dellawn Dr BUR . . . . . . . 164 U23
Dellview St CHL . . . . . . . . 233 N8
Delmar Ct DNV . . . . . . . . 123 J16
Delmont St CQT . . . . . . . 165 W32
Delmonte Cr DEL . . . . 204 F-G28
Delnova Dr DEL . . . . . . . . 204 G28
Delsey Pl SUR . . . . . . . . 246 S39
Delsom Ct DEL . . . . . 204 G-H28
Delta Av N BUR . . . . . . . 144 S23
Delta Av S BUR . . 144 S-T23 164 U23
Delta St CHL . . . . . . . . . . 233 K7
Delta St DEL . . . . 223 P16 243 Q16
Deltaport Way DEL . . . . . . . . . . . . .
. . . . 242 U13 243 T15-17 262 V13
Delview La DEL . . . . . . . . 204 F29
Delvista Dr DEL . . . . . . . . 204 F28
Delwood Ct BUR . . . . . . . 164 U25
Delwood Dr DEL . . . . 204 F-G28
Delwood Pl SUR . . . . . 205 F36-37
Demontigny Ct CHL . . . . 233 N6-7
Demorest Dr RMD . . . . . . 202 H13
Demorest Rd RMD . . . . . . 202 H13
Dempsey Rd DNV . . . 123 K19-20
Denbigh Av BUR . . 164 Y23 184 Z23
Denise Pl PCQ . . . . . . . . 166 X39
Deniza Av MAP . . . . . . . . 187 A48
Denman Ct CQT . . . . . . . 165 Y35
Denman St ABT . . . . . . 250 S-T72
Denman St VAN . . . 10 F34 142 R-S12
Dennett Pl DEL . . . . . 203 J19-20
Dennis Cr RMD . . . . . . . . 202 J14

Dennis Pl RMD . . . . . . . . 202 J14
Dennison Av CQT . . . . . . 165 W32
Dennison Dr DEL . . . . . . . 263 Y16
Dennison Pl DEL . . . . . . . 263 Y16
Dent Av BUR . . . 143 T22 163 U22
Denton St CQT . . . . . . . . 165 W31
Denver Ct CQT . . . . . . . . 165 V34
Depot Rd SQM . . . . . . . . . 301 B1-2
Derby Ct PCQ . . . . . . . . . 146 S41
Derby Pl DNV . . . . . . . . . 145 T37
Derby Pl DNV . . . . . . . 123 J-K15
Derbyshire Pl DNV . . . . . . 123 M22
Derbyshire Way DNV . . . . 123 M22
Derwent Cr DNV . . . . . . . 122 K14
Derwent Pl DEL . . . . . 204 F-G26
Derwent Way DEL . . . . . . . . . . . . . .
. . . . . 184 D27 204 E27-28 F25 G25-26
Desbrisay Av MIS . . . . . . 210 G74
Desmond Av ABT . . . . 250 U71-72
Desmond Av RMD . . . . . . 202 J9
Desmond Rd RMD . . . . 202 H-J9
Desswood Pl WVA . . . . . . 102 H13
Devon Cr ABT . . . . . . . . . 250 T77
Devon Rd CQT . . . . . . . . 146 S43
Devon Rd DNV . . . . . . . . 123 K15
Devon Rd PCQ . . . . . 146 T42-43
Devonshire Av CQT . . . . . 146 Q40
Devonshire Cr VAN . . . . 162 W12-13
Devonshire Dr SUR . . . . . 245 S38
Devoy St NEW . . 164 Y30 184 Z30
Dewar Way PCQ . . . . . . . 165 X38
Dewdney Av HOP . . . . . . 118 D44
Dewdney Ct RMD . . . . . . 202 E8-9
Dewdney Trunk Rd CQT . . . . . . . . .
. . . . . 145 T35-36 T37 165 U37
Dewdney Trunk Rd MAP 187 Z48-54
Dewdney Trunk Rd MIS . . . . . . . . . .
. . . . . 210 E72-74 G75-78
Dewsbury Ct RMD . . . . . . 203 E15
Dewsbury Dr RMD . . . . . . 203 E15
Dhaliwal Pl CHL . . . . . . . . 233 N6
Dhillon Way RMD . . . . . . . 204 E23
Diamond Av MIS . . . . . 210 J72-73
Diamond Cr ABT . . . . . . . 250 T73
Diamond Cr CHL . . . . . . . 213 H5
Diamond Cr CQT . . . . . . . 145 Q36
Diamond Cr MIS . . . . . . . 210 J73
Diamond Rd RMD . . . . . 202 H-J9
Diamond Rd SQM . . . . . . . 301 E3
Diamond St HHS . . . . . . . 155 R19
Diamond Head Rd SQM . . 301 E-F3
Dickens Pl BUR . . . . . . . . 164 Y24
Dickens St BUR . . . . . . . . 164 Y24
Dickenson St NEW . . 184 A30 A-B29
Dickinson Cr WVA . . . . . 122 K-L7
Diefenbaker Wynd DEL . . . 263 Z17
Dieppe Dr VAN . . . . . . . . 163 V20
Dieppe La VAN . . . . . . . . 162 U8
Dieppe Pl VAN . . . . . . . . 163 V20
Dieppe St CHL . . . . . . . . 233 M-N6
Dinah Av CHL . . . . . . . . . 213 F8
Dinmont Av VAN . . . . . . . 162 W14
Discovery St VAN 142 T7 162 U7 U-V7
Discovery Way SQM . . . . . 301 G2
Ditton St MAP . . . . . . . . 187 A-B48
Dixon Av RMD . . . . . . . . . 202 G13
Dixon Cr MIS . . . . . . . . . 210 G78
Dixon Pl DEL . . . . . . . . . 223 P17
Dixon St NEW . . . . . . . . 184 Z29-30
Dixon Pl PCQ . . . . . . . . . 165 U38
Dlugosh Av MIS . . . . 210 E75-76
Doble Ct CQT . . . . . 145 R36-37
Dock Rd DEL . . . . . . . . . 184 D28
Dockside Ct NEW . . . . . . 204 E26
Docksteader Cir MAP . . . . 167 V53
Docksteader Loop MAP . . . 167 V53
Doerksen Dr MIS . . . . . . . 210 G75
Doerksen Dr PTM . . . . . . 166 Y45
Dogwood CQT . . . . . 145 S-T38
Dogwood SUR . . . . . . . 266 V-W39
Dogwood Av MAP . . . . . . 167 X54
Dogwood Av VAN . . . . . . 182 Z12
Dogwood Cr ABT . . . . 250 U76-77
Dogwood Cr DNV . . . . . . 122 N14
Dogwood Dr ANM . . . . . . 145 Q34
Dogwood Dr CHL . . . . . . 233 K-L6
Dogwood Dr DEL . . . . . . . 263 Y16
Dogwood Dr HOP . . . . . . 118 E46
Dogwood Dr SUR . . . . . . 245 U31
Dogwood La DEL . . . . . . . 263 Y16
Dogwood La WVA . . . . . . . 121 L4
Dogwood Pl DEL . . . . . . . 263 Y16
Dogwood Pl PMD . . . . . . 145 M23
Dogwood Pl SQM . . . . . . . 301 B2
Dogwood Rd KNT . . . . . . 175 U18
Dogwood St CQT . . . . 165 U-V31
Dogwood St MIS . . . . . . . 210 G74

Dollar Rd DNV . . . . . 144 P25-26
Dollarton Hwy DNV . . . . . . . . . . . . .
. . . 143 P21-22 Q21 144 P23-24 Q25-26
Dollarton Hwy N DNV . . . 144 P26
Dolores Pl DNV . . . . . . . . 123 K16
Dolphin Av RMD . . . . . . . 202 H13
Dolphin Cr ABT . . . . . 270 V72-73
Dolphin Ct RMD . . . . . . . 202 H13
Dolphin St CQT . . . . . . . . 145 T37
Dolphin St WRK . . . . . . . 265 X38
Doman St VAN . . 163 Y20 183 Z20
Dominion Av PCQ . . . . 166 V41-42
Dominion Pl SUR . . . . . . . 205 H33
Dominion St BUR . . . . . . . . . . . . . . .
. . . . . 163 V21 V22 164 V23
Dominion St DNV . . . . . . 143 Q20
Don Moore Dr CQT . . . . . 146 R41
Donaghy Av CNV . . . . . . 123 N15
Donald Cr CHL . . . . . . . . 233 M6
Donald Rd RMD . . . . . . . 202 G11
Donald St CQT . . . . . . . . 165 W31
Donald St PCQ . . . . . 166 U-V39
Doncaster Cr DEL . . . . . . 204 G28
Doncaster Way VAN . . . . . 162 W7
Doneagle Pl ABT . . . . . . . 251 U79
Donegal Pl DNV . . . . . . . 123 L16
Donlyn Av ABT . . . . . . . . 250 S77
Donovan Av BUR . . . . . . . 164 X26
Donovan Av MAP . . . . 187 Z50-51
Doone Pl SUR . . . . . . . . 205 F33
Doran Rd DNV . . . . . 123 K19-20
Dorchester Dr BUR . . . . 164 W26-27
Doreen Pl CHL . . . . . . . . 233 M5
Dorell Pl CHL . . . . 213 J6 233 K6
Dorman Dr BUR . . . . . . . 164 U26
Dormel Ct CQT . . . . . . . . 146 Q39
Dormick Av ABT . . . . . . . 250 U72
Dorothea Ct MIS . . . . . . . 210 H75
Dorset Av PCQ . . . . . 146 T39-40
Dorset Pl ABT . . . . . . . . 250 I77
Dorset St BUR . . . . . . 184 Z23-24
Dorval Rd RMD . . . . . . . . 202 H I I
Dory St CQT . . . . . . . . . . 145 T37
Douglas Av MAP . . . . . . . 167 Y50
Douglas Cr I GC . . . . 227 N48-49
Douglas Cr RMD . . . . . 182 C-D11
Douglas Cr VAN . . . . . . . 162 V13
Douglas Dr CQT . . . . . . . 165 V36
Douglas Rd BUR . . . . . . . . . . . . . . . .
. . . . . 143 T21 164 U23 V-W24
Douglas Rd SUR . . . . . . . 185 B35
Douglas St ABT . . . . . . . 270 Z77
Douglas St HOP . . . . . . . 118 E44-45
Douglas St LGT . . . . . . . . 207 E54
Douglas St PMD . . . . . 145 S-T32
Douglas St RMD . . . . . . . 182 C13
Douglas St WVA . . . . . . . 101 G2
Douglas Ter PCQ . . . . . . . 166 X39
Doulton Av RMD . . . . . 202 H10-11
Doulton Pl RMD . . . . . . . 202 H11
Dove Pl DEL . . . . . . . . . 223 P17
Dove Pl SUR . . . . . . . . . 185 B37
Dover Cr RMD . . . . . . . . 202 E10
Dover Ct ABT . . . . . . . . . 251 U79
Dover Pl PCQ . . . . . . . . . 166 U40
Dover Rd MAP . . . . . . . . 187 Z51
Dover Rd RMD . . . . . . . . 202 F10
Dover St BUR . . . . . . . . . 164 Y23
Dover St CHL . . . . . . . . . 233 L5
Dover St MAP . . . . . . . . . 187 Z51
Dovercourt Rd DNV . . . . 123 K-L20
Dow Av BUR . . . . . 183 A22 Z22
Dowding Rd PMD . . . . . . 145 R34
Dowler Rd DEL . . . . . 223 N-P17
Downes Av CHL . . . . . . . . 213 H7
Downes Rd ABT . . . . . . . . . . . . . . . . .
. . . . . 249 R63 R67-70 250 R71-75
Downie St NEW . . . . . . . . 184 A27
Downs Rd DEL . . . . . . . . 204 F29
Dowsley Ct DNV . . . . 123 K-L17
Doyle St MIS . . . . . . . . . 210 E76
Drake Ct CQT . . . . . . . . . 165 X35
Drake St VAN 10 H-J36 11 J37 142 T13
Draper St MIS . . . . . 210 F77 G78
Drawbridge Cl PCQ . . . . . 166 Y39
Draycott Pl DNV . . . . . . . 123 L20
Draycott Rd DNV . . . 123 L20 L21
Draycott St CQT . . . . 165 V-W34
Drayton St DNV . . . . . . . 123 N19
Dresden Way DNV . . . . . 124 M23
Drew Dr WHS . . . . . . . . . 401 H2
Drewry Cr RMD . . . . . 202 F10-11
Drifter Pl WHS . . . . . . . . . 401 C3
Drifter Way WHS . . . . . . . 401 C3

Driftwood Av HHS . . . . . 155 P-Q20
Driftwood Cl WHS . . . . . 401 B-C3
Driftwood Dr MAP . . . 187 A51-52 Z51
Driftwood Pl BUR . . . . . . 163 W22
Drummond Dr VAN . . . . . 161 T-U6
Drummond Pl SUR . . . . . 205 F32
Dryden Rd SQM . . . . . . . 301 C2-3
Dryden Way DNV . . . . . . 123 L19
Dubbert St RMD . . . . . . 182 D13
Dublin Dr CHL . . . . . . . 193 C-D8
Dublin St NEW . . . . 184 A27 A-B26
Dubois St BUR . . . . . . . 183 Z21
Duchess Av ABT . . . . . . 250 T-U72
Duchess Av DNV . . . . . . 123 L18
Duchess Av WVA 122 M10-12 M12-13
Duchess St VAN . . . . . . 163 X18-19
Ducklow St CQT . . . . . . 165 U-V31
Dudley Rd DNV . . . . . . 123 K-L15
Dudley St VAN . . . . . . . 183 B20
Dueck Av ABT . . . . . . . 250 U72
Duff St VAN . . . . . . . . . 183 Z17
Dufferin Av BUR . . 164 Y24 184 Z24
Dufferin Av WVA . . . . . . . 101 G1
Dufferin St CQT . . . . . . 145 S-T37
Dufferin St NEW . . . . . . 184 A30
Duffy Pl DEL . . . . . . . . 223 P17
Duke St VAN . . . . . . . . 163 X18-19
Dumbarton Pl SUR . . . . 185 B36
Dumbarton Rd SUR . . . . 185 B36
Dumfries St VAN163 V17 W17 183 Z17
Dumont St VAN . . . 183 D15 203 E15
Dump Rd FRA . . . . . . . . 253 Q-R5
Dunavon Pl RMD . . . . . . 222 K9
Dunbar Div VAN . . . . . . 162 U-V8
Dunbar St MAP . . . . . . . 187 Z52
Dunbar St VAN 162 U9 V8-9 W8-9 X-Y8
Dunbar Way MIS . . . . . . 210 G73
Dunblane Av BUR . . . . . 184 Z23
Duncan Av ABT . . . . . . . 249 U67
Duncan Av BUR . . . . . . 144 S-T25
Duncan Av MIS . . . . . . . 230 K72
Duncan Dr DEL . . . . . 263 W-X18
Duncan Rd CHL . . . . . . . 233 P2
Duncan St CQT . . . . . 165 W-X34
Duncan St NEW . . . . . 184 C27-28
Duncan St WVA . . . . . . . 122 L11
Duncan Way LGC . . . 227 M48 M-N49
Duncliffe Rd RMD . . . . . 222 K9-10
Dundarave La WVA . . . . . 122 L9
Dundas St BUR . . . . . . . . . . . .
. . . . . 143 S21-22 S22 144 S23 S23-24
Dundas St VAN . . 143 S18 S18-19 S20
Dundee Pl ABT . . . . . . 250 R-S74
Dundee Pl CHL . . . . . . . 233 L-M6
Dundee St VAN . . . . . . . 163 X19
Dundonald Av BUR . . 164 W23-24
Dundonald Dr PMD . . . . 145 T31
Dundurn Av CHL . . . . . . 233 N6
Dunelm Av VAN . . . . . . 183 A20
Dunfell Rd RMD . . . . . . 222 K9-10
Dunford Rd RMD . . . . . . 222 K9
Dunkirk Av CQT . . . . . . 146 S39
Dunkirk St VAN . . . . . . . 162 W9
Dunlevy Av VAN . . 11 J41 143 S15 T15
Dunlewey Pl WVA . . . . . 122 J-K9
Dunlop Av BUR . . . . . . 144 T24
Dunlop Rd DEL . . . . . 204 G27-28
Dunlop Rd DEL . . . . . . 204 G28
Dunlop St CQT . . . . . . . 165 X31
Dunn Av MAP . . . . . . . . 187 Z47
Dunn Pl KNT . . . . . . . . 175 W20
Dunn St MIS . . . . . . . . 210 G77
Dunnedin St BUR . . . . . 144 T25
Dunoon Dr RMD . . . . . . 202 J12
Dunphy St PCQ . . . . . . 146 S40
Dunrobin Cr DNV . . . . 124 M-N23
Dunsany Pl RMD . . . . . . 202 H11
Dunsmuir Cr RMD . . . . . 202 F8
Dunsmuir Ct ABT . . . . . 250 S77
Dunsmuir Rd SUR . . . . . 245 T31
Dunsmuir St MIS . . . . . 210 H-J75
Dunsmuir St VAN . 11 G38 142 S13-14
Dunsmuir Viaduct VAN . . . . . . . .
. . . . . 11 H39-40 142 T14 143 T15
Dunsmuir Way ABT . . . 250 R-S77
Dunstone Pl DNV . . . . 124 M-N23
Dunvegan Ct BUR . . . . . 144 T26
Dupont Pl CQT . . . . . . . 145 S37
Duprez St WRK . . . . . . . 265 X36
Duranleau St VAN . . 10 K35 142 T12
Durant Dr CQT . . . . . . 145 R-S37
Durham Pl ABT . . 250 U78 270 V78
Durham Rd SUR . . . . . . 265 V38
Durham St NEW . . . . . 184 Z28-29
Durham St E NEW . 164 Y29 184 Z29
Durieu St MIS . . . . . 230 K74 K75

Durward Av VAN . . . . . . 163 X16
Duthie Av BUR . . . 144 S-T26 164 U26
Duval Ct CQT . . . . . . . . 165 V34
Duval Rd DNV . . . . . . . 123 L21
Dyck Rd DNV . . . . . . . 123 K19-20
Dyke Access MIS . . . . . 230 K73
Dyke Rd BTI . 186 B43-44 C43 D45-46
Dyke Rd CHL . . . . . 193 D5 213 E5
Dyke Rd DEL . . . . . . . 233 N4-5
Dyke Rd KNT . . . . . . . 175 W-X23
Dyke Rd RMD203 H19 204 F23-24 F25
. . . . . 222 L10 M11-14 223 L15
Dyke Rd SUR . . . . . . . . 184 B30
Dylan Pl RMD . . . . . . . 202 J10-11

## E

Eagle Av MAP . . . . . . . 187 Z53
Eagle Cr CHL . . . . . . . 194 C-D10
Eagle Cr MIS . . . . . . . . 210 H72
Eagle Cr PMD . . . . . . 145 Q-R33
Eagle Ct DNV . . . . . . . 103 H15
Eagle Dr PMD . . . . . . . 145 Q33
Eagle Dr WHS . . . . . . . 401 E3
Eagle Is WVA . . . . . . . . 121 J2
Eagle Pass PMD . . . . . 145 Q-R33
Eagle Pl SUR . . . . . . . . 185 B37
Eagle St ABT . . . . . . . 270 V74-75
Eagle St HHS . . . . . . . . 155 M8
Eagle Ter MIS . . . . . . . 210 H72
Eagle Way DEL . . . . . . 262 W15
Eagle Creek Av WVA . . . 122 M12
Eagle Harbour Rd WVA . 121 J2-3
Eagle Lake Access Rd WVA . . . . .
. . . . . 101 G4-5 121 J5
Eagle Mountain Dr ABT . 251 U79
Eagle Mountain Dr CQT . 145 Q36
Eagle Peak Dr ABT . . . . 251 U79-80
Eagle Peak La ABT . . . . 251 T79
Eagle Ridge Cr WHS . 401 F3 S-T21
Eagle Ridge Pl CHL . . . 213 F2
Eagle Run Dr SQM . . . . 301 C2
Eagle Summit Dr ABT . . 251 T79
Eagle View Pl ABT . . . . 251 U79-80
Eaglecrest Dr CQT . . . . 145 S36
Eaglecrest Pl ABT . . . . 251 U80
Eaglecrest Rd ANM . . . 125 N33
Eagleridge Dr CQT . . . . 145 S36
Eagleridge Dr WVA . . 101 H2 121 J2
Eagleridge Pl WVA . . . . 101 H2
Eagles Dr BUR . . . . . . . 164 Y25
Eagles Dr UEL . . . . . . . 161 V4
Eaglewind Blvd SQM . . . 301 J1
Earl St CHL . . . . . . . . 233 M6-7
Earl Finning Way VAN . . 163 U16
Earlmond Av RMD . . . . 202 H8-9
Earles St VAN . . . . . 163 X19 X-Y19
Earls Ct ABT . . . . . . . 250 T76-77
Earls Ct PCQ . . . . . . . . 166 X39
Easmont Ct PCQ . . . . . 166 U41
East Blvd VAN . . . . . . . . . . . .
. . . . . 162 V11 X-Y11 182 A11-12 Z11
East Ct BUR . . . . . . . . 144 T23
East Mall UEL . . . . . . . 161 U-V4
East Rd ANM . . . . . 145 P33 P-Q34
East Campus Rd BUR . . 144 S-T29
East Edwards St MIS . . . 210 F-G78
East Hemlock Dr ANM . 125 N33-34
East Lake Gt CQT . . . . . 165 V37
East Whalley Ring Rd SUR . . . . . .
. . . . . 185 C34 C-D34 D34
Eastbrook Pkwy BUR . . . 163 U-V22
Eastcot Rd WVA . . . . . . 122 L13
Easterbrook Rd RMD . . . 202 E9
Easterbrook St CQT . . . 165 V31-32
Eastern Av CNV . . 123 L17 M17 N17
Eastern Dr PCQ . . 165 X38 166 W39
Eastglen Cl SUR . . . . . 186 B-C40
Eastglen Pl SUR . . . . . . 186 C40
Easthope Av RMD . . . . . 222 L8
Eastlake Dr BUR . . . . 164 V28-29 V29
Eastlawn Dr BUR . . . . . 144 T23
Eastleigh Cr LGC . . . . 227 N48-49
Eastleigh La DNV . . . . 124 M-N26
Eastman Dr RMD . . . . . 202 J10
Eastmont Dr WVA . . . . . 101 H1
Eastridge Rd DNV . . . . 124 M27
Eastview Ct ABT . . . . . 250 T74
Eastview Pl ABT . . . . . 250 T74-75
Eastview Rd CNV . . . . 123 M-N19
Eastview St ABT . . . . . 250 T74
Eastwood St CQT . . . . . 145 S38
Easy St WHS . . . . . . . . 401 D-E3
Eaton Pl DEL . . . . . . . . 204 F26

Eaton Way DEL . . . . . . . 204 F25
Ebert Av CQT . . . . 164 V30 165 V31
Ebony St ABT . . . . . . . . 270 V76
Ebor Rd DEL . . . . . . . . 204 E29
Eburne Way RMD . . . . . 183 B15
Ebury Pl DEL . . . . . . . . 204 G26
Echo Av HHS . . . . . . . 155 P19-20
Echo Pl VAN . . . . . . . . 183 Z20
Eckersley Rd RMD . . . . 202 F13
Eckert St NEW . . . . . . . 184 D26
Edal St LGT . . . . . . . . 207 F53-54
Eddie Dr NEW . . . . . . . 184 Z29
Eddington Dr VAN . . . . 162 W10-11
Eddystone Cr DNV . . . . 144 P23
Eden Av CQT . . . . . . . 165 V33-34
Eden Cr DEL . . . . . . . . 263 X17-18
Eden Dr CHL . . . . . 213 J6 233 K6
Eden Pl DEL . . . . . . . . 263 X17-18
Eden Pl WVA . . . . . . . . 122 M12
Edenvale Av WVA . . . . . 121 K3
Edenvale Pl WVA . . . . . 121 K3
Edgar Av CQT . . . . . . . 165 X31-32
Edgar Cr VAN . . . . . . . 162 W10
Edge St VAN . . . . . . . . 183 B20
Edge St MAP . . . 167 X52 Y52 187 Z52
Edgedale Av MAP . . . . . 187 A49-50
Edgehill Av ABT . . . . . . 249 T70
Edgemont Blvd DNV . . . . . . . . .
. . . . 122 K-L14 123 L15 L-M15
Edgemont Pl CHL . . . . . 233 M8
Edgeview Pl ABT . . . . . 270 V78
Edgewater Access WHS . . 401 C3-4
Edgewater Cr SQM . . . . 301 F1-2
Edgewater Dr SQM . . . . 301 F2
Edgewood Av ABT . . . . 270 V74
Edgewood Dr SUR . . . . 266 V40
Edgewood Pl DNV . . . . 122 K14
Edgewood Rd DNV . . . . . . . . . .
. . . . 122 K14 123 K15 K16
Edinburgh Dr PMD . . . . 145 S-T35
Edinburgh Dr SUR . . . . 205 F33
Edinburgh Pl PMD . . . . 145 T35
Edinburgh Pl SUR . . . . 205 F33
Edinburgh St BUR . . . . 143 R21
Edinburgh St NEW . 184 A27 B26-27
Edinburgh St PCQ . . . . 146 T39
Edinburgh St VAN . . . 143 R20-21
Edison St BUR . . . . . . . 164 V26
Edith St BUR . . . . . . . . 144 S26
Edmonds Dr DEL . . . . . 243 Q15
Edmonds St BUR . . . . . . . . . . .
. . . . 164 Y27 184 A25-26 Z26-27
Ednor Cr BUR . . . . . . . 144 T26
Edson Av BUR . . . . . . . 183 A22
Edson Dr CHL . . . . . . . 233 L6
Edson Pl ABT . . . . . . . 251 S79
Education Rd UEL . . . . . 161 U3
Edward Cr PMD . . . . . . 145 T35
Edward St CHL . . . . 213 E6 F6
Edwards Dr HOP . . . . . . 118 G43
Edwards Rd SQM . . . . . 301 B2
Edwards St CQT . . . . 146 Q-R43
Edwards St MIS . . . . . . 210 G78
Edwin Ct CQT . . . . . . . 146 R41
Edworthy Way NEW . . . . 185 Z31
Eena Dr CHL . . . . . . . 233 M3-4
Egan Pl DEL . . . . . . . . 223 P17
Egglestone Av MIS . . . . 210 G73-74
Eglinton St BUR . . 164 W23-24 W-X24
Egmont Av CQT . . . . . . 165 U31
Egret Ct RMD . . . . . . . 222 K10
Ehkolie Cr DEL . . . 262 X15 263 X16
Eider St MIS . . . . . . . 210 H-J73
Eildon St PMD . . . . . . . 145 T31
El Camino Dr CQT . . . 146 Q-R39
El Casa Ct CQT . . . . . . 146 R39
Elan Pl CQT . . . . . . . . 145 R37
Elbow Pl PCQ . . . . . . . 166 U42
Elder Av CHL . . . . . . . . 213 H6
Elder Rd HOP . . . . . . . 118 G42
Eldon Rd DNV . . . . . . . 122 K14
Eldorado Pl ABT . . . . . . 270 V76
Eleanor Av ABT . . . . . . 270 V77
Eleanor St BUR . . . . . 184 A-B24
Electronic Av PMD . . . . 145 S-T34
Elementary Rd ANM . . . 145 P33
Elevator Rd SUR . . . . . 204 E28-29
Elford St BUR . . . . . . . 164 X-Y30
Elgin Av ABT . . . . 164 Y24 184 Z24
Elgin Av PCQ . . . . . . . 166 U39
Elgin Dr CHL . . . . . . . . 193 C8
Elgin Pl BUR . . . . . . . . 164 Y24
Elgin Rd SUR . . . . . 245 S35 S35-36

Elgin St NEW . . . . . . . . 184 A29
Elgin St PMD . . . . . . . . 145 T33
Elgin St VAN . . . 163 W-X16 X16 Y16
Elgon Ct ABT . . . . . . . . 250 T77
Elinor Cr PCQ . . . . . . . 165 W-X38
Elizabeth Av ABT . . . . . 230 N75
Elizabeth Dr CQT . . . 146 R39-40
Elizabeth Av MIS . . . . . 184 V27
Elizabeth Dr FRA . . . . . 253 R6
Elizabeth Way DNV . . . . 122 L14
Elk Pl CQT . . . . . . . . . 145 Q38
Elk Pl DEL . . . . . . . . . 224 K30
Elk Ter MIS . . . . . . . . 210 H73
Elk Valley Pl VAN . . . 183 A19 Z20
Elkford Dr ABT . . . . . . 250 S72
Elkhorn Av CQT . . . . . . 165 X35
Elkmond Rd RMD . . . . . 202 J8
Elkwood Pl BUR . . . . . . 164 U28
Ellen St CHL . . . . . . . . 233 M4
Ellendale Dr SUR . . . . . 185 B36
Ellerslie Av BUR . . 144 S25 164 V25
Ellerton Ct BUR . . . . . . 163 X22
Ellesmere Av N BUR . . . 144 S24
Ellesmere Av S BUR . . . . . . . . .
. . . . 144 S-T24 164 U24
Ellice Av CQT . . . . . . . 165 U31
Elliot Av ABT . . . . . . . 270 V77-78
Elliot St DEL . . . 223 P16 243 Q16
Elliot St NEW . . . . . . . 184 A29-30
Elliott Av CHL . . . . . . . 193 C8
Elliott St VAN . . . 163 Y18 183 A18 Z18
Ellis Dr PCQ . . . . . . . . 166 U41
Ellis St DNV . . . . . . . . 144 P23
Elm Ct CQT . . . . . . . . 145 S38
Elm Dr CHL . . . . . . . . . 213 F7
Elm Rd KNT . . . . . . . . 175 X21
Elm St ABT . . . . . . . . 270 U76
Elm St PMD . . . . . . . 145 S34-35
Elm St VAN . . . . 162 W-X10 X-Y10
Elm St WRK . . . . . . . 265 X36-37
Elm Vlg DEL . . . . . . . . 206 F39
Elmbridge Way RMD . . . 202 E11-12
Elmer St VAN . . . . . . . 164 Y30
Elmgrove Dr BUR . 163 W22 164 W23
Elmgrove Pl BUR . 163 W22 164 W23
Elmhurst Dr VAN . . . . . 183 Z19
Elmwood Dr ABT . . . . 250 S-T76
Elmwood Pl DNV . . . . . 122 N14
Elmwood St BUR . . . . . 163 W21
Elmwood St CQT . . . . . 165 U31
Elsdon Bay PMD . . . . . 145 Q33
Else Rd KNT . . . . . . . 175 V18-19
Elsmore Rd RMD . . . . . 202 G-H8
Elsom Av BUR . . . . . . . 163 X-Y22
Elspeth Pl PCQ . . . . . 166 W-X39
Elstree Pl DNV . . . . . . 123 L16
Elswick Pl CHL . . . . . . . 233 M4
Eltham St MAP . . . . . . . 187 A48
Elva Av CQT . . . . . . . . 165 W34
Elveden Row WVA . . . . . 122 J12
Elwell St BUR . . . . . . . . . . . . .
. . . . 164 X28 Y26 Y27 184 Z25 Z26
Elwood Pl ABT . . . . . . . 270 V78
Elwood Rd CHL . . . . . . 213 J6
Elwyn Dr BUR . . . . . . . 164 X25
Emerald Av ABT . . . . . . 270 V73
Emerald Av HHS . . . . . 155 R19-20
Emerald Dr CHL . . . . . . 193 C8
Emerald Dr DNV . . . . . 123 K-L15
Emerald Dr WHS . . . 401 A-B5
Emerald Pl RMD . . . . . . 202 F10
Emerald Pl WHS . . . . . . 401 B5
Emerald Rd HOP . . . . . 118 E47
Emerson Ct DNV . . . . . 124 N23
Emerson St ABT . 250 T-U73 270 V73
Emerson St BUR . . . . . 164 Y25
Emerson St CQT . . . . . 165 U31
Emerson Way DNV . . . . 124 N23
Emery Pl DNV . . . . . . . 123 M19-20
Emiry St MIS . . . . . . . 210 F73
Emory St NEW . . . . . . . 184 A29
Empire Dr BUR . . . . . . 144 S23
Empress Av BUR . . 164 Y25 184 Z25
Empress Dr ABT . . . . . . 251 T80
Empress La ABT . . . . . 251 T-U80
Empress La CHL . . . . . . 213 E7
Emwood Pl DEL . . . . . . 204 F30
Enderby Av DEL . . . . . . 263 W-X18
Enderby St ABT . . . . . . 270 V78
Endersby St BUR . . . . . 164 Y29
Engineering Rd UEL . . . 161 U-V4
English Av RMD . . . . . . 222 L8
English Pl SUR . . . . . . 225 K33
English St BUR . . . . . . 163 V22
English Bluff Ct DEL 262 Y15 263 Y16

English Bluff Rd DEL . . . . . . . . . .
. . . 262 X15 263 X16 Z16
Ennerdale Rd DNV . . . . 123 M19
Enterprise Av ABT . . . . 250 T75-76
Enterprise Dr CHL . . . . 213 H3-4
Enterprise Pl SQM . . . . 301 H1
Enterprise St ABT . . . . 164 V27
Enterprise Way SQM . . . 301 H1
Enterprise Way SUR . . . 226 M46
Entertainment Blvd RMD . . . . . . .
. . . 203 J17 223 K17
Entrance Ct CQT . . . . . 146 S39
Eperson Rd RMD . . . . . 202 G9
Epp Dr CHL . . . . . . . . 194 D9
Epping Ct BUR . . . . . . 164 W26
Epps Av DNV . . . . . . . . 124 N26
Epson Ct ABT . . . . . . . 250 S77
Epson La ABT . . . . . . . 250 S77
Epworth Ct ABT . . . . . . 251 T81
Eric Dr CHL . . . . . 193 C8 194 C9
Erickson Dr ABT . . . . . 164 V30
Erickson St MIS . . . . . . 210 E77
Erin Av BUR . . . . . . . . 164 X29
Erin Pl DEL . . . . . . . . 263 Y16
Erin Way DEL . . . . . . . 263 Y16
Errigal Pl WVA . . . . . . 122 K10
Errington Rd RMD . . . . 202 J12
Erskine Av MIS . . . . . . 210 J75
Erskine Pl PCQ . . . . . . 165 X38
Erskine St CQT . . . . . . 145 R37
Erwin Dr WVA . . . . . . . 121 L4-5
Escola Bay PMD . . . . . 145 Q33
Esmond Av BUR . . . . . . . . . . . .
. . . 143 R-S21 S-T21 T21 163 U21 V21
Esmond Av N BUR . . . 143 R-S21
Esperanza Dr CQT . . . . 146 S39
Esperanza Dr DNV . . . . 103 H15
Esplanade E CNV . . . . . 143 P17
Esplanade W CNV . 123 N16 143 P16
Esplanade Av HHS . . . 155 P18-20
Esplanade Av PMD . . . 145 S33-34
Esplanade Av WVA . . . 122 M11-12
Esquimalt Av WVA . . . . . . . . . .
. . . 122 M10-12 M12-13
Esquimalt Ter ABT . . . . 250 S73
Essendene Av ABT . . . . 250 U75-76
Essex Av PCQ . . . . . . . 146 S42
Essex Dr ABT . . . . . . . 270 V78
Essex Pl SUR . . . . . . . 265 V38
Essex Rd DNV . . . . . . . 123 K15
Estevan Ct ABT . . . . . . 251 T81
Estevan Pl WVA . . . . . . 121 K4
Ethel Av BUR . . . . . 184 A26-27
Eton Cr ABT . . . . . . . . 250 S77
Eton St BUR . . . . 143 S21-22 144 S23
Eton St VAN . . . 143 S18 S18-19 S20
Euclid Av VAN . . . . . . . 163 X19-20
Euclid Ct CQT . . . . . . . 165 X31
Eugene Cr SUR . . . . . . 225 P31
Euphrates Cr PCQ . . . . 166 V41
Eureka Av PCQ . . . . . . 166 X40
Eva Lake Rd WHS . . . . . 401 G2
Evancio Cr RMD . . . . . 202 H10
Evans Av VAN . . . . . . 143 T15-16
Evans Pkwy CHL . . . . . 213 H5
Evans Pl DEL . . . . . . . 204 H29
Evans Pl PCQ . . . 146 T42 166 U42
Evans Rd CHL . . . 213 H-J5 233 K-L5
Evans St MAP . . . 167 Y51 187 Z51
Eveleigh St VAN . . 11 F37 142 S13
Evelyn Dr WVA . . . . . . 122 M12
Evelyn St DNV 123 K19-20 K20-21 K21
Everall St WRK . . . . . 265 W-X37
Everett Cr BUR . . . . . . 144 T26
Everett Dr ABT . . . . . . 270 V78
Everett La MIS . . . . . . 210 G74
Everett Rd ABT . . . . . . 270 V78
Everett St ABT . . . . . . 270 V78
Everglade Pl DNV . . . . 123 K-L16
Evergreen Av WVA . . . . 121 L5
Evergreen Cr ANM . . . . 145 Q34
Evergreen Dr KNT . . . 175 W-X20
Evergreen Dr PMD . . . . 145 S32
Evergreen La DEL . . . . 243 Q16
Evergreen Pl DNV . . . . . . . . . .
. . . 123 K15-16 K-L16 L16-17
Evergreen St ABT . . . 250 T71-72
Evergreen St CHL . . . . . 193 C7
Evergreen St PCQ . . . 146 S-T41
Everson Pl ABT . . . . . . 270 V78
Ewart St BUR . . . . . . . 184 A24
Ewen Av NEW . . . 184 C27-28 D26-27
Ewen Av RMD . . . . . . . 222 L8
Ewen Rd RMD . . . . . . 203 F-G22
Ewert Av MIS . . . . . . . 210 G78
Ewson St WRK . . . 265 X38 266 X39

Exbury Av *ABT* . . . . . . . . . **250** S78
Exbury Pl *ABT* . . . . . . . . . **250** S78
Exegesis St *RMD* . . . . . . . **202** F-G10
Exeter Av *MAP* . . . . . . **167** Y50 Y51
Exmouth Rd *DNV* . . . . . . . **144** P23
Explorers Walk *VAN* . . . **183** A20 B19-20
Expo Blvd *VAN* . . . . . . . . . . . . .
. . . . **11** H39-40 J38 **142** T14 T14 **143** T15
Express St *ABT* . . . . . . . . **164** V27
Extrom Rd *CHL* . . . . . . . . **233** N8
Eyremount Dr *WVA* . . . . . . . . . . .
. . . . . . . . . **122** J11-12 J-K12 K12

**F**

Faber Cr *DEL* . . . . . . . **224** L28-29
Faber Cr *MAP* . . . . . . . . . **187** Z50
Fader St *NEW* . . . . **164** Y30 **165** Y31
Fair Wynd *DEL* . . . . . . . . . **223** M17
Fairbanks Cr *CHL* . . . . . . **193** C7-8
Fairbanks St *MIS* . . . . . . . **210** G73
Fairbrook Cr *RMD* . . . . . . . **202** G-H8
Fairbrook Rd *RMD* . . . . . . **202** G8
Fairchild Rd *VAN* . . . . . . **162** Y13
Fairdell Cr *RMD* . . . . . . . . **202** G8
Fairdell Pl *RMD* . . . . . . . . **202** G8
Fairfax Cr *RMD* . . . . . . . . **202** H8
Fairfax Pl *RMD* . . . . . . . . **202** H8
Fairfax St *CQT* . . . . . . . . **165** U33
Fairfield Av *PTM* . . . . . . . **187** Z47
Fairfield Pl *DEL* . . . . . . . . **204** J29
Fairfield Rd *CHL* . . . . . . . **194** B9-10
Fairfield Rd *DNV* . . . . . . . **144** P23
Fairford Pl *SUR* . . . . . . . . **225** K33
Fairhurst Rd *RMD* . . . . . . . **202** H8
Fairland Ct *BUR* . . . . . . . **164** V28
Fairlane Rd *RMD* . . . . . . . **202** H8
Fairlane St *ABT* . . . . . . . . **250** T-U74
Fairlawn Dr *BUR* . . **143** T22 **144** T23
Fairlight Cr *DEL* . . . . . . . . **224** N30
Fairmile Rd *WVA* . . . . . . . **122** K12
Fairmont Rd *DNV* . . . . . . . **123** L15
Fairmont St *VAN* . . . . . . . **163** X19
Fairview Av *UEL* . . . . . . . . **161** U4
Fairview Dr *CHL* . . . . . . . **193** C-D7
Fairview Pl *UEL* . . . . . . . . **161** U5
Fairview St *ABT* . . . . . . **270** V-W75
Fairview St *CQT* . . . . . . . . **165** V31
Fairway Dr *DNV* . . . . . . . . **144** P26
Fairway Dr *SUR* . . . . . . . . **226** M48
Fairway Dr *WHS* . . . . . . . **401** E-F3
Fairway Pl *DNV* . . . . . . **144** U25-26
Fairway Rd *RMD* . . . . . . . **202** H8
Fairway St *CQT* . . . . . . . . **165** W32
Fairway Views Wynd *DEL* . . . . . .
. . . . . . . . . . . . . . . . . **263** X17-18
Fairweather La *NEW* . . . . . **184** C28
Fairwood Dr *CHL* . . . . . . . **193** C8
Faith Rd *SQM* . . . . . . . . . . **301** B2
Falaise Av *CHL* . . . . . . . . **233** N5-6
Falaise Av *VAN* . . . . . . . . **163** V20
Falaise La *VAN* . . . . . . . . **162** U8
Falaise Pl *VAN* . . . . . . . . . **163** V20
Falcon Cr *CHL* . . . . . . . . **194** C-D10
Falcon Cr *MIS* . . . . . . . . **210** H72
Falcon Cr *WHS* . . . . . . . . **401** E3
Falcon Dr *CQT* . . . . . . . **145** S-T36
Falcon La *WHS* . . . . . . . . **401** E-F3
Falcon Pl *ABT* . . . . . . . . . **251** U80
Falcon Rd *WVA* . . . . . . . . **121** J2
Falcon Way *DEL* . . . **243** U15 **262** V15
Falkirk Dr *SUR* . . . . . . . . **205** E34
Falkland St *BUR* . . . . . . . **164** V26
Fallardeau Av *LGT* . . . . . . **207** E53
Fannin Av *VAN* . . . . . . . . . **161** T6
Fareham Av *BUR* . . . . . . . **164** X28
Farina Rd *ABT* . . . . . . . **251** U81-82
Farmer Rd *ABT* . . . **270** Y76-77 Y78
Farmleigh Rd *WVA* . . . . . . **122** K12
Farrant Cr *ABT* . . . . . . **250** U74-75
Farrell Av *DEL* . . . . . . . . **263** W18
Farrell Cr *DEL* . . . . . . . . . **263** W18
Farrington St *BUR* . . . . . . **163** X21
Farrow St *CQT* . . . . . . . **164** U-V30
Faulkner Rd *SUR* . . . . . . **184** B-C30
Fawcett Rd *CQT* . . . **165** Y35 **185** Z35
Fawn Ter *MIS* . . . . . . . **210** H72-73
Featherstone Way *RMD* . . . **223** K16
Fedoruk Rd *RMD* . . . . . . . **203** E20
Felix Ct *DNV* . . . . . . . . **124** N25-26
Fell Av *BUR* . . . . . . . . . . **144** S24
Fell Av *CHL* . . . . . . . . **123** M-N15
Fell Av N *BUR* . . . . . . . **144** S-T24
Fell Av S *BUR* . . . . **144** T24 **164** U24

Fellowes St N *VAN* . . **143** R21 R-S20
Felton Pl *DNV* . . . . . . . . . **144** P26
Felton Rd *DNV* . . . . . . . . **144** P26
Feniak St *CHL* . . . . . . . . . **193** D7
Fenmo Pl *MIS* . . . . . . . . **210** G77-78
Fennell La *MIS* . . . . . . . **210** F-G73
Fenton Dr *DEL* . . . . . . . . **223** P16
Fenton Rd *PTM* . . . . . . . . **166** U46
Fenton St *NEW* . . . . . . . . **184** C27
Fenwick Pl *PMD* . . . . . . . **145** T31
Fenwick St *BUR* . . . . . . . **184** C26
Fenwick Wynd *PMD* . . . . . **144** T30
Ferguson Av *MIS* . . . . . . **210** H77
Ferguson Ct *DEL* . . . . . . **263** X17-18
Ferguson Diversion *SUR* . . . . . . .
. . . . **184** D29 **185** B-C37 C37 **204** E29
Ferguson Pl *CHL* . . . . . . . **233** N8
Ferguson Rd *DEL* . . . . . . . **263** X17
Ferguson Rd *RMD* . . . . . **182** B8-9
Fern Av *BUR* . . . . . . **183** Z22 **184** Z23
Fern Cr *MAP* . . . . . . . . . . **167** X54
Fern Dr *ANM* . . . **125** N32 **145** P32
Fern Pl *HHS* . . . . . . . . . . **155** Q19
Fern St *ABT* . . . . . . . . . . **270** V76
Fern St *CHL* . . . . . . . . . **233** K-L5
Fern St *DNV* . . . . . . . . . **143** P20
Fern Ter *CQT* . . . . . . **165** W36-37
Fern Way *DEL* . . . . . . . . **204** F30
Ferndale Av *MIS* . . . . . . **210** E75-77
Ferndale Av *WVA* . . . . . . . **121** L5
Ferndale Rd *RMD* . . . . . . **202** F13-14
Ferndale St *VAN* . . . . . . **143** S17-18
Fernglen Ct *BUR* . . . . . . . **163** W22
Fernglen Dr *BUR* . . **163** W22 **164** W23
Fernglen Pl *BUR* . . . . . . . **163** W-X22
Fernhurst Pl *CQT* . . . . **165** W35-36
Fernridge Cr *LGT* . . . . . . **267** V47-48
Fernway Av *CHL* . . . . . . . **193** D6
Fernway Dr *PMD* . . . . . . . **145** P35
Fernwood Av *PCQ* . . . . . . **146** S41
Fernwood Cr *DNV* . . . . . . . **122** N14
Fernwood Pl *PMD* . . . . . . . **145** R35
Ferris St *CQT* . . . . . . . . . **165** W35
Ferry Rd *DEL* . . . . . . . . . **223** N16
Ferry Row *VAN* . . . . . . . . **162** U13
Ferry Landing Pl *HOP* . . . . **118** D44
Ferry Slip Rd *PTM* . . . . . . **166** W43
Festubert Rd *CHL* . . . . . . . **233** N5
Fetterly Pl *CHL* . . . . . . . . **233** N8
Fibish Pl *ART* . . . . . . . . . **250** T71
Field Pl *BUR* . . . . . . . . . . **164** X26
Fieldgate St *ABT* . . . . . . . **250** S71
Fielding Ct *BUR* . . . . . . . **164** V25
Fieldstone Av *VAN* . . . . **183** A19-20
Fieldstone Walk *PTM* . . . . **186** A46
Fiesta Av *CHL* . . . . . . . . . **193** C7
Fife Pl *ABT* . . . . . . . . . . . **250** S74
Filey Dr *DEL* . . . . . . . . . . **204** J29
Filuk Pl *ABT* . . . . . . . . . . **270** V78
Finch Ct *ABT* . . . . . . . . . . **164** U29
Finch Ct *CQT* . . . . . . . . **146** P-Q39
Finch Dr *SQM* . . . . . . . . . . **301** G3
Finch Hill *WVA* . . . . . . . **122** J-K10
Finch Pl *VAN* . . . . **183** A20 B19-20
Finch Ter *MIS* . . . . . . . . . **210** H73
Findlay Ct *MIS* . . . . . . . . **210** H73
Findlay St *VAN* . . . . . . . . **163** V17
Finlayson Ct *RMD* . . . . . . **182** C14
Finlayson Dr *RMD* . . . . . . **182** C14
Finley St *PCQ* . . . . . . . . . **146** S39
Finn Rd *RMD* . . . . **222** L11 L13
Finn Rd *RMD* . . . . . . . . **301** B2 C2-3
Finnigan St *CQT* . . . **165** X34-35
Fintry Pl *DNV* . . . . . . . . . **122** L14
Finuchi Rd *ABT* . . . . . . . . **251** R83
Fir CQT . . . . . . . . . . . . . . **145** S38
Fir Av *ABT* . . . . . . . . . . . **250** U72
Fir Rd *KNT* . . . . . . . . . **175** W-X19
Fir St *ABT* . . . . . . . . . . . **250** U72
Fir St *BUR* . . . . . . **163** W21 W21-22
Fir St *CHL* . . . . . . . . . . . **233** L7
Fir St *CNV* . . . . . . . . . . **123** M16
Fir St *FRA* . . . . . . . . . . . **253** R5
Fir St *MAP* . . . . . . . . . . . **187** A50
Fir St *MIS* . . . . . . . . . . . **210** H75
Fir St *PCQ* . . . . . . . . . . . **146** T42
Fir St *SQM* . . . . . . . . . . **301** J3-4
Fir St *VAN* . . . . . . . . . . . . . .
. . . . **10** K34 **142** T12 **162** U12 U12 U-V12
Fir St *WRK* . . . . . . **265** W-X37
Firbridge Way *RMD* . . . . **202** E-F12
Firbrook Pl *CQT* . . . . . . . **165** U38

Firby Ct *CQT* . . . . . . . . . **165** W33
Fircrest Dr *DEL* . . . . . . . . **204** F30
Fircrest Pl *DNV* . . . . . . . . **123** N20
Firdale Av *ABT* . . . . . . . . . **251** R79
Firdale St *CQT* . . . . . . . . . **165** V34
Firestone Pl *CQT* . . . **145** P38 **146** P39
Firhill Dr *ABT* . . . . . . . . **249** S-T70
Firth Av *BUR* . . . . . . . . . **184** B24
Firview Pl *PMD* . . . . . . . . **145** Q35
Fisher Ct *CQT* . . . . . . . . . **145** R38
Fisher Ct *RMD* . . . . . . . . **202** E14
Fisher Dr *RMD* . . . **182** D14 **202** E14
Fisher St *RMD* . . . . . . . . . **202** E14
Fisher Pl *MIS* . . . . . . . . . **210** G78
Fisher St *MAP* . . . . . . . . **187** A53
Fisher St *NEW* . . . . . . . . **184** Z29-30
Fisherman Rd *MAP* . . . . **187** C-D54
Fissile La *WHS* . . . . . . . . . **401** C3
Fitzgerald Av *BUR* . . . . . . **164** W24
Fitzsimmons Rd N *WHS* . . . **401** D-E4
Fitzsimmons Rd S *WHS* . . . **401** E4
Flagman Pl *ABT* . . . . . . . . **249** T63
Flagstaff Pl *VAN* . . . . . . . **183** A20
Flamingo Ct *RMD* . . . . . . **222** K10
Flamingo Pl *SUR* . . . . . . . **185** B37
Flavelle Dr *PMD* . . . . . . . **145** Q33
Fleet St *CQT* . . . . . . . . . **165** U36
Fleetwood Dr *SUR* . . . . . . **205** R34
Fleetwood Gn *SUR* . . **206** F-G39
Fleetwood Way *SUR* . . . . . **205** F37
Fleetwood Rose Gn *SUR* . . . . . . .
. . . . . . . **205** G38 **206** G39
Fleming Av *CQT* . . . . . **145** T37-38
Fleming Av *MIS* . . . . . . . . **210** J73
Fleming St *VAN* . . . . . . . . . . . .
. . **163** V17 V-W17 W-X17 X-Y17 **183** Z17
Fletcher Av *MIS* . . . . . . **210** J72-73
Fletcher St *CHL* . . . **193** D7 **213** E7
Fletcher St *MAP* . . . . . . . **187** Z53
Fletcher Way *PCQ* . . . . . . **165** X38
Flinn Ct *PMD* . . . . . . . . . **145** T35
Flint St *PCQ* . . . . . **146** T39 **166** U39
Flood-Hope Rd *HOP* . . . . **118** G41-44
Flora La *ABT* . . . . . . . . . **230** N72
Flora Pl *PCQ* . . . . **165** W38 **166** W39
Floralynn Cr *DNV* . . . . . . **123** M20
Florence Ct *ABT* . . . . . . . . **251** T81
Florence St *CQT* . . . . . . . . **165** V31
Florimond Rd *RMD* . . . . . **202** H-J8
Flower Rd *ABT* . . . . . . . . . **265** W38
Flowering Pl *BUR* . . . . . **164** U28-29
Floyd Av *CQT* . . . . . . . . . **165** V32
Floyd Av *RMD* . . . . . . . . **202** J10
Flury Dr *RMD* . . . . . . . . . **183** U16
Flute Pl *WHS* . . . . . . . . . . **401** E3
Flynn Cr *CQT* . . . . **146** R29-30 V-W29
Flynn Pl *DNV* . . . . . . . . . **122** M14
Foley St *VAN* . . . . . . . . . **163** U16
Folkestone Way *WVA* . . . . **122** K9
Folsom Ct *CQT* . . . . . . . . **165** V32
Fonteyn Way *DNV* . . . . . . **122** K14
Fooks Rd *ABT* . . . . . . . **251** U81-82
Fooks Rd *KNT* . . . . . . . . **175** W20
Foothills Ct *ABT* . . . . . . . **251** U80
Forbes Av *CNV* . **123** N16 N16 **143** P16
Forbes St *MIS* . . . . . . . . **210** G-H75
Ford Rd *PTM* . . . . . **186** Z41 Z43-46
Ford Rd Detour *PTM* . . . . . **186** Z42
Fore Rd *ABT* . . . . . . . . **230** M75-78
Foreman Dr *MAP* . . . . . **167** V53-54
Foreshore Walk *VAN* . **10** K35 **142** T12
Foress Dr *PMD* . . . **144** T30 **145** T31
Forest Av *ABT* . . . . . . . . . **250** U72
Forest Pl *BUR* . . . . . . . . . **164** W23
Forest Pl *DEL* . . . . . . . . . **204** E30
Forest Pl *MAP* . . . . . **167** Y50 **187** Z50
Forest St *BUR* . . **163** W21 **164** W23-24
Forest Walk *CQT* . . . . . . . **146** R40
Forest Way *DEL* . . . . . . . . **204** E30
Forest Grove Dr *BUR* . . . . . . . . . .
. . . . **164** U28-29 U29-30
Forest Grove Pl *PCQ* . . . . . **146** T42
Forest Hills Dr *DNV* . . . **123** K-L15
Forest Oaks Ct *ABT* . . . . . **251** S80
Forest Park Way *PMD* . . . **145** Q-R35
Forest Ridge Dr *WHS* . . . **401** C2-3
Forester St *DNV* . . . . . . **143** P-Q22
Forestgate Pl *CQT* . . . . . . **146** R40
Foresthill Pl *PMD* . . . . . . . **145** R34
Forestridge Pl *CQT* . . . . . **145** Q37
Forestview La *ANM* . . . . . . **145** P31
Forge Pl *RMD* . . . . . . . . **223** K15
Forglen Dr *BUR* . . . . . . . **144** P26
Forillon Pl *RMD* . . . **202** J12 **222** K12
Formby St *BUR* . . . . . . . . **164** Y26

Forrest Cr *HOP* . . . . . . **118** F46-47
Forrest Ter *ABT* . . . . . **270** V-W77
Forsman Av *DNV* . . **123** N20 **143** P20
Forsythe Cr *RMD* . . . . . . **202** E-F9
Fort St *HOP* . . . . . . . . **118** E44-45
Fort Fraser Rise *PCQ* . . . . **165** Y38
Fortress Ct *PCQ* . . . . . . . **165** Y38
Fortress Dr *PCQ* . . . . . . . **165** Y38
Fortune Av *RMD* . . . . . . . **202** J9
Foster Av *CQT* . . **164** V30 **165** V31-34
Foster Av *VAN* . . . . . . . . **163** X-Y20
Foster Rd *HOP* . . . . . . . . **118** H42
Foster Rd *RMD* . . . . . . . . **202** H12
Foster St *WRK* . . . . . . **265** W-X37
Fosters Way *DEL* . . . . . . . **204** F24
Foulds St *MIS* . . . . . . . . . **210** F71
Foundry Quay *VAN* . . . **162** U12-13
Foundry Row *NEW* . . . . . . **184** C28
Fountain Way *VAN* . . . . . . **162** U12
Fowler Ct *CQT* . . . . . . . . **165** U32
Fox St *CHL* . . . . . . . . . . . **193** D5
Fox St *PCQ* . . . . . . **145** T38 **165** U38
Fox St *WVA* . . . . . . . . . . **101** G2
Foxglove Av *CHL* . . . . . . **233** L6-7
Foxglove Cr *RMD* . . . . . . . **202** F9
Foxglove La *CQT* . . . . . . . **145** Q36
Foxhound Mews *VAN* . . . . **183** Z19
Foxwood Cr *PMD* . . . . . . **145** R34
Foxwood Dr *PMD* . . . . . . **145** R34
Foy St *ABT* . . . . . . . . . **270** V-W71
Frames Ct *DNV* . . . . . . . . **124** M25
Frames Pl *DNV* . . . . . . . . **124** M25
Frances St *BUR* . . . . . . **143** S21-22
. . . . **144** S23 S-T23 S-T24 S-T26 T25
Frances St *VAN* . . . . . . . . **143** S17
Francis Av *LGT* . . . . . . . . **207** F54
Francis Pl *PCQ* . . **165** W38 **166** W39
Francis Rd *RMD* . . . . . **202** H8-14
Francis Way *NEW* . . **184** A30 Z30
Francisco Ct *DNV* . . **103** H16 **123** J16
Franklin Av *ABT* . . . . . . . **270** W75
Franklin Rd *SUR* . . . . . . . **185** B34
Franklin St *CQT* . . . . . . . **145** R37
Franklin St *VAN* . . . **143** S17-19 S20
Fraser Av *CHL* . . . **193** D8 **213** E8
Fraser Av *HOP* . . . . . . . . . **118** E44
Fraser Av *PCQ* . . . . . . . . **166** U39-41
Fraser Cr *MIS* . . . . . . . . . **210** J73
Fraser Dr *KNT* . . . . . . . . . **175** W20
Fraser Hwy *ABT* . . . **249** T63 T67-68
Fraser Hwy *LGC* . . . **227** M-N47 **N48**
Fraser Hwy *LGT* . . . . . **248** T61-62
Fraser Hwy *SUR* . . . . . . . . . . . . .
. **205** E35 **206** G39 H-J41 J42 **226** L44-45
Fraser Pl *DEL* . . . . . . . . . **204** G27
Fraser St *ABT* . . . . . **250** U76-77
Fraser St *MAP* . . . . . . . . . **187** A52 Z52
Fraser St *PMD* . . . . . . . . **145** T35
Fraser St *VAN* . . . . . . . . . . . . . .
. . . **163** V-Y16 **183** A16 A-B15 Z15-16
Fraser Way *PTM* . . . . . . **186** B46
Fraser Dyke Rd *PTM* . . . . . . . . . .
. . . **166** U-V44 **186** A42-43
Fraser Park Dr *BUR* . . . . . . . . . . .
. . . . . . **183** C22 **184** C23 D23
Fraserbank Cr *RMD* . . . **204** E24-25
Fraserbank Pl *RMD* . . . . **204** E24-25
Fraserglen Dr *SUR* . . . . . . **186** C39
Fraserside Dr *RMD* . . . . . **204** E25
Fraserton Ct *BUR* . . . . . . **183** B21
Fraserview Dr *VAN* . . . . . **183** A18
Fraserview Pl *DEL* . . . **204** F-G26
Fraserview Pl *MIS* . . **210** J71 **230** K71
Fraserview St *MAP* . . . **187** A50 Z50
Fraserview St *PCQ* . . . . **166** X-Y39
Fraserwood Ct *BUR* . . . . . **183** B21
Fraserwood Pl *RMD* . . . **204** F23-24
Fraserwood Way *RMD* **204** E-F25 F24
Frederick Av *BUR* . . . . . . **183** Z22
Frederick Pl *DNV* . . . . . **123** K-L19
Frederick Rd *DNV* . . . . . **123** K-L19
Frederick St *VAN* . . . **163** Y15 **183** Z15
Freeland Ct *CHL* . . . . . . . **213** F3
Fremlin St *VAN* . **162** Y13 **182** A13 Z13
Fremont St *PCQ* . . . . . . . . . . . . .
. . . . **146** T42 **166** U42 V42 W42
French St *VAN* . . . . . . . . **182** A12
Frenice Cr *LGT* . . . . . . . . **207** E53
Freshwater Dr *RMD* . . **202** J9-10
Fresno Pl *CQT* . . . . . . . . **165** U34
Frew Rd *DEL* . . . . . . . . . **242** R10
Frey Pl *PCQ* . . . . . . . . . . **166** U40
Friar Ct *DNV* . . . . . . . . . **144** P26
Friedel Cr *SQM* . . . . . . . . **301** E4
Friesian Dr *SUR* . . . . . . **226** N41

Frigate Ct *RMD* . . . . . . . . **222** K9
Frigate Rd *DEL* . . . . . . . **223** N16
Friskie Av *PCQ* . . . . . . . . **146** T39
Frobisher Dr *RMD* . . . . . . **202** G9
Fromme Rd *DNV* . . . **123** K-L19 L-M19
Front St *DNV* . . . . . . **143** P-Q21 Q20
Front St *NEW* . . . . . **184** A-B30 B29
Frontenac St *VAN* . . **163** Y20 **183** Z20
Frost Ct *CQT* . . . . . . . . . **146** Q39
Frost Dr *HOP* . . . . . . . . . **118** E46
Fruno Pl *SUR* . . . . . . . . . **206** G45
Fuchsia Pl *CQT* . . . . . . . . **145** R36
Fujino St *MIS* . . . . . . . . . **210** G73
Fuller Av *MAP* . . . . . . . . **187** Z53
Fuller Cr *DEL* . . . . . . . **204** G28-29
Fuller Cr N *DEL* . . . . . . . **204** G29
Fuller Cr S *DEL* . . . . . . . **204** H29
Fuller St *ABT* . . . . . . . . . **250** U75
Fullerton Av *DNV* . . . . . . **122** M13
Fulmar St *MIS* . . . . . . . . **210** H72
Fulton Av *BUR* . . . . . . . . **184** Z26
Fulton Av *WVA* . . . **122** M10-11 M9-10
Fulton St *MAP* . . . . **167** Y53 **187** A53
Fulton St *NEW* . . . . . . . . **184** B27
Fulwell St *BUR* . . . . . . . . **164** V23
Fulwell St *BUR* . . . . . . . . **164** V24
Fundy Dr *RMD* . . . **202** J9 **222** K9
Fundy Gt *RMD* . . . . . . . . . **202** J9
Furness St *NEW* . . . . . . . **184** C28
Furukawa Pl *MAP* . . . . **187** A48 Z48

**G**

Gable Ct *ABT* . . . . . . . . . **251** U81
Gable Dr *BUR* . . . . . . . . . **163** V21
Gable Dr *CQT* . . . . . . **146** R39-40
Gables La *WVA* . . . . . . . **122** K-L7
Gabriola Cr *RMD* . . . . . . . **202** G8
Gabriola Ct *ABT* . . . . . . **250** S71-72
Gabriola Dr *CQT* . . . . . **146** R-S39
Gabriola Gt *RMD* . . . . . . . **202** G8
Gabriola Way *WHS* . . . . . **401** H-J2
Gaetz St *CHL* . . . . . . . . . **213** J6
Gage Rd *RMD* . . . . . . . . **182** C13
Gaglardi Way (Simon Fraser Hills)
. *BUR* . . . **144** T28 **164** U28-29 V-W29
Gagnon Pl *HOP* . . . . . . . . **118** H42
Gagnon Pl *RMD* . . . **182** C14 **183** C15
Gail Av *PCQ* . . . . . . . . . **145** T38
Gainsborough Dr *RMD* . . . **202** J11
Galbraith Av *NEW* . . . . . . **184** D26
Galbraith Cr *DEL* . . . . . . **223** P18
Galbraith Rd *SQM* . . . . . . . **301** K1
Galbraith St *DEL* . . . . . . **223** P18
Gale Av *CQT* . . . . . . . . . **165** W35
Gale Dr *DEL* . . . . . . . . . . **263** X16
Gale Pl *DEL* . . . . . . . . . . **263** X16
Gale St *MIS* . . . . . . . . . . **210** G75
Galer Way *PCQ* . . . . . . . . **146** S40
Galiano Ct *ABT* . . . . . . . . **250** S72
Galiano Dr *ABT* . . . . . . . . **250** S72
Galiano Rd *VAN* . . . . . . . **162** V9
Galiano St *CQT* . . . . . . . . **146** S39
Gallagher Pl *WVA* . . . . . . **121** J2-3
Gallant Av *DNV* . . . . . . . . **124** M26
Gallegos Cr *SUR* . . . . . . . **225** P31
Galleon Ct *RMD* . . . . . . . **222** K9
Galleon Pl *DEL* . . . . . . . . **223** N17
Gallette Av *CQT* . . . . . . . **146** Q39
Gallette Pl *CQT* . . . . . . . . **146** Q39
Galliford St *MIS* . . . . . . . **210** G71
Galloway Av *CQT* . . . . . . **146** R41
Galt St *VAN* . . . . . . . . . **163** W-X18
Galway Cr *SUR* . . . . . . **205** F-G33
Galway Dr *DEL* . . . . . . . . **263** Y16
Gamba Dr *RMD* . . . . . . . . **202** F9
Gambier Av *CQT* . . . . . . **146** R-S39
Gambier Av *SQM* . . . . . . . **301** H2
Gamma Av N *BUR* . . **144** R-S23 S23
Gamma Av S *BUR* . . . . . **144** S-T23
Gander Ct *RMD* . . . . . . . . **202** J9
Gander Dr *RMD* . . . . . . . . **202** J9
Gander Pl *RMD* . . . . . . . . **202** J9
Gander Pl *RMD* . . . . . . . . **222** K10
Ganymede Dr *BUR* . . . . . . **164** V29
Ganymede Pl *BUR* . . . . . . **164** V29
Garden Av *DNV* . . . **122** M13-14 N14
Garden Av *WVA* . . . . . . . . **122** K9
Garden Dr *CHL* . . . . . . . **213** E7-8
Garden Dr *VAN* . . . . . . . . . . . . . .
. . . . **143** S18 S-T18 **163** U-V18 V18
Garden Dr N *VAN* . . . . . **143** R-S18
Garden Pl *DEL* . . . . . . . . **263** W17
Garden Pl *KNT* . . . . . . . **175** W-X21

Garden Pl SQM . . . . . . . . 301 K3
Garden St ABT . . . . . . . 250 T-U73
Garden St MAP . . . . . . . . 187 Z52
Garden City Rd RMD . . . . . . . . . . .
. . . . 182 C-D13 202 E-J13 222 L-M13
Garden Grove Dr BUR . . . 164 W23
Gardena Dr CQT . . . . . . . 165 U31
Gardina CQT. . . . . . . . . 145 S-T38
Gardiner St SUR . . . . . . . 245 T31
Gardner Av ABT . . . . . . . . 249 T70
Gardner Ct ABT . . . . . . . . 249 T70
Gardner Ct BUR . . . 163 V22 164 V23
Gardner Ct CQT . . . . . . . 145 Q-R38
Gardner Dr HOP . . . . . . . 118 E46
Gardner Pl ABT . . . . . . . . 249 T70
Garfield Dr DEL. . . . . . . 204 H-J28
Garfield St NEW . . . . . . 164 X-Y30
Garibaldi Av SQM . . . . . . . 301 H1
Garibaldi Cr SQM . . . . . . . 301 E3
Garibaldi Dr ABT. . . . . . 250 T73-74
Garibaldi Dr DNV. . . . . . . 144 P24
Garibaldi Dr VAN. . . . . . . 183 Z20
Garibaldi Pl CQT . . . . . . . 145 Q36
Garibaldi Way SQM . . . . . 301 E-F3
Garibaldi Way WHS . . . . . . 401 G2
Garnet Ct CQT . . . . . . . . 145 Q36
Garnet Dr CHL . . . . . . . 213 H-J5
Garnet Dr RMD . . . . . . . 202 F10
Garnet Pl ABT . . . . . . . . 249 S69
Garratt Ct RMD . . . . . . . 204 E24
Garratt Dr RMD . . . . . . . 204 E24
Garrett Dr DEL . . . . . . . 204 H-J28
Garrett Pl DEL. . . . . . . 204 H-J28
Garrett St NEW . . . . . . . 165 Y31
Garrison Blvd CHL . . . . . . 233 M6
Garrison Ct PCQ . . . . . . 166 X-Y39
Garrison Ct RMD. . . . . . . 202 F10
Garrison Rd RMD . . . . . . 202 F10
Garrow Dr PMD . . . . . . . 144 T30
Garry St DEL . . . . . . . . . 243 Q16
Garry St RMD . . . . . . . . 222 K8-9
Gaspe Pl DNV . . . . . . . . 124 N24
Gaston St VAN . . . . . . . . 163 X20
Gatefield Av ABT . . . . . . . 250 R74
Gately Av PCQ. . . . . . . . 165 U38
Gatenby Av BUR . . . . . . 164 W-X23
Gatensbury Rd CQT . . . 165 U-W33
Gatensbury Rd PMD . . . . 145 T33
Gates Av RMD . . . . . . . . 204 E25
Gateway Dr SUR . . . . 185 B33-34
Gateway Dr WHS . . . . . . . 401 T21
Gateway Pl PCQ . . . . . . . 166 X39
Gatineau Pl BUR. . . . . . . 164 W30
Gatineau Pl VAN . . . . 183 A18 Z18
Gaunt Ct RMD . . . . 202 J10 222 K10
Gauthier Av CQT . . . . . 165 X31 X32
Gay Rd RMD . . . . . . . . . 202 H12
Gay St LGT . . . . . . . . . . 207 F53
Geal Rd RMD. . . . . . . . . 202 H10 H10
Gee St MAP . . . . . . . 167 Y53 187 Z53
General Currie Rd RMD. 202 G12-13
Genest Way CQT . . . . . . 145 R38
Geneva Av ABT . . . . . . . . 270 V73
Geneva Ct ABT . . . . . . . . 270 V73
Genoa Cr DNV . . . . . . . . 123 K16
George Av ABT . . . . . . 230 M-N75
George St CHL . . . . . . . . 193 D6
George St DNV . . . . . . . 123 M15
George St VAN . . . . . . . . 143 T16
George St WRK . . . . . . 265 W-X37
George Ferguson Way ABT . . . . . .
. . . . . . . 250 T72-74 U76-77
Georgeson Av CQT . . . . . 146 R39
Georgia St BUR . . . . . . . . . . . . . .
. . . . . . . 143 T21-22 144 T23 T25
Georgia St DEL . . . 223 P16 243 Q16
Georgia St RMD. . . . . . . 222 K8-9
Georgia St VAN. . . . . . . . . . . . . . .
. 10 E35-36 11 G37 H41 142 R12-13 S13
Georgia St E VAN . . . . . . . . . . . . .
. . 143 T15 T15-16 T16 T17 T18-20 T20
Georgia Wynd DEL . . . . . 263 Z16
Gerald Av BUR . . . . . . . 164 U26
Gerrard Pl RMD . . . . . . . 222 L8
Gerrit Pl KNT . . . . . . . . 175 X21
Ghent La VAN . . . . . . . . 162 U8
Ghum-Lye Rd DNV . . . . . 144 P23
Gibbard St MIS . . . . . . . 210 J75
Gibbons Dr RMD . . . . . . 202 E-F9
Gibson St BUR . . . . . . 164 U25-26
Giesbrecht Rd CHL . . . . . 233 N-P3
Gifford St NEW . . . . . . . 184 A29
Gifford St NEW . . . . . . . 184 D26
Gilbert Av CHL . . . . . . . . 193 C8
Gilbert Ct RMD . . . . . . . 202 J11
Gilbert Dr MAP . . . . . . . 167 V53-54

Gilbert Rd RMD 202 E-J11 222 K-M11
Gilchrist Dr DEL . . . . . . . 263 Y17
Gilchrist Pl DEL . . . . . . . 263 Y17
Gildwood Dr BUR . . . . 164 W29-30
Giles Pl BUR . . . . . 144 T26 164 U26
Gilford St VAN. . . . . . 10 F34 142 R12
Gilhurst Cr RMD . . . . . . . 202 J11
Gilhurst Gt RMD . . . . . . . 202 J11
Gilker Hill Rd MAP. . . . . . 187 B54
Gill Av MIS . . . . . . 210 J71 230 K71
Gillespie Pl PCQ . . . . . . 166 V41
Gillespie Rd DEL . . . . . 263 W-X18
Gillespie St PCQ . . . . . . 166 V41
Gilley Av BUR. 164 Y24 184 A-B24 Z24
Gilley Av MAP . . . . . . . . 187 A53
Gilley Rd RMD . . . . . . 204 E24-25
Gilley St NEW . . . . . . . . 184 B28
Gilley St SUR . . . . . . . . 245 T31
Gilleys Tr CQT . . . . . . . . 146 R43
Gillian Pl CHL . . . . . . . 233 M4-5
Gillis Av ABT . . . . . . . 270 W75-76
Gillis Pl MAP . . . . . . . . 187 A53
Gillnet Pl VAN . . . . . . . . 182 A11
Gilmon Av BUR . . . . . . . 164 W24
Gilmore Av BUR . . . 143 R-T21 163 U21
Gilmore Av N BUR. . . . . 143 R-S21
Gilmore Cr RMD . . . . . . . 182 C14
Gilmore Ct RMD . . . . . 182 B-C14
Gilmore Div BUR . . . . . . 163 V21
Gilmore Way BUR . . . . 163 V-W21
Gilmour Cr DEL . . . . . . . 204 J30
Gilmour Dr ABT . . . . . . . 270 V76
Gilpin Cr BUR . . . . . . . . 163 X22
Gilpin Ct BUR . . . . . . . . 163 X21
Gilpin St BUR . . . . . . . . . . . . . . .
. . . . 163 X21-22 164 X23-24 X25
Gilroy Cr CQT . . . . . . . . 164 U30
Gilston Rd WVA . . . . . . . 122 J12
Ginger Dr NEW . . . . . . . 184 Z29
Gingerhills Dr ABT. . . . . . 251 U79
Girard Av CQT . . . . . . . . 165 X31
Giroday Pl DEL . . . . . . . . 204 J30
Gisby St WVA . . . . . . . . 122 K8
Gislason Av CQT . . . . . . 146 R41
Givenchy Rd CHL . . . . . 233 N5
Glacier Cr RMD . . . . . . . 202 J12
Glacier Dr WHS . . . . 401 F4 T-U22
Glacier La WHS . . . . . 401 F4 U22
Glacier St CQT . . . . . . 165 X-Y36
Glacier Heights Pl SQM . . 301 E5
Glacier View Dr SQM . . . 301 D-E5
Glacier View Pl SQM . . . . 301 E5
Glade Ct PCQ . . . . . 166 U41-42
Gladstone Av CNV . . . . . 143 P19
Gladstone Av DNV . . . . . . . . . . . . .
. . . . . . 123 N19 N19 143 P19
Gladstone Dr SUR . . 185 A-B35 B36
Gladstone St VAN. . . . . . . . . . . . . .
. . . . 163 V-W18 W-X18 X18 X-Y18
. . . . . . . . . . . . . 183 A18 Z18
Gladwin Dr DNV. . . . . . . 122 L14
Gladwin Pl DNV . . . . . 123 L-M15
Gladwin Rd ABT . . . . . . . . . . . . . .
. . . . 230 M73-74 N-P74 250 Q-T77
. . . . . . . . . . . . . . . 270 V-Z74
Gladys Av ABT . . . 250 T-U76 270 V77
Gladys St CHL . . . . . . . . 193 C8
Glasgow Av BUR . . . . . . 144 R24
Glasgow Av MIS . . . . . 230 K74-75
Glasgow Rd CHL . . . . . . . 193 C8
Glasgow St PCQ . . . . . . . 146 T39
Glen WVA . . . . . . . . . . . 121 J4
Glen Ct NEW . . . . . . . . 184 Z29
Glen Dr CQT . . . . . . . 145 S37-38
Glen Dr VAN . . . . . . . . . . . . . . . .
. . 143 S-T16 T16 163 U16 U-V16 V-W16
Glen Abbey Dr BUR . . 144 T26-27
Glen Abbey La WHS . . . . 401 C4
Glen Abbey Pl DEL . . . 263 W16-17
Glen Avon Dr SUR . . 185 A36-37 B37
Glen Pine Ct CQT . . . . . 145 S38
Glenacre Ct PMD. . . . . . 145 T31
Glenacres Dr RMD . . . 202 H13-14
Glenaire Dr DNV . . . . . . . 122 M13
Glenaire Dr HOP . . . . . . 118 F46
Glenalder Pl SQM . . . . . 301 E-F3
Glenallan Dr RMD . . . . . . 202 H13
Glenallan Gt RMD . . . . . . 202 H13
Glenalmond Pl ABT. . . . . 250 T78
Glenavon Ct ABT. . . . . . . 250 T78
Glenavon St ABT. . . . . . . 250 T78
Glenayre Dr PMD . . . . . 145 S-T31
Glenbrook Ct RMD . . . . . . 202 H13
Glenbrook Dr NEW . . . 184 Z29-30
Glenbrook Dr RMD . . . . . 202 H13

Glenbrook Gr SUR . . . . . 186 C39
Glenbrook Pl DEL . . . . . . 204 J29
Glenbrook Pl SUR. . . . . . 186 C39
Glenbrook St CQT . . . . . 146 R40
Glencanyon Dr DNV . . . . 123 J-K16
Glencarin Dr BUR . . . . . 164 X25
Glencoe Dr PMD . . . 144 T30 145 T31
Glencoe Pl ABT . . . . . . . 250 T78
Glencoe St BUR . . . . . . . 164 X30
Glendale Av CQT . . . . . . 165 X34
Glendale Av DEL . . . . . . 243 Q16
Glendale Av LIO. . . . . . . 101 A23
Glendale Dr CHL . . . . . 233 M4-5
Glendale Pl ABT . . . . . . . 250 T78
Glendale St VAN. . . . . . . 163 W20
Glendalough Pl VAN . . . . 162 Y9
Glendower Dr PMD . . . 202 H13-14
Glendower Gt RMD . . . . . 202 H14
Gleneagles Cl WVA . . 101 H1 121 J1
Gleneagles Dr WVA . 101 H1 121 J1-2
Gleneagles Pl ABT. . . . . . 250 T78
Gleneagles Pl WVA . . . . 121 J1-2
Gleneden St CHL . . . . . . 233 K6
Glengarry Av ABT . . . 249 Q67-68
Glengarry Cr SUR . . . . 205 F32-33
Glengarry Cr WVA . . . . 102 H13-14
Glengarry Dr CHL . . . . . 233 L-M6
Glengyle St VAN . . . . 163 W17-18
Glenhaven Cr DNV . . . . . 144 P26
Glenholme St CQT . . . . . 165 W34
Glenhurst St MAP . . . 187 A54 Z54
Glenlyon Pkwy BUR . 183 B-C22 C22
Glenmaroon Rd WVA . . . 122 K12
Glenmoor St VAN . . . . . . 186 C40
Glenmoor Pl SUR . . . . 186 C39-40
Glenmore Dr CHL . . . . . 233 L-M6
Glenmore Dr WVA. . . . . . . . . . . . . .
. . . . . 102 H13 H14 122 J14
Glenmore Rd ABT. . . . . . . . . . . . . .
. . . . . . 230 M-P72 250 Q-R72
Glenn Mountain Dr ABT . . 250 U78
Glenora Av DNV. . . . . . . 123 L15
Glenrose Dr DEL . . . . . . 204 G27
Glenross Rd WVA . . . . . . 102 H13
Glenroy Dr CHL . . . . . . . 233 L6
Glenshiel Dr ABT. . . . . . . 250 T78
Glenside Ct SUR. . . . . . . 186 C40
Glenside Pl SUR . . . . . . . 186 C40
Glenthorne Ct RMD. . . . . 202 H14
Glenthorne Dr RMD . . . 202 H13-14
Glenview Cr DNV . . 123 K15-16 L15
Glenview Ct CQT . . . . 145 Q37-38
Glenwill Av ABT . . . . . . . 250 U76
Glenwood Av ABT . . . . . . 270 V72
Glenwood Av DNV. . . . . . 123 J15
Glenwood Av MAP . . 187 Z49-50 Z50
Glenwood Av PCQ . . . . . 146 T39
Glenwood Cl BUR . . . . 184 A-B24
Glenwood Cr E SUR . . . . 186 C40
Glenwood Cr N SUR. . . 186 C39-40
Glenwood Cr S SUR . . . . 186 C40
Glenwood Dr BUR . . . 184 C24-25
Glenwood Dr DEL . . . . . 262 Y15
Glenwood Dr KNT. . . . . 175 X21
Glenwood Dr SUR. . . . . . 186 C39
Glenwood Pl DEL . . 262 Y15 263 Y16
Glenwood St CHL . . . . . 213 F6
Glenwynd Pl WVA . . . . . 121 J1
Gloria Dr PCQ . . . . . . . . 166 X39
Gloucester Pl CQT. . . 165 X35-36
Gloucester St NEW. . . . . 184 B29
Glover Av NEW . . . . . . . 144 Z28
Glover Rd LGC . . . 227 M48-49 N48
Glover Rd LGT. 207 F53-54 G-H53 J51
. . . . . . . 227 K51 L50 L-M49
Glynde Av N BUR. . . . . . 144 S23
Glynde Av S BUR. . . . . . 144 S23
Goard Way BUR. . . . . . 163 V-W22
Godson Ct ABT. . . . . . . 270 V74
Godwin Av BUR. . . . . . 164 V-W24
Godwin Ct CQT. . . . . . . 165 X31
Goggs Av WRK265 W36 W38 266 W39
Golden Av ABT. . . . . . 250 S72-73
Golden Dr CQT . . . . . . . 165 Y36
Golden St BUR . . . . . . 164 U25-26
Golden Bear Pl WHS . . . 401 C3-4
Golden Link Cr VAN . . 183 Z19-20
Golden Spike La PMD . 145 T34-35
Goldeneye Pl RMD . . . . 222 K10
Goldenrod Av LIO . . . . . 101 A23
Goldenrod Blvd DEL . . . . 263 Y17
Goldenrod Cr DEL . . . 263 Y17-18
Goldfinch Pl ABT. . . . . . 249 S69
Goldfinch St BUR. . . . 249 S-T69
Goldhurst Ter BUR . . . 164 U-V29
Goldie Ct DNV . . . . . . . . 124 N25

Goldsmith Dr RMD . . . . 202 J10-11
Goldspring Pl CHL . . . . . 233 N8
Goldstream Cr CQT. . . . . 165 V36
Goldstream Dr ABT . . . 251 S-T79
Goldstream Dr RMD. . . . . 202 J12
Goldstream Pl RMD. . . . . 202 J12
Goleta Dr BUR. . . . . . . 164 U26
Goleta Pl BUR. . . . . . . 164 U26
Golf Dr DNV . . . . . . . 144 P-Q26
Golf Dr DNV . . . . . . . . 144 P26
Golf La MAP . . . . . . . . 187 A49
Golf Rd KNT . . . . . . . 155 S18-19
Golf Club Dr DEL . . . 263 W16-17
Golf Course Dr ABT . . . . 251 R80
Golf Course Rd HOP. . . . 118 D45
Golfer's App WHS . . . . . . 401 T21
Gondola Way WHS . . . . . . 401 H2
Goodall Pl CHL . . . . . . . 193 D8
Goodbrand Dr ABT. . . . 251 U79 U80
Goodchild St ABT . . . . 251 Q-R79
Goodlad St BUR. . . . . . 164 Y26-27
Goodrich Pl SUR. . . . . . . 205 J35
Gooseberry Pl CHL . . . . . 213 F-G1
Gordon Av BUR. . . . . 164 X25 Y26
Gordon Av CQT. . . . 145 T38 165 U38
Gordon Av PCQ. . . . . . . 165 U38
Gordon Av SUR . . . . . . 245 T-U31
Gordon Av WRK . . . . . . . 265 X36
Gordon Av WVA . . . . . . . . . . . . . . .
. . . . . 122 M10-11 M13 M9-10
Gordon Dr CHL . . . . . . . 213 J6
Gordon Dr HOP . . . . . . . 118 E46
Gordon Pl BUR . . . . . . . 164 Y26
Gordon Pl WVA. . . . . . . . 122 M13
Gordon Way RMD . . . . . 204 F23
Gore Av CHL . . . . . . . . . 213 E7
Gore Av VAN . . . . . 11 G-J41 143 S-T15
Gore St PMD . . . . . . . . 145 S32
Goring St BUR . . . . . . 164 U23-24
Gormond Rd RMD . . . . 202 H-J8
Gostick Pl CNV . . . 123 N15 143 P15
Gothard St VAN . . . . . . 163 W-X18
Goudy Pl DEL . . . . . . . 243 Q19
Goundrey St MIS . . . . . 210 F-G76
Government Rd BUR . . 164 W26-28
Government Rd SQM. . . . . . . . . . . .
. . . . 301 A1 B1-2 C2 E3 F1-3 G1
Government St BUR . . 164 W28-30
Governor Ct PCQ . . . . . . 166 X39
Governors Ct NEW . . . . . 184 Z30
Gower St RMD . . . . . 202 J13-14
Goyer Ct CQT . . . . . . . 165 W33
Grace Av ABT . . . . . . . 230 M75
Grace Av BUR . . . . . . . 164 W25
Grace Cr DNV . . . . . . . . 123 K15
Grace Rd SUR . . . . . 184 C-D30
Grace St MAP . . . . . . . 167 Y51
Gracemar Dr CHL . . . . . 194 D10
Grade Cr LGC . . . 227 P47 247 Q48-49
Grafton Ct BUR. . . . . . . 164 Y23
Grafton St BUR . . . 163 Y22 164 Y23
Graham Av BUR . . . . . . 184 Z27
Graham Ct MIS . . . . . . 210 G75
Graham Dr DEL . . . . . . 263 Z16
Graham St PCQ. . . . . . . 146 T39
Granada Cr DNV . . . . . . 123 K16
Grand Blvd CNV . . . 123 M18 N18
Grand St MIS . . . . . . . 210 H-J74
Grand View Dr CHL . . . 213 F2 G1-3
Grandview Cr ABT . . . . . 250 T71
Grandview Hwy BUR . . 163 V21-22
Grandview Hwy VAN . . 163 V19-20
Grandview Hwy N VAN . . . 163 U17
Grandview Hwy S VAN . . . 163 V18
Grandview Viaduct VAN. . . . . . . . . . .
. . . . . . 143 T16 163 U16-17
Grandy Rd RMD . . . . . . . 202 G11
Grange St BUR . . . . . . 163 Y21-22
Granite Av ABT . . . . . . 250 T72-73
Granite Ct CQT . . . . . . . 145 U34
Grant Av PCQ . . . . . . . 166 U39-40
Grant Ct PCQ . . . 146 T41 166 U41
Grant Pl BUR . . . . . . . . 144 T25
Grant Pl DEL . . . . . . . . 204 E30
Grant Pl PCQ . . . . 146 T41 166 U41
Grant Rd SQM . . . . . . . 301 C1-2
Grant St ABT . . . . 250 U72 270 V72
Grant St BUR . . . . . . 144 T21 T21-22
. . . . . . 144 T24 T24-25 164 U24
Grant St CHL . . . . . . . . . 193 C8
Grant St DNV . . . . . 145 T31 165 U31
Grant St PMD . . . . . . . . 145 T33
Grant St VAN . . . . . . . 143 T17-19
Grant McConachie Way RMD . . . . . .
. . . . . . . . . . . . . 182 C10-11

Grantham Pl DNV . . . . . 143 P21
Granville Av RMD . . . . . . 202 F8-14
Granville Cr RMD . . . . . . 202 F11
Granville Seawalk N VAN . . . . . . .
. . . . . . . . . 10 J35-36 142 T12
Granville St NEW . . . . 184 A29-30
Granville St VAN . . . . . . . . . . . . . . .
. . . . . 10 J36 142 T13 162 U12
Grassmere St BUR . 163 X22 164 X23
Grauer Bypass RMD . . . . 182 B11
Grauer Rd RMD . . . . . . 182 B-C12
Graveley St BUR. . . . . . . . . . . . . . .
. . . . . 143 T21 T21 T22 163 U21 U22
Graveley St DNV . . . . 122 M13 M14
Graveley St VAN . . . . . . . . . . . . . . .
. . . . . 143 T17-18 T19-20 T20
Graves St MAP . . . . . 187 A49 Z49
Gray Av BUR . . . . . . 183 A22 Z22
Gray Av UEL . . . . . . . . . 161 V5
Graybar Rd RMD . . . . . . 204 F23
Grayson Av CQT . . . . . . 165 X31
Graystone Dr ABT . . . . . 251 U80
Graystone La ABT . . . . . 251 U80
Great Canadian Way RMD . 182 C13
Great Northern Av ABT. . . 249 U69
Great Northern Way VAN 163 U15-16
Grebe Cr MIS. . . . . . . . 210 H73
Green Av ABT . . . . . . . 250 T77
Green Ct BUR . . . . . . . . 163 U22
Green Pl DEL . . . . . . . . 223 P17
Green Rd KNT. . . . . . . . 175 W20
Green Rd PTM . . . . . . . 166 Y44
Greenbriar Pl PMD . . . . 145 R35
Greenbriar Way DNV . . 122 K-L14
Greenbrier Pl CQT. . . . . 145 R36
Greenbrook Dr SUR . . . . 206 G41
Greenbrook Pl SUR. . . . . 206 G41
Greenchain VAN . . . . . . 162 U13
Greencrest Dr SUR . . . . 245 S35
Greendale Ct ABT . . . . . 249 S69
Greene Pl MIS . . . . . . . 210 F73
Greene St CQT . . . . . . . 165 U38
Greenfield Dr RMD . . . . 202 H13
Greenfield Gt RMD . . . 202 H-J13
Greenford Av BUR . . . . 184 Z25
Greenhaven Ct PTM . . . . 187 Z47
Greenhill Ct CQT . . . 145 R36-37
Greenhill Pl DEL . . . . . . 204 G29
Greenhouse La BUR . . 144 T28-29
Greenland Dr DEL . . . . 263 Z17
Greenland Dr RMD . . . . . 183 D16
Greenland Pl RMD . . . . . 183 D16
Greenleaf Ct PMD . . . 145 P-Q35
Greenleaf Dr PMD . . . . . 145 Q35
Greenleaf La WVA . . . . . 121 J3
Greenleaf Rd WVA. . . . . . 121 J3
Greenlees Rd RMD . . . . 202 H13
Greenmount Av PCQ. . . . 146 S40
Greenmount St CHL . . . . 233 K-L5
Greenock Pl DNV . . . . . 123 M20
Greenock Pl SUR. . . . . . . 205 F32
Greensboro Pl VAN . . . . 182 Z14
Greenside Dr E SUR . . . . 226 M46
Greenside Dr W SUR. . . . 226 M46
Greenstone Ct CQT . . . . 145 Q36
Greentree La DNV . . . . 122 K-L14
Greentree Pl BUR . 163 X22 164 X23
Greentree Rd WVA. . . . . 121 K2-3
Greenway Av DNV . . . 123 J-K16
Greenway Dr SUR. . . . . . 206 G41
Greenwell St MAP. . 167 Y53 187 Z53
Greenwood Dr CHL . . 213 J7 233 K7
Greenwood Dr HOP . . . . 118 E46
Greenwood Pl BUR . . . . 164 V26
Greenwood Pl WVA. . . . . 122 J12
Greenwood Rd WVA. . . . 122 J12-13
Greenwood St BUR . 164 V25 V26-27
Greenwood Way SQM . . . 301 D-E4
Greer Av VAN . . . . 10 J-K33 142 T11
Greer Pl PCQ . . . . 145 T38 146 T39
Greer St ABT . . . . . . . . 270 W75
Greer St LGT . . . . . . . . 207 E53
Greta St BUR . . . . . . . . 183 Z22
Grewall Cr MIS . . . . . . 210 H75
Greylynn Cr DNV. . . . . . 123 M20
Greystone Dr BUR . . . . . . . . . . . . . .
. . . . . . . . 144 T26-27 164 U27
Greystone Pl PMD. . . . . 145 R35
Griffen Rd MAP . . . . . . . 187 B54
Griffin Dr CHL . . . . . . . 233 K7
Griffiths Av BUR 164 Y25 184 A25 Z25
Griffiths Dr BUR . . . . . 184 A25-26

Street Index
Griffiths / Holly Park

Griffiths Pl NEW 164 Y30
Griffiths Rd ABT 270 V77
Griffiths Way VAN 11 H-J39 142 T14
Grimmer St BUR 184 Z23
Grizzly Pl CQT 145 Q38
Groat Av RMD 202 J9
Grosvenor Av N BUR 144 S23
Grosvenor Av S BUR 144 S23
Grosvenor Cr BUR 144 S23
Grosvenor Pl ABT 250 U77
Grosvenor Pl CQT 146 R40
Grosvenor Rd SUR 185 B34-35
Grosvenor Sq DEL 184 D27-28
Grouse Av MIS 210 H72
Grouse Ct ABT 250 U73
Grouse Walk VAN 163 X15
Grousewoods Cr DNV 103 H15
Grousewoods Dr DNV 103 H15
Grousewoods Pl DNV 103 H15
Grove Av BUR 144 S-T25
Grove Av CHL 233 N8
Grove Av DEL 223 P17-18
Grove Av MIS 210 G71-72
Grove Cr DEL 263 W18
Grove Cr SUR 185 D32
Grove Pl DEL 263 W18
Grove Pl DNV 123 M22
Groveland Ct WVA 122 J11
Groveland Pl WVA 122 J-K12
Groveland Rd WVA 122 J12
Grover Av CQT 165 U31-34
Groveridge Wynd DEL 263 Z17
Guelph St VAN 163 U-V15
Guest Pl PCQ 166 X39
Guest Ter MIS 210 H71
Guest Wynd PMD 145 R33-34
Guilby St CQT 165 W-X31
Guildford Dr PMD 145 S35-36
Guildford Dr SUR 185 C37
Guildford Way CQT 145 S36-38
Guilford Dr ABT 250 U77 270 V77
Guilford Dr SQM 301 K2-3
Guiltner St CQT 165 U-V31
Gulf Pl WVA 121 K2
Gulf View Wynd DEL 263 Z16
Gunderson Rd DEL 204 E29
Gwillim Cr VAN 183 Z20-21

## H

Habgood St WRK 266 W39 X39
Hachey Av CQT 165 X33
Hacienda Pl ABT 270 V73
Hacienda Pl CHL 233 M4
Hadden Dr WVA 122 K-L13
Hadden St LGT 207 F53
Haddon Ct RMD 202 J10
Haddon Dr RMD 202 J10
Haddon Pl RMD 202 J10
Haddon Rd SUR 185 B33
Hadway Dr HHS 155 R19-20
Haffner Ter MIS 210 G73
Haggart St VAN 162 W10
Haida Dr ABT 250 S73
Haida Dr VAN 163 V20
Haig Dr CHL 213 J5-6
Haig Hwy KNT 175 X21-22
Haig St MIS 210 J73
Haig St VAN 182 A12
Haig Station Rd HOP 118 D43
Hailey St CQT 165 U-V32
Hairy Chief Rd SQM 301 K2
Hajula Ct ABT 251 S79
Hale Rd PTM 146 T46 166 V-W46
Haley St MAP 167 W53
Halifax Av PCQ 146 S41
Halifax Pl SUR 225 N35
Halifax St BUR 163 U21-22 164 U23 U23-26
Hall Av BUR 184 Z26
Hall Av RMD 182 D14
Hall Pl CHL 213 H7-8
Hall Pl DEL 204 G30
Hall Pl RMD 182 D14
Hall Rd SUR 225 K34
Hall St MAP 187 Z51
Hallam Ct CQT 146 Q39
Hallert Rd ABT 230 P72 P76-78
Halley Av BUR 163 W22 X-Y22
Halligan St BUR 184 Z25-26
Halss Cr VAN 162 X-Y7 Y8
Halstead Pl SUR 185 D36
Halston Ct BUR 164 W29-30
Halston Ct WVA 122 K9
Hamber Ct DNV 124 N25
Hamber Pl DNV 124 N25
Hamber St RMD 202 F8
Hambry St BUR 184 Z24
Hamilton Av CNV 123 M-N15
Hamilton Rd KNT 175 X-Y17
Hamilton Rd RMD 204 F25
Hamilton St CHL 193 D5-6
Hamilton St NEW 184 A27 A27-28 B26 B26-27
Hamilton St PCQ 146 S42 T42
Hamilton St VAN 11 H38 J37 142 S-T14 T13
Hamlin Dr DEL 224 L29
Hammarskjold Dr BUR 144 S-T24
Hammersmith Gt RMD 223 K15
Hammersmith Way RMD 223 K-L15
Hammond Av CQT 165 W33-34
Hammond Rd MAP 187 A48 Z47
Hammond Rd PTM 186 Z46 187 Z47
Hammond St MIS 210 F74
Hamon Cr ABT 270 V78
Hamon Dr ABT 270 V78
Hampshire Ct SUR 246 T39
Hampshire Pl ABT 250 U77 270 V77
Hampshire Rd DNV 123 K15
Hampstead Cl DEL 204 F25
Hampstead Pl BUR 164 X-Y25
Hampton Blvd E SUR 225 L32
Hampton Blvd N SUR 225 L32
Hampton Ct SUR 225 L32
Hampton Dr CQT 145 P38
Hampton Gn CQT 145 P38 146 P39
Hampton Gt CQT 145 P38
Hampton Pl UEL 161 V5
Hampton St MAP 187 A-B48
Handel Av VAN 183 A20
Handley Av RMD 182 D11
Handley Cr PCQ 146 T42
Handsworth Rd DNV 122 J14 123 J15 J15-16
Hanes Av CNV 123 N15
Haney By-Pass MAP 187 A52 A-B53
Haney Pl MAP 187 Z52
Hankin Dr RMD 202 E8
Hanna Ct BUR 184 A25
Hansard Cr CQT 145 T37
Hanson Rd SUR 185 B34-35
Happy Valley La WVA 121 L2-3
Harbour Av DNV 143 P-Q20 Q20
Harbour Av MIS 230 K75
Harbour Dr CQT 165 U33-34
Harbour Pl PMD 145 R34
Harbour Rd DNV 143 Q21
Harbour St PCQ 166 X40
Harbour Stroll DEL 223 P16
Harbour View Pl SQM 301 J-K2
Harbourgreene Dr SUR 265 V31
Harbourside Dr CNV 143 P15
Harbourside Pl CNV 143 P15
Harbourview Rd BUR 144 R23
Hardie Av WRK 265 X36-37
Hardwick St BUR 164 W23-24
Hardy Cr DNV 123 N22
Hardy Pl DEL 204 F29
Hardy Rd DEL 204 E-F29
Hardy Rd KNT 155 T18 175 U18
Hardy St MAP 167 Y50
Harford St CHL 193 D7 213 E7
Hargitt Pl MIS 210 F73-74
Hargitt St ABT 230 L76
Harken Dr BUR 163 X22
Harkness Ct MAP 167 Y51
Harley Ct BUR 163 Y22 164 Y23
Harmony Bay SUR 266 V-W39
Harmony Ct ABT 250 S71
Harmony Ct WHS 401 G2
Harmony Pl SUR 265 V-W38
Harms St MIS 210 G75
Haro St VAN 10 E35 G36 142 R12 S13
Harold Rd DNV 123 L19 L20
Harold St VAN 163 Y20
Harper Ct BUR 163 X21
Harper Dr ABT 250 U78 251 U79
Harper Rd CQT 146 Q41
Harper Rd SUR 185 B34
Harrier Dr CQT 145 S36
Harriet St VAN 163 W16
Harris Av CQT 165 X32
Harris Av DNV 124 N26
Harris Pl DEL 263 X16-17
Harris Pl DNV 124 N26
Harris Rd ABT 230 N71-78
Harris Rd PTM 146 T45-46 166 U45-46 V45-46 X46 186 A46 Z46
Harris Rd SQM 301 E3
Harris St MIS 210 G73
Harrison Av CQT 165 U31
Harrison Av RMD 203 E15-16
Harrison Dr VAN 183 A17-18
Harrison St CHL 193 D6
Harrison St MAP 187 A53
Harrogate Dr DEL 204 G27-28
Hart St CQT 165 X31
Hartford Pl DNV 144 P23
Hartley Av CQT 165 Y34-35
Hartman Av MIS 210 E76
Hartnell Pl ABT 250 R78
Hartnell Rd RMD 223 K15-16
Harvard Dr PMD 145 S31-32
Harvard Pl CHL 213 G6
Harvest Dr ABT 251 S79-80
Harvest Dr DEL 243 Q17-18
Harvey St NEW 184 Z30
Harvie Rd SUR 206 F45 G-H44 H-J43
Harwood Av CQT 146 R39
Harwood Cr ABT 250 R-S74
Harwood Pl ABT 250 R74
Harwood St VAN 10 G34 H35 142 S12
Hashizume Ter MIS 210 G73
Hastings Pl PCQ 145 T38 146 T39
Hastings St BUR 143 S21-22 144 S23-26
Hastings St NEW 184 A30
Hastings St PCQ 146 T39 166 U39
Hastings St E VAN 11 H41 143 S16-20
Hastings St W VAN 11 F37 G39 142 R13 S14
Haszard St BUR 164 X25-26 Y25
Hatton Av BUR 144 T26
Haven Pl SUR 265 V31
Haverhill Pl DNV 123 L20
Haversley Av CQT 165 W33-35
Haviland St DEL 223 P16 243 Q16
Hawks Av VAN 143 S-T16
Hawkstream Dr SUR 205 H35
Hawksview Pl ABT 251 S80
Hawser Av CQT 145 T36
Hawstead Pl WVA 122 J13
Hawthorn Dr PMD 145 P-Q35
Hawthorne Av ABT 270 W74-75
Hawthorne Av MIS 210 G74
Hawthorne Av PCQ 165 V38 166 V39
Hawthorne Pl DEL 243 Q18
Hawthorne Pl KNT 175 X20
Hawthorne Pl WHS 401 F3
Hawthorne St MAP 187 Z54
Hawthorne Ter BUR 184 A25 Z25
Hayashi Ct RMD 222 K-L9
Hayes St WVA 121 L6
Hayle Pl SUR 225 K33
Hayne Ct RMD 182 D14
Hayseed Cl DNV 123 M22
Hayton Rd ABT 230 L77
Hayward La CQT 145 R37
Hayward Pl DEL 204 F30
Haywood Av WVA 122 L10-11 L11 L9-10
Hazel Cr MIS 210 G74
Hazel Ct DEL 223 P17
Hazel Ct SUR 186 C40
Hazel Dr CQT 146 P40
Hazel St BUR 163 Y22 164 Y23
Hazel St CHL 193 D8 213 E8 F8
Hazel St HOP 118 D44
Hazelbridge Way RMD 182 D12 202 E12
Hazellynn Pl DNV 123 M20
Hazelmere St BUR 164 Y26
Hazelnut Gr KNT 175 W20
Hazelnut Pl BUR 164 X29
Hazelton St VAN 143 T19-20
Hazelwood Av ABT 250 S76-77
Hazelwood Cr BUR 163 X21-22
Hazelwood St MAP 187 B48
Headland Cl WVA 121 K3
Headland Ct WVA 121 K3
Headland Dr WVA 121 J-K4 K3
Headland Pl WVA 121 K3
Health Sciences Rd UEL 161 U4
Hearthstone Ct ABT 250 R77-78
Heath Cr CQT 145 S36-37
Heath Cr DEL 204 J29
Heath Rd KNT 175 W-X21
Heathdale Ct BUR 144 T23-24
Heathdale Dr BUR 144 T23 164 U23
Heather Av HOP 118 G42
Heather Av MIS 210 H-J75
Heather Av PCQ 146 S40
Heather Dr ABT 270 V76-77
Heather Pl PMD 145 R35
Heather Pl RMD 202 J13
Heather St CHL 193 D7-8
Heather St RMD 202 G-H13
Heather St VAN 162 U-X13 182 A13 B13 Z13
Heatherstone Pl ABT 251 U80
Heatley Av VAN 143 S-T16
Hebb Av VAN 163 V19
Hecate Pl VAN 183 Z20-21
Heckbert Pl CQT 165 U37
Hedge Av BUR 184 Z27
Hedgestone Ct CQT 145 Q-R38
Hedley Av BUR 184 A25 Z25
Hedley St ABT 250 S72
Heffley Cr CQT 145 S38
Helc Pl SUR 245 T38
Helen Dr PCQ 165 X38
Helen Dr SUR 185 D32
Helm Pl WHS 401 G2
Helmcken St VAN 11 H37 142 S-T13
Helston Cr SUR 225 K32
Hemlock Av HOP 118 E44
Hemlock Av MAP 167 U54
Hemlock Av SQM 301 J-K3
Hemlock Cr ABT 250 U76
Hemlock Cr PCQ 146 T42
Hemlock Ct VAN 10 K36
Hemlock Dr ANM 125 N33
Hemlock Pl PMD 145 R36
Hemlock St ABT 250 U72 270 V72
Hemlock St CHL 193 D7
Hemlock St FRA 253 R5
Hemlock St MIS 210 H-J71
Hemlock St VAN 162 U-V12
Hendecourt Pl DNV 123 L19
Hendecourt Rd DNV 123 L19
Henderson Av CHL 193 D6 213 E6
Henderson Av CQT 165 X31-32
Henderson Av DNV 123 K-L20
Henderson St MIS 210 F-G74
Hendon St ABT 250 S77
Hendry Av DNV 123 N18-19
Hendry Pl NEW 184 D27
Hengestone Ct ABT 250 S77-78
Henley Av ABT 250 T-U77
Henley Av CHL 193 D6
Henley St NEW 184 A27
Henlow Rd WVA 122 J12
Hennepin Av VAN 183 Z20
Henning Dr BUR 163 U21
Henry Av MIS 210 G78
Henry St CHL 233 K7
Henry St PMD 145 T33
Henry St VAN 163 W-X16
Herar La MIS 210 G76
Herbert Rd RMD 202 H-J12
Hereford Pl SUR 226 M41
Heritage Blvd DNV 143 P21
Heritage Dr ABT 249 S69
Heritage Dr CHL 233 K6
Heritage Mountain Blvd PMD 145 R-S35
Heritage Peaks Tr WHS 401 J2
Hermitage Dr RMD 202 J9 222 K9
Hermon Dr VAN 163 U20
Hermosa Av DNV 123 K16
Hermosa Dr DEL 204 H28
Heron Av ABT 249 T70
Heron Pl VAN 183 A20
Heron Pl WHS 401 F3
Heron St MIS 210 H72
Heron Bay Cl DEL 223 P16
Herring Pl PTM 187 Z47
Herrmann St CQT 165 U37
Herron Av CHL 193 D6
Hersham Av BUR 164 Y26 184 Z26
Hertford St BUR 163 X21
Hett Creek Dr PMD 145 Q34
Hewitt St BUR 144 T26
Heywood St CNV 143 P19
Hialeah Ct CQT 145 S37
Hiawatha Dr WVA 122 M-N11
Hibbard Av CQT 165 U32
Hibiscus Ct ABT 251 U79
Hickey Dr CQT 165 W35-36
Hickory Ct BUR 164 W23
Hickory Dr PMD 145 P35
Hickory La ABT 251 U79
Hickory St PCQ 146 T41
Hideaway Bay SUR 266 W39
Hidhurst Pl WVA 122 K13
Hie Av CQT 165 X34
Hiebert St CHL 213 E8
Higgins Ct MAP 167 Y51
Higginson Cr ABT 270 W76
Higginson Rd CHL 233 K6-8
High Dr ABT 250 S-T78
High St CHL 233 M6
High St WRK 265 W36 X36
High St, The CQT 145 S38
High Park Av SUR 246 S39-40
High Point Dr WHS 401 H-J2
High Rock Passage WVA 121 K-L2
High View Pl PMD 145 T32
Highbury St VAN 142 T8 162 U-W8 W8 X8 X-Y8
Highfield Cr ABT 250 U77
Highfield Dr BUR 144 R-S24
Highgate St VAN 163 X18
Highland Av ABT 250 S74
Highland Blvd DNV 123 K15
Highland Cr ANM 125 N33
Highland Dr CQT 146 Q40-41
Highland Dr WVA 122 J12 K11-12 K12
Highland Pl DNV 123 K15-16
Highland Pl WVA 122 J11-12
Highland Way PMD 145 S35-36
Highlands Way N SQM 301 E4
Highlands Way S SQM 301 E-F4
Highlawn Dr BUR 143 T22 163 U22 164 U23
Highroad Cr CHL 233 N8
Highview Pl LIO 101 C23-24
Highview Pl MAP 167 Y51
Highview St ABT 270 W75
Highway WVA 121 L3-4
Hilary Pl DNV 123 N21
Hilda St BUR 184 Z27
Hill Av BUR 164 X27 Y28
Hill Av MIS 210 H74
Hill Dr BUR 184 A25
Hill Dr DNV 124 M23
Hill St NEW 184 A27
Hill-Tout St ABT 250 U71
Hillcrest Av ABT 250 U72-73
Hillcrest Av DNV 122 K14
Hillcrest Av MIS 210 J71-72
Hillcrest Dr CHL 194 C-D10
Hillcrest Dr WHS 401 G2-3
Hillcrest La WHS 401 G2
Hillcrest St CQT 165 V-W35
Hillcrest St WVA 121 K-L6
Hillier St CHL 193 D6
Hillkeep Pl CHL 213 G1
Hillside Av CQT 165 Y34
Hillside Cr DEL 224 L29
Hillside Dr ABT 250 U75
Hillside Pl BUR 164 U28
Hillside Rd SUR 225 N31
Hillside Rd WVA 122 J12
Hillside St MAP 167 Y52
Hillview Cr ABT 270 V78
Hillview Ct SUR 246 T42
Hillview Pl SUR 246 T42
Hillview St BUR 164 V25-26
Hilton Dr CHL 213 G7
Hilton Rd SUR 185 B33-34 B34
Hinch Cr MAP 167 Y52-53
Hipwell Dr CHL 233 M5
Hixon Ct DNV 124 M25
Hixon Pl DNV 124 M25
Hockaday Pl CQT 146 Q39
Hockaday St CQT 146 Q39
Hockin Rd HOP 118 G43
Hocking Av CHL 213 F6-7
Hodgins Av CHL 213 E5-6
Hodson Pl MIS 210 H75
Hoffmann Way PTM 186 B46
Hogarth Dr RMD 202 J11
Hogarth Pl RMD 202 J11 222 K11
Holborn St CQT 165 W32
Holdom Av N BUR 144 S24
Holdom Av S BUR 144 S-T24 164 U24
Holdsworth Pl CQT 146 R39-40
Holiday Av MIS 210 H72
Holland Av ABT 270 V75
Holland Av PCQ 166 W42
Holland St NEW 184 B27
Holland St VAN 162 X-Y8
Hollis Pl BUR 184 A23
Hollister Pl MIS 210 G76
Holly CQT 145 S38 146 S39
Holly Av NEW 184 C28
Holly Dr CQT 165 V-W37
Holly Dr PMD 145 Q35
Holly Rd KNT 175 W18-19
Holly St ABT 250 U72 270 V72
Holly St BUR 184 Z26
Holly St CHL 213 E8
Holly St MAP 167 Y50 187 A50 Z50
Holly Park Ct DEL 243 Q19

Holly Park Dr *DEL* . . . . . . 243 Q19
Holly Park La *SUR* . . . . . 185 C36-37
Holly Park Pl *DEL* . . . . . . 243 Q19
Holly Park Wynd *DEL* . . . . . 243 Q19
Hollybank Dr *RMD* . . . . . . 202 J10
Hollyberry Ct *ABT* . . . . . . 270 V76
Hollybridge Way *RMD* . . . . 202 E11
Hollybrook St *CQT* . . . . . . 146 R40
Hollycroft Dr *RMD* . . . . . . 202 J10
Hollycroft Gt *RMD* . . . . . . 202 J10
Hollyfield Av *RMD* . . . . . . 202 J10
Hollyhock La *VAN* . . 183 A20 B19-20
Hollymount Dr *RMD* 202 J10 222 K10
Hollymount Gt *RMD* . . . . . . 202 J10
Hollywell Dr *RMD* . . . . . . 202 J10
Hollywood Av *ABT* . . . . . 250 U73
Hollywood Dr *RMD* . . . . . . 202 J10
Holmbury Pl *WVA* . . . . . 122 K-L12
Holmes St *BUR* . . . . . . . 164 X30
Holmes St *NEW* . . . . . . . 164 X30
Holstein St *SUR* . . . . . . . 226 M41
Holt Av *RMD* . . . . . . . . . 202 F10
Holt Rd (120A St) *SUR* . . . 205 F31
Holtby St *CQT* . . . . . . . . 146 S41
Holyrood Av *MAP* . . . . . . 187 A53
Holyrood Rd *DNV* . . . . . . 123 L17
Homer Mews *VAN* . . . 10 K36 142 T13
Homer Pl *CHL* . . . . . . . . 213 F5
Homer St *VAN* 11 H38 J37 142 S14 T13
Homestead Cr *ABT* . . . . . 250 S71
Homesteader Ct *PCQ* . . . . 165 Y38
Homesteader Way *PCQ* . . . 165 Y38
Homeview St *ABT* . . . . . . 250 U75
Homfeld Pl *PCQ* . . . . . 166 V-W40
Honey La *SQM* . . . . . . . . 301 B2
Honeydew Dr *PTM* . . . . . . 187 Z47
Honeysuckle Dr *CHL* . . . . 213 F-G1
Honeysuckle La *CQT* . . . . 145 R36
Honeysuckle Pl *DNV* . . . . 103 H15
Hong Kong Dr *CHL* . . . . 233 N5-6
Hood Av *MIS* . . . . . . . . . 210 G73
Hood Rd *FRA* . . . . . . . . . 233 P8
Hood Rd *SQM* . . . . . . . . . 301 E3
Hood St *MAP* . . . . . . . . . 187 Z50
Hooge Rd *CHL* . . . . . . . . 233 N1
Hopcott Rd *DEL* . . . . . . . 203 J20
Hope Pl *HHS* . . . . . . . . . 155 R19
Hope Rd *DNV* . . . . . . . . . 122 M14
Hope Rd *SQM* . . . . . . . . . 301 B1
Hope St *HOP* . . . . . . . . 118 D-E44
Hope St *PMD* . . . . . 145 T32-33 T34
Hope River Rd *CHL*
. . . . . . . . . . . 193 C8 D7-8 194 C9-10
Hopedale Av *ABT* . . . . . . 250 T72
Hopedale Rd *CHL* . 213 J1 233 K-M1
Hopedale Rd E *CHL* . . . . . 233 N1
Hopedale Rd W *CHL* . . . . . 233 N1
Horizon St *ABT* . . . . . . . 270 V75
Horley St *VAN* . . . . . . . . 163 X19
Horn St *ABT* . . . . . . . . . 250 S74
Hornby Dr *DEL* . . . . . . 224 P26-29
Hornby St *CQT* . . . . . . . 146 R-S39
Hornby St *VAN* . . 10 H-J36 142 S-T13
Horne St *BUR* . . . . . . . . 164 W29
Horne St *MIS* 210 H74-75 J75 230 K75
Horseshoe Pl *RMD* . . . . . 223 L15
Horseshoe Way *RMD* . . . . 223 K-L15
Horstman La *WHS* . . . . 401 E5 S23
Horstman Pl *WHS* . . . . 401 E5 S-T23
Hoskins Pl *DNV* . . . . . . . 123 L20
Hoskins Rd *DNV* . . 123 J-K20 K-M20
Hoskins St *DEL* . . . . . . 203 H-J22
Hosmer Av *VAN* . . . . . . . 162 V11
Hosmer Ct *CQT* . . . . . . . 165 U38
Hospital La *UEL* . . . . . . . 161 U4
Hospital Pl *SQM* . . . . . . . 301 J-K2
Hospital St *NEW* . . . . . . 164 Y30
Hospital St *WRK* . . . . . . 265 W38
Hot Springs Rd *HHS* . . . . 155 P-Q19
Hot Springs Rd *KNT*.
. . . . . . . . . . 155 S-T19 175 U-V19
Hoult St *NEW* . . . . . . . 164 X-Y30
Housman Pl *RMD* . . . . . . 222 K11
Housman St *RMD* . . 202 J11 222 K11
Houston La *LGT* . . . . . . . 207 F53
Howard Av N *BUR* . . . . 144 S23-24
Howard Av S *BUR* .
. . . . . . . . 144 S23-24 T23 T23 164 U23
Howard Cr *CHL* . . . . . . . 213 F8
Howard Ct *WVA* . . . . . . . 121 K3
Howard Pl *DEL* . . . . . . . 224 L29
Howard Pl *RMD* . . . . . . . 202 E14
Howay St *NEW* . . . . . . . 184 A28

Howe St *VAN* . . 11 G38 H37 142 S13-14
Howe Sound La *WVA* . . . . 121 L2-3
Howell Ct *RMD* . . . . . . . 183 D15
Howes St *NEW* . . . . . . 184 D26-27
Howie Av *CQT* . . . . . . . . 165 W32-33
Howison Av *MAP* . . . . . . 187 Z51
Howse Pl *CQT* . . . . . . . . 165 W33
Hoy St *CQT* . . . 145 T37 165 U37 U38
Hoy St *VAN* . . . . . . . 163 W20 X20
Hoylake Av *VAN* . . . . . . . 183 A18
Huber Dr *PCQ* . . . . . . . . 146 S42
Hubert St *BUR* . . . . . . . . 184 Z26
Huckleberry La *DNV* . . . . 103 H15
Huckleberry La *PMD* . . 145 R34-35
Huckleberry Pl *CHL* . . . . . 213 F-G2
Huckleberry Pl *DNV* . . . . 103 H15
Hudson Av *RMD* . . . . . . . 182 C11
Hudson Ct *WVA* . . . . . . . 122 K9
Hudson Rd *CHL* . . . . . . . 233 M8
Hudson St *CQT* . . . . . . 145 R-S37
Hudson St *VAN*.
. . . . . 162 V-W12 X-Y12 182 A-B12 Z12
Hudson Bay St *HOP* . . 118 E44-45
Hudson Bay St *LGT* . . . . . 207 F54
Huff Blvd *DEL* . . . . . . . . 224 K29
Huggins Av *ABT* . . . . . . . 250 T75
Hugh St *PMD* . . . . . . . . 145 T34
Hughes Pl *PCQ* . . . . . . . 146 T39
Hughes Ter *MIS* . . . . . . . 210 H75
Hull Ct *CQT* . . . . . . . . . 145 T36
Hull St *VAN* . . . . . . . . 163 V17-18
Hum-Lu-Sum Dr *VAN* . . . . 162 Y8
Humber Cr *PCQ* . . . . . . . 166 W39
Humber Pl *DEL* . . . . . . 204 F26-27
Humberside Av *SUR* . . . . 246 S39
Hume Av *DEL* . . . . . . . . 223 K21
Hume St *NEW* . . . . . . . . 184 D26
Humm St *VAN* . . . . . . . . 183 Z18
Hummel St *BUR* . . . . . . . 164 U25
Hummingbird Dr *ANM* . . 145 Q34-35
Hummingbird Dr *RMD* . . . 222 K10
Hummingbird Pl *SUR* . . . . 185 B37
Hummingbird Pl *VAN* 183 A20 B19-20
Humphries Av *BUR* . 164 Y26 184 Z26
Humphries Ct *BUR* . . . . . 184 Z27
Humphries Pl *BUR* . . . . . 164 Y25
Humphrys Dr *HOP* . . . . . 118 N42
Hunt St *RMD* . . . . . . . . . 222 K8
Hunter Ct *BUR* . . . . . . 164 V-W27
Hunter Pl *MAP* . . . . . . . 187 Z49
Hunter Pl *SQM* . . . . . . . 301 J2
Hunter Pl *SUR* . . . . . . . . 226 M44
Hunter Rd *DEL* . . . . . . . 263 X17
Hunter St *BUR* . . . . . . 164 W27-28
Hunter St *DNV* . . . . . . . 143 P20
Huntingdon Cr *DNV* 124 N26 144 P26
Huntingdon Rd *ABT* . . 270 X71-75
Huntington Pl *PCQ* . . . . . 165 U38
Huntleigh Cr *DNV* . . . . 144 P23-24
Huntleigh Ct *DNV* . . . . . 144 P24
Huntley Av *SUR* . . . . . . 205 E33
Hurd St *MIS* . . . . . . . . 210 H-J72
Hurdle Cr *SUR* . . . . . . . 205 J32
Huron Ct *CQT* . . 145 T35 165 U35
Huron Mews *VAN* . . . 183 A19 Z19
Huron St *CHL* . . . . . . . . 213 J6
Hurst Av *VAN* . . . . . . . 183 Z20-21
Hurst Cr *ABT* . . . . . . . . 250 S77
Hurst Pl *VAN* . . . . . . . . 183 Z20
Hurst St *BUR* . . . 183 Z21 Z21-22
Huston Rd *DEL* . . . . . . . 203 H22
Hutcherson La *DEL* . . . . . 243 Q17
Hutchinson Pl *PCQ* . . 166 W39-40
Huxley Av *BUR* . . . . . . . 163 W22
Hyack Dr *VAN* . . . . . . . . 183 A20
Hyannis Dr *DNV* . . . . . . 124 M23
Hyannis Pt *DNV* . . . . . . 123 M22
Hyatt Pl *ABT* . . . . . . . . 250 U77
Hycrest Dr *BUR* . . . . . . . 164 U29
Hycrest Pl *ABT* . . . . . . . 250 U77
Hycroft Rd *WVA* . . . . . . 101 F-G1
Hycroft St *PMD* . . . . 145 R34-35
Hyde St *BUR* . . . . . . . . 164 V24
Hyde St *MIS* . . . . . . . . 210 H74
Hyde Park Pl *CQT* . . . . . 146 R40
Hylan Av *ABT* . . . . . . . 250 U72-73
Hyland Creek *LGT* . . . 207 F50-51
Hyland Dr *DEL* . . . . . . . 224 L30
Hyland Pl *DEL* . . . . . . . 224 L30
Hyland Rd *SUR* . . . 225 K-L34 L35 L37

Hymar Dr *CHL* . . . . . . . 193 C8
Hypwell Pl *CHL* . . . . . . . 233 M5
Hythe Av N *BUR* . . . . . . 144 S23
Hythe Av S *BUR* . . . . . . 144 S23

**I**

Idylwood Pl *WHS* . . . . . . 401 C2-3
Ihles Av *MIS* . . . . . . . . . 210 F75
Ikwikus Rd *WVA* . . . . . 122 M-N13
Immel St *ABT* . . . . . . . 250 S-T77
Imperial Av *PCQ* . . . . . . 166 W39
Imperial Av *WVA* . . . . . . 101 G1
Imperial Dr *RMD* . . . . . . 222 L10
Imperial Gt *DEL* . . . . . . 263 W16
Imperial Pl *ABT* . . . . . . 250 U71
Imperial St *ABT* . . . . . . 250 U71
Imperial St *BUR*.
. . . 164 Y26 183 Z21-22 184 Z23-24 Z26
Imperial St *CHL* . . . . . . 194 C10
Indian Rd *ABT* . . . . . . . 251 T83
Indian Fort Dr *SUR* . . . . 265 V31
Indian River Dr *DNV* . . . . 124 M25
Indian River Dr *DNV*.
. . . . . . . . 124 L27-28 L-M26 M-N25
Industrial Av *ABT* . . . . . 250 S76
Industrial Av *LGC* . . 227 M47 N48
Industrial Av *PCQ* . . . . . 166 W40
Industrial Av *VAN* . . 11 K41 163 V15
Industrial Rd *KNT* . . . . 175 W-X22
Industrial Rd *SUR* . . . . . 185 A31
Industrial Way *ABT* . . . . 270 Y77
Industrial Way *CHL* . . . . 213 H1-2
Industrial Way *SQM* . . . . 301 H1-2
Ingersoll Av *PMD* . . . . 145 T31-32
Ingleside Ct *BUR* . . . . . 164 V27
Ingleton Av *BUR*.
. . . . 143 R21 S-T21 163 U21 V21 W21
Inglewood Av *WVA*.
. . . . . . 122 L10-12 L12-13 L9-10
Inglewood Cr *CHL* . . . . 193 D7-8
Inglewood Pl *DEL* . . . . . 224 M30
Inglewood Pl *WVA* . . . . 122 L13
Inglis Dr *RMD* . . . . . . . 202 E10
Inkman Rd *KNT* . . . . . 175 W20
Inlet Cr *DNV* . . . . . . . . 124 N25
Inlet Dr *BUR* . . . . . . . . 144 S26
Inlet St *CQT* . . . . . . . . 145 S38
Inman Av *BUR* . . . . . 163 W21 X21
Inman Cl *BUR* . . . . . . . . 163 W21
Innsbruck Dr *WHS* . . . . . 401 H2
Innsmoor Pl *BUR* . . . . 164 X-Y27
Insley Av *CHL* . . . . . . . 233 L5
Institute Rd *DNV* . . . . . . 123 L20
Inter River Park Rd *DNV* 123 N20-21
International Av *ABT* . . . . 270 Z77
International Pl *RMD* . . . 203 E17
Invergarry Av *BUR* . . . . 144 S25
Inverness Pl *PCQ* . . . . . 146 T42
Inverness Pl *SUR* . . . . . 205 F33
Inverness St *ABT* . . . . . 250 S74
Inverness St *PCQ* . . . . 146 S-T42
Inverness St *VAN*.
. . . . . . 163 V-X16 X-Y16 183 A16 Z16
Ioco Rd *PMD* . . 145 Q31-32 R34 S35
Iona Dr *UEL* . . . . . . . . . 161 T3-4
Iona Pl *SUR* . . . . . . . . 205 E31
Ireland Av *MIS* . . . . . . . 210 G77
Irene Av *CHL* . . . . . . . . 233 L6
Irene Pl *DNV* . . . . . . . . 123 J21
Iris Av *BUR* . . . . . . . . . 164 W24
Iris Dr *CQT* . . . . . . . . . 165 V37
Iris Pl *CHL* . . . . . . . . . 233 M6
Iris Pl *SUR* . . . . . . . . . 265 V38
Irmin St *BUR*. 183 A21 A21-22 A22 A22
. . . . . . . . . . . 184 A23 A23 A24
Iron Ct *DNV* . . . . . . . 124 M-N25
Ironwood *CQT* . . . . . . . 146 S39
Ironwood Ct *PMD* . . 145 R35-36
Ironwood Pl *DEL* . . . . . . 263 Y18
Ironwork Passage *VAN* . . 162 U13
Irvine Av *CQT* . . . . . . . 166 V39
Irvine St *CQT* . . . . . . . 165 U38
Irving St *BUR* . . . 164 Y23 Y23-24
Irving St *MAP* . . . 167 Y48 187 Z48
Irwin Rd *DEL* . . . . . . 244 Q-R28
Isaac Ct *MAP* . . . 167 Y51 Y51-52
Isabel Pl *VAN* . . . . . . . 182 A11
Island Av *VAN* . . . . . . . 183 A17
Island Park Walk *VAN*.
. . . . . 10 K34-35 142 T12 162 U12
Isleview Pl *LIO* . . . . . . . 101 B23
Isleview Rd *WVA* . . . . . . 101 F1
Israel Av *MIS* . . . . . . . 210 H71

Ito Pl *MIS* . . . . . . . . . . 210 H74
Ivanhoe St *VAN* . . . . . . 163 X-Y19
Ivar Pl *BUR* . . . . . . . . 164 W-X23
Iverson Cr *DEL* . . . . . . . 204 G27
Ivy Av *BUR* . . . . . . . . . 183 B21
Ivy Av *CHL* . . . . . . . . . 233 K7
Ivy Av *CQT* . . . . . . . . . 165 V31
Ivy Ct *ABT* . . . . . . . . . 250 S78
Ivy Ct *MIS* . . . . . . . . . 210 H75
Ivywood Pl *DEL* . . . . . . 224 M30
Izon Ct *MAP* . . . . . . . . 167 Y52

**J**

Jacana Av *PCQ* . . . . . . 166 X39-40
Jack Adams Rd *MAP* . . . . 187 B47
Jack Bell Dr *RMD* . . 183 D16 203 E16
Jack Mahoney Pl *NEW* . . . 184 Z29
Jackson Av *VAN* . . 11 G-J41 143 S-T15
Jackson Cr *NEW* . . . . . . 164 Y29
Jackson St *ABT* . . . 270 V74 W74
Jackson St *CHL* . . . . . . 213 E5-6
Jackson St *CQT* . . . . . . 165 X31
Jackson Way *DEL* . . . . . 263 X18
Jacobs Rd *PMD* . . . . . . 145 R34
Jacobs Rd *WVA* . . . . . . 122 N13
Jacobson Way *RMD* . . . 223 K15-16
Jacombs Rd *RMD* . 183 D16 203 E16
Jade Ct *RMD* . . . . . . . . 202 F10
Jade Dr *ABT* . . . . . . . . 251 U79
Jade Manor *DEL* . . . . . . 223 P17
Jade Pl *CQT* . . . . . . . . 145 Q36
Jade Tree Ct *VAN* . . . . . 183 A20
James Av *CQT* . . . . . . . 165 X32
James Pl *DEL* . . . . . . 204 F28-29
James Rd *PMD* . . . . 145 T34-35
James Rd E *DNV* . . . . 123 L17-18
James St *ABT* . . . . . . . 250 U73
James St *BUR* . . . . . . . 163 Y21-22
James St *MIS* . . . . . . . . 210 J74
James St *VAN* . 162 X14 163 W15 X15
James Walk *VAN* . . . . . 162 X14
Jamieson Ct *NEW* . . 184 A30 Z30
Jane St *PCQ* . . . . . . . . 165 U38
Jane St *PMD* . . . . . . . 145 T33-34
Janis St *CHL* . . . . . . . . 233 M5
Janzen Av *MIS* . . . . . 210 G73-74
Janzen St *ABT* . . . . 250 U71-72
Japonica Pl *CQT* . . . . . . 145 Q37
Jardine St *NEW* . . . . . . 184 D26
Jarvis St *CQT* . . . . . . . 165 U32
Jaskow Dr *RMD* . . . . . . 202 H10
Jaskow Gt *RMD* . . . . . . 202 H10
Jaskow Pl *RMD* . . . . . . 202 H10
Jasmine Ct *CQT* . . . . . . 145 R36
Jasper Av *MIS* . . . . . . . 210 H77
Jasper Cr *VAN* . . . . . . . 183 A17
Jasper Ct *ABT* . . . . . . . 250 U73
Jasper Ct *CQT* . . . . . . . 165 W34
Jasper Dr *CHL* . . . . . . . 213 J5
Jasper Ter *MIS* . . . . . . . 210 H77
Jay Cr *SQM* . . . . . . . . . 301 D4
Jay Cr *SUR* . . . . . . . . . 185 B37
Jay Pl *SQM* . . . . . . . . . 301 D4
Jean Ct *ABT* . . . . . . . . 250 T71
Jedburgh Pl *SUR* . . . 205 F32-33
Jefferson Av *CQT* . . . . . 164 U30
Jefferson Av *WVA*.
. . . . . . . . 122 L10 L11 L11-12 L9-10
Jellicoe St *VAN* . . . . . . 183 A-B19
Jennings St *MIS* . . . . . . 210 G74
Jenny Lewis Av *LGT* . . . 207 E53
Jensen Av *PCQ* . . . . . . 146 T40
Jensen Dr *RMD* . . . . 203 E15-16
Jensen Gt *RMD* . . . 183 D16 203 E16
Jensen Pl *BUR* . . . . . . . 164 W27
Jensen St *NEW* . . . . . . 184 C28
Jericho Cir *VAN* . . . 142 T7 162 U7
Jericho Rd *RMD* . . . . 182 C-D10
Jerome Dr *DNV* . . . 123 J-K21
Jersey Av *BUR* . . . . . 163 X-Y21
Jersey Dr *SUR* . . . . . . 226 M41
Jervis Cr *ABT* . . . . . 250 S-T72
Jervis Ct *ABT* . . . . . 250 S-T72
Jervis Mews *VAN* . . 11 F37 142 R13
Jervis St *PCQ* . . . 145 T38 165 U38
Jervis St *VAN* . . 10 F36 G-H35 11 F37
. . . . . . . . . 142 R13 S12 S12-13
Jesmond Av *RMD* . . . . 202 H-J8
Jesperson Rd *CHL* . . . . 194 A12
Jewel Av *CHL* . . . . . . . 233 L6
Jewel Ct *ABT* . . . . . . . 251 U79
Jibset Bay *DEL* . . . . . . 223 N16
Jimmie Rd *CHL* . . . . . 213 F4-5

Joan St *ABT* . . . . . . . . 250 T72
Joe Sakic Way *BUR* . . . . 164 V25
Joffre Av *BUR* . . 183 A21 B21 Z21
John Pl *CHL* . . . . . . . 233 K7-8
John St *VAN* . . . . . . . . 163 W15
Johnson Av *RMD* . . . . . 202 F8
Johnson Ct *CQT* . . . . . . 145 R37
Johnson Rd *HOP* . . . . . 118 D48
Johnson Rd *KNT* . . . . . 175 X22
Johnson St *CHL* . . . . . . 193 D8
Johnson St *CQT* . . . 145 Q-T37
Johnson Wynd *DEL* . . . . 204 G27
Johnston Rd *WRK* . . . 265 W-X37
Johnston St *NEW* . . . . . 184 C27
Johnston St *VAN*.
. . . . . . . . 10 K35 142 T12 162 U12
Jones Av *CNV* . . . 123 L16 M-N16
Jones Av *DNV* . . . . . . . 123 L16
Jones Dr *CHL* . . . . . . . 194 C-D11
Jones Rd *RMD* . . . . . 202 G12-13
Jones Ter *MIS* . . . . . . . 210 F-G77
Jonquil Ct *ABT* . . . . . . 251 U79
Jordan Dr *BUR* . . . . . . 164 U25
Jordan La *WHS* . . . . . . 401 H1
Jordan St *CQT* . . . . . . 145 R37
Joseph Pl *PCQ* . . . . . . 146 S42
Joyce Av *ABT* . . . . . . . 270 V72
Joyce Dr *FRA* . . . . . . . 253 R6
Joyce St *CQT* . . . . . . . 165 W32
Joyce St *VAN* . . . 163 X20 Y19-20
Joyner Pl *PTM* . . 186 A46 187 A47
Jubilee Av *BUR* . . . 184 A23 Z23
Jubilee Ct *DNV* . . . . . . 124 N25
Judd Ct *CQT* . . . . . . . . 165 U38
Judd Rd *SQM* . . . . . . . 301 C1-3
Judd Ter *MIS* . . . . . . . 210 F73
Judith Av *CHL* . . . . . . . 233 L6
Judith St *MIS* . . . . . . . 210 G74
Julian Av *CQT* . . . . . . . 145 R38
Junction Av *ABT* . . . . . 249 T63
June Cr *PCQ* . . . . . . . . 165 X38
Juneau St *BUR* . . . . . . 163 U22
Juniper *CQT* . . . . . . . . 146 S39
Juniper Av *PCQ* . . . . . . 146 T41
Juniper Cr *ABT* . . . . . . 250 S76
Juniper Cr *SQM* . . . . . . 301 J3
Juniper Dr *RMD* . . . . . . 202 H11
Juniper Gt *RMD* . . . . . . 202 H11
Juniper Pl *DEL* . . . . . . 263 Y17
Juniper Pl *HHS* . . . . . . 155 Q19
Juniper Pl *PMD* . . . . . . 145 R36
Juniper Pl *WHS* . . . . . . 401 F3
Juniper St *CHL* . . . . . . 193 D7
Juniper St *MIS* . . . . . 210 H-J74
Jura Cr *SQM* . . . . . . . . 301 E4-5
Justice Way *ABT* . . . . 250 T-U72

**K**

K de K Ct *NEW* . . . . . . 184 B-C29
Kadenwood Dr *WHS* . . . 401 H2 J1-2
Kadlec Ct *WVA* . . . . . . 122 J-K9
Kadota Dr *DEL* . . . . . . 263 X16
Kahana Pl *ABT* . . . . . . 251 U79
Kaiser St *CQT* . . . . . 145 S36-37
Kalamalka Cr *RMD* . . . . 202 F11
Kalamalka Dr *CQT* . . . . 165 V37
Kaleigh Ct *ABT* . . . . . . 251 R79
Kalmar Rd *SUR* . . . 185 B34-35
Kalodon Rd *SQM* . . . . 301 E-F3
Kalyk Av *BUR* . . . . . . . 163 V-W21
Kalyna Dr *KNT* . . . . . . 175 X20
Kamloops Pl *PCQ* . . . . . 146 T41
Kamloops St *NEW* . . . . 184 B27-28
Kamloops St *VAN*.
. . . . . . 143 R-T18 163 U18 U-V18 V18 W18
Kamloops St N *VAN* . . . 143 R-S18
Kanaka St *LGT* . . . . . . 207 E53
Kanaka Way *MAP* . . . . . 187 B54
Kaptey Av *CQT* . . . 165 X34-35
Karen Cr *WHS* . . . . . . 401 H2
Karen Dr *CHL* . . . . . . . 213 F8
Karen Dr *FRA* . . . . . . . 253 R6
Karen St *BUR* . . . . . . . 164 U25
Karley Cr *CQT* . . . . . . 146 R39
Karp Ct *CQT* . . . . . . . 165 W33
Karr Pl *DEL* . . . . . . . . 204 G27
Karrman Av *BUR* . . . . . 164 Y29
Kartner Rd *RMD* . . . . 203 E-F20
Kaslo Ct *ABT* . . . . . . . 270 W75
Kaslo St *VAN* . 143 R-T19 163 U-W19
Kaslo St N *VAN* . . . . . 143 R-S19
Kaslo Ter *ABT* . . . . . . 270 W75
Kathleen Av *BUR* . . . . . 163 Y22

Kathleen Dr CHL . . . . . . . 233 M5
Kathleen Pl WHS . . . . . . 401 H1-2
Katzie Rd MAP . . . . 186 B46 187 B47
Katzie Rd PTM. . . . . . . . . . 186 A46
Kaw Rd HOP. . . . . . . . . . 118 D48
Kawkawa Lake Rd HOP. . . . . . . .
. . . . . . . . . . 118 D48 E45-47
Kawtin Rd WVA . . . . . . . . 122 N13
Kay Av ABT . . . . . . . . . . 270 V24
Kaylela Pl DNV . . . . . . . . 143 P20
Kaymar Dr BUR . . . . . . . . 183 A21
Ke Kait Pl VAN. . . . . . . . . 162 Y8
Keary St NEW . . . . 164 Y30 165 Y31
Keats Ct ABT . . . . . . . 270 W74-75
Keats Rd DNV . . . . . . . . 123 N22
Keats St ABT . . . . . . . . . 270 W75
Kebet Way PCQ . . . . . . 166 X40-41
Keefer Av RMD . . . . . . . . 202 G13
Keefer Pl VAN. . . . . . . 11 H39-40
Keefer St VAN. . . . . . . . . . . . .
. . . 11 H39-41 142 S14 143 S15-16 S16
Keeping Rd ABT . . . . . . . . 251 Q82
Keets Dr CQT . . . . . . . . . 146 R40
Keil Cr WRK . . . . . 265 X38 266 X39
Keil St WRK . . . . . 265 W38 266 W39
Keith Dr CQT . . . . . . . . . 146 R40
Keith Dr VAN. . . . . . . . . 163 U-V16
Keith Pl CQT . . . . . . . 146 R39-40
Keith Pl WVA . . . . . . . . . 122 M13
Keith Rd DNV . . . . . . . . . 123 M15
Keith Rd (Ambleside) WVA. . . . . .
. . . . . . . . . . . . . . 122 M11-13
Keith Rd (Cypress Park) WVA . . . .
. . 121 J3 J-K3 K4 K-L4
Keith Rd (Horseshoe Bay) WVA. . . .
. . . . . . . . . . . . . . . . 101 G2
Keith Rd E CNV. . . . . . . . . . . .
. . . . . . 123 N17 143 P17 P17-18
Keith Rd E DNV. . . . . . 143 P19-21
Keith Rd W CNV . . . . . 123 N16-17
Keith Rd W DNV . . . . . . . 122 M14
Keith St BUR . . . 183 B21 184 A23-24
Keith Wilson Rd CHL . . . . 233 M3-6
Kelleher St ABT . . . 210 J77 230 K77
Kelly Av PCQ . . . . 165 V38 166 V39
Kelly Dr DEL . . . . . . . . . 243 Q15
Kelly Pl DEL . . . . . . . . . 243 Q15
Kelly Rd ABT . . . . . . . . . 251 T83
Kelly Rd BEL . . . . . . . . . 124 N29
Kelly St NEW . . . . . . . . . 164 Y30
Kelmer Cr ABT . . . . . . . . 270 V76
Kelmore Rd RMD . . . . . . . 202 H8-9
Kelowna St VAN . . . . . . . 143 T19
Kelso Ct CQT . . . . . . . . . 165 W34
Kelvin St CQT . . . . . . . . 165 U32
Kelvin Grove Way LIO. . . . 101 C23
Kemi Pl MAP . . . . . . . . . 167 Y52
Kemp St BUR . . . . . . . . . 163 Y22
Kempley Ct ABT . . . . . . . 270 W75
Kempson Cr DEL . . . . . . . 224 L29
Kempton Pl VAN . . . . . 183 Z18-19
Kemsley Av CQT . . . . . . . 165 U31
Kendal Pl DNV. . . . . . . . 122 K14
Kendale Ct BUR . . . . . . . 164 U25
Kendale Pl ABT . . . . . . . 270 V73
Kendale Pl DEL . . . . . . . 204 E29
Kendale View DEL . . . . . . 204 E29
Kendale Way DEL . . . . . . 204 E29
Kendrick La MAP . . . . . . . 167 Y53
Kendrick Loop MAP . . . 167 Y52-53
Kendrick Pl MAP . . . . . . . 167 Y53
Keneng Ct CQT . . . . . . . . 165 V33
Kenmore Dr SUR . . . . . . . 205 E34
Kennard Av CNV . . . . . . . 143 P19
Kennard Av DNV . . . . . . . 143 P19
Kennedy Av DNV. . . . . . . 123 L15
Kennedy Pl RMD . . . . . . . 202 H10
Kennedy Pl (124A St) SUR . 205 F31
Kennedy Rd PTM . . . . . . . . . . .
. . . . . 166 W43 X42 X42-43
Kennedy St NEW . . . . . 184 A-B28
Kennedy St PCQ . . . . . . . 146 T40
Kenneth Av BUR . . . . . . . 184 Z24
Kenney Av MIS . . . . . . . 210 H71-72
Kenney St CQT . . . . . 146 Q-R39
Kenny Ct BUR. . . . . . . . 183 Z21-22
Kensington Av BUR . . . . . . . . . .
. . . . 144 S-T24 S-T25 T24 T25
. . . 164 U24 U25 V25 V-W25
Kensington Cr DNV. . . . . . 123 K17
Kensington Cr PCQ. . . . . . 166 X39
Kensington Cr WVA . . . . . 121 K2-3
Kensington Ct ABT . . . . . . 251 R81
Kensington Ct DEL . . . . . . 243 Q19
Kensington Pl DEL . . . . . . 243 Q19
Kensington Pl PCQ . . . . . . 166 X39
Kensington Rd DNV123 K-L17 L17-18

Kenswood Dr CHL . . . . 194 C11 D10
Kent Av ABT . . . . . . . . . . 250 T77
Kent Av PCQ . . . . . . . . 146 S40-41
Kent Av NE VAN . . . . . . . . . . .
. . . . . . 183 A15-17 A-B19 B20
Kent Av NW VAN. . . 182 A-B14 B13
Kent Av SE VAN. . . . . . . . . . . .
. 182 B14 183 A16 A-B15 A-B17 B19 B20
Kent Av SW VAN182 B13 B13-14 B14
Kent Cr DEL . . . . . . . . . . 224 L29
Kent Rd CHL. . . . . . . . . . 193 C8
Kent St MAP . . . . . . . . . 187 B48
Kent St NEW . . . . . . . . . 164 Y30
Kent St WRK . . . . . . . . 265 W-X38
Kentwood St BUR . . . . . . 164 W27
Kenward Pl PCQ . . . . . . . 146 T41
Kenwood Rd WVA . . . . . 122 J12-13
Kereluk Rd HOP . . . . . . . 118 D48
Keremeos Ct UEL . . . . . . . 161 U4-5
Kerfoot Rd WVA. . . . . . . 265 W35
Kermode Cr CHL . . . . . . . 233 N7
Kern Av BUR . . . . . . . . . 184 A25
Kerr Av CHL. . . . . . . . . . 213 G-H6
Kerr Bay DEL . . . . . . . . . 204 J30
Kerr St VAN. . . . . . . . . . . . . .
. . 163 X-Y19 Y19 183 A-B19 Z19
Kerria Dr CQT. . . . . . . . . 165 W37
Kerrstead Pl DNV . . . . . . 123 L20
Kerry Cr MAP . . . . . . . . 167 Y51-52
Kerry Dr DEL . . . . . . . . . 263 Y16
Kerry Pl DEL . . . . . . . . . 263 Y16
Kerry Pl DNV. . . . . . . . . 123 K-L16
Kerrywood Cr BUR. . . . . . 164 W27
Kersland Dr VAN . . . . . . . 162 X14
Kerwan Av CQT . . . . . . . . 165 V33
Kerwan Pl CQT . . . . . . . . 165 V33
Kestrel Ct SUR . . . . . . . . 145 S36
Kestrel Ct SUR . . . . . . . . 205 H35
Kestrel Dr RMD . . . . . . . 222 K10
Kestrel Pl ABT . . . . . . . . 249 T69
Keswick Av BUR . . . . . . 164 V-W29
Ketch Ct CQT . . . . . . . . . 165 Y33
Ketch Pl ABT . . . . . . . . . 270 W75
Ketch Pl DEL . . . . . . . . 223 N16-17
Kettle Cr E SUR . . . . . 225 M-N38
Kettle Cr N SUR . . . . . . . 225 M37
Kettle Cr W SUR. . . . . . 225 M-N37
Kettle Valley Rd HOP . . . . 118 E47
Kettles Rd DEL . . . . . . . . 242 R13
Kettley Pl MIS . . . . . . . 210 H75-76
Kevin Pl VAN . . . . . . . . . 162 W7
Kew Dr SUR . . . . . . . . . 185 A-B37
Kew Rd WVA. . . . . . . . . 121 K2
Kew Cliff Rd WVA . . . . . . 121 K2
Key Rd KNT . . . . . . . . . 175 W20
Keys Pl ABT. . . . . . . . . . 270 V76
Keystone Av MIS . . . . . . 210 E71-72
Keystone Pl CQT. . . . . . . 145 P38
Keystone St VAN . . . . . . . 183 A20
Khatsilano Rd WVA. . . . . 122 N13
Khyber La WHS . . . . . . 401 J1 J99
Kicking Horse Way PMD . 145 R34
Kidd Rd SUR . . . . . . . . . 245 T31
Kielder Cr VAN . . . . . . 183 A19-21
Kiernan Dr CHL . . . . . . . 213 G6-7
Kilburn Pl SUR . . . . . . 225 K32-33
Kilby Ct RMD. . . . . . . . . 182 D14
Kilby Dr RMD . . . . . . . . 182 D13-14
Kilby St RMD. . . . . . . . . 182 D13
Kildare Cl SUR . . . . . . . 225 M38
Kildare Ct SUR . . . . . . . 225 M37-38
Kildare Dr SUR . . . . . . . 225 M37-38
Kildare Ter ABT . . . . . . . 270 W75
Kildonan Rd WVA . . . . . 102 H12-13
Kilgour Pl RMD . . . . . . . 202 H10
Kilkee Dr SUR. . . . . . . . 225 M38
Kilkee Pl SUR . . . . . . . . 225 M38
Kilkenny Dr DEL . . . . . . . 263 Y16
Kilkenny Dr SUR . . . . . 225 N37-38
Kilkenny Rd DNV. . . . . . . 123 L20
Killarney Dr CHL . . . . . . . 193 C-D8
Killarney Dr SUR . . . . . 225 M37-38
Killarney Pl SUR . . . . . . 225 M38
Killarney St PCQ . . . . . . . 146 S42
Killarney St VAN . . . . . . . . . . .
. . . . 163 X19 X-Y19 183 Z19
Killdeer Pl VAN. . . 183 A20-21 B19-20
Kilmarnock Ct DNV . . . . . 123 M20
Kilmarnock Pl DNV . . . . . 123 M20
Kilmer Pl DNV . . . . . . . . 123 K20
Kilmer Rd DNV . . . . . . 123 K19-21
Kilmer St PCQ . . . . 146 T41 166 U41

Kilmore Cl SUR . . . . . . . 225 N38
Kilmore Cr E SUR . . . . . 225 N38
Kilmore Cr W SUR . . . . . 225 N38
Kilmore Ct SUR . . . . . . . 225 N38
Kilmore Pl SUR . . . . . . . 225 N38
Kilrea Cr BUR . . . . . . . 164 V26-27
Kilrea Pl BUR. . . . . . . . . 164 V26
Kim Pl CHL . . . . . . . . . . 233 M4-5
Kimball St MIS. . . . . . . . 210 G76
Kimberley Dr RMD . . . . . 222 K11
Kimberley St ABT . . . . . . 270 W75
Kimberly Pl CHL. . . . . . . 233 M4
Kincaid St BUR. . . . . . . . . . . . .
. . . 163 W21 164 W23-24 W24
Kindersley Dr SUR . . . . 185 B35-36
King Av CHL . . . . . . . . . . 193 D7
King Cr ABT . . . . . . . . . . 270 W76
King Rd ABT . . . . . . . . 270 W71-76
King Rd RMD . . . . . . . . 203 H-J15
King Rd SUR. . . . . . . . 185 A34-35
King St CQT. . . . . . . . . . 165 X32
King St DEL . . . . . . . . . . 243 R21
King St HOP. . . . . . . . . . 118 D-E44
King St LGT. . . . . . . . . . 207 F54
King Albert Av CQT. 165 W32-34 W35
King Edward Av UEL . . . . 162 W7
King Edward Av VAN. . . . 162 W11 W7
King Edward Av E VAN. 163 W15-17
King Edward Av W VAN. 162 W8-14
King Edward Pl DEL . . . 243 Q15-16
King Edward St CQT . . . 165 X-Y33
King George Hwy SUR. . . . . . . .
. . 185 A-B33 B32 D34 205 E34 H-J34
. . 225 K34 M34-35 N35 P35 245 T36 U37
. . . 265 V38 266 W39 X40
King George Hwy FG-E SUR . . . .
. . . . . . . . . . . . . . . 225 P36
King George Hwy FG-W SUR . . . .
. . . . . . . . . . . . . . . 225 P36
King Georges Way WVA . . . . . . . .
. . . . . . . 122 J13 K12 K12-13
Kingcome Av RMD. . . . . 203 H-J15
Kingcome Pl RMD. . . . . . 203 H15
Kingfisher Cr CQT. 145 P38 146 P39
Kingfisher Dr ABT . . . . . . 249 T70
Kingfisher Dr RMD . . . . . 222 K10
Kingfisher Pl ABT . . . . . . 249 T70
Kingfisher Pl DEL . . . . . . 263 Y17
Kinghorne Mews VAN . . . . . . . .
. . . . . . . . 10 J-K36 142 T13
Kings Av VAN. . . . . . . . . 163 W-X19
Kings Av WVA . . . . . . 122 L11 L9-10
Kings Ct PMD . . . . . . . . 145 S32
Kings Rd UEL . . . . . . . . . 161 U4
Kings Rd E DNV . 123 L17-18 L18-19
Kings Rd W DNV . . . . 123 L16-17
Kings Lynn St VAN . . . . . 163 Y20
Kingsborough St BUR. . . . 163 Y22
Kingsbridge Dr RMD. . . . . 203 H15
Kingsbrook Rd RMD. . . . . 203 H15
Kingsford Av BUR . . . . . . 164 U-V25
Kingsgrove Av RMD . . . . . 203 H15
Kingsland Ct BUR . . . . . . 164 U24
Kingsland Dr BUR . . . . . . 164 U24
Kingsley Cr HMD. . . . . . . 203 H15
Kingsley Ct RMD. . . . . . . 203 H15
Kingsley Ter ABT . . . . . . 270 W75
Kingston Pl SUR . . . . . . 205 G36
Kingston Rd UEL . . . . . . . 161 T4
Kingston St CQT . . . . . 146 Q-R41
Kingston St MAP. . . . . 187 A47 B48
Kingston St NEW. . . . . . . 184 A27
Kingsway BUR . . . . . . . . . . . . .
. . . . 163 Y21-22 164 Y23 Y23
. . . . 184 A27 Z24 Z25 Z27
Kingsway VAN. . . . . . . . . . . . . .
. . 163 V15-16 W17 X-W18 X19-20 Y20
Kingsway Av PCQ. . . . . . . . . . . .
. . 165 U38 166 U39 V39 V-W40 W42
Kinloch Pl ABT . . . . . . . . 251 R79
Kinloch Rd DNV . . . . . . . 124 N26
Kinross St VAN . . . . . . 183 A19-20 B20
Kinsac St CQT . . . . . . . . 165 U32
Kintyre Dr SQM . . . . . . . 301 E-F4
Kipling St ABT . . . . . . . . 270 W75
Kipp Av CHL . . . . . . . . . 213 E5-6
Kira Ct BUR. . . . . . . . . . 164 X23
Kirk Av ABT. . . . . . . . . . 270 W75
Kirk Pl DEL . . . . . . . . . . 243 Q16
Kirkland Rd DEL . . . . . . . 242 Q12
Kirkland St VAN . . . . . . . 163 Y20-21

Kirklyn St ABT. . . . . . . . . 270 W75
Kirkmond Cr RMD . . . . . . 202 J8
Kirkmond Rd RMD . . . . . . 202 H8
Kirkpatrick Av MIS . . . . 210 E76-77
Kirkpatrick Way WHS . . . . 401 D4
Kirkstone Pl DNV . . . . . . 123 M19
Kirkstone Rd DNV. . . . . . 123 M19
Kirkwood Dr DEL . . . . . . 263 W18
Kisbey Av BUR . . . . . . . . 164 Y24
Kitchen Rd CHL . . . . . . . 194 A-B10
Kitchen-Hall Rd CHL . . . . 194 A11
Kitchener Av PCQ . . 145 T38 146 T39
Kitchener St BUR . . . . . . . . . . .
. . . . 143 T21 T21-22 144 T24-26
Kitchener St VAN . . . . 143 T17-19
Kitcher Pl RMD . . . 182 D14 202 E14
Kite St MIS . . . . . . . . 210 H72-73
Kitsilano Div VAN . . . . . . 162 U10
Kittiwake Dr RMD . . . . . 222 K10
Kittson Pkwy DEL . . . . . . 224 L29
Klahanie Ct WVA . . . . . . 122 M13
Klahanie Dr PMD . . . 145 S35 T34-35
Klassen Ct PCQ. . . . . . . . 165 X38
Klassen Pl MAP. . . . . . . . 167 Y49
Klassen Rd HOP . . . . . . . 118 G41
Klenner Dr BUR . . . . . . . 164 X30
Knappen St PCQ . . . . . . . 166 W-X39
Kneale Pl BUR . . . . . . . . 164 V25
Knight Av MIS. . . . . . . . 210 H75-76
Knight Dr DEL . . . . . . . . 224 L30
Knight Rd CHL . . . . 213 H5-6 J6-7
Knight Rd RMD. . . . 183 C-D17 203 E17
Knight St VAN. . . . . . . . . . . . . .
. . . 163 V-Y17 183 A17 Z16 Z17
Knights Ct PCQ. . . . . . . . 166 X39
Knightswood Pl BUR . . . . 164 U27
Knockmaroon Rd WVA. . 122 K12-13
Knotts St MAP. . . . . . . . . 167 Y49
Knowle St PMD . . . . . . . . 145 S35
Knox Rd UEL . . . . . . . . . 161 T4
Knox St NEW . . . . . . . . . 164 Y30
Knox Ter ABT. . . . . . . . . 270 V78
Knox Way RMD . . . . . . 183 B17-18
Knudson Rd DEL . . . . . . . 204 E29
Koala Ct BUR . . . . . . . . . 164 Y26
Koerner Rd PTM. . . . . . 147 P47-48
Kokanee Pl VAN . . . . . . . 183 Z20
Kolthammer Cr WVA. . . . . 121 J2
Komarno Ct CQT. . . . . . . 165 U35
Kootenay Dr ABT . . . . . . 250 R78
Kootenay St VAN . . . . . . . . . . .
. . . . . . 143 S-T20 T20 163 U20 W20
Kootenay St N VAN. . . . . 143 R-S20
Kootenay Way WVA . . . . . . . . . .
. . . . . . 143 S-T20 T20 163 U20 W20
Korea Rd CHL. . . . . . . . . 233 N5
Kozier Dr RMD . . . . . . . . 202 J10
Kozier Gt RMD. . . . . . . . 202 J10
Kozier Pl RMD . . . . . . . . 222 K10
Kraft Cr BUR . . . . . . . . . 164 V26
Kraft Pl BUR . . . . . . . . 164 V26-27
Kristin Ct ABT . . . . . . . . 251 R79
Kudo Dr MIS . . . . . . . . . 210 G73
Kugler Av CQT . . . . . . 165 W34-35
Kullahun Dr VAN . . . . . . . 162 X7
Kuma Cr DEL . . . . . . . . . 262 X15
Kunimoto Ct MIS. 210 G75-76 H75-76
Kwantlen Ct NEW . . . . . . 184 Z30
Kwantlen Pl LGC . . . . . . . 227 M49
Kwantlen St RMD . . . . . . 202 E13
Kyle Ct WRK . . . . . . . . . 265 X38
Kyle St BUR. . . . . . . . . . 164 V26
Kyle St PMD . . . . . . . . . 145 T33
Kyle St (Garden Village) BUR. . . . .
. . . . . . . . . . . . . . . 163 W-X22

## L

Labelle Av CHL. . . . . . . . 213 F5-6
Labonte Av LGT. . . . . . . 207 H-J52
Laburnum Av ABT . . . 250 S78 S-T77
Laburnum Av PCQ . . . . . . 166 U41
Laburnum St VAN . 10 J-K33 142 T11
. . . . . . 162 X11 Y11 182 A11 Z11
Laburnum Park Pl DEL . 243 Q16-17
Lacerte La MIS . . . . . . . . 210 G73
Lacey Greene Way ABT . . . 251 U79
Lackner Cr RMD . . . . . . . 202 H10
Ladner Rd PTM . . . . . . 147 R49-50
Ladner St NEW . . . . . . . . 164 Y30
Ladner Trunk Rd DEL . . . . . . . . .
. . . . 223 P17 P18 P20 P21
. . . . 224 N30 P23-24 P28-29
. . . 243 Q17 Q18 Q20 Q21 244 Q23-24
Lafleur St PCQ. . . . . . . . 146 T39
Lagoon Dr VAN . . . 10 E34 142 R12

Laguna Ct NEW . . . . . . . 184 B-C28
Laidmore Rd RMD . . . . . . 202 H9
Laing Dr DNV . . . . . . . . 122 L14
Laird Pl VAN . . . . . . . . . 183 A19
Laity St MAP . . . . 167 Y50 187 Z50
Laka Dr RMD . . . . . . . . . 202 H10
Lakberg Cr HHS . . . . . . 155 Q19
Lake Dr CHL . . . . . . . . . 233 K7
Lake Way BUR . . . . . . . 184 Z24-25
Lake City Way BUR. . . . . . 164 V27
Lake Placid Rd WHS . . . . . 401 H1-2
Lakecrest La WHS . . . . . . 401 G2
Lakedale Av BUR. . . . . . 164 V-W28
Lakefield Dr BUR . . . . . 164 X26-27
Lakeland Dr BUR. . . . . . 164 V-W28
Lakeshore Dr CQT. . . . . . . 165 V33
Lakeshore Dr FRA . . . . . 253 R4-5
Lakeshore Dr WHS. . . . . . 401 A5
Lakeside Rd WHS . . . . . . 401 F-G2
Lakeview Av BUR . 164 Y25 184 Z25
Lakeview Cr ABT. . . . . . . 250 U74
Lakeview Cr HOP . . . . . . 118 E47
Lakeview Dr ABT. . . . . . . 251 T83
Lakeview St CQT . . . . . . 165 W35
Lakeview St VAN. . . . . . . . . . . .
. . . . . . . . . 143 S18 T18 163 U18
Lakewood Ct WHS . . . . . . 401 C3
Lakewood Dr VAN . . . . . . . . . . .
. . . . . . . 143 S18 T18 163 U18
Lakewood Dr N VAN . . . 143 S18
Lakewood Dr S VAN . . . . 163 V-W18
Lam Dr RMD . . . . . . . . . 202 F8
Lambert Cr DEL . . . . . . 224 L29-30
Lambert Way CQT . . 146 Q39-40
Lambeth Dr BUR . . . . . 164 Y25-26
Lamerton Av CQT . . . . . . 165 U33
Lamey's Mill Rd VAN. . . . 162 U12
Laminman Av MIS . . . . . 210 F73
Lamond Av ABT . . . . . . 250 U71-72
Lamond Av RMD . . . . . . 202 J8-9
Lamont Av MIS . . . . . . . 210 J72
Lampman Pl DNV . . . . . . 123 N22
Lamprey Dr PCQ . . . . . . . 166 W39
Lanark Pl SQM . . . . . . . . 301 E4
Lanark Pl SUR . . . . . . . . 205 F33
Lanark St CHL. . . . . . . . . 233 L5
Lanark St VAN. . . . . . . . . . . . . .
. . . 163 V-W17 W17 X17 X-Y17 183 Z17
Lancaster Cr RMD . . . . . 182 D11-12
Lancaster Ct CQT . . . . . . 146 Q40
Lancaster Dr CHL. . . . . . . 233 M4
Lancaster Pl PCQ . . 145 T38 165 U38
Lancaster Pl VAN . . . . . . 183 Z19
Lancaster St NEW. . . . . . . 184 A29
Lancaster St PCQ. . . 145 T38 165 U38
Lancaster St VAN . . . 163 Y19 183 Z19
Lancaster St WRK . . . . . . 265 W34
Lance Rd KNT . . . . . . . . 175 W20
Lancelot Pl RMD . . . . . . . 202 H9
Lancelot Dr RMD . . . . . 202 H9-10
Lancelot Gt RMD . . . . . . . 202 H9
Lancia Pl CQT . . . . . . . . 145 R37
Lancing Ct RMD . . . . . . . 202 G10
Lancing Pl RMD . . . . . . . 202 G10
Lancing Rd RMD . . . . . . . 202 G10
Landeau Pl ABT. . . . . . . . 250 T74
Landers Rd HOP . . . . . . 118 E43
Landmark Gt SUR . . . . . 226 M-N46
Landmark Way LGC . . . . . . . . . .
. . . . . . . . 226 M46 227 M47
Landmark Way SUR . . . . 226 M-N46
Landstrom Rd HOP. . . . . . 118 E43
Lane St BUR . . . . . . . . . 184 Z23
Lang Pl RMD. . . . . . . . . 202 G9
Langan Av PCQ . . . . . . . 166 W39-40
Langara Av VAN. . . . . . . 142 T7
Langara Ct CQT. . . . . . . . 145 T37
Langara St VAN. . . . . . . . 161 T6
Langdale Dr DNV. . . . . . . 122 J14
Langdon St ABT. . . . . . . 250 U72-73
Langford Av VAN . . . . . . 183 A20
Langley By-Pass LGC . . . . . . . . .
. . . 226 M46 227 M47-48 M-N49
Langley By-Pass SUR. . . 226 M-N46
Langley St BUR . . . . . . . 164 Y29
Langside Av CQT . . . . . . 165 V31
Langton Pl WVA . . . . . . . 122 J10
Langton Rd RMD . . . . . . 202 G10
Langtree Av RMD . . . . . . 202 K10
Langworthy St DNV . . . . 123 K20 K21
Lansdowne Dr CQT. . . . 145 Q-S36
Lansdowne Dr SUR. . . . . 185 A-B37
Lansdowne Rd RMD. . . . 202 E12-13
Larch Ct ANM. . . . . . . . . 145 Q34
Lantern Av DEL . . . . . . . 249 T63
Lapwing Cr MIS . . . . . . . 210 J72
Lapwing Cr RMD. . . . . . . 222 K10
Laramee Rd SQM . . . . . . 301 C1

Larch Av *CHL* . . . . . . . . . . 213 F7
Larch Av *MAP* . . . . . . . . . 167 W54
Larch St *ABT* . . . . . . . . 250 U76-77
Larch St *VAN* . . . . 162 U-V10 X-Y10
Larch Way *PCQ* . . . . . . . . 166 U41
Lariat Pl *ABT* . . . . . . . . . 250 T77
Lark Pl *SUR* . . . . . . . 185 B36-37
Lark Rd *CHL* . . . . . . . . . . 233 M6
Lark St *MIS* . . . . . . . . . 210 J72
Larkfield Dr *BUR* . . . . . . 164 U29
Larkhall Cr *DNV* . . . . . . 124 N23
Larkin Av *PCQ* . . . . . . . 145 T38
Larkin Ct *BUR* . . . . . . 164 U-V30
Larkin Dr *UEL* . . . . . . . . 161 V4
Larkspur Av *MIS* . . . . . . 210 E75
Larkspur Av *RMD* . . . . . 202 F9
Larkspur Ct *ABT* . . . . . . 251 U79
Larkspur Dr *PCQ* . . . . . . 166 U41
Larner Rd *SUR* . . . . . . . 185 B34
Laronde Dr *SUR* . . . 265 V-W33
Lars Rd *HOP* . . . . . . . . . 118 H42
Larson Cr *CNV* . . . . . . . 123 M16
Larson Pl *WVA* . . . . . . . 121 J2-3
Larson Rd *CNV* . . 123 L16 M-N16
Larson Rd *DEL* . . . . . . . 204 H29
Larson Rd *SUR* . . . . . . . 185 B31
Larter Av *CHL* . . . . . . . . 193 C7
Lasalle Ct *ABT* . . . . . 145 R-S37
LaSalle St *VAN* . . . . . . . 183 Z20
Lasko St *RMD* . . . . . . . 202 H-J10
Laslo Av *MIS* . . . . . . . . 210 E71
Lassam Rd *RMD* . . 202 J10 222 K10
Lasser Rd *PTM* . . . . . . . 186 B46
Latimer Av *CQT* . . . 165 W35-36
Latimer Pl *SUR* . . . . . . 226 M46
Latimer Rd *CHL* . . . . . . 194 D9
Latimer St *ABT* . . . . . 250 R-S78
Latta St *VAN* . . . . . . . . 163 Y20
Latvalla La *MAP* . . . . . . 187 A48
Lauder Dr *SUR* . . . . . . . 205 F34
Laura Cr *CHL* . . . . . . . . 233 M6
Lauralynn Dr *DNV* . . . . . 123 M20
Laurel Av *MIS* . . . . . . . 210 H75
Laurel Av *WRK* . . . . . . . 265 W35
Laurel Ct *CQT* . . . . . . . 165 U37
Laurel Dr *DEL* . . . . . . 223 N-P17
Laurel Dr *SUR* . . . . 205 E34-35
Laurel Gt *DEL* . . . . . . 223 N-P17
Laurel Pl *KNT* . . . . . 175 X21-22
Laurel Pl *PMD* . . . . . . . 145 R35
Laurel St *ABT* . . . . . . . 250 U76
Laurel St *BUR* 163 V21 164 V23-24 V24
Laurel St *NEW* . . . . . . . 164 Y29
Laurel St *VAN*
. . . . . . . 162 U13 V-W13 X13 Y13 Y13
. . . . . . . 182 A13 B13 Z13 Z13
Laurel Way *DEL* . . . . . . 223 P17
Laurelwood Ct *RMD* . . . . 202 G10
Laurelwood Pl *BUR* 163 W22 164 W22
Laurelwood Pl *CHL* . . . . 233 L5
Laurentian Cr *CQT* . . . 165 V-X34
Laurie Av *MAP* . . . . . . . 187 Z51
Laurie Cr *WVA* . . . . . . . 102 H13
Laurier Av *PCQ* . . 146 T39-41 T43
Laurier Av *VAN* . . . . . 162 W12-13
Laurnell Cr *ABT* . . . . . . 250 T75
Lauzon Rd *HOP* . . . . . . 118 E43
Laval Pl *VAN* . . . . . . . . 183 A20
Laval Sq *CQT* . . . . . . . 165 X33
Laval St *CQT* . . . . . . 165 W-X33
Lavender Ct *ABT* . . . . . . 251 U79
Lavender La *PMD* . . . 145 R34-35
Lavender Pl *CHL* . . . . . . 233 L7
Lawa Av *WVA* . . . . . . . 122 N13
Lawn Dr *CQT* . . . . . . . 165 W37
Lawrence Dr *BUR* . . . 164 V26-27
Lawrence La *MIS* . . . 210 G-H78
Lawrence Pl *DNV* . . . . . 123 K20
Lawrence St *BUR* . . . . . 164 V26
Lawrence St *NEW* . . . . 184 C-D27
Lawrence Way *WVA* . . . . 101 D4
Lawrie Cr *DEL* . . . . . . 224 L28
Lawson Av *WVA*
. . . . . . 122 L11 L11-12 L12 L13 L9
Lawson Dr *RMD* . . . . . . 202 J10
Lawson Rd *SQM* . . . . . . 301 C1
Laxton Av *MIS* . . . . . 210 F76-77
Laxton St *ABT* . . . . . . . 270 Y71
Layton Dr *DNV* . . . . . 123 M-N22
Lazenby Rd *CHL* . . . . . . 213 F5
Lazy A St *CQT* . . . . . . . 165 U37
Le Roi St *VAN* . . . . . . . 143 T19
Lea Av *CQT* . . . . . . . . 165 U31
Leacock St *PCQ* . . . 166 V-W39
Lealand Ct *BUR* . . . 164 V27-28
Lear Dr *CHL* . . . . . . . . 233 N8

Leary Cr *CHL* . . . . . . . . 213 J5
Leaside St *VAN* . . . . . . 183 A17
Leavens Rd *FRA* . . . . . . 253 R6
Lebleu St *CQT* . . . . . 165 W32 X32
LeClair Dr *CQT* . . . . . 165 W-X35
Ledger Av *BUR* . . . . . . 164 W24
Ledgeview Dr *ABT* . . . . . 251 S80
Leduc Av *CQT* . . . . . 165 W35-36
Ledunne Av *ABT* . . . . . 249 U63
Ledway Rd *RMD* . . . . . . 202 G10
Lee Av *MAP* . . . . . . . . 167 Y52-53
Lee St *BUR* . . . . . . . . 164 X-Y30
Lee St *MIS* . . . . . . . . . 210 J73
Lee St *WRK* . . . . 265 W38 X38
Leeder St *CQT* . . 165 Y35 185 Z35
Leeds Ct *BUR* . . . . . . 164 Y26-27
Leeside St *BUR* . . . . . . 184 A26
Leeward Ct *CQT* . . . . . 145 T36
Leeward Gt *RMD* . . . . 222 K9-10
Leg in Boot Sq *VAN* . . 162 U13-14
Legacy Ct *ABT* . . . . . . 250 S71
Legacy Way *WHS* . . . . . 401 J98
Leggatt Pl *PCQ* . . . 166 X-Y39
Lehman Pl *PMD* . . . 145 S35-36
Lehman Pl *PTM* . . . . . 186 B46
Leibly Av *BUR* . 164 Y25 Y26 184 Z26
Leigh Sq *PCQ* . . . . . . 166 U-V39
Leland Av *CQT* . . . . . . 165 U32
Lemax Av *CQT* . . . . . 165 V33 V34
Lemon Av *RMD* . . . . . . 204 F24
Lennox St *DNV* . . . . . . 123 N22
Lenora Cr *CHL* . . . . . . . 213 E5
Leonard Ct *RMD* . . . . . . 202 J12
Leonard Pl *RMD* . . . . . . 202 J12
Leonard Rd *RMD* . . . . . . 202 J12
Leopold Pl *NEW* . . . . . 184 A30
Leovista Av *DNV* . . . . . 123 K15
Leroy St *CQT* . . . . . . . 165 X35
Leslie Rd *RMD* . . . . 202 E12-13
Lester Pearson Way *ABT* . 251 Q82
Lethbridge Dr *ABT* . . . . 251 R-S79
Levi St *NEW* . . . . . . . . 184 B28
Levis St *CQT* . . . . . . . 165 U34
Levy Pl *SUR* . . . . . . . 225 K33
Lewis Av *CHL* . . . . . . . 193 D6-7
Lewister Rd *DNV* . . . . . . 122 K14
Leyland St *WVA* . . . . . 122 L-M12
Lholqwelwet Rd *CHL* . . . . 213 E4
Liard Pl *VAN* . . . . . . . . 183 Z20
Liberty Dr *ABT* . . . . . . 144 S23
Library Rd *DEL* . . . . . . 263 X17
Lickman Rd *CHL*.
. . . . . . . 213 F3-4 G-J3 233 K-M3
Lidster Pl *NEW* . . . . . . 184 Z29
Lien Rd *SUR* . . . . . . . 185 B31
Lightbody Ct *MIS* . . . . . 210 G73
Lightbody La *MIS* . . . . . 210 G73
Lighthall Ct *DNV* . . . . . 124 N25
Lighthouse Ct *CQT* . . . . 165 U36
Lighthouse La *MAP* . . 187 A51 Z51
Lighthouse Way *VAN* . . . 183 B19
Lila Pl *HOP* . . . . . . . . 118 E46
Lilac Cr *ABT* . . . . . . . 250 U73
Lilac Dr *SUR* . 265 V38 266 V39 W39
Lillian St *CQT* . . 145 T33 165 U33
Lillooet Av *HHS* . . . 155 P19-20
Lillooet La *DNV* . . . . 123 M-N21
Lillooet Pl *DNV* . . . . . 123 N21
Lillooet Rd *DNV*
. . . . . . . 123 K21 L-N21 143 P21
Lillooet St *VAN*
. . . . 143 S-T19 163 U19 U-V19 V-W19
Lily St *VAN* . . . . . . . 143 T17-18
Lima Rd *DNV* . . . . . . . 124 N26
Limbert Rd *KNT* . . . . 175 X17-18
Lime St *VAN* . . . . . . 162 Y10-11
Limerick Pl *DNV* . . . . . 123 M20
Limestone Ct *CQT* . . . 145 Q36
Limewood Pl *VAN* . . . 183 A20-21
Lincoln Av *CQT* 145 S-T38 146 T43-44
Lincoln Av *PCQ* . . . . . 145 T38
Lincoln Av *PCQ* . . 146 T40 T41-42
Lincoln Dr *DEL* . . . . . . 224 L29
Lincoln Dr *PCQ* . . . . . 146 S-T41
Lincoln Dr *SUR* . . . . . 185 C37
Lincoln Rd *ABT* . . . . 270 V75-76
Lincoln St *VAN* . . . . . 163 Y20
Lincoln Ter *HOP* . . . . . 118 F44
Lincoln Woods St *SUR* . 246 T39-40
Lindale St *ABT* . . . . . 250 U74
Linden Av *BUR* . . . . . 184 Z26
Linden Cr *UEL* . . . . . . 161 V5
Linden Ct *DEL* . . . . . 223 P17
Linden Ct *PMD* . . . . . 145 Q35
Linden Ct *SUR* . . . . . 186 C40
Linden Dr *DEL* . . . . 223 P16-17

Linden Pl *DEL* . . . . . . . 223 P17
Linden Rd *VAN* . . . . . . 162 X11
Lindrick Ct *BUR* . . . . . 144 T26
Lindsay Av *MAP* . . . . . 187 Z48
Lindsay Ct *RMD* . . . . . 202 G10
Lindsay Pl *MAP* . . 167 Y48 187 Z48
Lindsay Pl *SUR* . . . . . 205 F32
Lindsay Rd *RMD* . . . . . 202 G10
Lindsay St *ABT* . . . . . 250 R74
Lindsey Pl *DEL* . . . . . 204 F25
Lindys Rd *CHL* . . . . . . 233 M4
Linfield Gt *RMD* . . . . . 202 G10
Linfield Pl *BUR* . . . . 164 X26-27
Link Ct *ABT* . . . . . . . 250 S72
Link Rd *DNV* . . . . . . . 123 L19
Linkside Rd *WHS* . . . . . 401 F3
Linnae Av *DNV* . . 122 J14 123 J15
Linscott Ct *RMD* . . . . . 202 G10
Linscott Rd *RMD* . . . . . 202 G10
Linton St *CQT* . . . . . . 165 U32
Linton Way *SUR* . . . 225 K32-33
Linwood St *BUR* . . . . . 163 V21
Linwood St *CHL* . . . . . 193 D7
Lions Av *DNV* . . . . . 123 J-K15
Lions Way *PCQ* . . . . . 166 U39
Lions Bay Av *LIO* . . . 101 B-C23
Lions Gate Bridge Rd *VAN*.
. . . . . . . . . . . . . 142 P-Q12
Lisgar Ct *DNV* . . . . . . 123 K19
Lismer Av *RMD* . . . . 202 H11-12
Lismer Gt *RMD* . . . . 202 H11-12
Lissimore Av *MIS* . . . . 210 G73
Lister Ct *BUR* . . . . . . 163 W21
Lister St *BUR* . . . . . . 163 W21
Little La *KNT* . . . . . . 175 X21
Little St *VAN* . . . . . . . 163 X18
Little Ter *MIS* . . . . . . 210 H75
Littlemore Rd *RMD* . . . . 202 H9
Littlewood Av *BUR* . . . 164 W23
Liverpool Pl *PCQ* . . . . 146 S40
Liverpool Rd *SUR* . . . . 185 B31
Liverpool St *NEW* . . . . 184 A29
Liverpool St *PCQ* . . 146 S40 T40
Livingstone Av *ABT* . . 249 T-U70
Livingstone Gt *RMD* . . 202 F-G11
Livingstone Pl *RMD* . . . 202 G11
Lloyd Av *DNV* . . 123 L15 M15 N15
Loach Pl *DNV* . . . . . . 144 Q26
Locarno Cr *VAN* . . 142 T7 162 U7
Locarno Ct *ABT* . . 250 U78 251 U79
Locarno Dr *CQT* . . . . . 145 T37
Lochdale St *BUR* . . 164 U24-25 U25
Lock St *ABT* . . . . . . . 249 T-U68
Locke La *LGC* . . . . . . 227 N48
Lockehaven Pl *DNV* . . . 124 N27
Lockehaven Rd *DNV*. . 124 M-N27
Lockhart Rd *RMD* . . . 202 G8-9
Lockheed Pl *CHL* . . . . 213 G8
Locklin Ct *ABT* . . . . . . 249 U68
Lodge Dr *CQT* . . . . . 146 S39-40
Lodge Pl *CQT* . . . . . 146 S39-40
Lodge Rd *DNV* . . . . . 123 K15
Lodgepole Cr *CQT* . . . 145 Q38
Logan Av *LGC* . . . 227 M47-48 N48
Logan Av *MIS* . . . . . . 210 J73
Logan Dr *CHL* . . . . . . 213 H2
Logan Rd *KNT* . . . . . 175 X22
Logan St *CQT* . . . . . . 165 Y34
Logan St *VAN* . . . . . 182 A-B13
Loggers La *SQM* . . 301 G-H2 K1-2
Lolly La *CHL* . . . . . . . 233 M6
Lombard Av *ABT* . . . . 270 V71
Lombard Pl *SUR* . . . 225 N36
Lombard Rd *RMD* . . . . 202 G10
Lombardy Cr *CHL* . . . . 213 F7
Lombardy Cr *SQM* . . . 301 K3
Lombardy Dr *PCQ* . . 146 T41-42
Lomond Dr *SQM* . . . . 301 E4
Lomond St *CQT* . . . 165 U-V34
London Av *MIS* . . . . 230 K73-74
London Cr *DEL* . . . . . 243 Q19
London Ct *DEL* . . . . 243 Q19-20
London Dr *DEL* . . . . 243 Q19-20
London Gn *DEL* . . 223 P19 243 Q19
London Gt *DEL* . . . . 243 Q19
London La *DEL* . . . . . 243 Q19
London La *WHS* . . . . . 401 H2
London Mews *DEL* . . . 243 Q19
London Pl *NEW* . . . . 184 B25
London Rd *RMD* . . . 222 L-M11
London St *NEW* . . 184 A27 A-B26
Long Life Pl *VAN* . . . . 162 U14

Longlac St *CQT* . . . . . 165 U33
Longview Pl *ABT* . . . . 250 S71
Lonsdale Av *CNV*
. . . . . . 123 L-N17 143 P16-17 P17
Lonsdale Av *DNV* . . . 123 K-L17
Lonsdale Cr *ABT* . . . 270 V73
Lonzo Rd *ABT* . . . . . . 270 V77
Lookout La *WHS* . . . . . 401 H2
Lookout Pt *DNV* . . . . . 123 N27
Loraine Av *DNV* . . . 122 K-L14
Lord St *VAN* . . . . . . . 182 A13
Lorilawn Ct *BUR* . . . . 144 T23
Lorimer Rd *WHS* . 401 E3-4 S21-22
Loring Av *CHL* . . . . . 213 F7-8
Loring St *CQT* . . . . . . 165 X31
Lorne Av *MAP* . . 187 A48-49 B48
Lorne Ct *WRK* . . . . . . 265 X38
Lorne Dr *CHL* . . . . . . 233 K7
Lorne St *NEW* . . . . . . 184 B29
Lorne St *VAN* . . . . . . 163 U15
Lorraine Av *BUR* . . . . 163 X21
Lorraine Av *CQT* . . . 165 X34-35
Los Lenas Pl *WHS* . . . 401 H2
Lost Lake Dr *CQT* . . . 165 V36
Lost Lake Rd *WHS* . . . 401 E5
Lotus Ct *CQT* . . . . 145 R37-38
Louellen St *NEW* . . . . 184 B28
Lougheed Hwy *BUR* . . . . . .
. . 163 U21-22 164 U23-24 V26-28 W30
Lougheed Hwy *CQT*. . . . . .
. . . 145 T37 165 U-V37 X32-33
Lougheed Hwy *HOP*. . . 118 D42-43
Lougheed Hwy *KNT*. . . . . .
. . 175 U-V23 V19-20 W17-18 W21
Lougheed Hwy *MAP*. . . . . .
. . . . 187 A53 B54 C54 Z48-49
Lougheed Hwy *MIS* 210 H77 230 K72
Lougheed Hwy *PCQ* . 166 U39 V41
Lougheed Hwy *PTM* . . 166 X44-45
Lougheed Hwy *VAN* . . . 163 U20
Lougheed Meridian Rd *PCQ* 166 V40
Loughren Dr *SUR* . . . . 185 A37
Louie Cr *LGT* . . . . . . 187 B49
Louisburg Pl *RMD* . . 202 J9 222 K9
Low Level Rd *CNV* . 143 P-Q17 P-Q18
Lowell Ct *CQT* . . . . . 165 V34
Lower Mall *UEL* . . . . . 161 U3
Lower Bellevue Av *WVA*. . 122 L8-9
Lower Capilano Rd *WVA*
. . . . . . . . . 122 N13 142 P13
Lower Landing Rd *CHL* . . 193 D5
Lower Sumas Mountain Rd *ABT* . . .
. . . . . . . . 251 T81-82 U80-81
Lower Victoria Dr *PCQ* . . 146 S42
Lowland Dr *BUR* . . . . 184 C23
Lowry La *DNV* . . . . . . 144 P26
Lozells Av *BUR* . . . . . 164 W27
Lucas Rd *RMD* . . . . 202 H11-12
Lucern Cr *ABT* . . . . . 250 T-U78
Lucerne Dr *DNV* . . . . 123 K16
Lucerne Pl *RMD* . . . 202 G-H12
Lucerne Rd *RMD*. . . . . 202 G12
Lucille Starr Dr *CQT* . . 165 X33
Luckakuck Pl *CHL* . . . . 213 H5
Luckakuck Way *CHL* . . 213 H3-7
Lucking Pl *DNV* . . . 123 N19-20
Ludgate Rd *RMD* . . . . 202 G10
Ludlow Av *ANM* . . . . 145 P33
Ludlow Pl *RMD* . . . . . 202 G10
Ludlow Rd *RMD* . . . . 202 G10
Lumar Pl *ABT* . . . . . . 270 V77
Lumsden Rd *CHL* . . . . 233 P1
Lund Av *CQT* . . . . . . 165 W36
Lundy Rd *RMD* . . . . 202 G-H12
Lunen Rd *RMD* . . . . 202 H12
Lupine Ct *CQT* . . . . . 145 R36
Lurgan Rd *RMD* . . . 202 G-H12
Luton Rd *RMD* . . . . . 202 G12
Lutz Rd *CHL* . . . . . . 233 N8
Luxton Sq *CQT* . . 145 T33 165 U33
Lyardon Rd *FRA* . . . . 233 P8
Lyddon Rd *DNV* . . . . 123 L21
Lyn Ct *CQT* . . . . . . . 165 W33
Lynas La *RMD* . . . . 202 E-F10
Lynbrook Dr *VAN* . . . 183 Z18
Lyncean Dr *SUR* . . . . 186 D43
Lynden St *ABT* . 250 U73 270 V73
Lyndene Rd *DNV* . . . 122 L14
Lyndhurst St *BUR* . . . 164 V30
Lynham Rd *WHS* . . . . 401 H-J98
Lynmoor Pl *VAN* . . . . 183 A20
Lynn Av *ABT* . . . . . . 270 V75
Lynn Av *DNV* . . . . . . 143 P20

Lynn Cr *ABT* . . . . . . . 270 V75
Lynn Pl *DEL* . . . . . . . 243 Q16
Lynn Valley Rd *DNV*. . . . . .
. . . . . 123 K20-21 L-M19 M18
Lynndale Cr *BUR* . . . . 164 V-W26
Lynnmouth Av *DNV* . . 143 P19-20
Lynnwood Dr *RMD* . . . 202 G10
Lynwood Av *PCQ* . . 146 S41 S42
Lyon Pl *CNV* . . . . . . . 143 P18
Lyon Rd *DEL* . . . 224 K29 K30 L28
Lyons Ct *CQT* . . . . . 165 U34-35
Lyra Pl *ABT* . . . . . . . 164 V29
Lysander Cr *RMD* . . . 182 D11
Lysander La *RMD* . . . 182 C12
Lytham Pl *BUR* . . . . . 144 T26
Lythe Ct *WVA* . . . . . 122 K9-10
Lytton Pl *DNV* . . . . . . 123 N22
Lytton St *DNV* . . . 123 N22 143 P22

# M

Ma Murray La *ANM*. 125 N33 145 P33
MacBeth Cr *ABT* . . . . . 250 U78
MacBeth Cr *WVA*. . . . . 122 L13
MacBeth Pl *WVA* . . . 122 L-M13
MacDonald Av *BUR*. . . . . .
. . . . . . . 143 R-T21 163 U21 W21
MacDonald Av N *BUR* . 143 R-S21
MacDonald Pl *SQM* . . . 301 C2
MacDonald Rd *DEL* . 203 J19-20
Macdonald St *VAN* . . . 142 T10
. . 162 U10 U-W10 W-X10 Y10 182 Z10
MacGowan Av *DNV*. . . 122 M-N14
MacGregor Pl *CHL* . . . 233 M8
Machell St *MIS* . . . . 210 F-G73
Machrina Way *RMD*. . . . 223 L15
MacIntosh St *CQT* . . 165 U-V32
Mackay Av *CNV* . . . . 123 M15
Mackay Av *DNV* . . . . 123 M15
MacKay Cr *KNT* . . . 175 X20-21
Mackay Rd *DNV* . . . . 123 N15
Macken Av *CHL* . . . . 193 D8
Mackenzie Av *DEL* . . . 243 Q21
MacKenzie Pl *VAN*. . . 162 Y10
MacKenzie St *VAN*162 V10 W-X10 Y10
Mackie Ct *DEL* . . . . 204 H28
Mackie La *LGT* . . . . 207 F53
Mackie St *LGT* . . . . 207 F53
Mackie St *VAN*. . . . . 162 X14
MacLure Mews *VAN* . . 162 W-X11
Maclure Rd *ABT*. . . . . . . .
. 249 T63 T67-68 T70 250 T71-75 T76 T77
MacLure St *VAN* . . . 162 W-X11
MacPherson Av *BUR* . 184 A24 Z24
Maddams St *VAN* . . . 163 V17
Maddocks Rd *RMD* . . . 202 J14
Madeira Ct *DNV* . . . . 103 H16
Madeley Pl *WHS* . . . . 401 J98
Madeley Rd *DNV* . . . . 123 K17
Mader La *DEL* . . . . . 204 J29
Madera Ct *CQT* . . . . 165 V33
Madera Pl *ABT* . . . . 270 V72
Madill St *SQM* . . . . . 301 H1
Madison Av *BUR* . 143 S-T22 163 U22
Madison Av N *BUR* . . 143 R-S22
Madison St *CQT* . . . . 165 W34
Madley Pl *ANM* . . . . 125 N33
Madore Av *CQT* . . . 165 W31-34
Madrona Cr *RMD* . . . . 202 F11
Madrona Cr *WVA* . . . . 101 G1-2
Madrona Dr *SUR* . . . . 265 V38
Madrona Pl *CQT* . . . . 145 Q38
Madrona Pl *SUR* . . . . 265 V38
Madrona Pl *WVA* . . . . 101 G1-2
Magdalen Av *WRK* . . 265 W35-36
Magdalen Cr *WRK* . . . 265 X36
Magee St *SQM* . . . . . 301 H1-2
Magellan Ct *CQT* . . 165 X35-36
Magellan Pl *RMD* . . . . 202 G9
Magellan St *PCQ* . . . 166 W39
Maginnis Av *DNV* . . . 123 K-L20
Magnesia Springs Rd *LIO*. 101 A23
Magnolia Av *CHL* . . . 193 D7
Magnolia Cl *SUR* . . . 186 C40
Magnolia Cr *ABT* . . . 250 U73
Magnolia Cr *SQM* . . . 301 K3
Magnolia Ct *DEL* . . . 224 L28
Magnolia Dr *RMD* . . . 202 H11
Magnolia Estates *KNT* . . 175 X20
Magnolia Pl *CQT* . . . 145 Q-R35
Magnolia Pl *VAN* . . . 162 W11
Magnolia Ter *BUR* . . 184 A25 Z25
Magnolia Way *ANM* . 145 P32-33
Magnussen Pl *DNV*. . . 123 M19

Mahogany Dr *ABT*. . . . . . . . 251 U79
Mahon Av *BUR*. . . . . 164 W24 W-X24
Mahon Av *CNV*. 123 M17 N16 143 P16
Mahon Av *DNV*. . . . . . . . . 123 L16
Mahonia St *MIS*. . . . . . . 210 G75
Mahood Dr *RMD*. . . . . . . . 202 J9
Main Av *BEL*. . . . . . . . 124 N29-30
Main Mall *UEL*. . . . . . 161 U3-4 V4
Main St *CHL*. . . . . . . . . 213 E6
Main St *DEL*. . . . . . . . . 204 G27
Main St *DNV*. . . . . . . . . 143 Q20
Main St *SQM*. . . . . . . . . 301 K1
Main St *VAN*. . . . . . . . 11 H-K40
. . . . 143 S-T15 163 U-Y15 183 A15 Z15
Main St *WHS*. . . . . . 401 E4 S21
Main St *WVA*. . . . . . . . . 122 M12
Mainland Rd *RMD*. . . . . . 125 N33
Mainland St *VAN*. 11 J37 142 T13-14
Maitland Av *CHL*. . . . . . . 213 J6
Maitland Av *CNV*. . . . . . . 123 J22
Maitland St *BUR*. 163 Y22 164 Y23
Majestic Cr *ABT*. . . . . . . 270 V73
Major St *LGT*. . . . . . . . 207 F53
Major St *NEW*. . . . 164 Y30 165 Y31
Makinson St *MAP*. . 167 Y48 187 Z48
Malabar Av *WRK*. . . 265 W34 W35
Malabar Cr *WRK*. . . . 265 W-X36
Malahat Av *RMD*. . . . . . . 202 J12
Malahat Pl *ABT*. . . . . . . 250 S74
Malaspina Pl *DNV*. . . . 103 H15-16
Malcolm Pl *SUR*. . . . . . . 205 F32
Mali Av *VAN*. . . . . . . . . 162 Y7
Malibu Ct *CQT*. . . . . . . 145 R37
Malibu Dr *BUR*. . . . 144 S25-26
Malibu Pl *DEL*. . . . . . . . 263 X17
Malkin Av *VAN*. . . . . 11 J41 143 T16
Mall Av *RMD*. . . . . . . . 182 D14
Mallard Ct *CQT*. . . . . . . 146 P39
Mallard Dr *HOP*. . . . . . . 118 E45
Mallard Pl *MIS*. . . . . . . 210 H73
Mallard St *ABT*. . . . . . . 249 T70
Malory Ct *DNV*. . . . . . . 123 J20
Malta Av *VAN*. . . . . . . . 163 V20
Malta Pl *VAN*. . . . . . . . 163 V20
Malton Dr *DEL*. . . . . . . 204 J29
Malvern Av *BUR*. . . . . . . 164 Y25
Malvern Pl *DEL*. . . . . . . 263 X17
Malvern Pl *SUR*. . . . . . . 225 K33
Mamquam Rd *SQM*. . . . . . 301 F2-4
Mamquam Rd *SQM*. . . . . . 301 F4
Mamquam Forest Service Rd *SQM*
. . . . . . . . . . . . . . . . . 301 J5
Mamquam River Rd *SQM*. . . . . . .
. . . . . . . . . 301 J4-5 K3 K5
Manchester Ct *PCQ*. . . . 166 U40
Manchester Dr *BUR*. . . . 164 W30
Manchester Pl *CHL*. . . . . 233 M5
Mandeville Av *BUR*. 183 B22 184 B23
Mandy Av *BUR*. . . . . . . 183 721
Mang Rd *RMD*. . . . . . . 202 G11
Manitoba St *NEW*. . . . . . 184 A29
Manitoba St *VAN*. . . 11 K39 142 T14
. . . . 162 U-V14 W-V14 X-Y14 182 A14
Mann Park Cr *WRK*. . . . . 265 W36
Mannering Av *VAN*. . . . 163 X17-18
Manning Av *PCQ*. . . . . . 166 U39-40
Manning Cr *DNV*. . 124 N24 144 P24
Manning Ct *PCQ*. . . . . . 166 U41
Manning Ct *RMD*. . . . . 202 J11-12
Manning Pl *DNV*. . . . . . 144 P24
Manning Sq *PCQ*. . . . . . 166 U41
Manor Av *MAP*. . . . . . . 167 Y51
Manor Dr *CHL*. . . . . . . 233 K6-7
Manor St *BUR*. 163 V21 V21-22 164 V23
Manor St *VAN*. . . . . . . 163 X19
Mansfield Cr *PCQ*. . . 146 S41-42
Mansfield Pl *DNV*. . . . 143 P19-20
Manson Ct *BUR*. . . . . . 164 W28
Manson Dr *BUR*. . . . . . 164 V-W28
Manson St *MIS*. . . . . . . 210 G-H77
Manson St *VAN*. . . . . . . 162 X13
Manuel Rd *CHL*. . . . . . . 233 K6-7
Manufacturers Way *ABT*. . . 270 Y77
Manzanita Ct *CQT*. . . 145 Q36-37
Manzanita Pl *BUR*. . . . . . 164 X30
Maple *SUR*. . . . . . . . . 266 W39
Maple Av *CHL*. . . . . . . 213 E7-8
Maple Cr *DEL*. . . . . . . . 243 Q17
Maple Cr *KNT*. . . . . . 175 X21-22
Maple Cr *MAP*. . . . . . . 187 A48
Maple Cr *SQM*. . . . . . . . 301 C2
Maple Cr *VAN*. . . . . . . . 162 W11
Maple Ct *ANM*. . . . . . . 145 P33
Maple Ct *PMD*. . . . . . 145 Q35-36
Maple Dr *PMD*. . . . . . 145 P-Q35
Maple Dr *SQM*. . . . . . . . 301 K3

Maple La *MAP*. . . . . . 187 Z47-48
Maple La *WVA*. . . . . . . 122 K-L7
Maple Pl *PTM*. . . . 186 Z46 187 Z47
Maple Pl *RMD*. . . . . . . 202 H11
Maple Pl *SQM*. . . . . . . . 301 C2
Maple Pl *WVA*. . . . . . . . 121 J2
Maple Rd *RMD*. . . . . . 202 H10-11
Maple St *ABT*. . . . . . 250 T-U76
Maple St *CHL*. . . . . . . 233 L6-7
Maple St *FRA*. . . . . . . . 253 R5
Maple St *HHS*. . . . . . . 155 P19
Maple St *HOP*. . . . . . . 118 D44
Maple St *MIS*. . . . . . . . 210 J74
Maple St *NEW*. . . . . . . 184 A28
Maple St *PCQ*. . . 165 U38 166 U39
Maple St *SUR*. . . . . . . . 245 U31
Maple St *VAN*. . . 10 J-K33 142 T11
. . . . 162 U11 U-V11 W11 X11 Y11 182 Z11
Maple St *WRK*. . . . . 265 W-X38
Maple Grove Cr *BUR*. . . . 164 U29
Maple Meadows Way *MAP*. . . . . .
. . . . . . . . . . . 187 A47 Z47
Maple Tree La *MAP*. . . . . 183 A21
Maplebrook Pl *CQT*. . . 165 U38
Maplehurst Cir *BUR* 144 T26 164 U26
Mapleridge Dr *DNV*. . . . . 123 J15
Mapletree Cl *SUR*. . . . . 186 C40
Maplewood Cr *BUR*. . . . 163 X22
Maplewood Cr *DNV*. . . . 122 N14
Maplewood Ct *CQT*. . . 145 Q38
Maplewood Pl *ABT*. . . . 270 V74
Maplewood Pl *DEL*. . . 243 Q16-17
Maplewood Village *KNT*. . 175 X21
Maquinna Dr *VAN*. . . . . 183 A20
Mara Cr *RMD*. . . . . . . . 202 F11
Mara Dr *CQT*. . . . . . 165 V36-37
Marathon Ct *CQT*. . . 165 X33-34
Marble Ct *CQT*. . . . . . 145 Q36
Marble Hill Dr *ABT*. . . 250 T-U78
Marc Rd *MAP*. . . . . . . 167 V54
Marcellin Pl *CQT*. . . . 165 U37-38
Marcet Ct *ABT*. . . . . . 250 U78
March Pl *PCQ*. . . . . . . 146 S40
March Way *PCQ*. . . . . . 146 S40
Marchwood Pl *VAN*. . 183 A20-21
Marcliffe Pl *ABT*. . . . . . 250 T77
Mardale Rd *DNV*. . . . . . 122 L14
Margaree Pl *WVA*. . . . . . 122 M13
Margaret Av *CHL*. . . . . . 213 E7-8
Margate Pl *SUR*. . . . . . . 205 G38
Marguerite St *CQT*. . 146 Q40 R40
Marguerite St *VAN*. . . . . . . . . .
. . . 162 W11-12 X11-12 Y11-12 182 Z11
Maria La *KNT*. . . . . . . . 175 V23
Mariana Pl *CQT*. . . . . 165 X35-36
Marie Av *CHL*. . . . . . . 233 N6
Marie Pl *DNV*. . . . . . . 143 P20
Marie St *HOP*. . . . . . . 118 G-H42
Marigold Av *CHL*. . . . . . 233 L6
Marigold Av *DNV*. . . . . . 123 J15
Marigold Pl *DNV*. . . . . . 123 J15
Marigold St *CQT*. . . . . 146 R42-43
Marina Way *NEW*. . . . . 184 B26-27
Marinaside Cr *VAN*. . . . . . . . . .
. . . . . . . 11 K37-38 142 T13-14
Marine Av *BEL*. . . . . . . 124 N29
Marine Cr *CQT*. . . . . . . 165 U33
Marine Cr *VAN*. 162 Y10 Y10 182 Z10
Marine Dr *BUR*183 A22 184 A-B23 B25
Marine Dr *CNV*. . . . . . . 122 N13
Marine Dr *DNV*. . . . . . 122 N13-14
Marine Dr *NEW*. . . . . . 184 B-C26
Marine Dr *SUR*. . . . . 265 X33-34
Marine Dr *WRK*. . 265 X37 Y38 266 Y39
Marine Dr *WVA*. . . . . . . . . . . .
. . . . . 101 G1-2 H2 121 J2-3 K-L5 L3 L6
. . . . . . . . . 122 L8-9 M11-12 M13
Marine Dr, NW *UEL*. . . 161 S-T4 T-U3
Marine Dr, NW *VAN*. . . . . . . . . .
. . . . . . . . 142 T7 161 T6 162 U7
Marine Dr, SE *VAN*. . . . . . . . . .
. . . . . . . 183 A15-17 A19 A-B18
Marine Dr, SW *VAN*. . . . 162 Y9-10
. . . . 182 A11 A13-14 B12-13 183 A15
Marine Way *BUR*. . . . . . . . . . .
. . . 183 B21-22 184 B23-24 C25-26
Marine Way *VAN*. . . . . 183 B20
Mariner Cl *WVA*. . . . . . 121 K2-3
Mariner Pl *DEL*. . . . . . . 223 P18
Mariner Walk *VAN*. . 10 K34 142 T12
Mariner Way *CQT*. 145 T36 165 U-X36
Marinerview Cr *DNV*. . . . 123 J16
Mario Ct *BUR*. . . . . . . 164 V25
Marion Av *CHL*. . . . . . . 193 D7-8
Marion Rd *DNV*. . . . . . 123 J-K21
Mariposa Ct *RMD*. . . . . 202 F9-10

Maritime Mews *VAN*. 10 K35 142 T12
Mark Cr *BUR*. . . . . . . . 164 V26
Markel Dr *CHL*. . . . . . . 233 N8
Market Crsg *BUR*. . . . . 184 B24
Market Hill *VAN*. . . . . . 180 U13
Markham Pl *DNV*. . . . . . 123 L17
Marlborough Av *BUR*. . . . . . . . .
. . . . . . 164 Y23 184 Z23 Z23
Marlin Quay *VAN*. . . . . . 183 A18
Marlow St *CQT*. . . . . . 165 V-W33
Marlowe Pl *WVA*. . . . . . 122 J10
Marmion Av *VAN*. . . . 163 Y19-20
Marmont St *CQT*. . . . . 165 W33
Marmot Pl *WHS*. . . . . . . 401 H2
Marnac Av *CQT*. . . . . 165 U32
Marpole Av *PCQ*. . . . . . 166 V41
Marpole Av *VAN*. . . . . . 162 V12
Marquette Cr *VAN*. . . . . 183 A20
Marquis Ct *ABT*. . . . . 251 T-U80
Marr St *LGT*. . . . . . . . 207 E53
Marr Creek Ct *WVA*. . . . 122 K9
Marrington Rd *RMD*. . . . 202 F-G8
Mars Pl *PCQ*. . . . . . . 146 S42
Mars St *CQT*. . . . . . . 165 U-V34
Mars St *PCQ*. . . . . . . 146 S42
Marsden Ct *BUR*. . . . . 144 T26
Marsh Av *MIS*. . . . . . . 210 J72
Marshall Av *CHL*. . . . . . 193 D6
Marshall Av *PCQ*. . . 166 V-W39
Marshall Rd *ABT*. . . . . . . . . . .
. . . . 251 U80 270 V71 V72-78
Marshall Rd Diversion *ABT*. . . . .
. . . . . . . . . . . . 270 V71-72
Marshall St *VAN*. . . . 163 V-W18
Marshland Av *BUR*. . . . 184 C25
Marstrand Av *VAN*. . . . . 162 U11
Martens St *ABT*. . . . . . 270 V71
Martin Av *MIS*. . . . . . . 210 J72
Martin Ct *BUR*. . . . . . . 164 V30
Martin Ct *WVA*. . . . . . . 121 K3
Martin Dr *SUR*. . . . . . . 265 W37
Martin Pl *MIS*. . . . . . . 210 J72
Martin Rd *DEL*. . . . . 222 P10-11
Martin Rd *KNT*. . . . . . 175 X-Y21
Martin St *BUR*. . . . . . . 164 V30
Martin St *CQT*. . . . . . 146 P-Q40
Martin St *WRK*. . . . . . 265 W-X37
Martin Way *ABT*. . . . . . 230 N71
Martindale Cr *ABT*. . . . 250 U74
Martyniuk Gt *RMD*. . . . 202 H11
Martyniuk Pl *RMD*. . . 202 H10-11
Marvern Way *ABT*. . . 250 S-T78
Mary Av *BUR*. . . . . 184 Z26 27
Mary Av *LGT*. . . . . . . 207 F54
Mary Dr (125A St) *SUR*. . 185 D32
Mary St *CHL*. . . . . . . 213 E-F6
Mary St *MIS*. . . . . . 210 J75-76
Mary St *PMD*. . . . . . . 145 T33
Mary Hill By-Pass *PCQ*. . . . . . .
. . . 165 Y37-38 166 W41-42 X40
Mary Hill La *PCQ*. . . . 165 W-X38
Mary Hill Rd *PCQ*. . . . . . . . . .
. . . 165 W38 X Y38 166 V39 W39
Mary Kirk Pl *DNV*. . . . . 124 M23
Masefield Rd *DNV*. . . 123 L-M19
Maskall Dr *RMD*. . . . . . 202 H10
Mason Av *CQT*. . . . . . 146 R40
Mason Av *PCQ*. . . . . . 146 R40
Mason Ct *BUR*. . . . . . . 164 Y27
Mason Pl *DEL*. . . . . . . 224 L29
Masset Ct *CQT*. . . . . . 165 U34
Massey Dr *DEL*. . . . . . 243 Q16
Massey Pl *DEL*. . . . . . 175 X21
Massey Pl *NEW*. . 164 Y29 184 Z29
Mast Tower Rd *VAN*. 10 K35 142 T12
Matapan Cr *VAN*. . . . . 163 V20
Mathers Av *WVA*. . . . . . . . . . .
. . . 121 K6 122 K7-8 L12 L13 L9-11
Mathers Cr *WVA*. . . . . . 122 L8
Mathers Ct *WVA*. . . . . . 122 L10
Matheson Cr *VAN*. . . 183 A20 Z20
Matheson Rd *CHL*. . . . 233 L-M8
Mathissi Pl *BUR*. . . . . . 163 W22
Matsqui Pl *ABT*. . . . . . 249 T69
Matsqui St *CHL*. . . . . . 233 M5-6
Matterhorn Dr *WHS*. . . . . 401 C3
Matthews Av *VAN* 162 V12-13 W11-12
Maude Ct *PMD*. . . . . . . 145 R35
Maude Rd *PMD*. . . . 145 R35 S35
Maureen Cr *BUR*. . . . . 144 S26
Maureen Ct *BUR*. . . . 144 S25-26
Maurelle Ct *DNV*. . . . . 123 J16
Maurice St *CHL*. . . . . . . 193 D7
Mavis Av *LGT*. . . . . . . 207 F54
Mavis St *BUR*. . . . . 184 Z23-24
Mavis St *CHL*. . . . . . . . 213 E5

Mawhinney Cl *BUR*. . . . . 164 V25-26
Maxwell Cr *LGT*. . . . . . 227 K-L51
Maxwell Pl *PCQ*. . . . . . 166 U40
Maxwell St *CHL*. . . . . . . 213 E7
Maxwell St *VAN*. . . . 163 V-W17
May Pl *DEL*. . . . . . . . 224 K29
May St *MIS*. . . . . . . . 210 J72
Mayberry St *BUR*. . . . . 163 Y21-22
Maycrest Way *RMD* 183 D17 203 E17
Mayfair Av *ABT*. . . . . 270 V75-76
Mayfair Av *CHL*. . . . . . . 193 D8
Mayfair Av *VAN*. . . . . . 162 X9
Mayfair Ct *CQT*. . . . . 165 U33-34
Mayfield Pl *RMD*. . . . . . 183 D17
Mayfield St *BUR*. . . 164 Y26 Y26-27
Mayflower Dr *RMD*. . . . . 202 F9
Maynard Pl *MIS*. . . . . . 210 G73
Maynard Ter *MIS*. . . . 210 F-G73
Mayne Av *ABT*. . . . . . 250 S72
Mayne Cr *CQT*. . . . . . 146 S39
Mayo Pl *MAP*. . . . . . . 187 Z50
Maysfield Cr *LGT*. . . . . 247 Q49
Mayview Dr *ABT*. . . . . . 164 X26
Maywood Av *PCQ*. . . . 146 T41-42
Maywood Ct *ABT*. . . . 270 V77-78
Maywood St *BUR*. . . . . 183 Z22
McAdam Rd *ABT*. . . . . 250 U77
McAdam Rd *DEL*. . . . . 204 F28
McAllister Av *PCQ* 165 U38 166 U39
McAllister St *LGT*. . . . . 207 F54
McBain Av *VAN*. . . . 162 W10-11
McBeth Rd *SUR*. . 265 W38 266 W39
McBride Av *MIS*. . . . 210 G72-73
McBride Av *SUR*. . . . . . . 265 X38
McBride Blvd *NEW*. 184 A30 Z28-29
McBride Dr *SUR*. . . . . . . 185 A35
McBride Pl *NEW*. . . . . . 184 Z29
McBride St *ABT*. . . . . . 250 T78
McBride St *BUR*. . . . . 184 Z25-26
McBride St *DNV*. . . . . . 122 N14
McBride St *LGT*. . . . . . 207 F54
McBurney Ct *RMD*. . . . 202 G-H13
McBurney Dr *RMD*. . . 202 G13-14
McCabe Pl *ABT*. . . . . . 250 T78
McCaffrey Blvd *CHL*. . . 213 F7 F8
McCaffrey Rd *KNT*. . . . . 175 W20
McCallan Rd *RMD*. . . 202 E-F10 G10
McCallum Ct *MAP*. . . . . 167 Y50
McCallum Pl *ABT*. . . . . 250 T75
McCallum Rd *ABT*. . . . . . . . . .
. . . . 250 S-U75 270 V-Z75
McCallum Rd *KNT*. . . . . 175 U17-19
McCarthy Ct *BUR*. . . . . 164 X25
McCartney Cl *DNV*. . . . 144 P23
McCartney Rd *KNT*. . . 175 W-X22
McCartney Way *RMD*. . . 203 G21
McChessney St *PCQ*. . . 165 W38
McClary Av *ABT*. . . . . . 270 W77
McCleery St *VAN*. 162 Y10 182 Z10
McClinton Av *RMD*. . 204 E24-25
McColl Cr *RMD*. . . . . . 204 E25
McColl Ct *ABT*. . . . . . 250 T78
McCombs Dr *HHS*. . . 155 R19-20
McConachie Pl *ABT* 249 U70 250 U71
McConnell Ct *BUR*. . . . 164 W27
McConnell Dr *BUR*. . . . 164 W27
McConnell Rd *ABT*. . 270 X75-76 X77
McConnell Rd *CHL*. . . 194 C-D12
McCoomb Av *CQT*. . . . . 145 S37
McCord Ct *ABT*. . . . . . 250 T78
McCrae St *ABT*. . . . . . 250 T78
McCrimmon Dr *ABT*. . . 250 T76
McCullough Rd *KNT*. . . 175 X21
McCurdy Pl *ABT*. . . . . 249 T-U70
McCutcheon Av *CHL*. . . 213 F5-6
McCutcheon Pl *RMD*. 202 H11-12
McDermott St *BUR*. . . 164 U25-26
McDonald Av *WRK*. . . . 265 X36
McDonald La *KNT*. . . . . 175 X20
McDonald Pl *PCQ*. . . . . 166 X39
McDonald Rd *CHL*. . . . . 193 B-C8
McDonald Rd *PTM*. . . . . 146 T45
McDonald Rd *RMD*. . . 182 A-B10
McDonald Rd N *KNT*. . . 175 X20-21
McDonald Rd S *KNT*. . . 175 X21-23
McDonald St *NEW*. . . . . 164 Y30
McDougall Av *ABT*. . . 250 U75-76
McEwen Av *DNV*. . . . . 123 K-L21
McEwen Av *MIS*. . . . . . 210 G78
McEwen Pl *DNV*. . . . . . 123 K-L21
McEwen Pl *MIS*. . . . . . 210 G78
McEwen Ter *MIS*. . . . . . 210 G78
McFall Ter *MIS*. . . . . . 210 H71
McFarlane Av *MAP*. . . . 187 Z49
McGeer St *VAN*. . . . . . . 163 X20
McGill Dr *PMD*. . . . . . . 145 S32

McGill St *BUR*. . . . . . . 143 R21-22
McGill St *VAN*. 143 R18 R18-20 R-S20
McGillivray Pl *NEW*. . . . 184 C-D27
McGregor Av *BUR*. . . . . 184 A23
McGuigan Av *VAN*. . . . . 162 X13
McGuire Av *WVA*. . . . . 122 M-N13
McGuire Rd *CHL*. . . . . . 213 J8
McHardy St *VAN*. . . 163 X19-20 X20
McHugh Cl *PCQ*. . . . . . 165 W38
McInnes St *NEW*. . . . . 184 B28-29
McIntosh Av *MAP*. . 187 Z52 Z52-53
McIntosh Dr *CHL*. . . . . 213 F5-6
McIntosh La *MAP*. . . . . 187 Z52
McIntyre Ct *MAP*. . . . . 187 Z50
McIntyre Dr *VAN*. . . 183 X19 Z20
McIntyre St *MIS*. . . . . . 210 G74
McIvor Av *MAP*. . . . . . 167 Y48
McKay Av *BUR*. . . . . . . . . . . .
. . . . 163 Y22 Y22 183 A22 Z22
McKay Av *MAP*. . . . . . . 187 C54
McKay Dr *RMD*. . . . . . 182 D13-14
McKay Pl *RMD*. . . . . . 182 D13-14
McKay St *VAN*. . . . 164 Y29 184 Z29
McKechnie Av *WVA*. . . . . 121 L6
McKechnie Rd *PTM*. . . . 167 V-W47
McKee Dr *ABT*. . . . 250 S78 251 S79
McKee Dr *DEL*. . . . . . 224 N30
McKee Pl *ABT*. . . . . . . 251 S79
McKee Pl *BUR*. . . . . . . 184 A23
McKee Pl *CHL*. . . . . . . 213 F5
McKee Rd *ABT*. . . . . . 250 T-U77
McKee Rd *ABT*. . . . . . . . . . . .
. . . . 250 T78 251 Q-R81 S79 T79
McKee St *BUR*. . . . 183 A22 184 A24
McKeen Av *DNV*. . . 122 N14 142 P14
McKeevers Pl *WHS*. . . . 401 B-C3
McKenzie Av *SUR*. . . . . 245 T-U31
McKenzie Dr *DEL*. . . . . 224 L29
McKenzie Dr *WVA*. . . . . 121 K-L3
McKenzie Pl *PCQ*. . . . . 166 X39
McKenzie Rd *ABT*. . . . . . . . . .
. . . . 250 U76 270 V76 W-Z76
McKenzie Rd *RMD*. . . . 222 K12
McKenzie St *NEW*. . . . . 184 B29
McKercher Av *BUR*. 163 Y22 164 Y23
McKessock Av *RMD*. . . 182 C14
McKessock Pl *RMD* 182 C14 183 C15
McKim Way *RMD*. . . . . . 182 D13
McKinley Ct *ABT*. . . . . . 251 S79
McKinley Dr *ABT*. . . . . . 251 R-S79
McKinley Pl *ABT*. . . . . . 251 S79
McKinney Av *MAP*. . . . . 187 Z49
McKinnon Cr *LGT*. . . . . 187 D52
McKinnon St *CQT*. . . . . 165 X34
McKinnon St *VAN*. . . . . . . . . .
. . . 163 X19-20 Y19 Y19 183 Z19
McLallen St *VAN*. . . . . 122 M13-14
McLaren Ct *CQT*. . . . . 145 R37
McLaren Dr *CHL*. . . . . . 233 N4
McLaughlin Av *CQT*. . . . 145 R37
McLaughlin Ct *CQT*. . . . 145 R37
McLean Av *PCQ*. . . . . 166 V39-40
McLean Av *RMD*. . . . . . 204 E24
McLean Dr *VAN*. . . . . . . . . . .
. . . 143 S-T17 T17 T17 163 U17 U17
McLellan Av *RMD*. . . . . 146 R39
McLennan Av *RMD*. 182 C14 202 G14
McLennan Ct *PCQ*. . 165 X38 166 X39
McLennan Pl *RMD*. . . . . 182 C14
McLeod Av *ABT*. . . . . . 250 T78
McLeod Av *RMD*. . . . . . 182 C14
McLeod Ct *RMD*. . . . . . 182 C14
McLure Av *RMD*. . . . . . 202 G9
McLure St *MIS*. . . . . . . 210 J72
McMartin St *NEW*. . . . 184 B27-28
McMaster Ct *PMD*. . . . 145 S31-32
McMaster Rd *UEL*. . . . . . 161 U4
McMath Rd *RMD*. . . . . . 202 H12
McMillan Ct *ABT*. . . . . . 250 U78
McMillan Rd *ABT*. 250 T-U78 270 V78
McMillan Rd *SUR*. . 246 U44 266 V44
McMillan Way *RMD*. . . . 204 F23
McMullen Av *VAN*. . . . . 162 W10-11
McMurray Av *BUR*. . . . . 164 Y23
McMyn Av *PTM*. . . 166 Y46 186 Z46
McMyn Rd *PTM*. . . . . . 166 Y45
McNab Av *ABT*. . . . . . 250 T78
McNair Bay *PMD*. . . . 145 Q32-33
McNair Dr *DNV*. . . . . . 123 J20
McNair St *DNV*. . . . . 123 J19-20
McNamee Pl *SQM*. . . . 301 H-J1
McNaught Rd *CHL*. . . . . 194 D9
McNeeley's Way *DEL*. . . 223 P16
McNeely Dr *RMD*. 183 D16 203 E16
McNeely St *NEW*. . . . . 184 B29
McNeil Rd *PTM*. 146 T46 147 T47-48

McNicoll Av *VAN*..... 10 J33 142 T11
McPhaden St *NEW*...... 184 B28
McPherson Dr *PCQ*165 W38 166 W39
McPherson Rd *HHS*.... 155 S19-20
McPherson St *MIS*...... 210 G73
McQuarrie La *MIS*...... 210 G73
McQuarrie Rd *PTM*..... 166 U45
McRae Av *MIS*...... 210 H73
McRae Av *VAN*...... 162 V12
McRae Cr *PCQ* .... 145 T38 146 T39
McRae Rd *KNT*...... 175 V20
McRae St *RMD*...... 204 E24
McSpadden Av *VAN*...... 163 U17
McSween Rd *CHL*...... 194 A-C9
McTaggart St *MIS*...... 210 G78
McTavish Ct *CQT*...... 146 Q39-40
McTavish Pl *MAP*...... 167 Y49-50
McTavish Rd *PTM*...... 166 Y43-44
Mead St *NEW*...... 184 B26
Meadedale Dr *BUR*.... 144 T23-24
Meadfeild Cl *WVA*...... 121 K3
Meadfeild Ct *WVA*...... 121 K3
Meadfeild La *WVA*...... 121 J3
Meadfeild Pl *WVA*...... 121 K3
Meadfeild Rd *WVA*...... 121 K3
Meadfield Wynd *WVA*... 121 K3
Meadow Av *BUR*.... 184 B24 C25
Meadow Av *SQM*...... 301 C2
Meadow Dr *KNT*...... 175 X20
Meadow La *WHS*...... 401 B3
Meadow Pl *DEL*...... 243 Q19
Meadow Pl *MAP*...... 167 Y49
Meadow Brook Pl *MAP*.... 167 Y50
Meadow Gardens Way *PTM* .....
..... 166 Y46 167 Y47
Meadowbank Cl *DNV*.. 123 J-K20
Meadowbrook Dr *CHL*.. 213 F5-6
Meadowland Pl *VAN*... 183 A19 Z20
Meadowlands Av *ABT* .. 250 T74-75
Meadowlark Dr *MAP*.... 187 Z54
Meadowlark St *CHL*.... 213 J5
Meadowood Cl *BUR*.... 164 U27
Meadowood Dr *BUR*.... 164 U27
Meadowood Pk *BUR*.... 164 U27
Meadows St *ABT*...... 270 V72
Meadowtown Centre Way *PTM* ..
..... 187 Z47
Meadowview Ct *CQT*.... 145 Q37
Meadowvista Pl *CQT*... 145 Q37-38
Meares Av *VAN*...... 183 Z20-21
Medwin Pl *DNV*...... 124 N23
Meighen Pl *ABT*...... 251 Q81
Melan Ct *ABT*...... 270 Z78
Melbourne Av *DNV*...... 123 K15
Melbourne St *VAN*.. 163 X20 X-Y20
Melburn Ct *MIS*...... 210 G75-76
Melburn Dr *MIS*.. 210 G76 H75-76
Melfa Ct *UEL*...... 161 U5
Melfa Rd *UEL*...... 161 U5
Mellard Av *CHL*...... 193 D7 213 E7
Mellis Dr *RMD*...... 183 D15
Melmar Av *ABT*...... 270 V72
Melrose Dr *SUR*..... 185 A-B35 B36
Melville Pl *SUR*...... 205 E33
Melville St *CHL*...... 213 H-J7
Melville St *MAP*...... 187 A48
Melville St *VAN* .. 11 F37 142 R-S13 S13
Memorial Dr *NEW*...... 184 A30 Z30
Memorial Rd *UEL*...... 161 U3
Menchions Mews *VAN* ... 10 L36
Mendham St *ABT*...... 250 U77
Menholm Rd *CHL*...... 213 E-F6
Mentmore St *CQT*...... 165 W32
Menzies St *MIS*...... 193 D8
Mercantile Way *ABT*...... 270 V72
Mercer Av *PCQ*.. 166 W39-40
Mercer Pl *PCQ*...... 166 W40
Mercer St *NEW*...... 184 C27-28
Merchantman Pl *RMD*...... 222 K9
Mercier Rd *PMD*...... 145 T24
Meredith Pl *DEL*...... 263 Z19-20
Merganser Dr *RMD*...... 222 K10
Meridian Pl *BUR*...... 164 U28
Merivale St *NEW*...... 184 A-B29
Merklin St *WRK*...... 265 W-X37
Merlin Dr *ABT*...... 250 U77
Merlin Pl *ABT*...... 250 U77
Merlot Blvd *ABT*...... 249 U67
Merlynn Cr *DNV*...... 123 M20
Merritt Av *BUR*...... 184 Z24
Merritt Dr *CHL*...... 193 D7
Merritt St *ABT*...... 250 S72
Merritt St *CQT*...... 165 U33
Mersey Dr *RMD*... 202 J14 222 K14
Mershon St *MIS*...... 230 K74-75

Mesa Ct *BUR*...... 164 X-Y26
Messier Av *CQT*......... 165 X32
Metcalfe Way *CQT*...... 146 R40
Metheral Ct *RMD*...... 182 B-C14
Metta La *PMD*...... 145 S35
Metta St *PMD*...... 145 S35
Miami River Dr *HHS*.... 155 P-Q19
Mica Pl *CQT*...... 145 Q36
Michael Dr *CHL*...... 233 M44
Michaud Cr *LGC*...... 227 N47-48
Michel Pl *SUR*...... 185 C33
Michener Ct *DNV*...... 123 K19
Michener Way *DNV*...... 123 K19
Michigan Dr *CQT*...... 145 R-S37
Mid Way *SQM*...... 301 G-H2
Midas St *ABT*...... 250 U77
Midden Rd *BEL*...... 144 P28
Middle Beach Rd *SUR*.. 266 Y-Z40
Middleglen Cl *SUR*...... 186 C40
Middleglen Pl *SUR*.... 186 C39-40
Middleton Rd *PTM*..... 147 P-Q50
Midlawn Dr *BUR*...... 143 T22
Midlothian Av *VAN*.... 162 W-X14
Midvale St *CQT*...... 165 V-W34
Mierau Ct *ABT*...... 250 S77-78
Mierau St *ABT*...... 250 S77-78
Mila St *ABT*...... 270 V77-78
Milford Av *CQT*...... 165 V33-34
Milford Dr *RMD*...... 202 J14
Mill St *CHL*...... 213 E6-7
Mill St *DNV*...... 123 K19-20
Mill Lake Rd *ABT*...... 250 U74
Millar Cr *ABT*...... 250 R-S78
Millar Ct *ABT*...... 250 R-S78
Millar Rd *SUR*...... 184 D29-30
Millar Creek Rd *WHS*.. 401 H-J98
Millard Av *CQT*...... 146 R40
Millars Pond Cr *WHS* ..... 401 H1
Millbank Rd *VAN*...... 162 U13
Millbrook La *BUR*...... 164 W30
Millburn Ct *BUR*...... 164 W30
Millcarch St *RMD*...... 183 B15
Millcreek Ct *BUR*...... 183 B21
Millcross Av *VAN*.. 11 J40 143 T15
Miller Av *BUR*...... 164 Y23
Miller Av *CQT*...... 165 U31-32
Miller Cr *MIS*...... 210 G73
Miller Dr *CHL*...... 233 L-M6
Miller Rd *DNV*...... 182 C9-12
Miller St *MAP*...... 187 A48
Miller St *VAN*...... 163 W17
Millmore Rd *RMD*...... 202 H8
Millstone Ct *ABT*...... 250 S78
Millstone St *VAN*...... 183 A19
Millstone Way *ABT*...... 250 S78
Millstream Rd *WVA*.. 122 J11-12 J12
Millview St *CQT*...... 165 X33
Millyard *VAN*...... 162 U13
Milne St *CQT*...... 145 S37
Milross Av *VAN*.. 11 J40 143 T15
Milsom Wynd *DEL*...... 263 Y16
Milton Av *DNV*...... 123 L19
Milton Dr *SUR*...... 205 F-G37
Milton St *NEW*..... 184 B28-29
Milton St *VAN*...... 182 B12
Miner St *NEW*...... 184 Z30
Mingo Av *MIS*...... 210 F72
Minler Rd *RMD*...... 202 G-H11
Minoru Blvd *RMD*...... 202 E-G12
Minoru Gt *RMD*...... 202 F12
Minster Dr E *DEL*...... 204 J29
Minster Dr W *DEL*...... 204 J29
Minter St *ABT*...... 250 U72
Minto Cr *VAN*...... 162 X12
Mira Pl *BUR*...... 164 V29
Mirabel Ct *RMD*...... 202 G-H11
Miraun Cr *ABT*...... 250 U77
Mirus Dr *ABT*...... 270 V77
Mission Av *BUR*...... 184 A-B25
Mission Rd *CNV*...... 123 N16
Mission Way *MIS*.... 230 K73-74
Mission View St *ABT*.... 230 K76
Misuto Pl *MAP*...... 187 A48
Mitchell Av *MIS*...... 210 G73
Mitchell Pl *DEL*...... 204 J26
Mitchell Rd *PTM*.... 186 Z45-46
Mitchell Rd *RMD*.... 183 B15-17
Mitchell St *ABT*...... 250 U71
Mitchell St *CQT*...... 146 S42
Mitchell Way *DEL*...... 204 F30
Moberly Rd *VAN*.... 162 U13-14
Modesto Dr *DEL*.... 204 H27-28
Moffat Av *WRK*...... 265 X38
Moffatt Rd *RMD*...... 202 G12

Mohawk Av *CQT*...... 145 T35
Mohawk St *VAN*...... 163 W16-17
Molina Ct *DNV*...... 103 H15
Molina Rd *DNV*...... 103 H15
Mollie Nye Way *DNV* ... 123 M19
Mona Av *BUR*...... 164 X30
Monahan Ct *LGT*...... 247 Q50-51
Monarch Ct *ABT*...... 270 V71
Monarch St *BUR*.. 164 W23-24 W24
Monashee Ct *CQT*...... 165 X35
Monashee Dr *DNV*...... 123 N21
Monashee Dr *RMD* .. 202 J11 222 K11
Monashee St *ABT*...... 250 S78
Moncton St *RMD*...... 222 L8-10
Monkland Pl *SUR*.... 205 E-F35
Monmouth Av *VAN*...... 163 X20
Monroe Dr *DEL*.... 204 H28 H29
Mons Ct *WHS*...... 401 C4
Mons Dr *VAN*...... 163 X20
Mons Rd *WHS*...... 401 C4 D4
Mont Royal Sq *VAN*.... 183 Z19
Montana Dr *CHL*...... 193 B8
Montana Rd *RMD*...... 202 G9
Montcalm Rd *CHL*.... 233 L-M5
Montcalm St *VAN* .....
..... 162 V13 182 A12 A-B12 Z12
Montclair St *BUR*...... 164 U26
Monte Pl *CQT*...... 165 V36
Monte Bre Cr *WVA*...... 121 K3
Monte Bre Ct *WVA*...... 121 K3
Monte Bre Pl *WVA*...... 121 K3
Monte Vista Cr *ABT*.... 250 U71
Monte Vista Ct *DNV*.... 123 K17
Monte Vista Dr *CHL*.... 233 M4
Monte Vista St *MIS* .... 210 E75
Montebello Pl *WHS*...... 401 E4
Montecito Dr *BUR*...... 164 U26
Montego St *RMD*...... 183 D15
Monteith Rd *RMD*.... 222 K10-11
Monteray Av *DNV*.... 123 J-K16
Monteray Pl *ABT*...... 270 V78
Monterey Av *CQT*.... 165 X34-35
Montesina Pl *CHL*...... 233 M4
Montgomery Av *ABT*.... 270 V73
Montgomery St *CQT*.. 165 W-Y34
Montgomery St *VAN* .....
..... 162 X-Y12 Y12 182 Z12
Montiverdi Pl *WVA* ...... 121 K3
Monton Av *DNV*...... 122 L14
Montreal St *DEL*...... 243 Q21
Montrose Av *ABT*.... 250 U75-76
Montrose St *BUR*...... 143 R21
Montrose St *CQT*...... 165 U34
Montrose Way *SQM*...... 301 E4
Montroyal Blvd *DNV* .....
..... 123 J15-16 K16-17
Montroyal Pl *DNV*...... 123 J16
Montvue Av *ABT*...... 250 U76
Moody Av *CHL*...... 213 F5
Moody Av *CNV* .. 123 M-N18 143 P18
Moody Ct *PCQ*...... 166 Y39
Moody St *MAP*...... 167 Y51
Moody St *NEW*...... 184 B29
Moody St *PMD*...... 145 T33-34
Moorcroft Ct *BUR*...... 164 V25
Moore Av *BUR*...... 164 U25
Moore Av *CHL*...... 233 M4
Moore Pl *CQT*...... 146 Q39
Moore Rd *RMD*...... 202 H12
Moorland St *ABT*...... 250 U71
Moorside Pl *BUR*...... 164 U29
Moray St *PMD*...... 145 T34-35
Moreland Dr *BUR*...... 164 W23
Moresby Dr *RMD*...... 202 G8-9
Morey Rd *ABT*...... 250 T75-76
Morgan Av *PCQ*.... 166 W39-40
Morgan Cr *WVA*...... 121 L5
Morgan Dr *SUR*.... 226 M43-44
Morgan Pl *DEL*...... 243 Q16
Morgan Pl *SUR*...... 226 M43
Morgan Rd *DNV*.... 123 M18-19
Morgan Way *ABT*.... 250 S-T78
Morgan Creek Cr *SUR* .... 246 S39
Morgan Creek Pl *SUR* .. 246 S39-40
Morgan Creek Way *SUR* . 246 S-T39
Morioka Pl *SUR*.... 205 F-G37
Morley Dr *BUR*...... 164 Y26
Morley St *BUR* .. 164 Y25-26 Y26
Morning Cr *ABT*...... 250 T75
Morningside Dr *DEL*.... 263 Z17
Morningside La *BUR*.. 164 U-V29
Morningstar Cr *VAN*.... 183 B18
Morrey Ct *BUR*...... 164 V30
Morrill St *PCQ*...... 146 T39

Morris Cr *DEL*...... 263 X18
Morris St *MAP*.... 187 A50 Z50
Morrison Av *CQT*...... 165 U31
Morrison Cr *LGT*...... 207 J50
Morrison St *PCQ*...... 166 X40
Morrissey Rd *RMD*.... 145 S-T35
Morrow Rd *KNT*.... 175 X21 X22
Morse Cr *MAP*...... 167 Y52
Mortfield Ct *RMD*...... 222 K13
Mortfield Gt *RMD*...... 222 K13
Mortfield Pl *RMD*...... 222 K13
Mortfield Rd *RMD*.... 202 J13-14
Morton Av *VAN* .. 10 F34 142 R-S12
Morton Pl *CQT*...... 165 V37
Morton Rd *CHL*...... 233 N6
Morven Dr *WVA*.... 102 H13-14
Moscrop St *BUR* .....
..... 163 W-X21 W-X22 164 X23
Moscrop St *VAN*.... 163 W-X20
Mosquito Creek La *CNV*.. 123 N15
Moss La *MIS*...... 210 F76
Moss Ct *ABT*...... 270 V78
Moss Ct *CQT*...... 145 P38
Moss St *VAN*.... 163 W19 X19
Mossom Creek Dr *PMD* .. 145 Q32
Mott Cr *NEW*...... 184 Z29
Mouat Dr *ABT*...... 250 T72-73
Mouldstade Rd *ABT* 250 U76 270 V76
Mount St *HHS*...... 155 P20
Mount Blanchard Ct *ABT* .. 250 S78
Mount Blanchard Dr *ABT* .. 250 S78
Mount Blanchard Pl *ABT* .. 250 S78
Mount Crown Rd *DNV*.... 122 K14
Mount Fee Rd *WHS*..... 401 J98
Mount Hope Rd *HOP* ... 118 E46
Mount Lehman Rd *ABT* .. 249 Q-U69
Mount Royal Ct *PMD*.... 145 T31
Mount Royal Dr *PMD* .. 145 T31-32
Mount Royal Pl *PMD*.... 145 T31
Mount Seymour Pkwy *DNV* .....
..... 124 N24-26 143 P21-22
Mount Seymour Rd *DNV* .....
..... 124 L25-26 M-N25
Mount Waddington Av *ABT* .....
..... 250 T-U72
Mountain Dr *ABT*...... 251 U80
Mountain Dr *LIO*...... 101 A-B23
Mountain Hwy *DNV* .....
..... 123 J-N20 143 P-Q20
Mountain La *WHS*...... 401 F4
Mountain La *WHS*...... 401 T21
Mountain Pl *PTM*...... 147 S48
Mountain Pl *SQM*...... 301 D4
Mountain Sq *WHS*...... 401 T21
Mountain Ash Dr *HOP*.... 118 E46
Mountain Ayre La *ANM*.... 145 S35
Mountain Park Rd *CHL* .. 194 D9-10
Mountain View Blvd *DEL* .. 243 Q18
Mountain View Cr *HOP*.... 118 E47
Mountain View Cr *MAP*.... 187 Z51
Mountain View Dr *SUR* .. 245 T38
Mountain View Dr *WHS* ... 401 B3
Mountain View Rd *FRA* .. 253 R5-6
Mountain View Rd *KNT*.... 175 X19
Mountainview Ct *CQT*.... 145 Q37
Mountainview Way *CHL* .. 233 K-L5
Mountbatten St *BUR*.... 183 C22
Mountview Pl *ABT*...... 250 T75
Mountview Pl *BUR*...... 164 V30
Mountview Rd *ABT*.... 250 T-U75
Mowat Pl *DNV*...... 123 N22
Mowat St *LGT*...... 207 F54
Mowat St *NEW*...... 184 B28
Mowbray Ct *ABT*...... 270 V78
Mowbray Rd *RMD* .. 202 J12-13
Moyne Dr *WVA* .. 122 K13 K-L13
Muensch Tr *LGT*...... 207 E53-54
Mufford Cr *LGT*.... 227 L48 M49
Muir Dr *RMD*...... 204 E-F24
Muirfield Cr *WHS*...... 401 C4
Muirfield Dr *VAN* .. 183 A18 Z18
Muirfield La *WHS*...... 401 C4
Muirfield Pl *CQT*...... 145 P38
Mulberry Pl *BUR*...... 164 X29
Mulberry Pl *CQT*...... 145 P38
Mulberry Pl *KNT*...... 175 X20
Mulgrave Pl *WVA*...... 122 L13
Mulholland Pl *DEL*...... 204 F30
Mullins Rd *CHL*.... 233 M7-8
Munday Pl *CNV*...... 123 L18
Mundy St *CQT*.... 165 W-Y35
Munroe Av *FRA*...... 253 R4-5
Munroe Cr *VAN*...... 183 A19
Munster Av *DNV*...... 143 P21
Murchie Pl *PCQ*...... 145 T38
Murchie Rd *LGT*...... 267 Y54

Murchison Rd *RMD*........ 202 E9
Murphy Dr W *DEL* ...... 263 Z16
Murphy St *ABT* ...... 250 R74
Murray Av *ABT* ...... 250 U73
Murray Cr *LGT* ...... 247 Q51
Murray Dr *CHL* ...... 213 F5
Murray St *MIS* ...... 210 J75
Murray St *PMD* .. 145 S35 T34
Musgrave Cr *RMD* .... 202 E-F8
Musket Ter *PCQ* ...... 165 Y38
Musqueam Av *VAN* .. 162 Y7 182 Z7
Musqueam Cl *VAN* ...... 162 Y7
Musqueam Dr *SUR* .... 185 A31
Musqueam Dr *VAN* ...... 162 Y7
Mustang Pl *PCQ* ...... 166 W41
Muston Pl *DEL* ...... 204 J29
Mycon St *MIS* ...... 210 G78
Myhill Rd *RMD* ...... 202 H12
Myng Cr *HHS* ...... 155 R19
Myrnam St *CQT* .. 165 X34 Y34
Myron Ct *RMD* ...... 202 H13
Myrtle Av *MIS* ...... 210 H74
Myrtle St *BUR* .. 163 U-V21 V21
Myrtle Way *PCQ* ...... 146 S40
Myrtlewood Cr *SQM* .... 301 J4
Mystery Cr *DNV* ...... 124 M25
Mytko Cr *RMD* ...... 202 J10

**N**

Nacht Av *PCQ* ...... 165 W38
Nadeau Pl *ABT* ...... 250 S-T71
Nadina Ct *CQT* ...... 165 V36
Nadina Dr *CQT* ...... 165 V36
Nadine Cr *RMD* ...... 202 F11
Nairn Av *VAN* ...... 183 A20
Nairn Ct *DNV* ...... 144 P24
Nairn Pl *SUR* ...... 205 E33
Nairn Way *SQM* ...... 301 E4
Naismith Av *HHS* .. 155 P20 Q19
Nakiska Ct *ABT* ...... 251 R79
Nakusp Dr *ABT* .. 250 S72-73
Nanaimo Cl *ABT* ...... 250 S73
Nanaimo Ct *ABT* .. 250 R-S73
Nanaimo St *NEW* ...... 184 B27
Nanaimo St N *VAN* .. 143 R-S18
Nanaimo St *VAN* ...... 143 T18
.. 163 U-W18 X-Y18 183 A18 A-B18 Z18
Nancy Greene Dr *WHS* .... 401 E4
Nancy Greene Way *DNV* .....
..... 103 H15 122 J14 123 J15
Nanika Cr *RMD* ...... 202 F11
Nanika Gt *RMD* ...... 202 F11
Nanton Av *VAN* .. 162 W11-13
Nanton St *CQT* ...... 146 Q40
Naomi Pl *DNV* ...... 124 N27
Napanee St *NEW* .. 184 A-B28
Napier Pl *CQT* ...... 145 R37
Napier St *BUR* .....
.. 143 T21-22 T22 144 T24-25
Napier St *VAN* 143 T16-17 T17-19 T20
Naples Way *VAN* ...... 183 A20
Narvaez Dr *VAN* ...... 162 W-X10
Nash Dr *CQT* ...... 145 S37
Nash St *LGT* ...... 207 F53
Nassau Dr *VAN* ...... 183 Z17
National Av *RMD* .. 183 B17-18
National Av *VAN*11 J40-41 143 T15-16
Naughton Av *DNV* .... 124 M26
Nautilus Cr *VAN* ...... 162 U7
Neal St *VAN* .. 162 Y13 182 Z13 Z13
Neale Dr *MIS* ...... 210 F73
Neaves Rd *MAP* ...... 167 W49
Neaves Rd *PTM* .. 147 P-S49
Nechako Cr *PCQ* ...... 166 U42
Nechako Dr *DEL* .. 204 G-H27
Needles Dr *WHS* ...... 401 C3
Neill Pl *RMD* ...... 202 J11
Neilson Av *CNV* ...... 123 M15
Nelmes St *CHL* ...... 193 D6
Nelson Av *BUR* .....
.. 164 X-Y23 183 A22 B22 184 A23 Z23
Nelson Av *HOP* ...... 118 F44-45
Nelson Av (Horseshoe Bay) *WVA* .....
..... 101 G1-2
Nelson Av (Upper Levels) *WVA* .....
..... 122 L10-11 L9-10
Nelson Ct *ABT* ...... 250 T74
Nelson Pl *PCQ* ...... 165 W39
Nelson Rd *RMD* .. 183 C21 203 F-G21
Nelson St *CQT* ...... 165 W-Y32
Nelson St *MIS* ...... 210 G-H71
Nelson St *VAN* .. 10 E-F34 G35-36
..... 11 H37 142 R-S12 S12-13 T13-14

Nelson View *DEL* . . . . . . . . **204** F28
Nelson Way *BUR* . . . . . . . . **144** T29
Nelson Peak Rd *MAP* . . . . . **167** W53
Nepal Cr *WVA* . . . . . . . . . . **122** L11
Nepal Pl *WVA* . . . . . . . . . . **122** L11
Neptune Cr *BUR* . . . . . . . . **164** V29
Nesters Rd *WHS* . . . **401** D4 E3-4
Nestor St *CQT* . . . . . . . **146** R-S39
Netley Pl *WVA* . . . . . . . . . **122** L11
Neville St *BUR* . . **183** A22 **184** A23 A24
Nevis Dr *RMD* . . . . . . . . . **202** J12
New Brighton Rd *VAN* . . **143** H19-20
New McLellan Rd *SUR* . . . **225** N31
New Vista Pl *BUR* . . . . **184** Z26-27
Newark Pl *SUR* . . . . . . . . . **185** C36
Newberry St *PCQ* . . **146** T41 **166** U41
Newby Dr *CHL* . . . . . . . . . **233** N6
Newcastle Ct *ABT* . . . . . . **250** S72
Newcastle Ct *VAN* . . . . . **183** A19 Z20
Newcastle Dr *ABT* . . . . . . **250** S72
Newcastle Pl *PCQ* . . . . . . **166** U40
Newcombe St *BUR* . . . . . . **164** Y28
Newcroft Pl *WVA* . . . . . **122** L12-13
Newdale Ct *DNV* . . . . . **123** J16-17
Newdale Pl *WVA* . . . . . . . **122** L13
Newdale Rd *WVA* . . . . . **122** L12-13
Newlands Av *ABT* . . . . . **250** T74-75
Newlands Dr *LGC* . . . . . . **247** Q49
Newlands Pl *WVA* . . . . . . **122** L13
Newlands Rd *WVA* . . . . . . **122** L13
Newman Rd *CHL* . . . . . . . **213** E6
Newman St *SQM* . . . . . . . **301** K2
Newmarket Dr *DNV* . . . . . **123** L15
Newmond Rd *RMD* . . . . . . **202** H8
Newmore Av *RMD* . . . . . . **202** G8
Newport Av *SQM* . . . . . . . **301** H1
Newport Av *VAN* . . . . . **183** A17-18
Newport Dr *PMD* . . . . . . . **145** S35
Newport Pl *DEL* . . . . . . . **224** K29
Newport St *CQT* . . . . . . . **165** V34
Newport Ridge Dr *SQM* . . . **301** E3
Newton Ct *MIS* . . . . . . . . **210** H74
Newton St *BUR* . . . . . . . . **164** Y23
Newton Wynd *UEL* . . . . . . **161** T3-4
Nichol Rd *WRK* . . . . . . . . **265** W35
Nicholas Cr *LGI* . . . . . . **248** I62-63
Nichols Dr *BUR* . . . . . . . . **144** R29
Nicholson Rd *DEL* . . . . . . **224** K-L30
Nick Av *PCQ* . . . . . . . . . . **165** X38
Nicklaus Rd *PTM* . . . . . . . **147** P47
Nicklaus North Blvd *WHS* . **401** C3-4
Nico Wynd Dr *SUR* . **245** S34-35 S35
Nico Wynd Pl *SUR* . . . . . . **245** S35
Nicol Rd *CHL* . . . . . . . . . **233** N6
Nicola Av *CQT* . . . . . . . . **165** U31
Nicola Av *PCQ* . . . . . . . . **166** V41
Nicola Cl *ABT* . . . . . . . . . **250** S73
Nicola Pl *ABT* . . . . . . . . . **250** S73
Nicola St *ABT* . . . . . . . . . **250** S73
Nicola St *VAN* . **10** F-G35 G34 **142** S12
Nicolle Pl *RMD* . . . . . . . . **202** F9
Nicolum Cr *BUR* . . . . . . . **144** P24
Nicomekl Rd *SUR* . . . . . **245** R-S35
Nicomen Cr *CHL* . . . . . . . **233** M5
Nicomen Pl *ABT* . . . . . . . **251** S79
Nigel Av *VAN* . . . . . . . . . **162** W14
Nighthawk La *WHS* . . . . . **401** F3
Nightingale Av *MAP* . . . . . **187** Z54
Nightingale Dr *ABT* . . . . . **249** S69
Nikola St *PTM* . . . . . . . . . **166** Y45
Nile Gt *PCQ* . . . . . . . . . . **166** V42
Nishi Ct *RMD* . . . . . . . . . **202** J8
Nita La *WHS* . . . . . . . . . . **401** G2
Nita Lake Dr *WHS* . . . . . . **401** G-H1
Nithsdale St *BUR* . . . . . . . **163** W21
Nixon Av *DEL* . . . . . . . . . **263** Z16
No Name Rd *SQM* . . . . . . **301** F2
Noble Av *ABT* . . . . . . . . . **250** U72
Noble Ct *PMD* . . . . . . . . . **145** T33
Noble Rd *CHL* . . . . . . . . . **213** G6
Noel Dr *BUR* . . . . . . . . . . **164** V30
Noelani Pl *BUR* . . **164** Y26 **184** Z26
Nolan St *BUR* . . . . . **164** Y24 **184** Z24
Noons Creek Cl *PMD* . . **145** R35-36
Noons Creek Dr *CQT* . . **145** Q-R36
Noons Creek Dr *PMD* . . **145** R-S35
Nootka Cl *ABT* . . . . . . . . **250** S73
Nootka Pl *ABT* . . . . . . . . **250** S73
Nootka St *ABT* . . . . . . . . **250** S73
Nootka St *NEW* . . . . . . . . **164** X30
Nootka St *VAN* **143** T19 **163** U19 V-W19
Nootka Way *PMD* . . . . . **145** S-T35
Norbury Pl *CQT* . . . . . . . . **165** V37
Norcrest Ct *BUR* . . . . . . **164** U-V30
Norcross Way *DNV* . . . . . **122** L14
Nord Rd *CHL* . . . . . . . . . **233** N6

Nordby Pl *DNV* . . . . . . . . **123** K20
Nordel Ct *DEL* . . . . . . . . **204** H27
Nordel Way *DEL* . **204** G27-28 G29 H27
Nordic Dr *WHS* . . . . . **401** G2 H2-3
Nordic Pl *WHS* . . . . . . . . **401** G2
Nordsun Rd *SUR* . . . . . . . **185** B34
Norfolk Pl *MAP* . . . **167** Y50 **187** Z50
Norfolk Rd *SUR* . . . **265** V38 **266** V39
Norfolk St *BUR* . **163** V21 V22 **164** V23
Norfolk St *CQT* . . . . . . . . **165** U32
Norfolk St *PCQ* . . . . . . . . **146** T41
Norland Av *BUR* . . . **164** W-X24 W24
Norland St *CHL* . . . . . . . . **193** D6
Norman Av *CQT* . . . . . . . **145** T37
Norman Cr *CHL* . . . . . . . . **213** F7
Normanby Cr *WVA* . . . . . . **122** J13
Normandy Dr *CHL* . . . . . . **233** N6
Normandy Dr *VAN* . . . . . . **163** V-W20
Normandy Rd *VAN* . . . . . . **162** U7-8
Norquay St *VAN* . . . **163** W-X18
Norrish Av *CHL* . . . . . . . . **213** F7
Norrish Av *MIS* . . . . . . . . **210** H77
North Av *MAP* . . . . . . . . . **187** Z52
North Dr *SUR* . . . . . . . . . **266** V39
North Pl *SUR* . . . . . . . . . **266** V39
North Rd *CQT* . . . . . . **164** U-W30
North Bend St *CQT* . . . . . **165** Y36
North Bluff Rd *WRK* . . . **265** W36-37
North Dyke Rd *RMD* . . . . **182** A8-9
North Fraser Cr *BUR* . . . . **183** A-B22
North Fraser Ct *BUR* . . . . **183** C22
North Fraser Way *BUR* . . . . . . . . . . . .
. . . . . . . . **183** B21-22 **184** C24-25 C-D23
North Parallel Rd *ABT* . . . . **251** T83
North Railway Av *MIS* . . **210** J74-75
North Service Rd *RMD* . . . **182** C10
Northbrook Ct *BUR* . . . . . **183** B21
Northcliffe Cr *BUR* . . . **144** S25-26
Northcote Cr *MIS* . . . . . . . **210** J75
Northcote St *MIS* . . . . **210** J75
Northcoat Dr *SUR* . . . . . **245** T U35
Northdale Ct *ABT* . . . . . . **250** S71
Northern Av *CQT* . . . . **145** S37-38
Northern St *VAN* . . . . **11** K41 **143** T15
Northey Rd *RMD* . . . . . . . **182** D13
Northglen Cl *SUR* . . . . **186** C39-40
Northglen Pl *SUR* . . . . . . **186** C39
Northlands Blvd *WHS* **401** F-F4 G F-4 S21
Northlawn Dr *BUR* . . **143** I22 **144** I23
Northmount Av *MIS* . . . . . **210** H74
Northpark Cr *SUR* . . . . . . **225** M31
Northpark Pl *SUR* . . . . . . **225** M31
Northridge Dr *SQM* . . . . . **301** J3
Northumberland Av *VAN* . . **183** A20
Northview Cr *DEL* . . . . . . **224** K29
Northview Cr *SUR* . . . . . . **246** T40
Northview Ct *BUR* . . . . . . **163** X22
Northview Pl *ABT* . . . . . **250** T75
Northview Pl *DEL* . . . . **224** K-L29
Northview St *CHL* . . . . . . **193** D6
Northwest Marine Dr *UEL* . . . . . . . . . . . .
. . . . . . . . . . . . . **161** S-T4 T-U3
Northwest Marine Dr *VAN* . . . . . . . . . . .
. . . . . . **142** T7 **161** T6 **162** U7
Northwood Dr *WVA* . . . . . **121** J4
Norton Ct *DNV* . . . . . . . . **124** N25
Norton Ct *RMD* . . . . **204** E24-25
Norum Cr *DEL* . . . . . . . . **204** F28
Norum Pl *DEL* . . . . . . . . **204** F28
Norum Rd *DEL* . . . . . **204** F28-29
Norwood Av *DNV* . . . **123** K17 K-L17
Norwood Ct *CQT* . . . . . **125** N38
Nottingham Pl *PCQ* . . . . . **166** X39
Nottingham Rd *DNV* . . . . . **123** K20
Nova Scotia Av *PCQ* . . . . . **166** X39
Novak Dr *CQT* . . . . . . . . **146** R40
Nowell St *CHL* . . . . . . . . **213** E-F7
Nugget St *PCQ* . . . . . **166** X39-40
Nulelum Way *DEL* . . . . **263** V-W16
Nurseries Rd *UEL* . . . . . . **161** W5
Nursery St *BUR* . . . . . . . . **164** X26
Nuthatch Pl *DNV* . . . . . . . **103** H15

Oak Gt *SUR* . . . . . . . . . . **186** C40
Oak La *MIS* . . . . . . . . . . **210** J74
Oak Pl *DEL* . . . . . . . . . **243** Q16-17
Oak Pl *SQM* . . . . . . . . . . **301** C3
Oak St *CHL* . . . . . . . . . . **193** D7
Oak St *FRA* . . . . . . . . . . **253** R-S5
Oak St *NEW* . . . . . . . . . . **184** A29
Oak St *VAN* . **162** V-Y13 **182** A-B13 Z13
Oak Ter *PTM* . . . . . . . . . **166** Y46
Oakdale Rd *BUR* . . . . . . . **164** Y23
Oakdale St *PCQ* . . . . . . **146** S41-42
Oakglen Dr *BUR* . . . . . **164** X-Y23
Oakhill Pl *BUR* . . . . . . . . **164** Y25
Oakland Pl *BUR* . . . . . . . **164** Y23
Oakland St *BUR* . . . . . **164** Y23-25
Oakland St *NEW* . . . . . . . **184** A29
Oakmond Rd *RMD* . . . . . . **202** H8
Oakmount Cr *BUR* . . . . . . **164** Y23
Oakridge Ct *ABT* . . . . . . **270** V71
Oaktree Ct *BUR* . . . . . . . **164** X23
Oakview St *CQT* . . . . . . . **165** U32
Oakwood Cr *DNV* . . . **122** N13-14
Oakwood Dr *KNT* . . . . . . **175** X20
Oban Pl *SUR* . . . . . . . **205** E33
Oben St *VAN* . . . . . . . **163** X-Y20
Oboe Pl *WHS* . . . . . . . . . **401** E3
Ocean Pl *WVA* . . . . . . . . **121** J2
Ocean Breeze Pl *SUR* . **265** V31-32
Ocean Cliff Dr *SUR* . . . . . **265** V32
Ocean Forest Dr *SUR* . . . . **265** V32
Ocean Forest Pl *SUR* . . . . **265** V32
Ocean Park Rd *SUR* . . . . . . . . . . .
. . . . . . . . . . . **265** V-W31 V-W32
Ocean Surf Pl *SUR* . . . **265** V-W32
Ocean Tide Ct *SUR* . . . . . **265** V31
Ocean View La *SQM* . . **301** J2-3 K3
Ocean Wind Dr *SUR* . . . . . **265** V32
Oceanview Pl *LIO* . . . . . . **101** C23
Oceanview Rd *LIO* . . . **101** C23-24
Odd St *HOP* . . . . . . . . . **118** E44
Odlin Cr *RMD* . . . . . . . . **182** D13
Odlin Pl *RMD* . . . . . . . . **182** D13
Odlin Rd *RMD* . . . . . **182** D13-14
Odlum Ct *WVA* . . . . . . . . **101** G1
Odlum Dr *VAN* . . . . . . . . **143** T17
Officers Row *CHL* . . . . . . **233** M6
Ogdon St *CQT* . . . **145** T37 **165** U37
Ogilvie Cr *PCQ* . . . . . . . . **146** I39
Ogilvie St *SUR* . . . . . . . **118** E45
Ogilview Dr *HOP* . . . . . . **118** E47
Ohashi Ct *MIS* . . . . . . **210** G-H73
Okanagan Dr *ABT* . . . . . . **250** S73
Olafsen Av *RMD* . . . . . . **183** C15
Old Bridge Ct *VAN* . . . . **10** K35
Old Bridge St *VAN* . **10** K35 **162** U12
Old Bridge Walk *VAN* . . . . **10** K36
Old Clayburn Rd *ABT* . . . . . . . . . .
. . . . . . . . **250** T77 **251** R-S79
Old Dewdney Trunk Rd *PTM* . . . . .
. . . . . . . . **166** W44-45 X46
Old Dollarton Rd *DNV* . . **143** P-Q21
Old Gravel Rd *WHS* . . . . . **401** H1
Old Hope-Princeton Way *HOP* . . .
. . . . . . . . . . . . . **118** F44-46
Old Lillooet Rd *DNV* . . . . **143** P20
Old Marine Dr *UEL* . . . . . **161** W4
Old McLellan Rd *SUR* . . **226** M-N40
Old Mill La *WHS* . . . . . . . **401** G2
Old Riverside Rd *ABT* . . . . **250** S74
Old Yale Rd *ABT* . . . . . . . . . . . .
. . . **250** T71 U72 U76-77 U78 **251** V79
Old Yale Rd *HOP* . **118** G41-42 H42-43
Old Yale Rd *LGC* . . . . . **227** N-P49
Old Yale Rd *LGT* . . . . . **227** P49-50
. . . **247** Q51-52 Q-R53 R54 **248** T61
Old Yale Rd *SUR* . . **184** B30 B30
. . **185** B31 B-C31 B-C32 C32 C-D33 D34
Old Yale Rd E *SUR* . . . . . **226** K43
Oldfield Rd *RMD* . . . . . . **183** D15
Olds Dr *CHL* . . . . . . . . . **213** G7
Olive Av *BUR* . . . . . . . **163** Y21-22
Olive Ter *WHS* . . . . . . . . **401** H2
Olive Way *ABT* . . . . . . . . **270** V76
Oliver Cr *CHL* . . . . . . . . **233** M5
Oliver Cr *VAN* . . . . . . . . **162** W10
Oliver Dr *RMD* . . . . . . . . **204** E24
Oliver Rd *CQT* . . . . . . . . **146** R44
Oliver St *MIS* . . . . . . . **230** K71-72
Oliver St *NEW* . . . . . . . . **184** A29
Olsen Rd *SUR* . . . **184** B30 **185** B31
Olson Av *HOP* . . . . . . . **118** E45
Olson Av *MIS* . . . . . . . **210** F71-72
Olson Rd *SQM* . . . . . . . . **301** D3
Olund Cr *MAP* . . . . . . . . **187** A53

Olund Rd *ABT* . . . . . **249** Q69 Q70
Olympia Pl *ABT* . . **250** U78 **270** V78
Olympic St *VAN* . . . . . **162** X-Y8
Omineca Av *PCQ* . . . . . . **166** U42
Omineca Cr *PCQ* . . . . . . **166** U42
Omineca Ct *ABT* . . . . . . **251** S79
Omineca Pl *PCQ* . . . . . . **166** U42
Oneida Dr *CQT* . . . . . . . **145** T35
Onslow Pl *WVA* . . . . . **122** J-K13
Ontario Av *CHL* . . . . . . . **213** E6
Ontario Pl *VAN* . . **162** Y14 **163** Y15
Ontario St *DEL* . . . . . . . **243** Q21
Ontario St *NEW* . . . . **184** B28-29
Ontario St *VAN* . **11** K40 **142** T14
. . . . . . **162** U14 V-Y14 **182** A14 Z14
Onyx Pl *ABT* . . . . . . . . . **249** S69
Opal Pl *ABT* . . . . . . . . . **270** V73
Opal Pl *RMD* . . . . . . . . . **202** F10
Oranda Av *CQT* . . . . . . . **165** W35
Orchard Dr *ABT* . **250** U78 **270** V78
Orchard La *PTM* . . . . . . . **187** Z47
Orchard La *WVA* . . . . . . . **122** K9
Orchard Pl *ABT* . . . . . . . **250** U78
Orchard Rd *CHL* . . . . . . **213** F-G4
Orchard Way *WVA* . **122** K9-10 L9-10
Orchid Cr *MIS* . . . . . . . . **210** H74
Orchid Dr *CQT* . . . . . . . . **165** V37
Orchid Dr *MIS* . . . . . . . . **210** H74
Orchid Pl *MIS* . . . . . . . . **210** H74
Orchill Rd *WVA* . . . . . . . **101** H1-2
Oriole Av *MIS* . . . . . . . . **210** J72
Oriole Cr *ABT* . . . . . . . . **250** T73
Oriole Dr *SUR* . . . . . . . . **185** B37
Oriole Pl *PCQ* . . . . . . . . **146** T41
Oriole Walk *VAN* . **162** X14 **163** X15
Orion Pl *ABT* . . . . . . . . . **250** U78
Orion Pl *BUR* . . . . . . . . . **164** V29
Orkney Ct *CQT* . . . . . **165** V-W35
Orkney Pl *DNV* . . . . . . . . **124** N23
Orkney Way *SQM* . . . . . . **301** E4
Orland Dr *CQT* . . . . . . . . **165** V34
Orlohma Pl *DNV* . . . . . . . **124** N25
Ormidale St *VAN* . . . . . . **163** Y20
Orr Dr *PCQ* . . . . . . . . . . **165** Y38
Orr Rd *CHL* . . . . . . . . . . **213** H5
Ortona Av *UEL* . . . . . . . . **161** U5
Ortona Cr *VAN* . . . . . . . . **162** U8
Ortona La *VAN* . . . . . . . . **162** U8
Orwell St *DNV* . . . **143** P20 Q20
Osborne Av *NEW* . . . . . . **184** Z28
Osborne Rd *CHL* . . . . . . **193** C8
Osborne Rd E *DNV* . . . . **123** L17-18
Osborne Rd W *DNV* . . . . **123** L17
Osborne St *PCQ* . . . . . . **146** T39
Osgoode Dr *RMD* . . . . . . **202** H12
Osgoode Pl *RMD* . . . . . . **202** H12
Osler St *VAN* **162** V12-13 W13 X13 Y13
. . . . . . . . . . **182** A12-13 Z13
Osmond Av *RMD* . . . . . . **202** H9
Osoyoos Cr *UEL* . . . . . . . **161** V5
Osprey Ct *DNV* . . . . . **144** P24-25
Osprey Ct *RMD* . . . . . . . **222** L10
Osprey Dr *RMD* . . . . . **222** K-L10
Osprey Dr E *ABT* . . . . . . **249** T70
Osprey Dr W *ABT* . . . . . . **249** T69
Osprey Pl *PCQ* . . . . . . . **146** T42
Osprey Pl *WHS* . . . . . . . **401** F3
Osprey St *MIS* . . . . . . . . **210** J72
Ospring St *MAP* . . **187** A48 A-B47
Ostler Ct *DNV* . . . . . . . . **124** N26
Othello Rd *HOP* . . . . . . . **118** E48
Ottaburn Rd *WVA* . . . . . . **122** K-L11
Ottawa Av *WVA* . . . . . . . . . . . .
. . . . . . **122** L10-11 L11-12 L9-10
Ottawa Pl *WVA* . . . . . . . . **122** L10
Ottawa St *DEL* . . . . . . . **243** Q21
Ottawa St *PCQ* . . . . . . . **166** V41
Ottenbreit Rd *KNT* . . . . . **175** Y21
Otter Pl *RMD* . . . . . . . . . **202** H12
Otter St *ABT* . . . **250** U73 **270** V73
Oughton Dr *PCQ* . . . . . . **166** W39
Oval Dr *CHL* . . . . . . . . . **193** C8
Ovens Av *NEW* . . . . . . **184** Z28-29
Overstone Dr *WVA* . . . . . **101** H1
Owen Dr *MAP* . . . . . . . . **187** Z49
Owen St *MIS* . . . . . . . . . **210** G78
Owl Ct *DNV* . . . . . . . . . **124** N23
Owl Pl *HOP* . . . . . . . . . **118** G-H43
Oxbow Way *CQT* . . . **146** R39-40
Oxenham Av *WRK* . **265** W-X36 X38
Oxford Av *ABT* . . . . . . . **250** T76
Oxford Connector *PCQ* . **166** U39-40
Oxford Dr *PMD* . . . . . . . **145** S32
Oxford Pl *CQT* . . . . . . . **146** R40

Oxford Rd *CHL* . . . . . . . **233** K6
Oxford St *BUR* . **143** S21-22 **144** S23
Oxford St *CQT* . . . . . . **146** Q-R40
Oxford St *DNV* . . . . . . . **143** Q20
Oxford St *NEW* . . . . . . . **184** B28
Oxford St *PCQ* . **146** S-T40 **166** U40
Oxford St *VAN* . . . **143** S18-19 S20
Oxford St *WRK* . . . . . **265** W-X36
Oxley St N *WVA* . . . **121** K6 **122** K7
Oxley St S *WVA* . . . . . . . **121** L6
Oxtoby Pl *CQT* . . . . . . . **145** T37
Oyama Ct *UEL* . . . . . . . **161** U-V5
Oyama St *MIS* . . . . . . . . **210** H71
Ozada Av *CQT* . . . . . . . **146** S39

**O**

O'Flaherty Gt *PCQ* . . . . . **165** X-Y38
O'Hara La *SUR* . . . . . . . **245** T31

**P**

Pacemore Av *RMD* . . . . . . **202** G8-9
Pacific Av *WRK* . . **265** X37-38 **266** X39
Pacific Blvd *VAN* . . . . . . . . . . . . .
. . . . **11** J37-39 **142** T13-14 **143** T15
Pacific Ct *DEL* . . . . . . . . **262** X15
Pacific Dr *DEL* . . . . . . . . **262** X15
Pacific Hwy *SUR* . . . . . . . . . . . . .
**206** G-H42 **226** P42 **246** Q42 **266** V-W42
Pacific Pl *ABT* . . . . . . . . **250** T71
Pacific Pl *DEL* . . . . . . . . **262** X15
Pacific Pl *WRK* . . . . . . . **266** X39
Pacific St *ABT* . . . . . . . . **145** S37
Pacific St *VAN* . . . **10** H35 **142** S-T12
Packard Av *CQT* . . . . . . . **145** S37
Paco Rd *SQM* . . . . . . . . **301** F4
Paddock Dr *CQT* . . . . . . **145** P38
Page Rd *ABT* . . . . . . . **230** L75-78
Page Rd *DNV* . . . . . . . . **123** K20
Paige Pl *CHL* . . . . . . . . . **233** K5
Painted Cliff Rd *WHS* . **401** E5 F4 S23
Paisley Av *CHL* . . . . . . . **213** F5
Paisley Av *PCQ* . . . . . . . **146** S42
Paisley Pl *SQM* . . . . . . . **301** E4-5
Paisley Rd *DNV* . . . . . . . **122** L14
Paitsmauk Av *WVA* . . . . . **122** N13
Pakenham Pl *MIS* . . . **210** H77-78
Palace Ct *ABT* . . . . . . . . **250** T76
Palace Pl *BUR* . . . . . **164** Y25-26
Paladin Ter *PCQ* . **165** Y38 **166** Y39
Palermo St *CQT* . . . . . . . **145** T35
Palisade Cr *PCQ* . **165** Y38 **166** Y39
Palisade Ct *PCQ* . **165** Y38 **166** Y39
Palisade Dr *DNV* . . . . . . **123** J16
Palisade Pl *CQT* . . . . . . **146** R40
Pallicer Av *CQT* . . . . . **165** X34-36
Palm Av *BUR* . . . . . . . . **184** Z23
Palm Cr *ABT* . . . . . . . . . **250** T71
Palmberg Rd *RMD* . **203** J17 **223** K17
Palmdale St *CQT* . **145** T37 **165** U37
Palmer Av *CQT* . . . . . . . **145** T35
Palmer Dr *WHS* . . . . . . . **401** E3
Palmer Rd *RMD* . . . . . . . **202** H-J9
Palmerston Av *WVA* . . . . . . . . . .
. . . . **122** K-L8 L10 L11 L11-12 L9-10
Palmtree La *PTM* . . . . . . **186** A46
Palomino Cr *SUR* . . . . . . **226** M43
Pandora Av *ABT* . . . . . . . **270** V73
Pandora Dr *ABT* . . . . . . . **144** S26
Pandora Pl *ABT* . . . . . . . **270** V73
Pandora St *BUR* . . **144** S25 S26
Pandora St *CHL* . . . . . . . **213** E-F5
Pandora St *VAN* . . **143** S17-19 S20
Panorama Dr *ABT* . . . . . . **270** V78
Panorama Dr *CQT* . . . . **145** Q36-37
Panorama Dr *DNV* **124** M26-27 M-N26
Panorama Dr *PMD* . . . . . **145** Q35
Panorama Dr *SUR* . . . . **225** M-N37
Panorama Pl *LIO* . . . . . . **101** C23
Panorama Pl *PMD* . . . . . **145** Q35
Panorama Pl *SQM* . . . . **301** J2-3
Panorama Rd *LIO* . . . . . **101** C23
Panorama Ridge *WHS* . . **401** F-G3
Papuc Pl *DEL* . . . . . . . . **224** K30
Par Rd *WHS* . . . . . . . . . **401** E-F3
Paradise Av *CQT* . . . . . . **165** X35
Paradise Bay *SUR* . . . . . **266** W39
Paradise Pl *ABT* . . . . . . **250** R78
Paramount Cr *ABT* . . . . . **270** V71
Parana Dr *PCQ* . . . . . **166** U41-42
Parana Pl *PCQ* . . . . . . **166** U41-42
Parapet Ter *PCQ* . . . . . . **166** X39
Parc Ct *CQT* . . . . . . . . . **165** X34
Pare St *CHL* . . . . . . . . . **233** K5
Park Av *HOP* . . . . . . . . . **118** E47
Park Av *LGC* . . . . . . . . . **227** N48
Park Av *WRK* . . . . . . . . **265** W35
Park Cr *CQT* . . . . **145** T35 **165** U35

Park Cr *NEW* . . . . . . . . . . 184 Z29
Park Cr *SQM* . . . . . . . . . . 301 E3-4
Park Ct *DEL* . . . . . . . . . . 243 Q19
Park Dr *ABT* . . . . . . . . . . 250 U76
Park Dr *FRA* . . . . . . . . . . 253 S5-6
Park Dr *SUR* 185 B34-35 B35 266 W39
Park Dr *VAN* . . . . . . . . . . 182 A12 Z12
Park Dr (101B Av) *SUR* . . . . 185 D31
Park Dr (124A St) *SUR* . . . 185 D32
Park Dr (Chilliwack) *CHL* . . 213 F5-6
Park Dr (Squiaala IR) *CHL* . 213 F-G4
Park La *MAP* . . . . . . . . . . 167 W51
Park La *VAN* . . . . . . 10 E34 142 R11-12
Park La *WVA* . . . . . . . . . . 122 L7-8
Park Pl *RMD* . . . . . . . . . . 202 F13
Park Pl *SUR* . . . . . . . . . . 185 B35
Park Rd *PTM* . . . . . . . . . . 146 Y46
Park Rd *RMD* . . . . . . 202 F12 F13
Park Row *NEW* . . . . . . . . . 184 A29
Park St *HOP* . . . . . . . . . . 118 E44-45
Park St *KNT* . . . . . . . . . . 175 W21
Park St *MIS* . . . . . . . . . . 210 J73
Park Way *SQM* . . . . . . 301 E1-2
Parkcrest Dr *BUR* . . . . . . . 164 U24
Parkdale Dr *BUR* . . 164 U24-25 U25
Parkdale Pl *PMD* . . . . . 145 R34-35
Parker Pl *WRK* . . . . . . . . . 265 W38
Parker St *BUR* . . 143 T21-22 144 T23
Parker St *VAN* . . . . . . . . . . . . . . .
. . . 143 T16-17 T17-18 T18-19 T19-20
Parker St *WRK* . . . . . . . . . 265 X34
Parkeside Estate *DEL* . . . . 223 P16
Parkgate Av *DNV* . . . . . . . 124 N24
Parkglen Pl *PMD* . . . . . . . 145 R35
Parkgrove Cr *DEL* . . . . . 263 Z17-18
Parkhurst Rd *DNV* . . . . . . 143 P21
Parkland Dr *CQT* . . . . . 146 R-S40
Parkland Pl *CQT* . . . . . 146 S39-40
Parklane *ABT* . . . . . . 250 S-T76
Parklawn Dr *BUR* . . . . . . . 144 T23
Parkside Bay *SUR* . . . . . . 266 W39
Parkside Cl *SUR* . . . . . . . 225 M31
Parkside Cr *MAP* . . . . . 167 V53-54
Parkside Ct *PMD* . . . . . . . 145 Q34
Parkside Ct *SUR* . . . . . . . 225 M31
Parkside Dr *PMD* . . . . . 145 Q-R34
Parkside La *DNV* . . . . . 124 M-N26
Parkside Pl *SUR* . . . . . . . 225 M31
Parkside Rd *WVA* . . . . . 122 K-L12
Parkside Walk *PTM* . . . . . 186 A46
Parksville Dr *RMD* . . . . . . 202 H9
Parktree Cr *SUR* . . . . . . . 225 M31
Parktree Ct *SUR* . . . . . . . 225 M31
Parktree Pl *SUR* . . . . . 225 L-M31
Parkview La *PCQ* . . . . . . 165 V38
Parkview Pl *BUR* . . . . . 164 Y24-25
Parkview Pl *DEL* . . . . . 224 K29-30
Parkview Pl *SUR* . . . . . . . 186 C40
Parkview St *ABT* . . . . . . . 250 U72
Parkway Av *VAN* . . . . . . 162 V-W11
Parkway Blvd *CQT* . . . . . 145 P-R37
Parkway Dr *SUR* . . . . . 245 U37-38
Parkway Rd *SQM* . . . . . . 301 E3-4
Parkwood Av *BUR* . . . . . 163 X21-22
Parkwood Cr *BUR* . . . . . . 163 X22
Parkwood Dr *KNT* . . . . . . 175 X21
Parkwood Dr *SUR* . . . . . . 205 J32
Parkwood Dr *WHS* . . . . . . 401 B3
Parkwood Pl *DEL* . . . . . . . 204 J30
Parkwood Pl *PMD* . . . . 145 R34-35
Parkwood Pl *RMD* . . . . . . 203 E16
Parkwood Pl *SQM* . . . . . . 301 B1
Parkwood Way *RMD* . . . . . 203 E16
Parliament Cr *DNV* . . . . . 123 J-K15
Parmenter Rd *FRA* . . . . . 253 Q-R4
Parr Av *MIS* . . . . . . . . . . 210 G76
Parr Rd *CHL* . . . . . . . . . 213 G5-6
Parry St *VAN* . . . . . . . . . 202 G9
Parsons Dr *SUR* . . . . . . . 186 D43
Parsons Rd *RMD* . . . . . 202 J10-11
Parthenon Pl *WVA* . . . . 121 J2-3 K2
Parton Rd *SUR* . . . . . . . . 184 C30
Partridge Cr *SUR* . . . . . . 185 B37
Pasco Rd *WVA* . . . . . . . . 101 E3
Passage Dr *CQT* . . . . . . . 145 T36
Passaglia Pl *CQT* . . . . . . 146 R40
Pasture Cir *CQT* . . . . . . . 165 U37
Paterson Rd *DEL* . . . . . . . 224 K29
Paton Dr *DEL* . . . . . . . . 223 N17
Paton St *VAN* . . . . . . . 162 W-X10
Patricia Av *PCQ* . . . . . . . . . . . . . . .
. . . . . . . 145 T38 146 T39-40 T42
Patricia Dr *CHL* . . . . . . 233 K-L5
Patricia Dr *DEL* . . . . . . . 204 F29
Patrick Pl *BUR* . . . 183 A22 184 A23
Patrick Rd *PTM* . . . . . . . 146 T45

Patrick St *BUR* . . . . . . 184 A23-24
Patrick St *RMD* . . . . . . . 183 B18
Patten Av *CHL* . . . . . . . . 213 E6
Patterdale Dr *DNV* . . . . 122 J-K14
Patterson Av *BUR* . . . . . . . . . . . . . .
. . . . . 163 X21 Y21 183 A21 Z21
Patterson Av *MAP* . . . . . . 187 Z48
Patterson Rd *RMD* . . . . 182 C13-14
Patullo Cr *CQT* . . . . . 146 Q-R39
Patullo Pl *SUR* . . . . . . . . 185 B31
Paul Lake Ct *CQT* . . . . . . 165 V37
Paula Cr *CHL* . . . . . . . . 194 D9
Paula Pl *PCQ* . . . . . . . . 166 X39
Pauleshin Cr *RMD* . . . . . 202 H10
Pauline St *ABT* . . . . . . . 250 U75
Paulson Cr *ABT* . . . . . . . 270 V76
Paulus Cr *BUR* . . . 164 U25 U25-26
Paulus Ct *BUR* . . . . . . . . 164 U26
Pavilion Pl *MIS* . . . . . . . 210 E74
Payne St *VAN* . . . . . . . . 163 X20
Peace Park Dr (1 Av) *SUR* . 266 Z41
Peach Rd *CHL* . . . . . . . . 233 N4
Peach Tree La *MAP* . . . 187 Z53-54
Peacock Pl *MIS* . . . . . . . 210 G75
Peacock Pl *SUR* . . . . . . . 185 B37
Peacock St *MIS* . . . . . . . 210 G75
Peak Dr *WHS* . . . . . . . . . 401 F3
Pearce St *NEW* . . . . . . . . 184 B28
Peardonville Rd *ABT* . . . . . . . . . . . .
. . . . . . . . 249 U70 250 U71-73
Pearkes Dr *RMD* . . . . . . 202 F18
Pearkes La *UEL* . . . . . . . 161 U4-5
Pearkes Pl *PCQ* . . . . . . . 146 T41
Pearl Av *ABT* . . . . . . . . . 250 T77
Pearl Av *BUR* . . . . . . . . . 164 Y23
Pearl Ct *RMD* . . . . . . . . . 202 F10
Pearson St *CHL* . . . . . . . 213 F8
Pearson St *NEW* . . . . . . . 184 A29
Peebles Pl *SQM* . . . . . . . 301 D5
Pekin Pl *SUR* . . . . . . . . 185 D33
Pekrul Pl *PCQ* . . . . . . . 166 W40
Pelcher Ct *CQT* . . . . . . . 146 Q39
Pelican Ct *RMD* . . . . . . 222 K10
Pelletier Rd *HOP* . . . . . . 118 D43
Pelly Rd *DNV* . . . . . . . . 123 K15
Pelton Av *CQT* . . . . . . . 165 V32
Pemberton Av *DNV* . . . . . . . . . . . . . .
. . . . . . . 122 L14 M14 N14 142 P14
Pemberton Av *SQM* . . . . . 301 J1-2
Pemberton Cr *DEL* . . . . . 204 F29
Pemberton Pl *DEL* . . . . . 204 F29
Pembina St *NEW* . . . . . 184 C-D27
Pembroke Av *CQT* . . . . 165 W-X31
Pembroke Pl *RMD* . . . . 202 H9-10
Pender Pl *PCQ* . . . . . . . 166 U42
Pender St *BUR* . . 143 S21-22 144 S23
Pender St E *VAN* . . . . . . . . . . . . . .
. . . . 11 H40-41 143 S15-16 S16 S17-20
Pender St W *VAN* . . . . . . . . . . . . . .
. . 10 F36 11 F37 G38 H39 142 R-S13 S14
Pendlebury Rd *RMD* . . . 202 H-J9
Pendleton Av *RMD* . . . . . 202 H9
Pendrell St *VAN* . . . 10 F34 G35 H36
. . . . . . . . . 142 R12 R-S12 S12 S12-13
Pennant Bay *DEL* . . . . . . 223 N17
Penner Av *MIS* . . . . . . . 210 G77
Penner Dr *MIS* . . . . . . . 210 G77
Penner St *MIS* . . . . . . . 210 G77
Penny La *MAP* . . . . . . . . 187 Z49
Penny La *RMD* . . . . . . . 202 H12
Penny Pl *PCQ* . . . . . . . 166 V-W39
Penny Farthing Dr *VAN* . . . . . . . . . . .
. . . . . . . . . . . . . 10 K34 142 T12
Pennylane Pl *SQM* . . . . . . 301 J3
Pensnurst Ct *CQT* . . . . 165 X35-36
Penticton St *VAN* . . . . . . . . . . . . . .
. . . 143 R-T18 S18 U18 V18 V-W18 W18
Penticton St N *VAN* . . . . 143 R-S18
Pentland Ct *BUR* . . . . 164 W29-30
Pentland Way *SQM* . . . . 301 E4-5
Penzance Dr *BUR* . 143 S22 144 R23
Pepperidge Ct *BUR* . . . . . 164 U26
Percival Av *BUR* . . . . . . 164 W24
Percy Ct *DNV* . . . . . . . . 124 N25
Peregrine Ct *CQT* . . . . . . 145 S36
Periwinkle Ct *PMD* . . . . 145 R34
Periwinkle Pl *LIO* . . . . . . 101 C23
Perkins St *PCQ* . . . . . . . 166 W42
Perrot Mews *VAN* . . . . . . 183 Z19
Perry St *VAN* . . . . . . . . 163 W17
Perth Av *CHL* . . . . . . . . 233 K-L6
Perth Av *CQT* . . . . 164 V30 165 V31
Perth Dr *SQM* . . . . . . . . 301 E5
Perth Dr *SUR* . . . . . . . 185 A36-37
Perth Pl *SQM* . . . . . . . . 301 D5

Perth St *ABT* . . . . . . . . 250 S74
Petawawa Av *CHL* . . . . . 233 N5-6
Peter St *BUR* . . . . . . . . 183 Z21
Peter St *HOP* . . . . . . . . 118 G43
Peters Rd *DNV* . . . . . 123 L20-21
Petersham Av *VAN* . . . . . 163 Y20
Peterson Av *CQT* . . . . . . 165 X34
Peterson Dr *RMD* . . . . . . 202 J9
Peterson Rd *SQM* . . . . . . 301 B2
Peterson St *MIS* . . . . . . 210 J73
Petrie Ct *CQT* . . . . . . . . 165 X35
Petts Rd *RMD* . . . . . . 202 J11-12
Peveril Av *VAN* . . . . . . . 162 W14
Peytavin Pl *MIS* . . . . . . 210 H75
Pheasant Dr *SUR* . . . . . . 185 B37
Pheasant Pl *DNV* . . . . . . 123 J15
Pheasant St *CQT* . . . . . 145 T37-38
Phelps Av *MIS* . . . . . . . 210 G74
Philbert St *MIS* . . . . . . 210 H74
Philips St *NEW* . . 184 D26 204 E26
Phillip Av *DNV* . . . . . . . . . . . . . . .
. . . 122 L14 M14 M-N14 N14 142 P14
Phillips Av *BUR* . . . . . . . . . . . . . . .
. . . . . 144 T26 164 U26 V-W26
Phillips Pl *BUR* . . . . . . . 164 U26
Phoenix Dr *RMD* . . . . . . 222 L9
Phoenix St *WRK* . . . . . . 265 W35
Phyllis Rd *DNV* . . . . . . . 123 K21
Pia Rd *SQM* . . . . . . . . . 301 D4-5
Piccadilly St N *WVA* . . 121 K4 K-L4
Piccadilly St S *WVA* . . . 121 L3-4
Piccolo Dr *WHS* . . . . . . . 401 E3
Pickering Dr *RMD* . . . . . 202 J9
Picton Pl *ABT* . . . . . . . . 250 S77
Picton St *ABT* . . . . . . . . 250 S77
Picton St *VAN* . . . . . . 163 W-X19
Pier Dr *CQT* . . . . . . . 145 T36-37
Pier Pl *NEW* . . . . . . . . 204 E26
Pierard Rd *DNV* . . . . . . 123 L20
Pierce Pl *CQT* . . . . . . . 145 R37
Pierce Ter *ABT* . . 250 S78 251 S79
Piermond Rd *RMD* . . . . . 202 J8
Pierowall Pl *SQM* . . . . . . 301 D5
Pika Ct *CQT* . . . . . . . . 145 Q38
Pilot Dr *CQT* . . . . . . . 165 U36
Pilot House Rd *WVA* . . . 121 L3-4
Pimlico Pl *PCQ* . . . . . . 146 S41
Pimlico Way *RMD* . . . . . 202 F13
Pinda Dr *PMD* . . . . . . . 145 T35
Pinda Pl *MAP* . . . . . . . 187 A48
Pine Av *CHL* . . . . . . . . 213 E8
Pine Av *HHS* . . . . . . . . 155 Q19
Pine Cr *VAN* . . . . 162 V11-12 W11 X11
Pine Dr *SQM* . . . . . . . . 301 K3
Pine Rd *SUR* . . . . . . . . 184 C30
Pine St *ABT* . . . . . . 250 U75 U76
Pine St *BUR* . . . . . . 163 W21 W22
Pine St *FRA* . . . . . . . . 253 R5
Pine St *MAP* . . . . . . . . 187 A50
Pine St *MIS* . . . . . . . . 210 H75
Pine St *NEW* . . . . . . . . 184 A29
Pine St *VAN* . . . 10 K34 162 U-V12
Pine Ter *CQT* . . . . . . . 165 W37
Pinebrook Pl *CQT* . . . . 165 U38
Pinecrest Av *CQT* . . . . . 145 T35
Pinecrest Dr *WVA* . . . . . 122 J10
Pinegrove St *ABT* . . . 249 T68-69
Pinehurst Dr *BUR* . 144 T27 164 U27
Pinehurst Dr *VAN* . 162 Y14 182 Z14
Pinehurst Pl *CQT* . 125 N38 145 P38
Pinehurst Pl *DEL* . . . . 263 W16-17
Pinemont Av *PCQ* . . . . . 146 T42
Pinetree Cl *CQT* . . . . 145 P-Q38
Pinetree Cr *WVA* . . . . . 121 K3-4
Pinetree La *PTM* . . . . . 186 A46
Pinetree La *WHS* . . . . . 401 A5
Pinetree Pl *WHS* . . . . . 401 A5
Pinetree Way *CQT* . . 145 Q38 R-T38
Pineview Av *ABT* . . . . . 250 U72
Pinewell Cr *RMD* . . . . 202 J13-14
Pinewell Pl *RMD* . . . . . 202 J14
Pinewood Av *CQT* . . . . 145 R38
Pinewood Cr *BUR* . . . . 164 U26
Pinewood Cr *DNV* . . . . 122 N14
Pinewood Cr *SUR* . . 185 D31-32
Pinewood Dr *DEL* . . . . . 224 M30
Pinewood Dr *KNT* . . . . . 175 X21
Pinnacle Ct *VAN* . . . . . 183 Z20
Pinnacle Pl *ABT* . . . . . 250 S71
Pinnacle St *CQT* . . . . 165 U-V36
Pintail Dr *RMD* . . . . 222 K-L10
Pinyon Dr *PTM* . . . . . . 186 A46

Pinyon La *PTM* . . . . . . 186 A46
Pioneer Av *BUR* . . . . 163 X22 Y22
Pioneer Av *KNT* . . . . . 175 W19-21
Pioneer Ct *ABT* . . . . . . 250 Q78
Pioneer Dr *CHL* . . . . . . 233 K6
Pioneer Way *PCQ* . . . 165 X-Y38
Pioneer Way *SQM* . . . . . 301 G1-2
Pipeline Rd *CQT* . . . . . . . . . . . . . .
. . . 126 M-N39 145 R-S38 146 P-R39
Pipeline Rd *VAN* . . . . . 142 P-Q12
Piper Av *BUR* . . . 164 V-W27 W27
Piper Cr *CHL* . . . . . . . . 213 G7
Pitcairn Pl *WVA* . . . . . 121 K2-3
Pitlochry Way *SQM* . . . . 301 D4
Pitman Pl *DEL* . . . . . . 204 H29
Pitt St *BUR* . . . . . . . . 164 X-Y26
Pitt St *WVA* . . . . . . 101 G-H1 H2
Pitt River Rd *PCQ* . . . . . . . . . . . . . .
. . . . . . 165 V-W38 166 V-X39
Pixley La *KNT* . . . . . . 175 W-X22
Plane Tree Ct *CQT* . . . . 145 Q38
Planetree La *PTM* . . . . . 186 A46
Plateau Blvd *CQT* . . . . 145 P-Q38
Plateau Cr *CQT* . . . . . . 145 Q38
Plateau Cr *SQM* . . . . . 301 J3-4
Plateau Dr *DNV* . . . . . . 122 M14
Plateau Dr *SQM* . . . . . . 301 J3-4
Platinum La *CQT* . . . . . 145 P36
Platt Cr *DNV* . . . . . . . 123 L20
Plaxton Cr *ABT* . . . . 250 U74-75
Plaza St *MAP* . . . . . . . 187 Z52
Pleasant St *RMD* . . . . . . 222 K8
Pleasant St La *PMD* . . . . 145 S35
Pleasant Way *DEL* . . . 223 N-P17
Pleasantview Cr *MIS* . . . 210 J72
Plimsoll St *CQT* . 145 T36 165 U36
Plover Ct *RMD* . . . . 222 K-L10
Plover Dr *RMD* . . . . . . 222 K10
Plover St *MIS* . . . . . . 210 H72
Plum Av *BUR* . . . . . . . 184 A24
Plumridge Av *MIS* . . . 210 J74
Plumtree Cl *SUR* . . . . 236 C40
Plymouth Cr *PCQ* . . . 146 S41
Plymouth Dr *DNV* . . . . 144 P23
Plymouth Pl *DNV* . . . . 144 P23
Plywood Rd *SUR* . . . . 184 D29
Po Av *PCQ* . . . . . . . . 166 U41
Po Pl *PCQ* . . . . . . . 166 U41
Poel Pl *PCQ* . . . . . . 166 X39
Point Grey Rd *VAN* . . 142 T9-10
Poirier St *CQT* . . . . 165 U-W34
Polar Av *ABT* . . . . . . 249 R70
Polewe Pl *SQM* . . . . . 301 D5
Pollard St *CQT* . . . . . 146 R43
Pomona Way *SQM* . . 301 D4-5
Ponderay St *CHL* . . . . 193 B8
Ponderosa Blvd *PTM* . . 186 A46
Ponderosa Pl *ABT* . . . . 250 S71
Ponderosa Pl *PTM* . . . 186 A46
Ponderosa St *ABT* . . . 250 S-T71
Ponderosa St *CQT* . . . 145 T38
Pondside Rd *ANM* . . . 125 N33
Pooley Av *PCQ* . . . . 166 W39-40
Poplar Ct *ABT* . . . . . 251 R79
Poplar Dr *PTM* . . . . . 186 A46
Poplar Dr *SUR* . . . . 265 W38
Poplar Pl *PTM* . . . . . 186 A46
Poplar St *CQT* . . . . . 165 V34
Poplar St *HHS* . . . . 155 P-Q19
Poplar St *VAN* . . . . . 183 A15
Poplynn Dr *DNV* . . . . 123 M20
Poplynn Pl *DNV* . . . . 123 M20
Port View Pl *WVA* . . . 121 J4
Portage Av *CHL* . . . 193 D7-8
Portage Av *CQT* . . . 165 W35
Portage Pl *BUR* . . . 164 V-W26
Portage Rd *SUR* . 184 B30 185 B31
Porteau Pl *DNV* . . . 144 P24
Porter Dr *ABT* . . . . 249 T63
Porter St *CQT* . 165 U33 V32-33
Porter St *VAN* . . . . 163 V17
Portland St *BUR* . . . . . . . . . . . . . .
. . . 183 A21 A21-22 184 A23 A24
Portree Way *SQM* . . 301 E4-5
Portside Ct *VAN* . . . 183 A18
Portside Dr *VAN* . . . 183 A-B18
Portside Rd *RMD* . . 203 G19-20
Portview Pl *PMD* . . . 145 T35
Potter Rd *ABT* . . . . 270 X78
Powell Av *MAP* . . . 167 Y48-49
Powell Ct *ABT* . . . 270 V76
Powell St *VAN* . 11 G41 143 S15-17
Prairie Av *PCQ* . . 146 T39-43
Prairie St *ABT* . . . 250 R73
Prairie Central Rd *CHL* . 213 H7-8
Prairieview Dr *ABT* . 251 U81
Prasmount Pl *KNT* . . 175 X21

Pratt Cr *ABT* . . . . . . . 250 T76
Pratt St *ABT* . . . . . . . 250 T76
Preddy Dr *DEL* . . . . . 224 N30
Premier St *DNV* . . 123 N20 143 P20
Prenter St *BUR* . . 184 A24 A25 Z24
Prentis Av *MIS* . . . 210 H75-76
Prescott St *NEW* . . . . 184 A28
Prescott St *VAN* . . . . 182 Z9
Presidents Row *UEL* . . 161 U4-5
Prest Rd *CHL* . . . . . . 194 D9
Prestige Pl *SUR* . . 205 G37-38
Preston Ct *BUR* . . . . 144 T26
Prestwick Dr *VAN* . . . 183 Z17
Pretty Ct *NEW* . . . 184 D26 204 E26
Price Cr *BUR* . . . . . 163 X21-22
Price St *BUR* . . 163 X22 164 X24
Price St *VAN* . . . . . 163 W-X20
Prime Pl *DNV* . . . . 123 J-K20
Prime St *DNV* . . . . 123 J-K20
Primrose Dr *CHL* . . . 213 F-G2
Primrose La *CQT* . . . 145 S38
Primrose La *DNV* . . 123 J-K15
Primrose Pl *WVA* . . . 121 J2-3
Primrose St *ABT* . . . 270 V74
Primula Pl *BUR* . . . 164 X29
Prince St *PCQ* . . . 166 X40
Prince St *PMD* . . . 145 S32
Prince Albert St *VAN* . . . . . . . . . . . .
. 163 U-V16 V-X16 Y16 183 A16 Z16 Z16
Prince Charles Blvd *SUR* . . . . . . . . . .
. . . . . 205 E32-33 F32-33 F33
Prince Edward St *VAN* . . . . . . . . . . . .
. . . . . 163 U-Y15 183 A15 Z15
Princess Av *CHL* . . . 213 E5-7
Princess Av *DNV* . . 123 K-L18 L18
Princess Av *VAN* . 11 G-H41 143 S-T15
Princess Cr *CQT* . . . 145 S37-38
Princess Ct *ABT* . . 250 T71-72
Princess Dr *SUR* . . . 204 E29
Princess La *RMD* . . . 222 M11
Princess St *ABT* . . . 250 T71
Princess St *MAP* . . 187 A-B48
Princess St *NEW* . 184 A28 Z28-29
Princess St *RMD* . . 222 L-M11
Princeton Av *CQT* . 146 Q40 Q41
Princeton Av *PMD* . 145 S31-32
Princeton Av *RMD* . 202 H9-10
Prior Av *ABT* . . . . . 250 R77
Prior St *VAN* . . . 11 J40-41 143 T15-16
Priory Pl *DEL* . . . . . 204 J29
Pritchard Av *BUR* . . 164 V30
Probert Rd *KNT* . . . 175 W20
Procter Av *WVA* . . . 122 L7
Proctor St *MIS* . . . 210 J74
Production Blvd *SUR* . 226 N46
Production Way *BUR* . 164 V28-29
Production Way *LGC* . . . . . . . . . . . . .
. . . . 226 N46 227 M47 N47
Production Way *SQM* . . 301 G-H2
Progress Pl *DEL* . . . 203 J21-22
Progress Way *CHL* . 213 G2-3 H2
Progress Way *DEL* . . . . . . . . . . . . . .
. . . . . 203 J21 222 J23 K21
Progress Way *SQM* . . . 301 H2
Progressive Way *ABT* . . 249 U69
Promenade Mews *VAN* . 162 V14
Promontory Ct *ABT* . . 250 S71
Promontory Rd *CHL* . 233 M7 M-N8
Prospect Av *DNV* . . . 123 J15
Prospect Av *WRK* . . 265 X36-37
Prospect Cr *WRK* . . . 266 X39
Prospect Dr *DEL* . . . 224 K29
Prospect Rd *DNV* . . . 123 J-K17
Prospect St *ABT* . . . 250 T73
Prospect St *CQT* . . . 165 U34
Ptarmigan Dr *MIS* . . 210 H72-73
Ptarmigan Pl *DNV* . . 103 H15
Ptarmigan Pl *WHS* . . . 401 F3
Puffin Ct *RMD* . . . 222 K10
Puget Dr *VAN* . . . 162 V9 W9-10
Pugwash Pl *RMD* . . . 202 J9
Pullman Av *ABT* . . . 249 T63
Punnett Cl *BUR* . . . 164 Y25
Purcell Av *ABT* . . . 251 S-T79
Purcell Dr *CQT* . . 145 Q-R38
Purcell Way *DNV* . . 123 N20
Purdey Av *MAP* . . . 187 Z53
Pynford Ct *BUR* . . . 184 A24
Pyrford Rd *WVA* . . . 122 K12

**Q**

Quadling Av *CQT* . . 165 X31-33
Quadra Ct *CQT* . . 145 S38 146 S39
Quadra St *VAN* . . . . . 162 V9

Quail Av MIS . . . . . . . . . 210 J72
Quail Ct ABT . . . . . . . . 249 S69
Quail Run Estates WHS . . 401 G2
Qualicum Cl ABT . . . . . 250 R-S73
Qualicum Dr VAN . . . 183 A17-18
Qualicum Pl ABT . . . . . . 250 S73
Qualicum St ABT . . . . . . 250 S73
Quarry Av ABT . . . . . . 250 T77-78
Quarry Ct DNV . . . . . . . 123 K19
Quarry Rd CHL . . . . . . 194 C-D9
Quarry Rd CQT . . . . . . . 146 Q44
Quartz Pl CQT . . . . . . . 145 P36
Quatsino Dr VAN . . . . 183 Z20-21
Quay CT . . . . . . . . . . 145 T36
Quayside Ct VAN . . . . . . 183 B18
Quayside Dr NEW . . . . 184 B28-29
Quebec St CHL . . . . . 143 S-T15
. . . . 163 U-V15 V-W15 W15 W-X15 X-Y15
. . . . . . . . . . . . . . . . . . . 183 Z15
Quebec St NEW . . . . . 184 B28
Quebec St VAN . . . . . . 11 H-J40
Queen St CHL . . . . . 213 H-J7
Queen St HOP . . . . . 118 E44-45
Queen St LGT . . . . . . . 207 F54
Queen Mary Blvd SUR . . 205 F33
Queens Av NEW . . . 184 A-B29 B28
Queens Av VAN . . . 163 W-X19 X20
Queens Av WVA
. . . . . . 122 K9 K-L10 L10-11 L11-12
Queens Pl SUR . . . . . . 204 E29
Queens Rd E DNV . . . 123 L17 L18
Queens Rd W DNV . . . 123 L15-17
Queens St PMD . . . . . . 145 T33
Queens Way SQM . . . . . 301 G-H1
Queensbridge Dr BUR . 164 V25-26
Queensbury Av CNV
. . . . . . . . . . . 123 M18 143 P18
Queensland Rd UEL . . . 161 U6
Queenston Av CQT . . . . 146 Q41
Queenston Ct BUR . . . . 144 T26
Quesnel Dr VAN . . . . 162 V9 W9-10
Quilchena Cr VAN . . . . . 162 X11
Quilchena Pl VAN . . . . 162 W-X11
Quintette Cr CQT . 145 Q38 146 Q39
Quinton Av ABT . . . . . . 249 S63
Quinton Av CQT . . . . . . 165 V34
Quinton Pl DNV . . . . . . 123 K15

### R

Raab St HOP . . . . . . 118 E45 F44-45
Rabbit La WVA . . . 122 K13 K13-14
Rachael Pl FRA . . . . . . . 253 R6
Radcliffe Av WVA . . . . . . 122 L7
Radisson St VAN . . . 183 Z20-21
Rae Av VAN . . . . . . . . . 163 X20
Rae Rd SQM . . . . . . . . . 301 C1
Rae St PCQ . . . . . 146 T42 166 U42
Raeburn St DNV . . . . . . 124 N26
Rai Av MIS . . . . . . . . . . 230 K72
Railspur Alley VAN . . 10 K35 142 T12
Railway Av CHL . . . . . . 213 F6-7
Railway Av RMD . 202 G-J10 222 K10
Railway Av W ABT . . . . . 270 Z77
Railway Rd SUR . . . . . . 225 P32
Railway St DNV . . . . . . 143 Q20
Railway St VAN . . . . 11 G41 143 S15
Rainbow Av ABT . . . . . . 270 V75
Rainbow Ct BUR . . . . 164 V25-26
Rainbow Dr DNV . . . . . . 143 Q20
Rainbow Dr WHS . . . . . . 401 C3
Rainbow Plaza WHS . . . . 401 T21
Raindance Cr WVA . . . . . 122 N12
Raindance Ct WVA . . . . . 122 N12
Rainier Pl VAN . . . . . . 183 A-B20
Rainier St ABT . . . 250 U73 270 V73
Raintree Ct VAN . . . . . 183 A20-21
Rakanna Pl CQT . . . . . . 146 Q39
Raleigh Pl PCQ . . . 145 T38 165 U38
Raleigh St VAN . . . 163 Y19 183 Z19
Raleigh St WVA . . . . . . 101 G2
Ralph St DNV . . . . . . 123 K20-21
Ralston Ct CQT . . . . . . 165 U35
Rama Av NEW . . . . . . 204 E26
Ramage St NEW . . . . . 184 B29
Ramona Dr CHL . . . . . . 213 F8
Ramona Pl HHS . . . . . . 155 R19
Ramona Way DEL . . . . . 204 H28
Rampart Pl PCQ . . . . 166 X-Y39
Ramsay Av BUR . 164 Y26-27 184 Z27
Ramsay Ct CQT . . . 165 U32-33
Ramsay Rd DNV . . . . 123 J-K20
Ranch Park Way CQT . . . 165 U37

Ranchero Dr CHL . . . . . 213 J7
Rand Av VAN . . . . . . . 182 B12
Randolph Av BUR
. . . . . . 164 Y24 184 Z24 Z24
Ranelagh Av N BUR . . . 144 S23
Ranelagh Av S BUR . . . 144 S23
Ranger Av DNV . . . 103 H15 123 J16
Ranger Cr DNV . . . . . . 123 K16
Rannie Pl PTM . . . 147 P-Q49 S49
Ransford Gt RMD . . . . . 222 K9
Rathburn Dr BUR . . . . 164 U30
Rathburn Dr RMD . . . . 204 E24
Rathtrevor Ct ABT . . . 251 S-T79
Raven Av MIS . . . . . . . 210 J72
Raven Ct CQT . . . . . . . 145 S36
Raven Dr SQM . . . . . . . 301 G3
Raven La WHS . . . . . . . 401 H1
Raven Pl CHL . . . . . . . 213 J5
Raven Pl SUR . . . . . . . 185 B37
Raven Pl WVA . . . . . . . 121 J2
Raven Woods Dr DNV . . 144 P-Q25
Ravenswood Dr ANM . . . 145 P33
Ravine Av ABT . . . . . 250 U74-75
Ravine Dr PMD . . . . . 145 R34-35
Ravine Rd SUR . . . . . . 185 B33
Ravine St VAN . . . . . . 163 X19
Rawlins Cr DEL . . . . . 263 Y17
Rawlins Pl DEL . . . . . . 263 Y17
Rawlison Cr LGT . . 207 G53 G-H54
Rayburn Rd SQM . . . . . 301 B1
Raymond Av PCQ . . . . 146 S42
Raymond Av RMD . . . . 202 H8-9
Raymur Av VAN . . . . . 143 T16
Raynor St CQT . . . . . . 165 U31
Rayside Av BUR . . . . 164 X25-26
Read Ct SQM . . . . . 301 E3-4 F4
Read Pl SQM . . . . . . 301 E-F4
Rebekah Dr VAN . . . . 183 Z19-20
Red Alder Pl CQT . . . . 146 Q40
Reddington Ct CQT . . . 165 U37
Redfern Cr RMD . . . . . 202 F11
Redfern Pl CQT . . . . . 165 V37
Redfern Pl DNV . . . . . 123 L16
Redonda Dr CQT . . . 146 R-S39
Redonda Dr DNV . . . . 123 J16
Redtail Ct SUR . . . . . 205 H35
Redtail Pl SUR . . . . . . 205 H35
Redwood Av ABT . . . . 250 T77
Redwood Av CHL . . . . 233 L6
Redwood Av CQT . . . . 145 T38
Redwood Dr SUR . . . 266 V-W43
Redwood Pl DEL . . . . 224 L30
Redwood St DNV . . . . 122 N14
Reece Av CHL . . . . . . 193 D6-7
Reece Av CQT . . . . . . 165 U38
Reed Point Way PMD . . 145 R31
Reeder Rd RMD . . . . 202 H11-12
Rees Rd RMD . . . . . . . 183 D15
Rees Lake Rd LGT . . 247 T48-49
Reeve St PCQ . . . . . . 165 V38
Reeves Pl ABT . . . . . . 270 V76
Reeves Rd CHL . . . . . 194 B-C12
Reeves Rd RMD . . . . 202 E9-10
Regal Cr DNV . . . . . . 123 K18-19
Regal Dr SUR . . . . . . 204 E29
Regal Pkwy ABT . . . . 251 T-U80
Regan Av CQT . . . . . 165 U31-34
Regatta Way DEL . . . 223 N16-17
Regency Pl SQM . . . . 301 D-E3
Regency Pl WVA . . . . . 121 K4
Regent Av DNV . . . . 123 K-L18
Regent Pl SUR . . . . . 204 E29
Regent St BUR . . 163 V21 164 V23
Regent St CQT . . . . . 165 U33
Regent St RMD . . . . 222 K8-9
Regiment Sq VAN . 11 H39 142 S-T14
Regina Av RMD . . . . 182 C-D13
Regina St NEW . . . . . 184 A29
Regina St PCQ . . . . . 146 T41
Reichenbach Rd PTM . . 166 V-W44
Reid Av MAP . . . . . . 167 Y53
Reid Ct CQT . . . . . . 146 R39
Reid Rd CHL . . . . . . 233 K-L5
Reid Rd SQM . . . . . . 301 B2
Reid St VAN . . . . . 163 X19-20
Reigate Rd BUR . . 164 X27 X-Y26
Rekis Av RMD . . . . 202 H10-11
Rekis Gt RMD . . . . . 202 H-J11
Reliance Ct NEW . . . 184 B-C28
Remi Pl BUR . . . . . . 164 W26
Remington Cr CHL . . 233 M6-7
Rena Cr WVA . . . . . 122 K-L11
Renaissance Sq NEW . 184 B-C28
Renfrew St N VAN . 143 S-T19 163 U-V19
Renfrew St N VAN . . . 143 R19

Rennie Av LGT . . . . . . 207 F53
Rennie Pl NEW . . . . . . 184 C27
Renton Av PCQ . . . . . . 146 S40
Renton La ABT . . . . . 250 U76-77
Renton Pl WVA . . . . . . 122 K11
Renton Rd WVA . . . . 122 K-L11
Renton St ABT . . . . . 250 U76-77
Renton Way PCQ . . . . . 146 S40
Residence Way LGT . . 144 S27-28
Resolution Way SQM . . . 301 G-H1
Revelstoke Ct UEL . . . 161 U-V5
Reynolds Dr RMD . . . . . 202 J11
Reynolds Pl RMD . . . . . 202 J11
Rhine Cr PCQ . . . . . . 166 U41
Rhine Cr PCQ . . . . . . 166 U41
Rhodena Av CQT . . . . . 165 W34
Rhodes St VAN . . . 163 X-Y19
Rhum & Eigg Dr SQM . . 301 E5
Rialto Ct CQT . . . . . . 165 V34
Rialto Ct NEW . . . . . . 184 B28
Rialto Pl DNV . . . . . . 123 J15
Ricard Pl PCQ . . . . . . 166 X39
Rice Lake Rd DNV . . . . 123 K21
Rice Mill Rd RMD . . . . 223 K-L16
Richard St CQT . . . . . 165 W31
Richards Dr RMD . . . . 202 F8
Richards St VAN . 11 J37 142 S14 T13
Richardson Av CHL . . 213 J5
Richardson Gt DEL . . . 204 G28
Richardson Rd PTM . 146 T46 147 T47
Richelieu Av VAN . . . 162 V13
Richmond Dr HOP . . . 118 D-E45
Richmond Frwy RMD . . 203 E18-19
Richmond Pl PCQ . . . 146 S42
Richmond St DNV . . . . 143 Q20
Richmond St NEW
. . . . . . 164 Y30 Y30 184 Z30 Z30
Richmond St PCQ . . . 146 S42
Richmond St RMD . . . . 222 K8-9
Rickman Pl NEW . . . . . 164 Y29
Rideau Av CQT . . . . . 165 V34
Rideau Dr RMD . . . . . . 202 H12
Rideau Gt RMD . . . . . 202 H12
Rideau Pl RMD . . . . . 202 H12
Rideau St RMD . . . . . 250 U73
Ridge Cr SUR . . . . . 225 N35-36
Ridge Ct CQT . . . . . 165 U33
Ridge Dr BUR . . 144 S25-26 S26
Ridgecrest Dr DEL . . . 224 L30
Ridgelawn Dr BUR
. . . . . . 163 U22 164 U23 U23
Ridgemoor Pl BUR . . . 164 U29-30
Ridgeview Dr ABT . . 249 S70 250 S71
Ridgeview Dr BUR . . . 144 S26
Ridgeway Av CNV
. . . . . . 123 L-M18 M-N18 143 P18
Ridgeway Av CQT . . . 165 W32-33
Ridgeway Cr MAP . . . 167 Y51
Ridgeway Cr SQM . . . 301 E3-4
Ridgeway St ABT . . 250 U73 270 V73
Ridgewood Dr DNV . 122 L14 123 L15
Ridgewood Pl DEL . . . 224 K30
Ridley Dr BUR . . . . . 144 T26
Ridley Pl DEL . . . . . . 204 F-G25
Riel Pl VAN . . . . . . . 183 A20
Rietta Ct BUR . . . . . . 164 U30
Riley Pl DEL . . . . . . 243 Q15
Rimrock Estates WHS . . 401 G2
Rindall Av PCQ . . . 165 V38 166 V39
Ringwood Av VAN . . . 146 S40
Rio Pl SUR . . . . . . . 245 R-S35
Rippington Rd PTM . . . 166 V45
Ripple Pl WVA . . . . . 121 K5
Ripple Rd WVA . . . . . 121 K5
Rita Pl PCQ . . . . . . 166 W-X39
Ritchie Av MAP . . . . 187 A53
River Bend MAP . . . 187 A51-52
River Dr CQT . . . . . 146 K29
River Dr NEW . . . . 184 B26-27
River Dr RMD . . . . 182 B13-14 B-C14
River Pl MIS . . . . 210 J71 230 K71
River Rd DEL
. . . 203 H-J22 204 F28 G24-25 G27 G74
. . . . 223 K19-20 M18 M-N17 P16
River Rd LGT . . . . . 207 F54
River Rd MAP 187 A49 A51-52 B47 C54
River Rd PTM . . . . . 186 A46
River Rd RMD
. . 182 C13 D12 183 B18 C15 C20-22
. 184 D23 202 E8-11 204 E24-25
River Rd SQM . . . . . 301 H2
River Rd SUR . . . . . 184 D29-30
River Rd W DEL
. . . . . 242 Q13-14 S12 243 Q15
River Rd W. MAP . . 187 A48-49
River Reach DEL . . . 223 P16

River Way DEL . . . . . . 204 H23
River Wynd MAP . . . . 187 A50
River Wynde LGC . . . 227 N49
River Bend Rd CHL . . . 213 F2
Riverbank Pl DNV . . . 123 M22
Riverbend Dr BUR . . 184 C-D25 D24
Riverbend Dr CQT . . . 165 U38
Riverdale Dr RMD . . 202 E-F9
Riverfront St BUR . . . 184 D23
Rivergrove Pl DNV . . 123 M22
Riverport Way RMD . 223 K17-18
Rivers Dr WVA . . . . . 122 N13
Riverside Cl PCQ . . . . 166 U42
Riverside Dr CHL . . 193 D7-8
Riverside Dr DNV 123 M-N22 143 P22
Riverside Dr PCQ . . . 166 U42
Riverside Dr E DNV . . 143 Q21
Riverside Dr W DNV . . 143 Q21
Riverside Rd ABT . . 270 V-Z77
Riverside St ABT 230 L-P75 250 Q75
Riverside Way RMD . 223 K15-16
Riverview Cr CQT . . 165 W36-37
Riverview Dr HOP . . . 118 E46
Riverview St MIS . . . 210 J76
Riverway Pl BUR . . . . 184 B23
Riverwood Cr CHL . . . 233 N4
Riverwood Gt PCQ . . 166 U41
Riverwood Way VAN . . 183 B18
Riviere Pl DNV . . . . 122 K14
Roadhouse Mews VAN . 11 J-K37
Roan Pl SUR . . . . . . 226 N43
Rob Boyd Way WHS . . 401 H2
Roberts Av ABT . . . . 250 U75
Roberts St BUR . 164 W24-25 W25
Robertson Av CHL . . . 213 F7
Robertson Av PCQ . . 166 U40
Robertson Cr HOP . . 118 F46
Robertson Cr LGT . . 248 R60
Robertson Dr SUR . . 205 F32
Robertson Rd DEL . . 222 P10
Robin Cr MIS . . . . . 210 J72
Robin Cr SUR . . . . . 185 B37
Robin Dr ABT . . . . . 249 S69
Robin Dr SQM . . . . . 301 H3
Robin Pl PCQ . . . . 146 S40
Robin Hood Rd WVA . 122 J13
Robins Ct BUR . . . . 164 U29
Robinson Pl RMD . . . 202 H13
Robinson Rd DNV . . 123 K-L21 L21
Robinson Rd RMD . . 202 H12-13
Robinson St CQT . . 165 U-V31
Roblin Pl DNV . . . . 123 K-L18
Robson Ct RMD . . . . 202 F9
Robson Dr ABT . . . . 250 R-S77
Robson Dr CQT . . 145 Q38 146 Q39
Robson Dr RMD . . . 202 F8-9
Robson Pl DEL . . . . 263 Z16
Robson Rd BEL . . . 124 N28
Robson Rd SUR . . 184 D29 204 E29
Robson St CHL . . 193 D6 213 E6
Robson St VAN . . . 10 E35 F36
. . . 11 H37-38 142 R12-13 R-S13
Rochdale Dr RMD . . . 222 K14
Roche Pl DNV . . . . . 144 Q25
Roche Point Dr DNV
. . . 124 N25 144 P25 P-Q25
Rochester Av CHL . . 233 K5
Rochester Av CQT
. . . 164 W30 165 W31-33
Rochester St BUR . . 164 W30
Rockbank Pl WVA . . 121 K5
Rockcliff Rd DNV . . 124 M-N26
Rockcress Pl CQT . . 145 Q37
Rockend Pl WVA . . . 121 K5
Rocket Way CQT . . . 165 Y35
Rockford Pl DEL . . 224 K29
Rockhill Pl ABT . . 249 S-T70
Rockland Av ABT . . 270 V75-76
Rockland Rd E DNV . 123 K17
Rockland Rd W DNV . 123 K16-17
Rockland Wynd WVA . 101 G1
Rocklin St CQT . . . 146 S42
Rockpoole Dr VAN . 182 A14 Z14
Rockridge La CQT . . 145 Q37
Rockridge Pl MIS . . 210 H77
Rockridge Rd WVA . 121 K4 K4-5
Rockview Pl WVA . . 121 K6 122 K7
Rockwell Dr HHS . . 155 P20
Rockwood Ct CQT . . 145 Q37
Rockwood Pl CHL . . 233 N7
Rod Rd SQM . . . . . 301 C1
Roderick Av CQT . . 165 X31 X32

Rodger Av PCQ . . . . 166 X39-40
Rodgers St CHL . . . . 213 F8
Rodman Av MIS . . . 210 F71-72
Roe Dr PMD . . . . . 145 Q32-33
Rogate Av CQT . . . . 165 X36
Roger Av BUR . . . . 163 W22
Rogers Av ABT . . . . 250 S72
Rogers Av CNV . . . . 143 P16
Rogers Av MAP . . . . 167 Y53
Rogers Ct CNV . . . . 143 P16
Rogers La CNV . . . . 143 P16
Rogers St VAN . . . . 143 S16
Rogerson Dr CQT . . . 165 U35
Rolinde Cr CHL . . . . 213 F8
Rolls St MIS . . . . . 210 H77
Rolston Cr VAN . . 10 J36 142 T13
Romaniuk Dr RMD . . 202 H10-11
Romaniuk Pl RMD . . 202 H10-11
Ronayne Rd DNV . . 123 L19
Rondeau St CQT . . . 165 U33
Rondoval Cr DNV . . . 123 J17
Rook Cr MIS . . . . 210 H-J72
Roosevelt Cr DNV . . 123 N15
Roper Av WRK . 265 X36-38 266 X39
Rora Dr SUR . . . . 186 C43
Rosalie Ct CQT . . . 146 Q39
Rosamond Av RMD . 202 H8-9
Rose Av MIS . . . . 210 G74
Rose Cr WVA . . . . 121 K5
Rose Rd CHL . . . . 194 B11
Rose St VAN . . . . 143 T18
Rose Way CQT . . . . 165 V37
Rosebank Ct RMD . . 222 K12
Rosebank Ct RMD . . 222 K12
Rosebank Pl CHL . . 194 B10
Roseberry Av BUR 183 A21 A-B21 Z21
Roseberry Rd CHL . . 233 L5
Rosebery Av WVA
. . . 101 G1-2 122 K10 K7-8 K8-9
Rosebrook Rd RMD 202 J13 222 K13
Rosebury La VAN . . 182 Z13
Rosebury Walk VAN . 182 Z13
Rosecroft Cr RMD . . 202 J12-13
Rosedale Dr VAN . . 183 A18
Rosedene Cr RMD . . 202 J12-13
Rosedene Ct RMD . . 301 J13
Roseglen Ct BUR . . 164 V26-27
Rosehill Dr RMD . 202 J13 222 K12-13
Rosehill Wynd DEL . 263 Y-Z17
Roseland Gt RMD . . 222 K13
Roselea Cr RMD . . 202 J13 222 K13
Roselea Pl RMD . . . 222 K13
Roselynn Way PCQ . 166 X39
Rosemary Av RMD . 222 K13
Rosemary Heights Cr SUR
. . . . . . 245 S37-38 T38
Rosemary Heights Dr SUR
. . . . . . 245 S-T38
Rosemont Dr VAN . 183 A19-20 Z19
Rosetta Av MIS . . 210 F74
Rosetti Ct RMD . . 202 J11 222 K11
Rosevale Av KNT . . 175 X21
Rosevale Rd RMD . . 202 J13
Rosewell Av RMD . 202 J12 222 K12
Rosewood Av CNV . 122 N14
Rosewood Av HOP . 118 G42-43
Rosewood Dr ABT . 250 U75-76
Rosewood Dr DEL . . 224 M30
Rosewood Pl MAP . 187 Z49
Rosewood Pl SUR . . 186 C40
Rosewood St BUR 164 Y27 184 Z26
Rosewood St MAP . 187 Z49
Rosewood St PCQ . 166 U41
Roslin Pl SUR . . . 205 F34
Roslyn Av BUR . . 184 A23
Roslyn Blvd DNV . 144 P26 P-Q26
Ross Av CQT . . . . 165 V33
Ross Cr WVA . . . . 121 L4
Ross Dr NEW . . . 184 A30
Ross La WVA . . . . 121 L4
Ross Pl SUR . . . . 205 E32
Ross Rd ABT . . . . 249 Q-U67
Ross Rd DEL . . . . 203 J21
Ross Rd DNV . . . 123 L19-21
Ross Rd SQM . . . 301 A1-2 B2
Ross St VAN 163 W-X16 X-Y16 Y16 Y16
. . . . . . 183 A16 Z16 Z16
Rosser Av BUR . . 143 S-T22 163 U22
Rosser Av N BUR . . 143 S22
Rossland Pl ABT . . 250 U73
Rossland St VAN . . 143 T19
Rossmore Ct CQT . . 165 X34
Rosswood Pl BUR . 164 U28
Rotary Av CHL . . . 193 D7
Rothbury Pl BUR . 164 V26

| | | | |
|---|---|---|---|
| Roundhouse Dr *ABT* . . . . . **249** T63 | Sail Pl *CQT* . . . . . . . . . . . **145** T36-37 | Salt St *VAN* . . . . . . **11** K39-40 **142** T14 | Scales Pl *VAN* . . . . . . . . **163** X20-21 | Seavale Rd *RMD* . . . . . . . . **203** J15 |
| Roundhouse Mews *VAN* . . . . . | Sailes Av *LGT* . . . . . . . **207** E-F53 | Salt Spring Av *CQT* . . . . . . **146** S39 | Scantlings *VAN* . . . . . . . . **162** U13 | Seaview Dr *PMD* . . . . . . **145** T31-32 |
| . . . . . . . . . . **11** J-K37 **142** T13 | St. Albans Av *DNV* . . . . . . **123** K17 | Salter St *NEW* . . . . . . . . . | Scarboro Av *VAN* . . . **183** A17-18 A18 | Seaview Pl *LIO* . . . . . . **101** B-C23 |
| Rousseau St *NEW* . . . . . . **165** Y31 | St. Albans Rd *RMD* . . . . **202** G-H13 | . . . . . . **184** C28 D26 D27 D28 E26 | Scarborough Cr *PCQ* . . . . **166** W39 | Seaview Pl *WVA* . . . . . . . . **121** J2 |
| Routley Av *PCQ* . . . . . . **166** X39-40 | St. Albert Av *PCQ* . . . . . **166** U40 | Salton Rd *ABT* . . . . . **270** V76 W76 | Scarborough Dr *DEL*. . . . **204** J28-29 | Seaview Rd *DEL* . . . . . . **263** Z19-20 |
| Rowan Av *BUR* . . . . . . . **164** X24 | St. Alice St *HHS* . . . . . . . **155** P19 | Saltspring Ct *RMD* . . . . . . **202** G8 | Sceptre Cr *RMD* . . . . . . . **202** J8-9 | Seawalk *VAN* . . . . . . . . **11** F37-38 |
| Rowan Pl *RMD* . . . . . . . **183** D16 | St. Andrew's Way *WHS*. . . . **401** E53 | Salvador Ct *DNV* . . . . . . . **123** J16 | Schaefer Av *RMD* . . . . . **202** H11-12 | Seaward Ct *RMD* . . . **203** J15 **223** K15 |
| Rowat Av *CHL* . . . . . . . **213** F6-7 | St. Andrews Al *WHS* . . . . . **401** T21 | Samara Ct *BUR* . . . . . . . . **163** X22 | Schaefer Gt *RMD* . . . . . **202** H11-12 | Seaward Gt *RMD*. . . . . . . **223** K15 |
| Rowland St *PCQ* . . . . . . . **165** V38 | St. Andrews Av *CNV*. . . . . . | Sampson La *WVA* . . . . . . . **101** E3 | Scheldt Rd *CHL* . . . . . . . **233** M-N6 | Seaway Rd *RMD* . . . **203** J15 **223** K15 |
| Rowling Pl *RMD* . . . . . . . **204** E24 | . . . . . . . . **123** M-N17 **143** P17 | Samson Dr *NEW* . . . . . . . **184** B29 | Schmidt Cr *MAP* . . . . . **187** Z49-50 | Sechelt Dr *CQT* . . . . . . . **146** S39 |
| Roxburgh Cr *VAN* . . . . . . **162** X12 | St. Andrews Av *DNV*. . . . . **123** K-L18 | Samtree Pl *ABT* . . . . . . . . **251** T81 | School Av *VAN* . . . . . . **163** X-Y19 Y20 | Sechelt Dr *DNV* . . . **123** M22 **124** M23 |
| Roxburgh Rd *SUR*. . . . . . . **185** A36 | St. Andrews Av *LGT*. **207** F53 F53-54 | Samuel Ct *ABT* . . . . . . . . **250** S72 | School Gn *VAN* . . . . . . . . **162** U13 | Sechelt Ter *ABT*. . . . . . . . **250** S73 |
| Roxbury Rd *DNV*. . . . . . . **124** N27 | St. Andrews Ct *ABT* . . . . **251** S79-80 | Samuels Ct *CQT*. . . . **146** R-S39 | School La *CHL* . . . . . . . . **233** K7 | Secret Ct *CQT*. . . . . . . . . **146** S39 |
| Roxham St *CQT* . . . . . . . **165** W32 | St. Andrews Dr *SUR* . . . . . . **185** A36 | San Antonio Pl *CQT*. . . . . **165** X-Y35 | School Rd *HOP* . . . . . . . . **118** G43 | Sedge Ct *CQT* . . . . . . . . . **145** Q36 |
| Roxton Av *CQT* . . . . . . . **146** R41 | St. Andrews Pl *DEL* . . . . **263** W16-17 | San Juan Pl *CQT* . . . . . . . **165** X35 | School Rd *LGT* . . . . . . . . **207** F53 | Sedgemond Pl *RMD* . . . . . **202** J8 |
| Roy Av *CHL* . . . . . . . . . **233** K7 | St. Andrews Pl *WVA* **102** H13 **122** J13 | San Lucas Ct *CQT*. . . . . . **165** X35 | School St *CHL* . . . . . . . **213** E-F6 | Sefton St *PCQ*. . **146** S40 T40 **166** U40 |
| Roy St *BUR*. . . . . . . . **164** U23-24 | St. Andrews Rd *WVA* . . . . . | San Remo Dr *PMD*. . . . . . **145** R-S34 | School St *NEW* . . . . . . . . **164** Y30 | Seguin Dr *CQT* . . . . . . . . **165** X33 |
| Roy Vickers Ct *ABT* . . . . . **251** Q81 | . . . . . . . . **102** H13 **122** J12-13 J13 | Sandalwood Cr *ABT* . . . . . **270** V75 | Schoolhouse St *CQT* **165** U-W33 X33 | Selby Rd *DNV* . . . . . . . . **123** K20 |
| Royal Av *DNV* . . . . . . . . **123** L18 | St. Andrews St *NEW* . . . . **184** A-B28 | Sandbar Pl *DEL* . . . . . . . **263** Y19 | Schooner Ct *RMD*. . . . . . . **222** K10 | Seldon Rd *ABT*. . . . . . **250** Q-R75 |
| Royal Av *NEW* . . . . . . **184** A-B29 | St. Andrews St *PMD* . . . . **145** T32-34 | Sandberg St *ABT* . . . . . . **230** K-L78 | Schooner St *CQT* . . **165** Y34 **185** Z34 | Selkirk Av *ABT* . . . . . . . . **251** S79 |
| Royal Av *WRK* . . . . . . . **265** X37-38 | St. Anne Av *MAP* . . . . . . . **187** A52 | Sandborne Av *BUR*. . . . . . **184** A25 | Schooner Way *DEL* . . . . **223** N16-17 | Selkirk Av *MAP* . . . **187** Z51-52 Z52 |
| Royal Av *WVA* . . . . . . . . **101** G2 | St. Anne St *PCQ* . . . . . . . **146** T40 | Sandell St *BUR* . . . . . . . . **163** X-Y21 | Schou St *BUR* . . . . . . . . **164** V23 | Selkirk Bay *SUR* . . . . . . . **266** V39 |
| Royal Av E  *NEW* . . . . . . **184** A30 | St. Annes Dr *DNV* . . . . . . **122** L14 | Sanders St *BUR* . . . . . . . **164** Y23 | Schweyey Rd *CHL*. . . . . . **213** E-F4 | Selkirk Cr *CQT* . . . . . . . . **165** U34 |
| Royal Cr *SUR* . . . . . . . . **250** T72 | St. Annes Rd *DNV* . . . . . . **122** L14 | Sanderson La *DEL* . . . . . . **243** Q18 | Science Rd *BUR*. . . . . . **144** T28-29 | Selkirk Dr *SUR*. . . . . . . . **185** B34 |
| Royal Cr *MAP* . . . . . . . . **187** Z52 | St. Anton Way *WHS* . . . . . **401** F3 | Sanderson Way *BUR* . . . . . **163** W22 | Scotch Pine Av *CQT* . . . . . **146** Q40 | Selkirk St *CHL* . . . . . . . . **233** L5 |
| Royal Cr *SUR* . . **184** D29-30 **204** E29 | St. Brides Ct *RMD*. . . . . . . **202** J9 | Sandhurst Pl *WVA* . . . . . **122** J-K11 | Scotchbrook Rd *RMD* . . . . **202** H13 | Selkirk St *VAN* **162** V-W12 X12 Y12 Y12 |
| Royal Ct *ABT* . . . . . . . . **250** T72 | St. Brides Pl *RMD* . . . . . . . **202** J9 | Sandiford Dr *RMD* . . . . . . **202** J10 | Scotia St *VAN* . . . **11** K41 **163** U15 V15 | . . . . . . . **182** A12 A-B12 Z12 |
| Royal Pl *PCQ* . . . **165** X38 **166** X39 | St. Catherines St *VAN* . . . . . | Sandiford Pl *RMD* . . . . . . . **202** J10 | Scotsdale Av *RMD* . . . . . . **202** J9 | Sellers Av *BUR* . . . . . . . . **184** Z24 |
| Royal St *ABT* . . . . . . . . **250** T72 | . . . . . . **163** U-W16 X16 X-Y16 Y16 | Sandlewood Cr *BUR* . . . . . **164** W30 | Scotsdale Pl *RMD*. . . . . . . **202** J9 | Selma Av *DNV* . . . . . . . . **164** Y23 |
| Royal St *LGT* . . . . . . . . **207** F54 | St. Charles Pl *BUR* . . . . . . **184** Z24 | Sandlewood St *PCQ* . . . . . **166** U41 | Scott Av *MIS* . . . . . . . . . **210** J72 | Selman St *CQT* . . . . . . . . **165** W31 |
| Royal Oak Av *BUR* . . . . . . | St. Christophers Rd *DNV* . . . **123** L19 | Sandollar Pl *DEL* . . . . . . **263** Y17-18 | Scott Cr *SQM* . . . . . . . . . **301** K2 | Selonas Dr *CHL* . . . . . . . **233** L6 |
| . . . . **164** V23 W-Y23 **184** A23 Z23 | St. Clair Pl *VAN* . . . . . . . **162** Y8 | Sandon Dr *ABT* . . . . . . **250** U77-78 | Scott Dr *HOP* . . . . . . . . **118** F45 | Semana Cr *VAN* . . . . . . . . **162** X7 |
| Royal Oak Dr *DEL* . . . . . . **263** X17 | St. David St *CHL* . . . . . . . **193** D7 | Sandon St *ABT* . . . . . . . . **250** U78 | Scott Pl *PCQ* . . . . . . . . . **146** T39 | Semath Rd *ABT*. . . . . . . . **251** T83 |
| Royalmore Av *RMD* . . . . . **202** H8-9 | St. Davids Av *CNV* . . . . . . **143** P17 | Sandown Pl *DNV* . . . . . . **122** M13-14 | Scott Rd *DNV* . . . . . . . **123** L20 L21 | Semiahmoo Av *WRK* . . . . . **265** X38 |
| Roycroft Ct *BUR* . . . . . . . **164** V26 | St. Denis Av *DNV* . . . **123** N20 **143** P20 | Sandpiper Av *MAP* . . . . . . **187** Z54 | Scott Rd *KNT*. . . . . . . . **175** W22-23 | Semiahmoo Pl *SUR*. . . . . . **245** U37 |
| Ruby Av *DNV* . . . . **122** K14 **123** K15 | St. Denis Pl *WVA* . . . . . . . **122** L10 | Sandpiper Ct *CQT* . . . . . . **146** Q39 | Scott Rd *SUR* **184** D30 **185** B-C31 C31 | Semiahmoo Rd *SUR* . . . **185** C-D33 |
| Ruby St *VAN* . . . . . . . . **163** X20 | St. Denis Rd *WVA* . . . . . . . **122** L10 | Sandpiper Ct *RMD* . . . . . . **222** K10 | Scott St *NEW* . . . . . . . . . **164** Y29 | Semiahmoo Tr *SUR* . . . . . **245** T36 |
| Ruckle Ct *DNV* . . . . . . . **144** P24 | St. Edwards Dr *RMD* . . . . **182** C-D14 | Sandpiper Dr *ABT* . . . **249** S69 T70 | Scratchley Cr *RMD* . . . . . . **183** D15 | Semisch Av *CNV*. . . . **123** N16 **143** P16 |
| Rufus Av *CNV* . . . . . . . . **123** N19 | St. Gallen Way *ABT* . . . . . **250** U78 | Sandpiper Dr *MIS* . . . . . . **210** H72 | Sea Av N  *BUR* . . . . . . . . **144** S24 | Semlin Ct *RMD* . . . . . . . . **202** F8 |
| Rufus Dr *CNV* . . . . . . . **123** M-N19 | St. George St *NEW* . . . . . . **184** A29 | Sandpiper Pl *ABT* . . . . . . **249** T70 | Sea Av S  *BUR* . . . . . . . . **144** S24 | Semlin Dr *RMD* . . . . . . . . **202** F8 |
| Rugby St *BUR* . . . . . . . . **164** X25 | St. George St *PMD* . . . . **145** T32-34 | Sandpiper Pl *DEL* . . . . . **224** K29-30 | Sea Island Way *RMD* . . . . . **182** C13 | Semlin Dr *VAN* . . . . . . . . |
| Ruger Pl *CHL* . . . . . . . . **233** M6 | St. George St *VAN* . . . . . . **143** T16 | Sandpiper Pl *MIS* . . . . . . **210** H72 | Sea Ridge Bays *SUR* . . . . . **265** V38 | . . . . . . . **143** S-T18 T18 **163** U18 V17-18 |
| Rumble Av *VAN* . . . . . . . **183** A21 | **163** U16 U-V15 V-W15 W15 X15 Y15 Y15 | Sandra Way *PCQ*. . . . . . . **166** X39 | Sea Shell La *DNV* . . . . . **144** P-Q26 | Semlin Pl *ABT*. . . . . . . . **250** R-S77 |
| Rumble St *BUR* . **183** A21-22 **184** A24 | . . . . . . . . . **183** A15 Z15 Z15 | Sandringham Av *NEW*. . . . . **184** Z28 | Sea to Sky Hwy *LIO* . . . . . **101** A23 | Seneca Ct *ABT* . . . . . . . . **250** S78 |
| Runnel Dr *CQT* . . . . . . . **145** T36 | St. Georges Av *CNV*. . . . . . | Sandringham Cr *DNV* . . . . **123** K-L17 | Sea To Sky Hwy *SQM* **301** D-E3 G-H2 | Seney Pl *LGT* . . . . . . . . . **207** F53 |
| Runnymede Av *CQT* . . . . . **165** V32 | . . . . . . . . **123** M-N17 **143** P17 | Sandringham Dr *ABT* . . . . **251** T80-81 | Sea to Sky Hwy *WHS*. . . . . | Senkler Rd *BEL*. . . . . . . . **124** M30 |
| Runnymede Rd *DNV* . . . **123** K16-17 | St. Georges Av *DNV* . . . . . **123** K-L17 | Sandstone Cr *CQT* . . . . . . **145** Q36 | . . . . . . . . . . . **401** F-G3 H1 S-T21 | Senlac St *VAN* . . . . . . . . **163** Y20 |
| Rupert St *DNV* . . . . . . . . **143** P20 | St. Georges Av *WVA* . . . . . **101** H1 | Sandstone Ct *CQT* . . . . . **145** Q35-36 | Sea To Sky Hwy *WVA* . . . . . **101** G2 | Sennok Cr *VAN* . . . . . . . . **162** X7 |
| Rupert St *HOP* . . . . . . . **118** D44 | St. Georges Cr *WVA* . . . . . **101** H1 | Sandy Hill Cr *ABT* . . . . . . **251** R-S79 | Seabay Rd *RMD*. . . . . . . . **203** J15 | Sentinel Dr *ABT* . . . . . . **250** U77 |
| Rupert St *VAN* . . . . . . . . | St. Giles Rd *WVA* . . **102** H13 **122** J13 | Sandy Hill Rd *ABT* . . . . . . **251** R-S79 | Seabird Island Rd *KNT*. . . . . | Sentinel Dr *WVA* . . . . . . **122** L-M12 |
| . . . **143** S-T20 **163** U-X20 X-Y19 **183** Z19 | St. Ives Cr *DNV* . . . . . . . **123** L16 | Sangster Pl *NEW* . . . . . . **184** Z29 | . . . . . . . . **175** U22-23 V23 | Sentinel La *VAN* . . . . . . . **122** L12 |
| Rush Ct *DNV* . . . . . . . . **123** J20 | St. James Cr *WVA* . . . . . . **122** K13 | Santa Monica Dr *DEL* . . . **204** H27-28 | Seabreeze Walk *VAN* . . . . . | Sentinel Rd *PMD* . . . . . **145** S34-35 |
| Rushmoor Rd *RMD* . . . . . . **202** J12 | St. James Rd W  *DNV* . . . **123** L16-17 | Santa Monica Pl *DEL* . . . . **204** H28 | . . . . . . . . . **10** J35-36 **142** T12 | Sentinel St *MAP* . . . . . . . **187** Z48 |
| Ruskin Pl *DNV* . . . . . . . **123** J-K16 | St. James St *PCQ* . . . . . . . | Santiago St *CQT* . . . . . . **165** X35 | Seabright Rd *RMD* . . . . . . **203** J15 | Sepass Pl *CHL* . . . . . . . . **213** J7 |
| Ruskin Pl *RMD* . . . . . . . **202** J12-13 | St. John St *DEL* . . . . . . . **243** Q-R21 | Sapper St *NEW* . . . . . . . . **184** Z30 | Seabrook Cr *RMD* . . . . . . **203** J15 | Seppos Way *WHS* . . . . . . **401** E3 |
| Russ Baker Way *RMD* . **182** C12 D11 | St. Johns Pl *RMD* . . . . . . . **202** J9 | Sappers Way *CHL* . . . . . . **233** M5-6 | Seacastle Dr *RMD* . . . . . . **203** J15 | Sequoia Dr *SUR* . . . . . . **205** H37-38 |
| Russell Av *BUR* . . . . . . . **184** Z24 | St. Johns St *PMD* . . . . **145** T33-34 | Sapperton Av *BUR* . . . . . . **164** X30 | Seacliff Rd *RMD* . . . . . . . **203** J15 | Sequoia Rd *BUR* . . . . . . **164** X29-30 |
| Russell Av *DNV*. . . . . . . . **123** L18 | St. Julien Mews *VAN*. . . . . . **183** Z19 | Sapphire Dr *CHL* . . . . . . **213** H-J5 | Seacote Rd *RMD* . . . . . . **203** H-J15 | Serenity Gdns *SUR* . . . . . **206** G39 |
| Russell Av *WRK* . **265** W36 W37 W38 | St. Kilda Av *DNV* . . . . . . . **123** L18 | Sapphire Pl *ABT* . . . . . . . **249** S68 | Seacrest Ct *PMD* . . . . . . . **145** T31 | Serl Rd *ABT*. . . . . **250** U76 **270** V76 |
| Russell Ct *DNV* . . . . . . . **124** N26 | St. Laurence St *CQT* . . . . . **165** U34 | Sapphire Pl *CQT* . . . . . . **145** Q36 | Seacrest Dr *SUR* . . . . . . . **245** U31 | Service St *BUR* . . . . . . . . **164** Y24 |
| Russell Dr *DEL*. . . . . . . . **204** F29 | St. Lawrence St *NEW* . . . . . **163** W-X18 | Sapphire Pl *RMD*. . . . . . . **202** F10 | Seacrest Rd *RMD* . . . . . . **203** J15 | Sesame St *CHL* . . . . **213** J7 **233** K7 |
| Russet Pl *ABT*. . . . . **250** U77 **270** V77 | St. Margarets St *VAN* . . **163** X18 Y18 | Sapporo Dr *WHS* . . . . . . . **401** H2 | Seafair Dr *RMD*. . . . . . . . **202** H8 | Settebello Dr *WHS* . . . . . . **401** E4 |
| Russet Pl *WVA* . . . . . . . . **122** K9 | St. Marys Av *DNV* . . . . **123** K17 L17 | Sarajevo Dr *WHS* . . . . . . . **401** H2 | Seafield Cr *RMD* . . . . . . . **203** J15 | Settlers Ct *PCQ* . . . . . . **165** X-Y38 |
| Russet Way *WVA* . . . . . . . **122** K9 | St. Marys Pl *DNV* . . . . . **123** K17-18 | Saran Way *ABT* . . . . . . **270** X-Y77 | Seaford Cr *VAN* . . . . . . . **163** V20 | Severn Dr *RMD* . . . . . . . . **202** J13 |
| Ruth Cr *DNV* . . . . . . . . **123** K20 | St. Marys St *NEW* . . . . . . **184** A29 | Saratoga Ct *BUR* . . . . . . **163** X22 | Seaforth Cr *CQT* . . . . . . **165** X34 | Seville Pl *RMD* . . . . . . . . **202** J8 |
| Rutherford Cr *DNV* . . . . . **123** K-L18 | St. Matthews Way *ABT*. . **270** V77-78 | Saratoga Dr *DEL* . . . . . . **263** W16-17 | Seaforth Dr *VAN* . . . . . . . **163** V20 | Sexsmith Rd *RMD* . . . . **182** C-D13 |
| Ruthina Av *DNV* . . . . . . . **123** J15 | St. Michael St *PCQ* . . . . . **166** U40 | Sardis Cr *BUR* . . . . . . . . **164** Y23 | Seaforth Way *PMD* . . . . . **145** T32 | Seymour Av *WRK* . . . . . . **265** X36 |
| Rutland Ct *CQT* . . . . . . . **164** V30 | St. Moritz Cr *WHS*. . . . . . . **401** F3 | Sardis St *BUR*. . . . . . . . . | Seagrave Rd *RMD* . . . . . . **203** J15 | Seymour Blvd *DNV* . . . . . **143** P21 |
| Rutland Rd *WVA* . . . . . . . **121** K4 | St. Moritz Way *ABT*. . . . . . **250** U78 | . . . . . . . **163** X21-22 X-Y22 **164** Y23 | Seagull Pl *VAN*. . . . . . . . **183** A20 | Seymour Ct *DNV* . . . . . . . **143** P21 |
| Ryall Cr *DEL* . . . . . . . . **224** K-L29 | St. Olaf Av *ABT* . . . . . . . **230** M75 | Sargent Ct *CQT* . . . . . . . **165** V34 | Seaham Cr *RMD* . . . . . . . **203** J15 | Seymour Ct *NEW* . . . . . . **184** Z30 |
| Ryall Pl *DEL* . . . . . . . . **224** K-L29 | St. Patrick St *NEW* . . . . . . **184** A29 | Sarita Av *DNV* . . . . **103** H15 **123** J15 | Seahaven Pl *RMD* . . . . . . **203** J15 | Seymour Ct *CQT* . . . . . . **165** U35 |
| Ryan Cr *RMD*. . . . . **202** J13 **222** K13 | St. Patricks Av *CNV* . . . . . **143** P17 | Sarita Pl *DNV* . . . . . . . . **123** J15 | Seahaven Rd *RMD* . . . . . . **203** J15 | Seymour Mews *VAN*. . . . . . |
| Ryan Ct *RMD*. . . . . . . . **202** J13 | St. Pauls Av *DNV* . . . . . . . **123** K17 | Sarnia St *NEW* . . . . . . . **184** A30 | Seaholm Cr *CHL* . . . . . . . **193** C8 | . . . . . . . . . **10** J-K36 **142** T13 |
| Ryan Pl *RMD*. . . . . . . . **202** J13 | St. Regis La *VAN* . . . **11** G38 **142** S14 | Sasamat La *DNV* . . . . . . **142** S14 | Seal Way *ABT* . . . . . . . . **250** U73 | Seymour Pl *PCQ*. . . . **165** U38 **166** U39 |
| Ryan Rd *RMD* . . . . . . . **202** J12-13 | St. Stephens Pl *DNV* . . . **123** M19-20 | Sasamat Pl *VAN* . . . **142** T7 **162** U7 | Sealily Pl *RMD*. . . . . . . . . **203** J15 | Seymour Rd *VAN*. **11** H37 **142** S14 T13 |
| Ryan St *MIS* . . . . . . . . **210** J75 | St. Thomas St *PCQ* . . . **146** S42 T42 | Sasamat St *VAN* . . . **142** T62 **162** U-V7 | Sealord Rd *RMD*. . . . . . . . **203** J15 | Seymour View *ANM* . . . . . **145** P34 |
| Rydal Av *DNV* . . . . . . . **122** K14 | St. Vincents Ct *RMD*. . . . . . **202** J9 | Saskatchewan St *PCQ* . . . . **166** X39 | Sealord Rd *RMD* . . . . . . . **203** J15 | Seymour Mainline Forest Service |
| Ryder St *HOP* . . . . . . . **118** F45 | St. Vincents Pl *RMD* . . . . . . **202** J9 | Saturna Cr *ABT* . . . . . . **250** S-T72 | Seameadow Ct *RMD* . . . . **203** H-J15 | Rd *DNV* . . . . . . . . . . **123** J22 |
| | Salal Ct *CQT*. . . . . . . **145** Q36-37 | Saturna Dr *BUR* . . . . . . **164** V29 | Seamount Rd *RMD*. **203** J15 **223** K15 | Seymour River Pl *DNV* . . . **143** P21 |
| | Salal Dr *VAN* . . . . . . . . **162** U11 | Saturna Dr *WRK* . . . . . . **265** W36 | Seaport Av *RMD* . . . . . . . **203** J15 | Shackleton Dr *RMD* . . . . . **202** G9 |
| | Salal Pl *SUR*. . . . . . . . **205** E33 | Saturna Pl *RMD* . . . . . . . **202** G8 | Seascape Cl *WVA* . . . . . . **101** D4 | Shackleton Gt *RMD* . . . . . **202** G9 |
| | Salerno St *VAN* . . . . . . . **162** U8 | Sauder La *UEL* . . . . . . . **161** U3 | Seascape Cr *WVA* . . . . . . **101** D4 | Shadbolt Av *ABT* . . . . **251** Q80-81 |
| **S** | Salisbury Av *BUR* . . . . . . **184** Z25 | Saunders Rd *RMD* . . . . . **202** J12-14 | Seascape Dr *WVA* . . . . . . **101** D4 | Shadbolt La *WVA* . . . . . . **122** K9 |
| | Salisbury Av *PCQ* . . . . **146** T39 T40 | Sauve Ct *DNV* . . . . . . . . **123** K19 | Seascape La *WVA* . . . . . . **101** D4 | Shafton Pl *WVA* . . . . . . **122** K10 |
| Saab Pl *ABT* . . . . . . . . . **249** S69 | Salisbury Dr *SUR* . . . . . . **186** C41 | Sauve Pl *DNV* . . . . . . . . **123** K19 | Seascape Pl *WVA* . . . . . . **101** D4 | Shaftsbury Av *PCQ* . . . . . **145** T38 |
| Saanich St *ABT* . . . . . . **250** S-T73 | Salish Ct *BUR* . . . . **164** V-W29 W30 | Savage Rd *DEL* . . . **222** P11 **242** Q11 | Seascape Rd *WVA* . . . . . . **101** D4 | Shaftsbury Pl *PCQ* . . **145** T38 **146** T39 |
| Saba Rd *RMD* . . . . . . . . **202** F12 | Salish Dr *VAN* . . . . . . . **162** X7 Y7-8 | Savage Rd *RMD* . . . . . . . **183** B18 | Seascape Wynd *RMD* . . . . **203** J15 | Shakespeare Av *DNV* . . . . **123** L19 |
| Sable Av *RMD* . . . . . . . **202** J8-9 | Salish Rd *BEL* . . . . . . . . **124** N28 | Savary Av *CQT* . . . . . . . . **146** R39 | Seaside Bay *SUR* . . . . . . **266** W39 | Shakespeare Pl *SUR*. . . . . **205** G33 |
| Saddle La *VAN* . . . . . . . **183** A19 | Salish Rd *MAP* . . . **186** B46 **187** B47 | Saville Cr *DNV* . . . . . . . . **123** K16 | Seaside Pl *WVA* . . . . . . . **121** K2 | Shale Ct *CQT* . . . . . . **145** Q-R36 |
| Saddle St *ABT* . . . . . . . **250** S-T77 | Salish Rd *PTM*. . . . . . . . **186** A46 | Savoy St *DEL* . . . . . . . . **243** Q15 | Seaside Rd *WVA* . . . . . . . **121** K2 | Shaman Cr *DEL*. . . . . . . . **262** X15 |
| Saddle St *CQT* . . **145** T37 **165** U37 | Salish Way *CHL*. . . . . . . . **233** K7 | Saw-Cut *VAN*. . . . . . . . . **162** U13 | Seaton Av *CQT* . . . . . . . **165** U-V31 | Shamrock Dr *CHL* . . . . . **193** C-D7 |
| Safflower Cr *CHL* . . . . . . **233** L6 | Salmonberry Dr *CHL*. . . . . **213** G1 | Sawyer Av *MIS* . . . . . . . **210** J72 | Seaton Ct *RMD* . . . . . . . **203** J15 | Shamrock Pl *WVA* . . . . . . **122** K9 |
| Saffron Ct *BUR* . . . . . . . **164** U29 | Salsbury Av *MIS* . . . . . . **210** G73 | Sawyer Pl *PCQ* . . . **145** T38 **146** T39 | Seaton Pl *MAP* . . . . . . . . **187** Z51 | Shanghai Alley *VAN* . . . . . . |
| Sage Av *MIS* . . . . . . . . **210** H74 | Salsbury Dr *VAN*. . . . **143** S-T17 T17 | Sawyer's Rd *PTM* . . . . . . **186** B46 | Seaton Pl *RMD* . . . . . . . **203** J15 | . . . . . . . **11** H40 **142** S14 **143** S15 |
| Sage Pl *CQT* . . . . . . . . **165** V37 | Salt La *LGC* . . . . . . . . . **227** N48 | Saxbee Ct *ABT* . . . . . . . **270** V78 | Seaton Rd *RMD* . . . . . . . **203** J15 | Shannon Cr *DNV* . . . . . . **123** K-L16 |
| | | | | Shannon Ct *CQT*. . . . . . **165** U34 |

Shannon Dr ABT . . . . . . . 270 V76
Shannon Pl SUR . . . . . . . 226 N43
Shannon Rd RMD . . . . . . 182 B8
Shannon Way DEL . . . . . . 263 Y16
Sharon Dr WVA . . . . . . . 121 K-L6
Sharon Pl WVA . . . . . . . 121 K5-6
Sharpe Av RMD . . . . . . . 204 E-F24
Sharpe Rd PTM . . . . . . . 167 V-W48
Sharpe St CQT . . . . . . . 165 U37
Sharpe St MIS . . . . . . . 210 J75
Sharpe St NEW . . . . . . . 184 B27
Sharpewood Pl CQT . . 146 Q-R39
Shasta Ct CQT . . . . . . . 165 U34
Shaughnessy Pl CQT . . . 146 R39
Shaughnessy St CQT . . 146 R39-40
Shaughnessy St PCQ . . . . . . . . . 146 S-T39 166 U-V39
Shaughnessy St VAN . . 182 A13 B13
Shavington St CNV . . . . . 143 P19
Shaw Av CHL . . . . . . . . 213 J6
Shaw Av CQT . . . . . . 165 W31-32
Shaw St NEW . . . . . . . . 184 B28
Shawna Way CQT . . . . . 165 W35
Shawnee Pl VAN . . . . . . 183 Z19
Shawnigan Dr CHL . . . . . 233 M6
Shawnigan Pl RMD . . . . . 202 J11
Shearwater Dr ABT . . 251 Q-R79
Sheaves Ct DEL . . . . . . 204 G27
Sheaves Pl DEL . . . . . . 204 G27
Sheaves Rd DEL . . . . . . 204 G-H27
Sheaves Way DEL . . . . . 204 H27
Sheena Pl ABT . . . . . . . 251 R79
Sheffield Dr KNT . . . . . . 175 X21
Sheffield Pl DEL . . . . . . 224 K29
Sheffield Way CHL . 213 J6 233 K6
Shefield Way ABT . . . . . . 250 U76
Shelby St CQT . . . . . 164 W23-24
Sheldon Av MIS . . . . . . . 210 J74
Shell Rd RMD . . . . . . . . . . . . . . . 183 C-D15 203 E15 J15 223 K15
Shellbridge Gt RMD . . . . 102 D14
Shellbridge Way RMD . . . . . . . . 182 D14 183 D15
Shelley Av ABT . . . . . . . 270 W75
Shelley Pl DEL . . . . . 224 L28-29
Shelley Rd DNV . . . . . . . 123 N22
Shellmont St BUR . . . . 164 U27-28
Shelter Cr CQT . . . . . . . 146 S39
Shepherd Dr RMD . . 182 D14 202 E14
Shepherd St BUR . . 163 Y22 164 Y23
Shepherd Way DEL . . . . . . . . . . 204 F28-29 G28-29
Sherban Ct BUR . . . . . . 164 U24
Sherbrooke St NEW 164 Y30 165 Y31
Sherbrooke St VAN . . 163 X-Y16 Y16 . . . . . . . . . 183 A16 Z16 Z16
Sheridan Av CQT . . . . . . 165 X34
Sheridan Dr PTM . . . . . 147 S-T48
Sheridan Pl ABT . . . . . . 250 R-S78
Sheridan Rd RMD . . . . . 202 J11
Sheriff St CQT . . . . . . . 165 U32
Sherlock Av BUR . . . . . . . . . . . . 144 T26 164 U25-26 U26
Sherman St CQT . . . . . . 145 R37
Sherman St WVA . . . . . 121 K-L5
Sherwood Av CQT . . . . . 165 X32
Sherwood Blvd DEL . . . 263 Z17-18
Sherwood Cr ABT . . . . . 270 V72
Sherwood Dr CHL . . . . . 233 N7
Sherwood La WVA . . . 122 L-M10
Sherwood Pl DEL . . . . . 263 Z17
Shetland St SUR . . . 226 M43-44
Shiau Ct CQT . . . . . . . . 146 S41
Shields Av RMD . . . . . . 202 G14
Shikaze Ct MIS . . . . . . . 210 H74
Shiles St NEW . . . 164 Y30 184 Z30
Shiloh Ct CQT . . . . . . . 165 U38
Shiloh Pl CQT . . . . . 165 U37-38
Shimek St MIS . . . . . . . 210 G78
Shinglebolt Cr PTM . . . . 186 B46
Shirley Av BUR . . . . . . . 184 Z24
Shirley Av DNV . . . . . . . 123 J15
Shone Rd DNV . . . . . . . 124 N25
Shore Cr ABT . . . . . . . . 270 V76
Shoreline Dr PTM . . . . . 186 B46
Shoreline Cir PMD . . . 145 R31-32
Shorepine Walk VAN . . . 162 U12
Short Rd ABT . . . . . . 270 Y-Z74
Short St BUR . . . . . . 184 Z23-24
Short St PMD . . . . . . 145 S-T32
Shuswap Av CQT . . . . . 165 Y36
Shuswap Av RMD . . . . 222 K8-9
Shuswap Ct ABT . . . . 250 S73-74
Shuswap Ter ABT . . . . . 250 S73
Shuttle St ABT . . . . . . . 249 T63

Si-Lu Dr VAN . . . . . . . . 162 Y8
Sicamous Av CQT . . . . . 165 X35
Sicamous Pl CQT . 203 F-J16 223 X35
Sidaway Rd RMD . 203 F-J16 223 K16
Sidegrove Ct ABT . . . . . 250 S71
Sidley St BUR . . . . . 184 Z23 Z24
Sidney St CHL . . . . . . . . 193 D6
Sidney St VAN . . . 163 W17-18 W18
Sidoni Pl ABT . . . . . . . . 249 T70
Sidoni Pl ABT . . . . . . . . 249 T70
Sienum Pl VAN . . . . . . . 162 Y8
Sierpina Dr RMD . . . . . . 202 H13
Sierpina Pl RMD . . . . . . 202 H13
Sierra Dr BUR . . . . . 144 S25-26
Sierra Pl ABT . . . . . . . . 270 V78
Siesta Bay SUR . . . . . . 266 W39
Signal Ct ABT . . . . . 249 T-U63
Signal Ct CQT . . . . . . . 165 U36
Silica Pl CQT . . . . . . 145 P35-36
Sills Av RMD . . . . . . . . 182 C13
Silver Av BUR . . . 163 Y22 183 Z22
Silver Av CHL . . . . 213 J7 233 K6
Silver Way ABT . . . . . . . 251 S-T83
Silver Fox Ter MIS . . . . . 210 H72
Silver Lake Pl CQT . . . . 165 V37
Silver Skagit Rd HOP . . . 118 G-H42
Silver Springs Blvd CQT . 145 R38
Silver Valley Rd MAP . . . 167 V54
Silverado Pl DEL . . . . . . 263 W17
Silverberry Ct CQT . . . . 145 Q36
Silverdale Av MIS . . . . 210 H-J71
Silverdale Pl DNV . . . . . 123 K16
Silverdale Pl MIS . . . . . 210 H72
Silverhope Rd HOP . . . 118 G-H42
Silversmith Pl RMD . . . . 223 K15
Silverthorne Pl PTM . . . 187 A47
Silverthorne Pl CHL . . . . 233 L6
Silverthrone Dr CQT 145 Q38 146 Q39
Silvertree Ct ABT . . . . 250 T-U75
Silverview Rd HOP . . . . 118 G43
Silverwood Cr DNV . . . 122 N13-14
Sim Rd ABT . . 210 J78 230 K77 K78 L76
Simmons Rd CHL . . . . . 233 P1
Simon Av ABT . . . . . 250 T73-74
Simon St MIS . . . . . . . . 210 J72
Simon Fraser Ct PMD . . 145 S31
Simpson Av VAN . . 142 T7 161 T6
Simpson Rd ABT . 240 U63 U67 U60
Simpson Rd CHL . . . . . 233 L3-4
Simpson Rd RMD . . . . . 183 C15
Simpson Rd Ext ABT . 249 U67-68
Simpson St NEW . . . . . 184 Z30
Sinclair Av NEW . . . . . . 184 Z28
Sinclair Cr SUR . . . . . . 205 J32
Sinclair Ct WVA . . . . . . 122 L10
Sinclair Pl PCQ . . . . . . 166 X40
Sinclair St WVA . . . . 122 L-M10
Singh St LGT . . . . . 207 E53-54
Sininger Pl CHL . . . . . . 233 L6
Sirmac Av CQT . . 145 T32 165 U32
Siskin Ct ABT . . . . . . . 249 T69
Siskin St ABT . . . . . 249 S-T69
Sitka Av PCQ . . . . . . . . 146 T41
Sitka Sq VAN . . . . . . . . 162 U13
Skagit Av HOP . . . . . . . 118 E44
Skagit Dr ABT . . . . . . . 204 G27
Skagit Dr RMD . . 202 J8 222 K8
Skaha Cr RMD . . . . . . . 202 F11
Skana Dr DEL . . . . . . . 262 X15
Skana Dr VAN . . . . . 183 A20-21
Skawsten Rd WVA . . . . . 122 N13
Skeena Av ABT . . 250 S78 S78 251 T79
Skeena Bay SUR . . . . . 266 V39
Skeena Rd DNV . . . . . . 123 N21
Skeena St DEL . . . . . . . 262 X15
Skeena St PCQ . . 146 T42 166 U42
Skeena St VAN . . . . . . . . . . . . . . 143 S-T20 T20 163 U20 V20 W20
Skeena St N VAN . . . . . 143 S20
Skier's App WHS . . . . . . 401 T21
Skier's Plaza WHS . . . . . 401 T21
Skilift Pl WVA . . . . . . . 122 K8-9
Skilift Rd WVA . . . . . 122 K9-10
Skillen St MAP . . 167 Y49 Y49 187 Z49
Skipper Pl VAN . . . . . . 183 A18
Skowkale Cr CHL . . . . . 213 J7
Skway Rd CHL . . . . . . . 213 E4
Skye Pl PCQ . . . . . . . 146 S-T42
Skye Pl SUR . . . . . . . . 205 F33
Skylark Dr HOP . . . . . . 118 E46
Skylark La HOP . . . . . . 118 E46
Skyline Dr ABT . . . . 270 V77-78
Skyline Dr DNV . 123 J16 J-K16
Skyline Dr SQM . . . . . . 301 E3-4
Skyline Pl SQM . . . . . . 301 E4

Skyview Cr CHL . . . . . . 233 N8
Slager Av MAP . . . . . . . 187 Z54
Sleepy Hollow Rd CHL . . 233 P6
Sleepy Hollow Rd FRA . . 253 R6
Slocan Dr ABT . . . . . 250 S72-73
Slocan Pl ABT . . . . . 250 S72-73
Slocan Dr VAN . . . . . . . . . . . . . 143 R-T19 163 U-W19 W-X18 X18
Slocan St N VAN . . . 143 R-S19
Smallwood Av CQT . . 165 U32-33
Smallwood Pl RMD . . . 203 E16-17
Smith Av BUR . . . . . . . 163 V-X21
Smith Av CQT . . 164 V30 165 V31-34
Smith Cr LGT . . . . . 227 K50 K51
Smith Cr RMD . . 184 D25 204 E25
Smith Dr RMD . . . . . . . 204 E25
Smith Pl LGT . . . . . . . . 207 E53
Smith Rd CHL . . . . . . . 233 L1
Smith St BUR . . . . . 163 V21 V22
Smith St RMD . . . . . . . 182 C13
Smithe Mews VAN . 11 J39 142 T14
Smithe St VAN . . . . . . . . . . . . . 11 J37 H38 J38-39 142 S-T13 T14
Smoke Bluffs Rd SQM . . 301 J3
Smokehouse Rd CHL . . . 213 J7-8
Smokey Smith Pl NEW . . 184 Z29
Snow Valley Pl WHS . . . 401 H2
Snowberry Ct ABT . . 164 U29-30
Snowdon Av RMD . . . . 202 J13-14
Snowdon Pl SUR . . . . . 205 F33
Snowdrop Ct PMD . . . . 145 R34
Snowridge Cir WHS . . . . 401 H2
Snowridge Cr WHS . . . . 401 H2
Soball St CQT . . . . . 146 R-S41
Solar Ct CQT . . . . . . . . 165 X36
Solloway St MIS . . . . . . 210 H74
Solway Dr RMD . . . . . 202 J8-9
Somerset Av ABT . . . 250 T77-78
Somerset Cr DEL . . . . . 224 K29
Somerset Cr SUR . . . . . 246 S39
Somerset Cr VAN . . . . . 162 X12
Somerset Dr PTM . 186 Z46 187 Z47
Somerset La UEL . . . . . 161 U3
Somerset Pl PCQ . . . 146 S-T42
Somerset Pl SUR . 245 S38 246 S39
Somerset St CNV . . . . . 123 L18
Somerset St PCQ . . . 146 S-T42
Somerville St VAN . . . . . 163 X16
Sommeroot Cr RMD . . . 202 G13
Sonata Pl CHL . . . . . 233 M-N4
Sonora Dr CQT . . 145 T35 165 U35
Sonora Dr DNV . . 103 H15 123 J15
Sonora Pl DNV . . 103 H15 123 J15
Soowahlie Rd FRA . . . . 253 Q6
Sophia St VAN . . . . . . . . . . . . . 163 V-W15 W15 X15 Y15 . . . . . . . . . . . . . 183 A15 Z15 Z15
Sorenson Cr RMD . . . . . 202 E13
Sorenson Gt RMD . . . . . 202 D13
Sorenson St ABT . . . . 230 L-M74
Sorrel Dr RMD . . 202 J9 222 K9
Sorrel Pl SUR . . . . . . 226 L-M42
Sorrel St CQT . . . . . . . 165 W37
Sorrento Av CQT . . . . . 250 S72
Sorrento Dr CQT . . . . . 165 X35
Sorrento Pl CQT . . . . . 165 X35
Sotao Av VAN . . . . . 183 A-B19
South Arm Pl RMD . . . . 202 J13
South Campus Rd BUR . 144 T28-29
South Campus Rd UEL . . 161 W5
South Dyke Rd NEW . . . . . . . . . 184 D26 D27 204 E26
South Fraser Way ABT . . . . . . . 249 T69 U70 250 U71-75 U76 270 V76
South Fraser Way SUR . . 184 C-D30
South Fraser Perimeter Rd ABT . . . . . . 204 F27-28 G27 H24-25 223 L-M20
South Fraser Perimeter Rd SUR . . . . . . . . . . 185 A35-36 186 A40 B40-41
South Lake La WHS . . . 401 G2
South Parallel Rd ABT . . . . . . . . . . . . . . . 251 T83 270 W77-78
South Railway St MIS . . 210 J74-75
South Shore Cr VAN . . . 183 A-B18
South Sumas Rd CHL . . 233 L1-6
Southborough Dr WVA . . . . . . . . . . . . . . . . . . . 122 J13 K12-13
Southcrest Dr BUR . . . . 164 V26
Southdale Ct ABT . 250 U72 U73
Southdale Rd RMD . 202 J13 222 K13
Southdowne Pl CHL . . . . 233 K-L6
Southeast Marine Dr VAN . . . . . . . 183 A15-17 A19 A-B18
Southern Cr ABT . . 249 T70 250 T71
Southern Dr ABT . . 249 T70 250 T71
Southern Pl ABT . . 249 T70 250 T71

Southern St VAN . . . 11 K41 143 T15
Southgate Pl RMD . . . . 222 K14
Southgate Rd PTM . . . 187 A-B47
Southgate Rd RMD . 202 J14 222 K14
Southglen SUR . . . . . . 186 C39
Southglen Pl SUR . . . . 186 C39
Southlands Cr CHL . . . . 213 F-G7
Southlands Dr CHL . . . . 213 F7
Southlands Cr RMD . . . . 162 Y9
Southlawn Dr BUR . . . . . . . . . . . 143 T22 144 T23 164 U23
Southmere Cl SUR . . 265 V-W37
Southmere Cr SUR . . . . 265 W37
Southmere Cr E SUR 265 V37 V-W37
Southmere Cr W SUR . . 265 V36-37
Southmere Pl SUR . . . . 265 V37
Southoaks Cr BUR . . . . 184 Z25
Southpark Cl SUR . . . . 225 M31
Southpark Cr SUR . . . . 225 M31
Southpark Ct SUR . . . . 225 M31
Southpark Gr SUR . . . . 225 M31
Southpark Pl SUR . . . . 225 M31
Southpoint Dr BUR . 184 A26 A-B25
Southport Rd RMD . 202 J14 222 K14
Southridge Av WVA . . . 121 K6
Southridge Cr LGT . . . . 247 Q50
Southridge Ct DEL . . 224 K28-29
Southridge Dr BUR . . 184 B24-25
Southridge Dr SUR . . . 225 N32
Southridge Pl ABT . . . . 251 U80
Southridge Pl SUR . . 225 N-P32
Southridge Pl WVA . . . 121 K6
Southridge Rd DEL . . 224 K28-29
Southridge Rd RMD 202 J13 222 K13
Southside Dr VAN . . . 183 A17-18
Southview Dr SUR . . . . 225 N36
Southview Pl BUR . . . . 164 V26
Southview Pl LIO . . . . . 101 C23
Southwest Marine Dr VAN . . . . . . 162 Y9-10 182 A11 A13-14 B12-13 . . . . . . . . . . . . . . . . . . 183 A15
Southwood Pl BUR . . . . 183 A22
Southwood St BUR . . . . . . . . . . . 183 A21 A21-22 A22 184 A23
Southwynde Av BUR . . 184 A-B25
Sowden St DNV . . . . . . 122 N14
Spa-Ath Pl DNV . . . . . . 144 P23
Spa-Ath Rd DNV . . . . . 144 P23
Spadina Av CHL . . . . . . 213 E5-6
Spagnol St NEW . . . . . 204 E26
Spallin Av ABT . . . . . 249 Q68-69
Span Rd SUR . . . . . . . 185 C31
Spanish Corral CHL . . . 193 D6
Spanton Dr DEL . . . . . 243 Q16
Spanton Pl DEL . . . . . . 243 Q16
Spar Dr CQT . . . . . . . . 145 T36
Sparbrook Cr VAN . . . . 183 A20
Sparks Ct NEW . . . . . . 184 D26
Sparks Way ANM . . . . . 145 P34
Sparrow Ct CQT . . . . . 145 S36
Sparrow Dr ABT . . . . 249 S-T69
Sparrow La DNV . . . . . 144 Q25
Sparrow Pl VAN . 183 A20 B19-20
Sparrow Rd CHL . . . . . 233 N-P8
Spartan Cr CHL . . . . . . 213 F5-6
Sparwood Pl RMD . . . . 203 F17
Sparwood St ABT . . . . . 250 S72
Spearhead Dr WHS . . 401 E4-5 S23
Spearhead Pl WHS . . 401 E-F4 T23
Speen Rd SUR . . 184 C30 185 C31
Spence Av CQT . . . . . . 165 U32
Spence Rd ANM . . . . . 125 N33
Spencer Cl WVA . . . . . 122 K8
Spencer Cr WVA . . . . . 122 K7-8
Spencer Dr WVA . . . . . 122 K7-8
Spencer La MAP . . . . . 187 B54
Spencer St ABT . . . . . . 270 V78
Spencer St MIS . . . . . . 210 J72
Spencer St VAN . . . . 163 X19-20
Spender Ct RMD . 202 J10 222 K10
Spender Dr RMD . . . . 202 J10-11
Spenser Ct SUR . . . . . 205 G37
Spenser Dr SUR . . . . . 205 G37
Spenser Pl SUR . . . . . 205 G37
Sperling Av BUR . . . . . 144 T25 . . . . . . . 164 U25 V25 W25 X25 Y25 184 Z25
Spetifore Ct DEL . . . . . 263 Y17
Spicer Rd DNV . . . . . . 143 Q21
Spinnaker Bay DEL . . . 223 N17
Spinnaker Pl VAN . . . . 183 A20
Spires Gt RMD . . . . 202 F12-13
Spires Rd RMD . . . . . 202 F13
Spit Rd SQM . . . . . . . 301 G-H1
Spitfire Pl PCQ . . . . . . 166 X40
Spray Av CQT . . . . . 165 U33-34
Sprice Av CQT . . . 165 V31-34

Sprice St NEW . . . . . . 184 D26-27
Spring Av CQT . . . . . . 165 U32
Spring Av MAP . . . . . . 167 Y50
Spring Cr MAP . . . . . . 167 Y51
Spring St PMD . . . . . 145 T32-34
Spring Creek Dr WHS . . 401 J99
Springate Pl CHL . . . . . 233 N8
Springdale Ct BUR . . . . 144 T23
Springdale Dr PTM . . . . 187 Z47
Springer Av N BUR . . . . 144 S23
Springer Av S BUR . . . . . . . . . . . . 144 S-T23 164 U23
Springfield Ct RMD . . 202 J8 222 K8
Springfield Ct SUR . 205 G38 206 G39
Springfield Dr LGT . . 248 T62-63
Springfield Dr RMD . . . 202 J8-9
Springfield Gdns SUR . . . . . . . . . . . . . . 205 G38 206 G39
Springfield St CHL . . . . 233 M7
Springford Av RMD . . . . 202 J8
Springhill Cr RMD . . . . 202 J8
Springhill Ct ABT . . . . . 250 U71
Springhill Pl ABT . . . . . 250 U71
Springhill Pl RMD . . . . 202 J8
Springhill Rd ABT . . . . 250 U71
Springmont Dr RMD . . . 202 J8
Springside Gt RMD . 202 J8 222 K8
Springs La WHS . . . 401 F4 T21
Springside Cr SUR . . 186 B-C39
Springside Pl RMD . . . . 202 J8
Springthorne Cr RMD . 202 J8 222 K8
Springtree Dr VAN . . . . 162 W11
Springwood Cr RMD . 202 J8 222 K8
Springwood Gt RMD . 202 J8 222 K8
Sproatt Dr WHS . . . . . . 401 J1
Sprott St BUR . . . . . 164 W23-24
Sproule Av CQT . . . . . 165 U31
Spruce Av PCQ . . . . . . 146 T41
Spruce Ct PMD . . . . . . 145 Q35
Spruce Dr CHL . . . . . . 213 J5-6
Spruce Dr SQM . . . . . . 301 J3-4
Spruce Rd SUR . . . . . . 185 B31
Spruce St ABT . . . . . . 250 U76
Spruce St BUR . . . . . . . . . . . . . . 163 W21 W22 164 W23-24
Spruce St FRA . . . . . . 253 R5
Spruce St HHS . . . . . 155 P19-20
Spruce St NEW . . . . . . 185 Z31
Spruce St VAN . . . . . . 162 U13
Spruce Grove Cir WHS . . 401 D4
Spruce Grove La WHS . . 401 D4
Spruce Grove Way WHS . 401 D4
Sprucefeild Rd WVA . . . 121 K3
Spur Av ABT . . . . . . . 250 S71
Spur Rd BUR . . . . . 184 C25-26
Spur Rd SUR . . . . . . . 184 C30
Spuraway WVA . . . . . . 122 M13
Spuraway Av CQT . . . 165 U36-37
Spyglass Cr DEL . . . 263 W16-17
Spyglass Ct ABT . . . . . 251 U80
Spyglass Ct CQT . . 145 P38 146 P39
Spyglass La ABT . . . 251 U80-81
Spyglass Pl VAN . . . . . . . . . . . . 11 K38 142 T14 162 U14
Squamish Cr ABT . . . . . 250 S73
Squaw Valley Cr WHS . . 401 H1-2
Squiaala Rd CHL . . . . . 213 F-G5
Stadium Rd UEL . . . . . 161 V4
Stafford Av CQT . . . . . 165 V32
Stafford Av PCQ . 165 W38 166 W39
Staghorn Pl DNV . . . . . 103 H15
Stahaken Ct DEL . . . . . 262 X15
Stahaken Pl DEL . . . . . 262 X15
Stainsbury Av VAN . . 163 V17 W17-18
Stamford Pl DEL . . . . 204 H-J29
Stamford Pl SUR . . . . . 205 E33
Stamford St VAN . . . . . 163 Y20
Stamp's Ldg VAN . 11 K38 162 U13
Standish Dr DNV . . 123 M22 124 M23
Stanley Av DNV . . . . . 123 L16
Stanley Pl CQT . . . . . . 145 R37
Stanley St ABT . . . . . . 250 U71
Stanley St BUR . . 164 X-Y26 Y25
Stanley St CHL . . 193 D6 213 E6
Stanley St NEW . . . . . . 184 C27
Stanley Park Dr VAN . . . . . . . . . . 142 P-Q11 Q12-13 R11-12
Stanton Av CQT . . . . . . 165 U32
Stanton Av MAP . . . . . 187 Z48
Stanwood Av CQT . . . . 165 W35
Staples Cr DEL . . . . 224 K-L30
Star Cr NEW . . . . . . . 184 C28
Starboard Sq VAN . 11 K38 162 U14
Stardale Av CQT . . . . . 165 U32
Starflower Pl CQT . . . 145 Q36-37

Stark St RMD. . . . . . . . . 202 E10
Starlight Way CQT. . . . . . 165 U37
Starlight Way DNV. . . . . . 123 K17
Starling Av MIS . . . . . . . . 210 J72
Starret Rd HOP. . . . . . . 118 G41-42
Starview Pl SQM. . . . . . . 301 E3
Station Pl ABT. . . . . . . . 249 U63
Station Pl SUR. . . . . . . . 225 P32
Station Rd ABT. . . . . . . . 249 T-U63
Station Rd SUR . . . . . . . 225 N-P32
Station St DEL. . . . . . . . 243 Q15
Station St VAN. . . . . 11 J41 143 T15
Station Hill Ct BUR. . . . . 184 A25
Station Hill Dr BUR . . . . . 184 A25
Staulo Cr VAN . . . . . . . . 162 Y7
Stautlo Av VAN . . . . . . . 162 Y8
Stave Lake St MIS . . . . 210 F76 H-J75
Stawamus Rd SQM. . . . . . 301 K2
Stayte Rd WRK . . . . . . . 266 W-X39
Stearman Av WVA . . . . . . 121 L4
Steele Ct RMD. . . . . . . . 202 J11
Steelhead Ct ABT . . . . . . 249 S69
Steeple Ct CQT . . . . . . 145 R-S36
Steeple Dr CQT . . . . . . 145 S-R36
Steetaws Rd CHL . . . . . . 233 N6
Steeves St MAP . . . . . 187 A49 Z49
Stefanko Pl RMD. . . . . . . 202 J10
Stella Pl PCQ . . . . . . . . 166 W39
Stellar Ct ABT . . . . . . . . 249 S69
Stellar Ct CQT . . . . . . . 145 S36
Stellar Pl RMD. . . . . . . . 103 H15
Stephen Av CNV . . . . . . 123 N19
Stephen Leacock Dr ABT. . . . . . .
. . . . . . . . . . . . . . . . 251 Q80-81
Stephens Rd HOP . . . . . . 118 E48
Stephens St MAP . . . . . . 187 Z54
Stephens St VAN . 142 T10 162 U-V10
Sterling Ct DEL . . . . . . . 204 J30
Stevens Dr DEL . . . . . . . 263 Y16
Stevens Dr WVA122 J13 J-K13 L12-13
Stevens La DEL . . . . . . . 263 Y16
Stevens Pl DEL . . . . . . . 263 Y16
Stevens St ABT . . . . . . . 249 T68
Stevens St WRK . . . . . . 266 W-X39
Stevenson Rd CHL . . . . . 233 K5-6
Stevenson St ABT . . . . . . 270 V74
Stevenson St PCQ. . . . . . 146 T39
Steveston Hwy RMD . . . . . . .
. . . . . . . 222 K8-14 223 K15-17
Stewardson Way NEW . . 184 D27-28
Stewart Cr CQT . . . . . . 165 W32-33
Stewart Cr ABT . . . . . . . 250 U77
Stewart Cr MAP . . . . . . . 187 A48
Stewart Pl DEL . . . . . . . 224 K29
Stewart Pl PCQ . . . . . . 166 X39-40
Stewart Rd DEL. . . . . . . . 224 K29
Stewart Rd LIO. . . . . . . . 101 A-B23
Stewart St MIS . . . . . . . 210 H72
Stewart St VAN . . . . . . 143 S16-17
Stikine Pl VAN . . . . . . . . 183 A20
Still Creek Av BUR . . . . . . .
. . . . . . . . . 163 V21 164 V32 V30
Still Creek Dr BUR. . . . . . 163 V22
Stilmond Rd RMD . . . . . . 202 J8
Stirling Av CHL . . . . . . . 233 L5
Stirling Av PCQ . . . . . . . 146 T39
Stirling Av RMD. . . . . . . . 202 J11
Stirling St VAN. . 163 Y18 183 A18 Z18
Sto:lo Xalh Smemalt CHL . 233 L7-8
Stocker Ct WRK . . . . . . 265 X38
Stockton Cr ABT . . . . . . . 250 U77
Stokes Av MIS . . . . . . . . 210 G73
Stolberg St RMD. . . . . . . 182 D13
Stone Cr WVA . . . . . . . . 121 K4
Stone Ct WVA . . . . . . . . 121 K4
Stone Haven SQM . . . . . . 301 D2
Stone Ridge Pl CHL . . . . . 213 F2
Stonebridge Dr WHS . . . 401 F-G41
Stonebridge Pl WHS . . . . 401 F1
Stonecroft Dr ABT . . . . . . 251 U80
Stonecroft Pl ABT . . . . . . 251 U80
Stonecrop Ct CQT . . . . . 145 Q37
Stonegate Pl CHL . . . . . . 194 D9
Stonehaven Av DNV . . . . 124 N26
Stonehaven St CHL . . . . . 233 M8
Stonehouse Av MAP. 167 Y49-50 Y50
Stoneleigh Av ABT . . . . . 250 T77
Stoneridge La CQT . . . . . 145 Q36
Stoneridge Pl ABT. . . . . . 251 U80
Stoneview Dr CHL . . . . . 233 N7
Stoney Av MAP . . . . . . . 187 A49
Stoney Ct DEL . . . . . . . 224 K-L29
Stoney Creek Pl BUR . . . . 164 U30
Stores Rd UEL . . . . . . . . 161 U3-4
Storey Av CHL . . . . . . . . 213 J6
Storey Av MAP. . . . . . . . 187 Z53

Stormont Av BUR. . . . . . 164 W29
Strachan St MIS . . . . . 210 H-J73
Straiton Rd ABT. 250 Q78 251 Q79-80
Strand Av NEW . . . . . . . 184 Z30
Stratford Av N BUR . . . . . 144 S24
Stratford Av S BUR . . . . 144 S24 T24
Stratford Pl CHL . . . . . . . 233 M5
Stratford St PCQ . . 146 T41 166 U41
Strathaven Dr DNV . 124 N23 144 P23
Strathaven La DNV . . . . . 144 P23-24
Strathcona Ct ABT . . . . . 251 S79
Strathcona Pl DNV . . . . . 124 N27
Strathcona Rd CHL . . . . . 193 C7-8
Strathcona Rd DNV . 124 N26-27 N27
Strathcona Way DNV . . . . 124 N26
Strathearn Av BUR . . . . . 183 A22
Strathmore Av BUR. 164 Y26 184 Z26
Strathmore Mews VAN. . . . . . . .
. . . . . . . . . . . . . 10 K36 142 T13
Strauss Dr VAN. . . . . . . 183 A20-21
Strawson St BUR. . . . . . 164 Y25
Streamstone Walk PTM . 186 A46
Streng Av MAP . . . . . . . 167 Y52
Stride Av BUR . . . . . . 184 A26 B25
Strikers Cr KNT. . . . . . . 175 U19
Strong Av ANM . . . . . . . 145 P34
Stuart Cr SUR. . . . . . . . 205 E-F33
Stuart Pl SUR . . . . . . . . 205 E-F33
Stuart St HOP . . . . . . . . 118 D44
Student Union Blvd UEL. . . . 161 U4
Suffolk Av PCQ. . . . . . 166 U39-40
Suffolk Rd SUR . . . 265 V38 266 V39
Sugar Mountain Way ANM . 125 N33
Sugarpine Ct CQT . . . . . 145 P38
Sugarpine St ABT . . . . . . 250 U73
Sullivan Pl DEL . . . . . . . 204 G28
Sullivan St BUR . . . . . . . 164 Y30
Sullivan St SUR . . . . . . . 245 T-U31
Sultan Pl CQT . . . . . . 146 Q39-40
Sumac Pl DNV . . . . . . . . 103 H15
Sumac Pl MIS . . . . . . . . 210 H75
Sumac Pl PCQ. . . . . . . . 146 T42
Sumac Pl SUR. . . . . . . . 186 C40
Sumas Cr CHL . . . . . . . 233 M5
Sumas Dr BUR . . . . . . . 164 U22
Sumas St BUR . . . 163 U22 164 U24
Sumas Way ABT. . . . . . . . . . . . .
. . . . . . . 250 T76-77 U77 270 V-Z77
Sumas Central Rd CHL . . 213 J3-5
Sumas Mountain Rd ABT. . . . . . .
. . . . . . . . . . . 251 R82-83 S83 T82-83
Summer La WHS . . . . . . 401 A-B5
Summer Pl DEL . . . . . . . 263 Z17
Summer Pl WHS . . . . . . 401 A-B5
Summer Rd HOP . . . . . . 118 E48
Summer Way DEL . . . . . . 263 Z17
Summerhill Cr SUR . . . . . 265 W33
Summerhill Ct SUR . . . . . 265 W33
Summerhill Gr SUR . . . . . 265 W33
Summerhill Pl ABT . . . . . 250 T76
Summerhill Pl SUR . . . . . 265 W33
Summerside La DNV . . . 124 N26-27
Summit Av WVA . . . . . . . 101 H1
Summit Cr DEL . . . . . . . 224 L30
Summit Dr ABT . . . . . . . 249 S70
Summit Dr CQT . . . . . . . 165 U33
Summit La WHS . . . . . . . 401 F4
Summit Pl CHL . . . . . . . 213 F3
Summit Pl WVA . . . . . . . 101 H1
Sumner Av BUR. . . . . . . 163 V22
Sumpter Dr CQT . . . . . . 165 U35
Sunburst Pl CHL . . . . . . 213 F3
Sunbury Pl DEL . . . . . . . 204 G27
Suncrest Dr BUR. . . . . . . 183 A21
Suncrest Dr DEL . . 204 G28-29 G29
Suncrest Dr SUR . . . . . . 205 H35
Sundale Av SUR . . . . . 226 N45-46
Sundale Cl SUR. . . . . . . 226 N45
Sundale Ct SUR. . . . . . . 226 N45
Sundale Gr SUR. . . . . . . 226 N45
Sundale Pl SUR . . . . . . . 226 N45
Sundance Cr WVA . . . . . 122 N12
Sundance Ct WVA . . . . . 122 N12
Sundance Dr SUR . . . . 226 L-M44
Sundance Pl WHS . . . . . 401 H2
Sundew Pl ABT. . . . . . . . 251 U80
Sundew Pl CQT. . . . . . . 145 Q37
Sundial Cr WHS . . . . . . 401 T21
Sundial Pl WHS. . . . . . . 401 T21
Sunflower Av BUR. . . . . . 184 A23
Sunland Pl BUR. . . . . . . 183 A22
Sunningdale Rd BUR . . . 144 S23
Sunnybank Av RMD. . . . 202 H11-12
Sunnybridge Dr WVA . . . 122 V-26
Sunnycrest Dr DNV 123 K15-16 K-L15
Sunnycroft Rd RMD. . . . 202 G-H12

Sunnydene Rd RMD . . . . 202 G12
Sunnyholme Cr RMD. . . 202 G-H12
Sunnyhurst Rd DNV . . . . 123 L19
Sunnymede Cr RMD. . . . 202 G11-12
Sunnymede Gt RMD. . . . 202 G-H12
Sunnyside Blvd FRA . . . . 253 R5
Sunnyside Ct ABT. . . . . . 250 U71
Sunnyside Ct ABT. . . . . . 250 U71
Sunnyside Dr DNV. . . . . . 122 L14
Sunnyside Dr MIS . . . . . 210 G-H78
Sunnyside Pl ABT. . . . . . 250 U71
Sunnyside Pl PTM. . . . . . 187 Z47
Sunnyside Rd ANM . . . . . . . .
. . . . . . . . 125 N33 145 P32-33
Sunnyside St ABT. . . . . . 250 T-U71
Sunnyside View ABT. . . . . 250 U71
Sunnywood Dr RMD . . . 202 G-H11
Sunridge Ct WHS . . . . . . 401 F3
Sunridge Dr WHS . . . . . . 401 F3
Sunridge Pl DEL . . . . . . 204 G27
Sunridge Pl SUR . . . . . . 205 H35
Sunridge Pl WHS . . . . . . 401 F-G3
Sunrise Al WHS . . . . . . 401 T21
Sunrise Av SUR. . . . . . . 226 N45
Sunrise Bay SUR . . . . . . 266 W39
Sunrise Cr ABT . . . . . . . 250 U72
Sunrise Cr E SUR . . . . 226 M-N45
Sunrise Cr W SUR . . . . . 226 N45
Sunrise Dr CHL . . . . . . . 213 F3
Sunrise La DEL . . . . . . . 243 Q19
Sunrise Pl SQM . . . . . . . 301 E3
Sunrise Pl SUR . . . . . . . 226 N45
Sunrise Park Dr ABT. . . . . 251 U81
Sunset Av CQT . . . . . . . 165 X31
Sunset Bay SUR . . . . . . 266 W39
Sunset Blvd DNV. . 122 L14 123 K15
Sunset Cr ABT . . . . . . 249 R68-69
Sunset Dr CHL . . . . . . 213 E-F6
Sunset Dr CHL . . . . . . . 233 L6-7
Sunset Dr DEL. . . . . . . . 204 G27
Sunset Dr LIO . . . . . . . . 101 A23
Sunset Dr WRK . . . . . . 265 W-X35
Sunset La PTM . . . . . . . 187 Z47
Sunset La WRK . . . . . . 265 W-X36
Sunset La WVA . . . . . . . 121 L6
Sunset Ridge ANM . . . . 125 N33-34
Sunset St BUR. . . . 163 W21 164 W24
Sunshine Alley SUR. . . . . 245 T31
Sunshine Dr CHL. . . . . . 213 J5
Sunshine Dr DEL . . . . . . 224 L29
Sunshine Pl DEL . . . . . . 224 L29
Sunshine Pl WHS . . . . . . 401 T21
Sunshine Falls La DNV . . 124 K28-29
Sunslope Cr BUR . . . . . . 164 U28
Sunvalley Cr ABT . . . . . . 249 U67
Sunview Pl DEL . . . . . . 204 G27-28
Sunwood Dr DEL . . . . . . 224 L-M30
Sunwood Pl DEL . . . . . . 224 M30
Surf Cr CQT . . . . . . . . . 165 U36
Surrey Rd SUR . . . . . . . 185 A36
Surrey St NEW. . . . . . . . 164 Y30
Sussex Av BUR . . . . . . . . . . .
. . . . . . . 163 X22 Y22 183 A22 Z22
Sussex Cr DEL . . . . . . . 224 K29
Sussex Dr CHL . . . . . . 233 L-M6
Sussex Pl DEL . . . . . . . 224 K29
Sussex St ABT . . . . . . . 250 S78
Suter Brook Way PMD. . . 145 S-T35
Sutherland Av CNV. 123 N18 143 P18
Sutherland Av PCQ. . . . . 146 S-U41
Sutherland St PCQ. . . . . 146 S-T41
Sutliff St BUR . . . . . . . . 164 U26
Sutton Av PTM . . . . . . . 186 B46
Sutton Pl DEL . . . . . . . . 204 J29
Sutton Pl SUR . . . . . . . . 205 E33
Sutton Pl WVA. . . . . . . . 122 K11
Suzhou Alley VAN. . . . . . . . . .
. . . . . . . 11 H40 142 S14 143 S15
Suzuki St NEW . . . . 184 D26 204 E26
SW Marine Dr UEL. . 161 V-W4 X5-6
Swallow Cr CHL . . . . . . 194 C10
Swallow Dr RMD . . . . . . 222 K10
Swallow Dr SUR . . . . . . 185 B37
Swallow Pl ABT. . . . . . . 249 T70
Swallow Pl CHL . . . . . . . 194 D9
Swallow Pl HOP . . . . . . 118 E46
Swallow Pl VAN . . 183 A20 B19-20
Swan Av MIS . . . . . . . . 210 H73
Swan Cr SUR. . . . . . . . . 185 B37
Swan Pl CQT. . . . . . . . 165 V36-37
Swansacre VAN . . 183 A20 B19-20
Swansea Av VAN . . . . . . 183 A20
Swansea Dr RMD. . . . . . 202 J13-14
Swanson Dr DEL. . . . . . . 204 H-J29
Swanson Pl CQT. . . . . . . 166 U42
Swanson Pl SUR . . . . . . 225 L34

Swanson St ABT . . . . . . 230 L77
Swanson St CHL . . . . . . 233 K-L6
Sweatman Rd KNT. . . . . 175 W19
Sweden Way RMD . . . . . 183 C16
Sweetwater Pl LIO. . . . . . 101 C23
Sweltzer Creek Rd CHL . . 233 P6
Swenson Way DEL . . . . . 204 H27
Swensson Av ABT. . . . . . 249 U63
Swevillis Dr CHL . . . . . . 213 F5
Swift Av RMD. . . . . . . . . 202 J11
Swift Dr MIS . . . . . . . . 210 H-J72
Swift La RMD. . . . . . . . . 202 J11
Swiftsure Bay DEL . . . . . 223 N17
Swinburne Av DNV. 123 N21-22 N22
Swinton Cr RMD . . . . . . 202 J14
Swire Pl PCQ . . . . . . . . 146 S-T41
Switzer Av ABT . . . . . . . 250 U75
Swordfern Pl DNV . . . . . 103 H15
Sycamore Dr PMD . . . . 145 P-Q35
Sycamore Pl CHL . . . . . . 213 F7
Sycamore Rd DNV . . . . . 123 J-K15
Sydney Av CQT . . . . . . 165 W31
Sydney St NEW . . . . 184 A28-29
Sykes Rd DNV . . . . . . . 123 K-L19
Sykes St MIS. . . . . . . . . 210 H74
Sylvan Av DNV . . . . . . . 123 J16
Sylvan Dr BUR. . . . . . . . 184 Z26
Sylvan Dr CHL . . . . . . . 233 N8
Sylvan Pl ABT . . . . . . . . 250 S71
Sylvan Pl CQT . . . . . . 165 V-W37
Sylvia Av MIS. . . . . . . . . 210 G74
Sylvia Pl CQT . . . . . . . . 146 Q39
Symes Bay PMD. . . . . . 145 Q32-33
Symonds Rd DNV . . . . . 123 K20

**T**

Tabor Pl CQT. . . . . . . . 165 V36-37
Taft Av CQT . . . . . . . . . 165 Y35
Tahsis Av CQT. . . . . . . . 146 S39
Tait Ct RMD. . . . . . . . . 182 C14
Takaya Dr DNV . . . . . . . 144 P23
Takaya Pl DNV. . . . . . . . 143 P20
Takeda Dr BUR . . . . . . . 144 R28
Takla Pl RMD. . . . . . . . . 202 F10
Talbot Ct CQT . . . . . . . 145 R37
Talisman Av VAN. . . . . . . 162 W14
Tall Rd ABT . . . . . . . . . 230 L75
Tall Tree La DNV . . 122 K14 123 K15
Tallin Av BUR. . . . . . . . . 164 U25
Tallon Pl SUR . . . . . 205 E34-35
Talon Sq VAN. . . . . . . . 183 Z20
Taluswood Pl WHS . . . . . 401 H2-3
Tamarack La MAP. . . . . . 187 B54
Tamarack Pl CHL . . . . . . 213 F7
Tamarack Pl PCQ . . . . . . 166 U41
Tamarack Rd DNV. . . . . . 123 K17
Tamarind Dr VAN . . . . . 183 Z20-21
Tamath Cr VAN. . . . . . . 162 X-Y7
Tamboline Rd DEL . . . . . 242 Q11
Tamihi Way CHL . . . . . . 233 M6
Tanager Ct CQT . . 145 P38 146 P39
Tanager Pl DNV . . . . . . . 123 N21
Tanager St MIS . . . . . . . 210 H73
Tanaka Ter MIS . . . . . . . 210 G73
Tanglewood La CQT . . . 145 Q36-37
Tank Rd RMD . . . . . . . 182 A-B10
Tanner Pl MAP . . . . . . . 187 Z49
Tanner St VAN . . . . . . . 163 W-X20
Tannery Rd SUR . . . . . . 184 C30
Tantalus Ct CQT . . . . . . 145 Q38
Tantalus Dr WHS. . . . . . 401 F4 U21
Tantalus La VAN . . . . . 183 Z20-21
Tantalus Pl SQM . . . . . . 301 D-E3
Tantalus Rd DNV. . . . . . 123 N21
Tantalus Rd SQM. . . . . 301 D-E3
Tapley Pl WHS. . . . . . . . 401 E3
Taralawn Ct BUR. . . 144 T23 164 U23
Target St SUR . . . . . . . . 245 T31
Tarlton St MIS . . . . . . . 210 F73
Taseko Rd RMD . . . . . . 202 F11
Tasmania Cr UEL . . . . . . 161 U5-6
Tatla Pl CQT . . . . . . . . 165 U37
Tatlow Av DNV . . . . 122 M14 N14
Taulbut St MIS . . . . . . . 210 H74
Taunton St VAN. . . . . . . 163 X19-20
Tavernier Ter MIS . . . . . . 210 H75
Taylor Cr DEL . . . . . . . . 243 Q18
Taylor Dr WVA . . . . . . . . 101 H1
Taylor La SUR . . . . . . 245 T-U31
Taylor Pl BUR. . . . . . . . . 164 Y29
Taylor Pl WVA . . . . . . . 122 L-M12
Taylor St MIS . . . . . . . . 210 F77
Taylor St PCQ . . . . . . . 166 V-W40

Taylor St VAN. . . . . 11 H39-40 142 S14
Taylor Way ABT . . . . . . . 270 V76
Taylor Way DEL. . . . . . . 204 F28-29
Taylor Way WHS . . . . . . 401 H1
Taylor Way WVA . . . . . 122 L-M12
Taylor Creek Pl DNV . . . 124 M-N24
Taylorwood Pl WVA . . . . . 122 M12
Teakwood Pl VAN . . . . . 183 A20-21
Teal Av BUR . . . . . . . . . 164 W24
Teal Pl MIS . . . . . . . . . 210 H72
Teal St MIS . . . . . . . . . 210 H72
Teck St CQT . . . . . . . . 165 X33
Tecumseh Av VAN . . . . . 162 V12
Telegraph Tr LGT. . . . . . . . . .
. 186 D46 207 E47 F48 F49 G50 G51 H52
Telegraph Tr SUR . . 186 D46 206 E46
Telegraph Tr WVA . . . . . 121 J2-3
Telep Av MAP . . . . . . . . 167 Y48
Telford Av BUR . . . . . . . 183 Z22
Telosky Av MAP. . . . . . . 187 A53
Tempe Cr CNV. . . . . . . . 123 L18
Tempe Heights La CNV. . . 123 L18
Tempe Knoll Dr CNV . . . 123 L-M18
Temple Glen Dr CNV . . . 123 L-M18
Templeton Dr VAN . . . . . . . . .
. . . . . . 143 S18 T18 T18 163 U18 U-V18
Templeton Dr N VAN . . . 143 S18
Templeton St RMD . . . . 182 C11
Tenby St CQT . . . . . . . 165 X31
Tennyson Cr DNV . . . . . 123 L19
Tercel Ct CQT. . . . . . . 145 R-S36
Terepocki Ct MIS . . . . . . 210 J72
Terminal Av VAN . . . . . . 11 K41
Terminal Av VAN . . . . . 143 T15-16
Tern St MIS . . . . . . . . . 210 J72
Terra Ct PCQ. . . . . 146 T41 166 U41
Terra Vista Pl ABT. . . . 251 S79-80
Terra Vita Pl VAN . . . . . 143 T20
Terrace WVA . . . . . . . . 121 K3
Terrace Av DNV . . . . . . 122 L14
Terrace Ct ABT . . . . . . . 250 S78
Terrace Dr DEL . . . . . . 204 G27-28
Terrace Rd RMD . . . . . 182 C10-11
Terravista Pl PMD . . . . . 145 T34
Terris St MIS . . . . . . . . 210 G72
Terry Rd WRK . . . . . . . 265 X34-35
Terry Fox Av ABT . . . 250 T74-75
Terry Fox La BUR . . . . . 144 T28
Terry Fox Way VAN11 J38-39 142 T14
Teskey Ct CHL . . . . . . . 233 N7-8
Teskey Rd CHL . . . . . . 233 M-N8
Teslin Dr ABT. . . . . . . . 250 R78
Tessaro Cr ABT . . . . . . 250 U75
Teton Av CHL . . . . . . . 193 B8
Teviot Pl DNV . . . . 122 J14 123 J15
Texaco Dr BUR . . . . . . 144 R27-28
Texada St CQT . . . . . . . 146 S39
Thacker Av CQT . . . . . 165 U37-38
Thacker Rd DNV. . . . . 118 D44-45
Thacker Mountain Rd HOP . . . . .
. . . . . . . . . . . . . . . . 118 D-E45
Thames Cr PCQ. . . . . . . 166 V41
Thames Ct DNV. . . . . . . 123 K20
Thames St UEL. . . . . . . 161 V5
Thames Pl PCQ . . . . . . 166 U-V41
Thea Dr PCQ. . . . . . . . 166 W39
Thellaiwhaltun Av VAN . . 162 Y8
Theology Mall UEL . . . . . 161 T4
Theresa La CHL . . . . . . 213 F-G5
Thermal Dr CQT . . . . . . 165 U35
Therrien St CQT. . . . . 165 W-X33
Theta Ct DNV . . . . . . . 124 N25-26
Thetford Pl WVA . . . . . . 122 K13
Thetis Pl RMD . . . . . . . 202 F11
Thimbleberry Ct CQT . . . 145 Q36
Thirlmere Dr RMD . . . . . 202 F11
Thistle Pl CQT. . . . . . . 165 W37
Thistledown Pl DEL . . . 263 Y17-18
Thomas Av CQT . . . . . 165 X33 X34
Thomas Dr RMD . . . . . . 202 J10
Thomas Pl RMD. . . . . . . 202 J10
Thomas Rd CHL . . . . . 233 M6-7
Thomas St BUR . . . . . . 164 W25
Thompson Av CQT . . . . 165 U31
Thompson Av MIS . 210 J75 230 K75
Thompson Cr WVA . . . . . 122 K7
Thompson Gt RMD . . . . 184 D25
Thompson Pl WVA . . . . . 122 K7
Thompson Rd PTM. . . . 147 T49-50
Thompson Rd RMD 184 D25 204 E25
Thomson Rd ANM . . . . 145 P33-34
Thor Ct CQT . . . . . . . . 146 Q39
Thorburn Way PTM . . . . 186 B46
Thoreau Av ABT . . . . . . 250 S77
Thormanby Cr RMD. . . . 202 G8-9
Thorncliffe Dr DNV . . . . . 123 L15

Thorne Av *BUR* . . . . . . 184 C25
Thorne Av *MAP* . . . . . . 187 A48 A49
Thornhill Dr *VAN* . . . . . 183 A17
Thornhill Pl *ABT* . . . . . 250 S71-72
Thornhill St *CHL* . . . . . 233 M8
Thornton Av *MAP* . . . . . 167 Y50
Thornton Pl *ABT* . . . . . 250 R78
Thornton Pl *MAP* . . . . . 167 Y50
Thornton St *VAN* . . 11 J-K41 143 T15
Thornwood Pl *BUR* . . . . 164 W23
Thorpe Rd *RMD* . . . . . 183 D15
Thorpe St *MIS* . . . . . . 210 G73
Thrasher St *MIS* . . . . . 210 H73
Three Cedars Dr *VAN* . . 183 A20
Thrift Av *WRK* . 265 W36-38 266 W39
Thrift St *CQT* . . . . . 165 X31-32
Thrush Av *MIS* . . . . . . 210 J71-72
Thrush Pl *VAN* . 183 A20 B19-20
Thunderbird Blvd *UEL* . . 161 U-V4
Thunderbird Cr *BUR* . . . 164 V23
Thunderbird Ct *DEL* . . . 224 K29-30
Thunderbird Ridge *SQM* . 301 D-E5
Thurlow St *VAN* . . .
. . . . 10 G36 H35-36 142 R13-14 S12-13
Thurston Cl *PMD* . . . . 145 S35-36
Thurston Pl *ABT* . . . . . 250 S71
Thurston St *BUR* . . . . . 163 X21
Thurston Ter *PMD* . . . . 145 S35-36
Thyme Dr *CQT* . . . . . . 165 W37
Tiber Cl *PCQ* . . . . . . . 166 U-V41
Tiber Pl *PCQ* . . . . . . . 166 U39
Ticehurst La *PCQ* . 165 U38 166 U39
Tide Pl *CQT* . . . . . . . . 165 U37
Tidewater Bay *DEL* . . . . 223 N17
Tidewater Pl *VAN* . . . . 182 A11
Tidewater Way *LIO* . . . . 101 C23
Tiffany Blvd *RMD* . . . . 202 F10
Tiffany Pl *RMD* . . . . . . 202 F10
Tiffin Cr *RMD* . . . . . . . 202 F9
Tigris Cr *PCQ* . . . . . . 166 V41-42
Tilbury Av *CHL* . . . . . . 233 L6
Tilbury Pl *SUR* . . . . . . 186 B-C41
Tilbury Rd *DEL* . . . . . . 203 J20
Tillicum St *BUR* . . . . . 184 C-D23
Tilston Ct *CQT* . . . . . . 165 U33
Tilston St *CHL* . . . . . . 213 F8
Tilton Rd *RMD* . . . . . . 202 E9-10
Timber Ct *BUR* . . . . . . 164 U28
Timber Ct *CQT* . . . . . . 145 P-Q30
Timber La *WHS* . . . . . . 401 C3
Timber Ridge *CHL* . . . . 233 N8
Timber Ridge *WHS* . . . . 401 H1
Timbercrest Dr *PMD* . . . 145 R35
Timbercrest Pl *PMD* . . . 145 R34-35
Timberfeild Dr *WVA* . . . 121 J-K3
Timberfeild La *WVA* . . . 121 J3-4
Timberfeild Pl *WVA* . . . 121 J-K3
Timberlake St *MIS* . 210 J75 230 K75
Timberland Rd *SUR* . . . 184 B-C30
Timberlane Dr *ABT* . . . . 251 U80
Timberline Pl *CHL* . . . . 194 C10-11
Timberline Pl *DNV* . . . . 123 J15
Timbertop Dr *LIO* . . . . . 101 B24
Timbervalley Rd *DEL* . . . 263 Z17-18
Timberwood Av *MIS* 210 J75 230 K75
Timothy Av *CHL* . . . . . 233 M6
Tims Av *ABT* . . . . . . . 250 T72
Tims St *ABT* . . . . . . . . 250 T72
Tina Way *PCQ* . . . . . . 166 X39
Tindall Ter *MIS* . . . . . . 210 G78
Tinmore Pl *RMD* . . . . . 202 H8-9
Tipping Rd *RMD* . . . . . 183 B16
Tipton St *CQT* . . . . . . 165 V33
Tisdall St *VAN* . . . . . .
. . . . . . 162 Y13 Y13 182 Z13 Z13
Toad Hollow *WHS* . . . . 401 D-E3
Toba Dr *CQT* . . . . . . . 146 S39
Toba Pl *VAN* . . . . . . . 183 Z21
Tobena Rd *HOP* . . . . . 118 G41-42
Tobermory Way *SQM* . . . 301 D-E5
Tobruck Av *CNV* . . . . . 123 N15
Todd Cr *SUR* . . . . . . . 205 J35
Todd Ct *ABT* . . . . . . . 250 T78
Todd Pl *DEL* . . . . . . . 224 L30
Todd St *VAN* . . . . . . . 163 W-X19
Toderick St *VAN* . 163 Y20 183 Z20
Tolbooth La *VAN* . . . . . 183 A20
Tollcross Rd *DNV* . 124 N23 144 P23
Tolmie Av *CQT* . . . . . . 165 W35
Tolmie Rd *RMD* . . . . . . 202 F8
Tolmie St *VAN* . . . . . .
. . . . . 142 T7 161 U6 V6 162 U7 V7
Tom Berry Rd *VAN* . . . . 118 G42-43
Tom Thomson Ct *ABT* . . 251 Q80
Tomahawk Av *WVA* . . . 122 M-N12
Tomicki Av *RMD* . 182 D13 202 E13
Tompkins Cr *DNV* . . . . 124 M23

Toni Sailer La *WHS* . . . . 401 E4
Topaz Ct *CQT* . . . . . . 145 Q36
Topaz Dr *CHL* . . . . . . 213 H-J6
Topaz St *ABT* . . . . . . 270 V73
Topley La *WHS* . . . . . . 193 C7-8
Topper Ct *MIS* . . . . . . 210 H75
Topper Dr *MIS* . . . . . . 210 H75
Torbet St *SQM* . . . . . . 301 D5
Toronto Pl *PCQ* . . . . . 146 S40-41
Toronto Rd *UEL* . . . . . 161 U4-5
Toronto St *CQT* . . . . . 146 R-S41
Toronto St *PCQ* . 146 S-T41 166 U41
Torquay Av *DNV* . . . . . 123 M20
Tory Av *CQT* . . . . . . . 146 R39
Totem Ct *BUR* . . . . . . 163 U21-22
Totem Dr *SQM* . . . . . . 301 K2
Tourney Rd *DNV* . . . . . 123 J20
Tournier Pl *CHL* . . . . . 233 N7
Tower Ct *PCQ* . . . . . . 166 X-Y39
Tower Rd *BUR* . . . . . . 144 T29
Tower Rd *CHL* . . . . . . 193 B7
Tower Rd *KNT* . . . . . . 175 W-X22
Tower Hill Cr *WVA* . . . . 122 K8
Town Centre Blvd *CQT* . . 145 S38
Townley St *CQT* . . . . . 165 U-V32
Townley St *VAN* . . . . . 162 W10
Townline Rd *ABT* . . . . . 249 Q-70
Townsend Pl *NEW* . . . . 184 A29
Townshipline Av *MIS* . . 210 E71-72
Townshipline Rd *ABT* . . 230 P71-78
Tracey St *ABT* . . . . . . 270 W71
Trafalgar St *ABT* . . . . . 250 T74
Trafalgar St *VAN* . . . . .
. . . . 142 T10 162 U-W10 W-X10 Y10
Trail's End La *WHS* . . . . 401 J2
Tralee Cr *DEL* . . . . . . 263 Y16
Tralee Pl *DEL* . . . . . . 263 Y16
Tranmer Rd *KNT* . . . . . 175 X-Y22
Tranquille Pl *RMD* . . . . 202 F11
Trapp Av *BUR* . . 184 C25 C25-26
Trapp Rd *NEW* . . . . . . 184 C26
Trattle St *LGT* . . . . . . 207 F53
Travers Av *WVA* . . . . . 122 L7
Treetop Dr *ABT* . . . . . 251 S80
Treetop La *DNV* . . . . . 123 M22
Treetop La *WHS* . . . . . 401 E3
Treetops Dr *PMD* . . . . 145 R34
Trembath Av *MIS* . . . . . 210 J72
Trenant St *DEL* . . . . . . 223 P16
Trent Av *CQT* . . . . . . 165 V34
Trent St *CHL* . . . . . . . 233 L5
Trenton Pl *DNV* . . . . . 123 K16
Trenton St *PCQ* . . . . . 166 W42
Trepassey Dr *RMD* . . 202 J9 222 K9
Trestle Av *ABT* . . . . . . 249 T63
Tretheway Dr *BUR* . . . . 164 V25
Tretheway Av *CHL* . . . . 213 F6-7
Tretheway St *ABT* . . . . 250 S-T73
Triangle Rd *RMD* . . . . 203 J17-18
Tricouni Pl *WHS* . . . . . 401 H1
Triggs Rd *SUR* . . . . . . 186 C-D43
Trillium Pl *CQT* . . . . . . 145 R36
Trillium Pl *DNV* . . 123 N22 124 N23
Trim Rd *DEL* . . . . . . . 242 R12
Trimaran Dr *RMD* . . . . 222 K9
Trimaran Gt *RMD* . . . . 222 K9
Trimble St *VAN* . . 142 T7 162 U-V7
Trinity St *ABT* . . . . . . 250 U75-76
Trinity St *BUR* . . . . . . 143 R21
Trinity St *CQT* . . . . . . 165 W35
Trinity St *VAN* . . 143 R18-19 R20
Trites Rd *RMD* . . . . . . 222 L10
Trites Rd *SUR* . . . . . . 225 N35
Triumph St *BUR* . 143 S21-22 144 S23
Triumph St *VAN* . 143 S18-19 S20
Trolley St *VAN* . . . . . . 163 W18
Trounce Alley *VAN* 11 G39-40 142 S14
Trudy Ct *BUR* . . . . . . 144 T26
Trudy's Ldg *WHS* . . . . 401 B4
Trumond Av *RMD* . . . . 202 H8
Trumpeter Dr *RMD* . . . . 222 K10
Trunk Rd *PTM* . . . . . . 167 X47
Truro Dr *RMD* . . . . . . 202 J9
Trutch Av *CHL* . . . . . . 213 F5
Trutch Av *RMD* . . . . . . 202 F8
Trutch St *VAN* . . . . . . 162 U-V9
Tsawwassen Dr N *DEL* . . . . . .
. . . . . . 242 U14 262 V-W15
Tsawwassen Dr S *DEL* . . 262 W-X15
Tsawwassen Beach Rd *DEL* . . . .
. . . . . 262 X-Y15 Y15 Y-Z15
Tseil-Waututh Rd *DNV* . . 144 P23
Tuam Pl *VAN* . . . . . . . 183 Z20
Tuaq Dr *VAN* . . . . . . . 183 A20-21
Tucker Rd *RMD* . . . . . 202 F9

Tuckwell Ter *MIS* . . . . . 210 H75
Tudor Av *DNV* . . . . 123 K15-16
Tudor Ct *ABT* . . . . . . . 250 S77
Tudor Ct *DEL* . . . . . . . 263 Y17
Tugboat Pl *VAN* . . . . . 182 A11
Tulameen Pl *PCQ* . . . . 166 U42
Tulip Cr *ABT* . . . . . . . 250 U73
Tulip Dr *SUR* . . . . . . . 265 V-W38
Tulloch Rd *SUR* . . . . . 245 T-U32
Tully Cr *PTM* . . . . . . . 187 A-B47
Tulsy Cr *SUR* . . . . . . . 205 G33
Tulsy Cr E *SUR* . . . . 205 G33-34
Tulsy Pl *SUR* . . . . . . . 205 G33
Tum-Tumay-Whueton Dr *PMD* . . . .
. . . . . . . . . . . . 144 P28-30
Tum Tum Rd *HOP* . . . . 118 H42-43
Tumberry Cr *VAN* . 162 Y14 182 Z14
Tunbridge Av *MIS* . . . . 210 F73-74
Tunis Pl *SUR* . . . . . . . 205 G38
Tuohey Av *PCQ* . . . . . 145 T38
Tupper Av *CQT* . . . . . 165 X32
Tupper Blvd *MIS* . . . . . 210 G74
Tupper St *CHL* . . . . . . 213 E6
Tupper St *VAN* . . . . . . 162 V-W14
Turnberry La *CQT* . . . . .
. . . . . 125 N37 145 P37 P38
Turnbuckle Wynd *DEL* . . . . 223 P16
Turner Av *CQT* . . . . . . 146 Q39
Turner Pl *DEL* . . . . . . 204 H29
Turner St *ABT* . . . . . . 250 S-T76
Turner St *HOP* . . . . . . 118 F44
Turner St *MIS* . . . . . . . 210 J71
Turner St *PMD* . . . . . . 204 E24
Turner St *VAN* . 143 S-T18 S-T19 S-T20
Turner Creek Dr *PMD* . . . 145 R34-35
Turnill St *MIS* . . . . . . . 202 G13
Turquoise Dr *RMD* . . . . 202 F10
Turret Cr *CQT* . . . . . . 145 R36
Turtle Head Rd *BEL* . . . 124 N27-28
Tuttle Av *RMD* . . . . . . 182 D14
Tuxedo Dr *PMD* . . . . . 145 T31-32
Tuyttens Rd *KNT* . . . . 175 X20 X-Y19
Tweedsmuir Av *RMD* . . . 202 J12
Tweedsmuir Dr *ABT* . . . 251 S-T79
Twigg Pl *RMD* . . . . . . 183 B15
Twigg Rd *RMD* . . . . . . 183 B16
Twin Creek Pl *WVA* . . . 122 J9-10
Twintree Pl *RMD* . . . . 202 F10-11
Tye Ct *BUR* . . . . . . . . 144 T24
Tyee Ct *WVA* . . . . . . . 122 N12
Tyee Dr *WVA* . . . . . . . 122 N12
Tyler Av *PCQ* . . . . . . . 166 V-W39
Tyler St *MIS* . . . . . . . 210 F-H72
Tylney La *ABT* . . . . . . 271 S80
Tyndale Cr *BUR* . . . . . 164 V26-27
Tyndale Pl *BUR* . . . . . 164 V27
Tyndall St *CQT* . . . . . . 164 U30
Tyne Pl *SUR* . . . . . . . 266 V39
Tyne St *VAN* . . 163 Y20 183 Z20
Tynebridge La *WHS* . . . 401 J99
Tynehead Dr *SUR* . . 186 D40 D41-42
Tyner Av *MAP* . . . . . . 167 Y48-49
Tyner St *PCQ* . . . . . . . 166 V39
Tyrol Cr *WHS* . . . . . . . 401 F3
Tyrol Crt *WVA* . . . . . . 122 K10
Tyrol Pl *WVA* . . . . . . . 122 K10-11
Tyrol Rd *WVA* . . . . . . 122 K11
Tyson Pl *RMD* . . . . . . 202 F-G9
Tyson Rd *CHL* . . . . . . 233 L-M5
Tytahun Cr *VAN* . . . . . 162 X7-8

## U

Udy Rd *ABT* . . . . . . . 251 Q83
Udy Rd *RMD* . . . . . . . 202 G11
Ullsmore Av *RMD* . . . . 202 H8
Ulster St *BUR* . . . . . . 164 Y26
Ulster St *PCQ* . . . . 146 S41 T41
Ultra Ct *CQT* . . . . . . . 165 U35
Una Way *PCQ* . . . . . . 166 X39
Underhill Av *BUR* . . . . 164 U-V28
Underhill Dr *DEL* . . . . 263 X-Y16
Underwood Av *DNV* . . . 123 J20-21
Underwood Pl *DNV* . . . 123 J20-21
Unger Ct *MIS* . . . . . . . 210 F73
Ungless Way *PMD* . . . . 145 S35
Union Av *ABT* . . . . . . 250 U71-72
Union St *BUR* . . . . . . .
. . . . . 143 T21-22 144 T23 T25-26
Union St *PMD* . . . . . . 145 S35
Union St *VAN* . 11 J41 143 T15-16 T16
Union Bar Rd *HOP* . . . . 118 D-E46
United Blvd *CQT* . 165 X-Y36 Y32-34
University Blvd *SQM* . . . 301 E5

University Blvd *UEL* . . 161 U3-6
University Cr *BUR* . . . . 144 S-T29
University Dr E *BUR* 144 S29 T28-29
University Dr W *BUR* . . 144 S27-28
University La *LGT* . . . . 207 J52
University High St *BUR* . . 144 T29
Unsworth Rd *CHL* . . 233 K-L4 L-M3
Upland Cr *ABT* . . . . . . 250 T71
Upland Dr *DEL* . . . . . 263 W16-17
Upland Dr *VAN* . . . . . 183 Z17-18
Upland Pl *DEL* . . . . . . 263 W16
Upland Rd *SUR* . . . . . 225 L36
Uplands Ct *CQT* . . . . . 145 R36
Uplands Dr *ANM* . . . . . 125 N33
Uplands Dr *CHL* . . . . . 233 M7-8
Uplands Dr *HOP* . . . . . 118 H42
Uplands Dr *LGC* . . . . . 247 Q49
Uplands Rd *CHL* . . . . . 233 M8
Upper Levels Hwy *CNV* . 123 M16-17
Upper Bayview Rd *LIO* . . 101 B23-24
Upper Beach Rd *SUR* . . 266 Y40
Upper Bellevue Av *WVA* . 122 L8-9
Upper Canyon Rd *DEL* . . 224 K28-29
Upper Levels Hwy *DNV* . 123 N19
Upper Levels Hwy *WVA* . . . . .
101 H2-3 H3 121 J3 K6 122 K7-8 L11-13
Upper Maclure Rd *ABT* . . . . .
. . . . . 249 T70 250 T71
Upper Roper Av *WRK* . . 265 X36
Upton Rd *DNV* . . . . . . 123 L20
Ursus Cr *SUR* . . . . . . 205 F34

## V

Valdez Ct *CQT* . . . . . . 146 S39
Valdez Dr *ABT* . . . . . . 250 S72
Valdez Rd *VAN* . . . . . 162 V-W9
Vale Ct *DNV* . . . . . . . 123 L15
Valemont Cr *ABT* . . . . 250 U71
Valemont St *CHL* . . . . 193 D8
Valencia Av *DNV* . . . . 123 J-K16
Valencia Ct *ABT* . . . . . 270 V73
Valens St *PCQ* . . . . . . 166 W40
Valley Cr *ANM* . . . . . . 125 M-N33
Valley Dr *SQM* . . . . . . 301 K2
Valley Dr *VAN* . . . . . .
. . . . . 162 V-W10 W10-11 W-X11
Valley Dr *WHS* . . . . . . 401 B-C3
Valley Rd *ABT* . . . . . . 250 S75-76
Valley Rd *DNV* . . . . . 123 J-K20
Valleyview Ct *CQT* . . . . 145 Q-R37
Valleyview Rd *CHL* . . . . 233 N7-8
Valleyvista Dr *CQT* . . . . 145 Q37
Valmont Way *RMD* . . . . 183 B18
Valour Dr *PMD* . . . . . 145 T31
Vance Rd *FRA* . . . . . . 253 R-S6
Vancouver St *NEW* . . . . 184 A29-30
Vancouver St *SQM* . . . . 301 K1
Vanda *RMD* . . . . . . . 202 G13
VanDyke Pl *RMD* . . . . 183 B-C17
Vanessa Ct *CQT* . . . . . 165 V31
Vanguard Rd *RMD* . . . . 183 D15
VanHorne Way *RMD* . . . 182 B-C13
Vanier Av *CQT* . . . . . . 165 W33
Vanier Pl *RMD* . . . . . . 183 D16
Vanmar St *CHL* . . . . . 233 K7
Vanness Av *VAN* . 163 W18-19 X19-20
Vantage Pl *ABT* . 249 S70 250 S71
Vantage Pl *DEL* . . . . . 203 J22
Vantage Way *RMD* . . . . 203 J21-22
VanVelzen Av *MIS* . . . . 210 J72
Vardon Pl *DNV* . . . . . 263 W18
Varley La *WVA* . . . . . . 122 K9
Varley St *BUR* . . . . . . 164 Y26
Vasey Rd *ABT* . . . . . . 223 M18
Vauxhall Pl *RMD* . . . . 183 C16
Vedder Pl *PCQ* . . 146 T42 166 U42
Vedder Rd *CHL* . 213 H-J6 233 K-N6
Vedder Way *ABT* . . . . . 270 V77-78
Vedder Mountain Rd *CHL* . . . . .
. . . . . . . . 233 N-P5 P4
Vega Ct *BUR* . . . . . . . 164 V29
Velma Av *CHL* . . . . . . 213 H7-8
Venables St *BUR* 143 T21-22 144 T23
Venables St *VAN* . 143 T17-18 T18-20
Venice Av *CQT* . . . . . . 165 W35
Ventura Av *ABT* . . . . . 250 T-U74
Ventura Cr *DNV* . . . . . 123 J16-17
Venture Pl *CHL* . . . . . 213 H3
Venture St *BUR* . . . . . 164 V27
Venture St *DEL* . . . . . . 223 K21
Venture Way *SUR* . 205 G38 206 G39
Verbena Dr *CHL* . . . . . 233 K-L7
Verbena Pl *CQT* . . . . . 145 R36
Verdon Way *ABT* . . . . . 250 R73

Verdun Pl *RMD* . . . . . . 183 C17
Veres Ter *MIS* . . . . . . 210 G75
Vermilyea Ct *RMD* . . . . 202 E9-10
Vernon Av *MIS* . . . . . 210 F74-75
Vernon Dr *VAN* 143 S-T16 T16 163 U16
Vernon Ter *ABT* . . . . . 250 S78
Verona Pl *DNV* . . . . . . 123 K16
Veterans Way *ABT* . . . . 250 T73
Vicars St *CHL* . . . . . . 213 F5
Viceroy Pl *RMD* . . . . . 183 B-C18
Vickers Way *RMD* . . . . 183 C16
Vickery St *MIS* . . . . . . 210 F72
Victor St *CHL* . . . . . . 213 E7
Victor St *CQT* . . . . . . 165 V31
Victoria Av *CHL* . . . . . 213 E6-7
Victoria Av *WRK* . . . . . 265 X37-38
Victoria Div *VAN* . . . . . 163 V17
Victoria Dr *CQT* . . . . . 146 R42-43
Victoria Dr *PCQ* . . . . . 146 S41-42
Victoria Dr *VAN* . . . . . 143 S-T17
. . . . 163 U-V17 W-Y17 183 A17 Z17 Z17
Victoria Pl *CQT* . . . . . 146 S41
Victoria Pl *ABT* . . . . . . 250 T-U72
Victoria St *NEW* . . . . . 184 B29
Victoria St *SQM* . . . . . 301 J-K1
Victoria St *ABT* . . . . . 250 T-U72
Victory Blvd *ABT* . . . . . 270 V76
Victory Dr *PMD* . . . . . 145 T31
Victory St *BUR* . . . . . .
. . . . 183 Z21 Z22 Z22 184 Z23
Vidal St *WRK* . . . . . . 265 W37 X37
Vienna Cr *DNV* . . . . . . 123 K16
View Av *MIS* . . . . . . . 210 J73-74
View Cr *DEL* . . . . . . . 263 W17
View Ct *PMD* . . . . . . . 145 S32
View Pl *SQM* . . . . . . . 301 J2-3
View St *PMD* . . . . . . . 145 S32
Viewcrest Av *MIS* . . . . 210 G71-72
Viewgrove Pl *ABT* . . . . 270 V78
Viewlynn Dr *DNV* . . . . 123 M20
Viewmount Dr *PMD* . . . 145 T35
Viewmount Pl *ABT* . . . . 250 S71
Viewmount Pl *PMD* . . . 145 T35
Viewpoint Pl *CHL* . . . . 233 M8
Viewridge Pl *WVA* . . . . 121 K5-6
Viking Pl *RMD* . . . . . . 183 C17
Viking Way *RMD* . . . . . 183 C-D17
Villa Rosa Pl *CHL* . . . . 233 M4
Village Dr *BUR* . . 163 W22 164 W23
Village Dr *SQM* . . . . . 301 E-F5
Village Glen *ABT* . . . . . 251 U80
Village Gn *BUR* . . . . . 184 Z25
Village Gn *WHS* . . . . . 401 F4
Village Gn *WHS* . . . . . 401 T21
Village Ct *KNT* . . . . . . 175 X20
Village Knoll *ABT* . . . . . 251 U80
Village La *WHS* . . . . . . 401 T21
Village Sq *WHS* . . . . . 401 T21
Village St *CHL* . . . . . . 233 M6
Village Stroll *WHS* . . . . 401 T21
Village Gate Blvd *WHS* 401 F3-4 T21
Village Green Way *SQM* . . 301 J1
Village Greens Wynd *DEL* . 263 W17
Vimy Av *CHL* . . . . . . . 233 N6
Vimy Cr *VAN* . . . . . . . 163 V20
Vimy Rd *KNT* . . . . . . . 175 X21
Vincent St *PCQ* . 146 S-T40 166 U40
Vine Av *WRK* . . . . . . .
. . . . . 265 W35 W36-37 W38 266 W39
Vine St *VAN* . . . . . . .
. . . . . 10 K32 142 T11 162 U-V11 W11 X10 Y10
Vine Maple Dr *SUR* . . . 245 T33-34
Vinedale Rd *DNV* . . . . 123 M18-19
Vinemaple Pl *CQT* . . . . 145 Q-R37
Vines St *CHL* . . . . . . . 213 F5
Vineway St *PCQ* . . . . . 146 T42
Vinewood Pl *BUR* . . . . 164 U28
Vinmore Av *RMD* . . . . 202 H8
Vinson Creek Rd *WVA* . . 122 J11
Vintner St *PMD* . . . . . 145 T32-33
Viola Pl *MIS* . . . . . . . 210 G74
Viola St *CHL* . . . . . . . 233 N6
Violet *CQT* . . . . . . . . 165 W36
Vipond Pl *RMD* . . . . . 183 Z22
Virginia Cr *DNV* . . . . . 123 K15
Virtual Way *VAN* . . . . . 163 U19
Viscount Pl *CHL* . . . . . 213 G7
Viscount Pl *NEW* . . . . . 184 D27
Viscount Way *RMD* . . . . 183 C16
Vishloff St *MIS* . . . . . . 210 F73
Vista Cr *BUR* . . . . . . . 184 Z26
Vista Cr *SQM* . . . . . . . 301 J3
Vista Ct *ABT* . . . . . . . 250 S71
Vista Ct *CQT* . . . . . . . 165 U35
Vista Dr *WRK* . . . . . . 265 X38
Vista Pl *DEL* . . . . . . . 204 H28

Vista Pl WVA. . . . . . . . . . 121 K3-4
Vista Ridge Dr MAP. . . . . . 167 V53
Vistaview Ct CQT. . . . . . . 145 Q-R37
Vivaldi Pl VAN . . . . . . . . . . 183 A20
Vivian Dr VAN . . . . . . . . 183 A18-19
Vivian Pl PCQ . . . . . . . . . . 166 X39
Vivian St VAN. . . . . 163 Y19 183 Z19
Volkoff La UEL . . . . . . . . . 161 U3-4
Vonda Way CQT . . . . . . . . . 146 R40
Vosburgh Av MIS. . . . . . . 210 H77
Voyageur Way RMD. . . . . . 183 C15
Vulcan St NEW. . . . . . . . . 165 Y31
Vulcan Way RMD. . . . 183 B-C17 C16
Vye Rd ABT. . . . . . . . . . 270 X76-78

**W**

Waddell Av PCQ. . . . . . . . . 166 W39
Waddington Pl CQT. . . . . 145 Q-R38
Wade Rd DEL . . . . . . . . . . 224 L30
Wade Ter MIS . . . . . . . . . 210 H71
Wadham Dr DEL. . . . . . . 204 G-H28
Wagner Dr ABT. . . . . 249 S70 250 S71
Wagner Dr RMD. . . . . . . . 202 H13
Wagner Gt RMD. . . . . . . . 202 H13
Wagner Pl ABT . . . . . . . . . 250 S71
Wagon Wheel Cir CQT . . . . 165 U37
Wagon Wheel Cr LGT. . . . . 227 N54
Wagtail Av RMD . . . . . . . 222 K10
Wain Pl SQM . . . . . . . . . . 301 B-C2
Wakefield Ct BUR. . . . . . . 163 W21
Wakefield Ct LGT. . . . . . . 227 L47
Wakefield Dr LGT . 226 L46 227 L47
Wakely Ct BUR . . . . . . . . 164 V28
Walalee Dr DEL . . . . . . . . 262 X15
Walden St ABT . . . . . . . . 250 S77
Walden St VAN . . . . . 163 W-X15 X15
Wales St VAN . . . . 163 X-Y18 183 Z18
Walford St RMD . . . . . . . 182 C-D13
Walker Av BUR . . . 164 Y25 184 Z26
Walker Av DEL . . . . . . . . . 263 Z16
Walker Cr ABT . . . . . . . . . 270 V77-78
Walker Rd KNT . . . . . . . . 175 X20
Walker St CQT . . . . 165 W32 W-X31
Walker St VAN . . . . . . . . . 163 W18
Wall St VAN . . . . . . 143 R19 R-S18
Wallace Av DEL . . . . . . . . 263 Z16-17
Wallace Cr SUR. . . . . . . . 205 E32
Wallace Cr VAN. . . . . . . . 162 U8
Wallace Ct CQT . . . . . . . . 145 T37
Wallace Dr CHL . . . . . . . . 233 P6
Wallace Dr SUR . . . . . . . 185 A-B36
Wallace Pl DEL . . . . . . . . . 263 Z17
Wallace Pl VAN . . . . . . . . 162 Y8
Wallace Rd RMD . . . . . . . 202 J10
Wallace St ABT . . . . . . . . 230 M-N75
Wallace St HOP . . . . . . . . 118 E44-45
Wallace St VAN . . . . . . . . . . . . .
. . . . 142 T8 162 U8 U-V8 V-X8
Wallace Wynd PMD. . . . . . 145 T31
Waller Ct RMD. . . . . . . . . 202 J9
Waller Dr RMD. . . . . . . . . 202 J9
Walls Av CQT . . . . . . . . . 165 W32-33
Walmsley Av ABT . . . . . . 270 X71-72
Walmsley Ct BUR . . . . . . 164 Y26
Walmsley St NEW. . . . . . 184 A28-29
Walnut Av HHS . . . . . . . . 155 Q19
Walnut Av (Abbotsford) ABT 250 T76
Walnut Av (Huntingdon) ABT. . . .
. . . . . . . . . . . . . . . 270 Y-Z77
Walnut Cr SUR. . . . . . . . 186 B40
Walnut Cr CQT. . . . . . . : . . 165 V34
Walnut Cr MAP . . . . . . . . 187 Z48
Walnut Dr HOP . . . . . . . . 118 G42-43
Walnut Pl CQT. . . . . . . . 165 V34
Walnut Pl DEL . . . . . . . . 223 P17
Walnut St VAN . . . . . 10 J-K33 142 T11
Walnut Grove Dr LGT. . . 207 F-G49
Walpole Cr DNV. . . . 123 N22 124 N23
Walsh Av ABT. . . . . . . . 250 U74-75
Walter Pl BUR . . . . . . . . 164 V23
Walter Rd ABT . . . . . . . 251 T-U81
Walter Florence Rd PTM. . 187 B47
Walter Gage Rd UEL . . . . 161 T4 U3
Walter Hardwick Av VAN . . . . . . .
. . . . . . . 11 K39-40 142 T14
Walters St ABT . . . . . . . 210 J77
Walters St CHL . . . . . . . . 213 F8
Waltham Av BUR. . . 164 Y24 184 Z24
Walton Av CQT . . . . . . . 145 R37-38
Walton Rd RMD. . . . . . . 202 F10
Walton Way PMD . . . . . . 145 R33
Waneta Pl VAN . . . . . . . . 163 V19
Wansford Dr DEL. . . . . . 204 H-J29

Wanstead St MAP . . . 187 A48 B47-48
Warbler Av RMD. . . . . . . . 222 K10
Warbler La CQT. . . . . . . . 146 Q39
Ward Rd ABT. . . . . . . . . . 251 R83
Ward St NEW. . . . . . . . . . 164 Y30
Ward St VAN. . . . . 163 X18 X18-19
Wardance St WVA . . . . . 122 N12-13
Wardmore Pl RMD. . . . . . 202 H8
Wardrop St MIS . . . . 210 J73 230 K73
Ware St ABT . . . . . 250 U74 270 V74
Waresley St MAP. . . . . . . 187 A48
Warren Pl DEL . . . . . . . . 204 F30
Warren Pl LGT . . . . . . . 227 K-L47
Warren St BUR . . . . . . . . 163 X21
Warren St NEW . . . . . . . . 184 A29
Warrenton Av CQT. . . . . . 165 W35
Warrick St CQT . . . . . 165 X35 Y35
Warwick Av PCQ. . . 166 W39 W40
Warwick Av N BUR. . . . . . 144 S24
Warwick Av S BUR 144 S24 164 U24
Warwick Pl PCQ. . . . . . . 166 V-W39
Warwick Rd DEL. . . . . . . 204 J28-29
Wasco St CQT. . . . . . . . . 165 U34
Washington Dr PMD . . . 145 R-S32
Waska St LGT . . . . . . . . . 207 E53
Water Av HOP . . . . . . . . . 118 D-E44
Water La WVA . . . . . . . . 121 L3
Water St PMD . . . . . . . . . 145 R35
Water St VAN . . . . 11 G39-40 142 S14
Water Florence Rd MAP. . . 187 B47
Waterford Dr VAN . . . 182 A14 Z14
Waterford Pl CQT . . . . . . 145 Q38
Waterford Pl SUR . . . . . 205 G33-34
Waterfront Rd E VAN . . . . . . . . .
. . . . . . . 11 F-G39 G41 143 S15-16
Waterfront Rd W VAN . . . . . . . . .
. . . . 11 F-G39 G41 142 S14 143 S15
Waterleaf Pl ABT. . . . . . . 251 U80
Waterleigh Dr VAN. . . . . . 182 A14
Waterloo Dr PMD . . . . . . 145 S31-32
Waterloo St VAN . . . . 142 T9 162 U-V9
Waterside Av VAN . . . . . . 183 A17
Waterton Cr ABT . . . . . . . 251 R79
Waterton Dr RMD . . . . . . 222 K12
Watkins Av CQT . . . . . . . 146 Q40
Watkins Ter MIS . . . . . . . 210 H71
Watling St BUR . . . . . . . . . . . . . .
. . . . . . . 183 Z21 Z21-22 Z22 184 Z23
Watson Ct DEL . . . . . . . . 204 F29
Watson Dr DEL . . . . . . . . 204 F29
Watson Pl DEL. . . . . . . . 204 F29
Watson Rd ABT. . . . . . . . 249 Q63
Watson Rd BEL. . . . . 124 M-N30
Watson Rd CHL. . . . . . . . 233 M4-6
Watson St VAN . . . . 163 V15 W15
Watson Way WHS. . . . . . . 401 G2
Wavell La ABT. . . . . . . . . 270 V76
Waverley Av BUR . . . 183 A22 Z22
Waverley Av VAN . . . . . . . . . . . .
. . . . . . . 163 Y16 Y17-18 Y19-20
Waverly Pl SUR . . . . . . . 205 E33
Wavertree Rd DNV . . 123 K15-16
Waxberry Cr MIS. . . . . . 210 H75
Wayburne Cr LGT . . . . . . 227 L47
Wayburne Dr BUR . . . . . . . . . . .
. . . . . . . 163 W22 W-X22 164 V23 W23
Wayne Dr DNV . . . . . . . . 123 L16
Wayside La WHS. . . . . . . 401 G2
Weare St DEL . . . . . . . . . 243 Q15
Weather Ct BUR. . . . . 164 X25-26
Weatherby St WRK. . . . . . 265 W38
Weatherhead Ct MIS. . . . . 210 H75
Weaver Cr MIS . . . . . . . . 210 G78
Weaver Ct VAN . . . . . . . . 183 Z20
Weaver Dr DEL . . . . . . . . 263 Y16
Webb Av CHL . . . . . . . . . 213 J6
Webb Ct ABT. . . . . . . . . . 250 U78
Webber Av VAN . . . . . . . . 163 W15
Webster Av CQT . . . 164 V30 165 V31
Webster Ct ABT. . . . . . . . 270 V71
Webster Rd CHL. . . . . . . . 233 N4
Webster Rd DEL . . . . . . . 204 H23
Webster Rd RMD . . . . . . 202 F9-10
Wedge La WHS. . . . . . . . . 401 E3
Wedgeview Pl WHS. . . . . 401 C2-3
Wedgewood Dr CHL. . . . . 193 C8
Wedgewood St BUR. . . . . . . . . . .
. . . . . . 164 Y27 Y27-28 184 Z27
Wedgewood St PCQ . . . . . 146 S41
Weeden Dr CHL . . . . . . . . 233 N7
Weeden Pl CHL . . . . . . . . 233 N7
Welch St DNV. . . . . . . . . . 122 N14
Welch St VAN. . . . . . . . . . 122 N13
Welcher Av PCQ . . . 165 V38 166 V39
Weldon Ct PMD . . . . . . . . 144 T30

Wellburn Dr DEL. . . . . . . 223 N-P17
Wellington Av CHL . . . . . . 213 E6
Wellington Av VAN . . . . 163 W19 X20
Wellington Av WVA . . . . . 101 G1-2
Wellington Cr DNV. . . . . . 123 L15
Wellington Cr RMD. . . . . 182 C-D11
Wellington Cr SUR . . . . . . 185 A36
Wellington Ct CQT . . . . . . 146 R40
Wellington Dr DNV123 K17-18 K18-20
Wellington Dr SUR . . . . . . 185 A36
Wellington Pl DNV. . . . . . 123 K18
Wellington Pl WVA . . . . . . 101 G2
Wellington Rd DEL . . . . . 242 S14
Wellington St NEW . . . . . 184 A30
Wellington St PCQ146 S-T40 166 U40
Wellmond Rd RMD. . . . . . 202 H8
Wells Pl SUR. . . . . . . . 205 E-F32
Wells Rd CHL . . . . . . . . . 213 J5-6
Wells Rd KNT . . . . . . . . . 175 W17
Wells St MIS . . . . . . . . . 210 F75
Wells-Gray Av ABT . . . . . 251 T79
Wells-Gray Ct ABT . . . . . 251 S-T79
Wells-Gray Pl ABT . . . . . 251 S-T79
Wells Gray Pl NEW. . . . . 164 Y30
Wellsgreen Pl DEL . . . . . 263 Z17
Welsh St NEW . . . . . 184 A-B29
Welsley Dr BUR . . . . . . . . 164 Y26
Welton St MIS . . . . . . . . 210 E-F5
Welwyn St VAN. . . . . 163 V-W17 W17
Wembley Dr DNV . . . . . . 123 L20-21
Wembley Pl DNV. . . . . . . 123 L20-21
Wenda Pl SQM . . . . . . . . . 301 D3
Wendel Pl DNV . . . . . . . . 123 L19
Wenonah St VAN. . . . . . . 163 W18
Wentworth Av DNV. . . 123 K15-16
Wentworth Av WVA. . . . . 122 K9
Werks Dr VAN . . . . . . . . 183 A19 Z20
Wesbrook Cr UEL. . . . . . 161 T-U4
Wesbrook Mall UEL 161 T-U4 V4-5 W5
Wesbrook Vlg UEL . . . . . 161 V5
Wesley Pl DEL . . . . . . . . 262 X15
Wessex St VAN . . . . . . . 163 Y20
West Blvd VAN . . . 162 X-Y11 182 Z11
West Mall UEL . . . . . . . . 183 A20
West Rd BEL. . . . 124 N29 144 P29
West Rd RMD . . . . . . . . 182 C12
West St MAP . . . . . . . . 187 Z47
West Beach Av WRK. . . . . 265 X36
West Campus Rd BUR . . . 144 S28
West Edwards St MIS . . 210 F-G78
West Point Pl VAN . . . . . . 162 U7
West Railway St ABT . . . . . . . . . .
. . . . . . . 250 U76 270 V76
West Vista Ct WVA . . . . . 121 K3
West Whalley Ring Rd SUR. . . . . .
. . . . . . 185 B-C33 C33 C34 D33-34
Westbank Pl VAN . . . 183 A19 Z20
Westbury Av ABT . . . . . . 270 V75
Westbury La VAN. . . . . . 182 Z13
Westbury Walk VAN . . . . . 182 Z13
Westcot Pl WVA. . . . . . . 122 L12
Westcot Rd WVA . . . . . . 122 L12
Westcott St RMD. . . . . . 222 L10
Westdean Cr WVA. . . . . . 122 L10
Westerly St ABT . . . . . . . 250 U71
Western Av CNV . . . 123 L-M17
Western Cr UEL . . . . . . . 161 T4
Western Dr PCQ . . . 166 W-X39
Western Pkwy UEL . . . . 161 T-U4
Western Pl PCQ . . . . . . . 165 X38
Western St VAN . . 11 K40-41 143 T15
Westfield Av MAP. . . . . 187 A48-49
Westfield Ct LGT. . . . . . 247 Q54
Westham La DEL . . . . 243 Q16-17
Westham Island Rd DEL . . . . . . .
. . . 222 P10 242 Q10 Q11-12
Westhaven Ct WVA. . . . . 121 J3
Westhaven Pl WVA . . . . . 121 J3
Westhaven Rd WVA . . . . 121 J3
Westhaven Wynd WVA . . 121 J3
Westhill Cl WVA. . . . . . . 122 K10
Westhill Dr WVA . . . . . . 122 K10
Westhill Dr WVA . . . . . . 122 K10
Westhill Pl PMD. . . . . . . 145 S31
Westhill Pl WVA. . . . . . . 122 K10
Westhill Way WVA. . . . . 122 K10
Westhill Wynd WVA . . . 122 K10
Westholme Rd WVA. . . . 121 K-L6
Westhyde Pl DNV. . . . . 123 K-L16
Westlake Dr CQT. . . . . . 165 V36
Westlake Gt CQT. . . . . . 165 V36
Westlake Pl CQT. . . . . . 165 V36
Westlake St BUR . . . . . 164 V27-28
Westlawn Dr BUR . 143 T22 144 T23
Westley Av CQT . . . 164 U30 165 U31
Westminster Av BUR. 164 V23 V-W23
Westminster Av DEL. . . 223 P16-17

Westminster Av PCQ . . . . 166 U40
Westminster Ct DEL . . . . 223 P16
Westminster Dr ABT . . . . 251 R81
Westminster Hwy NEW. . . 184 D26
Westminster Hwy RMD . . . . . . . .
. . . 202 F8-14 203 F15-22 204 E24-25
Westminster Hwy N RMD . 204 F23
Westminster Hwy S RMD . . . . . . .
. . . . . . . 204 F23-24
Westminster La DEL . . . . 223 P16
Westmoreland Ct CNV . 123 M15-16
Westmount Ct WVA . . . . . 121 K6
Westmount Dr PMD. . . . . 145 T31
Westmount Pl WVA. . . . . 122 K7
Westmount Rd WVA . 121 K6 122 K7
Weston Ct BUR . . . . . . . 164 W26
Weston Pl SUR . . . . . . . 205 G37
Weston St CQT . . . . . . . 165 U34
Westover Dr DNV. . . . . . 123 L20-21
Westport Ct WVA . . . . . . 121 J3
Westport Pl WVA. . . . . 101 H3 121 J3
Westport Rd WVA . . . . 121 J3 J3-4
Westport Wynd WVA. . . . 121 J3
Westridge Av WVA . . . 121 K5 K6
Westridge La ANM . 125 N31 145 P31
Westside Dr DEL . . . . . . 204 H28
Westside Pl ABT . . . . . . . 250 T71
Westview Av CHL . . . . . 213 E-F5
Westview Av MIS. . . . . . 210 J72
Westview Cr CNV . . . . . . 123 L16
Westview Cr CNV . . . . . . 123 L-M16
Westview Dr DEL. . . . 224 K28 L28
Westview Pl CNV. . . . . . 123 L16
Westview Pl DEL . . . . . . 224 K28
Westview St CQT . . . . . . 165 W31
Westwater Dr RMD. . . . . 222 L9-10
Westway Av SQM . . . . . . 301 J4 K3
Westwood Dr CHL . . . . . 233 N7
Westwood Dr WVA . . . . . 121 J4
Westwood Pl WVA . . . . . 121 L-M19
Westwood St CQT145 S-T38 165 U38
Wethersfield Dr VAN 162 Y14 182 Z14
Weymoor Pl VAN . . . . . . 183 A20
Weymouth Dr DNV. . . . . 123 M18-19
Weymouth Pl DNV. . . . . 123 M18-19
Wharf St MAP. . 186 B46 187 B47-48
Wharton Pl MIS . . . . . . . 210 G75-76
Whatcom Pl ABT. . . . . . . 251 U80
Whatcom Rd ABT . . 251 S-T79 T-U80
Wheatley Av WRK . . . . . 265 W-X35
Wheel Av ABT. . . . . . . . . 249 U70
Wheeler Rd RMD. . . . . . 202 H13
Wheelhouse Sq VAN . . . . . . . . . .
. . . . 11 K38 142 T14 162 U14
Whelan Rd RMD . . . . . . . 202 J13
Whelen Ct BUR . . . . . . . 164 Y25
Whelpton Rd KNT . . . . 175 Y19-20
Whidden Av MIS . . . . . . . 210 G74
Whippoorwill Av MAP. . 187 Z54
Whiskey Cove La BEL . . 124 N28
Whisper Way CQT . . . . . 145 Q-R38
Whistle Dr ABT . . . . . . . 249 T63
Whistler Ct RMD. . . . . . 222 K11
Whistler Pl RMD. . . . . . 202 J11
Whistler Rd WHS . . . . . 401 G-H2
Whistler Ridge WHS . . . 401 G-H2
Whistler Way WHS . . 401 F4 T-U21
Whistler Cay Dr WHS . . . 401 E3
Whitby Pl DEL . . . . . . . . 204 J29
Whitby Rd WVA . . . . . . 122 K11
Whitchurch St DNV. 123 N19 143 P19
Whitcomb Pl DEL . . . . . 263 W18
White Av BUR . . . . . . . . 163 W22
White Pine Pl CQT . . . . . 145 R38
Whitebark Pl CQT. . . . . . 145 Q38
Whitehorn Ct CQT . 145 Q38 146 Q39
Whiteley Ct DNV. . . . . . 123 M19
Whiteoak Dr RMD. . . . . 202 H11
Whiteoak Gt RMD. . . . . 202 H-J11
Whitepine La DNV. . . . . 103 H15
Whitesail Pl CQT. . . . . . 165 V36-37
Whitespray Dr VAN . . 182 A14 Z14
Whitewood Pl DNV. . . . 122 N14
Whithorn Ct VAN. . . . . . 183 Z20
Whiting Way CQT . . . . . 164 V-W30
Whitman Av DNV. . . 123 M22 124 M23
Whitney Pl VAN . . . . . . 183 A20
Whitsell Av BUR . . . . . . 143 T22
Whitworth Cr N DEL. . . . 243 R16
Whitworth Cr S DEL. . . . 243 R16
Whonoak Rd WVA. . . . . 122 N13
Whorley Rd KNT . . . . . . 175 Y19
Whyte Av PCQ. . . . . . . . 165 U38
Whyte Av VAN. . . . 10 J33 142 T11
Wickenden Rd DNV . . . . 124 N27
Wickham Dr CQT . . . . . 165 U37
Wickham La SUR . . . . . 245 U31

Wickham Pl BUR. . . . . . . 164 Y26
Wicklow Way MAP . . . . . 187 Z51
Wicklund Av MAP. . . . . 187 Z49-50
Wickson Pl SUR . . . . . . 245 T31
Wickson Rd SUR. . . . . . 245 T31
Widgeon Av MIS . . . . . . 210 H73
Widmer Ct BUR. . . . . . . 184 C24
Wiggins Pl LGT . . . . . . 227 L47
Wiggins St BUR. . . 184 B23 C-D24
Wilberforce St BUR. . . 164 X29-30
Wilcox Rd PTM. . . . 187 A47 Z47
Wilderness Ct BUR . . . 164 U-V28
Wilding Cr LGT . . . . . . . 227 L47
Wilding Pl CNV. . . . . . . 123 M18
Wilding Way CNV . . . . . 123 M18
Wildwood Cr BUR . . . . . 163 X22
Wildwood Cr DEL . . . . . 263 W17
Wildwood Cr PTM. . . 186 A46 Z46
Wildwood Cr N PTM . . 187 A47 Z47
Wildwood Cr S PTM . . . . . . . . . .
. . . . . . . 186 A46 187 A47
Wildwood Dr ABT . . . . . 270 V75
Wildwood Dr KNT. . . . . 155 S-T19
Wildwood Dr LGT . . . . . 227 L47
Wildwood Dr PMD. . . . . 145 R35
Wildwood La WVA . . . . . 122 L12
Wildwood Pl PTM. . . . . 187 A47
Wildwood Pl SUR . . . . . 206 G41
Wildwood Pl WVA . . . . . 122 L12
Wildwood St ABT . . . . . 270 V74
Wilerose St ABT . . . . . . 270 V74
Wilkes Creek Dr PMD . . 145 R34
Wilkie Av CQT . . . . . . . 146 S41
Wilkins Dr CHL . . . . . . 233 M5
Wilkinson Rd RMD . . . . 202 J14
Willard St BUR. . . . . . 184 B-C25
Willband St ABT . . . . . 250 T75
Willerton Ct CQT . . . . . 146 Q40
Willet Pl MIS . . . . . . . . 210 H77
Willett Av RMD. . . . . . . 204 E25
William Av CNV . . . . 123 M-N19
William Av DNV . . . . 123 L-M19
William St BUR . . . . . 143 T21-22
William St NEW . . . . . . 164 Y29
William St VAN . . . . . . . . . . . . .
. . . 143 T16 T17 T18-19 T20
Williams Av DEL . . . . . 263 Z17
Williams Av MIS . . . . . 210 H-J73
Williams Rd CHL . . . . . 193 C-D7
Williams Rd RMD . . . . . . . . . . .
. . . 202 J8-14 203 J15 J17 J18
Williams St CHL . . . 193 D7 213 E7
Williams St PMD . . . . . 145 T34
Willingdon Av BUR . . . . . . . . . . .
. . . 143 S22 S-T22 163 U-Y22 183 Z21-22
Willingdon Av N BUR. . . 143 S22
Willingdon Cr ABT. . . . . 250 U73
Willingdon Gn BUR . . . 163 V22
Willoughby Av BUR. . . . 164 V30
Willoughby Ct LGT . . . . 227 L47
Willoughby Rd WVA . . . 122 K9
Willoughby Way LGT . . . . . . . . .
. . . . 226 L46 L46 227 L47
Willow Av HOP . . . . . . . 118 D44
Willow Cr SQM . . . . . . . 301 F3
Willow Dr CHL . . . . . . . 213 F7
Willow Gr SUR. . . . . . . 186 C40
Willow La ABT . . . . . . . 250 U76
Willow Pl DEL . . . . . . . 223 N-P17
Willow Pl WVA. . . . . . . 121 K4
Willow St ABT . . . . . . . 270 V76
Willow St FRA. . . . . . . . 253 R5
Willow St HOP. . . . . . . . 118 D44
Willow St MIS . . . . . . . 210 H75
Willow St VAN. . . . . . . . . . . . . .
. . . 162 U13 V13 W13 X-Y13 Y13
Willow Way CQT. . . . . . 165 U33
Willow Way PTM . . . . . 187 A47
Willow Creek Rd WVA. . . 121 K4
Willow Park Estates LGT. . 226 L46
Willowbrook Connector LGT . . . .
. . . . . . 227 L48-49
Willowbrook Dr LGT. . . . . . . . . .
. . . 226 L46 M46 227 L47 M47
Willowdale Pl BUR 163 W22 164 W23
Willowfield Dr RMD. . . . . 202 G9
Willowleaf Pl ABT . . . . . 164 U30
Willowtree La PMD . . . . 145 R34-35
Wilma St BUR . . . . . 184 A25 Z25
Wilmington Dr DEL . . . . 263 X16
Wilmot Cr CQT . . . . . . 165 V35
Wilson St PMD . . . . . . . 145 R31
Wilson Av BUR . . . . . . 163 Y21-22
Wilson Av DEL . . . . . . . 223 K21
Wilson Av PCQ. . . . 165 V38 166 V39
Wilson Av RMD . . . . . . 204 E24
Wilson Cr SQM. . . . . . . 301 J1-2
Wilson Ct DEL . . . . . . . 263 X16
Wilson Ct RMD . . . . . . 204 E24
Wilson Dr DEL . . . . . . . 263 Y16